Ibbotson® SBBI®
2012 Classic Yearbook

Market Results for
Stocks, Bonds, Bills, and Inflation
1926–2011

2012 Ibbotson® Stocks, Bonds, Bills, and Inflation® (SBBI®) Classic Yearbook

Published by:
Morningstar, Inc.
22 W. Washington Street
Chicago, Illinois 60602

Main (312) 696-6000
Product Sales (888) 298-3647
Fax (312) 696-6010
global.morningstar.com/SBBIYearbooks

ISBN 978-0-9849500-0-3
ISSN 1047-2436

The data in the 2012 Ibbotson SBBI Classic Yearbook is also available within many of Morningstar's software products. Statistics and graphs can be quickly accessed over any subperiod. For more information about Morningstar's software and data products for individuals, advisors, and institutions, see "Investment Tools and Resources" at the back of this book, or call (800) 735-0700.

Ibbotson Associates is a leading authority on asset allocation with expertise in capital market expectations and portfolio implementation. Approaching portfolio construction from the top-down through a research-based investment process, its experienced consultants and portfolio managers serve mutual fund firms, banks, broker-dealers, and insurance companies worldwide. Ibbotson Associates' methodologies and services address all investment phases, from accumulation to retirement and the transition between the two. Visit Ibbotson.com for contact information, published research, product fact sheets and other information.

Additional copies of the 2012 Ibbotson SBBI Classic Yearbook may be obtained for $175 per book, plus shipping and handling. Archived editions (2011 and prior) are available in limited quantities for $200 per book, plus shipping and handling. For purchasing or other information related to volume discounts or companion publications, please call (888) 298-3647, or write to the address above.

Table of Contents

Acknowledgements

We thank, foremost, Roger G. Ibbotson, Chairman and CIO of Zebra Capital Management, Professor in Practice at the Yale School of Management, and founder of Ibbotson Associates®, for his contributions to this book. Professor Ibbotson and Rex A. Sinquefield, a director of Dimensional Fund Advisors (Santa Monica, CA), wrote the two journal articles and four books upon which the Ibbotson® Stocks, Bonds, Bills, and Inflation® Classic Yearbook is based and formulated much of the philosophy and methodology. Dimensional Fund Advisors also provides the small stock returns, as it has since 1982.

We thank others who contributed to this book. Rolf W. Banz provided the small stock returns for 1926–1981. Thomas S. Coleman (Greenwich, CT), Professor Lawrence Fisher of Rutgers University, and Roger Ibbotson constructed the model used to generate the intermediate-term government bond series for 1926–1933. The pioneering work of Professors Fisher and James H. Lorie of the University of Chicago inspired the original monograph. We also wish to acknowledge the valuable role of Dr. Stan V. Smith, President of Smith Economics Group, Ltd. and former managing director of Ibbotson Associates, who originated the idea of the Yearbook. The Center for Research in Security Prices (CRSP®) at the University of Chicago contributed the data and methodology for the returns on the NYSE by capitalization decile used in Chapter 7, Firm Size and Return. Ken French, of Dartmouth College, and Eugene Fama, of the University of Chicago Booth School of Business, contributed the data and methodology for the returns on the growth and value portfolios. Chapter 9, Liquidity Investing, was written by Roger Ibbotson and Zhiwu Chen, both at the Yale School of Management. Michael Holmgren, of Holmgren Capital Management, helped develop the empirical results. William N. Goetzmann, Roger Ibbotson, and Liang Peng, all at the Yale School of Management, assembled the New York Stock Exchange database for the period prior to 1926, while James Licato converted the research into Chapter 12, Stock Market Returns from 1815–1925. James Licato also converted work originally authored by Peng Chen, president of Morningstar's global investment management division, into Chapter 11, Wealth Forecasting with Monte Carlo Simulation, created Chapter 13, International Equity Investing, and contributed to other chapters. Rod Bare contributed Chapter 14, "Lifecycle Investing". Paul Kaplan PhD, while at Ibbotson Associates, was the main contributor to Chapter 10, "Using Historical Data in Forecasting and Optimization", and more recently, created a set of monthly real stock market total returns going back a full 125 years in Chapter 12. Also, in Chapter 10, Paul Kaplan and Sam Savage, Consulting Professor of Management Science & Engineering at Stanford University, present new research and methodology that they have aptly dubbed "Markowitz 2.0" which promises to take traditional portfolio optimization into the supersonic age. Paul, now director of European quantitative research at Morningstar, Peng Chen, and Thomas Idzorek, chief investment officer and director of research at Morningstar Investment Management, all continue to provide valuable insights and analysis for the SBBI yearbook series.

We want to thank Laurence B. Siegel, research director of the Research Foundation of CFA Institute and senior advisor to Ounavarra Capital LLC, New York; from 1994 to 2009 he was director of research at the Ford Foundation and prior to that at Ibbotson Associates, James Harrington, formerly the senior editor of the SBBI Yearbooks at Morningstar, and Michael Barad, formerly of Ibbotson Associates and now senior vice president of the financial communications business at Morningstar, for their many contributions to the Yearbook.

Senior Editor	**Director of Design**	**Chairman and CEO**
Magdalena Mroczek	David Williams	Joe Mansueto
Contributing Editors	**Design Manager**	**President, Equity and**
Kevin Piccolo	Christopher Cantore	**Credit Research**
Roland Czerniawski		Catherine Odelbo
Yiteng Liu		
		Senior Vice President, Financial
		Communications Business
		Michael W. Barad

Who Should Read This Book

The Ibbotson® Stocks, Bonds, Bills, and Inflation® (SBBI®) Classic Yearbook is a history of the returns on the capital markets in the United States from 1926 to the present. It is useful to a wide variety of readers. Foremost, anyone serious about investments or investing needs an appreciation of capital market history. Such an appreciation, which can be gained from this book, is equally valuable to the individual and institutional investor. For students at both the graduate and undergraduate levels, this book is both a source of ideas and a reference. Other intended readers include teachers of these students; practitioners and scholars in finance, economics, and business; portfolio strategists; and security analysts.

Chief financial officers and, in some cases, chief executive officers of corporations will find this book useful. More generally, persons concerned with history may find it valuable to study the detail of economic history as revealed in more than eight decades of capital market returns.

To these diverse readers, we provide two resources. One is the data. The other is a thinking person's guide to using historical data to understand the financial markets and make decisions. This historical record raises many questions. This book represents our way of appreciating the past—only one of the many possible ways—but one grounded in real theory. We provide a means for the reader to think about the past and the future of financial markets.

How to Read This Book

Intended Reader	Most Important Chapters	Other Related Chapters, Graphs, Tables, and Appendices
Persons Concerned with Data	Chapters 1, 2, 3, 12, and 13	Chapters 4, 7, and 8; Graphs 2-1, 13-4, and 14-2; Tables 2-1, 13-1, 13-2, 14-2, and 14-6; and Appendices A, B, and C
Financial Planners, Asset Allocators, and Investment Consultants	Chapters 1, 2, 9, 10, 11, 12, 13, 14 and 15	Chapter 6; Graphs 2-1, 9-1, 10-4, 10-5, 11-1, 11-5, 13-4, and 14-2; and Tables 2-7, 6-6, 10-3, 10-6, 10-9, and 13-1
Individual Investors	Chapters 1, 2, 9, 10, and 12	Graph 2-1, 10-4, 10-5; and Tables 2-1, 9-1, 10-3, 10-6, 10-9, 12-9, 12-10, and 12-11
Institutional Investors, Portfolio Managers, and Security Analysts	Chapters 1 through 15	Graphs 2-1, 10-4, 10-5, 12-04, 13-4, and 14-2; Tables 2-7, 6-6, 7-1, 10-3, 10-6, 10-9, 13-1, 13-2, 14-2, and 14-6
Students, Faculty, and Economists	Chapters 2, 5, 6, 7, 8, 11, 12, 13, 14, and 15	Graphs 2-1, 13-4, and 14-2; Tables 6-6, 9-1, 13-1, 13-2, 14-2, and 14-6
Brokers and Security Sales Representatives	Chapters 1, 2, and 12	Graph 2-1; and Tables 2-1, 2-5, 12-9, 12-10, and 12-11
Investment Bankers and Security Sales Representatives	Chapters 2, 7, 8, 9, 14, and 15	Graph 9-1; and Table 2-1
Executives, Corporate Planners, Chief Financial Officers, Chief Executive Officers, and Treasurers	Chapters 1 and 2	Graph 2-1; and Table 2-1
Pension Plan Sponsors	Chapters 1, 2, 6, 9, 10, 11, 12 and 15	Graph 2-1, 9-1; and Tables 2-1 and 2-4

The Journal of Business published Roger G. Ibbotson and Rex A. Sinquefield's two companion papers on security returns in January 1976 and July 1976. In the first paper, the authors collected historical data on the returns from stocks, government and corporate bonds, U.S. Treasury bills, and consumer goods (inflation). To uncover the risk/return and the real/nominal relationship in the historical data, they presented a framework in which the return on an asset class is the sum of two or more elemental parts. These elements, such as real returns (returns in excess of inflation) and risk premia (for example, the net return from investing in large company stocks rather than bills), are referred to throughout the book as derived series.

In the second paper, the authors analyzed the time series behavior of the derived series and the information contained in the U.S. government bond yield curve to obtain inputs for a simulation model of future security price behavior. Using the methods developed in the two papers, they forecast security returns through the year 2000.

The response to these works showed that historical data are fascinating in their own right. Both total and component historical returns have a wide range of applications in investment management, corporate finance, academic research, and industry regulation. Subsequent work—the 1977, 1979, and 1982 Institute of Chartered Financial Analysts (ICFA) monographs; the 1989 Dow Jones-Irwin book; and the Ibbotson 1983 through 2012 Stocks, Bonds, Bills, and Inflation Classic Year-books—updated and further developed the historical data and forecasts. (All references to previous works used in the development of Stocks, Bonds, Bills, and Inflation [SBBI] data appear at the end of this introduction in the References section.)

In 1981, Ibbotson and Sinquefield began tracking a new asset class: small company stocks. This class consists of issues listed on the New York Stock Exchange (NYSE) that rank in the ninth and tenth (lowest) deciles when sorted by capitalization (price times number of shares outstanding), plus non-NYSE issues of comparable capitalization. This asset class has been of interest to researchers and investors because of its high long-term returns. Intermediate-term (five years to maturity) government bonds were added in 1988. Monthly and annual total returns, income returns, capital appreciation returns, and yields are presented.

The 2012 Ibbotson® Stocks, Bonds, Bills, and Inflation® Classic Yearbook

In the present volume the historical data are updated. The motivations are: 1) to document this history of security market returns; 2) to uncover the relationships between the various asset class returns as revealed by the derived series: inflation, real interest rates, risk premia, and other premia; 3) to encourage deeper understanding of the underlying economic history through the graphic presentation of data; and 4) to answer questions most frequently asked by subscribers. In keeping with the spirit of the previous work, the asset classes contained in this edition highlight the differences between targeted segments of the financial markets in the United States. Our intent is to show historical trade-offs between risk and return. International data was introduced in the 2002 edition.

In this book, the equity markets are segmented between large and small company stocks. Fixed income markets are segmented on two dimensions. Riskless U.S. government securities are differentiated by maturity or investment horizon. U.S. Treasury bills with approximately 30 days to maturity are used to describe the short end of the horizon; U.S. Treasury securities with approximately five years to maturity are used to describe the middle horizon segment; and U.S. Treasury securities with approximately 20 years to maturity are used to describe the long maturity end of the market. A corporate bond series with a long maturity is used to describe fixed income securities that contain risk of default.

Some indices of the stock and bond markets are broad, capturing most or all of the capitalization of the market. Our indices are intentionally narrow. The large company stock series captures the largest issues (those in the Standard & Poor's 500 Composite Index), while the small company stock series is composed of the smallest issues. By studying these polar cases, we identify the small stock premium (small minus large stock returns) and the premium of large stocks over bonds and bills. Neither series is intended to be representative of the entire stock market. Likewise, our long-term government bond and U.S. Treasury bill indices show the returns for the longest and shortest ends of the yield curve, rather than the return for the entire Treasury float. Readers and investors should understand that our bond indices do not, and are not intended to, describe the experience of the typical bond investor who is diversified across maturities; rather, we present returns on carefully focused segments of the market for U.S. Treasury securities.

Recent Changes and Additions

We are excited to provide our readers with a number of enhancements in the 2012 Ibbotson® SBBI® Classic Yearbook, including a new chapter on alternative investments, a new section in Chapter 6 that discusses the limitations of standard deviation as a measure of risk, and, back by popular demand, Chapter 2's basic series compound annual return data using various holding periods.

The new Chapter 10 in the 2012 Ibbotson SBBI Classic Yearbook, Alternative Investments, provides the latest trends and analyses of liquid alternatives. Alternative investments are commonly used to hedge traditional portfolio risk and can be an important component in portfolio allocation and optimization. The chapter covers the historical returns of various hedge fund and mutual fund alternative indices, as well as in-depth and useful quantitative information regarding their correlations, historical betas, and portfolio optimization.

Chapter 6, Statistical Analysis of Returns, provides an overview of the basic series' risk relationships through standard deviation and correlations across various time periods. While standard deviation is the most common measure of risk, it lacks essential qualities of risk from the standpoint of an investor of capital. The new section, Limitations of Standard Deviation, addresses fat tails, semi-variance and semi-standard deviation, as well as issues with relying solely on semi-variance.

After many requests for the five-, 10-, and 20-year holding period compound annual return tables previously in the 2009 Ibbotson® SBBI® Classic Yearbook, we have decided to reinstate them into Chapter 2. These tables illustrate the effects of time diversification during holding periods similar to those experienced by investors.

We continue to organize the impactful events of 2011 in Chapter 1 into more relevant sections for our readers. These sections include Economic Overview, Domestic and International Governmental Change, Selected Domestic and International Highlights, Natural and Environmental Disasters, Global Currencies, Commodities, and Sector Highlights, provided by Morningstar's equity analysts. We have added a table of annual sector returns to further support our Sector Highlights section

Your feedback is important to us and is the source of many ideas that keep Morningstar's products the best in the business. As always, we welcome your questions, comments, and ideas.

Magdalena Mroczek,
Senior Editor, *Ibbotson SBBI Classic Yearbook*
Financial Communications Business

The Ibbotson® SBBI® Data Series

The series presented here are total returns, and where applicable or available, capital appreciation returns and income returns for:

SBBI Data Series	Series Construction	Index Components	Approximate
1. **Large Company Stocks**	S&P 500 Composite with dividends reinvested. (S&P 500, 1957–Present; S&P 90, 1926–1956)	Total Return Income Return Capital Appreciation Return	N/A
2. **Small Company Stocks**	Fifth capitalization quintile of stocks on the NYSE for 1926–1981. Performance of the DFA U.S. 9-10 Small Company Portfolio January 1982–March 2001. Performance of the DFA U.S. Micro Cap Portfolio April 2001–Present.	Total Return	N/A
3. **Long-Term Corporate Bonds**	Citigroup Long-Term High Grade Corporate Bond Index	Total Return	20 Years
4. **Long-Term Government Bonds**	A One-Bond Portfolio	Total Return Income Return Capital Appreciation Return Yield	20 Years
5. **Intermediate-Term Government Bonds**	A One-Bond Portfolio	Total Return Income Return Capital Appreciation Return Yield	5 Years
6. **U.S. Treasury Bills**	A One-Bill Portfolio	Total Return	30 Days
7. **Consumer Price Index**	CPI—All Urban Consumers, not seasonally adjusted	Inflation Rate	N/A

References

Stocks, Bonds, Bills, and Inflation® Yearbook, annual.
1983, 1984, 1985, 1986, 1987, 1988, 1989,1990, 1991, 1992, 1993, 1994, 1995, 1996, 1997, 1998, 1999, 2000, 2001, 2002, 2003, 2004, 2005, 2006, 2007, 2008, 2009, 2010, 2011, 2012. Morningstar, Inc.

Banz, Rolf W.
"The Relationship Between Return and Market Value of Common Stocks,"
Journal of Financial Economics 9:3–18, 1981.

Brinson, Gary P., L. Randolph Hood, and Gilbert P. Beebower
"Determinants of Portfolio Performance," Financial Analysts Journal, July/August 1986.

Brinson, Gary P., Brian D. Singer, and Gilbert P. Beebower
"Determinants of Portfolio Performance II," *Financial Analysts Journal*, May/June 1991.

Coleman, Thomas S., Lawrence Fisher, and Roger G. Ibbotson
Historical U.S. Treasury Yield Curves 1926–1992 with 1994 update,
Ibbotson Associates, Chicago, 1994.

Coleman, Thomas S., Lawrence Fisher, and Roger G. Ibbotson
U.S. Treasury Yield Curves 1926–1988, Moody's Investment Service, New York, 1990.

Cottle, Sidney, Roger F. Murray, and Frank E. Block
"Graham and Dodd's Security Analysis," Fifth Edition, McGraw-Hill, 1988.

Cowles, Alfred
Common Stock Indices, Principia Press, Bloomington, 1939.

Goetzmann, William N., Roger G. Ibbotson, and Liang Peng
"A New Historical Database for the NYSE 1815 to 1925: Performance and Predictability,"
Journal of Financial Markets, December 2000.

Ibbotson, Roger G., and Rex A. Sinquefield
Speech to the Center for Research in Security Prices, May 1974.

Ibbotson, Roger G., and Paul D. Kaplan
"Does Asset Allocation Policy Explain 40, 90, or 100 Percent of Performance?,"
Financial Analysts Journal, January/February 2000.

Ibbotson, Roger G., and Peng Chen
"Long-Run Stock Returns: Participating in the Real Economy."
Financial Analysts Journal, January/February 2003.

Ibbotson, Roger G., and Rex A. Sinquefield (foreword by Jack L. Treynor)
*Stocks, Bonds, Bills, and Inflation: The Past (1926–1976) and the Future
(1977–2000)*, 1977 ed., Institute of Chartered Financial Analysts, Charlottesville, VA, 1977.

Ibbotson, Roger G., and Rex A. Sinquefield, (foreword by Laurence B. Siegel)
Stocks, Bonds, Bills, and Inflation: The Past and the Future, 1982 ed.,
Institute of Chartered Financial Analysts, Charlottesville, VA, 1982.

Ibbotson, Roger G., and Rex A. Sinquefield
Stocks, Bonds, Bills, and Inflation: Historical Returns (1926–1987), 1989 ed.,
Dow-Jones Irwin, Homewood, IL, 1989.

Ibbotson, Roger G., and Rex A. Sinquefield
Stocks, Bonds, Bills, and Inflation: Historical Returns (1926–1978),
Institute of Chartered Financial Analysts, Charlottesville, VA, 1979.

Ibbotson, Roger G., and Rex A. Sinquefield
"Stocks, Bonds, Bills, and Inflation: Year-By-Year Historical Returns (1926–1974),"
The Journal of Business 49, No. 1 (January 1976), pp. 11–47.

Ibbotson, Roger G., and Rex A. Sinquefield
"Stocks, Bonds, Bills, and Inflation: Simulations of the Future (1976–2000),"
The Journal of Business 49, No. 3 (July 1976), pp. 313–338.

**Ibbotson, Roger G., James Xiong, Robert P. Kreitler, Charles F. Kreitler,
and Peng Chen**
"National Savings Rate Guidelines for Individuals,"
Journal of Financial Planning, April 2007, pp. 50–61.

Ibbotson, Roger G., Siegel, Laurence B., and Diermeier, Jeffrey
"The Demand for Capital Market Returns," Financial Analysts Journal,
January/February 1984.

Ibbotson, Roger G.
"How did it happen?," *Wealth Manager Magazine*,
December 1, 2008. pp. 24–29. http://wealthmanagermag.com

Idzorek, Thomas M.
"Commodities and Strategic Asset Allocation," Chapter 6, *Intelligent Commodity Investing*,
Ed. by Till, Hilary and Eagleeye, Joseph. Risk Books, London, 2007.

Idzorek, Thomas M.
"Lifetime Asset Allocations: Methodologies for Target Maturity Funds"
Ibbotson Associates Research Paper, February 11, 2008

Kaplan, Paul D., Thomas Idzorek, Michele Gambera, Katsunari Yamaguchi, James Xiong, and David M. Blanchett.
"The History and Economics of Stock Market Crashes."
In Siegel, Laurence B., ed., Insights into the Global Financial Crisis, CFA Institute, Charlottesville, Va. 2009.

Levy, Haim, and Deborah Gunthorpe
"Optimal Investment Proportions in Senior Securities and Equities Under Alternative Holding Periods," *Journal of Portfolio Management*, Summer 1993, page 33.

Lewis, Alan L., Sheen T. Kassouf, R. Dennis Brehm, and Jack Johnston
"The Ibbotson-Sinquefield Simulation Made Easy,"
The Journal of Business 53, No. 2 (1980), pp. 205–214.

Markowitz, Harry M.
Portfolio Selection: Efficient Diversification of Investments,
John Wiley & Sons, New York, 1959.

Pierce, Phyllis, ed. 1982.
The Dow Jones Averages 1885-1980. Dow Jones Irwin, Homewood, IL

Poundstone, William
Fortune's Formula, Hill and Wang, 2005.

Savage, Sam
The Flaw of Averages, John Wiley & Sons, 2009.

Sharpe, William F.
"The Arithmetic of Active Management,"
Financial Analysts Journal, January/February 1991.

Sheikh, Abdullah Z. and Hongtao Qiao,
"Non-normality of Market Returns," J.P. Morgan Asset Management research paper, 2009.

Stevens, Dale H., Ronald J. Surz, and Mark E. Wimer
"The Importance of Investment Policy," *The Journal of Investing*, Winter 1999.

Xiong, James X, Ibbotson, Roger G., Idzorek, Thomas and Chen, Peng
"The Equal Importance of Asset Allocation and Active Management,"
Financial Analysts Journal, March/April, 2010.

Chapters

Chapter 1
Highlights of the 2011 Markets and the Past Decade

Events of 2011

A whirlwind of events shaped 2011, and these events triggered significant price volatility in the capital markets, from commodities and currencies to equities and bonds. The ebbs and flows of the global debt crisis, coupled with numerous uprisings in the Middle East and elsewhere brought much of this volatility. Dramatic austerity measures were taken by many European countries in an effort to turn the corner and get the eurozone back on track. Through this turbulence, the U.S. dollar was one of the more stable currencies. Total return on long-term corporate bonds, long-term government bonds, and intermediate government bonds were the clear victors over the S&P 500 and small-company stocks. There were bright spots, however, across the spectrum of sectors, such as utility, consumer defense, and healthcare. The Fed's Operation Twist and its buyback of bonds was a continued effort to keep U.S. interest rates low for the foreseeable future in an attempt to spur economic growth.

Unlike 2010, when the S&P 500 rallied 15.06 percent during a very difficult year globally, 2011 was a different story. The S&P 500 produced only a 2.11 percent total return in large part because of the perceived economic slowdown associated with these many global challenges. There are fears that Europe will hit a recession and that China and India will see continued slowdown in GDP. U.S. job creation has been sputtering along, but the country has not hit the low level of unemployment (9.4 percent in 2010 vs. 8.5 percent in 2011) combined with the high level of GDP growth (3.1 percent in 2010 versus 1.8 percent in 2011) necessary to decrease the U.S. national debt or debt levels on a state and local level. This debt will be concern well into 2012 and beyond.

Economic Overview[1]

The U.S. economy grew in 2011, but at a slower rate than many had hoped when the year began. The predicted 3.0 to 4.0 percent inflation-adjusted GDP growth for 2011 turned out to be a more modest 1.8 percent or so growth rate on a fourth-quarter-to-fourth-quarter basis. Even more surpris-

ing than the overall growth rate was the pattern of that growth rate throughout the year. Growth plunged to 0.4 percent in the first quarter and accelerated throughout the year, with the fourth quarter now likely to produce annualized growth of around of 3 percent.

A combination of poor weather, a shocking jump in oil and gas prices resulting from political unrest in the Middle East, and supply-chain disruptions related to the Japanese tsunami all contributed to the pitiful level of economic growth in the first half. As those factors reversed themselves in the second half, economic growth spiked. When the first half and second half are combined, the 1.8 percent overall growth rate seems to be more representative of the state of the U.S. economy than the first-half doldrums or the second-half spurt. Although the overall GDP for 2011 was below many forecasts, given all the first-half shocks followed by more severe sovereign debt issues in the second half, Morningstar economists are not that disappointed with the U.S. economic performance. Morningstar's experts may have started the year too bullish, but they didn't cave into the chorus of economists who were overly focused on manufacturing data and calling for another recession late this summer. Instead, they remained focused on the U.S. consumer, who continued to power ahead through 2011.

Real GDP

Real GDP for 2011 grew by an estimated 1.8 percent after surging 3.1 percent in 2010 and a basically flat performance in 2009. GDP growth could accelerate to between 2.0 percent and 2.5 percent in 2012, driven by a stronger consumer spending and improved construction sectors, both residential and commercial. Inventories and exports, the two big pluses so far in the recovery, are likely to be less influential in 2012.

Unemployment

The unemployment rate decreased to an estimated 8.5 percent at the end of 2011 from 9.4 percent in December 2010 and 9.9 percent at the end of 2009. A strong 2011 holiday season, improving employment growth at the end of 2011, and sharply falling initial claims for unemployment all point to job growth of 180,000 new private-sector jobs in 2012. This job growth rate, combined with a modestly lower participation rate, could drive unemployment to near 8 percent by late 2012.

Consumer Price Index

The CPI increased by 1.4 percent from December 2009 to December 2010 but leapt to 3 percent at the end of 2011, nearly killing the economic recovery. The good news is that the rate has fallen dramatically at the end of 2011, and the commodity bubble appears to have lost a little bit of air. Based on a potential recession in Europe and slowing emerging-markets growth, forecasts imply that inflation will slow to a more modest 2 percent growth rate in 2012, giving the U.S. consumer a little more room to spend. Lower inflation is not a sure thing, though, as producer prices, often a precursor of consumer prices, are still relatively near their peak, and they accelerated to a rate of 4.8 percent in 2011 from 3.8 percent for 2010.

Consumer Spending

Consumer consumption is the absolute key to economic growth, as consumption represents about 70 percent of U.S. GDP. Without decent prospects for consumer spending, businesses aren't going to invest and governments won't generate the tax revenue necessary to continue spending. On the surface, the consumption news in 2011 wasn't particularly good: Growth slipped to an estimated 1.8 percent rate in 2011 compared with a more robust 2.8 percent in 2010. However, a confluence of events, including an auto shortage, unusual weather, and rapidly rising gasoline prices drove consumers into their burrows, and consumption growth stalled out precariously close to zero early in the summer. Thankfully, consumers played catch-up in the last half of the year, as the same factors that hit the first half reversed. However, almost all of that consumption roller coaster was due to auto and fuel purchases. Excluding those categories consumers were on a more even keel than headline consumption figures suggested.

In 2011, consumers have remained cautious, frugal, and exceptionally price sensitive. Categories showing price increases often saw volumes collapse when price jumped and rocket when prices fell. Gasoline, autos, restaurant sales, apparel and even debit cards exhibited this price sensitive behavior in 2011. Given the recent retail sales growth levels, improving auto sales, the need to replace aging consumer goods and improved consumer confidence, it is suspected that consumption will grow 2.0–2.5 percent in 2012, slightly better than the 1.8 percent experienced in 2011.

Consumer Debt and Income

While consumer spending grew in 2011, albeit at a slower rate than 2010, inflation-adjusted disposable incomes fared even worse, registering basically no growth in 2011. So, where did the money come from? It appears that consumers dipped into savings, as the overall savings rate fell from 5.2 percent to 3.6 percent in 2011. While still comfortably above the 1.0 percent reached in 2005, economic growth cannot be sustained for very long on the back of a declining savings rate. For 2012, it is expected that the savings rate will remain basically unchanged, essentially eliminating an important economic tailwind that the U.S. experienced in 2011. Nevertheless, it is hopeful that the U.S. can achieve real personal disposable income growth of 2 percent or so as a result of lower inflation, higher employment growth, and higher Social Security payments. That is roughly in line with projected consumption growth.

While most consumer debts continued to decline in 2011, it is even more impressive that the ratio of all fixed consumer debt related payments continued to fall in 2011. The financial obligations ratio (which compares mortgage, auto, rent, and credit card payments with income) fell to an estimated 16.2 percent in 2011 from 16.7 percent in 2010 and down from its peak of 18.9 percent in 2007. Low mortgage rates, falling mortgage debt and increasing incomes should help this ratio to fall in 2012. In fact, it is suspected that the ratio will drop to a new record low (in 32 years of record keeping, the record low is 15.5 percent) sometime in 2012.

Non-Residential Corporate Investment Spending

Overall, business investment slowed to about 8 percent in 2011, following a more robust 2010 when in investment spending (equipment and software plus non-residential structures) increased almost 12 percent following declines in 2009. Beneath, the overall figure is an accelerating growth rate for business structures and a decline in equipment and software spending. Based on slowing in the overall business spending growth rates toward the end of 2011 and the completion of a lot of projects that were forgone during the recession, it is suspected that business capital spending growth in 2012 will drop into the more typical 6-8 percent range. The business investment category represents just 10 to 12 percent of overall GDP, so it won't be much of swing factor in 2012.

Housing Starts

Housing remains a real laggard in this recovery but at least modestly better news is expected in 2012. In 2011, housing starts moved from 585,000 to 607,000, hardly a move at all considering that starts were running at more than 2 million units per year as recently as 2005. The rate did improve toward the end of 2011, leading Morningstar analysts to believe that starts could increase to the 700,000 to 750,000 level in 2012. Improved housing data should be enough to offset the slowing in business investment and exports that are expected in 2012. Lower rates, higher affordability ratios and better employment levels form the basis of that optimism. Given that the housing market has been operating so far below what population growth would suggest, the potential housing recovery could extend the life of the recovery for several more years, even as other sectors begin to slow.

Government Spending

Combined federal, state, and local government spending comprises almost 20 percent of GDP, but these expenditures are very stable and hardly move the economic needle. Mandatory services, pension obligations, and pure momentum make large across-the-board cuts difficult. However, total spending (federal, state, and local) did decline by about 1.8 percent in 2011, weighing down GDP by about 0.3 percent. While not a huge number, a decline in government spending of any sort is highly unusual. As tax revenue continues to increase, the worst of the spending cuts should be behind us.

Developed Markets Soften

The sovereign debt crisis and various austerity measures meant to solve the problem have contributed to slowing growth rates in most of the developed world. Interestingly, while Europe appears to be falling into a recession and Japan continues to stumble along, growth in the U.S. appears to be accelerating. Fortunately, exports make up just 14% of the U.S. GDP, a relatively low figure compared with the rest of the world. Europe, the weakest of the bunch, accounts for just 3 percent of the U.S. GDP. Therefore, a slowdown there won't necessarily wreck the U.S. recovery. That is, unless the news in Europe become so bad as to bring down the whole financial system, an event that is viewed as unlikely, but still possible.

Emerging-Markets Highlights

Whether it's factory capital equipment or fast food, emerging markets remain important growth areas. Emerging markets boast growth rates that are 2 or 3 times higher than those in developed economies. A growing middle class further cements the opportunity in these markets. However, even a modest slowing of growth rates in China and elsewhere tends to move worldwide markets dramatically. Some of the worst days in the U.S. stock market this year happened when China's hot economy showed signs of slowing. Perhaps a stronger U.S. consumer will take some of the pressure off this fixation on growth in emerging markets.

U.S. Monetary Policy

The Federal Reserve Bank remained active in trying to help jump start the economy in 2011. As short term rates remained near zero, the Fed continued to try to bring down long term rates by the purchase of long term bonds and mortgages. The policy has been successful in bringing down long term rates, especially mortgage rates, which are now below 4%. However, tight lending standards, underwater mortgages, and high unemployment mean that low rates haven't really helped the economy very much. With the Fed's promise to keep rates low through 2013, and with the precarious financial conditions in Europe, it is suspected that interest rates will be little changed in 2012 despite an improving economic outlook for the U.S.

Domestic and International Governmental Change
Domestic | *U.S. Fiscal Deficit Debate*

The 2011 fiscal year budget debate witnessed its fair share of ups and downs. Congress had a strict April 8 deadline to reach an agreement on the budget in order to prevent a government shutdown. One of many major points brought up in this heated debate was the issue of raising the $14.3 trillion debt ceiling, which, at its present spending level, the government was projected to hit in August. Facing the imminent threat of a shutdown, Democrats and Republicans finally reached an agreement that raised the debt limit by $2.1 trillion and cut federal spending by $2.4 trillion just one day before the looming default. On Aug. 5, however, Standard & Poor's decided to cut the U.S. government long-term debt rating one notch from AAA to AA+. S&P claimed that the downgrade was a result of lack of stability and predictability of the U.S. government.

After months of deliberation following the downgrade, the Joint Select Committee on Deficit Reduction, also known as the Supercommittee, failed to reach an agreement on how to reduce the deficit, which might translate into automatic $1.2 trillion cuts beginning in 2013. As the fiscal uncertainty continues, however, both houses of Congress remain divided on the subject of government spending and further deficit reductions.

America Invents Act

After years of heated deliberations and extensive lobbying, the long-awaited America Invents Act patent bill was signed into law by the president in September. The bill aims to streamline the patent application process and reduce the large backlog of patent requests that are pending at the Patent and Trademark Office. The new law is based on the first-to-file system as opposed to the first-to-invent approach. In addition, the bill establishes a nine-month window for a post-grant review process that is designed to challenge new patents for any reason. Critics of the bill argue that the new system will favor large corporations with enough resources to file a bulk of patent requests, which might not necessarily spur the desired innovation.

Unemployment Extension

The year ended with a noteworthy Congressional drama, as both Republican and Democrats struggled to agree on how to extend the payroll tax cut and federal unemployment benefits that were to expire in January. The temporary extension bill found its approval in Senate earlier in December, while the House Republicans tried to push a yearlong action. Eventually both parties decided on a temporary resolution that keeps the payroll tax at 4.2 percent and extends the unemployment insurance to millions of Americans for two additional months. Congress announced that it will deliberate on a yearlong extension in January.

Operation Twist

In September, the Federal Reserve Bank announced a new monetary policy called "Operation Twist." The new program aims to put a downward pressure on long-term interest rates by selling $400 billion of short-term Treasury bonds and buying the same amount of long-term government securities. Operation Twist is another attempt by the central bank to repair the crippled economy just few months after the expiration of the second round

of quantitative easing program in June. The new policy intends to encourage long-term borrowing through affordable mortgages and business loans. As a result, 30-year fixed-rates hit an all-time low of 3.94 percent in October. The program is expected to last until June 2012.

International | *Death of Kim Jong-il*
The news of Kim Jong-il's death surprised the world as the North Korea's supreme leader died from a heart attack while riding on a train on Dec. 16. The "Dear Leader," as he was proclaimed after his father's death in 1994, led the country for more than 15 years. His rule was characterized by lavish lifestyle and ruthless pursuit of nuclear weaponry while many of his citizens starved to death. His youngest son, Kim Jong-un, is expected to take over his father's office. It is uncertain whether this development will bring any major political shifts to the communist nation, as North Korea remains one of the most isolated and secretive regions in the world.

Austerity Measures in Europe

As the European sovereign debt crisis unfolded, many troubled nations decided to implement various fiscal repairs to battle the crisis and ensure future prosperity. In addition to previous austerity packages, Greece decided on saving additional 28 billion euro, or 12 percent of its gross domestic product, over the next three years. The program was approved in June and will consist of cutting public jobs, social spending, and increasing the majority of taxes. Spain also decided to implement strict austerity measures this year by increasing taxes and cutting costs. The country also adopted so-called "Golden Rule," which limits the structural budget deficit to 0.4 percent of GDP. Similarly to Greece and Spain, Italy adopted an additional austerity package this year worth $65 billion over the next two years as the country struggled with its debt. Finally, Portugal approved series of measures that aimed at reducing its debt and budget deficit by increasing taxes on many necessities, such as electricity and gas. Moreover, under the new rules, Portugal's public workers will work an additional 30 minutes per day without extra pay.

Selected Domestic and International Highlights
Domestic | *Occupy Wall Street*
On Sept. 17, a group of about 1,000 people gathered in lower Manhattan to protest rising social inequality in the United States. The protests were aimed at the greed of the financial sector and the richest 1 percent of the population

Few weeks later about 700 people associated with the movement were arrested after blocking the Brooklyn Bridge, giving the protest mass media coverage. This, in turn, sparked a nationwide attention, and manifestations of the movement spread across the country to Washington, D.C., Los Angeles, Boston, Memphis, Minneapolis, and St. Louis, among other cities. As the demonstrations deepened, more people and organizations joined the protest, including celebrities, politicians, and labor unions. On Oct. 15, the protests spread worldwide, triggering Wall Street opposition movements in other parts of America, Asia, and Europe. As of Dec. 12, thousands of people continue to drive the movement and voice their frustrations about the influence of big banks in Washington D.C., and about their role in bringing up the Great Recession.

Death of Steve Jobs
The world was saddened to learn of the passing of Apple, Inc. chief executive officer and ex-chairman, Steve Jobs in October. The creator of the iPod, iPhone, and iPad transformed a private business venture started in his parents' garage into one of the most valuable companies in history. During Jobs' reign, the Apple's stock appreciated by more than 3,000 percent, making him one of the greatest innovators and CEOs of our time. Just few weeks before his death, Jobs resigned from his office and appointed Tim Cook as the new head of the company.

Corporate Scandals
In October, a derivatives trader and a primary broker-dealer MF Global was forced to file for Chapter 11 bankruptcy protection after series of bad bets on Europe resulted in large trading losses. Further investigation reveled that the firm might have misappropriated its clients' funds as $1.2 billion were missing from the books. MF Global's CEO Jon Corzine, a former New Jersey governor and former executive at Goldman Sachs, was asked to testify before Congress in attempt to track down the missing funds and explain the reasons behind the eight largest bankruptcy in U.S. history. As of Dec. 31, the investigation continues.

On the subprime mortgage front, six former executives of Fannie Mae and Freddie Mac, including the two former CEOs Daniel Mudd and Richard Syron, were charged for civil fraud. The Securities and Exchange Commission decided that the former leaders misled the government and the public about their firms' exposure to certain types of loans as well as about the risks of subprime lending.

During the financial crisis both Fannie Mae and Freddie Mac were rescued by the government as the housing bubble burst. It remains uncertain whether former executives will face any criminal charges.

International | *European Sovereign Debt Crisis*
Sovereign debt problems in Europe continued to leave their mark on the stability of global markets as, in addition to already indebted Greece and Ireland, other members of the monetary bloc, such as Portugal, Spain, and Italy, began to show signs of financial distress.

As the crisis deepened, several bailouts were paid out this year, in addition to a number of strict austerity measures that were imposed. In May, Portugal received a 78 billion euro bailout in return for slashing its government spending and selling some of its state assets. Two months later, Greece received the second bailout package—109 billion euros—in order to resolve its solvency issues and prevent further contagion. Then, in October, in order to ensure the availability of future bailout funds, European leaders decided to increase the European Financial Stability Facility vehicle, a fund that was designed to combat sovereign debt issues, to about 1 trillion euros.

In addition, the European financial crisis created a tremendous amount of political uncertainty, as a wave of high-profile resignations hit the region. First, Portugal's prime minister, Jose Socrates, resigned in March after the parliament rejected various austerity measures that he had proposed. In November, fueled by strong urges from the opposition as well as his own government cabinet, Greek prime minister, George Papandreou announced his official resignation. Following the resignation, Lucas Papademos took over as Greece's new interim prime minister. During the same month, the head of Italian government, Silvio Berlusconi, agreed to step aside after losing his parliamentary majority, and Mario Monti was appointed as his successor.

The political chaos and the lack of concise solution to the deep fiscal disorder did not pass unnoticed under the watchful eyes of the rating agencies. In June, Standard & Poor's downgraded Greek debt three notches from B to CCC on increased worries about the default, giving it the world's worst sovereign credit rating. A month later, following the Moody's downgrade, S&P decided to further slash Greece's credit rating to CC. In October, Moody's

Investor Service cut Spain's credit rating by 2 levels down to A1, while the country's unemployment rate exceeded a staggering 21 percent. During the same month, Moody's announced it had downgraded Italian debt to A2 from a previously slashed Aa2 rating. Finally, Fitch Ratings decided in November that it was appropriate to adjust Portugal's credit grade from BB+ to a junk BBB- rating.

Because of this fiscal, political, and financial instability, European bond yields skyrocketed, significantly increasing the troubled European countries' cost of borrowing. Following the Portugal's credit dip into junk territory, yields on two-year bonds reached 17.5 percent, which had not been seen in more than a decade. Four months later, the yields on Greek two-year bonds increased overwhelmingly to 107.16 percent, while Spanish yields more than doubled in just one month, peaking at a modest 5 percent. Finally, following Berlusconi's resignation, Italian 10-year yields soared above the critical 7 percent level, marking a 5.2 percent spread above the German bonds.

Moreover, the lingering debt crisis had a significant impact on the European currency, as Euro Trust ETF fell almost 15 percent after hitting its peak in early May. As in the case of most of the world's major currencies, the euro declined with respect to the U.S. dollar, falling below a crucial 1.300 level in December for first time since January.

Arab Spring

An unexpected wave of revolutionary protests hit the Arab world this year. Many demonstrations resulted in the abolishment of local regimes, marking a major political shift throughout the region. The movement began in December 2010 with the self-immolation of a street merchant in Tunisia, who sacrificed his life to protest social inequality and government corruption. Quickly after his death, a series of riots hit the country before spreading to other Arab nations such as Algeria, Egypt, Libya, Sudan, and Saudi Arabia, among other countries. As the protests and violent battles intensified, Tunisian president Ben Ali decided to step down and fled the country in January. Shortly after his departure, the uprising spread to other North African countries including Algeria, where a copycat suicide sparked a nationwide demonstration.

Following the January developments in Tunisia and Algeria, Egyptians crowded the streets of Cairo to protest rising food prices, government corruption, and high unemployment. The initial nonviolent demonstrations quickly turned

into fierce and often-deadly battles, initiating the so-called "Lotus Revolution." Under growing pressure from the opposition and ceaseless battles throughout the country, President Hosni Mubarak decided to step down on Feb. 11. Armed forces took control over the city and a few months later Mubarak was put on trail and was charged with ordering to kill protesters. In September, however, a new wave of demonstrations hit Cairo as people began to oppose the slow reform and the military rule.

The so-called Arab Spring did not, however, stop in Egypt. In February, civil protests against the government shook Libya's capital, Tripoli. The peaceful uprising was violently suppressed by forces of Libyan leader Muammar Gaddafi. Shortly after establishing a no-fly zone over Libya later in March, NATO decided to attack Gaddafi's crisis-stricken regime, initiating a multinational armed conflict. On Oct. 20, Muammar Gaddafi was captured and killed. Few days later Libya officially declared the nation's libration and Abdul Raheem al-Keeb was picked a new interim prime minister.

Meanwhile, in East Africa, Southern Sudan gained its independence from the Republic of Sudan after a peaceful referendum affirmed the split in January. The poll results were released a month later and showed unanimous agreement for the division, with more than 98 percent of Southern Sudanese people voting in favor of the split.

Finally, a major political and social breakthrough occurred in September, as Saudi women were given the right to vote and run in elections. In an official speech, King Abdullah announced that he refuses to remove women from various social and civic roles and that starting next term, women will be able to run as candidates for the royal advisory council, as well as in municipal elections. The reform marked a new era in the conservative kingdom where women citizens are still not allowed to drive or function on their own without male guardianship.

U.S. Troops Leave Iraq

On Dec. 17, after nearly nine years of deadly combats, the last U.S. troops left Iraq, officially ending the war. Operation Iraqi Freedom, initiated under the administration of George W. Bush in 2003, cost the United States some 4,500 lives along with the estimated total of $800 billion. More than 100,000 Iraqi lives were lost, and about 80 percent of those casualties were reported to be civilians. While many Iraqi citizens rejoiced the occupation-ending withdrawal, the future of the country remains uncertain because of looming political and economic instability. The United States is expected, however, to maintain its presence in the region in the form of diplomats, law enforcement officers, and various economic and agricultural experts.

Natural and Environmental Disasters
Earthquake in Japan
On March 11, a powerful (8.9 magnitude) earthquake and resultant tsunami struck the eastern coast of Japan and devastated some coastal cities. The death toll was reported to have exceeded 15,000 and the economic loss was estimated to be near $300 billion, or 5 percent of Japan's total GDP.

This disaster damaged several nuclear power plants and other nuclear facilities in Japan's Fukushima prefecture, causing a radiation leak and triggering a nuclear crisis. Japan enforced an evacuation zone in a radius of 20 kilometers, or 12.4 miles, from the Fukushima 1 nuclear reactor. This crisis prompted an international debate on nuclear safety and obscured the future of nuclear energy. Many countries have reignited efforts to reexamine the safety at their own nuclear plants, and some countries decided to shut down or temporarily suspended nuclear energy facilities that were in questionable condition.

The earthquake and tsunami caused major factories to be shut down, disrupting imports and exports globally. As such, all major indexes fell in the proceeding weeks. Major reinsurers, such as Munich Re and Swiss Re, felt the strongest hit among all companies, with the former expected to take on $2.1 billion in insured losses and latter $1.2 billion. AIG/Chartis and Hanover Re are also expected to take on losses totaling around $1 billion. In order to rebuild the devastated infrastructure and housing in the affected areas, Japanese government approved two stimulus packages totaling $78 billion and a third $156 billion supplementary budget. The Japanese stock market has declined more than 17 percent this year since the disaster occurred.

Midwest Tornados
Severe weather rocked the plains of the U.S. Midwest this year. Powerful tornadoes hit the states of Tennessee, Wisconsin, Iowa, Illinois, Missouri, and neighboring states. The storms reached their highest magnitude in April and May, when 1,245 tornados were reported during those two months. Joplin, Mo., experienced the greatest wreckage, when on May 22 a deadly tornado took 122 lives and left

more than 750 people wounded. According to witnesses, the winds reached speed of nearly 200 mph, and they destroyed some 2,000 homes, as well as local businesses, schools, and hospitals.

Drought in East Africa
Because of rapid climate changes and lack of adequate humanitarian support, some African countries, including Kenya, Ethiopia, and Somalia, face the most severe famine in more than 60 years. The crisis, which began in July, have claimed lives of tens of thousands of people so far. In addition, there were more than 13 million East African residents at risk of death in December. Young children are especially vulnerable to the famine and the unsanitary living conditions. According to UNICEF, there are 5,500 children under the age of five that die in Africa every day. United Nations requested $2.5 billion in donations, in an appeal that aims to provide humanitarian assistance to the famine-stricken regions, and about 68 percent of the funds have been collected to date.

Flooding in Thailand
The lives of 64 million people were surrounded by chaos as massive flooding inundated more 6 million hectares of land that included Bangkok and neighboring Pathum Thanai province this July. The disaster killed 600 people and caused an estimated $45 billion in property damage. Major hard-drive supply shortages were reported following the flooding—more than 1,000 factories belonging to manufacturing giants such as Western-Digital and Seagate were underwater. The shortages had a tremendous impact on the worldwide data storage devices industry, since Thailand accounts for almost 45 percent of the world's hard-drive production. As a result, prices of some of the electronic component have been seen to temporarily double. In the aftermath of the flooding, Thailand's economic growth is predicted to decrease this year from 3.54 percent to a mere 1.5 percent.

Hurricane Irene
On Aug. 28, a powerful hurricane caused extensive flood and property damage, leaving millions of U.S. residents without power. Some places experienced more than 16 inches of rainfall with winds reaching up to 85 miles per hour. Irene affected majority of the east coast states including North Carolina, New Jersey, and New York. There were more than 150 car crashes attributed to the hurricane, and about 10,000 flights were canceled across the country. The death toll was estimated at 46, making it one

Table 1-1: 2011 Currency Matrix

	USD B.O.Y	USD E.O.Y	AUD B.O.Y	AUD E.O.Y	BRL B.O.Y	BRL E.O.Y	CAD B.O.Y	CAD E.O.Y	CHF B.O.Y	CHF E.O.Y	CNY B.O.Y	CNY E.O.Y	EUR B.O.Y	EUR E.O.Y	GBP B.O.Y	GBP E.O.Y	HKD B.O.Y	HKD E.O.Y	INR B.O.Y	INR E.O.Y	JPY B.O.Y	JPY E.O.Y
1 USD	B.O.Y	E.O.Y	0.98	0.98	1.66	1.86	1.00	1.02	0.94	0.94	6.61	6.29	0.75	0.77	0.64	0.64	7.77	7.77	44.71	53.07	81.12	76.95
% Change	% Change			0.1%		12.0%		2.2%		0.3%		-4.7%		3.4%		0.5%		-0.1%		18.7%		-5.1%
1 AUD	1.02	1.02	B.O.Y	E.O.Y	1.70	1.82	1.02	1.00	0.96	0.92	6.76	6.16	0.76	0.76	0.66	0.63	7.95	7.60	45.75	51.92	83.01	75.29
	-0.1%		% Change		7.1%		-2.3%		-4.1%		-8.9%		-1.1%		-3.9%		-4.4%		13.5%		-9.3%	
1 BRL	0.60	0.54	0.59	0.53	B.O.Y	E.O.Y	0.60	0.55	0.56	0.50	3.98	3.38	0.45	0.42	0.39	0.35	4.68	4.17	26.91	28.51	48.83	41.34
	-10.8%		-10.6%		% Change		-8.8%		-10.5%		-15.0%		-7.7%		-10.3%		-10.8%		5.9%		-15.3%	
1 CAD	1.00	0.98	0.98	0.96	1.66	1.83	B.O.Y	E.O.Y	0.94	0.92	6.62	6.17	0.75	0.76	0.64	0.63	7.79	7.62	44.80	52.04	81.28	75.47
	-2.1%		-2.0%		9.7%		% Change		-1.8%		-6.7%		1.2%		-1.6%		-2.2%		16.2%		-7.1%	
1 CHF	1.07	1.07	1.05	1.04	1.78	1.98	1.07	1.09	B.O.Y	E.O.Y	7.06	6.71	0.80	0.82	0.68	0.69	8.31	8.28	47.80	56.58	86.74	82.04
	-0.3%		-0.2%		11.7%		1.9%		% Change		-5.0%		3.1%		0.2%		-0.4%		18.4%		-5.4%	
1 CNY	0.15	0.16	0.15	0.16	0.25	0.30	0.15	0.16	0.14	0.15	B.O.Y	E.O.Y	0.11	0.12	0.10	0.10	1.18	1.23	6.77	8.43	12.28	12.22
	5.0%		5.1%		17.6%		7.2%		5.3%		% Change		8.5%		5.5%		4.9%		24.6%		-0.4%	
1 EUR	1.34	1.29	1.31	1.27	2.22	2.41	1.34	1.32	1.25	1.21	8.84	8.15	B.O.Y	E.O.Y	0.86	0.83	10.40	10.05	59.83	68.68	108.56	99.60
	-3.3%		-3.2%		8.4%		-1.2%		-3.0%		-7.9%		% Change		-2.8%		-3.4%		14.8%		-8.3%	
1 GBP	1.56	1.55	1.53	1.52	2.59	2.89	1.56	1.58	1.46	1.46	10.32	9.78	1.17	1.20	B.O.Y	E.O.Y	12.14	12.07	69.79	82.44	126.64	119.54
	-0.5%		-0.4%		11.5%		1.7%		-0.2%		-5.2%		2.9%		% Change		-0.6%		18.1%		-5.6%	
1 HKD	0.13	0.13	0.13	0.13	0.21	0.24	0.13	0.13	0.12	0.12	0.85	0.81	0.10	0.10	0.08	0.08	B.O.Y	E.O.Y	5.75	6.83	10.44	9.91
	0.1%		0.2%		12.1%		2.2%		0.4%		-4.7%		3.5%		0.6%		% Change		18.8%		-5.1%	
1 INR	0.02	0.02	0.02	0.02	0.04	0.04	0.02	0.02	0.02	0.02	0.15	0.12	0.02	0.01	0.01	0.01	0.17	0.15	B.O.Y	E.O.Y	1.81	1.45
	-15.8%		-15.6%		-5.6%		-13.9%		-15.5%		-19.7%		-12.9%		-15.3%		-15.8%		% Change		-20.1%	
1 JPY	0.01	0.01	0.01	0.01	0.02	0.02	0.01	0.01	0.01	0.01	0.08	0.08	0.01	0.01	0.01	0.01	0.10	0.10	0.55	0.69	B.O.Y	E.O.Y
	5.4%		5.5%		18.1%		7.7%		5.7%		0.4%		9.0%		5.9%		5.3%		25.1%		% Change	

B.O.Y = Beginning of Year
E.O.Y = End of Year
Source: *Morningstar*

USD = US Dollar
AUD = Australian Dollar
BRL = Brazilian Real
CAD = Canadian Dollar
CHF = Swiss Franc
CNY = Chinese Yuan
EUR = Euro
GBP = British Pound Dollar
HKD = Hong Kong Dollar
INR = Indian Rupee
JPY = Japanese Yen

Table 1-2: 2011 Commodity Price Changes[1]

	Description	Exchange	2010	2011	% Change
Energy	Crude Oil	(NYMEX)	92.2	98.9	7.4%
	Unleaded Gas	(NYMEX)	241.5	265.3	9.9%
	Heating Oil	(NYMEX)	252.4	287.3	13.8%
	Natural Gas	(NYMEX)	4.6	3.3	-28.9%
Metals	*Industrial Metals*				
	Copper	(NYMEX), London	433.9	345.1	-20.5%
	Aluminum	(LME)	2470.0	2048.3	-17.1%
	Nickel	(LME)	24238.6	18734.5	-22.7%
	Precious Metals				
	Gold	(NYMEX), London	1419.7	1572.6	10.8%
	Silver	(NYMEX), London	30.7	28.0	-9.0%
	Platinum	(NYMEX), London	1778.2	1407.1	-20.9%

	Description	Exchange	2010	2011	% Change
Agriculture	*Grains & Softs*				
	Corn	(CBOT)	566.4	632.4	11.6%
	Soybeans	(CBOT)	1321.9	1213.0	-8.2%
	Wheat	(CBOT)	829.5	686.4	-17.2%
	Cocoa	LIFFE	2030.0	1411.4	-30.5%
	Coffee	(ICE)	221.2	231.8	4.8%
	Cotton	(ICE)	103.5	90.7	-12.4%
	Sugar	(ICE)	22.1	22.9	3.7%
	Meat & Livestock [2]				
	Lean Hogs	(CME)	84.6	89.4	5.6%
	Live Cattle	(CME)	109.5	124.8	14.0%
	Feeder Cattle	(CME)	123.6	150.9	22.1%

Source: *Morningstar*. [1] Uses twelve month average strip contracts through 12/31/2012, if available. If not available, the average maximum number of strip contracts in calendar year 2012 were used.
[2] Pork Bellies no longer trade as of July 15, 2011.

of the 30 most-deadly hurricanes in the U.S. history. The insured losses ranged between $2 and $3 billion, while the total damage was predicted to exceed $7 billion.

Earthquakes in Turkey

A series of devastating earthquakes shook eastern Turkey this year, leaving more than 600 dead and destroying, or severely damaging, some 25,000 structures throughout the region. The first, far more powerful, 7.2 magnitude earthquake occurred on Oct. 23, while a milder but still devastating aftershock (5.7 magnitude) followed two weeks later. The economic loss estimates range between $555 million and $2.2 billion. Many countries declared their unconditional financial support, and Saudi Arabia topped the list of donors with a generous $50 million gift.

Global Currencies

Government policies and economic conditions caused mixed results for most currencies in 2011. Table 1-1 shows the 2011 annual price changes of all the major currencies. Althought less than in 2010, Europe's debt crisis continued to raise fears among investors; causing the euro to depreciate against most of the currencies, excluding Brazil's real and India's rupee. In 2011, the rupee has suffered a triple misfortune of a slowing economy, high inflation, and a rapidly depreciating currency. The rupee dropped most significantly against the Japanese yen (20.1 percent) and the Chinese yuan (19.7 percent). Despite record-low interest rates in the U.S., the U.S. dollar was in strong demand versus a year prior. The dollar was up in seven of the ten currencies. However, the dollar did fall against the Hong Kong dollar (0.1 percent), the Chinese yuan (4.7 percent), and the Japanese yen (5.1 percent). The strongest-performing currency was the Japanese yen.

Commodities

Table 1-2 shows that 2011 commodity prices fluctuated substantially over 2010 prices across all major commodity groups. Following the financial crisis of late 2008, commodities were driven ever higher by bouts of substantial monetary debasement, a consistently uncertain global macroeconomic outlook, and the market's search for diversification. Through 2011, however, the asset class has not been nearly so flush. Energy commodities, excluding natural gas, increased by between 7 percent and 14 percent. Metal prices generally decreased significantly, with copper, aluminum, nickel, silver, and platinum falling between 9 percent and 22.7 percent, with gold increasing 10.8 percent because of continued flight to quality. Soybeans,

wheat, cocoa, and cotton felt tremendous downward pressure with those commodities decreasing from negative 8.2 percent to 30.5 percent. Corn, coffee, and sugar saw gains from 3.7 percent to 11.6 percent. Even though pork bellies pasted away and are no longer trading after 50 years, lean hogs, live cattle and feeder cattle performed very well increasing between 5.6 percent and 22.1 percent. The continued growing demand for commodities will play a central role in the tightening of the global food supply.

Table 1-3: Annual Total Returns by Sector

Sector	2009	2010	2011
Utilities	11.76	7.31	18.46
Consumer Defense	15.62	14.46	13.39
Healthcare	20.97	5.11	11.90
Real Estate	29.31	27.40	6.94
Energy	33.97	23.38	5.05
Consumer Cyclical	50.17	30.53	4.06
Communication Services	35.63	23.16	0.64
Technology	61.85	13.39	-0.38
Industrials	24.05	24.16	-0.71
Basic Materials	53.60	24.87	-14.12
Financial Services	14.55	11.81	-16.51

Data from 2009–2011.

Sector Highlights [2]

Below are the opinions and expectations of Morningstar's Equity Research sector teams regarding the highlights of 2011 and the outlook for 2012. These comments are to be used for informational purposes only and should not be construed as advice.

Financial Services

Banking

According to the Morningstar Financial Services Index, the financial services sector was the worst performing sector in the market (dropping over 16% during 2011 versus a flattish return for the S&P 500 Index - See Table 1-3). With gloomy headlines flooding the newswires, negative sentiment will weigh heavily on banking stocks, and the days of lofty valuations are not likely to return soon. In the United States, high-ground names with diversified business models, sound capital bases, and conservative underwriting standards are attractive targets, especially given that new regulations will hinder noninterest revenue. Investors should therefore focus their attention on stocks like Cullen/Frost, Bank of Hawaii, and Wells Fargo.

In addition, capital uncertainty, muted growth, and flat-to-slowly improving credit quality will be the themes driving returns in most of the developed world in coming quarters. Although developing economies face many of the same challenges, economic and credit growth prospects are somewhat brighter, and banks are likely to benefit from that. It is expected that uncertainty in many fronts will continue to depress bank stocks. Moreover, firms' current capital bases and ability to internally generate capital should be the name of the game. As a result, financial institutions with strong balance sheets and robust income statements will outperform in the long term. While some mouth-watering opportunities exist in several regions, investors will probably have to be patient in order to see these names outperform.

Life Insurance

Historically, if investors thought about the life insurance industry at all, they thought of it as a staid, safe business. But the industry's results throughout the financial crisis strongly suggested that this traditional view of the industry was no longer in sync with reality. Fundamentally, the life insurance industry suffers from poor competitive dynamics. That is, insurance, on the whole, is not a wide-moat business. But while the insurance industry is very competitive, life insurers are particularly badly placed. For whole and term life-insurance products, the entire industry uses essentially the same actuarial tables to price life insurance, and it therefore sells a straight commodity product. Any new product innovations, such as annuities, are not much help, as they are essentially just new contract structures that can be replicated by competitors the next day. It is because of the inability to differentiate their product lines that the life insurers' incentive to boost short-term returns through increased leverage and risky investments remains in place and could reassert itself over time. Also, as a result of the nature of the insurance industry, the negative effects of poor decisions made today might not hit a company for some time, which sets the stage for unpredictable shocks.

Asset Management

Asset managers continue to play out much of what expectations have been over the past couple of years, as investors once again fled equities in droves when the global markets turned south during the third quarter and part of the fourth quarter (and even took flight from taxable bonds in the aftermath of the political wrangling over the U.S. debt ceiling that ultimately led Standard & Poor's to downgrade the nation's debt rating). The theme of investors gradually

increasing their risk appetites during stable and expanding markets, while pulling back dramatically during market declines, will probably continue in the near term. As such, the more broadly diversified asset managers that have solid-performing funds across their different asset classes continue to hold the strongest hand, as shocks to any one asset class are likely to be offset by gains elsewhere. Firms that can either provide access to exchange-traded funds or have a fair amount of international business in their portfolios should get an added boost. With that being said, BlackRock, Franklin Resources, and Invesco seem to be the best-positioned asset managers in this environment.

Health Care

This may sound like a broken record, but the return of demand for non-acute health-care services appears to be directly tied to the improvement in the macro environment. A fairly muted economic recovery and stubborn unemployment levels have so far successfully suppressed any sort of pickup in demand for health-care services (particularly against the backdrop of the easy comps of 2010). With a larger portion of total health-care costs borne by patients (because of the sizable number of uninsured individuals and a trend toward greater out-of-pocket costs for commercial insurance plans), demand for health care has become more cyclical than in the past. A significant boost to consumer sentiment and a reduction in unemployment will be seemingly necessary to see a recovery in health-care consumption.

Negative foreign exchange pressures are set to weigh on 2012 Big Pharma earnings. Fourth quarter earnings were largely in-line with expectations, but 2012 guidance came in a little light. A key theme was the negative pressure foreign exchange is expected to have in 2012. The top line headwind will be partially offset by lower operating expenses since some expenses will be matched to the currency of revenue, however, it is still expected to be a net negative to pharma firms in 2012. The pharmaceutical industry is also facing major changes during the next decade. The upcoming patent cliff is the worst the industry has ever encountered, causing firms to cut costs and adapt to leaner infrastructures. Further, the payer dynamics are changing rapidly because of U.S. health-care reform and consolidation in the managed-care and pharmacy benefit manager industries. Offsetting some of these pressures, virtually untapped emerging markets present drug companies an avenue for geographic expansion and robust growth. In response to a more conservative FDA, drug firms are increasingly focusing on diseases with fewer treatment options, shifting away from the traditional primary-care markets and into more specialty disease areas that offer better reimbursement and a less crowded marketplace.

Energy

Troubles in euroland and renewed recession fears in the U.S. led to a sharp sell-off of stocks and commodities, hitting the oil patch particularly hard. However, short-term volatility seems to have clouded the market's view of the longer-term fundamentals that should continue to be the underlying drivers in the energy sector. Moreover, a double-dip recession here and in Europe certainly would reduce developed-market demand for oil, in a reprise of 2008-2009. This would help a market that has been undersupplied since the middle of 2010 come back into balance, suggesting that oil prices could settle into a new, lower equilibrium.

Four factors contributed to the view that higher oil prices are likely over the medium term. First, global crude oil supplies have been struggling throughout 2011. While OPEC production is now back to pre-Libya levels, thanks largely to efforts by Saudi Arabia, it is unclear whether this incremental production represents a short-term surge or something more sustainable. Second, major OPEC producers and Russia require oil prices around $90-$95 per barrel to balance national budgets, suggesting that exporters will again make efforts to defend oil prices in the face of a sustained downturn. Third, emerging-markets demand growth continues to consume greater than 100 percent of incremental supply growth. Fourth, while a "hard landing" in China would be enough to tank oil prices in the short run, it would also result in prices low enough to discourage investment in new production. This would lead to higher oil prices as natural production declines tighten supply in the absence of new investment.

Basic Materials

Agriculture

Agricultural markets remained strong toward the end of 2011. Historically tight supplies have kept crop prices elevated, lending demand and pricing support to crop inputs, especially fertilizers. PotashCorp, Mosaic, Agrium, and CF Industries all posted stellar results in the most recent quarter, as farmers used more fertilizer to boost yields and accepted higher prices upon the backdrop of excellent farmer economics. These dynamics will persist over the near term, as both fertilizer and crop supplies are expected to remain tight. On the crop side, the most recent estimates from the U.S. Department of Agriculture show that excessive heat in the Midwest has damaged yield potential for corn. As a result, production will be lower than expected, and prices are likely to remain elevated. With this year's corn crop not set up to alleviate supply pressure, 2012 could be a record year for planted acreage in the United States.

Metals and Mining

Mounting signs of weakness in the Organization for Economic Co-operation and Development economies seem likely to weigh on metals demand and prices in the near term, putting the onus on China and other emerging economies to support the global demand picture. There are significant doubts about the economy's ability to sustain such heady fixed-asset-investment growth rates for much longer without risking a sharp and wrenching rebalancing of the economy.

Coal

U.S. coal demand is largely stagnant as low natural gas prices steal power generation share. However, the export market is hitting multiyear highs, which should provide a tailwind for U.S. producers. Asian coal prices, especially for metallurgical coal, are currently very attractive. The coal sector stands at a critical inflection point. The tremors coming out of Europe and the slowing U.S. economy have certainly played their part in pushing down equity valuations, but the real battle will be fought in China. There is some mixed data on that front. On one hand, steel production has continued to be quite strong, and the economy is expanding. However, anecdotal evidence suggests that government efforts to curb real estate speculation and tamp down inflation are having some effect. For example, real estate price appreciation and auto sales have slowed. Of course, both are vital end markets for steel and hence metallurgical coal. Throughout the past two years, as metallurgical coal clearly outpaced thermal coal in price and profitability, the idea that metallurgical coal was in an extended secular bull market gained tremendous currency in the industry. Virtually all of the recent coal merger and acquisition activity in North America was predicated on this thesis. Plus, as costs rise and thermal coal prices stagnate, the industry is more reliant on metallurgical profits than ever before.

Technology

Weakness from large firms like Dell and HP are to be expected, given secular headwinds for PCs and ongoing pressure on public-sector budgets. However, even smaller, higher-growth companies with exposure to prominent secular trends, like Cavium, Riverbed, F5, and Juniper, provided a muted outlook relative to previous expectations. Software and services firms have yet to show signs of weakness, with Oracle's reasonably solid results serving as the most salient data point. However, Oracle's overarching strategy of providing complete and differentiated IT solutions, featuring software-plus-hardware components, should contribute to solid new software license growth and gross margin improvement in the hardware business. However, while the performance of the hardware business will remain volatile during the next few quarters, the core software business (which accounts for 68% of revenue) will continue to perform well in the near term.

At this point, it is beginning to feel like the market is experiencing a typical cyclical slowdown in tech—weakness in semiconductor firms and hardware companies first, with software vendors and services firms following later. This near-term uncertainty has created a number of buying opportunities across Morningstar's coverage, and investors should be currently finding the most value among large-cap firms with durable competitive advantages.

Communications Services

Sustainable competitive advantages in telecom are built on the scale and quality of a firm's network infrastructure, the intensity of the competitive environment, financial flexibility, and the regulatory situation. Few firms score well across each of these dimensions, which is why there are few wide-moat firms in the sector. Cable providers are often the best positioned of any firm in a given telecom market.

In the U.S., for example, Comcast has outperformed its cable peers along most penetration measures over the past year. The television business has been particularly impressive, with customer losses consistently improving during this period, something no other operator can claim. Threats to the traditional television business continue to emerge, but Comcast and other video distributors have done a good job of building new platforms to better meet customer demands. Critically, the strength of Comcast's networks remains on display in the Internet access and commercial services businesses, which are expected to drive cable results during the next several years. Comcast has begun investing in content at NBCU, a move that should augment the attractive cable networks segment while providing upside potential for the broadcast business. Comcast's networks provide a powerful competitive advantage that should endure in most of the markets for years to come. In the Internet access business, for example, the firm has added 80% more customers during the past year than AT&T and Verizon combined.

As expected, the iPhone took a massive bite out of AT&T's fourth-quarter earnings. Despite the loss of exclusivity early in 2011, the carrier remains far more beholden to the device than its competitors. A number of other charges, including the T-Mobile breakup fee and pension losses, muddied reported earnings, but the overall view of AT&T is unchanged after the first run through the numbers.

As Comcast claims a larger share of total telecom spending in a given neighborhood, it will be able to increasingly outspend rivals on network maintenance and upgrades while gaining operating cost efficiencies. In addition, Comcast's network should allow it to add capacity to meet customer demand at a far lower cost than the phone companies. Regulatory pressure on the U.S. cable business has also been light, as calls for increased oversight in recent years have met with a swift negative political reaction. The markets that Comcast serves are very mature, though, and rapid growth is unlikely for the firm.

Consumer Cyclical

Even though many of the consumer cyclical firms are still performing well, macro headwinds remain substantial, which leads us to only muster a "cautiously optimistic" outlook. The combination of inflation, selective pricing, and stabilizing (albeit high) unemployment levels should partially offset the risk of weaker pricing and volumes later this year, which provides a measure of confidence. Turning to 2012, lackluster economic growth remains a major concern, yet there are still ways for some firms to increase sales and maintain (or even improve) margins, which are currently sitting at or near peak levels.

Industrials

Orders for long-lasting items produced in the U.S. increased 17% from last year's period and almost 3% from November's revised result. It was the second extremely strong monthly increase after November's 4.3% growth.

Once again, the transportation segment was the outsized gainer, enjoying 42% annual growth in December before seasonal adjustments, driven by a 200% annual increase in nondefense aircraft and parts orders. With the volatile transportation segment stripped out, durable goods actually lost momentum in December, with last month's annual gain of 4.7% down from November's 7.5% and the lowest since December of 2009. The takeaway is that, as long as transportation orders hold up, overall durable goods orders will remain impressive and likely mask a slowing in most of the other durable goods areas.

The HSBC Flash China Manufacturing PMI increased only slightly to 48.8 in January from 48.7 in December, the third consecutive reading below 50. Per the report's authors, the reading suggests further moderation in growth, including likely destocking pressures for manufacturers. Still, the authors believe that the government will ease policy to stabilize growth.

Sales of new homes fell 7.3% from 2010 levels to 307,000 seasonally adjusted annual units in December 2011. More positively, inventories continue to be very low in the new home space, with December's level falling modestly to 157,000 units throughout the U.S., another record low. If and when new home sales pick up, these transactions won't be able to be satiated from existing inventory for long, as there isn't much of it around. As a result, once a turnaround does appear, it may do so with a more impressive volume increase than many expect.

Consumer Defensive

Significant macroeconomic headwinds face consumer defensive companies as the U.S. is poised for a multiyear period of anemic growth. Elevated fears surrounding fiscal austerity measures in Europe and domestically suggest that it will be more difficult for consumer goods firms to accelerate growth at a time when an increased number of consumers may be paring back spending.

Given the risks associated with more cautious consumer spending, and austerity measures likely lasting into 2012, recent market volatility could present investors with an opportunistic entry point for several best-in-class names. Several wide- or narrow-moat names that should offer investors value and relative stability in a volatile market include Anheuser-Busch, Kellogg, and Pepsi. Generally speaking, such companies possess a combination of economies of scale, pricing power to counterbalance a slowdown in volume growth, exposure to emerging markets (particularly China), resources to extend brand reach, and strong dividend growth potential.

Real Estate

Improved operating fundamentals, higher cash dividend payouts, and a brighter transactions market bid up Morningstar's aggregate price/fair-value estimate ratio of real estate stocks to 1.3 in late July. Since that peak, macroeconomic uncertainty and regulatory scrutiny on tenant revenue have taken their toll, dropping the sector to roughly fair value. But the decline has been uneven; inside the sector, there's been a flight to safety toward cyclically defensive property sectors owing to fears of a slowdown in the macro economy. Additionally, investors have favored stocks that bear less dependence on near-term access to capital markets.

Heading into the 2012, the lofty valuations afforded to the property classes in real estate investment trusts that have benefited from recent macroeconomic volatility are concerning. Still, while some sectors—especially those that renew leases on a near-term basis, such as lodging—could see a reversal in operating performance, the fundamental improvements seen in 2011 should hold in the near term. This bodes reasonably well for investors. Industrywide, REITs are currently yielding around 4 percent, and dividend payout as a percentage of funds from operation, in aggregate, is approximately 70 percent, according to NAREIT. The commercial real estate cycle continues to be in the early innings of improvement, and while there could be payout concerns on a granular company-by-company basis, the industry as a whole likely won't suffer rolling dividend cuts across the board.

Utilities

Change comes slowly in the utility industry, but it's about to ramp up. Not since deregulation in the late 1990s has the sector undergone the upheaval expected during the next year. Barring last-minute legal or political meddling, the U.S. Environmental Protection Agency's environmental regulations are set to reshape the sector. Utilities are hustling to position themselves for tightening regulations in 2012, 2014, and likely 2015 covering coal plant emissions, coal waste disposal, and water use.

Graph 1-1: The Decade: Wealth Indexes of Investments in U.S. Stocks, Bonds, Bills, and Inflation
Index (Year-End 2001 = $1.00)

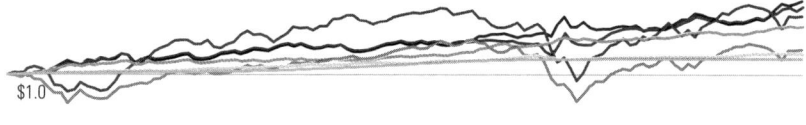

$10.0

$1.0

2001   2002   2003   2004   2005   2006   2007   2008   2009   2010   2011
Year-end

— LT Govt Bonds ($2.35 YE11)   — Large Company Stocks ($1.33 YE11)
— LT Corp Bonds ($2.22 YE11)   ⋯ T-Bills ($1.20 YE11)
— Small Company Stocks ($1.98 YE11)   ⋯ Inflation ($1.28 YE11)
— IT Govt Bonds ($1.76 YE11)

Data from 2001–2011.

Table 1-4: Compound Annual Rates of Return by Decade (%)

	1920s*	1930s	1940s	1950s	1960s	1970s	1980s	1990s	2000s	2011†
Large Company Stocks	19.2%	-0.1%	9.2%	19.4%	7.8%	5.9%	17.6%	18.2%	-0.9%	2.9%
Small Company Stocks	-4.5	1.4	20.7	16.9	15.5	11.5	15.8	15.1	6.3	7.0
LT Corporate Bonds	5.2	6.9	2.7	1.0	1.7	6.2	13.0	8.4	7.6	8.3
LT Government Bonds	5.0	4.9	3.2	-0.1	1.4	5.5	12.6	8.8	7.7	8.9
IT Government Bonds	4.2	4.6	1.8	1.3	3.5	7.0	11.9	7.2	6.2	5.8
Treasury Bills	3.7	0.6	0.4	1.9	3.9	6.3	8.9	4.9	2.8	1.8
Inflation	-1.1	-2.0	5.4	2.2	2.5	7.4	5.1	2.9	2.5	2.5

*Based on the period 1926-1929.
†Based on the period 2002–2011.

In response, utilities already have announced plans to close 32 gigawatts of coal plants, 10 percent of all coal plant capacity in the U.S. More importantly, the closures are concentrated in the eastern half of the U.S., dramatically altering the source and price of power in states that derive a large share of their power from coal plants like West Virginia (97 percent), Kentucky (93 percent), Indiana (90 percent), and Ohio (82 percent). Already utilities have mounted legal appeals, but political momentum in Washington is strong, and it is expected that the rules will hold mostly intact.

Despite these uncertainties, investors continue to flock to utilities. The Morningstar utilities index reached a three-year high ending 2011 at 18.46 percent total return, the best performing sector. Now more than ever, investors must choose their utilities carefully to capture the winners and avoid the losers as the sector changes rapidly.

Results of 2011 Capital Markets
Large Company Stocks

The market for U.S. large company stocks is represented here by the total return on the S&P 500 (the total return includes reinvestment of dividends). Large company stocks for the year produced a total return of 2.11 percent, down from 15.06 percent return of 2010. Six of the twelve months of 2011 produced positive returns. The month of October produced the highest return at 10.93 percent, while the month of September produced the lowest return at -7.03 percent.

An index of large company stock total returns, initialized at $1.00 on December 31, 1925, closed up from the previous year. The index increased to $3,045.22 by the end of 2011, compared with $2,982.24 a year earlier.

Small Company Stocks

Small company stocks produced a total return of negative 3.26 percent in 2011. Seven of the twelve months of 2011 produced negative returns. The month of September produced the lowest return at -10.58 percent, while the month of October produced the highest return at 15.43 percent.

The cumulative wealth index, initialized at $1.00 at the end of 1925, decreased to $15,532.07 at the end of 2011, compared with $16,054.70 at the end of 2010.

Long-Term Corporate Bonds

Long-term corporate bonds (with maturity near 20 years) posted a total return of 17.95 percent in 2011. Total returns were positive in eight of the twelve months during the year with September having the highest return of 5.75 percent, while November had the lowest return of -3.56.

The bond default premium, or net return from investing in long-term corporate bonds rather than long-term government bonds of equal maturity, was -8.02 percent in 2011, compared with 2.08 percent in 2010. One dollar invested in long-term corporate bonds at year-end 1925 rose to $157.32 by the end of 2011, compared with $133.38 at the end of 2010.

Long-Term Government Bonds

Long-term government bonds (with maturity near 20 years) returned 28.23 percent in 2011. This return was significantly higher than the 10.14 percent return seen in 2010 and the long-term average return (1926–2011) of 5.7 percent.

Eight of the months produced positive returns with August having the highest returns at 7.20 percent, and October having the lowest with return of -2.74 percent.

A wealth index of long-term government bonds, initialized at $1.00 at year-end 1925, increased to $119.18 by December 2011. The capital appreciation index of long-term government bond returns closed at $1.39 at year's end, down from $1.12 in 2010. This index reached its all-time high of $1.43 in early 1946.

Intermediate-Term Government Bonds

The total return on intermediate-term government bonds (with maturity near 5 years) in 2011 was 9.46 percent. This return was higher than the 7.12 percent return for 2010. The 2011 return was higher than the long-term average return (1926–2011) of 5.4 percent. Returns were positive for eight months of the year with August having the highest return of 2.17 percent while November had the lowest return of -1.27 percent.

The wealth index of intermediate-term government bonds, initialized at $1.00 at year-end 1925, increased to $92.08 at the end of 2011, up from $84.12 at year-end 2010.

Treasury Bills

An investment in bills with approximately 30 days to maturity returned 0.04 percent in 2011, less than the return in 2010 of 0.12 percent and below the long-term average (1926–2011) of 3.6 percent. The cumulative index of Treasury bill total returns ended the year at $20.56, compared with $20.55 a year earlier. Because monthly Treasury bill returns are nearly always positive, each monthly index value typically sets a new all-time high.

Inflation

Consumer prices increased to 2.96 percent in 2011, after dropping to 1.50 percent in 2010. The result is lower than the long-term historical average (1926–2011) of 3.0 percent. Inflation has remained below 5 percent for 29 of the last 30 years (the exception was the 6.11 percent rate seen in 1990).

A cumulative inflation index, initialized at $1.00 at year-end 1925, finished 2011 at $12.59, up from $12.23 at year-end 2010. That is, a "basket" of consumer goods and services that cost $1.00 in 1925 would cost $12.23 today. The two baskets are not identical, but are intended to be comparable.

A Graphic View of the Decade

Graph 1-1 shows the market results for the past decade—illustrating the growth of $1.00 invested on December 31, 2001 in stocks, bonds, and bills, along with an index of inflation. A review of the major themes of the past decade, as revealed in the capital markets, appears below.

The Decade in Perspective

The great stock and bond market rise of the 1980s and 1990s was one of the most unusual in the history of the capital markets. In terms of the magnitude of the rise, these decades most closely resembled the 1920s and 1950s. These four decades accounted for a majority of the market's cumulative total return over the past 85 years. While the importance of a long-term view of investing is noted consistently in this book and elsewhere, the counterpart of this observation is: To achieve high returns on your investments, you only need to participate in the few periods of truly outstanding returns. The bull markets of 1922 to mid-1929, 1949–1961 (roughly speaking, the Fifties), mid-1982 to mid-1987, and 1991–1999 were such periods. Over the past decade, 2002 to 2011, U.S. large company stocks returned an average 2.9 percent and small company stocks returned an average of 7.0 percent. Large company stocks performed extremely well in 2003 and continued positive returns through 2007, and again from 2009 to 2011. However, 2002 and 2008 posted negative returns, with 2008 being the highest at -37.0 percent. Small company stocks had negative returns in 2002, 2007, and 2008 but returned 60.70 percent in 2003, marking the highest return since 1967's 83.57 percent gain, and the 7th highest from 1926 to 2011.

Table 1-4 compares the returns by decade on all of the basic asset classes covered in this book. It is notable that either large company stocks or small company stocks were the best performing asset class in every full decade except for two (the 1930s and the 2000s).

It is interesting to place the decades of superior performance in historical context. The Twenties were preceded by mediocre returns and high inflation and were followed by the most devastating stock market crash and economic depression in American history. This sequence of events mitigated the impact of the Twenties bull market on investor wealth. Nevertheless, the stock market became a liquid secondary market in the Twenties, rendering that period important for reasons other than return. In contrast, the Fifties were preceded and followed by decades with

Table 1-5: Returns and Indices of Returns on Stocks, Bonds, Bills, and Inflation (%)

2011 Annual, Quarterly, and Monthly Market Results

	Year	Large Company Stocks	Small Company Stocks	Long-Term Corporate Bonds	Long-Term Government Bonds	Intermediate-Term Government Bonds	U.S. Treasury Bills	Inflation
2002-2011 Annual Returns	2002	-22.10	-13.28	16.33	17.84	12.93	1.65	2.38
	2003	28.68	60.70	5.27	1.45	2.40	1.02	1.88
	2004	10.88	18.39	8.72	8.51	2.25	1.20	3.26
	2005	4.91	5.69	5.87	7.81	1.36	2.98	3.42
	2006	15.79	16.17	3.24	1.19	3.14	4.80	2.54
	2007	5.49	-5.22	2.60	9.88	10.05	4.66	4.08
	2008	-37.00	-36.72	8.78	25.87	13.11	1.60	0.09
	2009	26.46	28.09	3.02	-14.90	-2.40	0.10	2.72
	2010	15.06	31.26	12.44	10.14	7.12	0.12	1.50
	2011	2.11	-3.26	17.95	28.23	9.46	0.04	2.96
2011 Quarterly Returns	I-11	5.92	8.12	-1.15	-0.91	0.04	0.03	1.96
	II-11	0.10	-2.43	2.82	4.26	3.89	0.01	1.01
	III-11	-13.87	-20.76	13.40	20.56	3.85	0.01	0.52
	IV-11	11.82	15.72	2.33	2.95	1.42	0.00	-0.54
2011 Monthly Returns	12-10	6.68	8.19	-0.36	-3.88	-1.71	0.01	0.17
	01-11	2.37	-1.09	-1.98	-1.96	0.62	0.01	0.48
	02-11	3.43	5.87	1.57	1.13	-0.53	0.01	0.49
	03-11	0.04	3.25	-0.72	-0.06	-0.05	0.01	0.98
	04-11	2.96	1.68	2.39	1.99	1.54	0.00	0.64
	05-11	-1.13	-1.92	2.57	3.55	1.79	0.00	0.47
	06-11	-1.67	-2.16	-2.10	-1.27	0.51	0.00	-0.11
	07-11	-2.03	-2.69	4.73	5.26	1.89	0.00	0.09
	08-11	-5.43	-8.93	2.40	7.20	2.17	0.01	0.28
	09-11	-7.03	-10.58	5.75	6.84	-0.24	0.00	0.15
	10-11	10.93	15.43	0.94	-2.74	1.67	0.00	-0.21
	11-11	-0.22	-0.60	-3.56	2.53	-1.27	0.00	-0.08
	12-11	1.02	0.86	5.12	3.24	1.04	0.00	-0.25
2002-2011 Annual Indices Year-End 1925=$1.00	2002	1778.910	6816.409	82.480	59.699	59.054	17.480	10.091
	2003	2289.182	10953.943	86.824	60.564	60.469	17.659	10.281
	2004	2538.292	12968.475	94.396	65.717	61.832	17.871	10.616
	2005	2662.972	13706.148	99.937	70.852	62.674	18.403	10.978
	2006	3083.570	15922.427	103.178	71.694	64.643	19.287	11.257
	2007	3252.980	15091.094	105.858	78.779	71.142	20.186	11.717
	2008	2049.448	9548.943	115.154	99.161	80.466	20.509	11.728
	2009	2591.824	12230.866	118.628	84.383	78.532	20.529	12.047
	2010	2982.240	16054.698	133.384	92.942	84.121	20.553	12.227
	2011	3045.218	15532.068	157.324	119.183	92.080	20.562	12.589
2011 Monthly Indices	12-10	2982.240	16054.698	133.384	92.942	84.121	20.553	12.227
	01-11	3052.924	15879.702	130.742	91.121	84.645	20.555	12.285
	02-11	3157.514	16811.840	132.801	92.152	84.196	20.557	12.346
	03-11	3158.770	17358.225	131.846	92.095	84.156	20.559	12.466
	04-11	3252.318	17649.843	134.997	93.929	85.453	20.560	12.546
	05-11	3215.504	17310.966	138.468	97.261	86.984	20.560	12.605
	06-11	3161.904	16937.049	135.566	96.022	87.427	20.561	12.592
	07-11	3097.607	16481.443	141.976	101.074	89.080	20.560	12.603
	08-11	2929.340	15009.650	145.378	108.355	91.013	20.562	12.638
	09-11	2723.410	13421.629	153.736	115.765	90.792	20.562	12.657
	10-11	3021.060	15492.586	155.178	112.589	92.305	20.562	12.631
	11-11	3014.384	15399.631	149.657	115.437	91.131	20.562	12.620
	12-11	3045.218	15532.068	157.324	119.183	92.080	20.562	12.589

Graph 1-2: Absolute Performance Comparison of Active Funds Versus Morningstar Indexes: Period Ending Dec. 31, 2011*

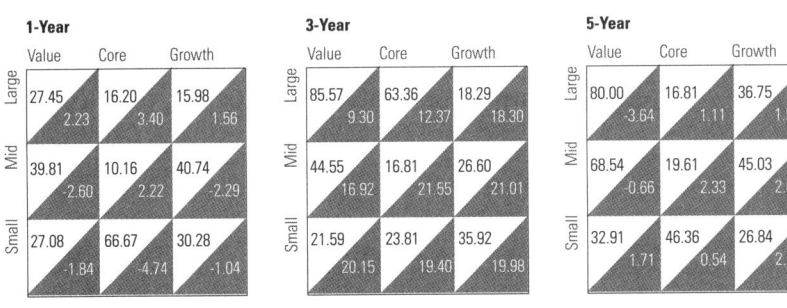

▷ Percent of Active Funds Outperforming Their Respective Morningstar Style Index[1]. ◢ Index Returns (%) as of Dec. 31, 2011.

[1] Includes the oldest share class for all U.S. diversified mutual funds. As of Dec. 31, 2011, there were 2,222 funds Morningstar classified into style categories based on the average style score (using the same 10-factor methodology as underlying benchmarks) of all available portfolio holdings.

roughly average equity returns. The Eighties were preceded by a decade of "stagflation" where modest stock price gains were seriously eroded by inflation and were followed by a period of stability in the Nineties.

The bond market performance of the Eighties and Nineties has no precedent. Bond yields, which had risen consistently since the 1940s, reached unprecedented levels in 1980–1981. (Other countries experiencing massive inflation have had correspondingly high interest rates.) Never before having had so far to fall, bond yields dropped further and faster than at any other time, producing what is indisputably the greatest bond bull market in history. Unfortunately, the boom came to an end in 1994. After falling to 21-year lows one year earlier, bond yields rose in 1994 to their highest level in over three years. Both long-term and intermediate-term government bond yields have generally fallen in the 2000s.

The historical themes of the past decade, as they relate to the capital markets, can be summarized in three observations. First, the 17 1/2 year period starting in mid-1982 and ending in 1999 comprised a rare span of time in which investors quickly accumulated wealth.

Second, the postwar aberration of ever-higher inflation rates ended with a dramatic disinflation in the early Eighties. In the Nineties, inflation was a relatively low 2.9 percent compound annual rate compared to the long term compound annual rate as of the end of that decade (1926–1999), which was 3.1 percent. The trend of relatively low inflation has continued in the 2000s through 2011, with the compound annual rate of 2.5 percent coming in below the long term average (1926–2011) compound annual rate of 3.0 percent.

Finally, participation in the returns of the capital markets since 1982 reached levels not approached in the Twenties, the Fifties, or even in the atypical boom period of 1967–1972. The growth in the importance of pension funds and 401(k)s since 1982, as well as the rapidly increasing popularity of stock and bond mutual funds as a basic savings vehicle have enabled more individuals to experience the returns of the capital markets than ever before.

Table of Market Results for 2002-2011

The 2002–2011 annual and 2011 quarterly and monthly total returns on the six basic asset classes and inflation, as well as cumulative indices of the returns, based on a starting value of $1.00 on December 31, 1925, are presented in Table 1-5. Over the 10 year period ending in 2011, both large and small company stocks have performed below their historical averages. Bonds produced returns that were above their long-term historical averages, while inflation rates fell slightly below their 86-year average.

Morningstar Style Indexes

Over the trailing five years, the odds are about even for an active fund to beat the Morningstar US Market Index or its respective Morningstar Style Index. Moreover, Morningstar Style Indexes have outperformed their active counterparts in eight of the nine domestic styles over the past one-year and seven of the nine domestic styles over the past three-years, as of Dec. 31, 2011. Blend funds are compared to the core indexes in the Morningstar Style Index Family. ▥

Endnotes

[1] Economic Overview: Robert Johnson, Director of Economic Analysis, data as of January 25, 2012

[2] Sector Highlights: Jim Sinegal (Financial Services); Alex Morozov, CFA (Health Care); Jason Stevens (Energy); Elizabeth Collins, CFA (Basic Materials); Grady Burkett (Technology); Michael Hodel, CFA (Communications Materials); Peter Wahlstrom, CFA and R.J. Hottovy, CFA (Consumer Cyclical); R.J. Hottovy, CFA and Erin Lash, CFA (Consumer Defense); Jason Ren (Real Estate); Eric Landry (Industrials); and Travis Miller (Utilities)

Chapter 2
The Long Run Perspective

Motivation

A long view of capital market history, exemplified by the 86-year period (1926–2011) examined here, uncovers the basic relationships between risk and return among the different asset classes including alternative investments and between nominal and real (inflation-adjusted) returns. The goal of this study of asset returns is to provide a period long enough to include most or all of the major types of events that investors have experienced and may experience in the future. Such events include war and peace, growth and decline, bull and bear markets, inflation and deflation, and other less dramatic events that affect asset returns.

By studying the past, one can make inferences about the future. While the actual events that occurred during 1926–2011 will not be repeated, the event-types of that period can be expected to recur. It is sometimes said that only a few periods are unusual, such as the crash of 1929–1932 and World War II. This logic is suspicious because all periods are unusual. Some of the most unusual events of the century—the stock market crash of 1987, the equally remarkable inflation of the 1970s and early 1980s, the more recent events of September 11, 2001, and most recently, the 2008–2009 financial crisis—took place over the last three decades. From the perspective that historical event-types tend to repeat themselves, an 86-year examination of past capital market returns reveals a great deal about what may be expected in the future.

Historical Returns on Stocks, Bonds, Bills, and Inflation

Graph 2-1 depicts the growth of $1.00 invested in large company stocks, small company stocks, long-term government bonds, Treasury bills, and a hypothetical asset returning the inflation rate over the period from the end of 1925 to the end of 2011. All results assume reinvestment of dividends on stocks or coupons on bonds and no taxes. Transaction costs are not included, except in the small stock index starting in 1982.

Each of the cumulative index values is initialized at $1.00 at year-end 1925. The graph vividly illustrates that large company stocks and small company stocks were the big winners over the entire 86-year period: investments of $1.00 in these assets would have grown to $3,045.22 and $15,532.07 respectively, by year-end 2011. This phenomenal

---

Graph 2-1: Wealth Indices of Investments in the U.S. Capital Markets

Index (Year-End 1925 = $1.00)

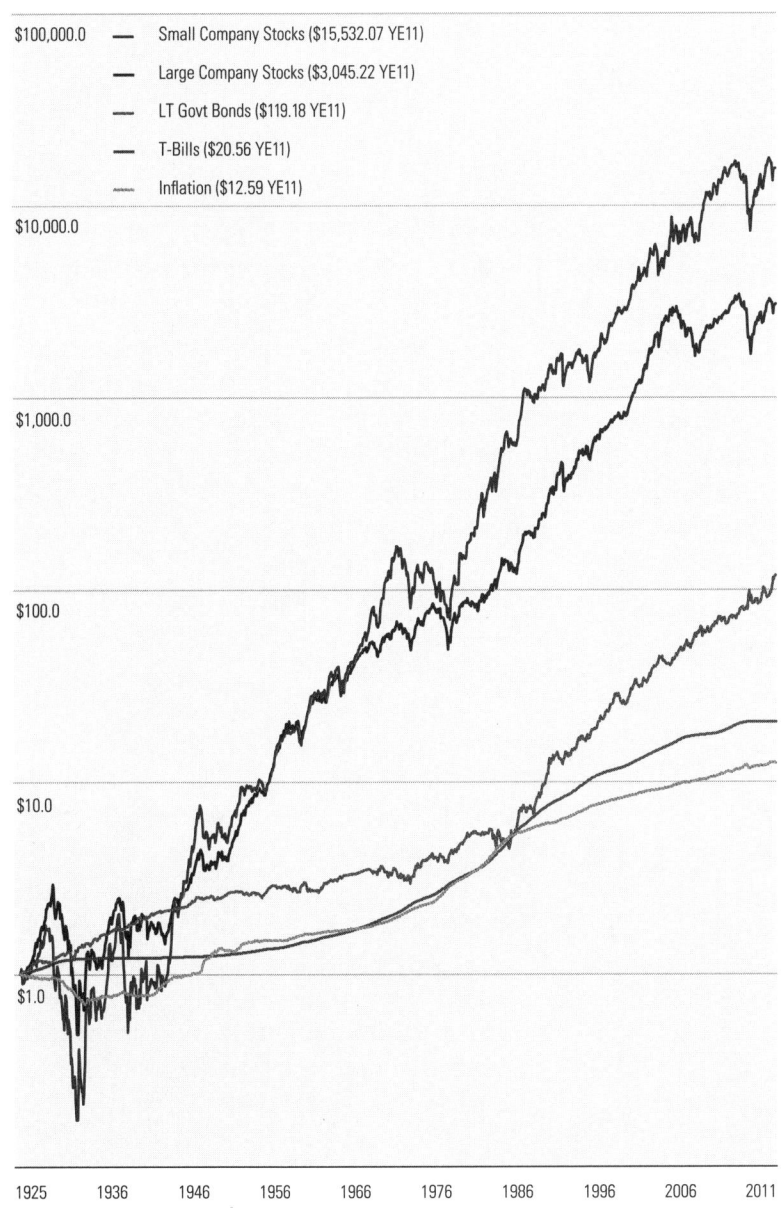

—	Small Company Stocks ($15,532.07 YE11)
—	Large Company Stocks ($3,045.22 YE11)
—	LT Govt Bonds ($119.18 YE11)
—	T-Bills ($20.56 YE11)
⋯	Inflation ($12.59 YE11)

$100,000.0

$10,000.0

$1,000.0

$100.0

$10.0

$1.0

1925　1936　1946　1956　1966　1976　1986　1996　2006　2011

Year-end

Data from 1925–2011.

growth was earned by taking substantial risk. In contrast, long-term government bonds (with an approximate 30-year maturity), which exposed the holder to much less risk, grew to only $119.18.

The lowest-risk strategy over the past 86 years (for those with short-term time horizons) was to buy U.S. Treasury bills. Since Treasury bills tended to track inflation, the resulting real (inflation-adjusted) returns were just above zero for the entire 1926–2011 period.

Logarithmic Scale on the Index Graphs

A logarithmic scale is used on the vertical axis of our index graphs. The date appears on the horizontal axis.

A logarithmic scale allows for the direct comparison of the series' behavior at different points in time. Specifically, the use of a logarithmic scale allows the following interpretation of the data: the same vertical distance, no matter where it is measured on the graph, represents the same percentage change in the series. On the log scale shown below, a 50 percent gain from $10 to $15 occupies the same vertical distance as a 50 percent gain from $100 to $150. On the linear scale, the same percentage gains look different.

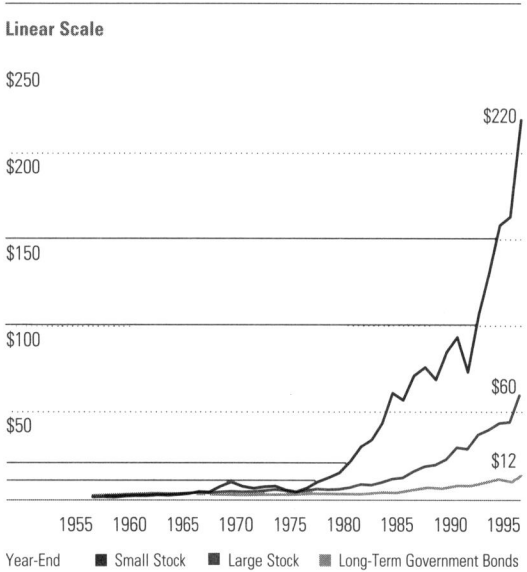

Year-End ■ Small Stock ■ Large Stock ■ Long-Term Government Bonds

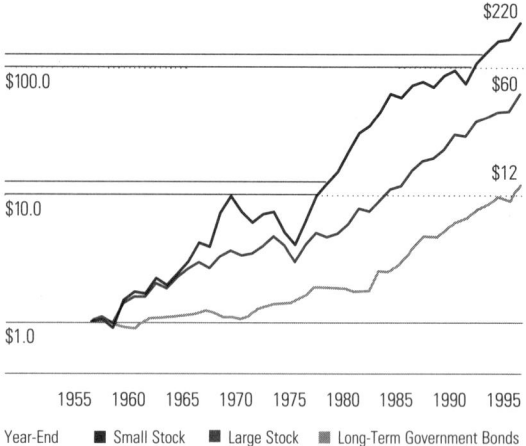

Year-End ■ Small Stock ■ Large Stock ■ Long-Term Government Bonds

A logarithmic scale allows the viewer to compare investment performance across different time periods; thus the viewer can concentrate on rates of return, without worrying about the number of dollars invested at any given time. An additional benefit of the logarithmic scale is the way the scale spreads the action out over time. This allows the viewer to more carefully examine the fluctuations of the individual time series in different periods.

Large Company Stocks

As noted above, an index of S&P 500 total returns, initialized on December 31, 1925, at $1.00, closed 2011 at $3,045.22, a compound annual growth rate of 9.8 percent. The inflation-adjusted S&P 500 total return index closed 2011 at a level of $241.89.

Small Company Stocks

Over the long run, small company stock returns surpassed the S&P 500, with the small company stock total return index ending 2011 at a level of $15,532.07. This represents a compound annual growth rate of 11.9 percent, the highest rate among the asset classes studied here.

Long-Term Corporate Bonds

Long-term corporate bonds outperformed both types of government bonds over the 1926–2011 period with a compound annual growth rate of 6.1 percent. One dollar invested in the long-term corporate bond index at year-end 1925 was worth $157.32 by the end of 2011. This higher return reflected the risk premium that investors require for investing in corporate bonds, which are subject to the risk of default.

Long-Term Government Bonds

The long-term government bond total return index, constructed with an approximate 20-year maturity, closed 2011 at a level of $119.18 (based on year-end 1925 equaling $1.00). Based on the capital appreciation component alone, the $1.00 index closed at $1.39, a 0.4 percent capital gain over the period 1926–2011. This indicates that more than all of the positive historical returns on long-term government bonds were due to income returns. The compound annual total return for long-term government bonds was 5.7 percent.

Intermediate-Term Government Bonds

One dollar invested in intermediate-term bonds at the end of 1925, with coupons reinvested, grew to $92.08 by year-end 2011, compared to $84.12 at year-end 2010. The compound annual total return for intermediate-term government bonds was 5.4 percent. Capital appreciation caused $1.00 to increase to $1.72 over the 86-year period, representing a compound annual growth rate of 0.6 percent.

Treasury Bills

One dollar invested in Treasury bills at the end of 1925 was worth $20.56 by year-end 2011, with a compound annual growth rate of 3.6 percent. Treasury bill returns followed distinct patterns, described on the next page. Moreover, Treasury bills tended to track inflation; therefore, the average annual inflation-adjusted return on Treasury bills (or real riskless rate of return) was only 0.6 percent over the 86-year period. This real return also followed distinct patterns.

Patterns in Treasury Bill Returns

During the late 1920s and early 1930s, Treasury bill returns were just above zero. (These returns were observed during a largely deflationary period.) Beginning in late 1941, the yields on Treasury bills were pegged by the government at low rates while high inflation was experienced.

Treasury bills closely tracked inflation after March 1951, when Treasury bill yields were deregulated in the U.S. Treasury-Federal Reserve Accord. (Treasury bill returns after that date reflect free market rates.) This tracking relationship has weakened since 1973. From about 1974 to 1980, Treasury bill returns were consistently lower than inflation rates. From 1981 to 2008, real returns on Treasury bills have been positive, with the exception of 2002–2005. Real treasury bill returns were also negative in 2009, 2010, and 2011.

Federal Reserve Operating Procedure Changes

The disparity between performance and volatility for the periods prior to and after October 1979 can be attributed to the Federal Reserve's new operating procedures. Prior to this date, the Fed used the federal funds rate as an operating target. Subsequently, the Fed de-emphasized this rate as an operating target and, instead, began to focus on the manipulation of the money supply (through nonborrowed reserves). As a result, the federal funds rate underwent much greater volatility, thereby bringing about greater volatility in Treasury returns.

In the fall of 1982, however, the Federal Reserve again changed the policy procedures regarding its monetary policy. The Fed abandoned its new monetary controls and returned to a strategy of preventing excessive volatility in interest rates. Volatility in Treasury bill returns from the fall of 1979 through the fall of 1982 was significantly greater than that which has occurred since.

Inflation

The compound annual inflation rate over 1926–2011 was 3.0 percent. The inflation index, initiated at $1.00 at year-end 1925, grew to $12.59 by year-end 2011. The entire increase occurred during the postwar period. The years 1926–1933 were marked by deflation; inflation then raised consumer prices to their 1926 levels by the middle of 1945. After a brief postwar spurt of inflation, prices rose slowly over most of the 1950s and 1960s. Then, in the 1970s, inflation reached a pace unprecedented in peacetime, peaking at 13.3 percent in 1979. The 1980s saw a reversion to more moderate, though still substantial, inflation rates averaging about 5 percent. Inflation rates continued to decline in the 1990s with a compound annual rate of 2.9 percent.

Summary Statistics of Total Returns

Table 2-1 presents summary statistics of the annual total returns on each asset class over the entire 86-year period of 1926–2011. The data presented in these exhibits are described in detail in Chapters 3 and 6.

Table 2-1: Basic Series: Summary Statistics of Annual Total Returns

Series	Geometric Mean (%)	Arithmetic Mean (%)	Standard Deviation (%)	Distribution (%)
Large Company Stocks	9.8	11.8	20.3	
Small Company Stocks*	11.9	16.5	32.5	
Long-Term Corporate Bonds	6.1	6.4	8.4	
Long-Term Government Bonds	5.7	6.1	9.8	
Intermediate-Term Government Bonds	5.4	5.5	5.7	
U.S. Treasury Bills	3.6	3.6	3.1	
Inflation	3.0	3.1	4.2	

-90   0   90

Data from 1926–2011. * The 1933 Small Company Stocks Total Return was 142.9 percent.

Note that in Table 2-1, the arithmetic mean returns are always higher than the geometric mean returns. The difference between these two means is related to the standard deviation, or variability, of the series. [See Chapter 6.]

The "skylines" or histograms in Table 2-1 show the frequency distribution of returns on each asset class. The height of the common stock skyline in the range between +10 and +20 percent, for example, shows the number of years in 1926–2011 that large company stocks had a return in that range. The histograms are shown in 5 percent increments to fully display the spectrum of returns as seen over the last 86 years, especially in stocks.

Riskier assets, such as large company stocks and small company stocks, have low, spread-out skylines, reflecting the broad distribution of returns from very poor to very good. Less risky assets, such as bonds, have narrow skylines that resemble a single tall building, indicating the tightness of the distribution around the mean of the series. The histogram for Treasury bills is one-sided, lying almost entirely to the right of the vertical line representing a zero return; that is, Treasury bills rarely experienced negative returns on a yearly basis over the 1926–2011 period. The inflation skyline shows both positive and negative annual rates. Although a few deflationary months and quarters have occurred recently, the last negative annual inflation rate occurred in 1954.

Capital Appreciation, Income, and Reinvestment Returns

Table 2-2 provides further detail on the returns of large company stocks, long-term government bonds, and intermediate-term government bonds. Total annual returns are shown as the sum of three components: capital appreciation returns, income returns, and reinvestment returns. The capital appreciation and income components are explained in Chapter 3. The third component, reinvestment return, reflects monthly income reinvested in the total return index in subsequent months in the year. Thus, for a single month the reinvestment return is zero, but over a longer period of time it is non-zero. Since the returns in Table 2-2 are annual, reinvestment return is relevant.

The annual total return formed by compounding the monthly total returns does not equal the sum of the annual capital appreciation and income components; the difference is reinvestment return. A simple example illustrates this point. In 1995, an "up" year on a total return basis, the total annual return on large company stocks was 37.58 percent. The annual capital appreciation was 34.11 percent and the annual income return was 3.04 percent, totaling 37.15 percent. The remaining 0.43 percent (37.58 percent minus 37.15 percent) of the 1995 total return came from the reinvestment of dividends in the market. For more information on calculating annual total and income returns, see Chapter 5.

Monthly income and capital appreciation returns for large company stocks are presented in Appendix A: Tables A-2 and A-3, respectively. Monthly income and capital appreciation returns are presented for long-term government

Table 2-2: Large Company Stocks, Long-Term Government Bonds, and Intermediate-Term Government Bonds
Annual Total, Income, Capital Appreciation, and Reinvestment Returns (%)

Year	Large Company Stocks				Long-Term Government Bonds					Intermediate-Term Government Bonds				
	Capital Apprec. Return	Income Return	Reinvestment Return	Total Return	Capital Apprec. Return	Income Return	Reinvestment Return	Total Return	Year-end Yield	Capital Apprec. Return	Income Return	Reinvestment Return	Total Return	Year-end Yield
1926	5.72	5.41	0.50	11.62	3.91	3.73	0.13	7.77	3.54	1.51	3.78	0.10	5.38	3.61
1927	30.91	5.71	0.87	37.49	5.40	3.41	0.12	8.93	3.16	0.96	3.49	0.07	4.52	3.40
1928	37.88	4.81	0.91	43.61	-3.12	3.22	0.01	0.10	3.40	-2.73	3.64	0.01	0.92	4.01
1929	-11.91	3.98	-0.49	-8.42	-0.20	3.47	0.15	3.42	3.40	1.77	4.07	0.18	6.01	3.62
1930	-28.48	4.57	-0.98	-24.90	1.28	3.32	0.05	4.66	3.30	3.30	3.30	0.11	6.72	2.91
1931	-47.07	5.35	-1.62	-43.34	-8.46	3.33	-0.17	-5.31	4.07	-5.40	3.16	-0.08	-2.32	4.12
1932	-15.15	6.16	0.80	-8.19	12.94	3.69	0.22	16.84	3.15	5.02	3.63	0.16	8.81	3.04
1933	46.59	6.39	1.01	53.99	-3.14	3.12	-0.05	-0.07	3.36	-0.99	2.83	-0.02	1.83	3.25
1934	-5.94	4.46	0.04	-1.44	6.76	3.18	0.09	10.03	2.93	5.97	2.93	0.09	9.00	2.49
1935	41.37	4.95	1.35	47.67	2.14	2.81	0.03	4.98	2.76	4.94	2.02	0.05	7.01	1.63
1936	27.92	5.36	0.64	33.92	4.64	2.77	0.10	7.52	2.55	1.60	1.44	0.02	3.06	1.29
1937	-38.59	4.66	-1.09	-35.03	-2.48	2.66	0.05	0.23	2.73	0.05	1.48	0.03	1.56	1.14
1938	25.21	4.83	1.07	31.12	2.83	2.64	0.06	5.53	2.52	4.37	1.82	0.04	6.23	1.52
1939	-5.45	4.69	0.35	-0.41	3.48	2.40	0.06	5.94	2.26	3.18	1.31	0.03	4.52	0.98
1940	-15.29	5.36	0.14	-9.78	3.77	2.23	0.09	6.09	1.94	2.04	0.90	0.02	2.96	0.57
1941	-17.86	6.71	-0.44	-11.59	-1.01	1.94	0.00	0.93	2.04	-0.17	0.67	0.00	0.50	0.82
1942	12.43	6.79	1.12	20.34	0.74	2.46	0.02	3.22	2.46	1.17	0.76	0.00	1.94	0.72
1943	19.45	6.24	0.21	25.90	-0.37	2.44	0.02	2.08	2.48	1.23	1.56	0.02	2.81	1.45
1944	13.80	5.48	0.47	19.75	0.32	2.46	0.03	2.81	2.46	0.35	1.44	0.01	1.80	1.40
1945	30.72	4.97	0.74	36.44	8.27	2.34	0.12	10.73	1.99	1.02	1.19	0.01	2.22	1.03
1946	-11.87	4.09	-0.29	-8.07	-2.15	2.04	0.01	-0.10	2.12	-0.08	1.08	0.00	1.00	1.12
1947	0.00	5.49	0.22	5.71	-4.70	2.13	-0.06	-2.62	2.43	-0.30	1.21	0.00	0.91	1.34
1948	-0.65	6.08	0.08	5.50	0.96	2.40	0.04	3.40	2.37	0.27	1.56	0.01	1.85	1.51
1949	10.26	7.50	1.03	18.79	4.15	2.25	0.06	6.45	2.09	0.95	1.36	0.01	2.32	1.23
1950	21.78	8.77	1.16	31.71	-2.06	2.12	0.00	0.06	2.24	-0.69	1.39	0.00	0.70	1.62
1951	16.46	6.91	0.65	24.02	-6.27	2.38	-0.04	-3.93	2.69	-1.63	1.98	0.01	0.36	2.17
1952	11.78	5.93	0.66	18.37	-1.48	2.66	-0.02	1.16	2.79	-0.57	2.19	0.01	1.63	2.35
1953	-6.62	5.46	0.18	-0.99	0.67	2.84	0.12	3.64	2.74	0.61	2.55	0.07	3.23	2.18
1954	45.02	6.21	1.39	52.62	4.35	2.79	0.05	7.19	2.72	1.08	1.60	0.01	2.68	1.72
1955	26.40	4.56	0.60	31.56	-4.07	2.75	0.03	-1.29	2.95	-3.10	2.45	0.00	-0.65	2.80
1956	2.62	3.83	0.11	6.56	-8.46	2.99	-0.12	-5.59	3.45	-3.45	3.05	-0.02	-0.42	3.63
1957	-14.31	3.84	-0.30	-10.78	3.82	3.44	0.20	7.46	3.23	4.05	3.59	0.20	7.84	2.84
1958	38.06	4.38	0.93	43.36	-9.23	3.27	-0.14	-6.09	3.82	-4.17	2.93	-0.05	-1.29	3.81
1959	8.48	3.31	0.16	11.96	-6.20	4.01	-0.07	-2.26	4.47	-4.56	4.18	-0.01	-0.39	4.98
1960	-2.97	3.26	0.19	0.47	9.29	4.26	0.23	13.78	3.80	7.42	4.15	0.19	11.76	3.31
1961	23.13	3.48	0.28	26.89	-2.86	3.83	0.00	0.97	4.15	-1.72	3.54	0.03	1.85	3.84
1962	-11.81	2.98	0.10	-8.73	2.78	4.00	0.11	6.89	3.95	1.73	3.73	0.10	5.56	3.50
1963	18.89	3.61	0.30	22.80	-2.70	3.89	0.02	1.21	4.17	-2.10	3.71	0.03	1.64	4.04
1964	12.97	3.33	0.18	16.48	-0.72	4.15	0.07	3.51	4.23	-0.03	4.00	0.07	4.04	4.03
1965	9.06	3.21	0.18	12.45	-3.45	4.19	-0.04	0.71	4.50	-3.10	4.15	-0.03	1.02	4.90
1966	-13.09	3.11	-0.08	-10.06	-1.06	4.49	0.22	3.65	4.55	-0.41	4.93	0.17	4.69	4.79
1967	20.09	3.64	0.25	23.98	-13.55	4.59	-0.23	-9.18	5.56	-3.85	4.88	-0.02	1.01	5.77
1968	7.66	3.18	0.22	11.06	-5.51	5.50	-0.25	-0.26	5.98	-0.99	5.49	0.03	4.54	5.96
1969	-11.36	2.98	-0.13	-8.50	-10.83	5.95	-0.19	-5.07	6.87	-7.27	6.65	-0.11	-0.74	8.29
1970	0.10	3.33	0.43	3.86	4.84	6.74	0.52	12.11	6.48	8.71	7.49	0.66	16.86	5.90

	Large Company Stocks				Long-Term Government Bonds					Intermediate-Term Government Bonds				
Year	Capital Apprec. Return	Income Return	Reinvest- ment Return	Total Return	Capital Apprec. Return	Income Return	Reinvest- ment Return	Total Return	Year- end Yield	Capital Apprec. Return	Income Return	Reinvest- ment Return	Total Return	Year- end Yield
1971	10.63	3.49	0.18	14.30	6.61	6.32	0.31	13.23	5.97	2.72	5.75	0.25	8.72	5.25
1972	15.79	2.95	0.25	18.99	-0.35	5.87	0.17	5.69	5.99	-0.75	5.75	0.16	5.16	5.85
1973	-17.37	2.86	-0.19	-14.69	-7.70	6.51	0.08	-1.11	7.26	-2.19	6.58	0.22	4.61	6.79
1974	-29.72	3.69	-0.44	-26.47	-3.45	7.27	0.54	4.35	7.60	-1.99	7.24	0.44	5.69	7.12
1975	31.55	5.37	0.31	37.23	0.73	7.99	0.47	9.20	8.05	0.12	7.35	0.36	7.83	7.19
1976	19.15	4.49	0.29	23.93	8.07	7.89	0.80	16.75	7.21	5.25	7.10	0.51	12.87	6.00
1977	-11.50	4.35	0.00	-7.16	-7.86	7.14	0.04	-0.69	8.03	-5.15	6.49	0.06	1.41	7.51
1978	1.06	5.33	0.18	6.57	-9.05	7.90	-0.03	-1.18	8.98	-4.49	7.83	0.14	3.49	8.83
1979	12.31	5.89	0.41	18.61	-9.84	8.86	-0.25	-1.23	10.12	-5.07	9.04	0.12	4.09	10.33
1980	25.77	5.74	0.99	32.50	-14.00	9.97	0.08	-3.95	11.99	-6.81	10.55	0.17	3.91	12.45
1981	-9.73	4.88	-0.08	-4.92	-10.33	11.55	0.64	1.86	13.34	-4.55	12.97	1.03	9.45	13.96
1982	14.76	5.61	1.18	21.55	23.95	13.50	2.91	40.36	10.95	14.23	12.81	2.06	29.10	9.90
1983	17.27	5.04	0.24	22.56	-9.82	10.38	0.09	0.65	11.97	-3.30	10.35	0.35	7.41	11.41
1984	1.40	4.57	0.31	6.27	2.32	11.74	1.42	15.48	11.70	1.22	11.68	1.12	14.02	11.04
1985	26.33	4.72	0.67	31.73	17.84	11.25	1.88	30.97	9.56	9.01	10.29	1.04	20.33	8.55
1986	14.62	3.92	0.13	18.67	14.99	8.98	0.56	24.53	7.89	6.99	7.72	0.43	15.14	6.85
1987	2.03	3.64	-0.41	5.25	-10.69	7.92	0.06	-2.71	9.20	-4.75	7.47	0.19	2.90	8.32
1988	12.40	3.99	0.22	16.61	0.36	8.97	0.34	9.67	9.18	-2.26	8.24	0.13	6.10	9.17
1989	27.25	4.03	0.40	31.69	8.62	8.81	0.68	18.11	8.16	4.34	8.46	0.49	13.29	7.94
1990	-6.56	3.43	0.03	-3.10	-2.61	8.19	0.61	6.18	8.44	1.02	8.15	0.56	9.73	7.70
1991	26.31	3.76	0.40	30.47	10.10	8.22	0.98	19.30	7.30	7.36	7.43	0.67	15.46	5.97
1992	4.46	2.98	0.17	7.62	0.34	7.26	0.45	8.05	7.26	0.64	6.27	0.28	7.19	6.11
1993	7.06	2.91	0.12	10.08	10.71	7.17	0.35	18.24	6.54	5.56	5.53	0.15	11.24	5.22
1994	-1.54	2.83	0.03	1.32	-14.29	6.59	-0.08	-7.77	7.99	-11.14	6.07	-0.08	-5.14	7.80
1995	34.11	3.04	0.43	37.58	23.04	7.60	1.03	31.67	6.03	9.66	6.69	0.45	16.80	5.38
1996	20.26	2.43	0.26	22.96	-7.37	6.18	0.26	-0.93	6.73	-3.90	5.82	0.18	2.10	6.16
1997	31.01	2.10	0.25	33.36	8.51	6.64	0.71	15.85	6.02	1.95	6.14	0.30	8.38	5.73
1998	26.67	1.67	0.24	28.58	6.89	5.83	0.34	13.06	5.42	4.66	5.29	0.25	10.21	4.68
1999	19.53	1.36	0.15	21.04	-14.35	5.57	-0.19	-8.96	6.82	-7.06	5.30	-0.01	-1.77	6.45
2000	-10.14	1.11	-0.07	-9.10	14.36	6.50	0.62	21.48	5.58	5.94	6.19	0.46	12.59	5.07
2001	-13.04	1.18	-0.03	-11.89	-1.89	5.53	0.06	3.70	5.75	3.23	4.27	0.12	7.62	4.42
2002	-23.37	1.39	-0.13	-22.10	11.69	5.59	0.56	17.84	4.84	8.65	3.98	0.30	12.93	2.61
2003	26.38	1.99	0.31	28.68	-3.36	4.80	0.01	1.45	5.11	-0.48	2.85	0.03	2.40	2.97
2004	8.99	1.76	0.13	10.88	3.26	5.02	0.23	8.51	4.84	-1.07	3.28	0.04	2.25	3.47
2005	3.00	1.84	0.07	4.91	3.02	4.69	0.10	7.81	4.61	-2.58	3.92	0.03	1.36	4.34
2006	13.62	2.01	0.17	15.79	-3.64	4.68	0.15	1.19	4.91	-1.51	4.54	0.11	3.14	4.65
2007	3.53	1.96	0.00	5.49	4.69	4.86	0.33	9.88	4.50	5.33	4.44	0.28	10.05	3.28
2008	-38.49	1.92	-0.43	-37.00	20.50	4.45	0.93	25.87	3.03	9.92	2.96	0.23	13.11	1.26
2009	23.45	2.48	0.53	26.46	-18.25	3.47	-0.12	-14.90	4.58	-4.42	2.01	0.00	-2.40	2.42
2010	12.78	2.02	0.26	15.06	5.89	4.25	0.00	10.14	4.14	5.16	1.92	0.04	7.12	1.70
2011	0.00	2.13	-0.01	2.11	23.74	3.81	0.68	28.23	2.48	7.79	1.58	0.09	9.46	0.59

Chapter 2: The Long Run Perspective

bonds in Appendix A: Tables A-7 and A-8; and for inter-mediate-term government bonds in Tables A-11 and A-12.

Annual Total Returns

Table 2-3 shows annual total returns for the six basic asset classes and inflation for the full 86-year time period. This table can be used to compare the performance of each asset class for the same annual period. Monthly total returns for large company stocks, small company stocks, long-term corporate bonds, long-term government bonds, intermediate-term government bonds, Treasury bills, and inflation rates are presented in Appendix A: Tables A-1, A-4, A-5, A-6, A-10, A-14, and A-15, respectively.

Rolling Period Returns

Tables 2-4, 2-5, and 2-6 show the compound annual total returns of the six basic classes and inflation for 5-, 10-, and 20-year holding periods. Often, these calculations are referred to as rolling period returns since they are obtained by rolling a data window of fixed length along each time series. They are useful for examining the behavior of returns for holding periods similar to those actually experienced by investors and show the effects of time diversification. Holding assets for long periods of time has the effect of lowering the risk of experiencing a loss in asset value.

The highest and lowest returns on the SBBI basic series, expressed as annual rates, are shown for 1-, 5-, 10-, and 20-year holding periods in Table 2-7. This exhibit also shows the number of times that an asset had a positive return, and the number of times that an asset's return was the highest among all those studied. The number of times positive (or times highest) is compared to the total number of observations—that is, 86 annual, 82 overlapping 5-year, 77 overlapping 10-year, and 67 overlapping 20-year holding periods.

Portfolio Performance

A portfolio is a group of assets, such as stocks and bonds, that are held by an investor. Because stocks, bonds, and cash generally do not react identically to the same econom-ic or market stimulus, combining these assets can often produce a more appealing risk-and-return tradeoff. By look-ing at Table 2-2, one notices that there are plenty of years in which stock returns were up at times when bond returns were down, and vice versa. These offsetting movements can assist in reducing portfolio volatility. Some recent examples include the years 2000 through 2002. Large com-pany stocks posted negative returns of -9.10, -11.89, and

-22.10 percent, while long-term government bonds posted positive returns of 21.48, 3.70, and 17.84 percent. This illus-trates the low correlation of stocks and bonds; that is, they tend to move independently of each other. (See Chapter 6 for a more detailed discussion of correlation).

While bond prices tend to fluctuate less than stock prices, they are still subject to price movement. By investing in a mix of asset classes such as stocks, bonds, and Treasury bills (cash), an investor may protect their portfolio from major downswings in a single asset class. One of the main advantages of diversification is that it makes investors less dependent on the performance of any single asset class.

Rolling Period Portfolio Returns

While Table 2-7 displays the performance of single asset classes over various rolling periods, Tables 2-8 through 2-11 show the performance of different portfolio alloca-tions over various periods. Once again, the table outlines the number of times that each portfolio has a positive return, and the number of times that each portfolio's return was the highest among all those studied. Maximum and minimum returns are also shown. The portfolios presented throughout the analysis are rebalanced so that the alloca-tions remain the same. The exception to this is Table 2-10, which contains portfolios that never rebalance for com-parison purposes. The data assumes reinvestment of all income and does not account for taxes or transaction costs.

The 1-year holding period results in Table 2-8 make it clear that 1933 was a great year for large com-pany stocks, while long-term government bonds shined in 1982. The 30% stock and 70% bond portfolio was the only portfolio that posted positive returns during all 5-year holding periods, while the 70% stock and 30% bond portfolio was never the highest returning portfolio during the 5-year holding periods. The 10-year holding period analysis shows that the 100% stock/100% bond, the 90% stock/10% bond, and the 100% bond portfolios were the only portfolios that posted negative 10-year hold-ing period returns. For the 20-year period, there were no negative holding period returns. The effects of time diver-sification are clearly evident. When portfolios, as well as individual asset classes, are held for longer periods of time, the possibility of losing portfolio value is lowered.

Table 2-3: Basic Series
Annual Total Returns (%)

Year	Large Comp. Stocks	Small Comp. Stocks	Long-Term Corp. Bonds	Long-Term Govt. Bonds	Inter-Term Govt. Bonds	U.S. Treasury Bills	Inflation	Year	Large Comp. Stocks	Small Comp. Stocks	Long-Term Corp. Bonds	Long-Term Govt. Bonds	Inter-Term Govt. Bonds	U.S. Treasury Bills	Inflation
1926	11.62	0.28	7.37	7.77	5.38	3.27	-1.49	1971	14.30	16.50	11.01	13.23	8.72	4.39	3.36
1927	37.49	22.10	7.44	8.93	4.52	3.12	-2.08	1972	18.99	4.43	7.26	5.69	5.16	3.84	3.41
1928	43.61	39.69	2.84	0.10	0.92	3.56	-0.97	1973	-14.69	-30.90	1.14	-1.11	4.61	6.93	8.80
1929	-8.42	-51.36	3.27	3.42	6.01	4.75	0.20	1974	-26.47	-19.95	-3.06	4.35	5.69	8.00	12.20
1930	-24.90	-38.15	7.98	4.66	6.72	2.41	-6.03	1975	37.23	52.82	14.64	9.20	7.83	5.80	7.01
1931	-43.34	-49.75	-1.85	-5.31	-2.32	1.07	-9.52	1976	23.93	57.38	18.65	16.75	12.87	5.08	4.81
1932	-8.19	-5.39	10.82	16.84	8.81	0.96	-10.30	1977	-7.16	25.38	1.71	-0.69	1.41	5.12	6.77
1933	53.99	142.87	10.38	-0.07	1.83	0.30	0.51	1978	6.57	23.46	-0.07	-1.18	3.49	7.18	9.03
1934	-1.44	24.22	13.84	10.03	9.00	0.16	2.03	1979	18.61	43.46	-4.18	-1.23	4.09	10.38	13.31
1935	47.67	40.19	9.61	4.98	7.01	0.17	2.99	1980	32.50	39.88	-2.76	-3.95	3.91	11.24	12.40
1936	33.92	64.80	6.74	7.52	3.06	0.18	1.21	1981	-4.92	13.88	-1.24	1.86	9.45	14.71	8.94
1937	-35.03	-58.01	2.75	0.23	1.56	0.31	3.10	1982	21.55	28.01	42.56	40.36	29.10	10.54	3.87
1938	31.12	32.80	6.13	5.53	6.23	-0.02	-2.78	1983	22.56	39.67	6.26	0.65	7.41	8.80	3.80
1939	-0.41	0.35	3.97	5.94	4.52	0.02	-0.48	1984	6.27	-6.67	16.86	15.48	14.02	9.85	3.95
1940	-9.78	-5.16	3.39	6.09	2.96	0.00	0.96	1985	31.73	24.66	30.09	30.97	20.33	7.72	3.77
1941	-11.59	-9.00	2.73	0.93	0.50	0.06	9.72	1986	18.67	6.85	19.85	24.53	15.14	6.16	1.13
1942	20.34	44.51	2.60	3.22	1.94	0.27	9.29	1987	5.25	-9.30	-0.27	-2.71	2.90	5.47	4.41
1943	25.90	88.37	2.83	2.08	2.81	0.35	3.16	1988	16.61	22.87	10.70	9.67	6.10	6.35	4.42
1944	19.75	53.72	4.73	2.81	1.80	0.33	2.11	1989	31.69	10.18	16.23	18.11	13.29	8.37	4.65
1945	36.44	73.61	4.08	10.73	2.22	0.33	2.25	1990	-3.10	-21.56	6.78	6.18	9.73	7.81	6.11
1946	-8.07	-11.63	1.72	-0.10	1.00	0.35	18.16	1991	30.47	44.63	19.89	19.30	15.46	5.60	3.06
1947	5.71	0.92	-2.34	-2.62	0.91	0.50	9.01	1992	7.62	23.35	9.39	8.05	7.19	3.51	2.90
1948	5.50	-2.11	4.14	3.40	1.85	0.81	2.71	1993	10.08	20.98	13.19	18.24	11.24	2.90	2.75
1949	18.79	19.75	3.31	6.45	2.32	1.10	-1.80	1994	1.32	3.11	-5.76	-7.77	-5.14	3.90	2.67
1950	31.71	38.75	2.12	0.06	0.70	1.20	5.79	1995	37.58	34.46	27.20	31.67	16.80	5.60	2.54
1951	24.02	7.80	-2.69	-3.93	0.36	1.49	5.87	1996	22.96	17.62	1.40	-0.93	2.10	5.21	3.32
1952	18.37	3.03	3.52	1.16	1.63	1.66	0.88	1997	33.36	22.78	12.95	15.85	8.38	5.26	1.70
1953	-0.99	-6.49	3.41	3.64	3.23	1.82	0.62	1998	28.58	-7.31	10.76	13.06	10.21	4.86	1.61
1954	52.62	60.58	5.39	7.19	2.68	0.86	-0.50	1999	21.04	29.79	-7.45	-8.96	-1.77	4.68	2.68
1955	31.56	20.44	0.48	-1.29	-0.65	1.57	0.37	2000	-9.10	-3.59	12.87	21.48	12.59	5.89	3.39
1956	6.56	4.28	-6.81	-5.59	-0.42	2.46	2.86	2001	-11.89	22.77	10.65	3.70	7.62	3.83	1.55
1957	-10.78	-14.57	8.71	7.46	7.84	3.14	3.02	2002	-22.10	-13.28	16.33	17.84	12.93	1.65	2.38
1958	43.36	64.89	-2.22	-6.09	-1.29	1.54	1.76	2003	28.68	60.70	5.27	1.45	2.40	1.02	1.88
1959	11.96	16.40	-0.97	-2.26	-0.39	2.95	1.50	2004	10.88	18.39	8.72	8.51	2.25	1.20	3.26
1960	0.47	-3.29	9.07	13.78	11.76	2.66	1.48	2005	4.91	5.69	5.87	7.81	1.36	2.98	3.42
1961	26.89	32.09	4.82	0.97	1.85	2.13	0.67	2006	15.79	16.17	3.24	1.19	3.14	4.80	2.54
1962	-8.73	-11.90	7.95	6.89	5.56	2.73	1.22	2007	5.49	-5.22	2.60	9.88	10.05	4.66	4.08
1963	22.80	23.57	2.19	1.21	1.64	3.12	1.65	2008	-37.00	-36.72	8.78	25.87	13.11	1.60	0.09
1964	16.48	23.52	4.77	3.51	4.04	3.54	1.19	2009	26.46	28.09	3.02	-14.90	-2.40	0.10	2.72
1965	12.45	41.75	-0.46	0.71	1.02	3.93	1.92	2010	15.06	31.26	12.44	10.14	7.12	0.12	1.50
1966	-10.06	-7.01	0.20	3.65	4.69	4.76	3.35	2011	2.11	-3.26	17.95	28.23	9.46	0.04	2.96
1967	23.98	83.57	-4.95	-9.18	1.01	4.21	3.04								
1968	11.06	35.97	2.57	-0.26	4.54	5.21	4.72								
1969	-8.50	-25.05	-8.09	-5.07	-0.74	6.58	6.11								
1970	3.86	-17.43	18.37	12.11	16.86	6.52	5.49								

Year	Large Comp. Stocks	Small Comp. Stocks	Long-Term Corp. Bonds	Long-Term Govt. Bonds	Inter-Term Govt. Bonds	U.S. Treasury Bills	Inflation
1926-30	8.68	-12.44	5.76	4.93	4.69	3.42	-2.10
1927-31	-5.10	-23.74	3.87	2.25	3.11	2.98	-3.75
1928-32	-12.47	-27.54	4.52	3.69	3.95	2.54	-5.42
1929-33	-11.24	-19.06	6.01	3.66	4.13	1.89	-5.14
1930-34	-9.93	-2.37	8.09	4.95	4.71	0.98	-4.80
1931-35	3.12	14.99	8.42	5.01	4.77	0.53	-3.04
1932-36	22.47	45.83	10.26	7.71	5.90	0.35	-0.84
1933-37	14.29	23.96	8.60	4.46	4.45	0.22	1.96
1934-38	10.67	9.86	7.75	5.61	5.33	0.16	1.29
1935-39	10.91	5.27	5.81	4.81	4.46	0.13	0.78
1936-40	0.50	-2.64	4.59	5.03	3.65	0.10	0.38
1937-41	-7.51	-13.55	3.79	3.71	3.13	0.08	2.02
1938-42	4.62	10.70	3.76	4.32	3.21	0.07	3.21
1939-43	3.77	18.71	3.10	3.63	2.54	0.14	4.44
1940-44	7.67	29.28	3.25	3.01	2.00	0.20	4.98
1941-45	16.96	45.90	3.39	3.90	1.85	0.27	5.25
1942-46	17.87	45.05	3.19	3.69	1.95	0.33	6.82
1943-47	14.86	35.00	2.17	2.49	1.75	0.37	6.77
1944-48	10.87	18.43	2.43	2.75	1.55	0.47	6.67
1945-49	10.69	12.66	2.15	3.46	1.66	0.62	5.84
1946-50	9.91	7.72	1.76	1.39	1.36	0.79	6.57
1947-51	16.70	12.09	0.87	0.60	1.23	1.02	4.25
1948-52	19.37	12.55	2.05	1.37	1.37	1.25	2.65
1949-53	17.86	11.53	1.91	1.41	1.64	1.45	2.23
1950-54	23.92	18.27	2.31	1.55	1.72	1.41	2.50
1951-55	23.89	14.97	1.98	1.28	1.44	1.48	1.43
1952-56	20.18	14.21	1.10	0.93	1.28	1.67	0.84
1953-57	13.58	10.01	2.10	2.15	2.49	1.97	1.27
1954-58	22.31	23.22	0.96	0.16	1.58	1.91	1.49
1955-59	14.96	15.54	-0.29	-1.67	0.96	2.33	1.90
1956-60	8.92	10.58	1.36	1.16	3.37	2.55	2.12
1957-61	12.79	15.93	3.77	2.53	3.83	2.48	1.68
1958-62	13.31	16.65	3.63	2.42	3.39	2.40	1.33
1959-63	9.85	10.11	4.55	3.97	4.00	2.72	1.30
1960-64	10.73	11.43	5.73	5.17	4.91	2.83	1.24
1961-65	13.25	20.28	3.82	2.63	2.81	3.09	1.33
1962-66	5.72	12.13	2.88	3.17	3.38	3.61	1.86
1963-67	12.39	29.86	0.30	-0.14	2.47	3.91	2.23
1964-68	10.16	32.37	0.37	-0.43	3.04	4.33	2.84
1965-69	4.96	19.78	-2.22	-2.14	2.08	4.93	3.82
1966-70	3.31	7.51	1.23	-0.02	5.10	5.45	4.54
1967-71	8.38	12.47	3.32	1.77	5.90	5.38	4.54
1968-72	7.50	0.47	5.85	4.90	6.75	5.30	4.61
1969-73	1.97	-12.25	5.55	4.72	6.77	5.65	5.41
1970-74	-2.39	-11.09	6.68	6.72	8.11	5.93	6.60
1971-75	3.21	0.56	6.00	6.16	6.39	5.78	6.90
1972-76	4.89	6.80	7.42	6.82	7.19	5.92	7.20
1973-77	-0.19	10.77	6.29	5.50	6.41	6.18	7.89
1974-78	4.35	24.41	6.03	5.48	6.18	6.23	7.94
1975-79	14.82	39.80	5.78	4.33	5.86	6.69	8.15
1976-80	14.02	37.35	2.36	1.68	5.08	7.77	9.21
1977-81	8.13	28.75	-1.33	-1.05	4.44	9.67	10.06
1978-82	14.12	29.28	5.57	6.03	9.60	10.78	9.46
1979-83	17.35	32.51	6.87	6.42	10.42	11.12	8.39
1980-84	14.80	21.59	11.20	9.80	12.45	11.01	6.53
1981-85	14.67	18.82	17.86	16.83	15.80	10.30	4.85
1982-86	19.87	17.32	22.51	21.62	16.98	8.60	3.30
1983-87	16.47	9.51	14.06	13.02	11.79	7.59	3.41
1984-88	15.31	6.74	15.00	14.98	11.52	7.10	3.53
1985-89	20.36	10.34	14.88	15.50	11.38	6.81	3.67
1986-90	13.19	0.58	10.43	10.75	9.34	6.83	4.13
1987-91	15.36	6.86	10.44	9.81	9.40	6.71	4.52
1988-92	15.88	13.63	12.50	12.14	10.30	6.31	4.22
1989-93	14.55	13.28	13.00	13.84	11.35	5.61	3.89
1990-94	8.70	11.79	8.36	8.34	7.46	4.73	3.49
1991-95	16.59	24.51	12.22	13.10	8.81	4.29	2.79
1992-96	15.22	19.47	8.52	8.98	6.17	4.22	2.84
1993-97	20.27	19.35	9.22	10.51	6.40	4.57	2.60
1994-98	24.06	13.16	8.74	9.52	6.20	4.96	2.37
1995-99	28.56	18.49	8.35	9.24	6.95	5.12	2.37
1996-00	18.33	10.87	5.79	7.49	6.17	5.18	2.54
1997-01	10.70	11.82	7.66	8.48	7.29	4.90	2.18
1998-02	-0.59	4.31	8.29	8.85	8.18	4.17	2.32
1999-03	-0.57	16.44	7.20	6.51	6.60	3.40	2.37
2000-04	-2.30	14.32	10.70	10.32	7.46	2.70	2.49
2001-05	0.54	16.44	9.30	7.72	5.22	2.13	2.49
2002-06	6.19	15.16	7.79	7.19	4.33	2.32	2.69
2003-07	12.83	17.23	5.12	5.70	3.79	2.92	3.03
2004-08	-2.19	-2.71	5.81	10.36	5.88	3.04	2.67
2005-09	0.42	-1.16	4.68	5.13	4.90	2.81	2.56
2006-10	2.29	3.21	5.94	5.58	6.06	2.23	2.18
2007-11	-0.25	-0.50	8.80	10.70	7.33	1.29	2.26

Table 2-5: Basic Series
Compound Annual Returns for 10-Year Holding Periods (% per annum)

Year	Large Comp. Stocks	Small Comp. Stocks	Long-Term Corp. Bonds	Long-Term Govt. Bonds	Inter-Term Govt. Bonds	U.S. Treasury Bills	Inflation	Year	Large Comp. Stocks	Small Comp. Stocks	Long-Term Corp. Bonds	Long-Term Govt. Bonds	Inter-Term Govt. Bonds	U.S. Treasury Bills	Inflation
1926-35	5.86	0.34	7.08	4.97	4.73	1.97	-2.57	1971-80	8.48	17.53	4.16	3.90	5.73	6.77	8.05
1927-36	7.81	5.45	7.02	4.95	4.50	1.66	-2.30	1972-81	6.50	17.26	2.95	2.81	5.80	7.78	8.62
1928-37	0.02	-5.22	6.54	4.08	4.20	1.37	-1.80	1973-82	6.72	19.67	5.93	5.76	8.00	8.46	8.67
1929-38	-0.89	-5.70	6.88	4.63	4.73	1.02	-1.98	1974-83	10.66	28.40	6.45	5.95	8.28	8.65	8.16
1930-39	-0.05	1.38	6.95	4.88	4.58	0.55	-2.05	1975-84	14.81	30.38	8.46	7.03	9.11	8.83	7.34
1931-40	1.80	5.81	6.49	5.02	4.21	0.32	-1.34	1976-85	14.34	27.75	9.84	8.99	10.31	9.03	7.01
1932-41	6.43	12.28	6.97	5.69	4.51	0.21	0.58	1977-86	13.85	22.90	9.95	9.70	10.53	9.14	6.63
1933-42	9.35	17.14	6.15	4.39	3.83	0.15	2.59	1978-87	15.29	18.99	9.73	9.47	10.69	9.17	6.39
1934-43	7.17	14.20	5.40	4.62	3.93	0.15	2.85	1979-88	16.33	18.93	10.86	10.62	10.97	9.09	5.93
1935-44	9.28	16.66	4.53	3.91	3.22	0.17	2.86	1980-89	17.55	15.83	13.02	12.62	11.91	8.89	5.09
1936-45	8.42	19.18	3.99	4.46	2.75	0.18	2.79	1981-90	13.93	9.32	14.09	13.75	12.52	8.55	4.49
1937-46	4.41	11.98	3.49	3.70	2.54	0.20	4.39	1982-91	17.59	11.97	16.32	15.56	13.13	7.65	3.91
1938-47	9.62	22.24	2.96	3.40	2.48	0.22	4.97	1983-92	16.17	11.55	13.28	12.58	11.04	6.95	3.81
1939-48	7.26	18.57	2.77	3.19	2.04	0.30	5.55	1984-93	14.93	9.96	14.00	14.41	11.43	6.35	3.71
1940-49	9.17	20.69	2.70	3.24	1.83	0.41	5.41	1985-94	14.38	11.06	11.57	11.86	9.40	5.76	3.58
1941-50	13.38	25.37	2.57	2.64	1.60	0.53	5.91	1986-95	14.88	11.90	11.32	11.92	9.08	5.55	3.46
1942-51	17.28	27.51	2.02	2.13	1.59	0.67	5.53	1987-96	15.29	12.98	9.48	9.39	7.77	5.46	3.68
1943-52	17.09	23.27	2.11	1.93	1.56	0.81	4.69	1988-97	18.05	16.46	10.85	11.32	8.33	5.44	3.41
1944-53	14.31	14.93	2.17	2.08	1.60	0.96	4.43	1989-98	19.21	13.22	10.85	11.66	8.74	5.29	3.12
1945-54	17.12	15.43	2.23	2.51	1.69	1.01	4.16	1990-99	18.21	15.09	8.36	8.79	7.20	4.92	2.93
1946-55	16.69	11.29	1.87	1.33	1.40	1.14	3.96	1991-00	17.46	17.49	8.96	10.26	7.48	4.74	2.66
1947-56	18.43	13.14	0.98	0.76	1.25	1.35	2.53	1992-01	12.94	15.58	8.09	8.73	6.73	4.56	2.51
1948-57	16.44	11.27	2.07	1.76	1.93	1.61	1.96	1993-02	9.34	11.58	8.75	9.67	7.29	4.37	2.46
1949-58	20.06	17.23	1.43	0.79	1.61	1.68	1.86	1994-03	11.07	14.79	7.97	8.01	6.40	4.18	2.37
1950-59	19.35	16.90	1.00	-0.07	1.34	1.87	2.20	1995-04	12.07	16.39	9.52	9.78	7.20	3.90	2.43
1951-60	16.16	12.75	1.67	1.22	2.40	2.01	1.77	1996-05	9.07	13.62	7.53	7.60	5.69	3.64	2.52
1952-61	16.43	15.07	2.43	1.73	2.55	2.08	1.26	1997-06	8.42	13.48	7.72	7.83	5.80	3.60	2.44
1953-62	13.44	13.28	2.86	2.29	2.94	2.19	1.30	1998-07	5.91	10.58	6.69	7.26	5.96	3.54	2.68
1954-63	15.91	16.48	2.74	2.05	2.78	2.31	1.40	1999-08	-1.38	6.44	6.50	8.42	6.24	3.22	2.52
1955-64	12.82	13.47	2.68	1.69	2.92	2.58	1.57	2000-09	-0.95	6.30	7.65	7.69	6.17	2.76	2.52
1956-65	11.06	15.33	2.58	1.89	3.09	2.82	1.73	2001-10	1.41	9.63	7.61	6.64	5.64	2.18	2.34
1957-66	9.20	14.02	3.33	2.85	3.60	3.05	1.77	2002-11	2.92	7.05	8.30	8.93	5.82	1.80	2.48
1958-67	12.85	23.08	1.95	1.13	2.93	3.15	1.78								
1959-68	10.00	20.73	2.44	1.75	3.52	3.52	2.07								
1960-69	7.81	15.53	1.68	1.45	3.48	3.88	2.52								
1961-70	8.16	13.72	2.51	1.30	3.95	4.26	2.92								
1962-71	7.04	12.30	3.10	2.47	4.63	4.49	3.19								
1963-72	9.92	14.22	3.04	2.35	4.59	4.60	3.41								
1964-73	5.99	7.77	2.93	2.11	4.89	4.98	4.12								
1965-74	1.22	3.20	2.13	2.20	5.05	5.43	5.20								
1966-75	3.26	3.98	3.59	3.03	5.74	5.62	5.71								
1967-76	6.62	9.60	5.35	4.26	6.54	5.65	5.86								
1968-77	3.58	5.50	6.07	5.20	6.58	5.74	6.24								
1969-78	3.15	4.48	5.79	5.10	6.47	5.94	6.67								
1970-79	5.87	11.49	6.23	5.52	6.98	6.31	7.37								

Table 2-6: Basic Series

Compound Annual Returns for 20-Year Holding Periods (% per annum)

Year	Large Comp. Stocks	Small Comp. Stocks	Long-Term Corp. Bonds	Long-Term Govt. Bonds	Inter-Term Govt. Bonds	U.S. Treasury Bills	Inflation	Year	Large Comp. Stocks	Small Comp. Stocks	Long-Term Corp. Bonds	Long-Term Govt. Bonds	Inter-Term Govt. Bonds	U.S. Treasury Bills	Inflation
1926-45	7.13	9.36	5.52	4.72	3.73	1.07	0.07	1971-90	11.17	13.35	9.01	8.71	9.08	7.66	6.26
1927-46	6.10	8.67	5.24	4.32	3.51	0.93	0.99	1972-91	11.91	14.58	9.43	9.00	9.40	7.72	6.24
1928-47	4.71	7.64	4.74	3.74	3.33	0.80	1.53	1973-92	11.35	15.54	9.54	9.12	9.51	7.70	6.21
1929-48	3.11	5.74	4.80	3.91	3.38	0.66	1.72	1974-93	12.78	18.82	10.16	10.10	9.85	7.49	5.91
1930-49	4.46	10.61	4.80	4.06	3.20	0.48	1.61	1975-94	14.60	20.33	10.00	9.42	9.25	7.29	5.44
1931-50	7.43	15.17	4.51	3.82	2.90	0.42	2.22	1976-95	14.61	19.57	10.58	10.45	9.69	7.28	5.22
1932-51	11.72	19.65	4.47	3.90	3.04	0.44	3.02	1977-96	14.57	17.84	9.71	9.54	9.14	7.28	5.14
1933-52	13.15	20.16	4.11	3.15	2.69	0.48	3.63	1978-97	16.66	17.71	10.29	10.39	9.51	7.29	4.89
1934-53	10.68	14.56	3.77	3.34	2.76	0.55	3.64	1979-98	17.76	16.04	10.86	11.14	9.85	7.17	4.52
1935-54	13.13	16.04	3.37	3.20	2.45	0.59	3.51	1980-99	17.88	15.46	10.66	10.69	9.53	6.89	4.00
1936-55	12.48	15.17	2.92	2.89	2.07	0.66	3.37	1981-00	15.68	13.33	11.49	11.99	9.97	6.62	3.57
1937-56	11.20	12.56	2.23	2.22	1.90	0.77	3.46	1982-01	15.24	13.76	12.13	12.09	9.88	6.09	3.21
1938-57	12.98	16.63	2.52	2.58	2.20	0.91	3.45	1983-02	12.71	11.57	10.99	11.12	9.15	5.65	3.13
1939-58	13.48	17.90	2.10	1.98	1.83	0.99	3.69	1984-03	12.98	12.35	10.94	11.16	8.89	5.26	3.04
1940-59	14.15	18.78	1.85	1.57	1.58	1.14	3.79	1985-04	13.22	13.69	10.54	10.82	8.30	4.83	3.00
1941-60	14.76	18.89	2.12	1.93	2.00	1.27	3.82	1986-05	11.94	12.76	9.41	9.74	7.37	4.59	2.98
1942-61	16.86	21.13	2.22	1.93	2.07	1.37	3.37	1987-06	11.80	13.23	8.60	8.61	6.78	4.53	3.06
1943-62	15.25	18.17	2.48	2.11	2.25	1.50	2.98	1988-07	11.82	13.48	8.75	9.27	7.14	4.49	3.04
1944-63	15.11	15.70	2.45	2.06	2.19	1.63	2.90	1989-08	8.43	9.78	8.65	10.03	7.48	4.25	2.82
1945-64	14.95	14.44	2.45	2.10	2.30	1.79	2.86	1990-09	8.21	10.61	8.00	8.24	6.69	3.83	2.73
1946-65	13.84	13.29	2.23	1.61	2.24	1.97	2.84	1991-10	9.14	13.49	8.28	8.44	6.56	3.45	2.50
1947-66	13.72	13.58	2.15	1.80	2.42	2.19	2.15	1992-11	7.81	11.23	8.19	8.83	6.27	3.17	2.49
1948-67	14.63	17.03	2.01	1.45	2.43	2.38	1.87								
1949-68	14.92	18.97	1.93	1.26	2.56	2.60	1.96								
1950-69	13.43	16.21	1.34	0.69	2.41	2.87	2.36								
1951-70	12.09	13.23	2.09	1.26	3.17	3.13	2.35								
1952-71	11.64	13.67	2.77	2.10	3.58	3.28	2.22								
1953-72	11.67	13.75	2.95	2.32	3.76	3.39	2.35								
1954-73	10.84	12.04	2.83	2.08	3.83	3.64	2.75								
1955-74	6.86	8.21	2.41	1.94	3.98	4.00	3.37								
1956-75	7.09	9.51	3.08	2.46	4.41	4.21	3.70								
1957-76	7.90	11.78	4.34	3.55	5.06	4.34	3.80								
1958-77	8.12	13.95	3.99	3.15	4.74	4.44	3.98								
1959-78	6.52	12.31	4.10	3.41	4.99	4.72	4.34								
1960-79	6.83	13.49	3.93	3.46	5.22	5.09	4.92								
1961-80	8.32	15.61	3.34	2.59	4.84	5.51	5.46								
1962-81	6.77	14.75	3.03	2.64	5.21	6.12	5.87								
1963-82	8.31	16.92	4.47	4.04	6.28	6.51	6.01								
1964-83	8.30	17.63	4.68	4.01	6.57	6.80	6.12								
1965-84	7.80	16.00	5.25	4.58	7.06	7.12	6.26								
1966-85	8.66	15.25	6.67	5.97	8.00	7.31	6.36								
1967-86	10.18	16.06	7.63	6.94	8.52	7.38	6.24								
1968-87	9.28	12.04	7.88	7.31	8.62	7.44	6.31								
1969-88	9.54	11.47	8.30	7.82	8.70	7.50	6.30								
1970-89	11.56	13.64	9.58	9.01	9.42	7.59	6.22								

Table 2-7: Basic Series

Maximum and Minimum Values of Compound Returns (%) for 1-, 5-, 10-, and 20-Year Holding Periods using data from 1926–2011

Annual Returns	Maximum Value Return and Year(s)		Minimum Value Return and Year(s)		Arithmetic Annualized Average	Times Positive (out of 86 years)	Times Highest Returning Asset
Large Company Stocks	53.99	1933	-43.34	1931	11.77	62	16
Small Company Stocks	142.87	1933	-58.01	1937	16.51	59	38
Long-Term Corporate Bonds	42.56	1982	-8.09	1969	6.26	69	6
Long-Term Government bonds	40.36	1982	-14.90	2009	6.14	64	11
Intermediate-Term Gov't Bonds	29.10	1982	-5.14	1994	5.54	77	3
U.S. Treasury Bills	14.71	1981	-0.02	1938	3.62	85	6
Inflation	18.16	1946	-10.30	1932	3.07	76	6

5-Year Rolling Period Returns	Maximum Value Return and Year(s)		Minimum Value Return and Year(s)		Arithmetic Annualized Average	Times Positive (out of 82 periods)	Times Highest Returning Asset
Large Company Stocks	28.56	1995-99	-12.47	1928-32	9.94	70	23
Small Company Stocks	45.90	1941-45	-27.54	1928-32	13.07	70	43
Long-Term Corporate Bonds	22.51	1982-86	-2.22	1965-69	6.00	79	7
Long-Term Government bonds	21.62	1982-86	-2.14	1965-69	5.63	76	5
Intermediate-Term Gov't Bonds	16.98	1982-86	0.96	1955-59	5.45	82	3
U.S. Treasury Bills	11.12	1979-83	0.07	1938-42	3.70	82	0
Inflation	10.06	1977-81	-5.42	1928-32	3.16	75	1

10-Year Rolling Period Returns	Maximum Value Return and Year(s)		Minimum Value Return and Year(s)		Arithmetic Annualized Average	Times Positive (out of 77 periods)	Times Highest Returning Asset
Large Company Stocks	20.06	1949-58	-1.38	1999-08	10.54	73	20
Small Company Stocks	30.38	1975-84	-5.70	1929-38	13.78	75	44
Long-Term Corporate Bonds	16.32	1982-91	0.98	1947-56	5.98	77	6
Long-Term Government bonds	15.56	1982-91	-0.07	1950-59	5.60	76	3
Intermediate-Term Gov't Bonds	13.13	1982-91	1.25	1947-56	5.48	77	2
U.S. Treasury Bills	9.17	1978-87	0.15	1933-42	3.78	77	1
Inflation	8.67	1973-82	-2.57	1926-35	3.41	71	1

20-Year Rolling Period Returns	Maximum Value Return and Year(s)		Minimum Value Return and Year(s)		Arithmetic Annualized Average	Times Positive (out of 67 periods)	Times Highest Returning Asset
Large Company Stocks	17.88	1980-99	3.11	1929-48	11.25	67	9
Small Company Stocks	21.13	1942-61	5.74	1929-48	14.42	67	57
Long-Term Corporate Bonds	12.13	1982-01	1.34	1950-69	5.79	67	0
Long-Term Government bonds	12.09	1982-01	0.69	1950-69	5.46	67	1
Intermediate-Term Gov't Bonds	9.97	1981-00	1.58	1940-59	5.50	67	0
U.S. Treasury Bills	7.72	1972-91	0.42	1931-50	4.04	67	0
Inflation	6.36	1966-85	0.07	1926-45	3.75	67	0

Table 2-8: Portfolios

Maximum and Minimum Values of Compound Returns (%) for 1-, 5-, 10-, and 20-Year Holding Periods using data from 1926–2011

Annual Returns	Maximum Value Return and Year(s)		Minimum Value Return and Year(s)		Arithmetic Annualized Average	Times Positive (out of 86 years)	Times Highest Returning Port
100% Large Stocks	53.99	1933	-43.34	1931	11.77	62	52
90% Stocks/10% Bonds	49.03	1933	-39.73	1931	11.18	63	0
70% Stocks/30% Bonds	38.68	1933	-32.31	1931	10.01	65	0
50% Stocks/50% Bonds	34.71	1995	-24.70	1931	8.87	67	0
30% Stocks/70% Bonds	34.72	1982	-16.96	1931	7.76	69	0
10% Stocks/90% Bonds	38.48	1982	-11.23	2009	6.67	67	0
100% Long-term Gov't Bonds	40.36	1982	-14.90	2009	6.14	64	34

5-Year Rolling Period Returns	Maximum Value Return and Year(s)		Minimum Value Return and Year(s)		Arithmetic Annualized Average	Times Positive (out of 82 periods)	Times Highest Returning Port
100% Large Stocks	28.56	1995-99	-12.47	1928-32	9.94	70	54
90% Stocks/10% Bonds	26.62	1995-99	-10.31	1928-32	9.66	74	1
70% Stocks/30% Bonds	22.75	1995-99	-6.31	1928-32	8.99	77	0
50% Stocks/50% Bonds	20.99	1982-86	-2.77	1928-32	8.19	77	3
30% Stocks/70% Bonds	21.30	1982-86	0.12	1965-69	7.27	82	2
10% Stocks/90% Bonds	21.53	1982-86	-1.38	1965-69	6.21	79	1
100% Long-term Gov't Bonds	21.62	1982-86	-2.14	1965-69	5.63	76	21

10-Year Rolling Period Returns	Maximum Value Return and Year(s)		Minimum Value Return and Year(s)		Arithmetic Annualized Average	Times Positive (out of 77 periods)	Times Highest Returning Port
100% Large Stocks	20.06	1949-58	-1.38	1999-08	10.64	73	52
90% Stocks/10% Bonds	18.52	1989-98	-0.25	1999-08	10.28	76	3
70% Stocks/30% Bonds	17.31	1982-91	1.74	1965-74	9.46	77	5
50% Stocks/50% Bonds	16.96	1982-91	1.98	1965-74	8.51	77	5
30% Stocks/70% Bonds	16.49	1982-91	2.13	1965-74	7.42	77	1
10% Stocks/90% Bonds	15.90	1982-91	1.81	1950-59	6.21	77	5
100% Long-term Gov't Bonds	15.56	1982-91	-0.07	1950-59	5.56	76	· 6

20-Year Rolling Period Returns	Maximum Value Return and Year(s)		Minimum Value Return and Year(s)		Arithmetic Annualized Average	Times Positive (out of 67 periods)	Times Highest Returning Port
100% Large Stocks	17.88	1980-99	3.11	1929-48	11.25	67	58
90% Stocks/10% Bonds	17.28	1980-99	3.58	1929-48	10.80	67	0
70% Stocks/30% Bonds	16.04	1979-98	4.27	1929-48	9.82	67	4
50% Stocks/50% Bonds	14.75	1979-98	4.60	1929-48	8.71	67	3
30% Stocks/70% Bonds	13.38	1979-98	3.62	1955-74	7.49	67	1
10% Stocks/90% Bonds	12.53	1982-01	1.98	1950-69	6.16	67	0
100% Long-term Gov't Bonds	12.09	1982-01	0.69	1950-69	5.46	67	1

Table 2-9, 2-10, and 2-11: Portfolios: Summary Statistics of Annual Returns
Always Rebalanced, Never Rebalanced, and by Decade

Table 2-9: Summary Statistics of Annual Returns (%)

Portfolio (Always Rebalance)	Geometric Mean	Arithmetic Mean	Standard Deviation
100% Large Company Stocks	9.8	11.8	20.3
90% Stocks/10% Bonds	9.6	11.2	18.3
70% Stocks/30% Bonds	9.0	10.0	14.5
50% Stocks/50% Bonds	8.3	8.9	11.3
30% Stocks/70% Bonds	7.4	7.8	9.3
10% Stocks/90% Bonds	6.3	6.7	9.1
100% Long-Term Gov't. Bonds	5.7	6.1	9.8

Data from 1926–2011.

Table 2-10: Summary Statistics of Annual Returns (%)

Portfolio (Never Rebalanced)	Ending Portfolio Large Company Stocks (% of Portfolio–12/10)	Ending Portfolio Bonds (% of Portfolio–12/10)	Geometric Mean	Arithmetic Mean	Standard Deviation
100% Large Company Stocks	100.0	0.0	9.8	11.8	20.3
90% Stocks/10% Bonds	99.6	0.4	9.6	11.5	19.3
70% Stocks/30% Bonds	98.4	1.6	9.3	10.8	17.5
50% Stocks/50% Bonds	96.3	3.7	8.9	10.1	15.8
30% Stocks/70% Bonds	91.8	8.2	8.4	9.3	14.0
10% Stocks/90% Bonds	74.4	25.6	7.3	7.8	11.1
100% Long-Term Gov't. Bonds	0.0	100.0	5.7	6.1	9.8

Data from 1926–2011.

Table 2-11: Compound Annual Rates of Return by Decade (%)

Portfolio (Always Rebalance)	1920s*	1930s	1940s	1950s	1960s	1970s	1980s	1990s	2000s	2002-11
100% Large Company Stocks	19.2	-0.1	9.2	19.4	7.8	5.9	17.6	18.2	-0.9	2.9
90% Stocks/10% Bonds	18.0	1.0	8.7	17.4	7.2	5.9	17.2	17.3	0.1	3.7
70% Stocks/30% Bonds	15.3	2.8	7.6	13.4	6.1	6.0	16.5	15.5	2.1	5.2
50% Stocks/50% Bonds	12.5	4.1	6.5	9.5	4.8	6.0	15.5	13.6	3.9	6.5
30% Stocks/70% Bonds	9.6	4.8	5.2	5.6	3.5	5.9	14.5	11.7	5.5	7.7
10% Stocks/90% Bonds	6.6	5.0	3.9	1.8	2.1	5.7	13.3	9.8	7.0	8.6
100% Long-Term Gov't. Bonds	5.0	4.9	3.2	-0.1	1.4	5.5	12.6	8.8	7.7	8.9

*Based on the period 1926–1929.

Summary Statistics of Portfolio Total Returns

Table 2-9 presents summary statistics of the annual total returns on each portfolio over the entire 86-year period of 1926 to 2011. The summary statistics presented are geometric mean, arithmetic mean, and standard deviation. As more fixed-income is added to the portfolio, the returns as well as the standard deviations decrease. Moving from a 100% stock portfolio to a 70% stock and 30% bond portfolio decreases the geometric mean by 0.9 percent but also decreases the standard deviation by 5.8 percent. This corresponds to the risk-return tradeoff. Large company stocks have a higher level of risk than long-term government bonds and are rewarded accordingly. One exception to the risk-return tradeoff is the return and standard deviation of the 100% bond portfolio compared to that of the 10% stock and 90% bond portfolio. This obviously defies the risk-return tradeoff and serves as an extreme case highlighting the benefits of diversification.

The portfolio's asset mix originally created by an investor inevitably changes as a result of differing returns among the various asset classes. As a result, the percentage allocated to the different asset classes will change. This change may have a dramatic effect on the risk of the portfolio. Table 2-10 presents summary statistics of the annual total returns of the portfolios that were never rebalanced and presents the new allocations that result. Since stocks have outperformed bonds over the long run, it only makes sense that the proportion allocated to stocks will inevitably grow over time as well. The 50% stock and 50% bond portfolio, after 86 years, turned into a 96.3% stock and 3.7% bond portfolio. The geometric mean slightly decreased from 9.0 percent to 8.9 percent, and the standard deviation also slightly decreased from 15.9 percent to 15.8 percent. Large company stocks are much more volatile than long-term government bonds.

Table 2-11 shows the compound returns by decade for the various portfolios. The 100% stock portfolio was the highest returning portfolio in every full decade except the 1930s, 1970s, and 2000s. The 100% bond portfolio was the top performer through the 2000s and the 2002–2011 period.

Real Estate Investment Trusts

Real estate investment trusts, commonly referred to as REITs, are companies that own and operate, as well as finance, income-generating real estate. To qualify as a REIT, a company is obligated to pay out at least 90 percent of its taxable profit to shareholders on an annual basis. This distribution comes in the form of dividends. By achieving REIT status, the real estate company avoids paying income taxes since it distributes almost all of its taxable income to shareholders. Taxes are paid by the shareholders. REITs were created by the United States Congress in 1960 to allow any investor, big or small, the opportunity to invest in large institutional-grade commercial real estate—pieces of property that may have been unaffordable any other way.

REITs have been an attractive investment vehicle to investors because they have traditionally had a relatively low and declining correlation to stocks and bonds. Though the reasons are not quite clear, this relationship changed after 2002 with REITs becoming increasingly correlated with stocks and bonds, though the overall level of correlation remains fairly low. A low correlation allows for the possibility of increased returns without a corresponding increase in risk. For instance, from 1972 to 2011, a portfolio (rebalanced annually) with a mix of 60% stocks and 40% bonds returned 10.0 percent with a standard deviation of 12.2 percent. If the portfolio is altered to include a 13% mix of REITs, the returns increase to 10.4 percent and the standard deviation decreases to 12.0 percent.

The number of REITs in the United States has grown dramatically in the last several decades; in 1971, there were 34 REITs in existence, but by the end of 2011, there were over 160 REITs. This growth has enabled a broader group of investors to add real estate to their portfolios and enjoy greater liquidity than they would otherwise be able. Graph 2-2 below displays the growth in market cap of REITs in the United States between 1971 and 2011.

Table 2-12: Portfolio Annual Total Returns (%)

Year	100% Large Comp. Stocks	Stocks %/Bonds % 90/10	70/30	50/50	30/70	10/90	100% Long-Term Govt. Bonds
1926	11.62	11.30	10.61	9.87	9.07	8.22	7.77
1927	37.49	34.45	28.49	22.69	17.06	11.60	8.93
1928	43.61	38.74	29.35	20.44	11.98	3.95	0.10
1929	-8.42	-6.76	-3.77	-1.19	0.97	2.71	3.42
1930	-24.90	-22.08	-16.33	-10.46	-4.48	1.59	4.66
1931	-43.34	-39.73	-32.31	-24.70	-16.96	-9.19	-5.31
1932	-8.19	-4.45	2.43	8.28	12.85	15.93	16.84
1933	53.99	49.03	38.68	27.89	16.80	5.56	-0.07
1934	-1.44	-0.13	2.38	4.76	6.99	9.05	10.03
1935	47.67	42.94	33.80	25.06	16.73	8.80	4.98
1936	33.92	31.15	25.69	20.35	15.12	10.02	7.52
1937	-35.03	-31.93	-25.44	-18.58	-11.34	-3.72	0.23
1938	31.12	29.24	24.93	19.99	14.51	8.61	5.53
1939	-0.41	0.65	2.51	4.00	5.09	5.77	5.94
1940	-9.78	-8.04	-4.65	-1.40	1.70	4.66	6.09
1941	-11.59	-10.33	-7.81	-5.30	-2.80	-0.31	0.93
1942	20.34	18.62	15.18	11.75	8.32	4.91	3.22
1943	25.90	23.43	18.54	13.73	9.00	4.37	2.08
1944	19.75	17.98	14.49	11.06	7.71	4.43	2.81
1945	36.44	33.72	28.39	23.18	18.11	13.16	10.73
1946	-8.07	-7.17	-5.42	-3.78	-2.23	-0.78	-0.10
1947	5.71	4.89	3.24	1.58	-0.10	-1.78	-2.62
1948	5.50	5.46	5.26	4.91	4.41	3.77	3.40
1949	18.79	17.55	15.07	12.60	10.13	7.68	6.45
1950	31.71	28.24	21.50	15.04	8.85	2.93	0.06
1951	24.02	20.97	15.05	9.36	3.88	-1.38	-3.93
1952	18.37	16.60	13.10	9.64	6.22	2.83	1.16
1953	-0.99	-0.50	0.47	1.41	2.32	3.21	3.64
1954	52.62	47.50	37.65	28.33	19.51	11.18	7.19
1955	31.56	27.98	21.02	14.32	7.89	1.70	-1.29
1956	6.56	5.42	3.08	0.68	-1.79	-4.31	-5.59
1957	-10.78	-8.99	-5.39	-1.75	1.92	5.61	7.46
1958	43.36	37.57	26.60	16.38	6.89	-1.93	-6.09
1959	11.96	10.49	7.59	4.72	1.90	-0.88	-2.26
1960	0.47	1.83	4.53	7.21	9.86	12.48	13.78
1961	26.89	24.10	18.65	13.38	8.29	3.37	0.97
1962	-8.73	-7.11	-3.90	-0.74	2.37	5.40	6.89
1963	22.80	20.52	16.03	11.66	7.40	3.25	1.21
1964	16.48	15.13	12.46	9.84	7.27	4.75	3.51
1965	12.45	11.26	8.89	6.53	4.19	1.86	0.71
1966	-10.06	-8.72	-6.02	-3.29	-0.53	2.25	3.65
1967	23.98	20.28	13.14	6.36	-0.10	-6.23	-9.18
1968	11.06	9.98	7.79	5.54	3.25	0.92	-0.26
1969	-8.50	-8.08	-7.28	-6.56	-5.91	-5.33	-5.07
1970	3.86	4.78	6.57	8.27	9.87	11.39	12.11
1971	14.3	14.29	14.21	14.04	13.78	13.44	13.23
1972	18.99	17.62	14.90	12.22	9.57	6.97	5.69
1973	-14.69	-13.31	-10.57	-7.83	-5.12	-2.44	-1.11
1974	-26.47	-23.66	-17.87	-11.82	-5.53	1.00	4.35
1975	37.23	34.30	28.51	22.84	17.29	11.86	9.20
1976	23.93	23.28	21.93	20.52	19.06	17.54	16.75
1977	-7.16	-6.50	-5.20	-3.90	-2.61	-1.33	-0.69
1978	6.57	5.86	4.40	2.88	1.30	-0.34	-1.18
1979	18.61	16.52	12.40	8.39	4.47	0.64	-1.23
1980	32.50	28.71	21.19	13.80	6.57	-0.49	-3.95
1981	-4.92	-4.16	-2.69	-1.30	0.02	1.27	1.86
1982	21.55	23.42	27.19	30.95	34.72	38.48	40.36
1983	22.56	20.24	15.68	11.25	6.92	2.71	0.65
1984	6.27	7.26	9.18	11.05	12.87	14.62	15.48
1985	31.73	31.72	31.65	31.53	31.35	31.11	30.97
1986	18.67	19.34	20.64	21.86	23.00	24.04	24.53
1987	5.25	5.07	4.24	2.83	0.93	-1.40	-2.71
1988	16.61	15.92	14.55	13.16	11.77	10.37	9.67
1989	31.69	30.37	27.70	25.00	22.26	19.50	18.11
1990	-3.10	-2.15	-0.26	1.61	3.46	5.28	6.18
1991	30.47	29.41	27.24	25.03	22.77	20.47	19.30
1992	7.62	7.69	7.81	7.91	7.98	8.04	8.05
1993	10.08	10.90	12.53	14.16	15.80	17.43	18.24
1994	1.32	0.40	-1.42	-3.25	-5.06	-6.87	-7.77
1995	37.58	37.02	35.88	34.71	33.51	32.29	31.67
1996	22.96	20.41	15.41	10.56	5.85	1.29	-0.93
1997	33.36	31.59	28.06	24.55	21.05	17.58	15.85
1998	28.58	27.33	24.60	21.59	18.33	14.86	13.06
1999	21.04	17.75	11.36	5.23	-0.63	-6.25	-8.96
2000	-9.10	-6.30	-0.53	5.46	11.70	18.16	21.48
2001	-11.89	-10.18	-6.85	-3.64	-0.58	2.32	3.70
2002	-22.10	-18.45	-10.90	-3.04	5.12	13.54	17.84
2003	28.68	25.86	20.27	14.77	9.36	4.06	1.45
2004	10.88	10.70	10.29	9.84	9.34	8.80	8.51
2005	4.91	5.28	5.96	6.58	7.12	7.60	7.81
2006	15.79	14.30	11.33	8.40	5.49	2.61	1.19
2007	5.49	6.03	7.03	7.95	8.79	9.54	9.88
2008	-37.00	-32.14	-21.55	-9.72	3.43	18.02	25.87
2009	26.46	21.86	12.97	4.49	-3.58	-11.23	-14.90
2010	15.06	14.97	14.52	13.70	12.53	11.02	10.14
2011	2.11	4.77	10.07	15.34	20.56	25.70	28.23

In 2001, Standard & Poor's added REITs to the most widely followed investment performance benchmark for the U.S. equity markets—the Standard & Poor's 500 Index. The addition to this famed index recognizes the significance of real estate in the overall economy.

Graph 2-2: All REITs Market Cap ($Mill)

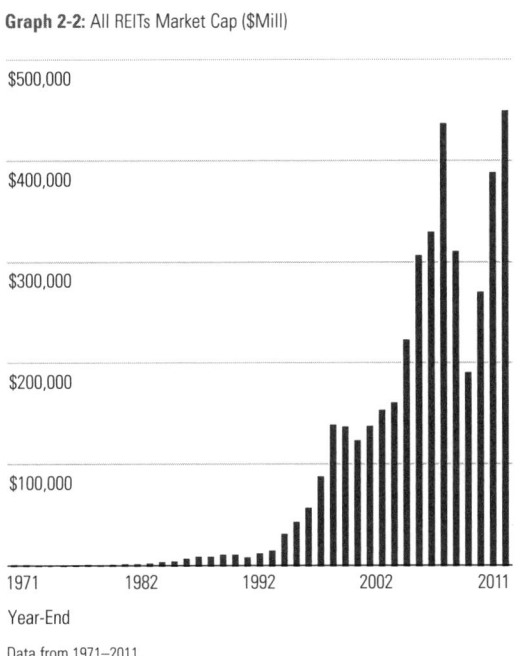

1971   1982   1992   2002   2011

Year-End

Data from 1971–2011.

Types of REITs

REITs can be categorized into three different types: equity, mortgage, and hybrid. Equity REITs are companies that own and operate income-generating real estate, while mortgage REITs invest in mortgages (loans secured by real estate). Hybrid REITs take both direct ownership in real estate and invest in mortgages. Of the 160 publicly-traded REITs in the United States as of December 31, 2011, 130 were equity and 30 were mortgage. NAREIT's Hybrid Index was discontinued in December 2010. In most cases these companies are traded on major stock market exchanges.

Investors can buy shares through a stock broker or by purchasing shares in a mutual fund, which is managed by a portfolio manager skilled in the real estate industry.

Equity REIT Index Construction Methodology

As discussed earlier, most REITs fall into the equity REIT category. The source of the data presented throughout this section, in commentary, graphs, and tables, is that of the National Association of Real Estate Investment Trusts® (NAREIT) Equity Index.

NAREIT Equity Index

NAREIT Equity Index data is based upon the last closing price of the month for all tax-qualified REITs listed on the New York Stock Exchange (NYSE), the NYSE Amex (AMEX), and the NASDAQ National Market System. The data is market-value-weighted. Prior to 1987, REITs were added to the index the January following their listing. Since 1987, newly formed or listed REITs are added to the index in the month in which they become public. Newly issued shares by existing REITs are added to the total shares outstanding figure in the month that the shares are issued. Only common shares issued by the REIT are included in the index. The total return calculation is based upon the weighting at the beginning of the period. Only those REITs listed for the entire period are used in the total return calculation. Dividends are included in the month based upon their payment date. There is no smoothing of income. Liquidating dividends, whether full or partial, are treated as income.

Historical Returns on Equity REITs

Graph 2-3 depicts the growth of $1.00 invested in equity REITs as well as U.S. small and large company stocks, long-term government bonds, Treasury bills, and a hypothetical asset returning the inflation rate over the period from the end of 1971 to the end of 2011. Of the asset classes shown, small company stocks accumulated the highest ending wealth. An investment of $1.00 in small company stocks at year-end 1971 would have grown to $127.92 by the end of December 2011, a compound return of 12.9 percent. Notice, however, that the same investment in equity REITs would have returned $90.39, a compound return of 11.9 percent. Equity REITs outperformed large company stocks, long-term government bonds, Treasury bills, and inflation during the time period.

Income Returns

REITs are obligated to pay out at least 90 percent of their taxable profit to shareholders on an annual basis. As a result, the income generated from REITs has proven to be steady and reasonably predictable.

Graph 2-3: Wealth Indices of Investments in Equity REITs and Basic Series
Index (Year-End 1971 = $1.00)

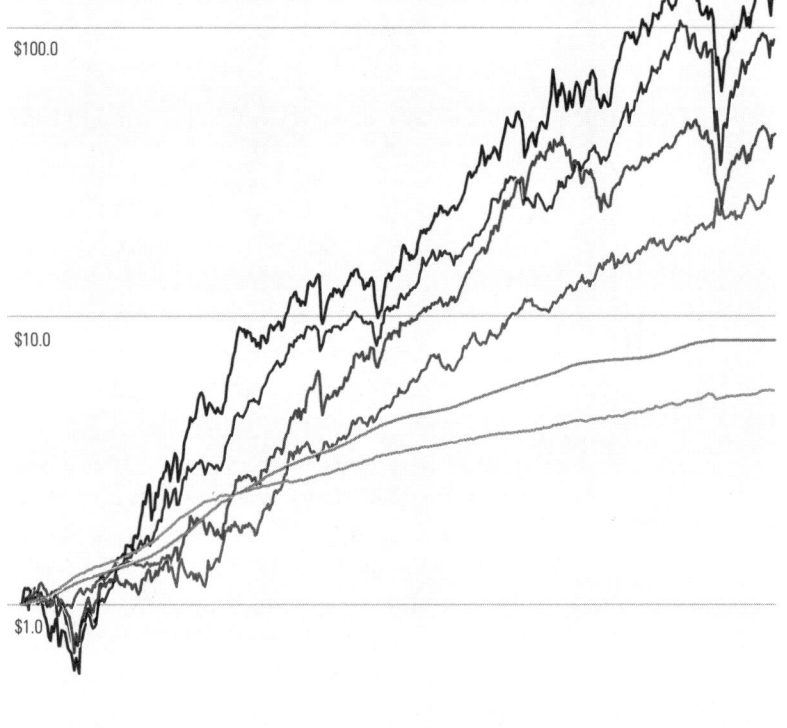

$1,000.0
- — Small Company Stocks ($127.92 YE11)
- — Equity REITS ($90.39 YE11)
- — Large Company Stocks ($42.71 YE11)
- — LT Govt Bonds ($30.43 YE11)
- — T-Bills ($8.26 YE11)
- — Inflation ($5.49 YE11)

$100.0

$10.0

$1.0

1971   1982   1992   2002   2011
Year-end

Data from 1971–2011.

Graph 2-4 shows both the income return and capital appreciation return of REITs on an annual basis from 1972 to 2011. REITs, similar to equity asset classes, can be quite volatile but offer the potential for price appreciation. However, price appreciation is by no means guaranteed (note the large negative price returns of 2007 and 2008). On the other hand, the income produced by REITs has been relatively stable since 1972. Equity REITs posted an average annual income return during that period of 7.7 percent. The highest annual income return was 18.8 percent in 1980, while the lowest was 3.8 percent in 2007.

Graph 2-4: Annual Returns on Equity REITs

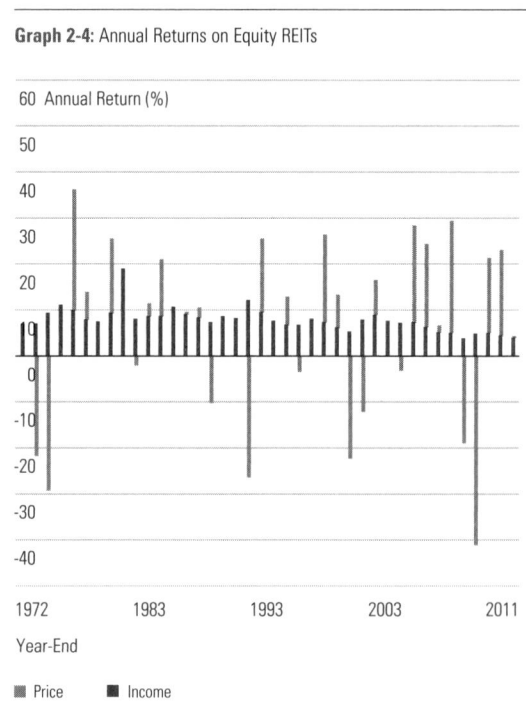

60 Annual Return (%)

50

40

30

20

10

0

-10

-20

-30

-40

1972   1983   1993   2003   2011
Year-End

■ Price   ■ Income

Data from 1972–2011.

Diversification

Along with the relatively predictable revenue stream provided by equity REITs, they can also offer another important advantage to investors—diversification. As the REIT industry has grown over time, REITs have exhibited characteristics similar to both bonds and stocks. REITs typically provide a consistent stream of dividend payments similar to bonds, and hold the potential for long-term capital appreciation, similar to stocks.

In addition, REIT returns have had a low and declining correlation to both stocks and bonds. The cross-correlation between two asset classes measures the extent to which they are linearly related. The correlation coefficient measures the sensitivity of returns on one asset class to the returns of another. A value of +1 indicates a perfectly positive relationship, −1 indicates a perfectly inverse relationship, and 0 indicates no relationship between the two asset classes. Correlation is discussed in greater detail in Chapter 6, Statistical Analysis of Returns.

Graph 2-5 shows the cross-correlations between large company stocks and equity REITs and between long-term government bonds and equity REITs for 60-month rolling periods. The first rolling period covered is January 1972 to December 1976. The graph illustrates that correlation between large company stocks and equity REITs generally fell throughout the 1990s, but steadily rose in the 2000s. The correlation between long-term government bonds and equity REITs generally fell throughout the 1990s (and actually was negative over some periods), but rose slightly in the 2000s.

Graph 2-5: Rolling 60-Month Correlations of Equity REITs

1.00 Correlation   — Large Company Stocks and Equity REITs
                      — LT Govt Bonds and Equity REITs

0.75

0.50

0.25

0.00

-0.25

1976   1988   1999   2011

60-Month Period Ending

Data from January 1972–December 1976 to January 2007–December 2011

Summary Statistics For Equity REITs and Basic Series
Table 2-13 shows summary statistics of annual total returns for REITs and the basic series over the period 1972 to 2011. The summary statistics presented are geometric mean, arithmetic mean, and standard deviation.

While small company stocks posted the highest geometric mean over the time period analyzed, it was accompanied by the highest amount of risk. When comparing equity REITs to large company stocks, equity REITs produced a higher return with only slightly higher risk.

Table 2-14 presents annual cross-correlations and serial correlations from 1972 to 2011 for equity REITs and the six basic asset classes plus inflation. The serial correlation, or the extent to which the return in one period is related to the return in the next period (discussed in greater detail in Chapter 6) of equity REITs suggests no strong pattern, and the return from period to period can best be interpreted as mostly random or unpredictable.

In conclusion, equity REITs have historically offered an attractive risk/return trade-off for investors. They have provided a current income stream along with the potential for long-term capital appreciation. The recent increase in correlation of REIT returns with other investments may lead to a decrease in the overall diversification benefit to investors, but they remain an attractive option.

Commodities Overview
2011 proved to be a volatile year for the capital markets, and the commodities market was no exception. A broad and practical definition of a commodity is any basic substance for which there is demand and supply and exhibits no differentiating qualitative characteristics. Examples of commodities include corn, soybeans, hogs, wheat, crude oil, gold, silver, and others. Investing in commodity futures is appealing to investors because commodities have low correlations to traditional asset classes, offer a hedge against inflation, and provide diversification through superior returns when they are needed most. Three ways investors can gain exposure to commodities are:

1. Direct physical investment
2. Investment in a basket of commodity-related stocks
3. Commodity futures

Table 2-13: Summary Statistics of Annual Returns (%)

	Geometric Mean	Arithmetic Mean	Standard Deviation
Equity REITs	11.9	13.6	18.7
Large Company Stocks	9.8	11.5	18.2
Small Company Stocks	12.9	15.4	23.3
Long-Term Corporate Bonds	8.8	9.3	10.3
Long-Term Government Bonds	8.9	9.6	12.2
Intermediate-Term Government Bonds	7.8	8.0	6.5
Treasury Bills	5.4	5.5	3.3
Inflation	4.4	4.4	3.1

Data from 1972-2011.

Table 2-14: Serial and Cross-Correlations of Annual Returns

	Equity REITs	Large Company Stocks	Small Company Stocks	LT- Corp. Bonds	LT- Gov't Bonds	IT- Gov't Bonds	T-Bills	Inflation
Equity REITs	1.00							
Large Company Stocks	0.57	1.00						
Small Company Stocks	0.79	0.72	1.00					
Long-Term Corporate Bonds	0.23	0.29	0.15	1.00				
Long-Term Government Bonds	-0.01	0.06	-0.09	0.89	1.00			
IT Government Bonds	0.00	0.09	-0.04	0.88	0.90	1.00		
Treasury Bills	-0.01	0.11	0.05	-0.01	0.01	0.30	1.00	
Inflation	-0.04	-0.09	0.06	-0.41	-0.35	-0.18	0.64	1.00
Serial Correlation	0.14	0.00	0.02	-0.06	-0.28	-0.03	0.85	0.73

Data from 1972-2011.

Direct physical investment in commodities is simply not practical in many cases because the majority of commodities are perishable and thus cannot be stored for long periods of time. One exception is precious metals, in which a direct physical investment is possible. Precious metals such as gold and silver are resistant to deterioration over time and therefore can be stored as an investment.

Commodity-related stocks are another way of gaining access to commodities; however, this method also provides exposure to the management skills, practices, and additional business lines of the companies represented in the portfolio.

Lastly, commodity futures constitute a third way of gaining exposure to commodities. Commodity futures may be accessed through a commodity trading advisor (CTA) or an investment in a passive or active investment product designed to track the performance of a commodity index.

Commodities as a Hedge Against Inflation

Investors often invest in commodities as a means to preserve asset values in periods of rising inflation. Gold is one example of a store-of-value asset that investors have historically turned to in order to protect wealth. Unlike stock and bond returns, commodity returns tend to increase in periods of high inflation. Table 2-15 includes the five highest and five lowest annual changes in the inflation rate since 1980 and the corresponding annual returns of large-company stocks, long-term government bonds, and commodities.[1] The change in the inflation rate is represented by the percentage change in the Consumer Price Index for All Urban Consumers (CPI-U).

As can be seen in the upper half of Table 2-15, commodities performed better than stocks and bonds in the five years that experienced the highest change in the inflation rate, with the exception of 2009. In the bottom half of Table 2-15, where the five years which experienced the lowest change in the inflation rate are displayed, stocks and bonds outperformed commodities; except in 2008, where commodities outperformed stocks. ∎

Table 2-15: Five Highest and Lowest Changes in Annual Inflation Rate and Corresponding Large Company Stock, Long-Term Government Bond, and Commodities Annual Total Returns (%) per Series

Top 5 Years of Percent Change in Inflation

Year	Large Company Stocks	Long-Term Government Bonds	Commodities	Change in Inflation
2009	26.5	-14.9	18.3	3,169%
1987	5.2	-2.7	22.1	290
2011	2.1	28.2	-5.3	98
2004	10.9	8.5	17.6	73
1999	21.0	-9.0	31.1	67

Bottom 5 Years of Percent Change in Inflation

Year	Large Company Stocks	Long-Term Government Bonds	Commodities	Change in Inflation
1991	30.5	19.3	-5.3	-50%
2001	-11.9	3.7	-23.1	-54
1982	21.4	40.4	5.6	-57
1986	18.5	24.5	-0.5	-70
2008	-37.0	25.9	-33.8	-98

Endnotes

[1] Commodity returns are represented by the Morningstar® Long-Only Commodity℠ Index. The Morningstar Commodity Index family consists of five indexes that employ different strategic combinations of long futures, short futures, and cash (referred to as flat positions). The index family is based on a transparent, rules-based methodology that is designed to serve investors seeking a passive approach to commodities and support investment product creation. For more information on the Morningstar Index family, please call 1 (312) 384-3735 or visit us on the web at: http://indexes.morningstar.com

Chapter 3
Description of the Basic Series

This chapter presents the returns for the seven basic asset classes and describes the construction of these returns. More detail on the construction of some series can be found in the January 1976 *Journal of Business* article, referenced at the end of the Introduction. Annual total returns and capital appreciation returns for each asset class are formed by compounding the monthly returns that appear in Appendix A. Annual income returns are formed by summing the monthly income payments and dividing this sum by the beginning-of-year price. Returns are formed assuming no taxes or transaction costs, except for returns on small company stocks that show the performance of an actual, tax-exempt investment fund including transaction and management costs, starting in 1982.

Large Company Stocks
Overview

One dollar invested in large company stocks at year-end 1925, with dividends reinvested, grew to $3,045.22 by year-end 2011; this represents a compound annual growth rate of 9.8 percent. [See Graph 3-1.] Capital appreciation alone caused $1.00 to grow to $98.56 over the 86-year period, a compound annual growth rate of 5.5 percent. Annual total returns ranged from a high of 54.0 percent in 1933 to a low of -43.3 percent in 1931. The 86-year average annual dividend yield was 4.1 percent.

Total Returns

From February 1970 to the present, the large company stock total return is provided by Standard and Poor's, which calculates the total return based on the daily reinvestment of dividends on the ex-dividend date. Standard and Poor's uses closing pricing (usually from the New York Stock Exchange) in their calculation. Prior to February 1970, the total return for a given month was calculated by summing the capital appreciation return and the income return as described below.

The large company stock total return index is based upon the S&P Composite Index. This index is a readily available, carefully constructed, market-value-weighted benchmark of large company stock performance. Market-value-weighted means that the weight of each stock in the index, for a given month, is proportionate to its market capitalization (price

times the number of shares outstanding) at the beginning of that month. Currently, the S&P Composite includes 500 of the largest stocks (in terms of stock market value) in the United States; prior to March 1957 it consisted of 90 of the largest stocks.

Capital Appreciation Return

The capital appreciation component of the large company stock total return is the change in the S&P 500 stock index as reported by Standard and Poor's from March 1928–Present, and in Standard and Poor's Trade and Securities Statistics from January 1926–February 1928.

Income Return

From February 1970 to present, the income return was calculated as the difference between the total return and the capital appreciation return. From January 1926 to January 1970, quarterly dividends were extracted from rolling yearly dividends reported quarterly in S&P's *Trade and Securities Statistics*, then allocated to months within each quarter using proportions taken from the 1974 actual distribution of monthly dividends within quarters.

Small Company Stocks
Overview

One dollar invested in small company stocks at year-end 1925 grew to $15,532.07 by year-end 2011. This represents a compound annual growth rate of 11.9 percent over the past 86 years. Total annual returns ranged from a high of 142.9 percent in 1933 to a low of -58.0 percent in 1937.

DFA U.S. Micro Cap Portfolio
(April 2001–December 2011)

For April 2001 to December 2011, the small company stock return series is the total return achieved by the DFA U.S. Micro Cap Portfolio net of fees and expenses. In April 2001, Dimensional Fund Advisors renamed the DFA U.S. 9–10 Small Company Portfolio (see below) the DFA U.S. Micro Cap Portfolio and changed some of the criteria. The fund is designed to capture the returns and diversification benefits of a broad cross-section of U.S. small companies on a market-cap weighted basis. The fund's target buy range includes those companies whose market capitalization falls in the lowest 5 percent of the market universe defined as the aggregate of the NYSE, NYSE AMEX and NASDAQ National Market System or companies smaller than the 1,500th largest U.S. company in the same market universe, whichever results in a higher market capitalization break.

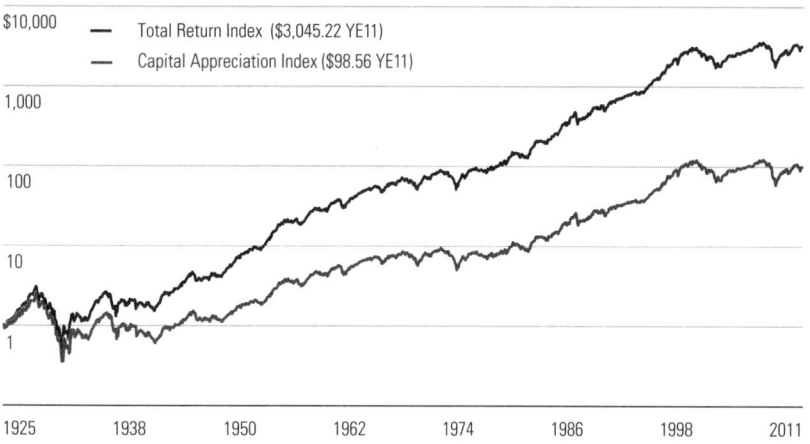

Graph 3-1: Large Company Stocks: Total Return and Capital Appreciation Indices

Index (Year-End 1925 = $1.00)

- — Total Return Index ($3,045.22 YE11)
- — Capital Appreciation Index ($98.56 YE11)

Year-End

Data from 1926–2011.

The market universe is examined on a dynamic basis to determine which issues are eligible for purchase or sale based on market capitalization. To minimize turnover, a hold or buffer range is created for issues that migrate above the buy range. The upper bound of the hold range is the 5th percentile of the market universe. Issues that migrate above the hold range are eligible for sale and proceeds are reinvested into the portfolio.

At year-end 2011, the DFA U.S. Micro Cap Portfolio contained 2,116 stocks, with a weighted average market capitalization of $611 million and the median market capitalization was $179 million.

DFA U.S. 9–10 Small Company Portfolio (January 1982–March 2001)

For January 1982–March 2001, the small company stock return series was the total return achieved by the DFA U.S. Small Company 9–10 (for ninth and tenth deciles) Portfolio. The fund's target buy range was a market-value-weighted universe of the ninth and tenth deciles of the New York Stock Exchange (NYSE), plus stocks listed on the NYSE Amex (AMEX) and NASDAQ National Market (NMS) with the same or less capitalization as the upper bound of the NYSE ninth decile. Since the lower bound of the tenth decile is near zero, stocks were not purchased if they were smaller than $10 million in market capitalization (although they were held if they fell below that level).

Stocks remained in the portfolio if they rose into the eighth NYSE decile, but they were sold when they rose into the seventh NYSE decile or higher. The returns for the DFA U.S. 9–10 Small Company Portfolio are net of transaction costs, fees and expenses, while the returns for the other asset classes and for pre-1982 small company stocks are before-transaction-cost returns and are not diminished by fees and expenses.

NYSE Fifth Quintile Returns (1926–1981)

The equities of smaller companies from 1926 to 1980 are represented by the historical series developed by Professor Rolf W. Banz (see reference section). This is composed of stocks making up the fifth quintile (i.e., the ninth and tenth deciles) of the New York Stock Exchange (NYSE); the stocks on the NYSE are ranked by capitalization (price times number of shares outstanding), and each decile contains an equal number of stocks at the beginning of each formation period. The ninth and tenth decile portfolio was first ranked and formed as of December 31, 1925. This portfolio was "held" for five years, with value-weighted portfolio returns computed monthly. Every five years the portfolio was rebalanced (i.e., all of the stocks on the NYSE were re-ranked, and a new portfolio of those falling in the ninth and tenth deciles was formed) as of December 31, 1930 and every five years thereafter through December 31, 1980. This method avoided survivorship bias by including the return after the delisting or failure of a stock in constructing the portfolio returns. (Survivorship bias is caused by studying only stocks that have survived events such as bankruptcy and acquisition.)

For 1981, Dimensional Fund Advisors, Inc. updated the returns using Professor Banz' methods. The data for 1981 are significant to only three decimal places (in decimal form) or one decimal place when returns are expressed in percent.

Long-Term Corporate Bonds
Overview

One dollar invested in long-term high-grade corporate bonds at the end of 1925 was worth $157.32 by year-end 2011. The compound annual growth rate over the 86-year period was 6.1 percent. Total annual returns ranged from a high of 42.6 percent in 1982 to a low of -8.1 percent in 1969.

Graph 3-2: Long-Term Government Bonds: Total Return and Capital Appreciation Indices and Returns
Index (Year-End 1925 = $1.00)

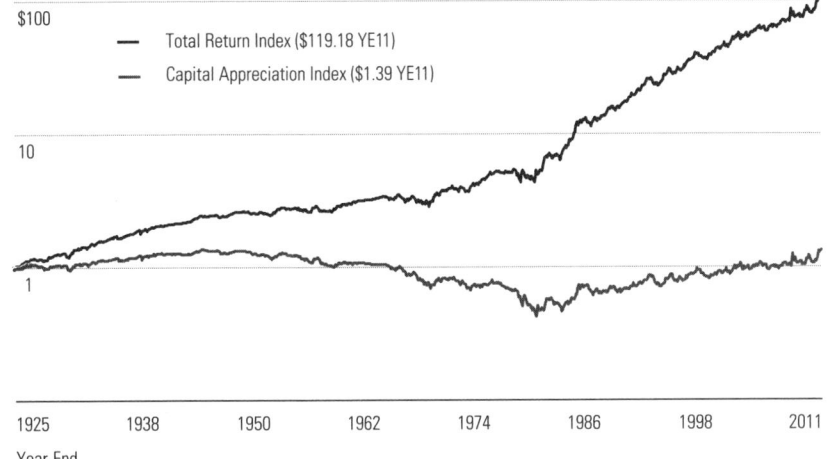

Total Return Index ($119.18 YE11)

Capital Appreciation Index ($1.39 YE11)

Total Annual Returns (%)

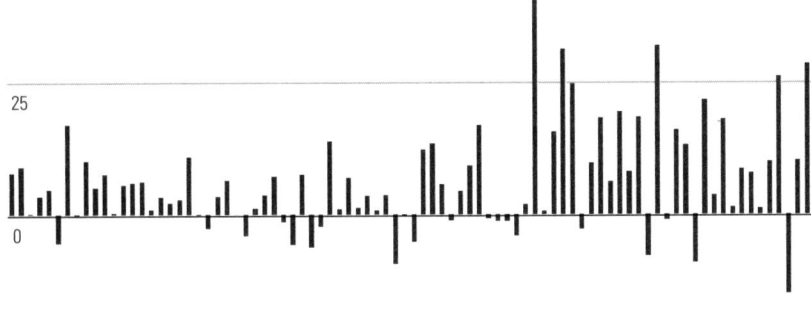

1926 1937 1947 1957 1967 1977 1987 1997 2011
Year-End
Data from 1926–2011.

Total Returns

For 1969–2011, corporate bond total returns are represented by the Citigroup Long-Term High-Grade Corporate Bond Index (formerly Salomon Brothers). Since most large corporate bond transactions take place over the counter, a major dealer is the natural source of these data. The index includes nearly all Aaa- and Aa-rated bonds. If a bond is downgraded during a particular month, its return for the month is included in the index before removing the bond from future portfolios.

Over 1926–1968, total returns were calculated by summing the capital appreciation returns and the income returns. For the period 1946–1968, Ibbotson and Sinquefield backdated the Salomon Brothers' index, using Salomon Brothers' monthly yield data with a methodology similar to that used by Salomon for 1969–2011. Capital appreciation returns were calculated from yields assuming (at the beginning of

each monthly holding period) a 20-year maturity, a bond price equal to par, and a coupon equal to the beginning-of-period yield.

For the period 1926–1945, Standard & Poor's monthly High-Grade Corporate Composite yield data were used, assuming a 4 percent coupon and a 20-year maturity. The conventional present-value formula for bond price was used for the beginning and end-of-month prices. (This formula is presented in Ross, Stephen A., and Randolph W. Westerfield, *Corporate Finance*, Times Mirror/Mosby, St. Louis, 1990, p. 97 ["Level-Coupon Bonds"]). The monthly income return was assumed to be one-twelfth the coupon.

Long-Term Government Bonds
Overview

One dollar invested in long-term government bonds at year-end 1925, with coupons reinvested, grew to $119.18 by year-end 2011; this represents a compound annual growth rate of 5.7 percent. [See Graph 3-2.] Returns from the capital appreciation component alone caused $1.00 to grow to $1.39 over the 86-year period, representing a compound annual growth rate of 0.4 percent. Total annual returns ranged from a high of 40.4 percent in 1982 to a low of -14.9 percent in 2009.

Total Returns

The total returns on long-term government bonds from 1977 to 2011 are constructed with data from The Wall Street Journal. The bond used in 2011 is the 5.375 percent issue that matures on February 15, 2031. The data from 1926–1976 are obtained from the Government Bond File at the Center for Research in Security Prices (CRSP) at the University of Chicago Graduate School of Business. The bonds used to construct the index are shown in Table 3-1. To the greatest extent possible, a one-bond portfolio with a term of approximately 20 years and a reasonably current coupon—whose returns did not reflect potential tax benefits, impaired negotiability, or special redemption or call privileges—was used each year. Where "flower" bonds (tenderable to the Treasury at par in payment of estate taxes) had to be used, we chose the bond with the smallest potential tax benefit. Where callable bonds had to be used, the term of the bond was assumed to be a simple average of the maturity and first call dates minus the current date. The bond was "held" for the calendar year and returns were computed.

Total returns for 1977–2011 are calculated as the change in the flat or and-interest price.[1] The flat price is the average of the bond's bid and ask prices, plus the accrued coupon.[2] The accrued coupon is equal to zero on the day a coupon is paid, and increases over time until the next coupon payment according to the formula below.

$$A = fC \qquad (1)$$

where,

A = accrued coupon;

C = semiannual coupon rate; and

$$f = \frac{\text{number of days since last coupon payment}}{\begin{array}{l}\text{number of days from last coupon payment}\\ \text{to next coupon payment}\end{array}}$$

Income Return

For 1977–2011, the income return is calculated as the change in flat price plus any coupon actually paid from one period to the next, holding the yield constant over the period. As in the total return series, the exact number of days comprising the period is used. For 1926–1976, the income return for a given month is calculated as the total return minus the capital appreciation return.

Capital Appreciation or Return in Excess of Yield

For 1977–2011, capital appreciation is taken as the total return minus the income return for each month. For 1926–1976, the capital appreciation return (also known as the return in excess of yield) is obtained from the CRSP Government Bond File.

A bond's capital appreciation is defined as the total return minus the income return; that is, the return in excess of yield. This definition omits the capital gain or loss that comes from the movement of a bond's price toward par (in the absence of interest rate change) as it matures. Capital appreciation, as defined here, captures changes in bond prices caused by changes in the interest rate.

Yields

The yield on the long-term government bond series is defined as the internal rate of return that equates the bond's price (the average of bid and ask, plus the accrued coupon) with the stream of cash flows (coupons and principal) promised to the bondholder. The yields reported for 1977–2011 were calculated from *The Wall Street Journal* prices for the bonds listed in Table 3-1. For noncallable bonds, the maturity date is shown. For callable bonds, the first call date and the maturity dates are shown as in the following example: 10/15/47–52 refers to a bond that is first callable on 10/15/1947 and matures on 10/15/1952. Dates from 47–99 refer to 1947–1999; 00–16 refers to 2000–2016. For callable bonds trading below par, the yield to maturity is used; above par, the yield to call is used. The yields for 1926–1976 were obtained from the CRSP Government Bond File.

Intermediate-Term Government Bonds
Overview

One dollar invested in intermediate-term government bonds at year-end 1925, with coupons reinvested, grew to $92.08 by year-end 2011. [See Graph 3-3.] This represents an 86-year compound annual growth rate of 5.4 percent. Total annual returns ranged from a high of 29.1 percent in 1982 to a low of -5.1 percent in 1994.

Capital appreciation caused $1.00 to increase to $1.72 over the 86-year period, representing a compound annual growth rate of 0.6 percent. This increase was unexpected: Since yields rose on average over the period, capital appreciation on a hypothetical intermediate-term government bond portfolio with a constant five-year maturity should have been negative. An explanation of the positive average return is given at the end of this chapter.

Total Returns

Total returns of the intermediate-term government bonds for 1987–2011 are calculated from *The Wall Street Journal* prices, using the coupon accrual method described above for long-term government bonds. [See Equation (1).] The bond used in 2011 is the 3.25 percent issue maturing on July 31, 2016. Returns over 1934–1986 are obtained from the CRSP Government Bond File. The bonds used to construct the index over 1934–2011 are shown in Table 3-1.

Chapter 3: Description of the Basic Series

As with long-term government bonds, one-bond portfolios are used to construct the intermediate-term government bond index. The bond chosen each year is the shortest noncallable bond with a maturity not less than five years, and it is "held" for the calendar year. Monthly returns are computed. (Bonds with impaired negotiability or special redemption privileges are omitted, as are partially or fully tax-exempt bonds starting with 1943.)

Over 1934–1942, almost all bonds with maturities near five years were partially or fully tax-exempt and selected using the rules described above. Personal tax rates were generally low in that period, so that yields on tax-exempt bonds were similar to yields on taxable bonds.

Over 1926–1933, there are few bonds suitable for construction of a series with a five-year maturity. For this period, five-year bond yield estimates are used. These estimates are obtained from Thomas S. Coleman, Lawrence Fisher, and Roger G. Ibbotson, *Historical U.S. Treasury Yield Curves: 1926–1992 with 1995 update* (Ibbotson Associates, Chicago, 1995). The estimates reflect what a "pure play" five-year Treasury bond, selling at par and with no special redemption or call provisions, would have yielded had one existed. Estimates are for partially tax-exempt bonds for 1926–1932 and for fully tax-exempt bonds for 1933. Monthly yields are converted to monthly total returns by calculating the beginning and end-of-month flat prices for the hypothetical bonds. The bond is "bought" at the beginning of the month at par (i.e., the coupon equals the previous month-end yield), assuming a maturity of five years. It is "sold" at the end of the month, with the flat price calculated by discounting the coupons and principal at the end-of-month yield, assuming a maturity of 4 years and 11 months. The flat price is the price of the bond including coupon accruals, so that the change in flat price represents total return. Monthly income returns are assumed to be equal to the previous end-of-month yield, stated in monthly terms. Monthly capital appreciation returns are formed as total returns minus income returns.

Income Return and Capital Appreciation

For the period 1987–2011, the income return is calculated according to the methodology stated under "Long-Term Government Bonds." Monthly capital appreciation (return in excess of yield) over this same period is the difference between total return and income return.

For 1934–1986, capital appreciation (return in excess of yield) is taken directly from the CRSP Government Bond File. The income return is calculated as the total return minus the capital appreciation return. Prior to 1934, the income and capital appreciation components of total return are generated from yield estimates as described earlier under Total Returns.

Yields

The yield on an intermediate-term government bond is the internal rate of return that equates the bond's price with the stream of cash flows (coupons and principal) promised to the bondholder. The yields reported for 1987–2011 are calculated from *The Wall Street Journal* bond prices listed in Table 3-1. For 1934–1986, yields were obtained from the CRSP Government Bond File. Yields for 1926–1933 are estimates from Coleman, Fisher, and Ibbotson, *Historical U.S. Treasury Yield Curves: 1926–1992 with 1995 update*.

U.S. Treasury Bills
Overview

One dollar invested in U.S. Treasury bills at year-end 1925 grew to $20.56 by year-end 2011; this represents a compound annual growth rate of 3.6 percent. Total annual returns ranged from a high of 14.7 percent in 1981 to a low of 0.0 percent for the period 1938 to 1940.

Total Returns

For the U.S. Treasury bill index, data from *The Wall Street Journal* are used for 1977–2011; the CRSP U.S. Government Bond File is the source until 1976. Each month a one-bill portfolio containing the shortest-term bill having not less than one month to maturity is constructed. (The bill's original term to maturity is not relevant.) To measure holding period returns for the one-bill portfolio, the bill is priced as of the last trading day of the previous month-end and as of the last trading day of the current month.

The price of the bill (**P**) at each time (**t**) is given as:

(2)

$$P_t = \left[1 - \frac{rd}{360} \right]$$

where,

r = decimal yield (the average of bid and ask quotes) on the bill at time **t**; and,

d = number of days to maturity as of time **t**.

Table 3-1: Long-Term and Intermediate-Term Government Bond Issues

Long-Term Government Bonds

Period Bond is Held in Index	Coupon (%)	Call/ Maturity Date
1926–1931	4.25	10/15/47–52
1932–1935	3.00	9/15/51–55
1936–1941	2.875	3/15/55–60
1942–1953	2.50	9/15/67–72
1954–1958	3.25	6/15/78–83
1959–1960	4.00	2/15/80
1961–1965	4.25	5/15/75–85
1966–1972	4.25	8/15/87–92
1973–1974	6.75	2/15/93
1975–1976	8.50	5/15/94–99
1977–1980	7.875	2/15/95–00
1981	8.00	8/15/96–01
1982	13.375	8/15/01
1983	10.75	2/15/03
1984	11.875	11/15/03
1985	11.75	2/15/05–10
1986–1989	10.00	5/15/05–10
1990–1992	10.375	11/15/07–12
1993–1996	7.25	5/15/16
1997–1998	8.125	8/15/19
1999–2001	8.125	8/15/21
2002	6.25	8/15/23
2003–2004	7.50	11/15/24
2005	6.875	8/15/25
2006	6.75	8/15/26
2007	6.375	8/15/27
2008	5.50	8/15/28
2009	5.25	2/15/29
2010–2011	5.375	2/15/31

Intermediate-Term Government Bonds

Period Bond is Held in Index	Coupon (%)	Call/ Maturity Date
1934–1936	3.25	8/01/41
1937	3.375	3/15/43
1938–1940	2.50	12/15/45
1941	3.00	1/01/46
1942	3.00	1/01/47
1943	1.75	6/15/48
1944–1945	2.00	3/15/50
1946	2.00	6/15/51
1947	2.00	3/15/52
1948	2.00	9/15/53
1949	2.50	3/15/54
1950	2.25	6/15/55
1951–1952	2.50	3/15/58
1953	2.375	6/15/58
1954	2.375	3/15/59
1955	2.125	11/15/60
1956	2.75	9/15/61
1957–1958	2.50	8/15/63
1959	3.00	2/15/64
1960	2.625	2/15/65
1961	3.75	5/15/66
1962	3.625	11/15/67
1963	3.875	5/15/68
1964	4.00	2/15/69
1965	4.00	8/15/70
1966	4.00	8/15/71
1967	4.00	2/15/72
1968	4.00	8/15/73
1969	5.625	8/15/74
1970	5.75	2/15/75
1971	6.25	2/15/76
1972	1.50	10/01/76
1973	6.25	2/15/78
1974	6.25	8/15/79
1975	6.875	5/15/80
1976	7.00	2/15/81
1977	6.375	2/15/82
1978	8.00	2/15/83
1979	7.25	2/15/84
1980	8.00	2/15/85

Intermediate-Term Government Bonds (Continued)

Period Bond is Held in Index	Coupon (%)	Call/ Maturity Date
1981	13.50	2/15/86
1982	9.00	2/15/87
1983	12.375	1/01/88
1984	14.625	1/15/89
1985	10.50	1/15/90
1986	11.75	1/15/91
1987	11.625	1/15/92
1988	8.75	1/15/93
1989	9.00	2/15/94
1990	8.625	10/15/95
1991–1992	7.875	7/15/96
1993	6.375	1/15/99
1994	5.50	4/15/00
1995	8.50	2/15/00
1996	7.75	2/15/01
1997	6.375	8/15/02
1998	5.75	8/15/03
1999	7.25	8/15/04
2000	6.50	8/15/05
2001	6.50	10/15/06
2002	6.125	8/15/07
2003	5.625	5/15/08
2004	5.50	5/15/09
2005	5.75	8/15/10
2006	5.00	8/15/11
2007	4.875	2/15/12
2008	3.625	5/15/13
2009	4.25	8/15/14
2010	4.125	5/15/15
2011	3.25	7/31/16

Chapter 3: Description of the Basic Series

Graph 3-3: Intermediate-Term Government Bonds: Total Return and Capital Appreciation Indices

Index (Year-End 1925 = $1.00)

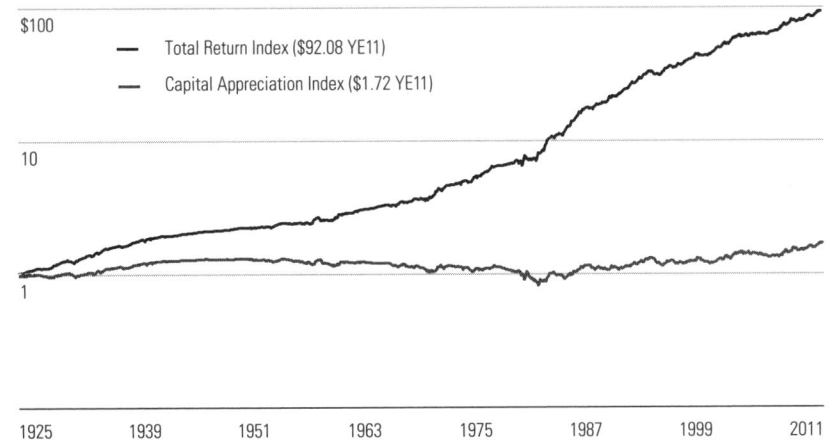

- Total Return Index ($92.08 YE11)
- Capital Appreciation Index ($1.72 YE11)

Year-End

Data from 1926–2011.

The total return on the bill is the month-end price divided by the previous month-end price, minus one.

Negative Returns on Treasury Bills

Monthly Treasury bill returns (as reported in Appendix A-14) were negative in February 1933, and in 12 months during the 1938–1941 period. Also, the annual Treasury bill return was negative for 1938. Since negative Treasury bill returns contradict logic, an explanation is in order.

Negative yields observed in the data do not imply that investors purchased Treasury bills with a guaranteed negative return. Rather, Treasury bills of that era were exempt from personal property taxes in some states, while cash was not. Further, for a bank to hold U.S. government deposits, Treasury securities were required as collateral. These circumstances created excessive demand for the security, and thus bills were sold at a premium. Given the low interest rates during the period, owners of the bills experienced negative returns.

In 2008, yields on U.S. Treasury bills fell from a little over 3.0 percent at the beginning of the year to approximately 0.0 percent by the end of the year, but the dynamics were different than those just described for the 1938–1941 period. In the wake of the 2008 financial crisis, investors' behavior could be described as an extreme flight to safety; investors were willing to accept little (if anything) in return for the assurance that they would get their principal back.

In 2011, U.S. Treasury bill yields remained near historical lows near 0.0 percent. These low yields can be partially explained by the Federal Funds target rate, which has remained unchanged between 0.0 and 0.25 percent throughout 2011.

Inflation
Overview

A basket of consumer goods purchased for $1.00 at year-end 1925 would cost $12.61 by year-end 2011. Of course, the exact contents of the basket has changed over time. This increase represents a compound annual rate of inflation of 3.0 percent over the past 86 years. Inflation rates ranged from a high of 18.2 percent in 1946 to a low of -10.3 percent in 1932.

Inflation

The Consumer Price Index for All Urban Consumers (CPI-U), not seasonally adjusted, is used to measure inflation, which is the rate of change of consumer goods prices. Unfortunately, the CPI is not measured over the same period as the other asset returns. All of the security returns are measured from one month-end to the next month-end. CPI commodity prices are collected during the month. Thus, measured inflation rates lag the other series by about one-half month. Prior to January 1978, the CPI (as compared with CPI-U) was used. For the period 1978 through 1987, the index uses the year 1967 in determining the items comprising the basket of goods. Following 1987, a three-year period, 1982 through 1984, was used to determine the items making up the basket of goods. All inflation measures are constructed by the U.S. Department of Labor, Bureau of Labor Statistics, Washington.

Positive Capital Appreciation on Intermediate-Term Government Bonds

The capital appreciation component of intermediate-term government bond returns caused $1.00 invested at year-end 1925 to grow to $1.72 by the end of 2011, representing a compound annual rate of 0.6 percent. This is surprising because yields, on average, rose over the period.

An investor in a hypothetical five-year constant maturity portfolio, with continuous rebalancing, suffered a capital loss (that is, excluding coupon income) over 1926–2011. An investor who rebalanced yearly, choosing bonds according to the method set forth above, fared better. This investor would have earned the 0.6 percent per year capital gain recorded here.

This performance relates to the construction of the inter-mediate-term bond series. For 1926–1933, the one-bond portfolio was rebalanced monthly to maintain a constant maturity of five years. For the period 1934–2011, one bond (the shortest bond not less than five years to maturity) was chosen at the beginning of each year and priced monthly. New bonds were not picked each month to maintain a constant five years to maturity intra-year.

There are several possible reasons for the positive capital appreciation return. Chief among these reasons are convexity of the bond portfolio and the substitution of one bond for another at each year-end.

Convexity

Each year, we "bought" a bond with approximately five years to maturity and held it for one year. During this period, the market yield on the bond fluctuates. Because the duration of the bond shortens (the bond becomes less interest-rate sensitive) as yields rise and the duration lengthens as yields fall, more is gained from a fall in yield than is lost from a rise in yield. This characteristic of a bond is known as convexity.

For example, suppose an 8 percent coupon bond is bought at par at the beginning of a year; the yield fluctuates (but the portfolio is not rebalanced) during the year; and the bond is sold at par at the end of the year. The price of the bond at both the beginning and end of the year is $100; the change in bond price is zero. However, the fluctuations will have caused the gains during periods of falling yields to exceed the losses during periods of rising yields. Thus the total return for the year exceeds 8 percent. Since our measure of capital appreciation is the return in excess of yield, rather than the change in bond price, capital appreciation for this bond (as measured) will be greater than zero.

In 1992, the yield for intermediate-term government bonds started the year at 5.97 percent, rose, fell, and finally rose again to end at 6.11 percent, slightly higher than the starting point. In the absence of convexity, the capital appreciation return for 1992 would be negative. Because of the fluctuation of yields during the year, however, the capital appreciation return on the intermediate-term government bond index was positive 0.64 percent.

It should be noted that the return in excess of yield, or capital gain, from convexity is caused by holding, over the year, a bond whose yield at purchase is different than the current market yield. If the portfolio were rebalanced each time the data were sampled (in this case, monthly), by selling the old bond and buying a new five-year bond selling at par, the portfolio would have no convexity. That is, over a period where yields ended where they started, the measured capital appreciation would be zero. However, this is neither a practical way to construct an index of actual bonds nor to manage a bond portfolio.

Bond Substitution

Another reason why the intermediate-term government bond series displays positive capital appreciation even though yields rose is the way in which bonds were removed from the portfolio and replaced with other bonds. In general, it was not possible to replace a bond "sold" by buying one with exactly the same yield. This produces a spurious change in the yield of the series—one that should not be associated with a capital gain or loss.

For example: Suppose a five-year bond yielding 8 percent is bought at par at the beginning of the year; at that time, four-year bonds yield 7 percent. Over the year, the yield curve rises in parallel by one percentage point so that when it comes time to sell the bond at year-end, it yields 8 percent and has four years to maturity. Therefore, at both the beginning and end of the year, the price of the bond is $100.

The proceeds from the sale are used to buy a new five-year bond yielding 9 percent. While the bond price change was zero over the year, the yield of the series has risen from 8 percent to 9 percent. Thus it is possible, because of the process of substituting one bond for another, for the yield series to contain a spurious rise that is not, and should not be expected to be, associated with a decline in the price of any particular bond. This phenomenon is likely to be the source of some of the positive capital appreciation in our intermediate-term government bond series.

Other Issues

While convexity and bond substitution may explain the anomaly of positive capital appreciation in a bond series with rising yields, there are other incomplete-market problems that may also help explain the capital gain. For example, intermediate-term government bonds were scarce in the 1930s and 1940s. As a result, the bonds chosen for this series occasionally had maturities longer than five years, ranging as high as eight years when bought. The 1930s and the first half of the 1940s were bullish for the bond market. Longer bonds included in this series had higher yields and substantially higher capital gain returns than bonds with exactly five years to maturity might have had if any existed. This upward bias is particularly noticeable in 1934, 1937, and 1938.

In addition, callable and fully or partially tax-exempt bonds were used when necessary to obtain a bond for some years. The conversion of the Treasury bond market from tax-exempt to taxable status produced a one-time upward jump in stated yields, but not a capital loss on any given bond. Therefore, part of the increase in stated yields over 1926–2011 was a tax effect that did not cause a capital loss on the intermediate-term bond index. Further, the callable bonds used in the early part of the period may have commanded a return premium for taking this extra risk. ▐▌

Endnotes

[1] "Flat price" is used here to mean the unmodified economic value of the bond, i.e., the and-interest price, or quoted price plus accrued interest. In contrast, some sources use flat price to mean the quoted price.

[2] For the purpose of calculating the return in months when a coupon payment is made, the change in the flat price includes the coupon.

Chapter 4
Description of the Derived Series

Historical data suggests that investors are rewarded for taking risks and that returns are related to inflation rates. The risk/return and the real/nominal relationships in the historical data are revealed by looking at the risk premium and inflation-adjusted series derived from the basic asset series. Annual total returns for the four risk premia and six inflation-adjusted series are presented in Table 4-1 of this chapter.

Geometric Differences Used to Calculate Derived Series

Derived series are calculated as the geometric differences between two basic asset classes. Returns on basic series **A** and **B** and derived series **C** are related as follows:

(3)

$$\left(1+C\right)=\left[\frac{1+A}{1+B}\right]$$

where the series **A**, **B**, and **C** are in decimal form (i.e., 5 percent is indicated by 0.05). Thus **C** is given by:

(4)

$$C=\left[\frac{1+A}{1+B}\right]-1\approx A-B$$

As an example, suppose return **A** equals 15%, or 0.15; and return **B** is 5%, or 0.05. Then **C** equals (1.15 / 1.05) − 1 = 0.0952, or 9.52 percent. This result, while slightly different from the simple arithmetic difference of 10 percent, is conceptually the same.

Definitions of the Derived Series

From the seven basic asset classes—large company stocks, small company stocks, long-term corporate bonds, long-term government bonds, intermediate-term government bonds, U.S. Treasury bills, and consumer goods (inflation)—10 additional series are derived representing the component or elemental parts of the asset returns.

Two Categories of Derived Series

The 10 derived series are categorized as risk premia, or payoffs for taking various types of risk; and as inflation-adjusted asset returns. The risk premia series are the bond horizon premium, the bond default premium, the equity risk premium, and the small stock premium. The inflation-adjusted asset return series are constructed by geometrically subtracting inflation from each of the six asset total return series.

These 10 derived series are:

Risk Premia Series	Derivation
Equity Risk Premium	$\dfrac{(1 + \text{Large Stock TR})}{(1 + \text{Treasury Bill TR})} - 1$
Small Stock Premium	$\dfrac{(1 + \text{Small Stock TR})}{(1 + \text{Large Stock TR})} - 1$
Bond Default Premium	$\dfrac{(1 + \text{LT Corp Bond TR})}{(1 + \text{LT Govt Bond TR})} - 1$
Bond Horizon Premium	$\dfrac{(1 + \text{LT Govt Bond TR})}{(1 + \text{Treasury Bill TR})} - 1$

Inflation-Adjusted Series	Derivation
Large Company Stock Returns	$\dfrac{(1 + \text{Large Stock TR})}{(1 + \text{Inflation})} - 1$
Small Company Stock Returns	$\dfrac{(1 + \text{Small Stock TR})}{(1 + \text{Inflation})} - 1$
Corporate Bond Returns	$\dfrac{(1 + \text{Corp Bond TR})}{(1 + \text{Inflation})} - 1$
Long-Term Government Bond Returns	$\dfrac{(1 + \text{LT Govt Bond TR})}{(1 + \text{Inflation})} - 1$
Intermediate-Term Government Bond Returns	$\dfrac{(1 + \text{IT Govt Bond TR})}{(1 + \text{Inflation})} - 1$
Treasury Bill Returns (Real Riskless Rate of Returns)	$\dfrac{(1 + \text{Treasury Bill TR})}{(1 + \text{Inflation})} - 1$

TR = Total Return

Equity Risk Premium

Large company stock returns are composed of inflation, the real riskless rate, and the equity risk premium. The equity risk premium is the geometric difference between large company stock total returns and U.S. Treasury bill total returns.

Because large company stocks are not strictly comparable with bonds, horizon and default premia are not used to analyze the components of equity returns. (Large company stocks have characteristics that are analogous to horizon and default risk, but they are not equivalent.)

The monthly equity risk premium is given by:

$$\frac{\left(1 + \text{Large Stock TR}\right)}{\left(1 + \text{Treasury Bill TR}\right)} - 1 \tag{5}$$

Small Stock Premium

The small stock premium is the geometric difference between small company stock total returns and large company stock total returns. The monthly small stock premium is given by:

$$\frac{\left(1 + \text{Small Stock TR}\right)}{\left(1 + \text{Large Stock TR}\right)} - 1 \tag{6}$$

Bond Default Premium

The bond default premium is defined as the net return from investing in long-term corporate bonds rather than long-term government bonds of equal maturity. Since there is a possibility of default on a corporate bond, bondholders receive a premium that reflects this possibility, in addition to inflation, the real riskless rate, and the horizon premium.

The monthly bond default premium is given by:

$$\frac{\left(1 + \text{LT Corp Bond TR}\right)}{\left(1 + \text{LT Govt Bond TR}\right)} - 1 \tag{7}$$

Components of the Default Premium

Bonds susceptible to default have higher returns (when they do not default) than riskless bonds. Default on a bond may be a small loss, such as a late or skipped interest payment; it may be a larger loss, such as the loss of any or all principal as well as interest. In any case, part of the default premium on a portfolio of bonds is consumed by the losses on those bonds that do default.

The remainder of the default premium—over and above the portion consumed by defaults—is a pure risk premium, which the investor demands and, over the long run, receives for taking the risk of default. The expected return on a corporate bond, or portfolio of corporate bonds, is less than the bond's yield. The portion of the yield that is expected to be consumed by defaults must be subtracted. The expected return on a corporate bond is equal to the expected return on a government bond of like maturity, plus the pure risk premium portion of the bond default premium.

Callability Risk is Captured in the Default Premium

Callability risk is the risk that a bond will be redeemed (at or near par) by its issuer before maturity, at a time when market interest rates are lower than the bond's coupon rate. The possibility of redemption is risky because it would prevent the bondholder of the redeemed issue from reinvesting the proceeds at the original (higher) interest rate. The bond default premium, as measured here, also inadvertently captures any premium investors may demand or receive for this risk.

Bond Horizon Premium

Long-term government bonds behave differently than short-term bills in that their prices (and hence returns) are more sensitive to interest rate fluctuations. The bond horizon premium is the premium investors demand for holding long-term bonds instead of U.S. Treasury bills.

The monthly bond horizon premium is given by:

$$\frac{\left(1 + \text{LT Govt Bond TR}\right)}{\left(1 + \text{Treasury Bill TR}\right)} - 1 \tag{8}$$

Graph 4-1: Large Company Stocks: Real and Nominal Return Indices

Index (Year-End 1925 = $1.00)

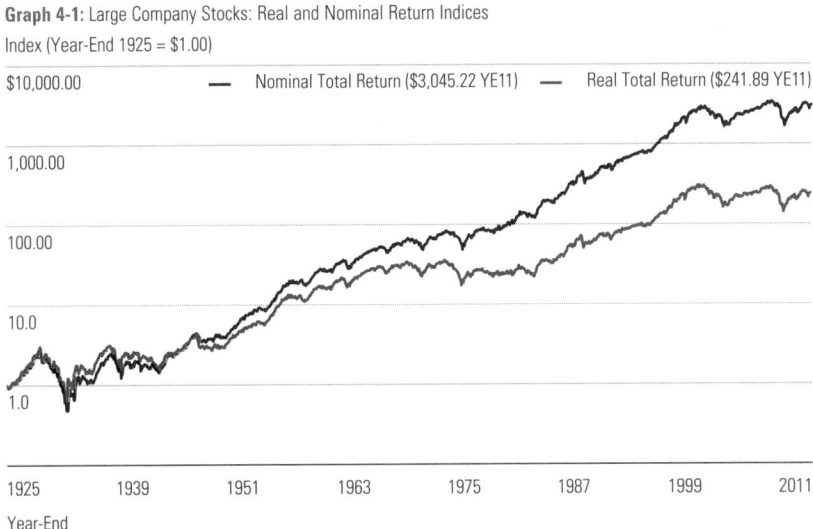

— Nominal Total Return ($3,045.22 YE11)   — Real Total Return ($241.89 YE11)

Year-End
Data from 1926–2011.

Graph 4-2: Small Company Stocks: Real and Nominal Return Indices

Index (Year-End 1925 = $1.00)

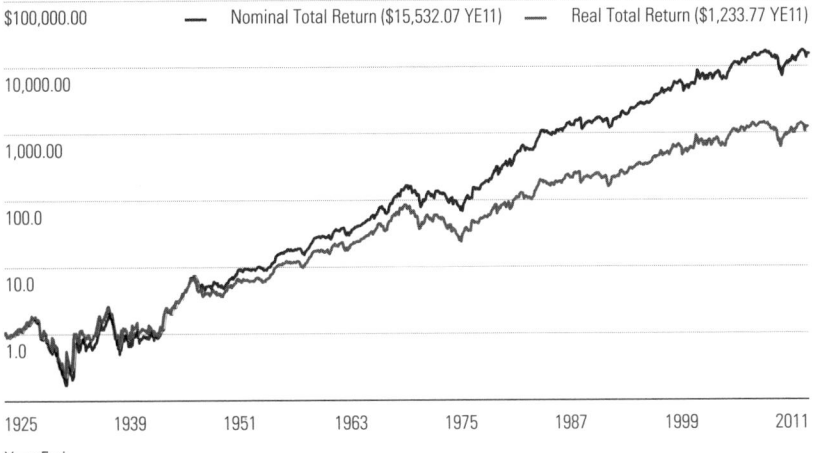

— Nominal Total Return ($15,532.07 YE11)   — Real Total Return ($1,233.77 YE11)

Year-End
Data from 1926–2011.

Long-term rather than intermediate-term government bonds are used to derive the bond horizon premium so as to capture a "full unit" of price fluctuation risk. Intermediate-term government bonds may display a partial horizon premium, which is smaller than the difference between long-term bonds and short-term bills.

Does Maturity or Duration Determine the Bond Premium?

Duration is the present-value-weighted average time to receipt of cash flows (coupons and principal) from holding a bond, and can be calculated from the bond's yield, coupon rate, and term to maturity. The duration of a given bond determines the amount of return premium arising from differences in bond life. The bond horizon premium is also referred to as the "maturity premium," based on the

observation that bonds with longer maturities command a return premium over shorter-maturity bonds. Duration, not term to maturity, however, is the bond characteristic that determines this return premium.

Why a "Horizon" Premium?

Investors often strive to match the duration of their bond holdings (cash inflows) with the estimated duration of their obligations or cash outflows. Consequently, investors with short time horizons regard long-duration bonds as risky (due to price fluctuation risk), and short-term bills as riskless. Conversely, investors with long time horizons regard short-term bills as risky (due to the uncertainty about the yield at which bills can be reinvested), and long-duration bonds as riskless or less risky.

Empirically, long-duration bonds bear higher yields and greater returns than short-term bills; that is, the yield curve slopes upward on average over time. This observation indicates that investors are more averse to the price fluctuation risk of long-duration bonds than to the reinvestment risk of bills.

Bond-duration risk is thus in the eye of the beholder, or bondholder. Therefore, rather than identifying the premium as a payoff for long-bond risk (which implies a judgment that short-horizon investors are "right" in their risk perceptions), it is better to go directly to the source of the return differential (the differing time horizons of investors) and use the label "horizon premium."

Inflation-Adjusted Large Company Stock Returns Overview

Large company stock total returns were 9.8 percent compounded annually over the period 1926–2011 in nominal terms. [See Graph 4-1.] In real (inflation-adjusted) terms, stocks provided a 6.6 percent compound annual return. Thus, a large company stock investor would have experienced a substantial increase in real wealth, or purchasing power, over the 86-year period.

Graph 4-3: Long-Term Corporate Bonds: Real and Nominal Return Indices

Index (Year-End 1925 = $1.00)

$1,000.00	— Nominal Total Return ($157.32 YE11)	— Real Total Return ($12.50 YE11)

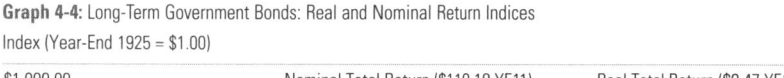

100.00

10.0

1.0

| 1925 | 1939 | 1951 | 1963 | 1975 | 1987 | 1999 | 2011 |

Year-End

Data from 1926–2011.

Graph 4-4: Long-Term Government Bonds: Real and Nominal Return Indices

Index (Year-End 1925 = $1.00)

$1,000.00	— Nominal Total Return ($119.18 YE11)	— Real Total Return ($9.47 YE11)

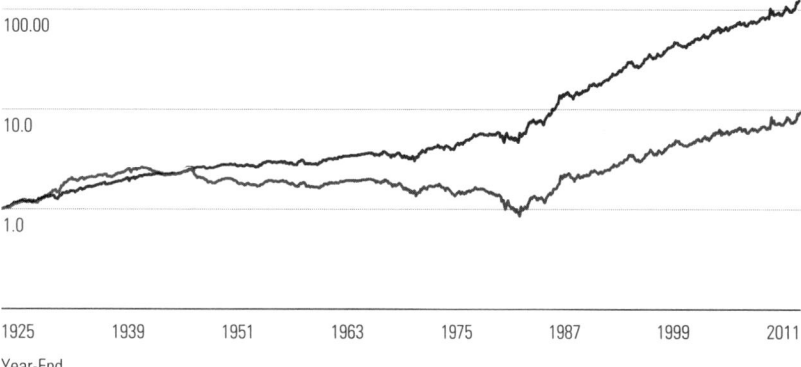

100.00

10.0

1.0

| 1925 | 1939 | 1951 | 1963 | 1975 | 1987 | 1999 | 2011 |

Year-End

Data from 1926–2011.

Construction

The inflation-adjusted return is a geometric difference and is approximately equal to the arithmetic difference between the large company stock total return and the inflation rate. The monthly inflation-adjusted large company stock return is given by:

$$\frac{\left(1+\text{Large Stock TR}\right)}{\left(1+\text{Inflation}\right)}-1 \tag{9}$$

The inflation-adjusted large company stock return may also be expressed as the geometric sum of the real riskless rate and the equity risk premium:

$$\left[\left(1+\text{Real Riskless Rate}\right)\times\left(1+\text{Equity Risk Premium}\right)\right]-1 \tag{10}$$

Inflation-Adjusted Small Company Stock Returns

Overview

Small company stock total returns were 11.9 percent compounded annually over the period 1926–2011 in nominal terms. [See Graph 4-2.] In real terms, small company stocks provided a 8.6 percent compound annual return. Thus, long-term a small company stock investor would have experienced a substantial increase in real wealth, or purchasing power, over the 86-year period.

Construction

The inflation-adjusted return is a geometric difference and is approximately equal to the arithmetic difference between the small company stock total return and the inflation rate. The monthly inflation-adjusted small company stock return is given by:

$$\frac{\left(1+\text{Small Stock TR}\right)}{\left(1+\text{Inflation}\right)}-1 \tag{11}$$

Inflation-Adjusted Long-Term Corporate Bond Returns

Overview

Corporate bonds returned 6.1 percent compounded annually over the period 1926–2011 in nominal terms, and a 3.0 percent compound annual return in real (inflation-adjusted) terms. [See Graph 4-3.] Thus, corporate bonds have outpaced inflation over the past 86 years.

Construction

The inflation-adjusted return is a geometric difference and is approximately equal to the arithmetic difference between the long-term corporate bond total return and the inflation rate. The monthly inflation-adjusted corporate bond total return is given by:

$$\frac{\left(1+\text{Corp Bond TR}\right)}{\left(1+\text{Inflation}\right)}-1 \tag{12}$$

Graph 4-5: Intermediate-Term Government Bonds: Real and Nominal Return Indices

Index (Year-End 1925 = $1.00)

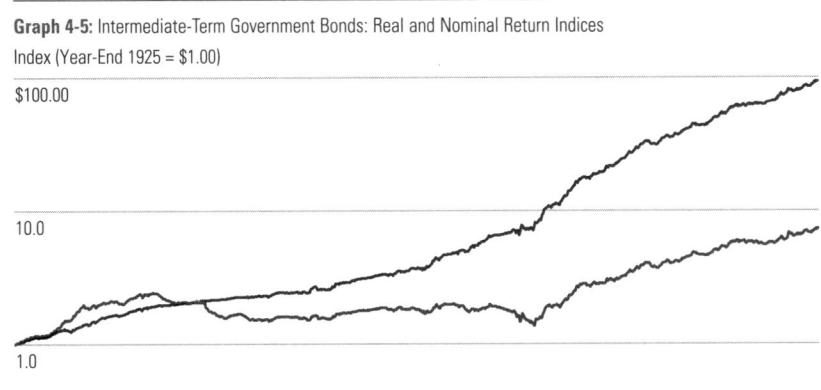

— Nominal Total Return ($92.08 YE11)   — Real Total Return ($7.31 YE11)

Year-End

Data from 1926–2011.

Graph 4-6: U.S. Treasury Bills: Real and Nominal Return Indices

Index (Year-End 1925 = $1.00)

— Nominal Total Return ($20.56 YE11)   — Real Total Return ($1.63 YE11)

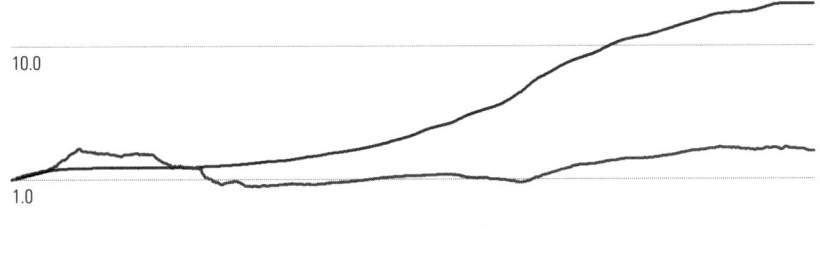

Year-End

Data from 1926–2011.

Inflation-Adjusted Long-Term Government Bond Returns

Overview

Long-term government bonds returned 5.7 percent compounded annually over the period 1926–2011 in nominal terms, and a 2.6 percent compound annual return in real (inflation-adjusted) terms. [See Graph 4-4.] Thus, long-term government bonds have outpaced inflation over the past 86 years despite falling bond prices over most of the period.

Construction

The inflation-adjusted return is a geometric difference and is approximately equal to the arithmetic difference between the long-term government bond total return and

the inflation rate. The monthly inflation-adjusted long-term government bond total return is given by:

$$\frac{\left(1+\text{LT Govt Bond TR}\right)}{\left(1+\text{Inflation}\right)}-1 \quad (13)$$

Since government bond returns are composed of inflation, the real riskless rate, and the horizon premium, the inflation-adjusted government bond returns may also be expressed as:

$$\left[\left(1+\text{Real Riskless Rate}\right)\times\left(1+\text{Horizon Premium}\right)\right]-1 \quad (14)$$

Inflation-Adjusted Intermediate-Term Government Bond Returns

Overview

Intermediate-term government bonds returned 5.4 percent compounded annually over the period 1926–2011 in nominal terms, and 2.3 percent in real (inflation-adjusted) terms. [See Graph 4-5.]

Construction

The inflation-adjusted return is a geometric difference and is approximately equal to the arithmetic difference between the intermediate-term government bond total return and the inflation rate. The monthly inflation-adjusted intermediate-term government bond return is given by:

$$\frac{\left(1+\text{IT Govt Bond TR}\right)}{\left(1+\text{Inflation}\right)}-1 \quad (15)$$

Inflation-Adjusted U.S. Treasury Bill Returns (Real Riskless Rates of Return)

Overview

Treasury bills returned 3.6 percent compounded annually over 1926–2011, in nominal terms, but only a 0.6 percent compound annual return in real (inflation-adjusted) terms. [See Graph 4-6.] Thus, an investor in Treasury bills would have barely beaten inflation over the 86-year period.

Construction

The real riskless rate of return is the difference in returns between riskless U.S. Treasury bills and inflation. This is given by:

$$\frac{\left(1 + \text{Treasury Bill TR}\right)}{\left(1 + \text{Inflation}\right)} - 1 \tag{16}$$

Graph 4-7 shows the levels, volatility, and patterns of real interest rates over the last 86 years.

Graph 4-7: Annual Real Riskless Rates of Return (%)

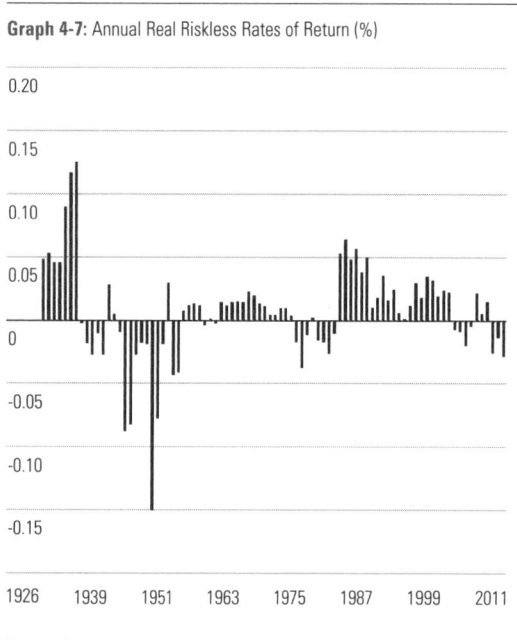

Year-end
Data from 1926–2011.

Returns on the Derived Series

Annual returns for the 10 derived series are calculated from monthly returns in the same manner as the annual basic series. Table 4-1 presents annual returns for each of the 10 derived series. Four of the derived series are risk premia and six are inflation-adjusted total returns on asset classes. ▐▌

Table 4-1: Annual Returns of Derived Series (%)

Year	Equity Risk Premia	Small Stock Premia	Default Premia	Horizon Premia	Inflation-Adjusted Large Company Stocks	Small Company Stocks	Long-Term Corp. Bonds	Long-Term Govt. Bonds	Intermed. Govt. Bonds	U.S. Treasury Bills
1926	8.09	-10.17	-0.37	4.36	13.31	1.79	9.00	9.40	6.97	4.83
1927	33.32	-11.19	-1.36	5.63	40.41	24.69	9.73	11.24	6.74	5.31
1928	38.67	-2.73	2.73	-3.34	45.01	41.06	3.84	1.08	1.90	4.57
1929	-12.57	-46.89	-0.14	-1.27	-8.59	-51.45	3.07	3.22	5.81	4.54
1930	-26.66	-17.64	3.17	2.20	-20.08	-34.18	14.90	11.38	13.56	8.98
1931	-43.94	-11.33	3.65	-6.31	-37.37	-44.46	8.48	4.66	7.96	11.71
1932	-9.07	3.05	-5.15	15.73	2.35	5.47	23.54	30.26	21.30	12.55
1933	53.53	57.72	10.46	-0.37	53.21	141.63	9.82	-0.58	1.31	-0.21
1934	-1.60	26.04	3.47	9.85	-3.40	21.75	11.58	7.84	6.83	-1.83
1935	47.42	-5.06	4.41	4.81	43.39	36.13	6.44	1.94	3.91	-2.73
1936	33.68	23.06	-0.72	7.32	32.32	62.83	5.47	6.23	1.83	-1.02
1937	-35.23	-35.37	2.51	-0.08	-36.98	-59.27	-0.35	-2.78	-1.50	-2.71
1938	31.14	1.28	0.57	5.55	34.87	36.59	9.16	8.55	9.27	2.84
1939	-0.43	0.76	-1.86	5.92	0.07	0.83	4.46	6.45	5.02	0.50
1940	-9.79	5.13	-2.54	6.08	-10.64	-6.05	2.41	5.08	1.99	-0.94
1941	-11.64	2.93	1.78	0.87	-19.42	-17.06	-6.37	-8.01	-8.40	-8.80
1942	20.02	20.08	-0.60	2.94	10.11	32.23	-6.12	-5.55	-6.73	-8.25
1943	25.46	49.62	0.73	1.73	22.04	82.60	-0.32	-1.04	-0.34	-2.73
1944	19.36	28.37	1.87	2.48	17.28	50.55	2.57	0.69	-0.31	-1.74
1945	35.99	27.25	-6.01	10.37	33.43	69.79	1.78	8.30	-0.03	-1.88
1946	-8.39	-3.87	1.83	-0.45	-22.20	-25.21	-13.91	-15.46	-14.52	-15.07
1947	5.18	-4.53	0.29	-3.11	-3.03	-7.42	-10.41	-10.67	-7.43	-7.80
1948	4.65	-7.22	0.71	2.57	2.72	-4.69	1.39	0.67	-0.84	-1.85
1949	17.50	0.80	-2.95	5.29	20.97	21.95	5.21	8.40	4.20	2.96
1950	30.16	5.34	2.05	-1.12	24.50	31.15	-3.47	-5.42	-4.81	-4.34
1951	22.19	-13.07	1.29	-5.34	17.14	1.82	-8.09	-9.26	-5.21	-4.14
1952	16.44	-12.96	2.33	-0.49	17.33	2.13	2.62	0.27	0.74	0.77
1953	-2.76	-5.55	-0.22	1.78	-1.60	-7.07	2.77	2.99	2.59	1.19
1954	51.32	5.21	-1.68	6.27	53.39	61.38	5.91	7.72	3.20	1.37
1955	29.52	-8.45	1.80	-2.82	31.07	19.99	0.10	-1.66	-1.02	1.19
1956	4.00	-2.13	-1.30	-7.85	3.59	1.38	-9.41	-8.21	-3.19	-0.39
1957	-13.50	-4.25	1.17	4.19	-13.40	-17.08	5.52	4.31	4.67	0.11
1958	41.19	15.01	4.13	-7.52	40.88	62.03	-3.91	-7.72	-3.00	-0.22
1959	8.75	3.97	1.32	-5.06	10.30	14.68	-2.43	-3.70	-1.86	1.43
1960	-2.14	-3.74	-4.14	10.83	-0.99	-4.70	7.48	12.12	10.13	1.17
1961	24.25	4.10	3.81	-1.13	26.04	31.21	4.12	0.30	1.17	1.44
1962	-11.16	-3.48	0.99	4.04	-9.83	-12.97	6.64	5.59	4.29	1.49
1963	19.09	0.62	0.97	-1.85	20.81	21.56	0.54	-0.43	-0.01	1.44
1964	12.50	6.04	1.22	-0.03	15.11	22.07	3.54	2.29	2.82	2.32
1965	8.20	26.06	-1.16	-3.10	10.33	39.08	-2.33	-1.19	-0.89	1.97
1966	-14.15	3.39	-3.33	-1.06	-12.98	-10.03	-3.06	0.29	1.29	1.36
1967	18.97	48.07	4.66	-12.85	20.32	78.15	-7.76	-11.86	-1.97	1.13
1968	5.57	22.43	2.84	-5.20	6.05	29.84	-2.05	-4.76	-0.18	0.46
1969	-14.16	-18.09	-3.18	-10.94	-13.77	-29.37	-13.38	-10.54	-6.45	0.45
1970	-2.50	-20.50	5.59	5.24	-1.55	-21.73	12.21	6.27	10.78	0.98

Table 4-1: Annual Returns of Derived Series (%) (Continued)

Year	Equity Risk Premia	Small Stock Premia	Default Premia	Horizon Premia	Inflation-Adjusted Large Company Stocks	Small Company Stocks	Long-Term Corp. Bonds	Long-Term Govt. Bonds	Intermed. Govt. Bonds	U.S. Treasury Bills
1971	9.50	1.92	-1.96	8.47	10.59	12.71	7.41	9.55	5.19	0.99
1972	14.59	-12.24	1.49	1.78	15.07	0.99	3.72	2.20	1.69	0.41
1973	-20.22	-19.01	2.27	-7.52	-21.59	-36.49	-7.04	-9.10	-3.85	-1.72
1974	-31.92	8.87	-7.11	-3.38	-34.46	-28.65	-13.60	-6.99	-5.80	-3.74
1975	29.70	11.36	4.99	3.21	28.23	42.80	7.13	2.04	0.76	-1.13
1976	17.93	26.99	1.62	11.11	18.24	50.15	13.20	11.40	7.69	0.26
1977	-11.68	35.04	2.41	-5.53	-13.04	17.43	-4.74	-6.99	-5.02	-1.55
1978	-0.57	15.85	1.12	-7.80	-2.25	13.24	-8.34	-9.36	-5.08	-1.69
1979	7.46	20.96	-2.98	-10.52	4.68	26.62	-15.43	-12.83	-8.13	-2.59
1980	19.12	5.56	1.24	-13.65	17.89	24.45	-13.48	-14.54	-7.55	-1.03
1981	-17.11	19.78	-3.04	-11.20	-12.73	4.53	-9.34	-6.50	0.47	5.30
1982	9.95	5.31	1.57	26.97	17.02	23.23	37.25	35.13	24.28	6.42
1983	12.64	13.96	5.57	-7.49	18.07	34.56	2.37	-3.03	3.48	4.82
1984	-3.26	-12.18	1.20	5.12	2.23	-10.22	12.42	11.08	9.68	5.67
1985	22.28	-5.36	-0.67	21.58	26.94	20.13	25.36	26.21	15.96	3.81
1986	11.78	-9.96	-3.76	17.30	17.34	5.66	18.51	23.14	13.85	4.98
1987	-0.20	-13.82	2.51	-7.76	0.81	-13.13	-4.48	-6.82	-1.44	1.01
1988	9.65	5.37	0.94	3.13	11.67	17.67	6.02	5.03	1.61	1.85
1989	21.51	-16.33	-1.59	8.99	25.84	5.29	11.07	12.87	8.26	3.56
1990	-10.13	-19.05	0.57	-1.51	-8.68	-26.08	0.64	0.07	3.42	1.61
1991	23.55	10.86	0.49	12.98	26.59	40.33	16.32	15.75	12.03	2.46
1992	3.97	14.62	1.24	4.39	4.59	19.87	6.31	5.01	4.17	0.59
1993	6.98	9.90	-4.28	14.91	7.13	17.74	10.16	15.08	8.26	0.14
1994	-2.49	1.76	2.18	-11.24	-1.32	0.42	-8.22	-10.17	-7.62	1.20
1995	30.29	-2.27	-3.39	24.69	34.17	31.13	24.06	28.41	13.91	2.98
1996	16.87	-4.34	2.35	-5.83	19.01	13.84	-1.86	-4.12	-1.18	1.82
1997	26.70	-7.94	-2.51	10.07	31.13	20.72	11.06	13.91	6.57	3.49
1998	22.62	-27.91	-2.04	7.83	26.54	-8.78	9.00	11.27	8.46	3.19
1999	15.63	7.23	1.67	-13.04	17.88	26.39	-9.87	-11.34	-4.34	1.95
2000	-14.16	6.06	-7.09	14.72	-12.08	-6.75	9.17	17.50	8.90	2.42
2001	-15.13	39.33	6.70	-0.13	-13.23	20.89	8.96	2.11	5.97	2.24
2002	-23.36	11.33	-1.28	15.93	-23.91	-15.29	13.63	15.10	10.31	-0.71
2003	27.38	24.88	3.76	0.42	26.31	57.73	3.32	-0.42	0.51	-0.84
2004	9.56	6.77	0.19	7.22	7.39	14.66	5.29	5.09	-0.97	-1.99
2005	1.88	0.74	-1.80	4.69	1.45	2.20	2.37	4.25	-1.99	-0.42
2006	10.49	0.32	2.03	-3.45	12.93	13.29	0.69	-1.32	0.59	2.20
2007	0.79	-10.16	-6.63	4.99	1.36	-8.94	-1.43	5.57	5.74	0.56
2008	-37.99	0.43	-13.58	23.89	-37.06	-36.78	8.68	25.76	13.00	1.51
2009	26.34	1.28	21.06	-14.98	23.11	24.69	0.29	-17.16	-4.99	-2.56
2010	14.92	14.08	2.08	10.01	13.37	29.33	10.78	8.52	5.54	-1.35
2011	2.07	-5.26	-8.02	28.18	-0.83	-6.04	-14.55	24.54	6.31	-2.84

Chapter 5
Annual Returns and Indices

Returns and indices are used to measure the rewards investors earn for holding an asset class. Indices represent levels of wealth or prices, while returns represent changes in levels of wealth. Total returns for specific asset classes consist of component returns that are defined by the nature of the rewards being measured. For example: The total return on a security can be divided into income and capital appreciation components. The income return measures the cash income stream earned by holding the security, such as coupon interest or dividend payments. In contrast, the capital appreciation return results from a change in the price of the security. The method for computing a return varies with the nature of the payment (income or capital appreciation) and the time period of measure (monthly or annual frequency). Indices are computed by establishing a base period and base value and increasing that value by the successive returns. Indices are used to illustrate the cumulative growth of wealth from holding an asset class. This chapter describes the computation of the annual returns and indices.

The first generation of stock indices was created to assess the market's general direction. One of the oldest and most recognizable market indices is the Dow Jones Industrial Average (DJIA), first published on May 26, 1896. When Charles Dow initially calculated the DJIA, which originally consisted of only twelve stocks[1], the process was simple: Add up the share prices of the stocks in the index and then divide this result by the number of stocks in the index. In this type of index, which is known as a price-weighted index, higher-priced stocks have a greater influence than lower-priced stocks.

Most modern indices, however, are market weighted. With market-weighted indices, companies with greater overall market capitalization (share price times number of shares outstanding) have a larger influence than companies with lesser market capitalization. Market weighting has a strong theoretical motivation because the capital asset pricing model (CAPM) implies that every investor should hold every security in proportion to its market capitalization. In contrast, price weighting lacks any theoretical motivation so it is rarely used outside of the Dow Jones Averages (Dow Jones uses market weighting for all of its other indexes). Market weighting is widely considered to be the central organizing principle of good index construction. Its practical advantage is that the weights adjust automatically as share prices fluctuate, eliminating the need for the frequent and expensive rebalancing that can occur with other weighting schemes.

Market weighting is usually implemented with a "float" adjustment that subtracts the number of closely-held and illiquid shares from the number of shares outstanding. A float-adjusted market-cap weighted portfolio is macroconsistent, meaning that if all investors held such a portfolio, all available shares of its constituent stocks would be held, with none left over. With all other weighting schemes, it is mathematically impossible for all investors to hold the index portfolio.

While there is wide agreement on the general principles of equity index construction, index providers differ in their methodologies in the process by which stocks are selected for inclusion, the number of stocks to include, and other details. Table 5-3 summaries the construction methodologies of the major broad indexes of the U.S. equity market.

Annual and Monthly Returns
Returns on the Basic Asset Classes
Summary statistics of annual total returns of the seven basic asset classes are presented in Table 2-1 in Chapter 2. The monthly total returns on the asset classes and inflation appear in Appendix A: Tables A-1, A-4, A-5, A-6, A-10, A-14, and A-15.

Calculating Annual Returns
Annual returns are formed by compounding the 12 monthly returns. Compounding, or linking, monthly returns is multiplying together the return relatives, or one plus the return, then subtracting one from the result. The equation is denoted as the geometric sum as follows:

$$r_{year} = \left[(1+r_{Jan})(1+r_{Feb})\cdots(1+r_{Dec})\right]-1 \qquad (17)$$

where,

r_{year} = the compound total return for the year;

and,

$r_{Jan}, r_{Feb}, \ldots, r_{Dec}$ = the returns for the 12 months of the year.

The compound return reflects the growth of funds invested in an asset. The following example illustrates the compounding method for a hypothetical year:

Month	Return (%)	Return (Decimal)	Return Relative
January	1	0.01	1.01
February	6	0.06	1.06
March	2	0.02	1.02
April	1	0.01	1.01
May	-3	-0.03	0.97
June	2	0.02	1.02
July	-4	-0.04	0.96
August	-2	-0.02	0.98
September	3	0.03	1.03
October	-3	-0.03	0.97
November	2	0.02	1.02
December	1	0.01	1.01

The return for this hypothetical year is the geometric sum:

$$(1.01 \times 1.06 \times 1.02 \times 1.01 \times 0.97 \times 1.02 \times 0.96 \times 0.98 \times 1.03 \times 0.97 \times 1.02 \times 1.01) - 1 = 1.0567 - 1 = 0.0567$$

or a gain of 5.67 percent. One dollar invested in this hypothetical asset at the beginning of the year would have grown to slightly less than $1.06. Note that this is different than the simple addition result, $(1 + 6 + 2 + 1 - 3 + 2 - 4 - 2 + 3 - 3 + 2 + 1) = 6$ percent.

Calculation of Returns From Index Values

Equivalently, annual returns, r_t, can be formed by dividing index values according to:

$$r_t = \left[\frac{V_t}{V_{t-1}} \right] - 1 \tag{18}$$

where,

r_t = the annual return in period **t**;
V_t = the index value as of year-end **t**; and,
V_{t-1} = the index value as of the previous year-end, **t** − 1.

The construction of index values is discussed later in this chapter.

Calculation of Annual Income Returns

The conversion of monthly income returns to annual income returns is calculated by adding all the cash flows (income payments) for the period, then dividing the sum by the beginning period price:

$$r_I = \frac{(I_{Jan} + I_{Feb} \ldots + I_{Dec})}{P_0} \tag{19}$$

where,

r_I = the income return for the year;
$I_{Jan}, I_{Feb}, \ldots, I_{Dec}$ = the income payments for the 12 months of the year; and,
P_0 = the price of the security at the beginning of the year.

The following example illustrates the method for a hypothetical year:

Month	Beginning of Month Price ($)	Income Return (Decimal)	Income Payment ($)
January	100	0.006	0.60
February	102	0.004	0.41
March	105	0.002	0.21
April	101	0.001	0.10
May	99	0.005	0.50
June	103	0.004	0.41
July	105	0.003	0.32
August	103	0.002	0.21
September	105	0.003	0.32
October	103	0.004	0.41
November	106	0.001	0.11
December	105	0.002	0.21

Sum the income payments (not the returns), and divide by the price at the beginning of the year:

$$(0.60 + 0.41 + 0.21 + 0.10 + 0.50 + 0.41 + 0.32 + 0.21 + 0.32 + 0.41 + 0.11 + 0.21) / 100 = 0.0381$$

or an annual income return of 3.81 percent.

Annual income and capital appreciation returns do not sum to the annual total return. The difference may be viewed as a reinvestment return, which is the return from investing income from a given month into the same asset class in subsequent months within the year.

Index Values

Index values, or indices, represent the cumulative effect of returns on a dollar invested. For example: One dollar invested in large company stocks (with dividends reinvested) as of December 31, 1925 grew to $1.12 by December 1926, reflecting the 11.6 percent total return in 1926.

[See Table B-1 in Appendix B.] Over the year 1927, the $1.12 grew to $1.53 by December, reflecting the 37.5 percent total return for that year. By the end of 2011, the $1.00 invested at year-end 1925 grew to $3,045.22. Such growth reveals the power of compounding (reinvesting) one's investment returns.

Year-end indices of total returns for all six basic asset classes plus inflation are displayed in Table 5-1 (see next page). This table also shows indices of capital appreciation for large company stocks as well as long- and intermediate-term government bonds. Indices of the inflation-adjusted return series are presented in Table 5-2. Monthly indices of total returns and, where applicable, capital appreciation returns on the basic asset classes are presented in Appendix B: Tables B-1 through B-10.

Graphs of index values, such as Graph 2-1 "Wealth Indices of Investments in the U.S. Capital Markets," depict the growth of wealth. The vertical scale is logarithmic so that equal distances represent equal percentage changes anywhere along the axis.

The inflation-adjusted indices in Table 5-2 are notable in that they show the growth of each asset class in constant dollars, or (synonymously) in real terms. Thus an investor in large company stocks, with dividends reinvested, would have multiplied his or her wealth in real terms, or purchasing power, by a factor of 241.9 between the end of 1925 and the end of 2011.

Calculation of Index Values

It is possible to mathematically describe the nature of the indices in Tables 5-1 and 5-2 precisely. At the end of each month, a cumulative wealth index (V_n) for each of the monthly return series (basic and derived) is formed. This index is initialized as of December 1925 at $1.00 (represented by $V_0 = 1.00$). This index is formed for month n by taking the product of one plus the returns each period, as in the following manner:

(20)

$$v_n = v_0 \left[\prod_{t=1}^{n} (1 + r_t) \right]$$

where,

V_n = the index value at end of period **n**;
V_0 = the initial index value at time **0**; and,
r_t = the return in period **t**.

Using Index Values for Performance Measurement

Index values can be used to determine whether an investment portfolio accumulated more wealth for the investor over a period of time than another portfolio, or whether the investment performed as well as an industry benchmark. In the following example, which produced more wealth—the "investor portfolio" or a hypothetical S&P 500 index fund returning exactly the S&P total return? Each index measures total return and assumes monthly reinvestment of dividends.

	Investor Portfolio	S&P 500
January 1990 (%)	-5.35	-6.71
February 1990 (%)	0.65	1.29
March 1990 (%)	0.23	2.65
Accumulated wealth of $1	$0.955	$0.970

Taking December 1989 as the base period, and using the computation method described above, the S&P 500 outperformed the investor portfolio.

Computing Returns for Non-Calendar Periods

Index values are also useful for computing returns for non-calendar time periods. To compute the capital appreciation return for long-term government bonds from the end of June 1987 through the end of June 1988, divide the index value in June 1988, 0.661, by the index value in June 1987, 0.683, and subtract 1. [Refer to Table B-6 in Appendix B.] ▬

This yields:

(0.661/ 0.683) − 1 = -0.0322, or -3.22 percent.

Endnotes

[1]Of the original twelve companies listed in the DJIA, General Electric is the only company that remains a component of the average. The total number of companies listed in the DJIA has not changed since 1928 when the number of companies in the index was increased to thirty. For more information on the historical make up of the DJIA, please visit the Dow Jones website at http://www.dowjones.com.

Table 5-1: Basic Series

Indices of Year-End Cumulative Wealth Over Past 10 Years (Year-End 1925 = $1.00)

	Large Stocks		Small Stocks	LT-Corp Bonds	LT-Govt Bonds		IT-Govt Bonds		U.S. T-Bills	
Year*	Total Returns	Capital Apprec	Total Returns	Total Returns	Total Returns	Capital Apprec	Total Returns	Capital Apprec	Total Returns	Inflation
2002	1,778.910	68.953	6,816.409	82.480	59.699	1.039	59.054	1.453	17.480	10.091
2003	2,289.182	87.143	10,953.944	86.824	60.564	1.004	60.469	1.446	17.659	10.281
2004	2,538.293	94.980	12,968.476	94.396	65.717	1.037	61.832	1.431	17.871	10.616
2005	2,662.973	97.830	13,706.149	99.937	70.852	1.069	62.674	1.394	18.403	10.978
2006	3,083.570	111.154	15,922.429	103.178	71.694	1.030	64.643	1.373	19.287	11.257
2007	3,252.981	115.078	15,091.095	105.858	78.779	1.078	71.142	1.446	20.186	11.717
2008	2,049.448	70.789	9,548.944	115.154	99.161	1.299	80.466	1.589	20.509	11.728
2009	2,591.824	87.390	12,230.866	118.628	84.383	1.062	78.532	1.519	20.529	12.047
2010	2,982.240	98.560	16,054.698	133.384	92.942	1.124	84.121	1.598	20.553	12.227
2011	3,045.218	98.557	15,532.068	157.324	119.183	1.391	92.080	1.722	20.562	12.589

*For additional data dating back to 1926, see Appendix B.

Table 5-2: Inflation-Adjusted Series

Indices of Year-End Cumulative Wealth (Year-End 1925 = $1.00)

	Inflation-Adjusted Large Company Stocks	Small Company Stocks	Long-Term Corporate Bonds	Long-Term Government Bonds	Intermediate Government Bonds	U.S. Treasury Bills
1925	1.000	1.000	1.000	1.000	1.000	1.000
1926	1.133	1.018	1.090	1.094	1.070	1.048
1927	1.591	1.269	1.196	1.217	1.142	1.104
1928	2.307	1.790	1.242	1.230	1.164	1.154
1929	2.109	0.869	1.280	1.270	1.231	1.207
1930	1.685	0.572	1.471	1.414	1.398	1.315
1931	1.056	0.318	1.596	1.480	1.509	1.469
1932	1.080	0.335	1.971	1.928	1.831	1.654
1933	1.655	0.810	2.165	1.917	1.855	1.650
1934	1.599	0.986	2.415	2.067	1.982	1.620
1935	2.292	1.342	2.571	2.107	2.059	1.576
1936	3.033	2.185	2.712	2.238	2.097	1.560
1937	1.912	0.890	2.702	2.176	2.065	1.517
1938	2.578	1.216	2.950	2.362	2.257	1.561
1939	2.580	1.226	3.082	2.514	2.370	1.568
1940	2.305	1.152	3.156	2.642	2.417	1.554
1941	1.858	0.955	2.955	2.430	2.214	1.417
1942	2.046	1.263	2.774	2.295	2.065	1.300
1943	2.496	2.306	2.765	2.271	2.058	1.264
1944	2.928	3.472	2.836	2.287	2.052	1.242
1945	3.907	5.895	2.887	2.477	2.051	1.219
1946	3.039	4.409	2.485	2.094	1.753	1.035
1947	2.947	4.081	2.227	1.871	1.623	0.955
1948	3.027	3.890	2.258	1.883	1.609	0.937
1949	3.662	4.744	2.375	2.042	1.677	0.965
1950	4.560	6.221	2.293	1.931	1.596	0.923
1951	5.341	6.335	2.107	1.752	1.513	0.885
1952	6.267	6.469	2.162	1.757	1.524	0.891
1953	6.166	6.012	2.222	1.809	1.564	0.902
1954	9.458	9.703	2.354	1.949	1.614	0.914
1955	12.397	11.642	2.356	1.917	1.597	0.925
1956	12.843	11.803	2.134	1.759	1.547	0.922
1957	11.122	9.788	2.252	1.835	1.619	0.923
1958	15.669	15.859	2.164	1.694	1.570	0.921
1959	17.283	18.187	2.112	1.631	1.541	0.934
1960	17.111	17.333	2.270	1.829	1.697	0.945
1961	21.567	22.741	2.363	1.834	1.717	0.958
1962	19.447	19.792	2.520	1.937	1.791	0.973
1963	23.494	24.060	2.534	1.928	1.790	0.987
1964	27.044	29.370	2.623	1.972	1.841	1.010
1965	29.838	40.848	2.562	1.949	1.825	1.029
1966	25.964	36.751	2.484	1.955	1.848	1.043
1967	31.239	65.471	2.291	1.723	1.812	1.055
1968	33.129	85.005	2.244	1.641	1.808	1.060
1969	28.567	60.042	1.944	1.468	1.692	1.065
1970	28.124	46.993	2.181	1.560	1.874	1.075

| | Inflation-Adjusted | | | | | |
	Large Company Stocks	Small Company Stocks	Long-Term Corporate Bonds	Long-Term Government Bonds	Intermediate Government Bonds	U.S. Treasury Bills
1971	31.101	52.968	2.343	1.709	1.971	1.086
1972	35.788	53.492	2.430	1.746	2.005	1.091
1973	28.062	33.971	2.259	1.587	1.927	1.072
1974	18.391	24.238	1.951	1.476	1.815	1.032
1975	23.583	34.612	2.091	1.506	1.829	1.020
1976	27.884	51.971	2.366	1.678	1.970	1.023
1977	24.247	61.029	2.254	1.561	1.871	1.007
1978	23.701	69.108	2.066	1.415	1.776	0.990
1979	24.810	87.502	1.747	1.233	1.632	0.964
1980	29.248	108.894	1.512	1.054	1.508	0.954
1981	25.526	113.831	1.371	0.985	1.515	1.005
1982	29.870	140.278	1.881	1.332	1.884	1.069
1983	35.268	188.759	1.926	1.291	1.949	1.121
1984	36.055	169.470	2.165	1.434	2.138	1.184
1985	45.768	203.588	2.714	1.810	2.479	1.230
1986	53.704	215.106	3.216	2.229	2.822	1.291
1987	54.137	186.867	3.072	2.077	2.782	1.304
1988	60.456	219.893	3.257	2.182	2.826	1.328
1989	76.077	231.516	3.617	2.462	3.060	1.375
1990	69.473	171.148	3.641	2.464	3.164	1.397
1991	87.944	240.179	4.235	2.852	3.545	1.431
1992	91.977	287.908	4.502	2.995	3.693	1.440
1993	98.539	338.990	4.959	3.447	3.998	1.442
1994	97.239	340.412	4.552	3.096	3.693	1.459
1995	130.467	446.387	5.647	3.976	4.207	1.503
1996	155.264	508.167	5.542	3.812	4.157	1.530
1997	203.600	613.460	6.155	4.342	4.430	1.584
1998	257.633	559.617	6.709	4.832	4.805	1.634
1999	303.690	707.326	6.047	4.284	4.597	1.666
2000	266.998	659.578	6.601	5.033	5.006	1.706
2001	231.668	797.394	7.193	5.140	5.305	1.745
2002	176.279	675.462	8.173	5.916	5.852	1.732
2003	222.658	1,065.441	8.445	5.891	5.882	1.718
2004	239.104	1,221.615	8.892	6.191	5.824	1.683
2005	242.564	1,248.459	9.103	6.454	5.709	1.676
2006	273.916	1,414.400	9.165	6.369	5.742	1.713
2007	277.633	1,287.986	9.035	6.724	6.072	1.723
2008	174.755	814.233	9.819	8.455	6.861	1.749
2009	215.148	1,015.290	9.847	7.005	6.519	1.704
2010	243.909	1,313.068	10.909	7.601	6.880	1.681
2011	241.894	1,233.774	12.497	9.467	7.314	1.633

Table 5-3: The Major Capitalization and Style Indexes of the U.S. Equity Market*

	Index Family				
	Morningstar	DJ/Wilshire	MSCI	Russell	S&P/Citigroup
Broad Market Index	Morningstar US Market Index	Dow Jones Wilshire 5000 Composite	MSCI Investable Market	Russell 3000	S&P Composite 1500**
Percent U.S. Market Cap Coverage for Broad Market Index	97%	>99%	>99%	98%	90%
Total Number of Stocks	1,700+	5,000	2,500	3,000	1,500
Transparent, Rule-based Methodology	Yes	Yes	Yes	Yes	No
Eligibility	Stocks of companies domiciled in U.S. listed on the NYSE, NYSE Amex, or NASDAQ	Stocks of U.S. domiciled companies for which prices are available and listed on a U.S. exchange	Stocks of companies domiciled in U.S. listed on the NYSE, NYSE Amex, or NASDAQ	Stocks of the largest 3,000 companies domiciled in the U.S. listed on a U.S. exchange or the NASDAQ	Stocks of U.S. domiciled companies listed on the NYSE, NYSE Amex, or NASDAQ chosen for market size, liquidity, and industry group representation by the S&P Index Committee
Exclusion Criteria	ADRs Limited Partnerships, Investment Trusts (except REITs), Tracking Stocks and Holding Companies	ADRs Over the Counter Issues	ADRs Limited Partnerships , Investment Trusts (except REITs), Mutual Funds, Equity Derivatives , and Royalty Trusts and LLCs	ADRs Limited Partnerships, Closed-end mutual funds, Price < $1, and Royalty Trusts and LLCs	ADRs Limited Partnerships, Investment Trusts (except REITs), Tracking Stocks, Holding Companies and Royalty Trusts and LLCs
Market Cap Cut-off Method	Market Cap Percent	Fixed Number of Stocks	Fixed Number of Stocks	Fixed Number of Stocks	Fixed Number of Stocks
Unique Cap Classification	Yes	No, stocks may be included in more than one cap index	Yes	Yes	Yes
Unique Style Classification	Yes	Yes	No, stocks may be included in more than one style index	No, stocks may be included in more than one style index	No, stocks may be included in more than one style index
Core Style Index	Yes	No	No	No	No
Reconstitution Frequency	Semi-Annual	Semi-Annual	Semi-Annual	Annual	Ad hoc

*The broad market indices shown in Table 5-3 can be disaggregated into capitalization and style indices. For example, the S&P Composite 1500 can be disaggregated into the S&P 500 (large-cap stocks), the S&P 400 (mid-cap stocks), and the S&P 600 (small-cap stocks).

**The market for U.S. large company stocks is represented by the S&P 500 throughout the Ibbotson® SBBI® Yearbook series.

Chapter 6
Statistical Analysis of Returns

Statistical analysis of historical asset returns can reveal the growth rate of wealth invested in an asset or portfolio, the riskiness or volatility of asset classes, the comovement of assets, and the random or cyclical behavior of asset returns. This chapter focuses on arithmetic and geometric mean returns, standard deviations, and serial and cross-correlation coefficients, and discusses the use of each statistic to characterize the various asset classes by growth rate, variability, and safety.

Calculating Arithmetic Mean Returns

The arithmetic mean of a series is the simple average of the elements in the series. The arithmetic mean return equation is:

$$r_A = \frac{1}{n}\sum_{t=1}^{n} r_t \tag{21}$$

where,

r_A = the arithmetic mean return;

r_t = the series return in period t, that is, from time $t-1$ to time t; and,

n = the inclusive number of periods.

Calculating Geometric Mean Returns

The geometric mean of a return series over a period is the compound rate of return over the period. The geometric mean return equation is:

$$r_G = \left[\prod_{t=1}^{n} (1+r_t) \right]^{\frac{1}{n}} - 1 \tag{22}$$

where,

r_G = the geometric mean return;

r_t = the series return in period t; and,

n = the inclusive number of periods.

The geometric mean return can be restated using beginning and ending period index values. The equation is:

$$r_G = \left[\frac{V_n}{V_0} \right]^{\frac{1}{n}} - 1 \tag{23}$$

where,

r_G = the geometric mean return;

V_n = the ending period index value at time n;

V_0 = the initial index value at time 0; and,

n = the inclusive number of periods.

The annualized geometric mean return over any period of months can also be computed by expressing n as a fraction. For example: starting at the beginning of 1996 to the end of May 1996 is equivalent to five-twelfths of a year, or 0.4167. V_n would be the index value at the end of May 1996, V_0 would be the index value at the beginning of 1996, and n would be 0.4167.

Geometric Mean Versus Arithmetic Mean

A simple example illustrates the difference between geometric and arithmetic means. Suppose $1.00 was invested in a large company stock portfolio that experiences successive annual returns of +50 percent and -50 percent. At the end of the first year, the portfolio is worth $1.50 and at the end of the second year, it is worth $0.75. The annual arithmetic mean is 0.0 percent, whereas the annual geometric mean is -13.4 percent. Both are calculated as follows:

$$r_A = \frac{1}{2}\left(0.50 - 0.50\right) = 0.0, \text{ and}$$

$$r_G = \left[\frac{0.75}{1.00} \right]^{\frac{1}{2}} - 1 = -0.134$$

The geometric mean is backward-looking, measuring the change in wealth over more than one period. On the other hand, the arithmetic mean better represents a typical performance over single periods.

In general, the geometric mean for any time period is less than or equal to the arithmetic mean. The two means are equal only for a return series that is constant (i.e., the same return in every period). For a non-constant series, the difference between the two is positively related to the variability or standard deviation of the returns. For example, in Table 6-7, the difference between the arithmetic and geometric mean is much larger for risky large company stocks than it is for nearly riskless Treasury bills.

Calculating Standard Deviations

The standard deviation of a series is a measure of the extent to which observations in the series differ from the arithmetic mean of the series. For a series of asset returns, the standard deviation is a measure of the volatility, or risk, of the asset.

In a normally distributed series, about two-thirds of the observations lie within one standard deviation of the arithmetic mean; about 95 percent of the observations lie within two standard deviations; and more than 99 percent lie within three standard deviations.

For example, the standard deviation for large company stocks over the period 1926–2011 was 20.3 percent with an annual arithmetic mean of 11.8 percent. Therefore, roughly two-thirds of the observations have annual returns between -8.5 percent and 32.1 percent (11.8 ± 20.3); approximately 95 percent of the observations are between -28.8 percent and 52.4 percent (11.8 ± 40.6).

The equation for the standard deviation of a series of returns (σ_r) is:

$$\sigma_r = \sqrt{\frac{1}{n-1}\sum_{t=1}^{n}(r_t - r_A)^2} \tag{24}$$

where,
  r_t = the return in period **t**;
  r_A = the arithmetic mean of the return series **r**; and,
  n = the number of periods.

The scaling of the standard deviation depends on the frequency of the data; therefore, a series of monthly returns produces a monthly standard deviation. For example, using the monthly returns for the hypothetical year on Page 68, a monthly standard deviation of 2.94 percent is calculated applying equation (24):

$$\left[\frac{1}{12-1}\left((0.01-0.005)^2 + (0.06-0.005)^2 + (0.02-0.005)^2 + \right.\right.$$
$$(0.01-0.005)^2 + (-0.03-0.005)^2 + (0.02-0.005)^2 +$$
$$(-0.04-0.005)^2 + (-0.02-0.005)^2 + (0.03-0.005)^2 +$$
$$\left.\left.(-0.03-0.005)^2 + (0.02-0.005)^2 + (0.01-0.005)^2\right)\right]^{\frac{1}{2}} = 0.0294$$

It is sometimes useful to express the standard deviation of the series in another time scale. To calculate the annualized monthly standard deviations (σ_n), one uses equation (25).[1]

$$\sigma_n = \sqrt{\left[\sigma_1^2 + (1+\mu_1)^2\right]^n - (1+\mu_1)^{2n}} \tag{25}$$

where,
  n = the number of periods per year, e.g. 12 for monthly, 4 for quarterly, etc.;
  σ_1 = the monthly standard deviation; and,
  μ_1 = the monthly arithmetic mean.

Applying this formula to the prior monthly standard deviation of 2.94 percent results in an annualized monthly standard deviation of 10.78 percent. The annualized monthly standard deviation is calculated with equation (25) as follows:

$$\sqrt{\left[0.0294^2 + (1+0.005)^2\right]^{12} - (1+0.005)^{2(12)}} = 0.1078$$

This equation is the exact form of the common approximation:

$$\sigma_n \approx \sqrt{n}\,\sigma_1$$

The approximation treats an annual return as if it were the sum of 12 independent monthly returns, whereas equation (25) treats an annual return as the compound return of 12 independent monthly returns. [See Equation (17).] While the approximation can be used for "back of the envelope" calculations, the exact formula should be used in applications of quantitative analysis. Forming inputs for mean-variance optimization is one such example. Note that both the exact formula and the approximation assume that there is no monthly autocorrelation.

Limitations of Standard Deviation[2]

Using the statistical measure of standard deviation of returns is clearly the easiest and most elegant way to mathematically express the concept of risk. However, practitioners and academics alike have made the criticism that, while elegant, standard deviation does not express important and essential qualities of risk from the standpoint of an investor of capital.

One limitation of standard deviation as a measure of risk is the tacit assumption that returns can be described by a measure that assumes a normal distribution of returns, while it is empirically acknowledged that many financial market returns exhibit excess kurtosis relative to the normal (Gaussian) distribution. This characteristic is referred to as a leptokurtic or "fat-tailed" return distribution. Fat-tailed outcomes reflect market movements far larger than one would reasonably expect from a normal distribution of returns. One of the most extreme examples of a fat-tailed return profile occurred on Oct. 19, 1987, when the Dow Jones Industrial Average declined by 22.68%, or more than 20 standard deviations. The magnitude of the deviation from normal returns can be understood when considering that a normal distribution would predict such a move once in more than 4.5 billion years. More recently, 2008 had 11 days with declines greater than 4 standard deviations, and on May 6, 2010, the Dow Jones Industrial Average declined by 9% in a matter of minutes on an intraday basis, a move that on a daily basis would have been among the top 10 declines in recorded history. Clearly, an awareness of the nature of statistical descriptions of market moves beyond standard deviation is helpful in developing a representative profile of market risk.

Semi-Variance and Semi-Standard Deviation

Given academic and practitioner concerns about variance, various approaches have been taken to attempt to more appropriately measure risk. We take a moment here to briefly discuss investor perception of risk and to review another measure—semi-variance.

One criticism of variance and standard deviation is that an investor is less worried about bidirectional variation in value (the essence of the standard deviation measure) than he is about an ultimately unrecoverable shortfall in investment capital. In considering risk from this point of view, two cases stand out as the most salient: 1) suffering a realized or mark-to-market loss of capital such that one is prevented from fulfilling one's goal or mandate over

one's investment timeframe and 2) allocating capital in investments that appreciate too little to fulfill one's goal or mandate over one's investment timeframe. The former case involves an excess of variation in an unacceptable direction; the latter case involves a paucity of variation to an acceptable magnitude.

Of these two cases mentioned here, most academic work has focused on developing a framework to accurately measure and analyze directionally-specific variance. Foremost in this attempt has been the concept of semi-variance.

Semi-variance characterizes the downside risk of a distribution and focuses on the portion of risk that is below (to the left of) the mean or a specific target. For example, if your target return is 4%, the semi-variance describes the variance of the data points below (to the left of) the specified target return of 4%. The semi-variance below the mean uses the mean return as the target return. The semi-standard deviation is simply the square-root of the semi-variance. The semi-variance (standard deviation) is always lower than the total variance (standard deviation) of the distribution.

$$SV_m = \frac{1}{n} \times \sum_{r_t < r_A}^{n} \left(r_A - r_t \right)^2$$

$$SV_t = \frac{1}{n} \times \sum_{r_t < r_T}^{n} \left(r_T - r_t \right)^2$$

$$SSTD_m = \sqrt{SV_m}$$

$$SSTD_t = \sqrt{SV_t}$$

where,

SV_m	= the semi-variance below mean;
SV_t	= the semi-variance below target;
r_A	= the arithmetic mean return;
r_t	= the series return in period **t**;
r_T	= the target selection return;
n	= the inclusive number of periods;
$SSTD_m$	= the semi-standard deviation below mean;
$SSTD_t$	= the semi-standard deviation below target;

Issues Regarding Semi-Variance

While it is clear that semi-variance seems to intuitively address issues regarding directionality, it does have empirical, theoretical, and practical issues. Empirically, when returns are measured over relatively short time frames, distributions tend to be symmetric. As such, using semi-variance for short time frames effectively gives one no extra explanatory power (since semi-variance simply equates to one half of the variance) and, in fact, limits the data available for analysis (since the calculation of semi-variance discards any positive return observations). When returns are measured over relatively longer time frames (on the order of a year or more), asset returns tend to follow a distribution that is positively skewed. As such, for investors with longer time horizons, semi-variance has less explanatory power since the data set is limited to the less germane case, while the richer part of the data set is discarded.

From a theoretical standpoint, the assumption implicit in the calculation of semi-variance—that investors do not care about positive variance—has repercussions regarding investor utility functions. Namely, ignoring positive variation implies that an investor is indifferent when presented with the choice between making an uncertain but positive-return bet and making a bet that is certain to generate the expected payoff from the uncertain bet. For example, investors would, under the assumptions of semi-variance, be agnostic between a 50-50 bet of generating either 5% or 10% and a sure bet paying 7.5%.

Practically speaking, ignoring upside variation means that we ignore the second aspect of risk mentioned above—a paucity of magnitude. In other words, if one attempts to minimize semi-variance, without regard to the degree to which an asset or allocation has upside potential, one runs the risk of generating returns which, while low in downside variance, are also low in upside variance. In this case, one has protected oneself from one class of risk by taking on yet another. Given these issues, semi-variance has met with limited acceptance among academics and practitioners alike.

Volatility of the Markets

The volatility of stocks and long-term government bonds is shown by the bar graphs of monthly returns in Graph 6-1. The stock market was tremendously volatile in the first few years studied; this period was marked by the 1920s boom, the crash of 1929–1932, and the Great Depression years. The market settled after World War II and provided more stable returns in the postwar period. In the 1970s and 1980s, stock market volatility increased, but not to the extreme levels of the 1920s and 1930s. In the 1990s and 2000s, volatility was relatively moderate.

Bonds present a mirror image. Long-term government bonds were extremely stable in the 1920s and remained so through the crisis years of the 1930s, providing shelter from the storms of the stock markets. Starting in the late 1960s and early 1970s, however, bond volatility soared; in the 1973–1974 stock market decline, bonds did not provide the shelter they once did. Bond pessimism (i.e., high yields) peaked in 1981 and subsequent returns were sharply positive. While the astronomical interest rates of the 1979–1981 period have passed, the volatility of the bond market remains higher.

Table 6-1: Annualized Monthly Standard Deviations by Decade (%)

	1920s*	1930s	1940s	1950s	1960s
Large Company Stocks	23.9	41.6	17.5	14.1	13.1
Small Company Stocks	24.7	78.6	34.5	14.4	21.5
Long-Term Corp Bonds	1.8	5.3	1.8	4.4	4.9
Long-Term Govt Bonds	4.1	5.3	2.8	4.6	6.0
Inter-Term Govt Bonds	1.7	3.3	1.2	2.9	3.3
Treasury Bills	0.3	0.2	0.1	0.2	0.4
Inflation	2.0	2.5	3.1	1.2	0.7

	1970s	1980s	1990s	2000s	2002-11
Large Company Stocks	17.2	19.4	15.9	16.3	16.6
Small Company Stocks	30.8	22.5	20.2	26.1	23.7
Long-Term Corp Bonds	8.7	14.1	6.9	11.7	12.2
Long-Term Govt Bonds	8.7	16.0	8.9	12.4	13.2
Inter-Term Govt Bonds	5.2	8.8	4.6	5.2	5.1
Treasury Bills	0.6	0.9	0.4	0.6	0.5
Inflation	1.2	1.3	0.7	1.6	1.5

Data from 1926–2011.
*Based on the period 1926–1929.

Changes in the Risk of Assets Over Time

Another time series property of great interest is change in volatility or riskiness over time. Such change is indicated by the standard deviation of the series over different sub-periods. Table 6-1 shows the annualized monthly standard deviations of the basic data series by decade beginning in 1926 and illustrates differences and changes in return volatility. In this table, the '20s cover the period 1926–1929. Equity returns have been the most volatile of the basic series, with volatility peaking in the 1930s due to the instability of the market following the 1929 market crash. The significant bond yield fluctuations of the '80s caused the fixed income series' volatility to soar compared to prior decades.

Table 6-2 (see Page 80) displays the annualized standard deviation of the monthly returns on each of the basic and derived series from 1926 to 2011. The estimates in this table and in Table 6-1 are not strictly comparable to

Table 2-1 and Table 6-7 and 6-8, where the 86-year period standard deviation of annual returns around the 86-year annual arithmetic mean is reported. The arithmetic mean drifts for a series that does not follow a random pattern. A series with a drifting mean will have much higher deviations around its long-term mean than it has around the mean during a particular calendar year.

Graph 6-1: Month-by-Month Returns on Stocks and Bonds
Monthly Return (%)

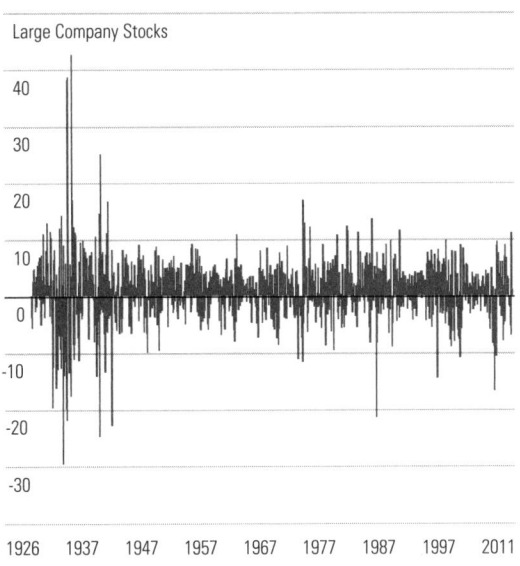

Large Company Stocks

1926 1937 1947 1957 1967 1977 1987 1997 2011
Year-end

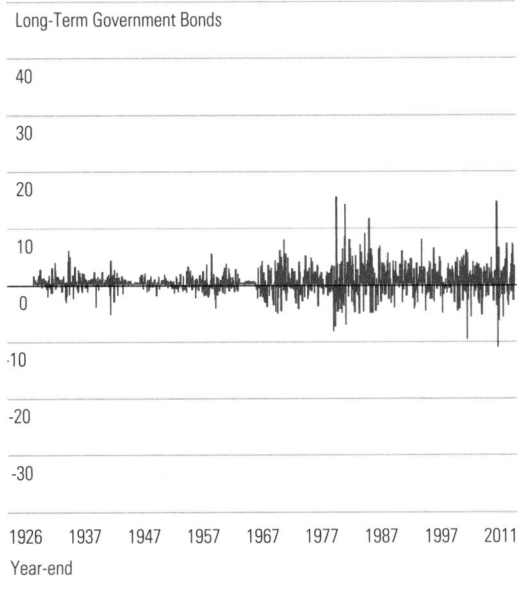

Long-Term Government Bonds

1926 1937 1947 1957 1967 1977 1987 1997 2011
Year-end

Data from 1926–2011.

As shown in Table 6-2, large company stocks and equity risk premia have virtually the same annualized monthly standard deviations because there is very little deviation in the U.S. Treasury bill series. The series with drifting means (U.S. Treasury bills, inflation rates, and inflation-adjusted U.S. Treasury bills) all tend to have very low annualized monthly standard deviations, since these series are quite predictable from month to month. As seen in Tables 6-7 and 6-8 (see Pages 83 and 84), however, there is much less predictability for these series over the long term. Since it is difficult to forecast the direction and magnitude of the drift in the long-term mean, these series have higher standard deviations over the long term in comparison to their annualized monthly standard deviations.

While equity investors may have the impression that the 2008–2009 crisis was mainly one of the equity markets, a careful look at Table 6-2 will show the much greater effect the crisis had on the price fluctuation of bonds in general and long-term corporate bonds in particular. The annualized standard deviation of long-term corporate bonds recorded an historic high value of 25.5% per annum in 2008, a year which saw the collapse of storied investment banks Lehman Brothers and Bear Sterns. The previous record standard deviation for long-term bonds of 20.2% per annum—measured during 1981—is more than one fifth lower than the 2008 value, and more than twice the Depression era record of 11.7% per annum, recorded in 1933. In contrast, the peak in large-capitalization stocks clearly falls early in the series (99.8% per annum in 1933), dwarfing 2009's recorded value of 28.5% per annum. Despite the large number of record-breaking daily index point movements during 2009, this year only represents the eighth most volatile year in our series. Even removing Depression-era records, 2009 only turns up as the second most volatile year on record, behind 1987 (34.2% per annum) and just ahead of 1998 (27.9% per annum). Another mark of the severity of bond price fluctuations can be seen by noting that the annualized standard deviations for long-term bonds in 2008 were only three percentage points shy of the annualized standard deviations for the S&P 500 in 2009.

Table 6-2: Basic and Derived Series
Annualized Monthly Standard Deviations (%)

Year	Basic Series							Derived Series				
	Large Company Stocks	Small Company Stocks	Long-Term Corporate Bonds	Long-Term Govt Bonds	Intermediate-Term Govt Bonds	U.S. Treasury Bills	Inflation	Equity Risk Premia	Small Stock Premia	Bond Default Premia	Bond Horizon Premia	Inflation-Adjusted T-Bills
1926	13.10	16.89	0.96	1.88	1.02	0.32	2.03	12.73	9.74	1.63	1.68	2.06
1927	17.90	21.19	1.49	2.88	1.05	0.11	2.78	17.35	11.13	2.90	2.76	3.03
1928	24.62	28.68	1.87	3.21	1.27	0.32	1.72	23.65	14.48	2.74	3.06	1.84
1929	30.55	18.35	2.42	6.56	2.82	0.21	1.62	29.16	7.76	6.79	6.20	1.62
1930	21.19	25.55	2.38	2.34	2.43	0.30	2.03	20.65	11.68	2.45	2.12	2.31
1931	30.04	45.35	5.91	5.24	3.72	0.16	1.35	29.72	27.44	5.25	5.18	1.75
1932	83.36	147.23	7.71	9.50	2.94	0.29	1.74	82.72	41.92	12.69	9.35	2.40
1933	99.82	286.56	11.74	5.11	3.70	0.10	4.24	99.27	72.06	7.67	5.06	4.15
1934	22.64	73.85	3.10	4.50	4.07	0.04	2.03	22.59	42.03	2.52	4.46	1.94
1935	23.73	36.09	2.53	2.88	2.78	0.01	2.18	23.69	15.08	1.36	2.88	2.05
1936	19.06	66.23	1.18	2.25	1.27	0.02	1.55	19.02	37.72	1.78	2.25	1.51
1937	16.33	21.81	1.99	5.04	2.44	0.05	1.74	16.28	16.46	3.93	5.01	1.63
1938	58.87	114.31	2.38	2.35	2.48	0.07	1.78	58.85	30.94	1.89	2.31	1.89
1939	31.09	95.06	5.36	8.59	5.06	0.02	2.26	31.07	43.55	8.40	8.59	2.24
1940	25.56	46.88	2.02	5.20	3.25	0.02	1.09	25.55	25.68	3.92	5.19	1.07
1941	12.95	29.10	1.67	3.71	1.50	0.03	2.30	12.92	20.75	3.59	3.70	1.90
1942	17.67	37.55	0.73	1.42	0.79	0.03	1.39	17.60	25.78	1.16	1.42	1.17
1943	19.59	71.56	0.90	0.65	0.51	0.01	2.35	19.53	33.94	0.58	0.65	2.21
1944	9.30	28.75	1.34	0.37	0.29	0.01	0.97	9.27	15.14	1.11	0.37	0.94
1945	17.64	37.50	1.42	2.97	0.50	0.01	1.32	17.59	16.92	1.92	2.96	1.26
1946	17.72	27.25	2.15	2.73	0.94	0.00	6.65	17.65	12.20	1.74	2.72	4.66
1947	10.15	18.24	2.13	2.86	0.52	0.07	3.34	10.09	10.58	3.26	2.90	2.79
1948	21.49	24.11	2.20	1.95	0.59	0.07	2.90	21.30	6.44	1.92	1.96	2.73
1949	12.02	18.75	2.17	1.83	0.47	0.02	1.63	11.89	6.72	2.44	1.80	1.71
1950	13.99	20.58	1.07	1.45	0.34	0.03	1.81	13.83	8.82	1.35	1.44	1.62
1951	15.04	16.02	3.92	3.03	1.91	0.05	1.79	14.80	6.12	2.67	2.95	1.63
1952	13.32	9.66	2.85	3.24	1.32	0.08	1.15	13.11	3.78	3.82	3.23	1.14
1953	9.32	10.90	5.53	5.16	3.26	0.11	1.01	9.21	8.74	3.50	5.07	0.95
1954	19.27	20.02	2.35	3.47	1.93	0.06	0.74	19.08	10.08	2.32	3.42	0.77
1955	16.11	7.70	2.17	3.60	1.65	0.14	0.67	15.91	8.83	2.36	3.47	0.71
1956	15.86	8.39	3.00	4.28	2.64	0.10	1.08	15.50	7.87	2.60	4.15	1.00
1957	11.48	10.42	9.40	8.26	5.57	0.07	0.66	11.13	9.98	5.48	8.00	0.65
1958	8.74	15.44	4.56	6.29	4.50	0.27	0.90	8.47	7.99	3.73	6.16	0.88
1959	8.91	10.34	3.91	3.25	2.72	0.18	0.65	8.67	7.31	3.35	3.18	0.59
1960	13.63	13.37	3.93	6.45	4.99	0.27	0.71	13.36	7.07	3.85	6.22	0.80
1961	11.16	19.02	3.63	3.55	1.57	0.07	0.51	10.94	7.72	3.93	3.51	0.50
1962	18.97	21.58	2.27	3.70	2.15	0.08	0.67	18.46	8.38	2.17	3.63	0.70
1963	11.91	13.47	1.25	0.72	0.60	0.08	0.55	11.54	7.26	1.28	0.72	0.55
1964	4.63	7.05	1.46	0.91	0.78	0.06	0.41	4.47	3.78	1.84	0.87	0.38
1965	9.56	20.55	1.96	1.51	1.83	0.08	0.67	9.26	11.19	1.09	1.47	0.64
1966	9.96	17.80	4.80	8.08	4.13	0.11	0.71	9.50	13.76	5.39	7.66	0.73
1967	14.89	36.96	7.33	6.58	3.81	0.16	0.44	14.24	17.30	5.14	6.27	0.54
1968	14.49	28.29	7.39	7.93	3.50	0.09	0.42	13.76	16.40	3.57	7.52	0.40
1969	12.10	18.71	6.93	9.95	5.54	0.22	0.62	11.35	9.73	7.39	9.34	0.63
1970	21.43	27.68	11.28	15.07	7.05	0.22	0.44	20.17	13.26	9.22	14.11	0.47

Chapter 6: Statistical Analysis of Returns

Table 6-2: Basic and Derived Series (Continued)
Annualized Monthly Standard Deviations (%)

	Basic Series							Derived Series				
Year	Large Company Stocks	Small Company Stocks	Long-Term Corporate Bonds	Long-Term Govt Bonds	Intermediate-Term Govt Bonds	U.S. Treasury Bills	Inflation	Equity Risk Premia	Small Stock Premia	Bond Default Premia	Bond Horizon Premia	Inflation-Adjusted T-Bills
1971	15.74	29.73	11.12	10.67	6.98	0.19	0.57	15.07	14.50	6.12	10.15	0.63
1972	7.28	16.60	3.21	5.85	1.97	0.17	0.41	7.00	11.36	3.97	5.61	0.42
1973	12.57	21.94	7.57	8.38	4.99	0.37	1.53	11.66	13.83	5.12	7.71	1.34
1974	18.93	20.15	11.45	8.64	5.73	0.36	0.91	17.69	21.83	5.76	8.05	0.89
1975	24.35	46.28	11.49	9.13	5.68	0.21	0.78	22.96	19.59	4.43	8.55	0.77
1976	17.34	50.83	5.21	5.43	4.24	0.13	0.48	16.42	27.60	1.55	5.15	0.45
1977	8.85	17.05	4.57	5.69	2.73	0.19	0.77	8.38	13.50	1.56	5.41	0.85
1978	17.92	42.56	4.45	4.45	2.07	0.36	0.67	16.73	27.21	1.66	4.21	0.78
1979	16.00	34.71	10.43	10.81	7.31	0.29	0.53	14.48	15.59	2.16	9.77	0.60
1980	23.94	39.80	20.12	21.16	16.77	0.98	1.45	22.02	14.48	4.57	18.60	1.18
1981	12.33	21.37	20.21	23.25	11.84	0.51	1.15	10.75	15.65	5.23	20.23	1.00
1982	23.36	21.97	17.80	14.40	8.91	0.78	1.64	21.54	7.80	5.37	13.37	1.42
1983	12.21	21.83	10.86	11.43	5.72	0.18	0.73	11.30	14.80	3.98	10.52	0.67
1984	14.99	14.57	12.97	13.34	7.17	0.34	0.61	13.62	4.41	1.92	11.97	0.61
1985	15.62	18.10	13.28	15.78	6.69	0.18	0.33	14.44	6.29	2.56	14.56	0.35
1986	21.27	15.49	9.71	21.58	6.53	0.20	1.03	20.01	6.52	9.54	20.26	1.17
1987	34.17	34.45	9.67	10.09	4.93	0.23	0.68	32.50	11.31	3.03	9.49	0.64
1988	11.70	16.08	9.10	11.03	5.00	0.36	0.57	11.08	11.31	2.45	10.45	0.64
1989	16.17	11.65	7.13	9.53	6.07	0.23	0.63	14.93	6.91	2.36	8.73	0.67
1990	18.28	16.85	7.55	9.89	4.75	0.18	1.16	16.95	6.80	2.67	9.18	1.16
1991	20.49	22.50	5.08	7.33	3.49	0.17	0.54	19.40	9.77	2.13	6.99	0.51
1992	7.98	21.58	5.77	7.62	5.83	0.14	0.54	7.75	19.96	2.32	7.38	0.53
1993	6.65	11.43	5.53	8.38	4.44	0.05	0.57	6.48	8.29	2.38	8.15	0.57
1994	10.76	10.38	6.70	8.12	4.50	0.24	0.47	10.33	6.35	2.27	7.77	0.62
1995	6.99	12.65	7.37	9.70	3.94	0.13	0.60	6.67	8.41	1.88	9.11	0.64
1996	13.25	21.06	7.62	9.33	3.89	0.09	0.61	12.63	15.18	2.14	8.87	0.62
1997	21.09	22.13	8.00	10.44	4.10	0.13	0.53	20.01	16.45	2.30	9.91	0.60
1998	27.90	25.76	5.91	7.70	4.63	0.16	0.30	26.69	6.81	4.35	7.24	0.31
1999	15.78	26.31	4.57	5.25	3.45	0.10	0.77	15.02	19.21	1.90	5.00	0.77
2000	16.02	40.42	5.88	6.92	3.43	0.17	0.99	15.14	44.92	4.10	6.58	1.06
2001	18.15	34.55	8.17	9.69	5.00	0.39	1.25	17.52	21.21	6.02	9.31	0.99
2002	16.90	20.14	8.82	12.36	6.77	0.04	0.83	16.64	18.02	4.50	12.15	0.79
2003	14.47	25.04	13.47	14.82	6.22	0.04	1.21	14.33	10.89	2.77	14.66	1.17
2004	8.06	18.81	9.13	9.73	4.88	0.12	1.14	7.90	10.58	1.03	9.61	1.17
2005	8.31	16.11	8.56	9.66	3.76	0.19	1.96	8.03	8.78	1.38	9.39	1.97
2006	6.46	16.09	8.23	8.82	2.46	0.11	1.55	6.18	9.96	2.19	8.38	1.61
2007	10.20	11.57	5.49	7.95	5.33	0.19	1.19	9.70	6.03	4.81	7.64	1.10
2008	14.20	19.83	25.50	22.57	6.94	0.18	3.20	13.93	12.23	11.16	22.36	3.07
2009	28.52	42.42	14.88	14.47	4.85	0.02	1.02	28.48	14.48	16.44	14.45	0.96
2010	22.43	32.44	9.12	13.04	4.20	0.01	0.49	22.40	9.82	7.72	13.02	0.49
2011	16.51	23.35	12.24	14.43	4.15	0.01	1.34	16.51	8.54	8.21	14.43	1.26

Correlation Coefficients: Serial and Cross-Correlations

The behavior of an asset return series over time reveals its predictability. For example, a series may be random or unpredictable; or it may be subject to trends, cycles, or other patterns, making the series predictable to some degree. The serial correlation coefficient of a series determines its predictability given knowledge of the last observation. The cross-correlation coefficient (often shortened to "correlation") between two series determines the predictability of one series, conditional on knowledge of the other.

Serial Correlations

The serial correlation of a return series, also known as the first-order autocorrelation, describes the extent to which the return in one period is related to the return in the next period. A return series with a high (near one) serial correlation is very predictable from one period to the next, while one with a low (near zero) serial correlation is random and unpredictable.

The serial correlation of a series is closely approximated by the equation for the cross-correlation between two series, which is given in equation (26). The data, however, are the series and its "lagged" self. For example, the lagged series is the series of one-period-old returns:

Year	Return Series (X)	Lagged Return Series (Y)
1	0.10	undefined
2	-0.10	0.10
3	0.15	-0.10
4	0.00	0.15

Cross-Correlations

The cross-correlation between two series measures the extent to which they are linearly related.[3] The correlation coefficient measures the sensitivity of returns on one asset class or portfolio to the returns of another. The correlation equation between return series **X** and **Y** is:

$$\rho_{X,Y} = \left[\frac{Cov(X,Y)}{\sigma_X \, \sigma_Y} \right] \tag{26}$$

where,

Cov (X,Y) = the covariance of **X** and **Y**, defined below;
σ_X = the standard deviation of **X**; and,
σ_Y = the standard deviation of **Y**.

The covariance equation is:

$$Cov(X,Y) = \frac{1}{n-1} \sum_{t=1}^{n} (r_{X,t} - r_{X,A})(r_{Y,t} - r_{Y,A}) \tag{27}$$

where,

$r_{X,t}$ = the return for series **X** in period **t**;
$r_{Y,t}$ = the return for series **Y** in period **t**;
$r_{X,A}$ = the arithmetic mean of series **X**;
$r_{Y,A}$ = the arithmetic mean of series **Y**; and,
n = the number of periods.

Correlations of the Basic Series

Table 6-3 presents the annual cross-correlations and serial correlations for the seven basic series. Long-term government and long-term corporate bond returns are highly correlated with each other but negatively correlated with inflation. If inflation is unanticipated, it has a negative effect on fixed income securities. In addition, U.S. Treasury bills and inflation are reasonably highly correlated, a result of the post-1951 "tracking" described in Chapter 2. Lastly, both the U.S. Treasury bills and inflation series display high serial correlations.

Table 6-3: Basic Series:
Serial and Cross Correlations of Historical Annual Returns

Series	Large Co Stocks	Small Co Stocks	LT-Corp Bonds	LT-Govt Bonds	Inter Govt Bonds	U.S. T-Bills	Inflation
Large Co Stocks	1.00						
Small Co Stocks	0.79	1.00					
LT-Corp Bonds	0.16	0.06	1.00				
LT-Govt Bonds	0.01	-0.08	0.89	1.00			
IT-Govt Bonds	-0.01	-0.11	0.88	0.89	1.00		
U.S. Treasury Bills	-0.01	-0.09	0.16	0.18	0.45	1.00	
Inflation	0.00	0.05	-0.16	-0.14	0.00	0.41	1.00
Serial Correlations	0.02	0.06	0.08	-0.11	0.13	0.91	0.64

Data from 1926–2011.

Correlations of the Derived Series

The annual cross-correlations and serial correlations for the four risk premium series and inflation are presented in Table 6-4. Notice that inflation is negatively correlated with the horizon premium. Increasing inflation causes long-term bond yields to rise and prices to fall; therefore, a negative horizon premium is observed in times of rising inflation.

Table 6-5 presents annual cross-correlations and serial correlations for the inflation-adjusted asset return series. It is interesting to observe how the relationship between the asset returns are substantially different when these returns are expressed in inflation-adjusted terms (as compared with nominal terms). In general, the cross-correlations between asset classes are higher when one accounts for inflation (i.e., subtracts inflation from the nominal returns.)

Table 6-4: Risk Premia and Inflation:
Serial and Cross Correlations of Historical Annual Returns

Series	Equity Risk Premia	Small Stock Premia	Default Premia	Horizon Premia	Inflation
Equity Risk Premia	1.00				
Small Stock Premia	0.28	1.00			
Default Premia	0.28	0.17	1.00		
Horizon Premia	0.03	-0.08	-0.50	1.00	
Inflation	-0.06	0.11	0.00	-0.27	1.00
Serial Correlations	0.02	0.37	-0.30	-0.14	0.64

Data from 1926–2011.

Table 6-5: Inflation-Adjusted Series:
Serial and Cross Correlations of Historical Annual Returns

Inflation Adjusted Series	Inflation-Adjusted Large Co Stocks	Small Co Stocks	LT-Corp Bonds	LT-Gov't Bonds	Inter-Gov't Bonds	T-Bills*	Inflation
Large Co Stocks	1.00						
Small Co Stocks	0.79	1.00					
LT-Corp Bonds	0.22	0.09	1.00				
LT-Govt Bonds	0.09	-0.04	0.92	1.00			
IT-Govt Bonds	0.08	-0.06	0.92	0.92	1.00		
T-Bills*	0.10	-0.06	0.54	0.51	0.70	1.00	
Inflation	-0.19	-0.07	-0.56	-0.50	-0.60	-0.73	1.00
Serial Correlations	0.01	0.03	0.19	-0.02	0.21	0.66	0.64

Data from 1926–2011.
*Real Interest Rates

Serial Correlation in the Derived Series: Trends or Random Behavior?

The risk/return relationships in the historical data are represented in the equity risk premia, the small stock premia, the bond horizon premia, and the bond default premia. The real/nominal historical relationships are represented in the inflation rates and the real interest rates. The objective is to uncover whether each series is random or is subject to any trends, cycles, or other patterns.

The one-year serial correlation coefficients measure the degree of correlation between returns from each year and the previous year for the same series, as seen in Table 6-6. Highly positive (near 1) serial correlations indicate

trends, while highly negative (near -1) serial correlations indicate cycles. There is strong evidence that both inflation rates and real riskless rates follow trends. Serial correlations near zero suggest no patterns (i.e., random behavior); equity risk premia and bond horizon premia are random variables. Small stock premia and bond default premia fall into a middle range where it cannot be determined that they either follow a trend or behave randomly.

Table 6-6: Interpretation of the Annual Serial Correlations

Series	Serial Correlation	Interpretation
Equity Risk Premia	0.02	Random
Small Stock Premia	0.36	Likely Trend
Bond Default Premia	-0.30	Likely Trend
Bond Horizon Premia	-0.14	Random
Inflation Rates	0.64	Trend
Real Interest Rates	0.66	Trend

Data from 1926–2011.

Summary Statistics for Basic and Inflation-Adjusted Series

Table 6-7 presents summary statistics of annual total returns, and where applicable, income and capital appreciation, for each asset class. The summary statistics presented here are arithmetic mean, geometric mean, standard deviation, and serial correlation. Table 6-8 presents summary statistics for the six inflation-adjusted total return series.

Table 6-7: Total Returns, Income Returns, and Capital Appreciation of the Basic Asset Classes: Summary Statistics of Annual Returns

Series	Geometric Mean	Arithmetic Mean	Standard Deviation	Serial Correlation
Large Company Stocks				
Total Returns	9.8	11.8	20.3	0.02
Income	4.1	4.1	1.6	0.90
Capital Appreciation	5.5	7.4	19.6	0.01
Small Co Stocks (Total Returns)	11.9	16.5	32.5	0.06
LT-Corp Bonds (Total Returns)	6.1	6.4	8.4	0.08
LT-Gov't Bonds				
Total Returns	5.7	6.1	9.8	-0.11
Income	5.1	5.2	2.6	0.96
Capital Appreciation	0.4	0.8	8.7	-0.23
Intermediate-Term Gov't Bonds				
Total Returns	5.4	5.5	5.7	0.13
Income	4.6	4.6	2.9	0.96
Capital Appreciation	0.6	0.7	4.6	-0.17
Treasury Bills (Total Returns)	3.6	3.6	3.1	0.91
Inflation	3.0	3.1	4.2	0.64

Data from 1926–2011.

Total return is equal to the sum of three component returns; income return, capital appreciation return, and reinvestment return. Annual reinvestment returns for select asset classes are provided in Table 2-2.

Highlights of the Summary Statistics

Table 6-7 shows that over 1926–2011 small company stocks were the riskiest asset class with a standard deviation of 32.5 percent, but provide the greatest rewards to long-term investors, with an arithmetic mean annual return of 16.5 percent. The geometric mean of the small stock series is 11.9 percent. Large company stocks, long-term government bonds, long-term corporate bonds, and intermediate-term government bonds are progressively less risky, and have lower average returns. Treasury bills were nearly riskless and had the lowest return. In general, risk is rewarded by a higher return over the long term.

Inflation-adjusted basic series summary statistics are presented in Table 6-8. Note that the real rate of interest is close to zero (0.6 percent) on average. For the 86-year period, the geometric and arithmetic means are lower by the amount of inflation than those of the nominal series.

The standard deviations of large company stock and small company stock returns remain approximately the same after adjusting for inflation, while inflation-adjusted bonds and bills are more volatile (i.e., have higher standard deviations.)

Table 6-8: Inflation-Adjusted Series Summary Statistics of Annual Returns

Inflation Adjusted Series	Geometric Mean (%)	Arithmetic Mean (%)	Standard Deviation (%)	Serial Correlation
Large Company Stocks	6.6	8.6	20.3	0.01
Small Company Stocks	8.6	13.1	31.9	0.03
LT-Corp Bonds	3.0	3.4	9.5	0.19
LT-Gov't Bonds	2.6	3.2	10.8	-0.02
Inter-Term Gov't Bonds	2.3	2.6	6.8	0.21
U.S. T-Bills*	0.6	0.6	3.9	0.66

Data from 1926–2011.
*Real Riskless Rates of Returns

Rolling Period Standard Deviations

Rolling period standard deviations are obtained by rolling a view window of fixed length along each time series and computing the standard deviation for the asset class for each window of time. They are useful for examining the volatility or riskiness of returns for holding periods similar to those actually experienced by investors. Graph 6-2 graphically depicts the volatility. Monthly data are used to maximize the number of data points included in the standard deviation computation.

The upper graph places the 60-month rolling standard deviation for large company stocks, small company stocks, and long-term government bonds on the same scale. It is interesting to see the relatively high standard deviation for small company stocks and large company stocks in the 1930s, with an apparent lessening of volatility for 60-month holding periods during the 1980s. Note also how the standard deviation for long-term government bonds reaches the level of both common stock asset classes during part of the 1980s. The lower graph places the 60-month rolling standard deviation for long- and intermediate-term government bonds, and Treasury bills on the same scale.

Graph 6-2: Rolling 60-Month Standard Deviation (%)

Small Company Stocks, Large Company Stocks, Long-Term Government Bonds

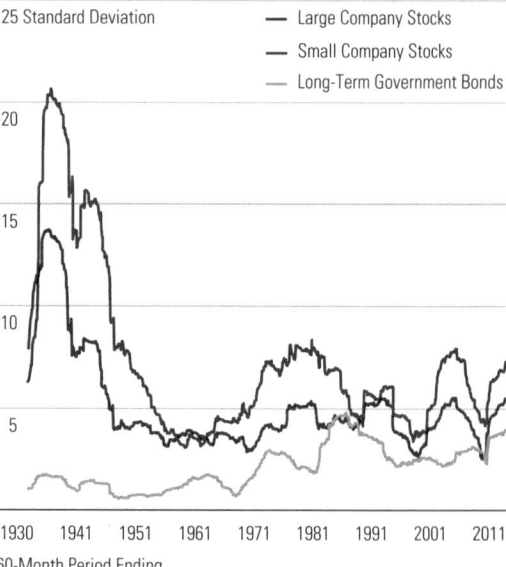

60-Month Period Ending

Long-Term Government Bonds, Intermediate-Term Government Bonds, Treasury Bills

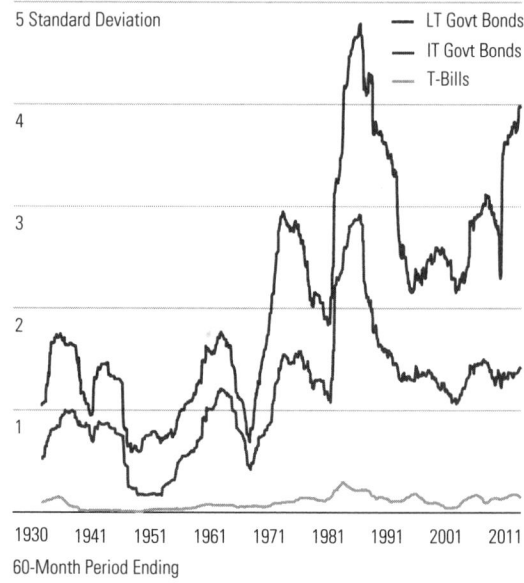

60-Month Period Ending

Data from January 1926–December 1930 to January 2007–December 2011.

Rolling Period Correlations

Rolling period correlations are obtained by moving a view window of fixed length along time series for two asset classes and computing the cross-correlation between the two asset classes for each window of time. They are useful for examining how asset class returns vary together for holding periods similar to those actually experienced by investors. Monthly data are used to maximize the number of data points included in the correlation computation.

Graph 6-3 shows cross correlations between two asset classes for 60-month holding periods. The first rolling period covered is January 1926–December 1930, so the graphs begin at December 1930. The top graph shows the volatility of the correlations between large company stocks and long-term government bonds. There are wide fluctuations between strong positive and strong negative correlations over the past 86 years. The lower graph shows the correlation between Treasury bills and inflation. These asset classes also show wide fluctuations in correlation over the past 86 years.

The True Impact of Asset Allocation on Returns

The importance of asset allocation has been the subject of considerable debate and misunderstanding for decades. An article recently written by Thomas Idzorek in Morningstar Advisor Magazine, "Asset Allocation is King", pinpoints one of the primary sources of confusion surrounding the importance of asset allocation.[4] How much of a portfolio's level of return comes from a fund's asset-allocation policy? The rest of this section has been written by Thomas Idzorek and adapted from his article.

BHB Starts the Debate

The seminal work on the importance of asset allocation, the catalyst of a 25-year debate, and unfortunately the source of what is arguably the most prolific misunderstanding among investment professionals, is the 1986 article "Determinants of Portfolio Performance," by Gary Brinson, Randolph Hood, and Gilbert Beebower (BHB).[5] BHB regressed the time series returns of each fund on a weighted combination of indexes reflecting each fund's asset-allocation policy. In one of the many analyses that BHB carried out (and probably one of the least important ones), they found that the policy mix explained 93.6% of the average fund's return variation over time (as measured by the R-squared of the regression)—the keyword being variation.

Unfortunately, this 93.6% has been widely misinterpreted. Many practitioners incorrectly believe the number means that 93.6% of a portfolio's return level (for example, a fund's 10-year annualized return) comes from a fund's asset-allocation policy. Not true. The truth is that in aggregate 100% of portfolio return levels comes from asset-allocation policy.

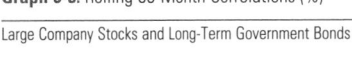

Graph 6-3: Rolling 60-Month Correlations (%)

Large Company Stocks and Long-Term Government Bonds

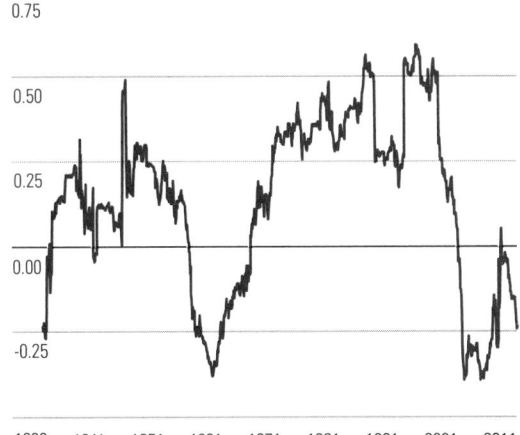

60-Month Period Ending

Treasury Bills and Inflation

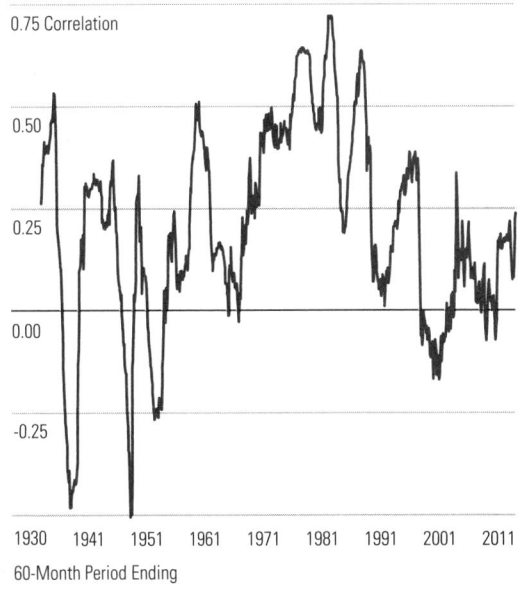

60-Month Period Ending

Data from January 1926–December 1930 to January 2007–December 2011.

Return 'Levels' Versus Return 'Variations'

It is imperative to distinguish between return levels and return variations. In the big picture, investors care far more about return levels than they do return variation. The often-cited 93.6% says nothing about return levels, even though that is what so many practitioners mistakenly believe. It is possible to have a high R-squared, indicating that the return variations in the asset-class factors did a good job of explaining the return variations of the fund in question, yet see the weighted-average composite asset-allocation policy benchmark produce a significantly different return level than the fund in question. This is the case in BHB's study. Despite the high average 93.6% R-squared of their 91 separate time-series regressions, the average geometric annualized return of the 91 funds in their sample was 9.01% versus 10.11% for the corresponding policy portfolios.

So even though 93.6% is the number that seems to be stuck in everyone's mind, 112% (10.11% divided by 9.01%) of return levels in the study's sample came from asset-allocation policy. To put it bluntly, when it comes to returns levels, asset allocation is king. In aggregate, 100% of return levels come from asset allocation before fees and somewhat more after fees. This is a mathematical truth that stems from the concept of an all-inclusive market portfolio and the fact that active management is a zero-sum game. This fundamental truth is somewhat boring; therefore, it is often lost in the debate, even though it is by far the most important result.

Relative Importance of Asset Allocation

This discussion leads us to a much more interesting question for most investors—even if in the bigger picture of realized return levels it is far less important. Among funds in a particular peer group and over a time period, what causes certain funds to underperform and others to over-perform? In contrast with the "100% number" that stems from a mathematical identity, the answer to this question is an empirical one. This also brings us back to our new article, "The Equal Importance of Asset Allocation and Active Management."[6, 7]

To help answer the relative importance of asset allocation among funds as it pertains to return variations, researchers use cross-sectional regression rather than a time-series regression. For example, in Roger Ibbotson and Paul Kaplan's 2000 article, "Does Asset Allocation Policy Explain 40, 90, or 100 Percent of Performance?" the "40%" number comes from a cross-sectional regression, the "90%" comes from a time-series regression, and the "100%" comes from the ratio of realized policy return to fund return.[8] More recently, in a 2007 article, Raman Vardharaj and Frank Fabozzi performed a series of cross-sectional regressions in which the ensuing R-squareds varied widely (a result they inaccurately attribute mostly to style drift).[9]

Before our new article, researchers and investors mis-interpreted the results of cross-sectional regressions. Historically, these cross-sectional regressions have been performed on total returns; because of this, some may have mistakenly interpreted the R-squared as a statement about total returns and the overall importance of asset alloca-tion. We show that a cross-sectional regression performed on total returns is equivalent to a cross-sectional regres-sion performed on "market-excess" returns, because the cross-sectional regression procedure naturally removes the common "market" return that is inherent in the peer group of funds being analyzed. The term "market" is used loosely to describe the peer-group-specific common return, but the results would not change significantly with a more-generic market definition. After we identify the inherent market return as the weighted average return of the funds being analyzed, we convert total returns into market-excess returns by subtracting the peer-group-specific market return. When one performs a cross-sectional regression, it does not matter which type of returns one uses—total returns or excess-market returns. The beta coefficient and R-squared from the cross-sectional regressions are the same; only the intercepts are different. This is proof that a cross-sectional regression naturally removes the common market factor and, more importantly, that the R-squared from a cross-sectional regression is never a statement about the overall importance of asset allocation.

Why Results May Vary

Building upon this clarification related to the "40%" number associated with cross-sectional analysis, our article makes two additional important contributions.

First, by running a series of rolling cross-sectional regression analyses (in which the return of each fund in question is regressed against its corresponding asset allocation policy) and graphing the residual error, the cross-sectional fund return dispersion, and the resulting R-squared at each point in time, we pinpoint that dramatic changes over time in cross-sectional fund return dispersion explain why different researchers may get very different cross-sectional results. Most researchers have simply run one cross-sectional regression and present the corresponding regression results, rather than a series of cross-sectional regressions results. In Graph 6-4, we link each of these separate cross-sectional regression results. The red line represents the cross-sectional fund return dispersion at each point in time for U.S. equity funds. The gray line represents the standard deviation in the unexplained residual returns. Taking the information in Graph 6-4 and recalling that the formula for R-squared is 1 minus the variance in the unexplained residual returns divided by the cross-sectional fund return variance, we plot the rolling cross-sectional regression R-squareds in Graph 6-5. The average of the rolling regressions is around 40% (the bold line), indicating that variations in asset allocation in excess of market movement explain 40% of the excess-market return variations.

Next, in Graph 6-6, by performing a time-series analysis on excess-market returns, we put time-series regression analysis and cross-sectional regression analysis on an even playing field for the first time. The R-squareds from a time-series regression on excess-market returns and cross-sectional regression on either type of return (total or excess-market) give us consistent answers. The frequency in the vertical axis is rescaled for 4,641 time-series regressions and 120 cross-sectional regressions so that the cumulative distribution adds up to 100% for both sets of regressions. Empirically, after adjusting for the overall movement of the market, detailed asset- allocation decisions and active management are about equally important, although this result varies significantly over time.

Graph 6-4: Cross-Sectional Regressions on Monthly Returns for U.S. Equity Funds

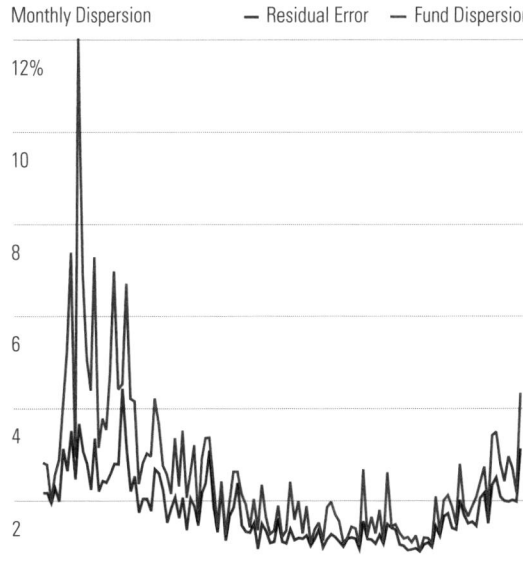

Data from May 1999–April 2009.

Market Movement

Finally, returning to that dreaded "90 percent" number that comes from a time-series regression on total returns, some researchers—especially our own Roger Ibbotson—think that it is important to recognize that much of the "90 percent" in return variations comes from the market's overall movement, while a much smaller amount comes from the return variations coming from the granular asset-allocation decisions. This was an important contribution from Ibbotson and Kaplan (2000) that was largely overlooked, and it is a point made even more clear by our new research.

Graph 6-5: Cross-Sectional R-Squared on Monthly Returns for U.S. Equity Funds

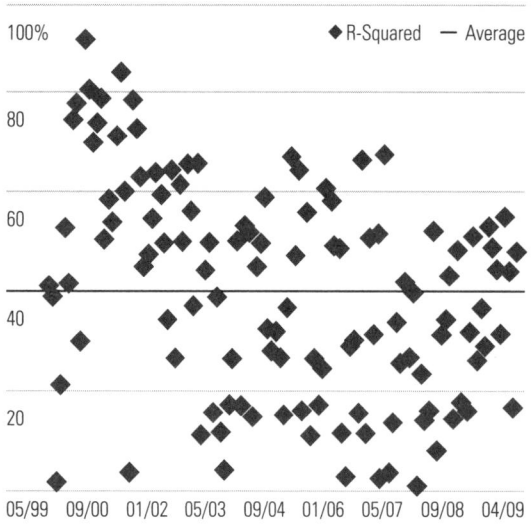

Data from May 1999–April 2009.

Graph 6-6: Cross-Sectional and Time-Series R-Squared Distributions

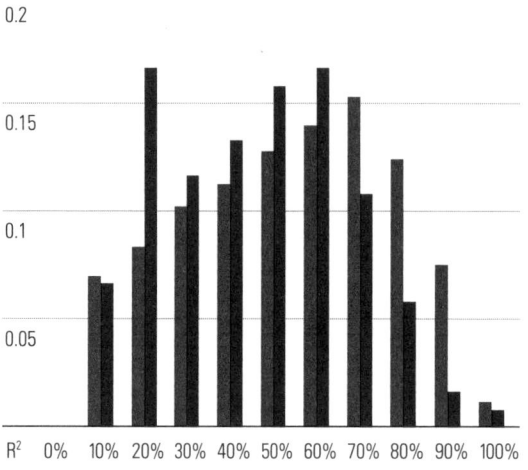

Data from May 1999–April 2009.

The "90 percent" number comes from a time-series regression, typically on multiple asset-class factors. Switching from a somewhat granular list of asset-class factors to a single explanatory variable, such as the S&P 500 (single factor regression), typically leads to only a minor decrease in the average R-squared.

Graph 6-7: Decomposition of Total Return Variations

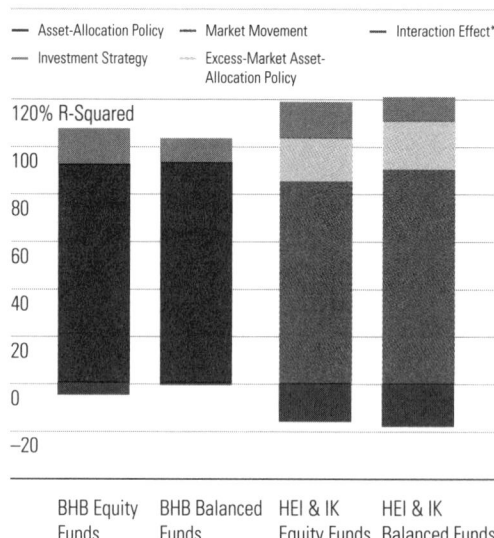

*The interaction effect is a balancing term that makes the three return components of R-squared add up to 100%.

In Graph 6-7, the left two bars illustrate the BHB time-series regression analysis for both equity and balanced funds in which the bulk of the return variations are attributed to what is usually identified as asset-allocation policy. In contrast, the right two bars illustrate the arguments put forth in Hensel, Ezra, and Ilkiw (1991) and Ibbotson and Kaplan (2000) (HEI & IK)—that market movement dominates time-series regressions on total returns.[8, 10]

The two right bars give a more detailed decomposition of total return and its parts: the applicable market return, asset-allocation policy return in excess of the market return, and the return from active portfolio management. Taken together, market return and asset-allocation return in excess of market return dominate active portfolio management. This affirms that market return plus asset-allocation return in excess of market return are the dominant determinants of total return variations.

Chapter 6: Statistical Analysis of Returns

Long Live Asset Allocation

Investors understand that asset allocation is important, but the answer to the question of how important is complicated. Unfortunately, BHB's landmark article unintentionally created the fallacy that 90% of return levels come from asset allocation. Investors would do well to forget the 90% number. In aggregate, 100% of return levels come from asset allocation. Return variations are dominated by the common market factor embedded in the funds being analyzed. After removing this common market factor, on average for typical funds about half of the return variations comes from detailed asset-allocation decisions in excess of the market movement and about half of the return variations comes from active management, although this 50/50 result dramatically changes from one period to the next. Our research clarifies the contribution of each and highlights the significant contribution from market movement. ▥

Endnotes

[1] The equation appears in Haim Levy and Deborah Gunthorpe, "Optimal Investment Proportions in Senior Securities and Equities Under Alternative Holding Periods," *Journal of Portfolio Management*, Summer 1993, page 33.

[2] The Limitations of Standard Deviation, the Semi-Variance and Semi-Standard Deviation, and the Issues Regarding Semi-Variance sections were written by Erik Kobayashi-Solomon and Philip Guziec.

[3] Two series can be related in a non-linear way and have a correlation coefficient of zero. An example is the function $y = x^2$, for which $\rho_{x,y} = 0$.

[4] Idzorek, Thomas M. "Asset Allocation is King," *Morningstar Advisor*, April/May, 2010, pp. 28-31.

[5] Brinson, Gary P., L. Randolph Hood, and Gilbert L. Beebower"Determinants of Portfolio Performance," *Financial Analysts Journal*, July/August, 1986, pp. 39–44.

[6] Xiong, James X., Roger G. Ibbotson, Thomas M. Idzorek, and Peng Chen., "The Equal Importance of Asset Allocation and Active Management," *Financial Analysts Journal*, March/April, 2010.

[7] Ibbotson, Roger G., "The Importance of the Asset Allocation Decision," *Financial Analysts Journal*, March/April, 2010.

[8] Ibbotson, Roger G., and Paul Kaplan "Does Asset Allocation Policy Explain 40, 90, or 100 Percent of Performance?," *Financial Management*, January/February, 2000, pp. 26–33.

[9] Vardharaj, Raman and Frank J. Fabozzi., "Sector, Style, Region: Explaining Stock Allocation Performance," *Financial Analysts Journal*, May/June, 2007, pp. 59–70.

[10] Hensel, Chris R., D. Don Ezra, and John H. Ilkiw., "The Importance of the Asset Allocation Decision," *Financial Analysts Journal*, July/August, 1991, pp. 65–72.

Chapter 7

Firm Size and Return

The Firm Size Phenomenon

One of the most remarkable discoveries of modern finance is the finding of a relationship between firm size and return.[1] On average, small companies have higher returns than large ones. Earlier chapters document this phenomenon for the smallest stocks on the New York Stock Exchange (NYSE). The relationship between firm size and return cuts across the entire size spectrum; it is not restricted to the smallest stocks. In this chapter, the returns across the entire range of firm size are examined.

Construction of the Size Decile Portfolios

The portfolios used in this chapter are those created by the Center for Research in Security Prices (CRSP) at the University of Chicago's Booth School of Business. CRSP has refined the methodology of creating size-based portfolios and has applied this methodology to the entire universe of NYSE/AMEX/NASDAQ-listed securities going back to 1926.

In 1993, CRSP changed the method used to construct these portfolios, thereby causing the return and index values in Table 7-2 and 7-3 to be significantly different from those reported in previous editions of the Yearbook. Previously, some eligible companies had been excluded or delayed from inclusion when the portfolios were reformed at the end of each calendar quarter. Also, while in prior editions of the Yearbook we used NYSE-listed securities only in the composition of size decile portfolios, starting with the 2001 edition we use the entire population of NYSE, NYSE Amex, and NASDAQ-listed securities for use in the firm size chapter.

The New York Stock Exchange universe excludes closed-end mutual funds, preferred stocks, real estate investment trusts, foreign stocks, American Depository Receipts, unit investment trusts, and Americus Trusts. All companies on the NYSE are ranked by the combined market capitalization of all their eligible equity securities. The companies are then split into 10 equally populated groups or deciles. Eligible companies traded on the NYSE, the NYSE Amex (AMEX), and the Nasdaq National Market (NASDAQ) are then assigned to the appropriate deciles according to their capitalization in relation to the NYSE breakpoints. The portfolios are rebalanced using closing prices for the last trading day of March, June, September, and December. Securities added during the quarter are assigned to the appropriate portfolio when two consecutive month-end prices are available. If the final NYSE price of a security that becomes delisted is a month-end price, then that month's return is included in the quarterly return of the portfolio. When a month-end NYSE price is missing, the month-end value is derived from merger terms, quotations on regional exchanges, and other sources. If a month-end value is not available, the last available daily price is used.

In October 2008, NYSE Euronext acquired the American Stock Exchange (AMEX) and rebranded the index as NYSE Amex. To ease confusion, we will continue to refer to this index as AMEX throughout this chapter.

Base security returns are monthly holding period returns. All distributions are added to the month-end prices. Appropriate adjustments are made to prices to account for stock splits and dividends. The return on a portfolio for one month is calculated as the weighted average of the returns for the individual stocks in the portfolio. Annual portfolio returns are calculated by compounding the monthly portfolio returns.

Aspects of the Firm Size Effect

The firm size phenomenon is remarkable in several ways. First, the greater risk of small stocks does not, in the context of the Capital Asset Pricing Model, fully account for their higher returns over the long term. In the CAPM, only systematic, or beta risk, is rewarded. Small company stocks have had returns in excess of those implied by the betas of small stocks. Secondly, the calendar annual return differences between small and large companies are serially correlated. This suggests that past annual returns may be of some value in predicting future annual returns. Such serial correlation, or autocorrelation, is practically unknown in the market for large stocks and in most other capital markets.

In addition, the firm size effect is seasonal. For example, small company stocks outperformed large company stocks in the month of January in a large majority of the years. Again, such predictability is surprising and suspicious in the light of modern capital market theory. These three aspects of the firm size effect (long-term returns in excess of risk, serial correlation and seasonality) will be analyzed after the data are presented.

Presentation of the Decile Data

Summary statistics of annual returns of the 10 deciles and size groupings from 1926–2011 are presented in Table 7-1. Note from this exhibit that the average return tends to increase as one moves from the largest decile to the smallest. (Because securities are ranked quarterly, returns on the ninth and tenth deciles are different than those suggested by the small company stock index presented in earlier chapters. A detailed methodology for the small company stock index is included in Chapter 3.) The total risk, or standard deviation of annual returns, also increases with decreasing firm size. The serial correlations of returns are near zero for all but the smallest decile.

Table 7-2 is a year-by-year history of the returns for the different size categories. Table 7-3 shows the growth of $1.00 invested in each of the categories at year-end 1925.

The sheer magnitude of the size effect in some years is noteworthy. While the largest stocks actually declined in 2001, the smallest stocks rose more than 30 percent. A more extreme case occurred in the depression-recovery year of 1933, when the difference between the first and tenth decile returns was far more substantial. The divergence in the performance of small and large company stocks is evident. In 28 of the 86 years since 1926, the difference between the total returns of the largest stocks (decile 1) and the smallest stocks (decile 10) has been greater than 25 percent.

Table 7-1: Size-Decile Portfolios of the NYSE/AMEX/NASDAQ Summary Statistics of Annual Returns

Decile	Geometric Mean	Arithmetic Mean	Standard Deviation	Serial Correlation
1-Largest	9.0	10.8	19.2	0.07
2	10.4	12.8	22.2	0.01
3	10.8	13.4	23.7	-0.04
4	10.7	13.8	25.9	-0.03
5	11.3	14.6	26.7	-0.04
6	11.2	14.8	27.3	0.02
7	11.2	15.1	29.6	0.00
8	11.4	16.3	34.2	0.04
9	11.5	16.9	36.3	0.04
10-Smallest	12.9	20.6	44.8	0.14
Mid Cap	10.9	13.7	24.8	-0.04
Low Cap	11.3	15.2	29.2	0.02
Micro	12.0	18.0	38.9	0.07
NYSE/AMEX/ NASDAQ Total Value Weighted Index	9.6	11.6	20.3	0.02

Data from 1926–2011. Source: Morningstar and CRSP. Calculated (or Derived) based on data from CRSP US Stock Database and CRSP US Indices Database ©2012 Center for Research in Security Prices (CRSP®), The University of Chicago Booth School of Business. Used with permission.

Results are for quarterly re-ranking for the deciles. The small company stock summary statistics presented in earlier chapters comprise a re-ranking of the portfolios every five years prior to 1982.

Table 7-2: Size-Decile Portfolios of the NYSE/AMEX/NASDAQ

Annual Returns

	Decile 1	Decile 2	Decile 3	Decile 4	Decile 5	Decile 6	Decile 7	Decile 8	Decile 9	Decile 10
1926	0.1358	0.0637	0.0247	0.0209	-0.0236	0.0522	-0.0143	-0.1085	-0.0815	-0.0526
1927	0.3436	0.3051	0.3102	0.3887	0.3427	0.2553	0.3468	0.2834	0.2567	0.2606
1928	0.3939	0.3748	0.3844	0.3471	0.5516	0.2716	0.3485	0.3156	0.3983	0.6894
1929	-0.1094	-0.0796	-0.2195	-0.3432	-0.2510	-0.4037	-0.3726	-0.4019	-0.4976	-0.5266
1930	-0.2456	-0.3749	-0.3527	-0.3488	-0.3578	-0.3639	-0.3624	-0.4931	-0.4463	-0.4834
1931	-0.4141	-0.5114	-0.4596	-0.4609	-0.4695	-0.5174	-0.4881	-0.4928	-0.5029	-0.4942
1932	-0.1096	0.0252	-0.0374	-0.1264	-0.1378	0.0726	-0.1440	0.0242	-0.0093	0.3981
1933	0.4599	0.7625	1.0087	1.1243	0.9505	1.0247	1.1045	1.7322	1.7477	2.1845
1934	0.0208	0.0583	0.0852	0.1845	0.0929	0.1951	0.1434	0.3076	0.2156	0.3489
1935	0.4170	0.5630	0.3705	0.3753	0.6521	0.5091	0.6677	0.6459	0.5849	0.8226
1936	0.2990	0.3436	0.2736	0.4170	0.4952	0.4928	0.5413	0.5028	0.8772	0.8546
1937	-0.3189	-0.3699	-0.3808	-0.4371	-0.4852	-0.4664	-0.4930	-0.5278	-0.5231	-0.5645
1938	0.2501	0.3401	0.3423	0.3512	0.5040	0.4189	0.3574	0.4344	0.3385	0.0540
1939	0.0480	-0.0387	-0.0279	0.0042	0.0157	0.0603	0.0482	-0.0425	-0.0526	0.1737
1940	-0.0702	-0.0884	-0.0837	-0.0404	-0.0079	-0.0580	-0.0574	-0.0634	-0.0491	-0.3114
1941	-0.1069	-0.0778	-0.0590	-0.0984	-0.1197	-0.0990	-0.0890	-0.0886	-0.1253	-0.1798
1942	0.1337	0.2365	0.2026	0.2031	0.2097	0.2463	0.2912	0.2971	0.4429	0.8021
1943	0.2350	0.3526	0.3343	0.4049	0.4949	0.4129	0.7226	0.7146	0.8725	1.3764
1944	0.1719	0.2539	0.2294	0.3308	0.4003	0.4405	0.3841	0.4886	0.5655	0.7003
1945	0.2950	0.4758	0.5448	0.6365	0.5341	0.6106	0.6509	0.6895	0.7690	0.9554
1946	-0.0446	-0.0439	-0.0781	-0.1268	-0.1022	-0.0617	-0.1485	-0.1535	-0.0972	-0.1833
1947	0.0555	0.0076	-0.0020	0.0207	0.0342	-0.0335	-0.0217	-0.0323	-0.0356	-0.0088
1948	0.0371	0.0016	0.0253	-0.0207	-0.0253	-0.0345	-0.0329	-0.0659	-0.0741	-0.0520
1949	0.1858	0.2521	0.2595	0.1953	0.1861	0.2329	0.2177	0.1652	0.1979	0.2489
1950	0.2881	0.2892	0.2672	0.3137	0.3703	0.3387	0.3786	0.3995	0.4132	0.5514
1951	0.2141	0.2286	0.2116	0.1663	0.1442	0.1372	0.1811	0.1511	0.1125	0.0685
1952	0.1428	0.1293	0.1216	0.1190	0.1107	0.1010	0.1039	0.0768	0.0852	0.0230
1953	0.0115	0.0169	0.0033	-0.0136	-0.0293	-0.0095	-0.0241	-0.0772	-0.0494	-0.0818
1954	0.4833	0.4825	0.5892	0.5081	0.5673	0.5955	0.5738	0.5287	0.6373	0.6863
1955	0.2846	0.1877	0.1834	0.1932	0.1771	0.2265	0.1843	0.2023	0.2053	0.2553
1956	0.0794	0.1108	0.0741	0.0902	0.0805	0.0594	0.0830	0.0522	0.0589	-0.0165
1957	-0.0932	-0.0869	-0.1285	-0.1079	-0.1384	-0.1821	-0.1677	-0.1855	-0.1424	-0.1679
1958	0.4071	0.4981	0.5406	0.5964	0.5583	0.5627	0.6814	0.6527	0.7144	0.6975
1959	0.1236	0.0967	0.1363	0.1524	0.1994	0.1516	0.1987	0.1799	0.2011	0.1542
1960	0.0037	0.0548	0.0482	0.0128	-0.0165	-0.0087	-0.0586	-0.0511	-0.0380	-0.0786
1961	0.2627	0.2710	0.2898	0.2933	0.2853	0.2699	0.3043	0.3377	0.3030	0.3202
1962	-0.0878	-0.0959	-0.1194	-0.1296	-0.1638	-0.1793	-0.1640	-0.1476	-0.1701	-0.1460
1963	0.2249	0.2141	0.1647	0.1712	0.1273	0.1853	0.1782	0.1997	0.1280	0.1117
1964	0.1599	0.1428	0.1997	0.1625	0.1623	0.1666	0.1597	0.1714	0.1532	0.2094
1965	0.0893	0.1925	0.2483	0.2425	0.3217	0.3776	0.3373	0.3190	0.3194	0.4315
1966	-0.1027	-0.0574	-0.0507	-0.0623	-0.0721	-0.0452	-0.0955	-0.0864	-0.0589	-0.1008
1967	0.2197	0.2079	0.3169	0.4564	0.5145	0.5343	0.6472	0.8133	0.9064	1.1416
1968	0.0753	0.1654	0.1979	0.1829	0.2759	0.3047	0.2673	0.4047	0.3711	0.6136
1969	-0.0584	-0.1295	-0.1172	-0.1662	-0.1808	-0.1871	-0.2445	-0.2471	-0.3158	-0.3290
1970	0.0231	0.0182	0.0330	-0.0699	-0.0601	-0.0593	-0.0973	-0.1614	-0.1526	-0.1785

Source: Morningstar and CRSP. Calculated (or Derived) based on data from CRSP US Stock Database and CRSP US Indices Database
©2012 Center for Research in Security Prices (CRSP®), The University of Chicago Booth School of Business. Used with permission.

	Decile 1	Decile 2	Decile 3	Decile 4	Decile 5	Decile 6	Decile 7	Decile 8	Decile 9	Decile 10
1971	0.1484	0.1328	0.2011	0.2472	0.1890	0.2244	0.2018	0.1735	0.1647	0.1853
1972	0.2212	0.1278	0.0938	0.0881	0.0863	0.0695	0.0632	0.0205	-0.0229	-0.0057
1973	-0.1274	-0.2266	-0.2278	-0.2680	-0.3217	-0.3191	-0.3702	-0.3534	-0.3897	-0.4203
1974	-0.2803	-0.2441	-0.2458	-0.2834	-0.2167	-0.2694	-0.2558	-0.2423	-0.2635	-0.2715
1975	0.3169	0.4573	0.5363	0.6168	0.5966	0.5675	0.6326	0.6579	0.6649	0.7579
1976	0.2073	0.3045	0.3811	0.4008	0.4363	0.4808	0.5018	0.5690	0.5101	0.5516
1977	-0.0884	-0.0367	0.0109	0.0376	0.1126	0.1408	0.1754	0.2261	0.2022	0.2310
1978	0.0637	0.0229	0.1084	0.0974	0.1207	0.1637	0.1705	0.1632	0.1605	0.2815
1979	0.1519	0.2871	0.3061	0.3516	0.3557	0.4888	0.4206	0.4638	0.4594	0.4158
1980	0.3275	0.3442	0.3186	0.3043	0.3193	0.3141	0.3623	0.3233	0.3823	0.3071
1981	-0.0833	0.0059	0.0372	0.0403	0.0484	0.0677	-0.0040	0.0055	0.0802	0.0856
1982	0.1964	0.1749	0.2081	0.2566	0.3076	0.2940	0.2919	0.2955	0.2608	0.2855
1983	0.2057	0.1686	0.2662	0.2633	0.2626	0.2589	0.2727	0.3721	0.3130	0.3690
1984	0.0840	0.0770	0.0253	-0.0458	-0.0269	0.0248	-0.0426	-0.0745	-0.0896	-0.1951
1985	0.3137	0.3770	0.2910	0.3390	0.3115	0.3097	0.3255	0.3651	0.3077	0.2582
1986	0.1801	0.1816	0.1628	0.1732	0.1512	0.0874	0.1248	0.0387	0.0570	0.0041
1987	0.0504	0.0037	0.0393	0.0170	-0.0382	-0.0508	-0.0861	-0.0808	-0.1262	-0.1492
1988	0.1486	0.1982	0.2126	0.2237	0.2138	0.2339	0.2394	0.2854	0.2285	0.2105
1989	0.3295	0.3008	0.2629	0.2308	0.2423	0.2107	0.1785	0.1788	0.1058	0.0550
1990	-0.0088	-0.0853	-0.1015	-0.0875	-0.1409	-0.1849	-0.1532	-0.1979	-0.2460	-0.3128
1991	0.3039	0.3463	0.4140	0.3883	0.4811	0.5326	0.4421	0.4707	0.5066	0.4807
1992	0.0474	0.1577	0.1387	0.1249	0.2613	0.1878	0.1920	0.1287	0.2495	0.3398
1993	0.0732	0.1319	0.1614	0.1562	0.1694	0.1726	0.1900	0.1853	0.1658	0.2558
1994	0.0174	-0.0174	-0.0423	-0.0098	-0.0166	0.0034	-0.0252	-0.0308	-0.0309	-0.0298
1995	0.3940	0.3527	0.3533	0.3276	0.3324	0.2692	0.3264	0.2935	0.3500	0.3047
1996	0.2375	0.1962	0.1714	0.1883	0.1366	0.1737	0.1965	0.1720	0.2064	0.1722
1997	0.3486	0.3012	0.2512	0.2610	0.1566	0.2864	0.3003	0.2538	0.2554	0.2204
1998	0.3515	0.1272	0.0758	0.0724	0.0054	0.0116	-0.0090	0.0098	-0.0503	-0.1155
1999	0.2450	0.2018	0.3404	0.2966	0.2595	0.3492	0.2570	0.3886	0.3430	0.2809
2000	-0.1359	-0.0030	-0.0620	-0.0997	-0.0710	-0.1028	-0.1068	-0.1300	-0.1331	-0.1291
2001	-0.1529	-0.0881	-0.0411	-0.0096	-0.0214	0.0952	0.1226	0.2111	0.3168	0.3676
2002	-0.2246	-0.1736	-0.1934	-0.1771	-0.1778	-0.2122	-0.2297	-0.1994	-0.1870	-0.0550
2003	0.2568	0.3738	0.4029	0.4438	0.4090	0.4877	0.5074	0.5761	0.6783	0.9245
2004	0.0794	0.2013	0.1796	0.1874	0.1734	0.2206	0.1904	0.2196	0.1518	0.1857
2005	0.0371	0.1221	0.1237	0.1059	0.1011	0.0306	0.1058	0.0753	0.0216	0.0591
2006	0.1561	0.1559	0.1453	0.1164	0.1557	0.1504	0.1627	0.1761	0.1713	0.1948
2007	0.0718	0.0747	0.0362	0.0436	0.0785	0.0498	-0.0159	-0.0559	-0.0647	-0.0992
2008	-0.3508	-0.4190	-0.4034	-0.3683	-0.3539	-0.3998	-0.3620	-0.3574	-0.3685	-0.4736
2009	0.2255	0.3839	0.3780	0.4594	0.4367	0.4153	0.4362	0.4877	0.5023	0.8179
2010	0.1338	0.2209	0.3006	0.2123	0.2958	0.2780	0.3154	0.3289	0.2899	0.2946
2011	0.0222	0.0025	-0.0210	0.0118	-0.0098	-0.0160	-0.0475	-0.0670	-0.0712	-0.1399

Source: Morningstar and CRSP. Calculated (or Derived) based on data from CRSP US Stock Database and CRSP US Indices Database
©2012 Center for Research in Security Prices (CRSP®), The University of Chicago Booth School of Business. Used with permission.

Table 7-3: Size-Decile Portfolios of the NYSE/AMEX/NASDAQ
Year-End Index Values (Year-End 1925 = $1.00)

	Decile 1	Decile 2	Decile 3	Decile 4	Decile 5	Decile 6	Decile 7	Decile 8	Decile 9	Decile 10
1925	1.000	1.000	1.000	1.000	1.000	1.000	1.000	1.000	1.000	1.000
1926	1.136	1.064	1.025	1.021	0.976	1.052	0.986	0.892	0.919	0.947
1927	1.526	1.388	1.343	1.418	1.311	1.321	1.328	1.144	1.154	1.194
1928	2.127	1.909	1.859	1.910	2.034	1.679	1.790	1.505	1.614	2.018
1929	1.895	1.757	1.451	1.254	1.524	1.002	1.123	0.900	0.811	0.955
1930	1.429	1.098	0.939	0.817	0.978	0.637	0.716	0.456	0.449	0.493
1931	0.837	0.536	0.507	0.440	0.519	0.307	0.367	0.231	0.223	0.250
1932	0.746	0.550	0.488	0.385	0.447	0.330	0.314	0.237	0.221	0.349
1933	1.088	0.969	0.981	0.817	0.873	0.668	0.660	0.648	0.608	1.111
1934	1.111	1.026	1.065	0.968	0.954	0.798	0.755	0.847	0.739	1.499
1935	1.574	1.604	1.459	1.331	1.576	1.204	1.260	1.394	1.171	2.732
1936	2.045	2.155	1.858	1.886	2.356	1.798	1.941	2.094	2.197	5.067
1937	1.393	1.358	1.151	1.062	1.213	0.959	0.984	0.989	1.048	2.206
1938	1.741	1.819	1.545	1.434	1.825	1.361	1.336	1.418	1.403	2.326
1939	1.825	1.749	1.502	1.440	1.853	1.443	1.401	1.358	1.329	2.729
1940	1.697	1.594	1.376	1.382	1.839	1.359	1.320	1.272	1.264	1.880
1941	1.515	1.470	1.295	1.246	1.619	1.225	1.203	1.159	1.105	1.542
1942	1.718	1.818	1.557	1.499	1.958	1.526	1.553	1.504	1.595	2.778
1943	2.122	2.459	2.078	2.106	2.927	2.157	2.675	2.579	2.987	6.602
1944	2.487	3.083	2.554	2.803	4.099	3.107	3.702	3.838	4.675	11.225
1945	3.220	4.550	3.946	4.587	6.288	5.003	6.112	6.485	8.271	21.950
1946	3.077	4.350	3.638	4.005	5.645	4.695	5.205	5.490	7.467	17.926
1947	3.247	4.383	3.630	4.088	5.838	4.538	5.092	5.312	7.201	17.768
1948	3.368	4.390	3.722	4.004	5.691	4.381	4.924	4.962	6.668	16.844
1949	3.994	5.496	4.688	4.786	6.750	5.401	5.997	5.782	7.988	21.036
1950	5.144	7.086	5.940	6.287	9.249	7.231	8.267	8.092	11.288	32.636
1951	6.245	8.705	7.197	7.333	10.583	8.223	9.764	9.314	12.558	34.871
1952	7.137	9.831	8.072	8.205	11.755	9.054	10.778	10.030	13.629	35.673
1953	7.219	9.997	8.099	8.093	11.410	8.968	10.518	9.256	12.956	32.754
1954	10.708	14.820	12.871	12.205	17.884	14.309	16.553	14.149	21.213	55.233
1955	13.755	17.602	15.232	14.564	21.051	17.550	19.604	17.011	25.568	69.335
1956	14.847	19.553	16.361	15.878	22.747	18.593	21.230	17.899	27.076	68.193
1957	13.464	17.854	14.258	14.165	19.599	15.207	17.670	14.580	23.221	56.742
1958	18.945	26.748	21.967	22.613	30.541	23.765	29.710	24.096	39.810	96.319
1959	21.287	29.335	24.961	26.060	36.630	27.368	35.613	28.430	47.817	111.172
1960	21.366	30.943	26.164	26.393	36.025	27.128	33.525	26.978	46.000	102.433
1961	26.979	39.328	33.747	34.135	46.302	34.449	43.725	36.089	59.940	135.228
1962	24.610	35.558	29.716	29.713	38.719	28.274	36.555	30.761	49.742	115.483
1963	30.143	43.170	34.612	34.799	43.648	33.514	43.068	36.902	56.106	128.379
1964	34.962	49.335	41.524	40.455	50.734	39.098	49.946	43.225	64.702	155.258
1965	38.083	58.833	51.832	50.265	67.054	53.861	66.795	57.014	85.371	222.249
1966	34.171	55.455	49.202	47.136	62.222	51.426	60.414	52.090	80.339	199.850
1967	41.678	66.984	64.794	68.648	94.237	78.902	99.515	94.457	153.162	427.993
1968	44.817	78.066	77.615	81.201	120.233	102.941	126.119	132.679	210.006	690.608
1969	42.198	67.956	68.519	67.709	98.500	83.685	95.279	99.892	143.692	463.384
1970	43.174	69.190	70.783	62.976	92.584	78.721	86.008	83.772	121.764	380.688

Source: Morningstar and CRSP. Calculated (or Derived) based on data from CRSP US Stock Database and CRSP US Indices Database
©2012 Center for Research in Security Prices (CRSP®), The University of Chicago Booth School of Business. Used with permission.

	Decile 1	Decile 2	Decile 3	Decile 4	Decile 5	Decile 6	Decile 7	Decile 8	Decile 9	Decile 10
1971	49.582	78.380	85.019	78.544	110.084	96.390	103.365	98.304	141.813	451.246
1972	60.549	88.400	92.996	85.463	119.582	103.087	109.900	100.320	138.561	448.673
1973	52.838	68.365	71.812	62.555	81.109	70.189	69.218	64.866	84.561	260.087
1974	38.026	51.679	54.159	44.825	63.532	51.282	51.514	49.149	62.283	189.465
1975	50.075	75.310	83.204	72.474	101.434	80.386	84.101	81.481	103.694	333.057
1976	60.457	98.244	114.912	101.522	145.692	119.033	126.303	127.842	156.591	516.784
1977	55.114	94.641	116.161	105.340	162.096	135.795	148.457	156.753	188.254	636.174
1978	58.623	96.810	128.757	115.602	181.663	158.018	173.769	182.335	218.469	815.247
1979	67.529	124.608	168.171	156.247	246.280	235.265	246.858	266.896	318.844	1154.203
1980	89.642	167.495	221.752	203.790	324.928	309.150	336.293	353.172	440.733	1508.688
1981	82.171	168.486	230.000	212.012	340.658	330.086	334.956	355.111	476.060	1637.806
1982	98.309	197.961	277.862	266.417	445.453	427.119	432.737	460.051	600.204	2105.324
1983	118.536	231.336	351.823	336.573	562.436	537.709	550.745	631.240	788.094	2882.280
1984	128.496	249.156	360.708	321.152	547.328	551.050	527.300	584.194	717.520	2319.945
1985	168.799	343.079	465.674	430.017	717.830	721.717	698.952	797.490	938.290	2918.990
1986	199.203	405.372	541.507	504.509	826.375	784.763	786.180	828.328	991.802	2930.952
1987	209.237	406.864	562.767	513.077	794.795	744.859	718.467	761.390	866.642	2493.635
1988	240.323	487.505	682.400	627.867	964.734	919.100	890.492	978.714	1064.661	3018.511
1989	319.517	634.137	861.817	772.773	1198.484	1112.769	1049.459	1153.680	1177.323	3184.493
1990	316.696	580.036	774.312	705.157	1029.606	906.966	888.732	925.311	887.722	2188.421
1991	412.940	780.876	1094.907	978.935	1524.998	1390.054	1281.599	1360.883	1337.401	3240.359
1992	432.528	904.053	1246.792	1101.211	1923.542	1651.164	1527.706	1535.982	1671.149	4341.570
1993	464.200	1023.276	1448.020	1273.167	2249.452	1936.090	1818.024	1820.666	1948.174	5452.331
1994	472.281	1005.505	1386.834	1260.636	2212.120	1942.657	1772.157	1764.589	1887.894	5289.982
1995	658.354	1360.139	1876.818	1673.588	2947.424	2465.680	2350.677	2282.491	2548.704	6902.067
1996	814.721	1626.941	2198.551	1988.737	3350.013	2893.890	2812.472	2675.160	3074.639	8090.904
1997	1098.728	2116.959	2750.825	2507.894	3874.475	3722.689	3657.082	3354.002	3859.974	9874.270
1998	1484.945	2386.193	2959.244	2689.548	3895.300	3765.924	3624.257	3386.763	3665.743	8733.362
1999	1848.820	2867.706	3966.538	3487.400	4906.053	5081.009	4555.730	4702.836	4923.248	11186.740
2000	1597.583	2859.238	3720.436	3139.817	4557.657	4558.894	4069.294	4091.354	4267.999	9742.548
2001	1353.311	2607.248	3567.403	3109.557	4460.000	4993.107	4568.166	4954.981	5620.110	13323.510
2002	1049.390	2154.621	2877.420	2558.865	3667.100	3933.746	3518.738	3966.994	4569.073	12590.514
2003	1318.847	2960.002	4036.603	3694.589	5166.919	5852.310	5304.257	6252.256	7668.054	24230.073
2004	1423.611	3555.873	4761.488	4386.977	6062.734	7143.115	6314.087	7625.189	8832.170	28730.582
2005	1476.498	3990.023	5350.498	4851.512	6675.503	7361.863	6982.197	8199.603	9022.881	30428.623
2006	1707.026	4612.246	6128.086	5416.218	7715.172	8469.343	8118.430	9643.387	10568.327	36357.297
2007	1829.638	4957.001	6349.776	5652.208	8320.755	8890.975	7989.212	9104.422	9884.069	32751.548
2008	1187.843	2880.007	3788.227	3570.509	5376.004	5336.079	5097.073	5850.762	6241.739	17239.988
2009	1455.713	3985.621	5220.170	5210.781	7723.646	7552.012	7320.243	8704.258	9376.984	31340.641
2010	1650.490	4866.065	6789.352	6317.254	10008.562	9651.235	9628.913	11567.273	12095.416	40575.107
2011	1687.186	4878.388	6646.606	6391.607	9910.859	9496.585	9171.424	10792.122	11234.376	34900.635

Source: Morningstar and CRSP. Calculated (or Derived) based on data from CRSP US Stock Database and CRSP US Indices Database
©2012 Center for Research in Security Prices (CRSP®), The University of Chicago Booth School of Business. Used with permission.

Chapter 7: Firm Size and Return

Table 7-4: Size-Decile Portfolios of the NYSE/AMEX/NASDAQ
Mid-, Low-, Micro-, and Total Capitalization Returns and Index Value

Year	Total Return				Index Value			
	Mid-Cap Stocks	Low-Cap Stocks	Micro-Cap Stocks	Total Value Weighted NYSE/ AMEX/ NASDAQ	Mid-Cap Stocks	Low-Cap Stocks	Micro-Cap Stocks	Total Value Weighted NYSE/ AMEX/ NASDAQ
1925					1.000	1.000	1.000	1.000
1926	0.0144	-0.0042	-0.0721	0.0924	1.014	0.996	0.928	1.092
1927	0.3394	0.2912	0.2576	0.3339	1.359	1.286	1.167	1.457
1928	0.4040	0.3057	0.4685	0.3886	1.908	1.679	1.714	2.023
1929	-0.2623	-0.3925	-0.5044	-0.1455	1.407	1.020	0.849	1.729
1930	-0.3521	-0.3898	-0.4555	-0.2854	0.912	0.622	0.462	1.236
1931	-0.4615	-0.5040	-0.5028	-0.4354	0.491	0.309	0.230	0.698
1932	-0.0794	-0.0077	0.0890	-0.0869	0.452	0.306	0.250	0.637
1933	1.0294	1.1752	1.8695	0.5709	0.917	0.666	0.718	1.001
1934	0.1159	0.1990	0.2509	0.0428	1.024	0.799	0.899	1.043
1935	0.4181	0.5860	0.6484	0.4432	1.452	1.267	1.481	1.506
1936	0.3594	0.5101	0.8749	0.3226	1.973	1.913	2.777	1.992
1937	-0.4200	-0.4874	-0.5340	-0.3469	1.145	0.981	1.294	1.301
1938	0.3756	0.4029	0.2625	0.2809	1.575	1.376	1.634	1.666
1939	-0.0095	0.0360	0.0021	0.0286	1.560	1.425	1.637	1.714
1940	-0.0553	-0.0588	-0.1236	-0.0708	1.473	1.342	1.435	1.592
1941	-0.0835	-0.0934	-0.1373	-0.1003	1.350	1.216	1.238	1.433
1942	0.2042	0.2705	0.5247	0.1604	1.626	1.545	1.888	1.662
1943	0.3868	0.5728	1.0007	0.2838	2.255	2.430	3.776	2.134
1944	0.2950	0.4323	0.6040	0.2131	2.920	3.481	6.057	2.589
1945	0.5704	0.6418	0.8265	0.3807	4.586	5.715	11.064	3.575
1946	-0.0986	-0.1126	-0.1260	-0.0586	4.134	5.072	9.669	3.365
1947	0.0128	-0.0296	-0.0266	0.0358	4.187	4.922	9.412	3.486
1948	0.0000	-0.0413	-0.0660	0.0211	4.187	4.719	8.790	3.559
1949	0.2243	0.2127	0.2149	0.2022	5.126	5.722	10.679	4.279
1950	0.3027	0.3655	0.4591	0.2961	6.677	7.814	15.583	5.546
1951	0.1830	0.1546	0.0977	0.2068	7.900	9.022	17.105	6.693
1952	0.1186	0.0966	0.0647	0.1342	8.836	9.894	18.212	7.591
1953	-0.0084	-0.0290	-0.0598	0.0067	8.762	9.607	17.122	7.642
1954	0.5604	0.5747	0.6523	0.4998	13.673	15.128	28.291	11.461
1955	0.1850	0.2078	0.2211	0.2521	16.202	18.273	34.546	14.351
1956	0.0803	0.0653	0.0346	0.0826	17.503	19.466	35.741	15.537
1957	-0.1242	-0.1783	-0.1505	-0.1005	15.329	15.996	30.361	13.975
1958	0.5611	0.6186	0.7092	0.4502	23.931	25.891	51.894	20.267
1959	0.1536	0.1726	0.1868	0.1267	27.608	30.359	61.588	22.835
1960	0.0243	-0.0339	-0.0500	0.0116	28.279	29.331	58.506	23.100
1961	0.2899	0.2951	0.3084	0.2695	36.477	37.986	76.547	29.324
1962	-0.1315	-0.1683	-0.1650	-0.1018	31.682	31.593	63.920	26.340
1963	0.1593	0.1867	0.1193	0.2098	36.731	37.490	71.547	31.866
1964	0.1813	0.1652	0.1834	0.1613	43.392	43.685	84.672	37.004
1965	0.2608	0.3499	0.3798	0.1446	54.708	58.971	116.833	42.356

Source: Morningstar and CRSP. Calculated (or Derived) based on data from CRSP US Stock Database and CRSP US Indices Database
©2012 Center for Research in Security Prices (CRSP®), The University of Chicago Booth School of Business. Used with permission.

Table 7-4: Size-Decile Portfolios of the NYSE/AMEX/NASDAQ (Continued)
Mid-, Low-, Micro-, and Total Capitalization Returns and Index Value

	Total Return				Index Value			
Year	Mid-Cap Stocks	Low-Cap Stocks	Micro-Cap Stocks	Total Value Weighted NYSE/ AMEX/ NASDAQ	Mid-Cap Stocks	Low-Cap Stocks	Micro-Cap Stocks	Total Value Weighted NYSE/ AMEX/ NASDAQ
1966	-0.0586	-0.0710	-0.0825	-0.0874	51.502	54.785	107.189	38.654
1967	0.3994	0.6387	1.0344	0.2874	72.070	89.779	218.063	49.763
1968	0.2108	0.3182	0.5015	0.1414	87.261	118.343	327.422	56.800
1969	-0.1469	-0.2216	-0.3236	-0.1091	74.445	92.116	221.456	50.601
1970	-0.0201	-0.0987	-0.1681	0.0000	72.947	83.027	184.224	50.602
1971	0.2123	0.2032	0.1767	0.1615	88.437	99.899	216.771	58.772
1972	0.0906	0.0558	-0.0138	0.1684	96.451	105.476	213.778	68.668
1973	-0.2594	-0.3435	-0.4078	-0.1806	71.432	69.247	126.594	56.263
1974	-0.2513	-0.2587	-0.2676	-0.2704	53.483	51.335	92.715	41.051
1975	0.5709	0.6092	0.7150	0.3875	84.016	82.609	159.003	56.960
1976	0.3979	0.5074	0.5335	0.2676	117.447	124.528	243.838	72.203
1977	0.0385	0.1708	0.2177	-0.0426	121.973	145.792	296.917	69.128
1978	0.1075	0.1663	0.2245	0.0749	135.081	170.033	363.563	74.303
1979	0.3298	0.4626	0.4369	0.2262	179.631	248.690	522.404	91.113
1980	0.3144	0.3310	0.3464	0.3281	236.104	330.995	703.379	121.011
1981	0.0409	0.0305	0.0818	-0.0365	245.761	341.091	760.892	116.596
1982	0.2443	0.2939	0.2723	0.2100	305.799	441.333	968.104	141.082
1983	0.2644	0.2882	0.3410	0.2198	386.645	568.525	1298.236	172.086
1984	-0.0103	-0.0224	-0.1403	0.0451	382.659	555.814	1116.057	179.849
1985	0.3115	0.3283	0.2833	0.3217	501.840	738.313	1432.191	237.703
1986	0.1637	0.0877	0.0320	0.1619	583.976	803.032	1478.083	276.188
1987	0.0130	-0.0689	-0.1381	0.0167	591.583	747.687	1273.886	280.801
1988	0.2167	0.2476	0.2192	0.1803	719.777	932.794	1553.116	331.423
1989	0.2479	0.1923	0.0815	0.2886	898.199	1112.149	1679.745	427.084
1990	-0.1053	-0.1779	-0.2744	-0.0596	803.585	914.340	1218.755	401.636
1991	0.4191	0.4865	0.5005	0.3467	1140.359	1359.121	1828.732	540.871
1992	0.1612	0.1738	0.2814	0.0980	1324.133	1595.389	2343.256	593.865
1993	0.1627	0.1824	0.2010	0.1114	1539.505	1886.336	2814.214	660.004
1994	-0.0263	-0.0152	-0.0314	-0.0006	1499.087	1857.587	2725.976	659.604
1995	0.3404	0.2947	0.3320	0.3679	2009.376	2405.034	3630.877	902.300
1996	0.1685	0.1804	0.1926	0.2135	2348.036	2838.819	4330.072	1094.950
1997	0.2329	0.2804	0.2402	0.3140	2894.819	3634.907	5370.151	1438.759
1998	0.0591	0.0051	-0.0817	0.2429	3065.774	3653.462	4931.268	1788.242
1999	0.3107	0.3290	0.3165	0.2527	4018.318	4855.359	6491.852	2240.054
2000	-0.0755	-0.1100	-0.1302	-0.1141	3714.844	4321.148	5646.670	1984.392
2001	-0.0280	0.1324	0.3399	-0.1115	3610.715	4893.280	7566.103	1763.231
2002	-0.1850	-0.2158	-0.1386	-0.2115	2942.738	3837.458	6517.072	1390.376
2003	0.4161	0.5173	0.7786	0.3161	4167.126	5822.500	11591.112	1829.916
2004	0.1807	0.2110	0.1670	0.1197	4919.965	7051.111	13526.855	2048.888
2005	0.1136	0.0677	0.0366	0.0616	5478.654	7528.428	14021.280	2175.152
2006	0.1387	0.1617	0.1810	0.1547	6238.765	8745.681	16558.950	2511.620
2007	0.0474	-0.0012	-0.0794	0.0583	6534.381	8734.751	15244.556	2658.067
2008	-0.3815	-0.3760	-0.4147	-0.3670	4041.416	5450.428	8921.939	1682.567
2009	0.4176	0.4415	0.6119	0.2882	5728.968	7856.969	14381.027	2167.539
2010	0.2737	0.3044	0.2907	0.1791	7296.919	10248.601	18562.218	2555.655
2011	-0.0088	-0.0401	-0.1015	0.0077	7232.592	9837.317	16678.586	2575.381

Source: Morningstar and CRSP. Calculated (or Derived) based on data from CRSP US Stock Database and CRSP US Indices Database
©2012 Center for Research in Security Prices (CRSP®), The University of Chicago Booth School of Business. Used with permission.

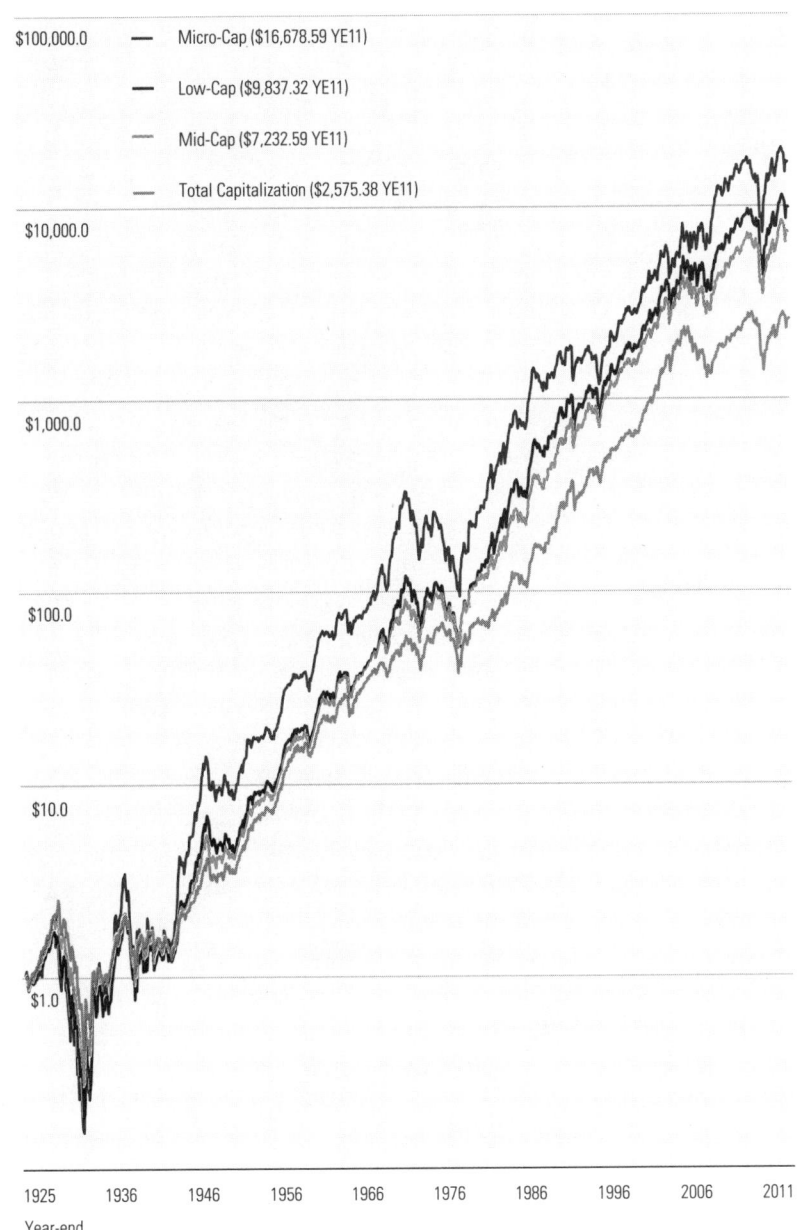

Graph 7-1: Size-Decile Portfolios of the NYSE/AMEX/NASDAQ
Wealth Indices of Investments in Mid-, Low-, Micro-, and Total Capitalization Stocks
Index (Year-End 1925 = $1.00)

— Micro-Cap ($16,678.59 YE11)

— Low-Cap ($9,837.32 YE11)

— Mid-Cap ($7,232.59 YE11)

— Total Capitalization ($2,575.38 YE11)

$100,000.0

$10,000.0

$1,000.0

$100.0

$10.0

$1.0

1925   1936   1946   1956   1966   1976   1986   1996   2006   2011

Year-end

Data from 1925–2011.

In Table 7-4, the decile returns and index values of the NYSE/AMEX/NASDAQ population are broken down into mid-cap, low-cap, and micro-cap stocks. Mid-cap stocks are defined here as the aggregate of deciles 3–5. Based on the most recent data, as shown in the bottom section of Table 7-5, companies within this mid-cap range have market capitalizations at or below $6,896,389,000 but greater than $1,620,860,000. Low-cap stocks include deciles 6–8, and currently include all companies in the NYSE/AMEX/NASDAQ with market capitalizations at or

below $1,620,860,000 but greater than $422,811,000. Micro-cap stocks include deciles 9–10, and include companies with market capitalizations at or below $422,811,000. The returns and index values of the entire NYSE/AMEX/NASDAQ population are also included. All returns presented are value-weighted based on the market capitalizations of the deciles contained in each sub-group. Graph 7-1 graphically depicts the growth of $1.00 invested in each of these capitalization groups.

Size of the Deciles

Table 7-5 reveals that most of the market value of the stocks listed on the NYSE/AMEX/NASDAQ is represented by the top three deciles. Approximately two-thirds of the value is represented by the first decile, which currently consists of 163 stocks. The smallest decile represents just under one percent of the market value of the NYSE/AMEX/NASDAQ. The data in the second column of Table 7-5 are averages across all 86 years. Of course, the proportions represented by the various deciles vary from year to year.

In columns three and four are the number of companies and market capitalization. These present a snapshot of the structure of the deciles near the end of 2011.

The lower portion of Table 7-5 shows the largest firm in each decile and its market capitalization.

Long-Term Returns in Excess of Risk

The Capital Asset Pricing Model (CAPM) does not fully account for the higher returns of small company stocks. Table 7-6 shows the returns in excess of the riskless rate over the past 86 years for each decile of the NYSE/AMEX/NASDAQ.

The CAPM can be expressed as follows:

$$k_s = r_f + (\beta_s \times ERP)$$ (28)

where,

k_s = the expected return for company **s**;

r_f = the expected return of the riskless asset;

β_s = the beta of the stock of company **s**; and,

ERP = the expected equity risk premium, or the amount by which investors expect the future return on equities to exceed that on the riskless asset.

Table 7-5: Size-Decile Portfolios of the NYSE/AMEX/NASDAQ
Bounds, Size, and Composition

Decile	Historical Average Percentage of Total Capitalization	Recent Number of Companies	Recent Decile Market Capitalization (in Thousands)	Recent Percentage of Total Capitalization
1-Largest	63.24%	163	8,865,444,654	62.30%
2	13.94	181	2,044,297,841	14.37
3	7.53	196	1,063,677,148	7.47
4	4.71	201	664,148,153	4.67
5	3.24	200	449,181,802	3.16
6	2.39	238	369,281,218	2.60
7	1.76	301	297,500,544	2.09
8	1.32	333	208,267,900	1.49
9	1.03	450	156,980,841	1.10
10-Smallest	0.83	1,212	111,034,220	0.78
Mid-Cap 3-5	15.48	597	2,177,007,103	15.30
Low-Cap 6-8	5.47	872	875,049,662	6.15
Micro-Cap 9-10	1.86	1,662	268,015,061	1.88

Data from 1926–2011. Source: Morningstar and CRSP. Calculated (or Derived) based on data from CRSP US Stock Database and CRSP US Indices Database ©2012 Center for Research in Security Prices (CRSP®), The University of Chicago Booth School of Business. Used with permission.

Historical average percentage of total capitalization shows the average, over the last 86 years, of the decile market values as a percentage of the total NYSE/AMEX/NASDAQ calculated each month. Number of companies in deciles, recent market capitalization of deciles and recent percentage of total capitalization are as of September 30, 2011.

Decile	Recent Market Capitalization (in Thousands)	Company Name
1(Largest)	$354,351,912	Apple Inc.
2	15,408,314	Marathon Oil Corp.
3	6,896,389	Waters Corp.
4	3,577,774	Solera Holdings Inc.
5	2,362,532	Pandora Media Inc.
6	1,620,860	Cabot Corp.
7	1,090,515	Vitamin Shoppe Inc.
8	682,750	Stepan Co.
9	422,811	Boyd Gaming Corp.
10 (Smallest)	206,795	Miller Industries

Source: Morningstar and CRSP. Calculated (or Derived) based on data from CRSP US Stock Database and CRSP US Indices Database ©2012 Center for Research in Security Prices (CRSP®), The University of Chicago Booth School of Business. Used with permission. Market capitalization and name of largest company in each decile as of September 30, 2011.

The amount of an asset's systematic risk is measured by its beta. A beta greater than 1 indicates that the security is riskier than the market, and according to the CAPM equation, investors are compensated for taking on this additional risk. However, based on historical return data on the NYSE/AMEX/NASDAQ decile portfolios, the smaller deciles have had returns that are not fully explainable by the CAPM. This return in excess of CAPM grows larger as one moves from the largest companies in decile 1 to the smallest in decile 10. The excess return is especially pronounced for micro-cap stocks (deciles 9–10). This size related phenomenon has prompted a revision to the CAPM that includes the addition of a size premium.

The CAPM is used here to calculate the CAPM return in excess of the riskless rate and to compare this estimate to historical performance. According to the CAPM, the return on a security should consist of the riskless rate plus an additional return to compensate for the systematic risk of the security. Table 7-6 uses the 86-year arithmetic mean income return component of 20-year government bonds as the historical riskless rate. (However, it is appropriate to match the maturity, or duration, of the riskless asset with the investment horizon.) This CAPM return in excess of the riskless rate is β (beta) multiplied by the realized equity risk premium. The realized equity risk premium is the return that compensates investors for taking on risk equal to the risk of the market as a whole (estimated by the 86-year arithmetic mean return on large company stocks, 11.77 percent, less the historical riskless rate, 5.15 percent). The difference between the excess return predicted by the CAPM and the realized excess return is the size premium, or return in excess of CAPM.

This phenomenon can also be viewed graphically, as depicted in the Graph 7-2. The security market line is based on the pure CAPM without adjusting for the size premium. Based on the risk (or beta) of a security, the expected return should fluctuate along the security market line. However, the expected returns for the smaller deciles of the NYSE/AMEX/NASDAQ lie above the line, indicating that these deciles have had returns in excess of their risk.

For additional information regarding size premia or a more detailed breakdown of the size effect over size-decile portfolios please reference Chapter 7 of the *Ibbotson® SBBI® Valuation Yearbook.*

Table 7-6: Size-Decile Portfolios of the NYSE/AMEX/NASDAQ
Long-Term Returns in Excess of CAPM

Decile	Beta*	Arith-metic Mean Return	Actual Return in Excess of Riskless Rate** (%)	CAPM Return in Excess of Riskless Rate† (%)	Size Premium (Return in Excess of CAPM) (%)
Mid-Cap, 3-5	1.12	13.70	8.55	7.41	1.14
Low-Cap, 6-8	1.23	15.16	10.01	8.13	1.88
Micro-Cap, 9-10	1.36	18.04	12.88	8.99	3.89

Data from 1926–2011. Source: Morningstar and CRSP. Calculated (or Derived) based on data from CRSP US Stock Database and CRSP US Indices Database ©2012 Center for Research in Security Prices (CRSP®), The University of Chicago Booth School of Business. Used with permission.

*Betas are estimated from monthly returns in excess of the 30-day U.S. Treasury bill total return, January 1926–December 2011.

**Historical riskless rate measured by the 86-year arithmetic mean income return component of 20-year government bonds (5.15 percent).

†Calculated in the context of the CAPM by multiplying the equity risk premium by beta. The equity risk premium is estimated by the arithmetic mean total return of the S&P 500 (11.77 percent) minus the arithmetic mean income return component of 20-year government bonds (5.15 percent) from 1926–2011.

Graph 7-2: Security Market Line Versus Size-Decile Portfolios of the NYSE/AMEX/NASDAQ

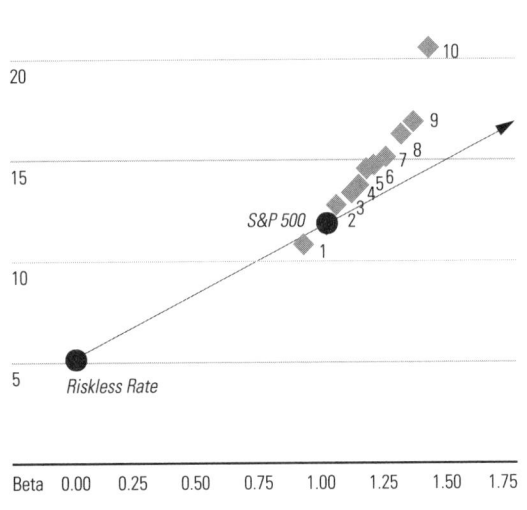

Data from 1926–2011.

Serial Correlation in Small Company Stock Returns

The serial correlation, or first-order autocorrelation, of returns on large capitalization stocks is near zero. [See Table 7-1.] If stock returns are serially correlated, then one can gain some information about future performance based on past returns. For the smallest stocks, the serial correlation is near or above 0.1. This observation bears further examination.

Table 7-7: Size-Decile Portfolios of the NYSE/AMEX/NASDAQ
Serial Correlations of Annual Returns in Excess of Decile 1 Returns

Decile	Serial Correlations of Annual Returns in Excess of Decile 1 Return
2	0.22
3	0.27
4	0.25
5	0.25
6	0.33
7	0.27
8	0.34
9	0.29
10	0.39

Data from 1926–2011. Source: Morningstar and CRSP. Calculated (or Derived) based on data from CRSP US Stock Database and CRSP US Indices Database ©2012 Center for Research in Security Prices (CRSP®), The University of Chicago Booth School of Business. Used with permission.

To remove the randomizing effect of the market as a whole, the returns for decile 1 are geometrically subtracted from the returns for deciles 2 through 10. The result illustrates that these series differences exhibit greater serial correlation than the decile series themselves. Table 7-7 above presents the serial correlations of the excess returns for deciles 2 through 10. These serial correlations suggest some predictability of smaller company excess returns. However, caution is necessary. The serial correlation of small company excess returns for non-calendar years (February through January, etc.) do not always confirm the results shown here for calendar (January through December) years. The results for the non-calendar years (not shown in this book) suggest that predicting small company excess returns may not be easy.

Table 7-8: Size-Decile Portfolios of the NYSE/AMEX/NASDAQ: Returns in Excess of Decile 1 (%)

Decile	Jan	Feb	Mar	Apr	May	Jun	Jul	Aug	Sep	Oct	Nov	Dec	Total (Jan–Dec)
2	0.84	0.51	-0.01	-0.17	0.11	-0.10	-0.10	0.17	0.02	-0.32	0.12	0.38	1.51
	65	57	41	33	44	42	37	44	45	40	49	47	
3	1.12	0.39	0.10	0.01	-0.09	-0.15	-0.10	0.33	-0.11	-0.37	0.49	0.31	1.98
	62	55	42	33	39	37	43	51	41	36	48	49	
4	1.33	0.61	-0.01	-0.16	0.11	-0.09	-0.15	0.25	0.05	-0.78	0.33	0.53	2.12
	63	54	42	36	42	41	37	49	44	31	46	49	
5	2.14	0.62	-0.01	-0.10	-0.12	0.01	-0.10	0.25	0.03	-0.75	0.30	0.38	2.78
	63	53	40	38	38	41	43	48	44	35	49	47	
6	2.41	0.46	-0.03	0.03	0.30	-0.10	-0.20	0.46	0.14	-1.19	0.21	0.30	2.93
	63	54	46	37	42	39	43	49	46	36	45	46	
7	3.01	0.64	-0.04	-0.01	0.15	-0.31	-0.09	0.20	0.24	-1.03	0.15	0.09	3.03
	64	55	45	37	37	34	38	41	47	31	45	42	
8	4.13	0.67	-0.22	-0.24	0.39	-0.42	0.06	0.11	0.04	-1.03	0.14	-0.13	3.86
	63	50	40	34	36	38	40	39	45	36	39	39	
9	5.32	0.88	-0.06	-0.06	0.29	-0.42	-0.01	0.04	-0.05	-1.17	0.02	-0.79	4.28
	63	47	45	34	37	34	37	44	41	35	37	36	
10	8.70	0.90	-0.69	0.06	0.60	-0.59	0.52	-0.20	0.52	-1.41	-0.57	-1.44	7.22
	78	44	37	36	37	35	40	32	42	31	32	33	

First row: Average excess return in percent   Second row: Number of times excess return was positive (in 86 years)

Data from 1926–2011. Source: Morningstar and CRSP. Calculated (or Derived) based on data from CRSP US Stock Database and CRSP US Indices Database ©2012 Center for Research in Security Prices (CRSP®), The University of Chicago Booth School of Business. Used with permission.

Seasonality

Unlike the returns on large company stocks, the returns on small company stocks appear to be seasonal. In January, small company stocks often outperform larger stocks by amounts far greater than in any other month.

Table 7-8 shows the returns of capitalization deciles 2 through 10 in excess of the return on decile 1. This table segregates excess returns into months. For each decile and for each month, the exhibit shows both the average excess return as well as the number of times the excess return is positive. These two statistics measure the seasonality of the excess return in different ways. The average excess return illustrates the size of the effect, while the number of positive excess returns shows the reliability of the effect.

Virtually all of the small stock effect occurs in January. The excess outcomes of the other months are on net, mostly negative for small company stocks. Excess returns in January relate to size in a precisely rank-ordered fashion. This "January effect" seems to pervade all size groups. ▥

Endnotes

[1] Rolf W. Banz was the first to document this phenomenon. See Banz, Rolf W., "The Relationship Between Returns and Market Value of Common Stocks," *Journal of Financial Economics,* Volume 9 (1981), pp. 3–18.

Chapter 8
Growth and Value Investing

Discussion of Style Investing

The concept of equity investment style has come into being over the past 30 years or so. Investment style can broadly be defined as an overarching description of groups of stocks or portfolios based on shared characteristics. Probably the first discussion and consideration of style concerned large-company versus small-company investing, and even this distinction was not prominent until the 1960s. Styles of investing are now broken down into more detail and used for performance measurement, asset allocation, and other purposes. Mutual funds and other investment portfolios are often measured against broad growth or value benchmarks. In some cases, investment-manager-specific style benchmarks are constructed to separate pure stock-selection ability from style effects.

Most investors agree on the broad definitions of growth and value, but when it comes to specifics, definitions can vary widely. In general, growth stocks have high relative growth rates in regard to earnings, sales, or return on equity. Growth stocks usually have relatively high price-to-earnings and price-to-book ratios. Value stocks will generally have lower price-to-earnings and price-to-book values and often have higher dividend yields. Value stocks are often turnaround opportunities, companies that have had disappointing news, or companies with low growth prospects. Value investors generally believe that a value stock has been unfairly beaten down by the market, leading the stock to sell below its "intrinsic" value. Therefore, they buy the stock with the hope that the market will realize the stock's full value and eventually bid the price up to its fair value.

Different Ways of Measuring Growth and Value

In order to objectively measure the performance of value and growth stocks, several different data providers have constructed value and growth indexes. Each index provider may use a different methodology to draw the line between growth and value and may use different techniques for constructing portfolios, but all of the methodologies generally start with some combination of accounting data, analyst growth estimates, and market capitalization.

Growth and value stocks have certainly been around for as long as stocks have been traded, but much of the accounting data that is readily available today was not available in years past or was of poor quality. However, Eugene Fama and Ken French constructed growth and value data from both Compustat and hand-collected data for the early years of the series. This chapter places a heavy emphasis on the Morningstar growth and value indexes[1], but it also presents the Fama-French data in order to provide a high-level look at trends in growth/value over longer time periods.

Morningstar Growth and Value Series

The following commentary and corresponding data make use of the Morningstar growth and value data series.

Morningstar Index Construction Methodology

The Morningstar Index family consists of 16 indexes that track the U.S. market by capitalization and investment style and are based on the same methodology as the Morningstar Style Box.[2]

The Morningstar Style Indexes include U.S.-based, U.S.-traded companies listed on the New York Stock Exchange (NYSE), the NYSE Amex (AMEX), and the National Association of Securities Dealers Automated Quotations (NASDAQ). American Depository Receipts (ADRs), fixed-dividend shares, convertible notes, warrants, rights, unit investment trusts, limited partnerships, closed-end funds, holding companies, and other non-equity listed securities are excluded.

We calculate a liquidity score for each security in this universe. Liquidity is defined as the average monthly trading volume over the past six months and the lowest two months' total trading volume over the same period. Stocks that fall in the bottom quartile are not eligible for inclusion in the indexes.

Sixteen portfolios are then formed based on size and style. The top 70 percent of market cap are defined as large-cap stocks, the next 20 percent are mid cap and the next 7 percent represent small-cap stocks. The bottom 3 percent of stocks is excluded from the index. Historically, the large-cap, mid-cap, and small-cap indexes comprise around 200, 600, and 1,000 companies, respectively. Each of these portfolios is then divided into style classifications based on a 10-factor model consisting of five value factors and five growth factors. Half of each score is based on a forward-looking factor and the other half is based on historical factors.

For example, half of the value score is based on the one-year forward price-to-earnings ratio. The other four value factors, which are historical and equal weighted, are price-to-book, price-to-sales, price-to-cash flow, and dividend yield. Alternatively, the growth score is based on the long-term earnings growth rate. The other four growth factors, also historically and equal weighted, are book value growth, sales growth, cash-flow growth, and trailing earnings growth. The threshold levels for the value, core, and growth styles are set so that over time the average of each style represents roughly one-third of the investable universe within the capitalization band.

Portfolios are rebalanced semi-annually on the third Friday of June and the third Friday of December. Each stock is weighted according to its free float value, which is the product of the number of free float shares and the most recent traded price. All of these indexes are calculated daily. The inception date of the style indexes is June 1997, based on data availability. The cap indexes and overall U.S. Market Index have an inception date of December 1991.

The Morningstar Style Box
Graph 8-1 shows a nine-square grid called the Morningstar Style Box. The Morningstar Style Box classifies stocks by size along the vertical axis and by value and growth characteristics along the horizontal axis.[3] Different investment styles often have different levels of risk and lead to differences in returns.

Graph 8-1: Morningstar Style Index Family

US Market Index	US Value Index	US Core Index	US Growth Index
Large Cap Index	Large Value Index	Large Core Index	Large Growth Index
Mid Cap Index	Mid Value Index	Mid Core Index	Mid Growth Index
Small Cap Index	Small Value Index	Small Core Index	Small Growth Index

Graph 8-2 shows the stock market performance of the Morningstar Style Index Family from June 1997 to December 2011. Over this period, small-value stocks were the best performers, with an 8.93 percent return, while large-growth stocks were the worst performers, returning only 1.00 percent. Historically, small-value stocks have outperformed large-growth stocks.[4]

Graph 8-2: Morningstar Style Index Family: Compound Annual Total Return

4.68	5.48	5.68	2.14
3.72	4.48	4.77	1.00
6.94	7.80	7.68	4.78
6.91	8.93	8.64	3.31

Data from June 1997 to December 2011.

Graph 8-3 displays the annual standard deviation for the Morningstar Style Index Family. Small-growth stocks had the highest risk, at 30.38 percent, while large-value stocks tended to exhibit the lowest risk.

Note that small-value stocks not only had significantly higher return over the period than large-growth stocks, but they also did so with lower risk.

Graph 8-3: Morningstar Style Index Family: Annualized Standard Deviation

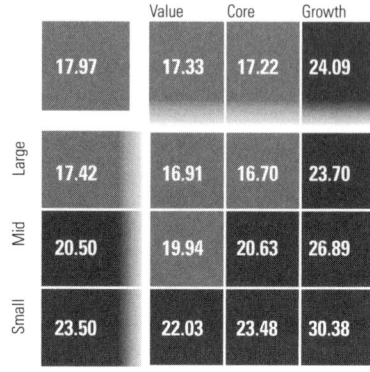

	Value	Core	Growth
	17.97	17.33	17.22	24.09
Large	17.42	16.91	16.70	23.70
Mid	20.50	19.94	20.63	26.89
Small	23.50	22.03	23.48	30.38

Data from June 1997 to December 2011.

The Morningstar Market Barometer
The Morningstar Market Barometer[5] provides at-a-glance insight into past stock market performance by segmenting the market by investment style and market capitalization. These images illustrate the annual returns for each market segment, as defined and tracked by the Morningstar Style Indexes.

The lighter the colored shading, the better the return; the darker colored red worse return.

Graph 8-4 (see next page) offers a vivid example of how the Morningstar Market Barometer imparts a visual, high-level perspective by presenting the Market Barometers as of year-end 2008, 2009, 2010, and 2011. The images illustrate the end of a U.S. equity bull market that was fueled by rapidly rising housing wealth and profligate consumer spending. The market collapse in 2008 was indiscriminate in terms of style as the entire U.S. financial system fell into severe distress. In 2009, however, U.S. equities rallied across the spectrum. This rally carried over to 2010 with more modest but still high returns. 2011, on the other hand, saw low returns in the overall market without a particular index faring much better or worse than another.

Fama-French (FF) Growth and Value Series
The following commentary and corresponding data make use of the Fama-French growth and value data series.

Fama-French Index Construction Methodology
Fama-French use all stocks traded on the New York Stock Exchange (NYSE) to set both growth/value and small/large breakpoints. They then apply these breakpoints to all stocks traded on NYSE, NYSE Amex, and NASDAQ to construct each index.

The market capitalization breakpoint between small and large stocks is set as the median market capitalization of NYSE stocks. This breakpoint is then applied to all stocks traded on NYSE, NYSE Amex, and NASDAQ.

To define value and growth, Fama-French use the book value of equity (BE) divided by market capitalization (ME), which is the inverse of how much investors are willing to pay for a dollar of book value. Value companies will have a high book-to-market ratio, while growth companies will have a low book-to-market ratio. Fama-French used Compustat as their data source to calculate book value from 1963 forward, and hand-collected data for 1928 to 1962.

Book value was calculated as follows:

$$BV = SE + DT + ITC - PS \tag{29}$$

where,
- BV = Fama-French book value;
- SE = book value of stockholders' equity;
- DT = balance sheet deferred taxes;
- ITC = investment tax credit (if available); and,
- PS = book value of preferred stock. Depending on availability, either redemption, liquidation, or par value (in that order) is used to estimate book value of preferred stock.

Stocks are put into three groups based on book-to-market: low, medium, or high. The definition of low, medium, and high is based on the breakpoints for the bottom 30 percent, middle 40 percent, and top 30 percent of the value of book-to-market for NYSE stocks. These breakpoints are then applied to all NYSE, NYSE Amex, and NASDAQ stocks. For the growth/value analysis shown in this chapter, only the low and high portfolios are used. The medium portfolios, which are blends of growth and value, are not shown.

Firms with negative book values are not used when calculating the book-to-market breakpoints or when calculating size-specific book-to-market breakpoints. Also, only firms with ordinary common equity (as classified by CRSP) are included in the portfolios. This excludes ADRs, REITs, and unit trusts.

The four size-specific style indices used in this chapter are small value, small growth, large value, and large growth. These portfolios are defined as the intersections of the two size groups and the low and high book-to-market groups.

Graph 8-4: Morningstar Market Barometer

Overview

The Morningstar Market Barometer™ provides an at-a-glance perspective of the U.S. equity market, allowing instant analysis of performance trends. This analysis helps identify investment opportunities and explain the long-term benefits of diversification. The four years represented below illustrate the end of a U.S. equity bull market fueled by rapidly rising housing wealth and profligate consumer spending. The market collapse in 2008 was indiscriminate in terms of style. However, the rebound in 2009 and 2010 clearly benefited growth-oriented firms, as well as small- and mid-cap shares.

2008

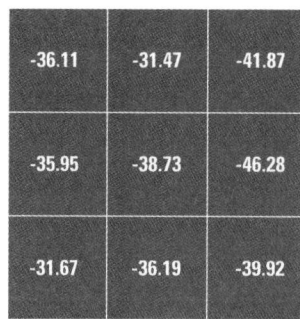

2009

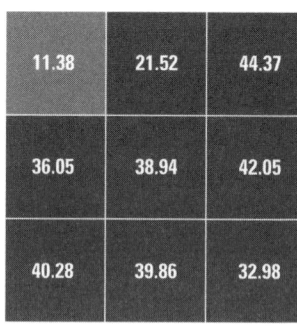

The U.S. housing market collapse in 2008 shattered the financial services sector, which sparked a global credit crisis that impacted equities across the board. The US Market Index dropped 37.0 percent in 2008 and there was no place to hide, according to the Market Barometer. Value did trump growth; the US Growth Index dropped 42.6 percent in 2008, 6.8 percentage points farther than the US Value Index. Little was gained by a flight to "large-cap safety" as the Large Cap and Small Cap Indexes both ended down 36 percent.

After a painful 2008, equity investors were rewarded handsomely in 2009 as the Morningstar US Market Index posted a gain of 28 percent. There was a massive divergence across investment styles—growth stocks rose 43% for the year, while value stocks were up a more modest 18 percent. Mid-cap and small-cap stocks outperformed the broader market, increasing 39 percent and 38 percent, respectively.

2010

14.69	12.93	12.91
20.61	26.46	27.67
25.96	27.77	31.26

2011

2.23	3.40	1.56
-2.60	2.22	-2.29
-1.84	-4.74	-1.04

Still recovering from 2008, 2010 did not exhibit as high returns as 2009 but they are all still well above the average annual returns shown in Graph 8-2. The US Market Index had a return of 17 percent in 2010. The Growth Index and the Value Index both rose by the same amount, 17 percent. Large-cap stocks had the lowest return of 13 percent while, just like in 2009, mid-cap and small-cap stocks beat the US Market with returns of 25 percent and 28 percent, respectively.

In 2011, none of the nine style indices had great gains or loses. The US Market Index ended the year flat at 1.58 percent in 2011. Both the Growth and Value Indices struggled to grow and ended the year with annual returns of 0.74 percent and 0.92 percent, respectively. The Core Index grew the most, ending the year at 2.67 percent. Large-cap stocks came in at a close second with an annual return of 2.61 percent. On the other hand, small-cap stocks had the lowest return of -2.57 in 2011.

Graph 8-5: FF Small Value Stocks, FF Small Growth Stocks, FF Large Value Stocks, FF Large Growth Stocks Index (Year-End 1927 = $1.00)

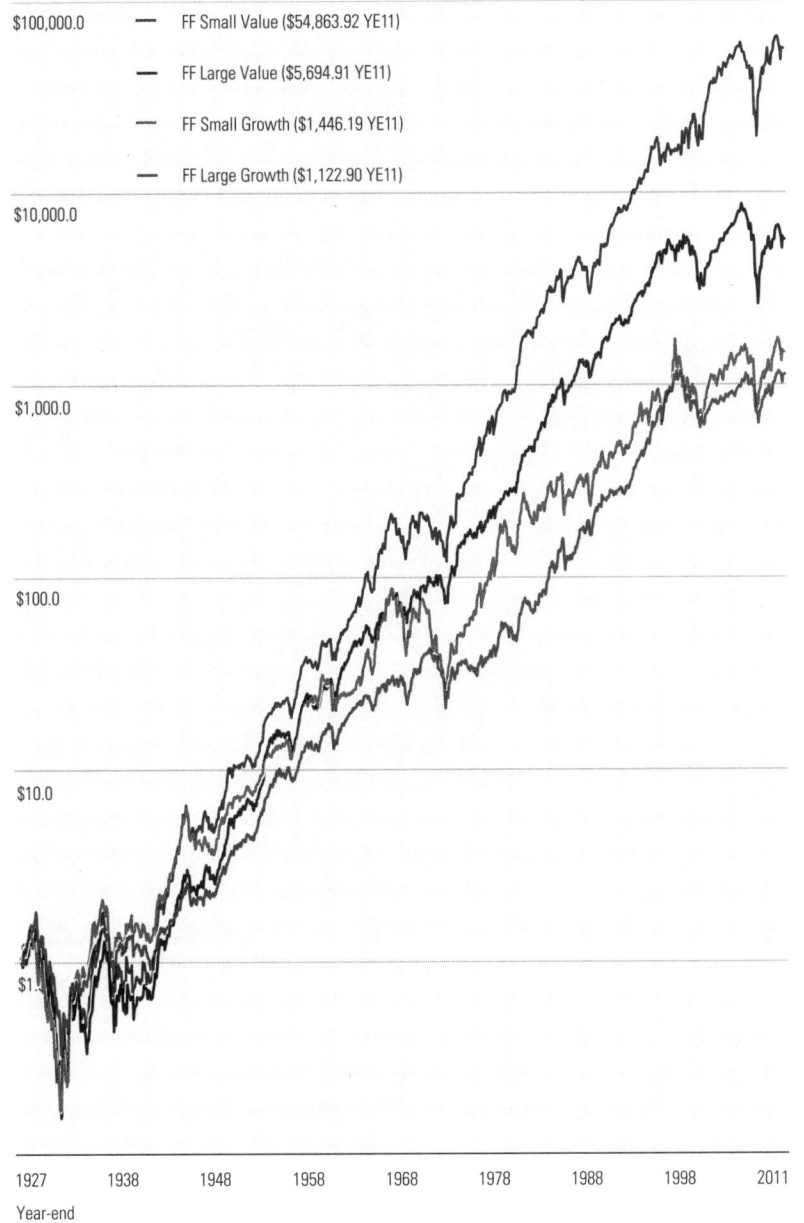

- — FF Small Value ($54,863.92 YE11)
- — FF Large Value ($5,694.91 YE11)
- — FF Small Growth ($1,446.19 YE11)
- — FF Large Growth ($1,122.90 YE11)

$100,000.0

$10,000.0

$1,000.0

$100.0

$10.0

$1.

1927   1938   1948   1958   1968   1978   1988   1998   2011

Year-end

Data from 1927–2011.

Historical Returns of FF Growth and Value Series

Using the Fama-French series, Graph 8-5 depicts the growth of $1.00 invested in FF small growth, small value, large growth, and large value stocks from the end of 1927 to the end of 2011. All results assume reinvestment of dividends and exclude transaction costs. The top two performers during this time period were small value and large value stocks followed by small growth and large growth stocks. Over the period from 1928 to 2011, small value stocks outperformed all other stock series in the graph. One dollar invested in small value stocks at the end of 1927 grew to $54,863.92 by the end of 2011, rising from $59,017.28 at the end of 2010.

Summary Statistics for FF Growth and Value Series

Table 8-1 shows summary statistics of annual total returns for the Fama-French growth and value series from 1928 to 2011. The summary statistics presented are geometric mean, arithmetic mean, and standard deviation.

Value significantly outperformed growth across the market capitalization spectrum. In the large capitalization arena, the extra return of value over growth was at the expense of increased risk, as the standard deviation of large value was 27.8 percent versus 20.2 percent for large growth. Between the small cap series, small value significantly outperformed small growth and did so with lower volatility (32.8 percent versus 33.2 percent).

Table 8-1: FF Growth and Value Series
Summary Statistics of Annual Returns

Series	Geometric Mean (%)	Arithmetic Mean (%)	Standard Deviation (%)
FF Large Growth Stocks	8.7	10.7	20.2
FF Large Value Stocks	10.8	14.4	27.8
FF Small Growth Stocks	9.0	13.7	33.2
FF Small Value Stocks	13.9	18.6	32.8

Data from 1928–2011.

Table 8-2: FF Growth and Value Series

Compound Annual Rates of Return by Decade (%)

	1920s*	1930s	1940s	1950s	1960s	1970s	1980s	1990s	2000s	02–11
FF Large Growth Stocks	8.1	1.5	7.3	17.6	7.9	3.4	15.8	19.9	-1.8	3.3
FF Large Value Stocks	9.0	-5.5	17.2	22.2	10.7	12.2	20.2	13.9	0.3	0.9
FF Small Growth Stocks	-13.3	7.4	11.6	17.7	10.7	5.8	10.8	15.0	-1.1	4.0
FF Small Value Stocks	-4.8	-0.3	21.0	20.0	15.4	15.0	21.1	14.5	10.6	9.3

*Based on the period 1928–1929.
Data from 1928-2011.

Table 8-3: FF Growth and Value Series

Serial and Cross Correlations of Historical Annual Returns

Series	FF Large Growth Stocks	FF Large Value Stocks	FF Small Growth Stocks	FF Small Value Stocks	FF U.S. Treasury Bills	Inflation
FF Large Growth Stocks	1.00					
FF Large Value Stocks	0.81	1.00				
FF Small Growth Stocks	0.81	0.81	1.00			
FF Small Value Stocks	0.74	0.90	0.87	1.00		
U.S. Treasury bills	-0.01	-0.03	-0.10	-0.08	1.00	
Inflation	-0.01	0.06	0.00	0.05	0.41	1.00
Serial Correlations	0.03	-0.07	0.01	0.03	0.91	0.63

Data from 1928–2011.

Returns by Decade for FF Growth and Value Series

Table 8-2 shows the compound returns by decade for the growth and value series. Small value stocks beat small growth stocks in all decades except the 1930s and the 1990s. It is also interesting to note that in any decade small value stocks were never the worst performing among all four stock series.

Correlation of FF Growth and Value Series

Table 8-3 presents the annual cross-correlations and serial correlations for the growth and value series.

Presentation of Annual FF Growth and Value Returns

Table 8-4 shows year-by-year total annual returns for the Fama-French growth and value series from 1928 to 2011. This table compares the performance of large growth, large value, small growth, and small value.

Conclusion

What can explain this value effect? Readers of Graham and Dodd's Security Analysis,[6] first published in 1934, would say that the outperformance of value stocks is due to the market coming to realize the full value of a company's securities that were once undervalued. The Graham and Dodd approach to security analysis is to do an independent valuation of a company using accounting data and common market multiples, then look at the stock price to see if the stock is under- or overvalued. Several academic studies have shown that the market overreacts to bad news and underreacts to good news. This would lead us to conclude that there is more room for value stocks (which are more likely to have reported bad news) to improve and outperform growth stocks, which already have high expectations built into them.

Possibly a larger question is what does the future hold as far as growth and value investing goes? Advocates of growth investing would argue that technology- and innovation-oriented companies will continue to dominate as the Internet changes the way the world communicates and does business. Stalwarts of value investing would argue that there are still companies and industries that continue to be ignored and represent long-term investment bargains. Only time will tell. ▥

Endnotes

[1] The Ibbotson Associates (IA) Growth and Value Series has been discontinued.

[2] To learn more about Style Indexes, including Morningstar growth and value indexes, or for more information on the entire Morningstar Index family, please visit http://indexes.morningstar.com/

[3] To learn more about the Morningstar Style Box, please visit http://global.morningstar.com/StyleBoxMethodology

[4] For current total returns on the 16 Morningstar Style Indexes, please visit http://global.morningstar.com/MorningstarIndexData

[5] The Morningstar Market Barometer provides a visual perspective of the U.S. equity market by depicting the performance of major economic spheres while placing them in context of the overall market. iShares offers exchange-traded funds based on Morningstar Style Indexes. For more information, please visit www.iShares.com

[6] Cottle, Sidney, Murray, Roger F., and Block, Frank E. "Graham and Dodd's Security Analysis," Fifth Edition, McGraw-Hill, 1988.

Table 8-4: Fama-French (FF) Growth and Value Series:
Annual Total Returns

	FF Large Growth Stocks	FF Large Value Stocks	FF Small Growth Stocks	FF Small Value Stocks		FF Large Growth Stocks	FF Large Value Stocks	FF Small Growth Stocks	FF Small Value Stocks
1928	0.4805	0.2363	0.3486	0.4096	1971	0.2394	0.1255	0.2586	0.1447
1929	-0.2107	-0.0393	-0.4423	-0.3577	1972	0.2132	0.1862	0.0039	0.0728
1930	-0.2644	-0.4316	-0.3585	-0.4638	1973	-0.2179	-0.0367	-0.4507	-0.2723
1931	-0.3696	-0.5824	-0.4270	-0.5187	1974	-0.2924	-0.2340	-0.3190	-0.1902
1932	-0.0793	-0.0326	-0.0525	0.0135	1975	0.3444	0.5590	0.6132	0.5712
1933	0.4465	1.1691	1.5941	1.1869	1976	0.1754	0.4462	0.3820	0.5913
1934	0.1106	-0.2151	0.3589	0.0851	1977	-0.0946	0.0164	0.1935	0.2382
1935	0.4222	0.5114	0.4834	0.5316	1978	0.0700	0.0348	0.1765	0.2212
1936	0.2646	0.4812	0.3710	0.7319	1979	0.1659	0.2267	0.4884	0.3833
1937	-0.3412	-0.4107	-0.4864	-0.5147	1980	0.3520	0.1645	0.5266	0.2228
1938	0.3320	0.2520	0.4381	0.2621	1981	-0.0713	0.1280	-0.1153	0.1768
1939	0.0773	-0.1251	0.1072	-0.0355	1982	0.2148	0.2767	0.1972	0.3986
1940	-0.0981	-0.0262	0.0057	-0.0983	1983	0.1467	0.2692	0.2212	0.4758
1941	-0.1267	-0.0088	-0.1734	-0.0482	1984	-0.0072	0.1617	-0.1284	0.0752
1942	0.1317	0.3371	0.1676	0.3500	1985	0.3264	0.3175	0.2891	0.3212
1943	0.2204	0.4402	0.4508	0.9182	1986	0.1438	0.2182	0.0195	0.1450
1944	0.1611	0.4198	0.4123	0.4971	1987	0.0743	-0.0276	-0.1224	-0.0712
1945	0.3195	0.4906	0.6428	0.7461	1988	0.1253	0.2596	0.1663	0.3076
1946	-0.0829	-0.0829	-0.1240	-0.0736	1989	0.3611	0.2970	0.2058	0.1570
1947	0.0410	0.0866	-0.0838	0.0534	1990	0.0106	-0.1275	-0.1774	-0.2513
1948	0.0335	0.0509	-0.0716	-0.0230	1991	0.4333	0.2735	0.5473	0.4056
1949	0.2331	0.1871	0.2352	0.2104	1992	0.0641	0.2357	0.0582	0.3476
1950	0.2311	0.5522	0.3101	0.5216	1993	0.0238	0.1951	0.1264	0.2941
1951	0.2005	0.1436	0.1626	0.1227	1994	0.0195	-0.0578	-0.0436	0.0321
1952	0.1338	0.1954	0.0855	0.0859	1995	0.3716	0.3768	0.3513	0.2769
1953	0.0229	-0.0704	-0.0068	-0.0692	1996	0.2125	0.1335	0.1236	0.2071
1954	0.4779	0.7732	0.4320	0.6343	1997	0.3161	0.3188	0.1529	0.3729
1955	0.2850	0.2978	0.1395	0.2347	1998	0.3464	0.1623	0.0304	-0.0863
1956	0.0652	0.0337	0.0765	0.0598	1999	0.2943	-0.0022	0.5475	0.0559
1957	-0.0914	-0.2272	-0.1699	-0.1590	2000	-0.1363	0.0580	-0.2415	-0.0080
1958	0.4162	0.7230	0.7522	0.6967	2001	-0.1559	-0.0118	0.0016	0.4024
1959	0.1315	0.1882	0.2142	0.1742	2002	-0.2150	-0.3253	-0.3087	-0.1241
1960	-0.0236	-0.0856	-0.0178	-0.0602	2003	0.2629	0.3507	0.5320	0.7469
1961	0.2643	0.2889	0.2220	0.3085	2004	0.0653	0.1891	0.1254	0.2659
1962	-0.1089	-0.0309	-0.2233	-0.0947	2005	0.0282	0.1217	0.0545	0.0353
1963	0.2188	0.3235	0.0798	0.2834	2006	0.0888	0.2261	0.1167	0.2176
1964	0.1448	0.1916	0.0813	0.2290	2007	0.1408	-0.0645	0.0736	-0.1521
1965	0.1336	0.2242	0.3999	0.4250	2008	-0.3371	-0.4903	-0.4156	-0.4439
1966	-0.1077	-0.1021	-0.0532	-0.0776	2009	0.2792	0.3915	0.3445	0.7054
1967	0.2917	0.3174	0.8842	0.6755	2010	0.1587	0.2161	0.3066	0.3354
1968	0.0403	0.2708	0.3273	0.4581	2011	0.0414	-0.0904	-0.0432	-0.0704
1969	0.0288	-0.1639	-0.2368	-0.2584					
1970	-0.0565	0.1063	-0.2025	0.0662					

Chapter 9
Liquidity Investing

This chapter is written by Roger Ibbotson and Zhiwu Chen, using research developed at Zebra Capital Management, LLC.[1]

What is Liquidity?

Liquidity has many different, but similar meanings. In every case it is related to the ease of movement. Even within the context of financial markets, liquidity has several different meanings. In the banking system, liquidity measures the degree to which loans are made. In the securities markets, liquidity is the ease with which transactions can be made. In valuation, this liquidity impacts value, so that the more liquidity an asset has the more value it has, all other things being equal. The absence of liquidity lowers the value of the asset by the amount of an liquidity discount.

In this chapter, we focus on liquidity as the ease of executing securities in general, especially equities. We focus on liquidity's impact on valuation and in particular its impact on security returns. We will demonstrate that less-liquid securities have higher expected returns.

Valuation as Present Value of Cash Flows

In equilibrium, an asset has a value that equals its present value, or the discounted sum of its expected cash flows. These future cash flows are unobservable, except for risk-free assets. For stocks, there is great disagreement as to what these expected cash flows might be. This disagreement is the primary reason that stocks are traded. A secondary reason is that they are bought or sold to meet liquidity needs.

The other component of a present value calculation is the discount rate. Similar to the expected cash flows, these discount rates are unobservable. We can usually observe the riskless discount rates from a term structure of riskless bonds, which we unravel from U.S. government discount bonds. But there are usually other premiums that we would add to the riskless term structure. The most common one is an equity risk premium, which is often modified by a beta in the CAPM framework. We might also add a premium for size and another one for value (or distress). We argue here that another premium should be added for lack of liquidity.

The difference of opinion that investors have about expected cash flows leads to the additional risk of a security. The risk of the security reflects not only the changing economy and company cash-flow expectations, but also the divergence of opinion that changes from moment to moment. This risk reduces the value of a security. Ironically though, this divergence of opinion also leads to most of the trading of a security, thereby making the security more liquid for trades, whether they be active or liquidity traders. The higher liquidity increases the security's value.

We do not mean to imply that most investors actually make these present value calculations. Instead investors rely on simple metrics, such as the price/earnings ratio (PE ratio), trying to buy stocks with relatively high but unspecified cash flow projections, at relatively low PE ratios. Or they may simply feel that a stock's price is too low or high relative to its estimated value, leading them to buy or sell a security.

The Liquidity Premium

Most conventional present value calculations ignore the liquidity premium. These calculations usually implicitly assume that securities are perfectly liquid. If they are somewhat liquid, an liquidity discount is often made to the present value, at the end of the calculation. Thus, a liquid stock is priced at the present value of the expected cash flows, discounted by the riskless rate and various other risk premiums, such as a beta adjusted equity risk premium, a size premium, and a value premium. The final present value is then reduced by some percentage due to its lack of liquidity.

The other way to calculate a present value is to add a liquidity premium into the discount rate. Less liquid securities would then have their cash flows discounted at higher rates. The benefit of this approach is that this liquidity premium can be thought of as causing a higher discount rate. These discount rates are equivalent, under certain conditions, to the expected return that an investor receives for investing in less liquid securities.

The liquidity premium is the extra return an investor would demand in order to hold a security that cannot costlessly be traded. This premium is not exactly a risk premium, since it more reflects a transaction cost. We can think of the premium as related to risk however, because it is the risk of having to buy or sell a security quickly. The less liquid and more hurried the transaction, the more the cost.

The liquidity premium is potentially interesting to investors who can afford to hold a security over time, instead of continuously trading it. For investors with longer-term horizons, the trading costs become trivial because they happen so infrequently. The liquidity premium is a benefit to the longer-term investor. It means that the less-liquid securities will have higher returns and these higher returns are not likely to be affected by trading costs.

It is sometimes argued that part of the expected return that is demanded from real estate, private equity, or venture capital comes from their relative liquidity.[2] In addition to any of their return for other risk characteristics, investors want an extra return for holding an illiquid asset. Thus, investors would only want to invest in alternative illiquid assets if they thought they would receive extra compensation for their lack of liquidity.

The liquidity premium also is substantial within publicly traded securities. There is a difference in the return of the more highly traded securities versus the less traded securities, even though most all public securities can be readily traded. The remainder of this chapter examines the relative impact of liquidity across publicly traded stocks on the NYSE, NYSE Amex, and NASDAQ.

Liquidity and Stock Returns

In the U.S. stock market, liquidity has substantial impact on stock returns. We examine the monthly data for the largest 3,500 U.S. stocks by capitalization over the period 1972 through 2011. These stocks are traded on either the New York Stock Exchange, the NYSE Amex, or NASDAQ. All are publicly traded and relatively liquid, but of course some are more liquid than others.

We separate the stocks into four quartiles separated from the prior year by the turnover rate. The turnover rate is the number of shares traded during the year divided by the number of shares outstanding for the stock. The stocks with the highest turnover rates are the most liquid, and the stocks with the lowest turnover rates the least liquid. The return, share volume, and capitalization data are from the Center for Research in Security Prices, at the University of Chicago Booth School of Business.

Table 9-1 summarizes the results for the four liquidity quartiles. The table illustrates the historical magnitude of the liquidity premium over the 40-year period from 1972–2011. Note that there is a substantial difference in the returns of the least-liquid quartile versus the most-liquid quartile, as well as a continual progression of higher returns as we move to less-liquid quartiles. The less-liquid stocks are not necessarily more risky. Measured by the standard deviation, risk seems to increase with liquidity.

Table 9-1: Liquidity Quartiles of the NYSE/AMEX/NASDAQ: Annualized Returns (%)

Quartile	Geometric Mean	Arithmetic Mean	Standard Deviation
1-Less Liquid	14.93%	16.75%	20.00%
2	14.15	16.21	21.27
3	11.88	14.33	22.98
4-More Liquid	7.84	11.48	27.74

Data from 1972–2011. Source: Roger G. Ibbotson and Zhiwu Chen, Zebra Capital Management, LLC. All rights reserved. www.zebracapm.com

Graph 9-1 shows the same four quartiles of liquidity, but here presented as indices of cumulative wealth. The quartiles consist of equally weighted portfolios with all dividends reinvested. The least-liquid quartile of stocks is at the top of the graph, and $1 invested at the end of 1971 grows to $261.08 by the end of 2011. One dollar invested in the second-least-liquid quartile grows to $198.85 over the period. One dollar invested in the third-least-liquid quartile (the second-most-liquid quartile) grows to $88.99 over the

Graph 9-1: Wealth Indices of Investments in Low to High Quartiles of Liquidity in NYSE/AMEX/NASDAQ Stocks Cumulative Total Returns: Index (Year-End 1971 = $1.00)

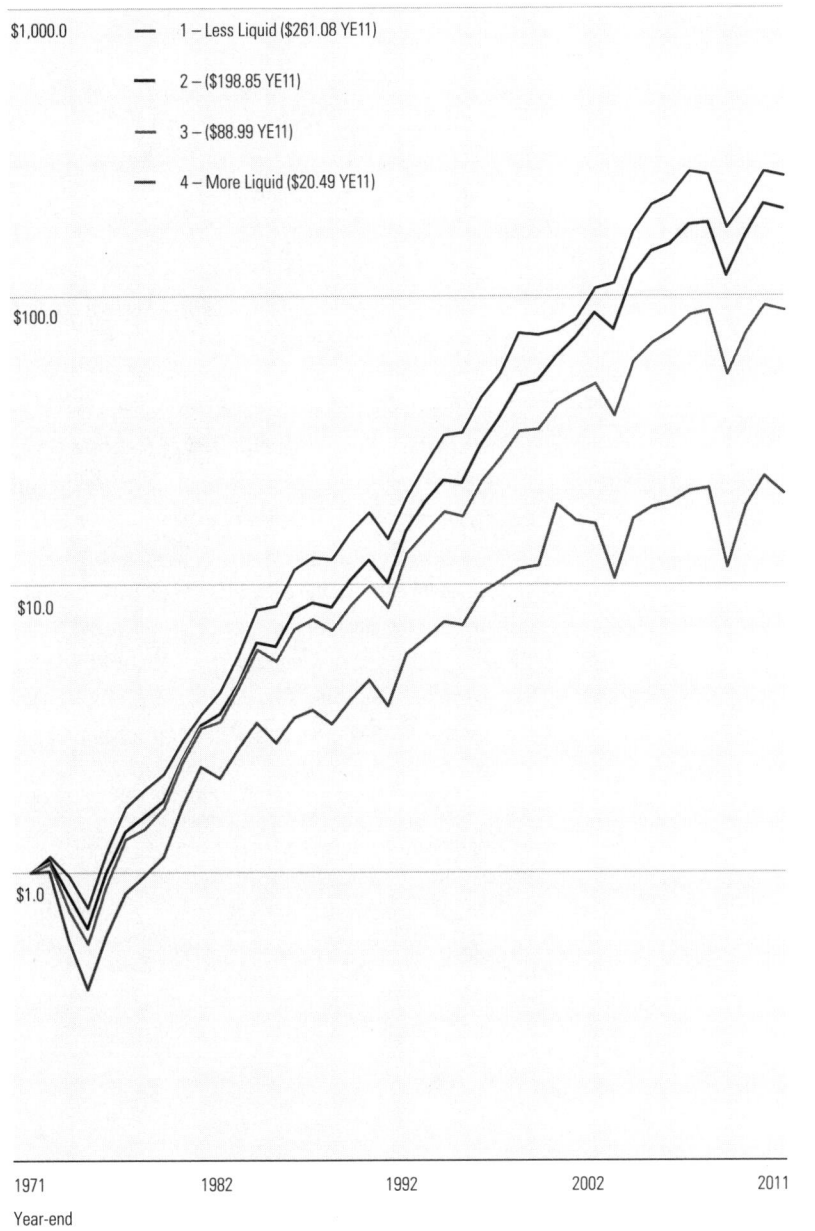

$1,000.0 ——— 1 – Less Liquid ($261.08 YE11)

——— 2 – ($198.85 YE11)

——— 3 – ($88.99 YE11)

——— 4 – More Liquid ($20.49 YE11)

$100.0

$10.0

$1.0

1971   1982   1992   2002   2011

Year-end

Data from 1972–2011.

stocks. In this way, liquidity can be thought of as another risk factor, with a risk premium. There are some years in which each style outperforms, as well as some years of underperformance. But each style has a long-run positive payoff for investing in it.

Returns on stocks typically are greater than the returns on riskless (or default free) bonds. This extra expected return is called the equity risk premium. The styles of investing can also add or detract from the investor's return. In fact, styles explain about half of the cross-sectional variation in equity mutual funds, with stock selection, market timing, and fees explaining the other half. Styles seem to explain more of the variation in mutual fund portfolio returns than do industry sectors.[3]

The premiums in the equity market are as follows:

Equity Risk Premium: The excess return of stocks relative to risk-free (default-free) government bonds. This premium can be measured over various bond horizons, and the bonds may themselves contain a horizon premium.

Size Premium: The excess return on small stocks versus the return on larger stocks.

Value Premium: The excess return on value stocks versus growth stocks.

Liquidity Premium: The excess return on less-liquid stocks versus more-liquid stocks.

Liquidity Versus Size
It is natural to think that liquidity and size would be related. The total number of shares of a company that are traded in a given period (say a year) are the number of shares outstanding times the turnover rate. Turnover is a measure of liquidity, adjusted for the number of shares outstanding.

period. One dollar invested at year-end 1971 into the most-liquid quartile only grows to $20.49 over the period. These large differences in terminal wealth reflect investments at different share turnover rates, but include most types of companies in each liquidity quartile.

Liquidity as an Investment Style
Similar to small versus large or value versus growth, liquidity versus illiquidity can be viewed as an investment style. Returns are on average higher for small, value, or illiquid

Table 9-2 breaks the universe of stocks into four turnover quartiles and four size-capitalization quartiles, each independently sorted. The numbers in the table are the compound annual (geometric mean) rate of returns for each category. Note that small stocks tend to outperform large stocks in general, but not for the most-liquid stocks. In fact, for the most-liquid stocks shown in column four, the pattern is reversed. The poorest performing category is the highly liquid stocks that are the smallest in size, i.e. that upper-right quartile with a return of only 2.57 percent per year.

The best-performing category is column 2, which represents less-liquid stocks. The worst-performing category is column 4, the most-liquid stocks. There is a clear pattern of decreasing returns as the liquidity of the stocks increase. The best-performing category is the small, less-liquid stocks, with a 17.24 percent return.

As shown in the low minus high liquidity column, the impact of liquidity is strongest for the smallest companies and weakest for the largest companies. However, the impact of liquidity is strong and consistent across all categories. Liquidity appears to be a much better predictor of returns than does size. Note the mixed results for size shown in the bottom small minus large row.

Table 9-2: Size and Liquidity Quartiles of the NYSE/AMEX/NASDAQ: Stocks Independently Sorted Each Year
Compound Annual Returns (%)

| Size | Liquidity | | | | Low Minus |
	1-Low	2	3	4-High	High Liquidity
1-Small	16.22%	17.24%	10.71%	2.57%	13.65%
2	15.86	14.26	12.25	6.44	9.42
3	14.05	13.19	12.40	8.43	5.62
4-Large	11.61	11.33	11.06	9.09	2.52
Small Minus Large	4.60	5.91	-0.35	-6.52	

Data from 1972–2011.

Liquidity Versus Value/Growth

As noted from Chapter 8, value tends to outperform growth over time. In this chapter, less-liquid stocks are shown to outperform more-liquid stocks. In this section, we examine how liquidity and value/growth interact.

The stocks are ranked by turnover rates and separated into quartiles. Similarly, the stocks are ranked by the earnings to price ratios and separated into quartiles. The high earnings to price companies are considered value companies, while the low earnings to price companies are growth

companies. The inverse, of course is, the PE ratio, with the growth companies having high PE ratios, and the value companies having low PE ratios.

The earnings used are the trailing reported earnings. The earnings data is from Compustat, owned by Standard & Poors. The portfolios are rebalanced once per year with the earnings lagged by two months to reflect delays in compiling the accounting earnings. Note that in Chapter 8, the value and growth measures use market to book instead of the E/P measures we use in this chapter. The two types of measures are roughly comparable.

Table 9-3 presents the quartile results for the different levels of liquidity and value/growth. Note that both liquidity and value/growth have a strong impact on stock market returns across all categories. The results appear to be additive. There is an excess return for investing in either low-liquidity or value stocks, and the best return of all was earned by investing in the upper-left category: high-value low-liquidity stocks, which have a realized return of 19.19 percent. The worst category is the lower right corner, high-liquidity growth stocks, which have a return of 3.18 percent.

Table 9-3: Value vs. Growth and Liquidity Quartiles of the NYSE/AMEX/NASDAQ: Stocks, Independently Sorted Each Year
Compound Annual Returns (%)

| Value/Growth | Liquidity | | | | Low Minus |
	1-Low	2	3	4-High	High Liquidity
1-Value	19.19%	17.16%	15.56%	10.63%	8.56%
2	14.95	14.30	12.34	11.01	3.94
3	12.65	12.36	10.96	7.76	4.89
4-Growth	10.54	11.80	8.20	3.18	7.36
Value Minus Growth	8.66	5.36	7.36	7.45	

Data from 1972–2011.

International Liquidity Premiums

Liquidity seems to impact realized and expected returns across all types of securities and across all locations. Liquidity is valuable in any security, and the market seems to be willing to pay a high price for it. This high price for liquidity usually corresponds with a lower return, in most markets.

We separate the returns from 1996–2010 into quartiles for the U.S., U.K., European Monetary Union (E.M.U.), and Japan. The international returns data and the trading volume data are from International Data Corporation, and the earnings data is from Worldscope.

In Table 9-4, the returns for each market are shown for the first and fourth quartiles, showing the most-liquid and least-liquid stocks, ranked by turnover. The universe is the largest- capitalization stocks in each market, with 3,500 stocks in the U.S., 500 stocks in the U.K., 1,000 stocks in Japan and 1,000 stocks in E.M.U. In each market, there is a substantially higher return for the less-liquid stocks compared with the most-liquid stocks. Note that because of a lag in the availability of international data, this table shows data through 2010.

Table 9-4: Liquidity Quartiles Based Upon Turnover
Compound Annual Returns (%)

Country/ Number of Stocks	Liquidity		Benchmark	Return
	Low	High		
U.S. (3,500)	12.43%	6.06%	S&P 500	6.76%
U.K. (500)	8.70	5.01	MSCI U.K.	6.52
E.M.U. (1,000)	13.26	6.33	MSCI E.M.U.	7.91
Japan (1,000)	1.62	-1.22	MSCI JP.	-0.79

Data from 1996–2010. Source: Roger G. Ibbotson and Zhiwu Chen, Zebra Capital Management, LLC. All rights reserved. www.zebracapm.com

Conclusion

The results confirm that liquidity impacts returns across styles and locations. Investing in less liquid securities generates higher returns. Liquidity seems to be an investment style that is different from size or value. This result seems to hold up in almost any equity market subset and in any location. ▮▮

Endnotes

[1] Roger G. Ibbotson is Chairman and CIO of Zebra Capital Management, Professor in Practice at Yale School of Management, and founder and former Chairman of Ibbotson Associates, Inc. which was acquired by Morningstar Inc. Zhiwu Chen is Professor at Yale School of Management. Michael Holmgren, of Holmgren Capital Management, helped develop the empirical results.

[2] Ibbotson, Roger, Siegel, Laurence B., and Diermeier, Jeffrey "The Demand for Capital Market Returns," *Financial Analysts Journal*, January/ February 1984.

[3] Xiong, James X., Roger G. Ibbotson, Thomas M. Idzorek, and Peng Chen., "The Equal Importance of Asset Allocation and Active Management," *Financial Analysts Journal,* March/April, 2010.

Chapter 10
Alternative Investments

Ten years ago, the investing world could be easily compartmentalized into stocks, bonds, and cash. Since then, however, hedge funds have transformed the investment landscape with sophisticated trading strategies that simply do not fit into the traditional Morningstar Style Box™. Morningstar launched its hedge fund database in 2005, creating categories based upon the underlying asset classes and trading strategies, rather than traditional style box metrics. The hedge fund database now actively tracks more than 5,000 single manager funds in 21 categories, and more than 2,500 hedge fund of funds in 6 categories. Over time, many of these hedge fund strategies found their way into registered mutual funds and exchange-traded funds, prompting Morningstar to expand its research efforts. Morningstar now has 15 different alternative mutual fund and ETF categories, up from one in 2006, tracking several hundred funds and billions in assets.

The defining characteristic of an alternative investment is that it generates a risk/return profile different from traditional stocks and bonds. This can be accomplished in three ways: one, by investing in nontraditional asset classes, such as commodities or currencies; two, by using a nontraditional investment strategy such as shorting or hedging; or three, by investing in illiquid instruments such as private equity or private debt. It's important to note that what is considered an alternative investment today may not be tomorrow. Once an investment becomes mainstream (emerging market stocks or listed REITs, for example), it is no longer alternative. Furthermore, the definition of "alternative" no longer hinges upon the structure of an investment. A mutual fund or exchange-traded fund can be alternative, while a hedge fund can be traditional.

The Birth of "Liquid" Alternatives
Although liquid alternative investment vehicles, namely mutual funds and exchange traded funds, have been around since the late 1980's, the largest wave developed in response to the 2008 financial crisis. [See Graph 10-1]. Many of the products were launched by firms previously running alternative strategies in vehicles such as hedge funds or separately managed accounts. These new liquid

Graph 10-1: Alternative Mutual Fund and ETF Launches by Year

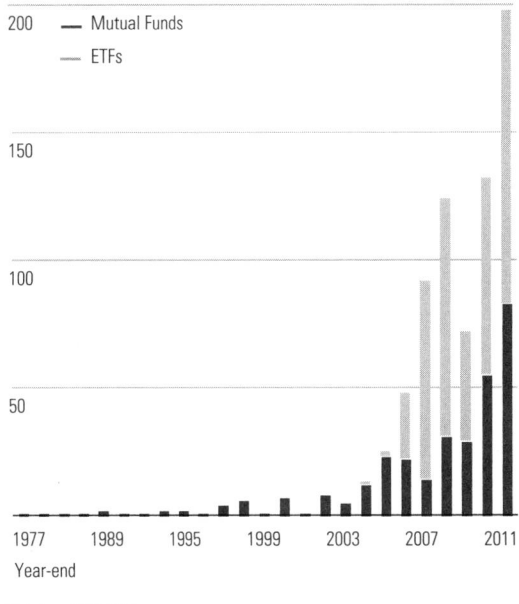

Data from 1977–2011.

Graph 10-2: Growth of Assets in Alternative Mutual Fund and ETFs

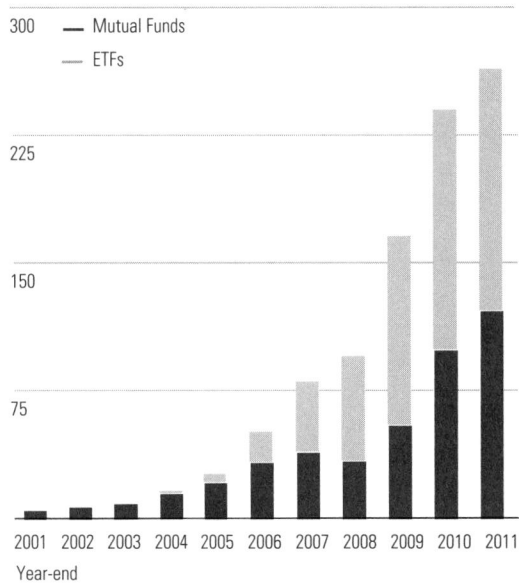

Data from 2001–2011.

alternative products served the dual purpose of meeting individual investors' demand for diversification beyond traditional investing, which failed miserably during the crisis, and hedge funds' need for a wider and more stable investor base. As of the end of December, 2011, total assets in alternative mutual funds topped $122 billion, while total assets in alternative ETFs exceeded $142 billion

Graph 10-3: Morningstar Alternative Investment Classification Scheme

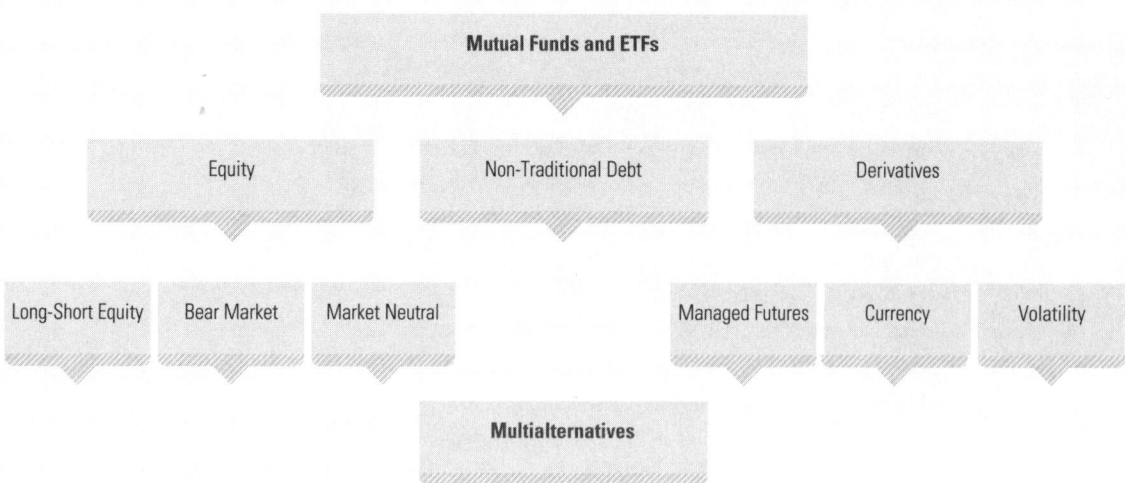

[See Graph 10-2]. Even though assets in liquid alternatives have grown exponentially, they still represent less than 1% of the total assets invested in traditional stock and bond mutual funds. Financial advisors, the primary consumer of alternative mutual funds and ETFs, cite lack of understanding as a major hurdle to this investment, per the 2010 Morningstar Barron's Alternative Investment Survey.

Alternative Investments, Deconstructed

Morningstar classifies alternative investments similarly across investment vehicle. Both the underlying holdings and the trading strategy determine which category an alternative investment falls under. There are more alternative categories for hedge funds than there are mutual funds and ETFs, because not every alternative investment strategy has made its way into liquid investment vehicles. Graph 10-3 breaks down the eight major mutual fund and ETF categories: Equities for Long-short, Bear Market, and Market Neutral; Non-Traditional Debt; and Derivatives for Managed Futures, Currency, and Volatility; and Multialternative. The seven "trading" categories are not depicted in Graph 10-3. These categories include Trading—Leveraged Equity, Commodity, or Debt; Trading—Inverse Equity, Commodity, or Debt; and Trading—Miscellaneous. Funds in the trading categories are designed for short-term tactical trading, rather than long-term strategic investment.

Long-short equity funds take on muted stock market exposure relative to long-only stock funds, as measured by

beta to the major stock indexes (generally 0.3 to 0.8). Bear market funds take a short bet on the direction of the stock market, as measured by a beta of less than -0.3. Market neutral funds, which include equity market neutral and arbitrage strategies, are relatively immune to the movements of the broad stock market, as measure by a beta between -0.3 and 0.3.

Nontraditional debt, Morningstar's newest alternative category, was designed to capture funds which fall outside of the fixed-income Morningstar Style Box™. That is, in addition to buying bonds, they short or hedge interest rate (duration) and/or credit risk, either by shorting bonds or using derivative debt instruments.

Alternative strategies using primarily derivatives include managed futures, currency, and volatility. Managed futures strategies take long and short bets on futures contracts in various asset classes, attempting to profit from momentum. Currency strategies primarily short the U.S. dollar, although there are some long-U.S. dollar and non-U.S. dollar strategies as well. Volatility strategies, which are available primarily in ETFs, bet on volatility through VIX (the CBOE Volatility Index) futures contracts.

Finally, multialternative funds combine more than one of the above strategies and asset classes into one alternative solution. They can be internally managed or use a multiple-manager (fund or separate account) structure.

Table 10-1: Morningstar MSCI Hedge Fund Index Annual Returns

	2002	2003	2004	2005	2006	2007	2008	2009	2010	2011
Asia Pacific	5.83	21.56	7.39	15.04	10.83	15.01	-27.12	24.99	8.36	-10.26
Composite AW	2.10	13.61	7.24	7.67	11.74	10.40	-13.17	14.68	10.38	-2.72
Emerging Markets	7.42	26.61	12.35	13.75	16.91	18.59	-33.37	37.52	13.99	-11.75
Europe	-0.10	7.01	6.54	11.41	13.54	4.05	-11.55	14.00	10.99	-5.91
Multi-Process Group	0.79	18.12	10.12	7.98	12.02	9.71	-19.56	26.88	11.11	-5.36
North America	-0.46	17.60	7.92	6.13	11.07	7.99	-18.74	25.42	12.16	-3.13
Specialist Credit	5.17	24.60	13.18	7.62	12.82	7.30	-22.17	20.43	12.70	-0.17
Systematic Trading	14.35	10.78	1.51	3.88	7.17	7.68	19.31	0.43	11.26	-4.77
Relative Value N Am	7.18	6.06	3.37	2.00	10.00	4.19	-15.06	20.47	9.11	2.94
Currencies	2.92	14.22	-1.31	3.91	4.72	3.35	2.69	3.12	6.92	-6.78
Short Bias All Size	24.06	-17.28	-3.93	6.65	-5.25	4.26	21.46	-9.26	-4.32	16.95
MSCI World NR USD	-19.89	33.11	14.72	9.49	20.07	9.04	-40.71	29.99	11.76	-5.54
BarCap Global Aggregate TR USD	16.52	12.51	9.27	-4.49	6.64	9.48	4.79	6.93	5.54	5.64

Data from 2002-2011.

Table 10-2: Annual Returns of Morningstar Mutual Fund Category Averages

	2002	2003	2004	2005	2006	2007	2008	2009	2010	2011
Bear Market	28.87	-30.33	-14.16	-4.41	-8.88	-6.03	29.95	-33.88	-24.28	-10.85
Currency	17.89	19.43	8.59	-4.10	4.47	5.50	-2.38	-1.73	-0.02	-3.33
Market Neutral	8.82	0.37	2.72	2.88	4.78	2.03	-0.33	-1.18	-2.00	-0.30
Long/Short Equity	2.05	8.46	5.06	4.77	7.23	4.42	-15.40	10.46	4.13	-2.81
Managed Futures[1]	N/A	N/A	N/A	N/A	N/A	N/A	8.33	-5.80	3.77	-6.92
HF Systematic Futures	19.80	18.51	6.90	5.11	8.66	14.16	18.10	1.65	11.55	-6.18
Multialternative	-22.74	16.59	7.38	1.63	8.73	3.49	-22.14	14.20	5.51	-2.79
Nontraditional Bond	4.83	15.36	5.92	4.36	6.08	1.97	-16.76	19.00	5.44	-1.29
S&P 500 TR	-22.10	28.68	10.88	4.91	15.79	5.49	-37.00	26.46	15.06	2.11
BarCap US Agg Bond TR USD	10.26	4.10	4.34	2.43	4.33	6.97	5.24	5.93	6.54	7.84

Data from 2002–2011. [1]Managed Futures data is from April 2007 to December 2011.

Historical Returns and Risk Exposures of Alternative Strategies

Morningstar tracks alternative investments in mutual funds, ETFs, separately managed accounts, and hedge funds. In the mutual fund, ETF, and separate account databases, category averages can give investors a feel for historical risk and return characteristics. In the hedge fund database, the Morningstar MSCI Hedge Fund Indexes can be used as historical benchmarks. The hedge fund indexes correct for survivorship and backfill bias, while the mutual fund and ETF category averages do not. The hedge fund indexes are subject to selection bias, however, the index constituents are limited to the voluntary nature of hedge fund database reporting.

Table 10-1 below shows the calendar year returns of selected Morningstar MSCI Hedge Fund Indexes, which correspond to the Morningstar mutual fund category averages in Table 10-2. Because there are more hedge fund strategies, there is more than one hedge fund index representing long-short equity (Asia Pacific, Emerging Markets, Europe, and North America). The other Morningstar MSCI hedge fund indexes can be compared to the mutual fund category averages as follows: the Multi-process Hedge Fund Index is most similar to the multialternative mutual fund category; the Systematic Futures Hedge Fund Index is most similar to the managed futures mutual fund category; the Specialist Credit Hedge Fund Index is most similar to the nontraditional bond mutual fund category; the Short Bias All Sizes is most similar to the bear market mutual fund category; the Currencies Index is most similar to the currency mutual fund category; and finally, the Relative Value North America Hedge Fund Index is most similar to market

Table 10-3: Annualized Returns of Indexes

Morningstar MSCI Hedge Fund Indexes	Total Ret 1 Yr	Total Return Annualized		
		3 Yr	5 Yr	10 Yr
Asia Pacific	-10.26	6.72	0.37	6.02
Composite AW	-2.82	7.15	3.35	5.84
Emerging Markets	-12.64	11.05	1.59	8.20
Europe	-5.84	6.01	1.86	4.68
Multi-Process Group	-5.63	9.98	3.26	6.41
North America	-3.10	10.88	3.65	5.94
Specialist Credit	-0.13	10.67	2.51	7.38
Systematic Trading	-4.95	2.03	6.41	6.92
Relative Value N Am	2.68	10.51	3.62	4.65
Currencies	-9.87	-0.21	1.07	2.91
Short Bias All Size	15.63	0.13	4.92	2.39
MSCI World NR USD	-5.54	11.13	-2.37	3.62
BarCap Global Aggregate TR USD	5.64	6.04	6.46	7.16
Morningstar Alternative Mutual Fund Categories				
Bear Market	-10.85	-26.85	-14.35	-10.07
Currency	-3.33	1.83	1.06	5.41
Market Neutral	-0.30	0.06	0.39	2.10
Long/Short Equity	-2.81	6.27	-0.22	4.56
Managed Futures[1]	-6.92	-6.60	NA	NA
Multialternative	-2.79	5.22	-0.91	-0.65
Nontraditional Bond	-1.29	7.74	2.82	4.83
S&P 500 TR	2.11	14.11	-0.25	2.92
BarCap US Agg Bond TR USD	7.84	6.77	6.50	5.78

Data through December 2011. [1]Managed Futures data is from April 2007 to December 2011.

neutral mutual fund category. While there is no alternative mutual fund composite index, there is a Morningstar MSCI Composite (Asset Weighted) Hedge Fund Index.

Table 10-3 displays the annualized returns over the one-, three-, five- and 10-year period for hedge funds and alternative mutual funds, respectively.

On a 10-year total return basis, hedge fund have outperformed the respective strategies in mutual fund structures, with the exception of currency mutual funds, which outperformed hedge funds, and managed futures strategies, which did not exist in mutual fund form. Over the past five year, even currency mutual fund strategies underperformed their hedge fund counterparts. Looking at the last three years, currency and nontraditional bond mutual fund strategies outpaced their hedge fund counterparts, while the other alternative mutual fund categories fell behind on average. In the last year, currency and multialterna-

tive mutual funds beat their hedge fund equivalents. It is important to note that unlike hedge funds, mutual funds have limits on leverage and illiquidity, which can hinder returns. In years such as 2008, however, the combination of leverage and illiquidity can be fatal, causing many hedge funds to close. The underperformance (relative to mutual funds) in 2008, however, was not enough to drag down hedge funds' overall performance when comparing alternative mutual fund or the broad stock market indexes.

Morningstar Risk-Adjusted Returns

When comparing any investments, it is important to consider risk-adjusted returns (See Table 10-4). However, different aspects of portfolio theory suggest various interpretations of the phrase "risk-adjusted." As the term is most commonly used, to "risk adjust" the returns of two funds means to equalize their risk levels through leverage or de-leverage before comparing them. Hence, a fund's score is not sensitive to its proportion of risk-free assets

Table 10-4: Risk-Adjusted Return Statistics

Morningstar MSCI Hedge Fund Indexes	Sharpe Ratio			Morningstar Risk-Adj		
	3 Yr	5 Yr	10 Yr	Ret 3 Yr	Ret 5 Yr	Ret 10 Yr
Asia Pacific	0.73	-0.03	0.51	5.69	-2.07	3.28
Composite AW	1.38	0.36	0.80	6.76	1.64	3.61
Emerging Markets	0.97	0.09	0.66	9.56	-1.36	5.10
Europe	0.93	0.11	0.53	5.46	0.10	2.43
Multi-Process Group	1.42	0.28	0.73	9.35	1.29	4.02
North America	1.41	0.32	0.62	10.15	1.59	3.50
Specialist Credit	2.16	0.20	0.95	10.30	0.66	5.02
Systematic Trading	0.27	0.61	0.59	1.27	4.29	4.13
Relative Value N Am	3.18	0.41	0.63	10.28	1.90	2.49
Currencies	0.24	0.23	0.32	-0.64	-0.48	0.71
Short Bias All Size	0.04	0.43	0.10	-0.67	2.77	-0.36
MSCI World NR USD	0.61	-0.08	0.19	6.57	-7.81	-1.37
BarCap Global Aggregate TR USD	0.90	0.75	0.83	5.45	4.60	4.74

Morningstar Alternative Mutual Fund Categories						
Bear Market	-1.01	-0.45	-0.38	-20.01	-17.96	-15.75
Currency	0.27	0.08	0.44	-1.98	-1.44	2.33
Market Neutral	-0.05	-0.19	0.07	-1.71	-1.76	-0.61
Long/Short Equity	0.49	-0.06	0.28	-3.33	-2.08	-0.25
Managed Futures[1]	-0.68	N/A	N/A	-1.09	N/A	N/A
MultiAlternative	0.58	-0.17	-0.16	-2.82	-1.40	-2.48
Nontraditional Bond	1.52	0.26	0.53	0.86	0.40	2.12
S&P 500 TR	0.79	0.01	0.14	-6.34	-2.81	-1.65
BarCap US Agg Bond TR USD	2.30	1.38	1.01	5.74	4.00	3.65

Data through December 2011. [1]Managed Futures data is from April 2007 to December 2011.

or its amount of leverage. The Sharpe ratio is consistent with this interpretation of risk-adjusted.

Many practitioners use the Sharpe ratio, which measures excess return (above cash) divided by volatility. But, the Sharpe ratio does not always produce intuitive results. If two funds have equal positive average excess returns, the one that has experienced lower return volatility receives a higher Sharpe ratio score. However, if the average excess returns are equal and negative, the fund with higher volatility receives the higher score, because it experienced fewer losses per unit of risk. While this result is consistent with portfolio theory, many retail investors find it counterintuitive. Unless advised appropriately, they may be reluctant to accept a fund rating based on the Sharpe ratio, or similar measures, in periods when the majority of the funds have negative excess returns.

Morningstar Risk-Adjusted Return (MRAR) is similar to the Sharpe ratio, but goes a step further by penalizing downside risk. (Also, one can compare negative values of Morningstar Risk-Adjusted Returns, while negative Sharpe ratios do not make sense).

MRAR is the guaranteed return that provides the same level of utility to the investor as the specific combination of returns exhibited by the fund. The formal equation for Morningstar Risk-Adjusted Return uses the parameter gamma to describe the model investor's sensitivity to risk. Morningstar sets that value equal to two, so MRAR is calculated as follows:

$$MRAR = \left[\frac{1}{T} \sum_{t=1}^{T} (1+ER_t)^{-2} \right]^{-\frac{12}{2}} - 1$$

where:
MRAR = Morningstar Risk-Adjusted Return;
ER_t = the geometric excess return for the fund for month **t**;
T = number of months in the period (e.g., three, five, or ten years).

The section inside the brackets determines the investor's average utility from this fund's monthly excess returns over 36, 60 or 120 months. Then, that level of utility is converted into a return by taking it to the power of −1/2. Lastly, Morningstar annualizes the result by taking it to the power of 12.

When considering only the Sharpe ratio, traditional bonds (as represented by the BarCap Global Aggregate) have outperformed all but one (relative value, or market neutral) hedge fund strategies by a wide margin over the last three- and five-year period. When considering downside risk (the Morningstar Risk-Adjusted Return), however, long-short emerging market equity, long-short U.S. equity, and relative value (market neutral) have outperformed over the last three years, and managed futures (systematic trading) has outperformed over the last five years. Over the past 10 years, long-short debt strategies (specialist credit) have outperformed long-only global bond strategies.

Table 10-5: Morningstar Alternative Mutual Fund Category Average Correlation Matrix

Investment Name	1	2	3	4	5	6	7	8
1. BarCap US Agg Bond TR USD								
2. S&P 500 TR	0.12							
3. Bear Market	-0.15	-0.98						
4. Currency	0.03	0.50	-0.48					
5. Long/Short Equity	0.11	0.95	-0.93	0.59				
6. Market Neutral	0.06	0.09	-0.10	0.26	0.29			
7. Managed Futures[1]	-0.33	-0.22	0.20	0.07	-0.16	0.06		
8. Multialternative	0.21	0.94	-0.92	0.48	0.95	0.14	-0.17	
9. Nontraditional Bond	0.18	0.73	-0.70	0.29	0.78	0.11	-0.31	0.83

Data from January 2002–December 2011. [1]Managed Futures data is from April 2007 to December 2011.

Table 10-6: Morningstar MSCI Hedge Fund Index Correlation Matrix

Investment Name	1	2	3	4	5	6	7	8	9	10	11	12
1. Asia Pacific												
2. Composite AW	0.84											
3. Emerging Markets	0.91	0.87										
4. Europe	0.77	0.88	0.81									
5. Multi-Process Group	0.87	0.93	0.92	0.88								
6. North America	0.82	0.90	0.88	0.86	0.96							
7. Specialist Credit	0.70	0.81	0.81	0.73	0.86	0.84						
8. Systematic Trading	0.16	0.40	0.13	0.16	0.15	0.12	0.01					
9. Relative Value N Am	0.65	0.72	0.70	0.64	0.77	0.78	0.79	-0.03				
10. Currencies	0.26	0.41	0.24	0.21	0.27	0.24	0.21	0.69	0.11			
11. Short Bias All Size	-0.49	-0.53	-0.47	-0.52	-0.59	-0.63	-0.51	0.01	-0.39	-0.14		
12. MSCI World NR USD	0.76	0.75	0.80	0.75	0.83	0.88	0.67	0.02	0.58	0.20	-0.64	
13. BarCap Global Aggregate TR USD	0.28	0.28	0.31	0.09	0.23	0.21	0.16	0.34	0.24	0.36	0.02	0.30

Data from January 2002–December 2011.

Alternative mutual funds have not kept up with hedge funds in terms of risk-adjusted returns. Many alternative mutual fund strategies generated losses on average over the past three, five, and ten years, resulting in negative risk-adjusted returns. Although the Morningstar risk-adjusted return of the stock market (as represented by the S&P 500) was more negative than many of the mutual fund categories over the past five and ten years, the story is not very compelling. As most of the alternative mutual fund offerings have launched in the last three years however, the historical category averages may not represent the future for these funds. The exception is bear market funds. These funds, which are mostly passively-managed inverse and leveraged-inverse index funds, do not provide good long term investment options, similar to other "tail risk" hedging products.

Besides looking at total and risk-adjusted returns, investors should consider the merits of an alternative investment based upon its correlation (see Table 10-5 and Table 10-6) and beta. According to modern portfolio theory, adding an asset with low correlation and a positive (even a small, positive) risk-adjusted return will improve the overall risk-adjusted return of the overall portfolio. When selecting alternative strategies, investors should choose investments with lower correlations to their existing portfolio, as well as to other alternative investments. Long-short equity, multi-alternative, and non-traditional bond mutual funds on average tend to have higher correlations to equities than other alternative categories, but within those categories, investors can find lower-correlating strategies. The only strategies that appear to exhibit negative correlation to stocks and bonds are managed futures (systematic trading) and bear market (short bias) strategies.

Table 10-7: Beta of Morningstar MSCI Hedge Fund Indexes to Various Market Indexes

	MSCI World NR Stock Index	Barcap Global Aggregate Bond Index	Morningstar Long-only Commodity Index	Nominal Broad US Dollar Index
Asia Pacific	0.38	0.37	0.25	(0.92)
Composite AW	0.22	0.22	0.17	(0.51)
Emerging Markets	0.47	0.48	0.33	(1.18)
Europe	0.24	0.08	0.13	(0.42)
Multi-Process Group	0.30	0.23	0.19	(0.66)
North America	0.34	0.22	0.21	(0.71)
Specialist Credit	0.23	0.15	0.16	(0.49)
Systematic Trading	0.01	0.48	0.16	(0.36)
Relative Value N Am	0.15	0.17	0.12	(0.36)
Currencies	0.06	0.30	0.04	(0.29)
Short Bias All Size	(0.35)	0.04	(0.09)	0.46

Data from January 2002-December 2011.

Table 10-8: Beta of Morningstar Alternative Mutual Fund Category Averages to Various Market Indexes

	S&P 500 Index	Barcap US Aggregate Bond Index	Morningstar Long-only Commodity Index	Nominal US Broad Dollar Index
Bear Market	(1.19)	0.04	(0.34)	1.92
Currency	0.06	0.29	0.08	(0.48)
Market Neutral	(0.04)	0.14	0.03	(0.08)
Long/Short Equity	0.30	0.09	0.18	(0.71)
Managed Futures[1]	(0.12)	(0.89)	0.02	0.15
Multialternative	0.53	(0.15)	0.16	(0.82)
Nontraditional Bond	0.19	0.44	0.09	(0.42)

Data from January 2002-December 2011. [1]Managed Futures data is from April 2007 to December 2011.

Even though some alternative strategies, for example long-short equity strategies, exhibit high correlations to the overall stock market, their betas are relatively low (typically less than 0.4 on average for both hedge funds and mutual funds). This generally means that they will underperform during equity rallies and outperform in downturns. Investors should also consider correlations and betas to non-stock and non-bond indexes—exposures to commodities or non-U.S. dollar currencies, for example. [See Table 10-7 and Table 10-8].

Incorporating Alternative Investments in a Portfolio

Alternative investments should not be judged on a stand-alone basis. They should be judged as tools to diversify a portfolio. Incorporating them into a portfolio, however, can be difficult. Investors can go one of three routes. They can use an optimizer, such as the ones found in Morningstar Direct or Morningstar EnCorr, which will tell them how much to allocate to which alternatives for various levels of risk. They can decide how much to allocate to an "alternatives" bucket, and divide the assets within that bucket equally among a few alternative strategies. Finally, investors can simply allocate the whole bucket to a multi-alternative mutual fund or hedge fund of funds manager that makes strategic and tactical alternative investment allocation decisions.

Graph 10-4: Efficient Frontier: Traditional Optimization

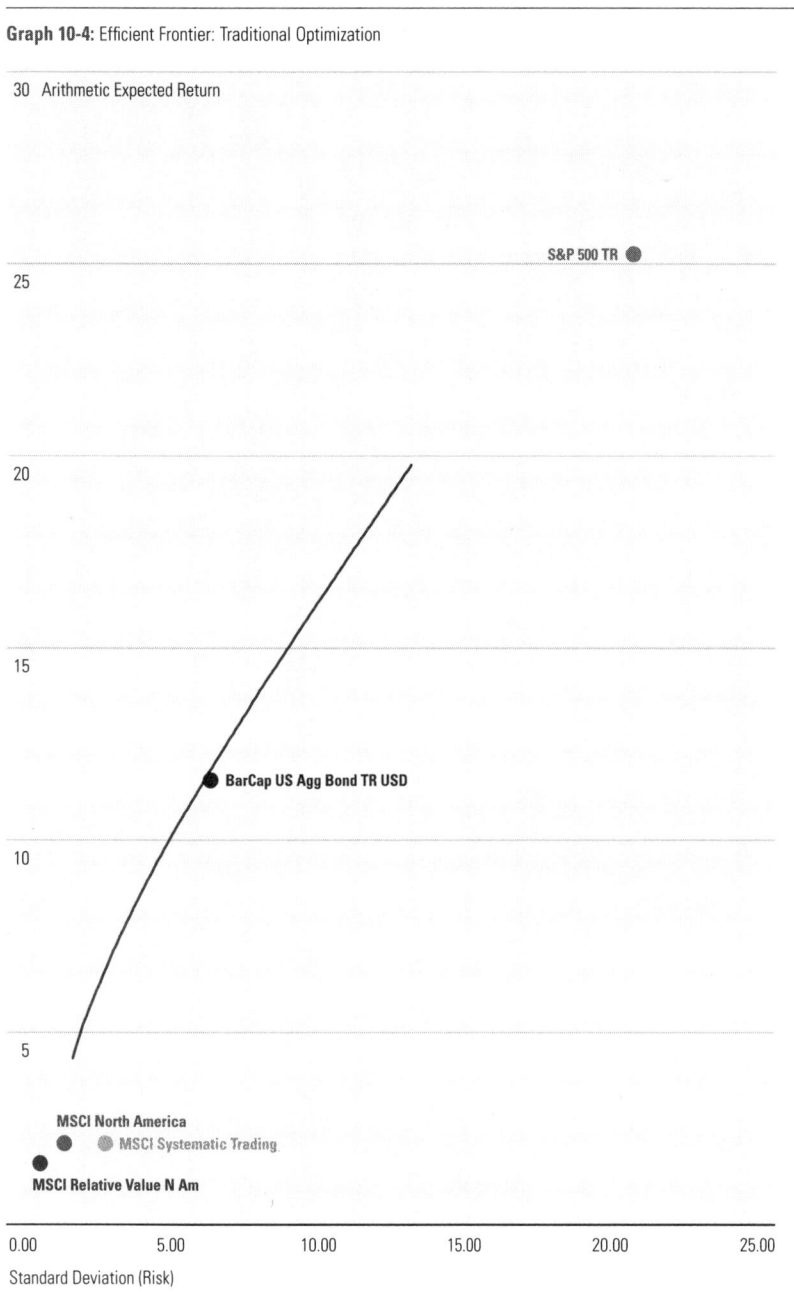

30 Arithmetic Expected Return

S&P 500 TR ●

25

20

15

● BarCap US Agg Bond TR USD

10

5

MSCI North America
●   ● MSCI Systematic Trading
MSCI Relative Value N Am

0.00   5.00   10.00   15.00   20.00   25.00

Standard Deviation (Risk)

Optimizers are no crystal ball into the future, but they can provide valuable input as to how to weight various asset classes and alternative strategies within a portfolio at different levels of desired risk. Graph 10-4 and Graph 10-5, for example show the results of a very simple resampled mean-variance optimization in Morningstar EnCorr with two traditional asset classes (the S&P 500 index to represent stocks, and the BarCap US Agg Bond to represent bonds) and three alternative investments (the Morningstar MSCI North America Hedge Fund Index to represent long-short equity, the Morningstar MSCI Relative Value North America Hedge Fund Index to represent market neutral, and the Morningstar MSCI Systematic Trading Hedge Fund Index to represent managed futures). Stocks were capped at 60%, bonds were capped at 40%, and the alternatives were constrained to a 25% allocation each. The historical standard deviations and returns were used for alternatives, while Morningstar Ibbotson's projected expected return and standard deviations were used for stocks and bonds. Historical correlations were used for all indexes.

Graph 10-4 displays the standard efficient frontier chart generated by optimizers, demonstrating the optimal portfolio at each level of risk (levels 1-100). The frontier area graph in Graph 10-5 is a better way to see the optimal portfolio, as it shows breakdown of the allocation at each risk level. The frontier area graph recommends that for low levels of desired risk, higher levels of alternatives are recommended, while at the higher level of desired risk, lower levels of alternatives are optimal. An allocation to managed futures (the Morningstar Systematic Trading Hedge Fund Index) appears to be optimal at most levels of risk, based upon the strategy's negative correlation. Investors should be careful when relying on optimizers, however, as they are only as good as their inputs (i.e. garbage in, garbage out).

Table 10-9: Effect of Equally Weighted Alternatives Allocation on a Traditional Portoflio

| | Total Return Annualized | | | Standard Deviation | | | Morningstar Risk-Adj Ret | | |
Investment Name	3 Yr	5 Yr	10 Yr	3 Yr	5 Yr	10 Yr	3 Yr	5 Yr	10 Yr
Sample Traditional Portfolio	11.74	3.03	4.55	11.32	11.50	9.53	10.22	0.32	1.65
Sample Equally Weighted 20% Alts Portfolio	10.42	3.97	5.12	8.22	8.49	6.95	9.57	1.88	2.65
Sample Equally Weighted 10% Alts Portfolio	11.09	3.52	4.85	9.75	9.98	8.22	9.94	1.14	2.18
Sample Equally Weighted 5% Alts Portfolio	11.42	3.28	4.70	10.53	10.74	8.87	10.09	0.74	1.92

Data through December 2011.

Graph 10-5: Efficient Frontier: Area Graph

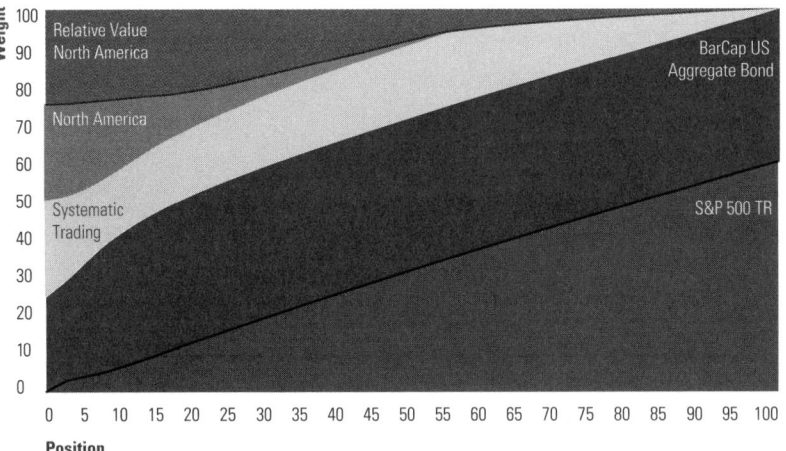

For those that choose to opt out of optimization, due to its many uncertainties, perhaps a better solution is to equally weight a few alternatives strategies in a slice of a traditional portfolio. Because most traditional portfolios are heavily skewed towards equities (historically, a 60% allocation to equities has generated 90% of the risk), allocating out of equities is a good place to start. Table 10-9 demonstrates the historical results of a 5%, 10% and 20% equally-weighted and quarterly rebalanced allocation to the three alternative strategies (long-short equity, managed futures, and market neutral) used in Graph 10-4. In all three cases, the risk-adjusted return of the portfolio improved.

Finally, investors who are confounded by the prospect of selecting and putting together an alternatives portfolio can turn to a multialternative or fund of fund manager. Many hedge funds of funds and multialternative mutual fund strategies have performed poorly, however, due to both their costs (two layers of management fees, plus two layers of performance fees in hedge funds) and their surprising high exposure to equities (the beta of the average multialternative mutual fund in Table 10-8 is slightly higher than the beta of the average long-short equity mutual fund). Nevertheless, there are usually good options in every category of funds. ▮▮

Endnotes

[1] Nadia Papagiannis, CFA — Director of Alternative Fund Research, Morningstar, Inc

Chapter 11
Using Historical Data in Forecasting and Optimization

Probabilistic Forecasts

When forecasting the return on an asset or a portfolio, investors are (or should be) interested in the entire probability distribution of future outcomes, not just the mean or "point estimate." An example of a point estimate forecast is that large company stocks will have a return of 13 percent in 2012. It is more helpful to know the uncertainty surrounding this point estimate than to know the point estimate itself. One measure of uncertainty is standard deviation. The large company stock return forecast can be expressed as 13 percent representing the mean and 20 percent representing the standard deviation.

If the returns on large company stocks are normally distributed, the mean (expected return) and the standard deviation provide enough information to forecast the likelihood of any return. Suppose one wants to ascertain the likelihood that large company stocks will have a return of -25 percent or lower in 2012. Given the above example, a return of -25 percent is $[13 - (-25)]/20 = 1.9$ standard deviations below the mean. The likelihood of an observation 1.9 or more standard deviations below the mean is 2.9 percent (This can be looked up in any statistics textbook, in the table showing values of the cumulative probability function for a normal distribution). Thus, the likelihood that the stock market will fall by 25 percent or more in 2012 is 2.9 percent. This is valuable information, both to the investor who believes that stocks are a sure thing and to the investor who is certain that they will crash tomorrow.

In fact, the historical returns of large company stocks are not exactly normally distributed, and a slightly different method needs to be used to make probabilistic forecasts. The actual model used to forecast the distribution of stock returns is described later in this chapter.

Some people are wary of probabilistic forecasts because they seem too wide to be useful—the most widely quoted forecasters, after all, make very specific predictions. However, the forecast of a probability distribution actually reveals much more than the point estimate. The point estimate reflects what statisticians call an "expected value", but the actual return will likely be higher or lower than the point estimate. By knowing the extent to which actual returns are likely to deviate from the point estimate, the investor can assess the risk of every asset, and thus compare investment opportunities in terms of their risks as well as their expected returns. As Harry Markowitz showed nearly a half-century ago in his Nobel Prize-winning work on portfolio theory, investors care about avoiding risk as well as seeking return. Probabilistic forecasts enable investors to quantify these concepts.

The Lognormal Distribution

In the lognormal model, the natural logarithms of asset return relatives are assumed to be normally distributed. A return relative is one plus the return. That is, if an asset has a return of 15 percent in a given period, its return relative is 1.15.

The lognormal distribution is skewed to the right. This means that the expected value, or mean, is greater than the median. Furthermore, if return relatives are lognormally distributed, returns cannot fall below negative 100 percent. These properties of the lognormal distribution make it a more accurate characterization of the behavior of market returns than does the normal distribution.

In all normal distributions, moreover, the probability of an observation falling one standard deviation below the mean equals the probability of falling one standard deviation above the mean; both probabilities are about 34 percent. In a lognormal distribution, these probabilities differ and depend on the parameters of the distribution.

Forecasting Wealth Values and Rates of Return

Using the lognormal model, it is fairly simple to form probabilistic forecasts of both compound rates of return and ending period wealth values. Wealth at time **n** (assuming reinvestment of all income and no taxes) is:

$$W_n = W_0(1+r_1)(1+r_2)...(1+r_n) \tag{30}$$

where,

W_n = the wealth value at time **n**;

W_0 = the initial investment at time **0**; and,

r_1, r_2, etc. = the total returns on the portfolio for the rebalancing period ending at times 1, 2, and so forth.

The compound rate of return or geometric mean return over the same period, r_G, is:

$$r_G = \left(\frac{W_n}{W_0}\right)^{\frac{1}{n}} - 1 \qquad (31)$$

where,

r_G = the geometric mean return;
W_n = the ending period wealth value at time **n**;
W_0 = the initial wealth value at time **0**; and,
n = the inclusive number of periods.

By assuming that all of the $(1+r_n)$'s are lognormally distributed with the same expected value and standard deviation and are all statistically independent of each other, it follows that W_n and $(1+r_G)$ are lognormally distributed. In fact, even if the $(1+r_n)$'s are not themselves lognormally distributed but are independent and identically distributed, W_n and $(1+r_G)$ are approximately lognormal for large enough values of **n**. This "central-limit theorem" means that the lognormal model can be useful in long-term forecasting even if short-term returns are not well described by a lognormal distribution.

Calculating Parameters of the Lognormal Model

To use the lognormal model, we must first calculate the expected value and standard deviation of the natural logarithm of the return relative of the portfolio. These parameters, denoted **m** and **s** respectively, can be calculated from the expected return (μ) and standard deviation (σ) of the portfolio as follows:

$$m = \ln(1+\mu) - \left(\frac{s^2}{2}\right) \qquad (32)$$

$$s = \sqrt{\ln\left[1+\left(\frac{\sigma}{1+\mu}\right)^2\right]} \qquad (33)$$

where,

l_n = the natural logarithm function.

To calculate a particular percentile of wealth or return for a given time horizon, the only remaining parameter needed is the z-score of the percentile. The z-score of a percentile

ranking is that percentile ranking expressed as the number of standard deviations that it is above or below the mean of a normal distribution. For example, the z-score of the 95th percentile is 1.645 because in a normal distribution, the 95th percentile is 1.645 standard deviations above the 50th percentile or median, which is also the mean. Z-scores can be obtained from a table of cumulative values of the standard normal distribution or from software that produces such values.

Given the logarithmic parameters of a portfolio (**m** and **s**), a time horizon (**n**), and the z-score of a percentile (**z**), the percentile in question in terms of cumulative wealth at the end of the time horizon (**W_n**) is:

$$e^{\left(mn + zs\sqrt{n}\right)} \qquad (34)$$

Similarly, the percentile in question in terms of the compound rate of return for the period (r_G) is:

$$e^{\left(m + z\frac{s}{\sqrt{n}}\right)} - 1 \qquad (35)$$

Mean-Variance Optimization

One important application of the probability forecasts of asset returns is mean-variance optimization. Optimization is the process of identifying portfolios that have the highest possible expected return for a given level of risk, or the lowest possible risk for a given expected return. Such a portfolio is considered "efficient," and the locus of all efficient portfolios is called the efficient frontier. An efficient frontier constructed from large company stocks, long-term government bonds, and Treasury bills is shown in Graph 11-1. All investors should hold portfolios that are efficient with respect to the assets in their opportunity set.

The most widely accepted framework for optimization is Markowitz or mean-variance optimization (MVO), which makes the following assumptions: 1) the forecast mean, or expected return, describes the attribute that investors consider to be desirable about an asset; 2) the risk of the asset is measured by its expected standard deviation of returns; and 3) the interaction between one asset and another is captured by the expected correlation coefficient of the two assets' returns. MVO thus requires forecasts of the return and standard deviation of each asset, and the correlation of each asset with every other asset.[1]

In the 1950s, Harry Markowitz developed both the concept of the efficient frontier and the mathematical means of constructing it (mean-variance optimization).[2] Currently, there are a number of commercially available mean-variance optimization software tools available, including Morningstar *EnCorr*®.[3] This advanced analytical software unites proven financial models, sophisticated Ibbotson methodologies, and comprehensive Morningstar investment data.

Graph 11-1: Efficient Frontier
Large Company Stocks, Long-Term Government Bonds, and U.S. Treasury Bills

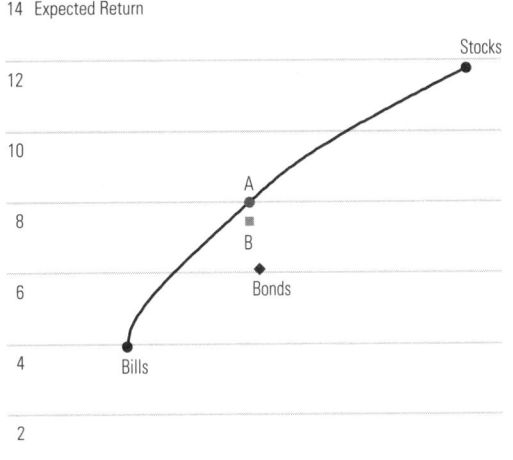

Standard Deviation (Risk)

Data from 1926–2011.

Estimating the Means, Standard Deviations, and Correlations of Asset Returns

To simulate future probability distributions of asset and portfolio returns, one typically estimates parameters of the historical return data. The parameters that are required to simulate returns on an asset are its mean and standard deviation. To simulate returns on portfolios of assets, one must also estimate the correlation of each asset in the portfolio with every other asset. Thus, the parameters required to conduct a simulation are the same as those required as inputs into a mean-variance optimization.[4]

To illustrate how to estimate the parameters of asset class returns relevant to optimization and forecasting, we construct an example using large company stocks, long-term government bonds, and Treasury bills. The techniques used to estimate these parameters are described below. These are similar techniques as those used in Morningstar *EnCorr*® software.

Means, or Expected Returns

The mean return (forecast mean, or expected return) on an asset is the probability-weighted average of all possible returns on the asset over a future period. Estimates of expected returns are based on models of asset returns. While many models of asset returns incorporate estimates of GNP, the money supply, and other macroeconomic variables, the model employed in this chapter does not. This is because we assume (for the present purpose) that asset markets are informationally efficient, with all relevant and available information fully incorporated in asset prices. If this assumption holds, investor expectations (forecasts) can be discerned from market-observable data. Such forecasts are not attempts to outguess, or beat, the market. They are attempts to discern the market's expectations, i.e., to read what the market itself is forecasting.

For some assets, expected returns can be estimated using current market data alone. For example, the yield on a riskless bond is an estimate of its expected return. For other assets, current data are not sufficient. Stocks, for example, have no exact analogue to the yield on a bond. In such cases, we use the statistical time series properties of historical data in forming the estimates.

To know which data to use in estimating expected returns, we need to know the rebalancing frequency of the portfolios and the planning horizon. In our example, we will assume an annual rebalancing frequency and a twenty-year planning horizon. The rebalancing frequency gives the time units in which returns are measured.

With a twenty-year planning horizon, the relevant riskless rate is the yield on a twenty-year coupon bond. This riskless rate is the baseline from which the expected return on every other asset class is derived by adding or subtracting risk premia.

Large Company Stocks

The expected return on large company stocks is the riskless rate, plus the expected risk premium of large company stocks over bonds that are riskless over the planning horizon. With a twenty-year planning horizon, this risk premium is 6.62 percent, shown as the long-horizon expected equity risk premium in Table 11-1. Hence, the expected return on large company stocks is 2.48 (the riskless rate) plus 6.62 (the risk premium) for a total of 9.10 percent.

Bonds and Bills

For default-free bonds with a maturity equal to the planning horizon, the expected return is the yield on the bond; that is, the expected return is the riskless rate of 2.48 percent. For bonds with other maturities, the expected bond horizon premium should be added to the riskless rate (for longer maturities) or subtracted from the riskless rate (for shorter maturities). Since expected capital gains on a bond are zero, the expected horizon premium is estimated by the historical average difference of the income returns on the bonds.[5]

For Treasury bills, the expected return over a given time horizon is equal to the expected return on a Treasury bond of a similar horizon, less the expected horizon premium of bonds over bills. The long-term horizon premium is estimated by the historical average of the difference of the income return on bonds and the return on bills. From Table 11-1, this is 1.73 percent. Subtracting this from the riskless rate (2.48 percent) gives us an expected return on bills of 0.75 percent. Of course, this forecast typically differs from the current yield on a Treasury bill, since a portfolio of Treasury bills is rolled over (the proceeds of maturing bills are invested in new bills, at yields not yet known) during the time horizon described.

Standard Deviations

Standard deviations are estimated from historical data as described in Chapter 6. Since there is no evidence of a major change in the variability of returns on large company stocks, we use the entire period 1926–2011 to estimate the standard deviation of these asset classes. For bonds and bills, we use the period 1970–2011.

Correlations

Correlations between the asset classes are estimated from historical data as described in Chapter 6. Correlation coefficients for stocks, bonds, and bills are derived from 1926–2011. Correlations between major asset classes change over time. Graph 11-2 shows the historical correlation of annual returns on large company stocks and long-term bonds over 20 year rolling periods from 1926–1945 through 1992–2011.

Generating Probabilistic Forecasts

For large company stocks in Table 11-2, the logarithmic parameters are calculated to be $m = 0.0950$ and $s = 0.1801$ based on equations (32) and (33). The z-scores of the 95th, 50th, and 5th percentile are 1.645, 0, and -1.645, respectively. Using these parameters, we can calculate the 95th, 50th, and 5th percentiles of cumulative wealth and compound returns over various time horizons using equations (34) and (35). Graph 11-3 shows percentiles of compound returns over the entire range of one to twenty year horizons in graphical form. This type of graph is some-

Table 11-1: Building Blocks for Expected Return Construction

Yields (Riskless Rates)[†]	Value (%)
Long-Term (20-year) U.S. Treasury Coupon Bond Yield	2.48
Intermediate-Term (5-year) U.S. Treasury Coupon Note Yield	0.59
Short-Term (30-day) U.S. Treasury Bill Yield	0.01

Fixed Income Risk Premia[†, ‡]	
Expected default premium: *long-term corporate bond total returns minus long-term government bond total returns*	-0.19
Expected long-term horizon premium: *long-term government bond income returns minus U.S. Treasury bill total returns**	1.73
Expected intermediate-term horizon premium: *intermediate-term government bond income returns minus U.S. Treasury bill total returns**	1.10

Equity Risk Premia [†, ◊]	
Long-horizon expected equity risk premium: *large company stock total returns minus long-term government bond income returns*	6.62
Intermediate-horizon expected equity risk premium: *large company stock total returns minus intermediate-term government bond income returns*	7.15
Short-horizon expected equity risk premium: *large company stock total returns minus U.S. Treasury bill total returns**	8.15
Small Stock Premium: *small company stock total return minus large company stock total return*	4.74

[†] As of December 31, 2011. Maturities are approximate.

[‡] Expected risk premia for fixed income are based on the differences of historical arithmetic mean returns from 1970–2011.

[◊] Expected risk premia for equities are based on the differences of historical arithmetic mean returns from 1926–2011.

[*] For U.S. Treasury bills, the income return and total return are the same.

times called a "trumpet" graph because the high and low percentile curves taken together make the shape of a trumpet. The "mouthpiece" of the trumpet is on the right side of the graph because for long time horizons, all percentiles converge to the median (50th percentile).

Graph 11-2: Twenty Year Rolling Period Correlations of Annual Returns Large Company Stocks and Long-Term Government Bonds

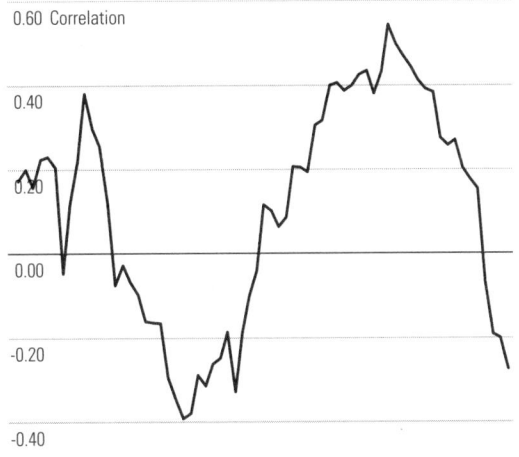

0.60 Correlation

0.40

0.20

0.00

-0.20

-0.40

| 1945 | 1956 | 1967 | 1978 | 1989 | 2000 | 2011 |

Twenty-Year Period Ending

Data from 1926–1945 through 1992–2011.

Graph 11-3: Forecast Total Return Distribution
100 Percent Large Stocks

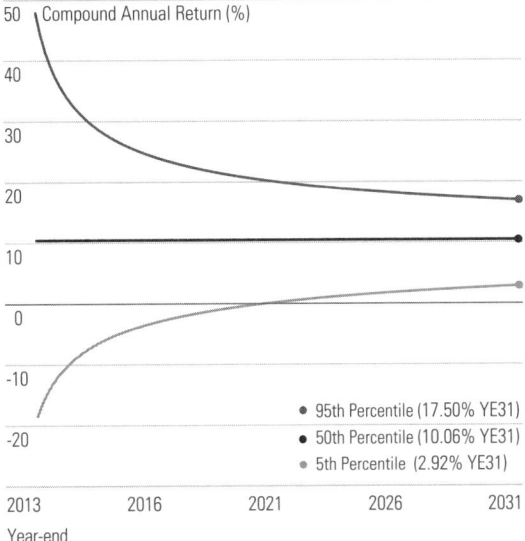

50 Compound Annual Return (%)

40

30

20

10

0

-10

-20

- 95th Percentile (17.50% YE31)
- 50th Percentile (10.06% YE31)
- 5th Percentile (2.92% YE31)

| 2013 | 2016 | 2021 | 2026 | 2031 |

Year-end

Data from 2012–2031.

Table 11-2: Optimization Inputs: Year-End 2011 Large Company Stocks, Long-Term Government Bonds, and U.S. Treasury Bills (%)

| | Expected Return | Standard Deviation | Correlation with | | |
			Stocks	Bonds	Bills
Stocks	11.8	20.3	1.00		
Bonds	6.1	9.8	0.01	1.00	
Bills	3.6	3.1	-0.01	0.18	1.00

Data from 1926-2011.

Graph 11-4 is a graph showing percentiles of cumulative wealth over the entire range of zero to twenty year time horizons, along with the back history of the portfolio's performance. The past and forecasted (future) values on the graph are connected by setting the wealth index to $1.00 at the end of 2011. The past index values show how much wealth one would have had to hold in large company stocks to have $1.00 at the end of 2011; the percentiles of future value show the probability distribution of future growth of $1.00 invested in large company stocks. This type of graph is sometimes called a "tulip" graph because of its overall shape.

Graph 11-4: Forecast Distribution of Wealth Index Value
100 Percent Large Stocks

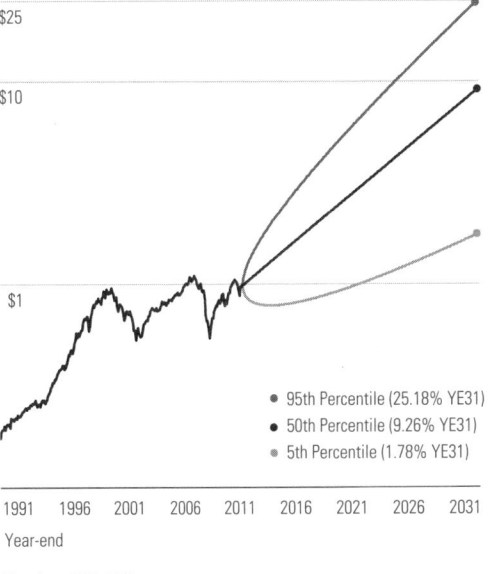

$25

$10

$1

- 95th Percentile (25.18% YE31)
- 50th Percentile (9.26% YE31)
- 5th Percentile (1.78% YE31)

| 1991 | 1996 | 2001 | 2006 | 2011 | 2016 | 2021 | 2026 | 2031 |

Year-end

Data from 1991–2031.

Table 11-3 shows (in the top panel) the probability distribution of compound annual returns on large company stocks over the next 20 years. The top line shows the 95th percentile or optimistic case, the middle line the 50th percentile or median case, and the bottom line the 5th percentile or pessimistic case. The bottom panel shows the same projections, redrawn as cumulative values of $1.00 invested at the beginning of the period simulated. Simulations such as these are used for asset allocation, funding of liabilities, and other portfolio management-related applications; Morningstar *EnCorr*® mean-variance optimization software can produce these forecasts.

Table 11-3: Forecast Distributions of Compound Annual Returns and End of Period Wealth – Large Company Stocks

| | Compound Annual Return (%) | | | | |
Percentile	2013	2016	2021	2026	2031
95th	35.60	25.55	20.77	18.71	17.50
90th	29.47	21.93	18.30	16.72	15.80
75th	19.84	16.11	14.28	13.48	13.00
Expected Value	10.87	10.33	10.15	10.09	10.06
25th	0.92	4.15	5.83	6.57	7.02
10th	-6.59	-0.82	2.23	3.61	4.44
5th	-10.82	-3.68	0.14	1.87	2.92

| | End of Period Wealth ($1 Invested on 12/31/11) | | | | |
Percentile	2013	2016	2021	2026	2031
95th	1.84	3.12	6.60	13.11	25.18
90th	1.68	2.70	5.37	10.17	18.79
75th	1.44	2.11	3.80	6.66	11.52
Expected Value	1.25	1.74	3.04	5.31	9.26
25th	1.02	1.23	1.76	2.60	3.89
10th	0.87	0.96	1.25	1.70	2.38
5th	0.80	0.83	1.01	1.32	1.78

Data from Year-end 2011.

Constructing Efficient Portfolios

A mean-variance optimizer uses the complete set of optimizer inputs (the expected return and standard deviation of each asset class and the correlation of returns for each pair of asset classes) to generate an efficient frontier. The efficient frontier shown in Graph 11-1 was generated from the inputs described above and summarized in Table 10-2. Each point on the frontier represents a portfolio mix that is mean-variance efficient. The point labeled **A** represents a portfolio that contains 38 percent in large company stocks, 51 percent in long-term bonds, and 11 percent in Treasury bills (Recall that other asset classes were not considered in this example). From the location of point **A** on the grid, we can find its expected return (8.00 percent) and standard deviation (9.28 percent).

Using Inputs to Form Other Portfolios

Given a complete set of inputs, the expected return and standard deviation of any portfolio (efficient or other) of the asset classes can be calculated. The expected return of a portfolio is the weighted average of the expected returns of the asset classes:

$$r_p = \sum_{i=1}^{n} x_i r_i \tag{36}$$

where,

r_p = the expected return of the portfolio **p**;
n = the number of asset classes;
x_i = the portfolio weight of asset class **i**, scaled such that:

$$\sum_{i=1}^{n} x_i = 1$$

and,

r_i = the expected return of asset class **i**.

The point labeled **B** in Graph 11-1 represents a portfolio that contains 45 percent large company stocks (asset class 1), three percent in long-term bonds (asset class 2), and 52 percent in Treasury bills (asset class 3). Applying the above formula to this portfolio using the inputs in Table 11-2, we calculate the expected return to be 7.36 percent as follows:

$$(0.45 \times 11.8) + (0.03 \times 6.1) + (0.52 \times 3.6) = 7.36^*$$
*difference due to rounding

The standard deviation of the portfolio depends not only on the standard deviations of the asset classes, but on all of the correlations as well. It is given by:

$$\sigma_p = \sqrt{\sum_{i=1}^{n} \sum_{i=1}^{n} x_i x_j \sigma_i \sigma_j \rho_{ij}} \tag{37}$$

where,

σ_p = the standard deviation of the portfolio;
x_i and x_j = the portfolio weights of asset classes **i** and **j**;
σ_i and σ_j = the standard deviations of returns on asset classes **i** and **j**; and,
ρ_{ij} = the correlation between returns on asset classes **i** and **j**.
(Note that ρ_{ij} equals one and that ρ_{ij} is equal to ρ_{ji}).

	Stocks (asset class 1)	Bonds (asset class 2)	Bills (asset class 3)
Stocks	$x_1^2 \sigma_1^2 \rho_{1,1} =$ $(0.45)^2(0.203)^2(1) =$ 0.008345	$x_1 x_2 \sigma_1 \sigma_2 \rho_{1,2} =$ $(0.45)(0.03)(0.203)$ $(0.098)(0.01) =$ 0.000003	$x_1 x_3 \sigma_1 \sigma_3 \rho_{1,3} =$ $(0.45)(0.52)(0.203)$ $(0.031)(-0.01) =$ -0.000015
Bonds	$x_1 x_2 \sigma_1 \sigma_2 \rho_{1,2} =$ $(0.03)(0.45)(0.098)$ $(0.203)(0.01) =$ 0.000003	$x_2^2 \sigma_2^2 \rho_{2,2} =$ $(0.03)^2(0.098)^2(1) =$ 0.000009	$x_2 x_3 \sigma_2 \sigma_3 \rho_{2,3} =$ $(0.03)(0.52)(0.098)$ $(0.031)(0.18) =$ 0.000009
Bills	$x_1 x_3 \sigma_1 \sigma_3 \rho_{1,3} =$ $(0.52)(0.45)(0.031)$ $(0.203)(-0.01) =$ -0.000015	$x_2 x_3 \sigma_2 \sigma_3 \rho_{2,3} =$ $(0.52)(0.03)(0.031)$ $(0.098)(0.18) =$ 0.000009	$x_3^2 \sigma_3^2 \rho_{3,3} =$ $(0.52)^2(0.031)^2(1) =$ 0.000260

The standard deviation for point **B** in Graph 11-1 (containing three asset classes) would be calculated as shown above.

By summing these terms and taking the square root of the total, the result is a standard deviation of 9.28 percent.

Enhancements to Mean-Variance Optimization

Ibbotson Associates was an early adopter of the use of mean-variance optimization to develop asset class model guidelines and continues to assist the industry in the development of enhancements to the traditional mean-variance approach as well as the state-of-the-art techniques described later in the chapter. Over the last-half century, the Markowitz mean-variance optimization (MVO) framework has become the textbook approach for creating these optimal asset allocations, but the approach has several shortcomings.

Shortcomings of Traditional Optimization Techniques

One notable shortcoming is that the output (optimal asset allocation weights) is very sensitive to the inputs (expected returns, standard deviations, and correlations). Input sensitivity oftentimes can lead to highly concentrated allocations in only a small number of the available asset classes. For example, if a typical optimization starts with around 10 asset classes to choose from, it wouldn't be uncommon to see just a few of these asset choices ending up in the resulting optimal allocation, with the remaining asset choices not even getting a mention. An example of this is shown in Graph 11-5, where only two of the nine asset classes originally considered made it into the final optimized mix (point **A**).

Graph 11-5 highlights the potential pitfalls of blindly following mean-variance optimization results. Mean-variance optimization is a powerful tool, but it needs to be used with caution. For instance, basing mean-variance optimization inputs on shorter time periods, as was done in Graph 11-5, can contribute to the extreme results. Basing the mean-variance optimization inputs on longer time periods, such as those presented elsewhere in this book, can help mitigate the extreme asset allocations mixes. The reason that longer time periods are preferred is that with longer time periods there is usually a more consistent ratio of return to risk amongst the different asset classes.

In addition to basing inputs on longer term histories, the most common solution to the problem of the highly concentrated asset allocations is to place maximum and minimum allocation constraints on each asset. For instance, in the example shown in Graph 11-5, we could specify a minimum allocation of 5 percent and a maximum allocation of 15 percent for each of the nine asset choices. This would ensure that each asset gets represented in the final allocation and also that no single asset completely dominates in the final allocation mix. Unfortunately, these artificial minimums and maximums are arbitrary, and usually end up limiting the ability of the optimizer to properly act on the information contained in the inputs.

Two Popular Enhancements to Traditional Optimization Techniques

Two popular enhancements to traditional optimization techniques have emerged in recent years that can help overcome these difficulties. While both of these methods can help develop well-diversified asset allocations, they approach the problem in very different ways. The first of these, the Black-Litterman model, attempts to create better inputs. The second, resampled mean-variance optimization, attempts to build a better optimizer.

The Black-Litterman model was created by Fischer Black and Robert Litterman in the late 1980s. The Black-Litterman model combines investors' views regarding expected returns and the expected returns predicted by the capital asset pricing model (CAPM) to form a single blended estimate of expected returns. When this new combined estimate is used as an input within a traditional mean-variance optimization framework, it produces well-diversified portfolios that include not only market-based asset allocations but also allocations in assets that received favorable views.

Graph 11-5: Efficient Frontier: Traditional Optimization*

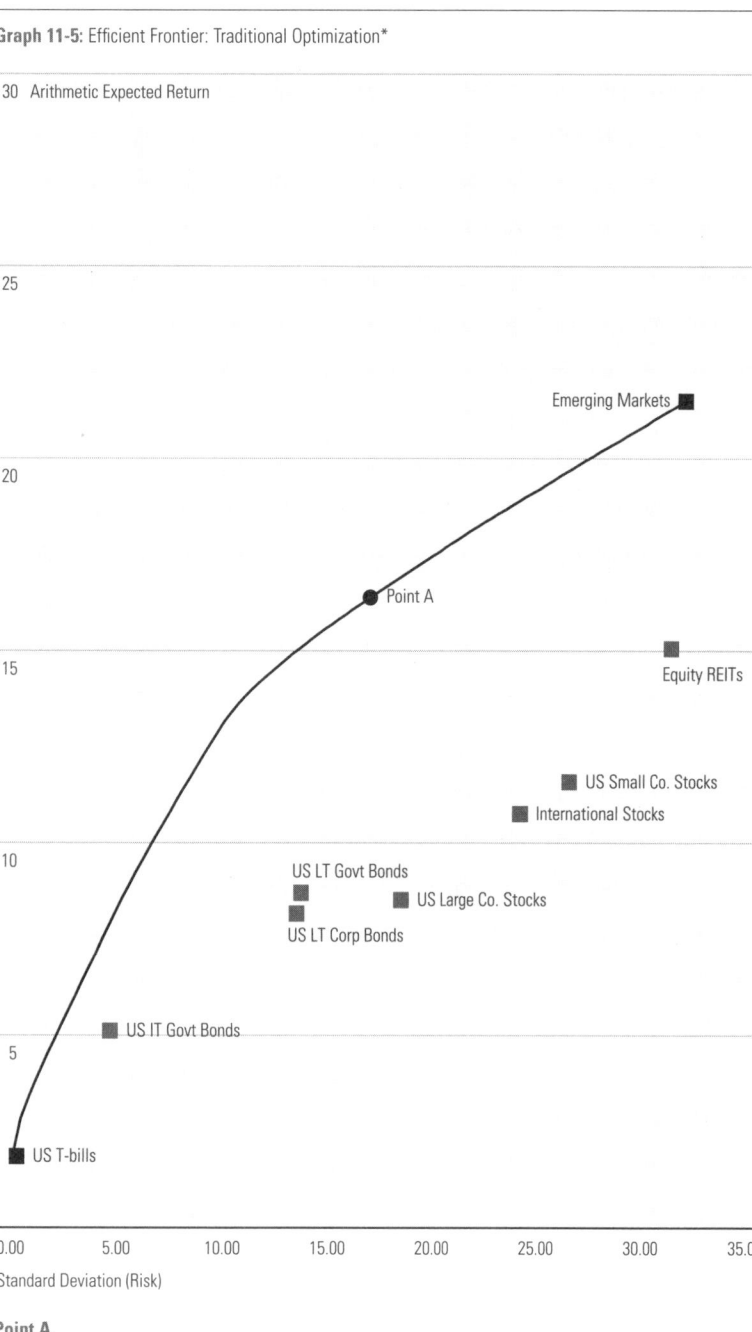

Point A.

■ Emerging Markets		60%
▨ U.S. Long-Term Gov't Bonds		40%

Data from 2002–2011

* The inputs for Graph 11-5 were estimated using 10 years of quarterly data.

** International stocks are represented by the Morgan Stanley Capital International Europe, Australasia, and Far East (EAFE®) Index; REITs are represented by the FTSE NAREIT Equity REIT Index®; emerging markets are represented by the Morgan Stanley Capital International Emerging Markets Index.

The second approach, resampled mean-variance optimization, is an attempt to build a better optimizer. Resampling grew out of the work of a number of authors, but is most closely associated with the work of Richard Michaud. While traditional mean-variance optimization treats the capital market assumptions as if they were known with 100 percent certainty, resampled mean-variance optimization recognizes that the capital market assumptions are forecasts, and are therefore not known with 100 percent certainty.

Conceptually, resampled mean-variance optimization is a combination of Monte Carlo simulation[6] and the more traditional Markowitz mean-variance optimization approach. The simulation randomly resamples possible returns from a forecasted return distribution or randomly resamples possible returns from a historical distribution. The simulated returns lead to a simulated set of capital market assumptions that are used in a traditional mean-variance optimizer, and the asset allocations are recorded. After combining the asset allocations from the numerous intermediate optimizations, the resulting asset allocations are those that, on average, are predicted to perform best over the range of potential outcomes implied by the capital market assumptions. Research has shown that asset allocations selected from a resampled efficient frontier may outperform those from a traditional efficient frontier.[7]

In addition to the problem of getting results that are highly concentrated in just a few of the assets available, there are two more criticisms of the traditional mean-variance optimization framework.

First, the traditional approach focuses on a subset of the total portfolio. Traditionally, the focus is on finding a mix of asset classes that maximizes the expected return, subject to a risk constraint. However, because the purpose of most asset portfolios is to fund a specified future cash-flow stream—a liability—the true risk for the portfolio is not the standard deviation of the assets or the performance of the assets relative to that of peers—the true risk is not being able to fund the future liability.

An asset allocation approach that takes the future liability into account is called liability-relative optimization (or surplus optimization). The usual method employed to accomplish this is to constrain the optimizer to hold an asset class representing the liability short.

Second, the traditional mean-variance optimization framework assumes that the returns of the assets in the optimization are normally distributed. As illustrated in Table 2-1, the return distributions of different asset classes do not always follow a standard, symmetrical bell-shaped curve. Some assets have distributions that are skewed to the left or right, while others have distributions that are skinnier or fatter than others. These more complicated characteristics are called skewness and kurtosis, respectively. The next wave of enhancements to the traditional mean-variance optimization are frameworks that incorporate these additional types of non-normalities into the optimization.

Markowitz 1.0

In 1952, Harry Markowitz, invented portfolio optimization. His genius was based on three principles; risk, reward and the correlation of assets in a portfolio. Over the years, technologies advanced, markets crashed, but the portfolio optimization models used by many investors did not evolve to compensate. This is surprising in light of the fact that Markowitz was a pioneer of technological advancement in the field of computational computer science. Furthermore, he did not stand idly by in the area of portfolio modeling, but continued to make improvements in his own models and to influence the models of others. Few of these improvements, however, were picked up broadly in practice.

Going Supersonic

Because Markowitz's first effort was so simple and powerful, it attracted a great number of followers. The greater the following became, the fewer questioners debated its merits. Markowitz's original work is synonymous with modern portfolio theory and has been taught in business schools for generations and not surprisingly, is still widely used today.

Then came the crash of 2008, and people are starting to ask questions at last. The confluence of the recent economic trauma and the technological advances of the past few decades make today the perfect moment to describe the supersonic models that can be built around Markowitz's fundamental principles of risk, reward and correlation. In a recent paper, we assert that Markowitz's original work remains the perfect framework for applying the latest in economic thought and technology. We dub our updated model "Markowitz 2.0."

Markowitz 2.0
The Flaw of Averages

The 1952 mean-variance model of Harry Markowitz was the first systematic attempt to cure what Savage [2009] calls the "flaw of averages". In general, the flaw of averages is a set of systematic errors that occur when people use single numbers (usually averages) to describe uncertain future quantities. For example, if you plan to rob a bank of $10 million and have one chance in 100 of getting away with it, your average take is $100,000. If you described your activity before hand as "making $100,000" you would be correct on average. But this is a terrible characterization of a bank heist. Yet as Savage [2009] discusses, this very "flaw of averages" is made all the time in business practice, and helps explain why everything is behind schedule, beyond budget, and below projection, and was an accessory to the economic catastrophe that culminated in 2008.

Harry Markowitz's 1952 mean-variance model distinguished between different investments that had the same average (expected) return but different risks, measured as variance or its square root (standard deviation). This breakthrough systematic attempt to cure the flaw of averages ultimately garnered a Nobel Prize for its inventor. However, the use of standard deviation and covariance introduces a higher order version of the flaw of averages, in that these concepts are themselves a version of averages.

Adding Afterburners to Traditional Portfolio Optimization

By taking advantage of the very latest in economic thought and computer technology, we can, in effect, add more thrust to the original framework of the Markowitz portfolio optimization model. The result is a dramatically more powerful model that is more aligned with 21st century investor concerns, markets, and financial instruments such as options.

Traditional portfolio optimization, commonly referred to as mean-variance optimization (MVO), suffers from several limitations which can easily be addressed with today's technology. Our discussion here will focus on five practical enhancements:

1. First, we use a scenario-based approach to allow for fat-tailed distributions. "Fat-tailed" return distributions are not possible within the context of traditional mean-variance optimization, where return distributions are assumed to be adequately described by mean and variance.

2. Second, we replace the single period expected return with the long-term forward-looking geometric mean (GM), as this takes into account accumulation of wealth.

3. Third, we substitute conditional value at risk (CVaR), which only looks at tail risk, for standard deviation, which looks at average variation.

4. Fourth, the original Markowitz model used a covariance matrix to model the distribution of returns on asset classes; we replace this with a scenario-based model that can be generated with Monte Carlo simulation, and can incorporate any number of distributions.

5. Finally, we exploit new statistical technologies pioneered by Savage in the field of Probability Management. Savage invented an astonishing new technology called the Distribution String, or DIST™, which encapsulates thousands of trials as a single data element or cell, thus eliminating the main disadvantage of the scenario-based approach—the need to store and process large amounts of data.

The Scenario Approach
versus Lognormal Distributions

One of the limitations of the traditional mean-variance optimization framework assumes that the distribution of returns of the assets in the optimization can be adequately described simply by mean and variance alone. The most common depiction of this assumption is to draw the distribution of each asset class as a symmetrical bell-shaped curve, which is not always the case.

Over the years, various alternatives have been put forth to replace mean-variance optimization with an optimization framework that takes into account the non-normal features of return distributions. Some researchers have proposed using distributions curves that exhibit skewness and kurtosis (i.e., have fat tails) while others have proposed using large numbers of scenarios based on historical data or Monte Carlo simulation.

The scenario-based approach has two main advantages over a distribution curve approach: (1) it is highly flexible; for example, non-linear instruments such as options can be modeled in a straight forward manner, and (2) it is mathematically manageable; for example, portfolio returns under the scenarios are simply weighted averages of asset class returns within the scenarios. In this way, the distribution of a portfolio can be derived from the distributions of the assets classes without working complicated equations that might lack analytical solutions; only straight-forward portfolio arithmetic is needed.

In standard scenario analysis, there is no precise graphical representation of return distributions. Histograms serve as approximations such as those shown in Graph 2-1. We augment the scenario approach by employing a smoothing technique so that smooth curves represent return distributions. For example, Graph 11-6 shows the distribution curve of annual returns of large company stocks under our scenario-based approach. Comparing Graph 11-6 with the large company stock histogram in Graph 2-1, we can see that the smooth distribution curve retains the properties of the historical distribution while showing the distribution in a more esthetically pleasing and precise form. Further, our model can bring all of the power of continuous mathematics to the scenario approach. This was previously enjoyed only by models based on continuous distributions.

In Graph 11-6, the solid gray line represents the distribution of annual returns of large company stocks when our smoothed scenario-based approach is used and the red line represents the distribution curve of annual returns of large company stocks when traditional mean-variance analysis is used and we assume that returns follow a lognormal distribution.

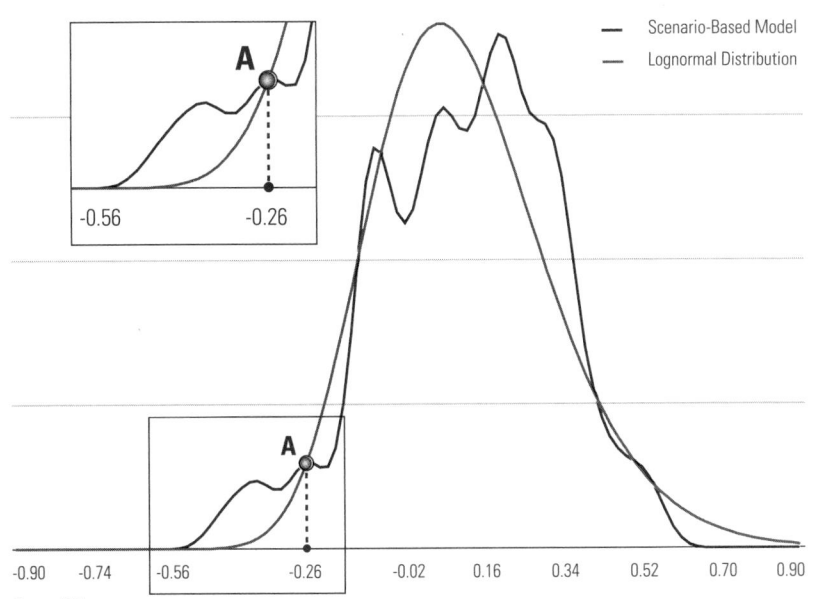

Return (%)
Data from 1926–2009

As Kaplan et al. [2009] discuss, "tail events" have occurred often throughout the history of capital markets all over the world, but the probabilities associated with them may be systematically underestimated within the context of traditional mean-variance analysis, where return distributions are assumed to be lognormal. The scenario-based model proposed by Kaplan and Savage is a real step forward as it better models the non-trivial probabilities associated with tail events. For a more detailed discussion of tail events and their non-triviality, see Chapter 13. In Chapter 13, Kaplan introduces a new set of monthly real stock market total returns going back a full 124 years, and uses these new returns to demonstrate that the severity of the financial crisis of 2008 was not unique, but was merely the latest chapter in a long history of market meltdowns.

Geometric Mean (GM) versus Single Period Expected Return

In MVO, reward is measured by expected return which is a forecast of arithmetic mean. However, over long periods of time, investors are not concerned with simple averages of return; rather they are concerned with the accumulation of wealth. We use forecasted long-term geometric mean (GM) as the measure of reward because investors who plan on repeatedly reinvesting in the same strategy over an indefinite period would seek the highest rate of growth for the portfolios as measured by geometric mean.[8]

Conditional Value at Risk (CVaR) versus Standard Deviation

As for risk, much has been written about how investors are not concerned merely with the degree of dispersion of returns (as measured by standard deviation), but rather with how much wealth they could lose. A number of "downside" risk measures have been proposed to replace standard deviation as the measure of risk in strategic asset allocation. While any one of these could be used, our preference is to use Conditional Value at Risk (CVaR).

If we extend a vertical line from Point A down to the x-axis, the area to the left (and underneath) each of the curves represents the occurrences of annual returns equal to or less than, in this case, −26 percent. Since these are cumulative distributions, we can calculate the probability that the annual returns of large company stocks will be less than or equal to −26 percent by dividing the area underneath each of the curves by the total area underneath each of the curves as a whole.

For example, looking to the scenario-based model, the area to the left of the vertical line under the scenario-based distribution represents 5 percent of the total area underneath this entire distribution line. This implies that the probability of large company stocks having a return of −26 percent or less is 5 percent. Correspondingly, the area to the left of the vertical line for the lognormal distribution represents 1.6 percent of the total area under the entire lognormal distribution line. This implies that the probability of large company stocks having a return of −26 percent or less using the traditional mean-variance model is 1.6 percent.

CVaR is related to Value at Risk (VaR). VaR describes the left tail in terms of how much capital can be lost over a given period of time. For example, a 5 percent VaR answers a question of the form: Having invested $10,000 there is a 5 percent chance of losing $X or more in 12 months. (The "or more" implications of VaR are sometimes overlooked by investors with serious implications.) Applying this to idea to returns, the 5 percent VaR is the negative of the 5th percentile of the return distribution. For example, the 5th percentile of the distribution shown in Graph 11-6 is −25.8 percent so its 5 percent VaR is 25.8 percent. This means there is a 5 percent chance of losing $2,850 or more on a $10,000 investment. CVaR is the expected or average loss of capital should VaR be breached. Therefore CVaR is always greater than VaR. For example, the 5 percent CVaR for the distribution shown in Graph 11-6 is 35.8 percent, or $3,580 on a $10,000 investment.

Scenarios versus Correlation

In mean-variance analysis, the covariation of the returns of each pair of asset classes is represented by a single number, the correlation coefficient. This is mathematically equivalent to assuming that a simple linear regression model is an adequate description of how the returns on the two asset classes are related. In fact, the r-square statistic of a simple linear regression model for two series of returns is equal to the square of the correlation coefficient.

However, for many pairs of asset classes, a linear model misses the most important features of the relationship. For example, during normal times, non-U.S. equities are considered to be good diversifiers for U.S. equity investors. But during global crises, all major equity markets move down together.

Furthermore, suppose that the returns on two asset classes indices were highly correlated, but instead of including direct exposures to both in the model, one was replaced with an option on itself. Instead of having a linear relationship, we now have a nonlinear relationship which cannot be captured by a correlation coefficient.

Fortunately, these sorts of nonlinear relationships between returns on different investments can be handled in a scenario-based model. For example, in scenarios that represent normal times, returns on different equity markets could be modeled as moving somewhat apart from each other; while scenarios that represent global crises could model the markets as moving downward together.

Ultrasonic Statistical Technology

Since it may take thousands of scenarios to adequately model return distributions, until recently, a disadvantage of the scenario-based approach has been that it requires large amounts of data to be stored and processed. Even with the advances in computer hardware, the conventional approach of representing scenarios with large tables of explicit numbers remained problematic.

The phenomenal speed of computers has given rise to the field of Probability Management, an extension of data management to probability distributions, rather than numbers. The key component of Probability Management is the Distribution String, or DIST™, that can encapsulate thousands of trials as a single data element. The use of DISTs greatly saves on storage and speeds up processing time, so that a Monte Carlo simulation consisting of thousands of trials can be performed on a personal computer in an instant. Monte Carlo simulations that use DISTs are also very adaptable, allowing for almost any return distribution or underlying probability model, rather than being contained by parameters. While not all asset management organizations are prepared to create the DISTs needed to drive GM-CVaR optimization, some outside vendors, such as Morningstar Ibbotson, can fulfill this role.

Another facet of Probability Management is interactive simulation technology, which can run thousands of scenarios through a model before the sound of your finger leaving the <Enter> key reaches your ear. These supersonic models allow much deeper intuition into the sensitivities of portfolios, and encourage the user to interactively explore different portfolios, distributional assumptions, and potential black swans. A sample of such an interactive model is available for download from http://www.ProbabilityManagement.org.

Finale: The New Efficient Frontier

Putting it all together, we form an efficient frontier of forecasted geometric mean (GM) and conditional value at risk (CVaR) as shown in Graph 11-7,[9] incorporating our scenario approach to covariance and new statistical technology. We believe that this efficient frontier is more relevant to investors than the traditional expected return vs. standard deviation frontier of MVO because it shows the trade-off between reward and risk that is meaningful to investors; namely, long-term potential growth vs. short-term potential loss.

Graph 11-7: Geometric Mean – Conditional Value at Risk Efficient Frontier

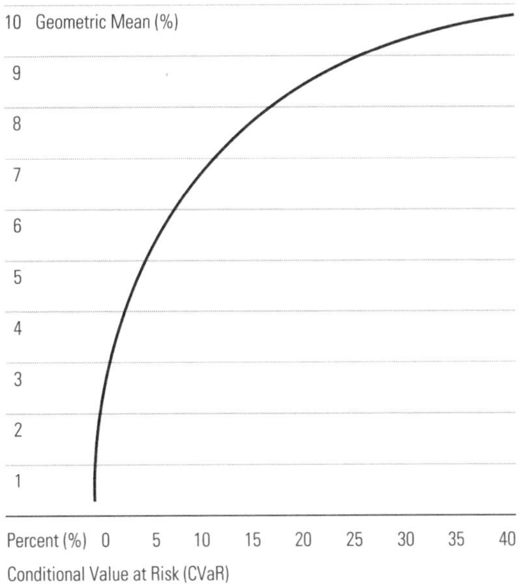

Approaches to Calculating the Equity Risk Premium

The expected return on stocks over bonds, the equity risk premium, has been estimated by a number of authors who have utilized a variety of different approaches. Such studies can be categorized into four groups based on the approaches they have taken. The first group of studies derive the equity risk premium from historical returns between stocks and bonds. Supply side models, using fundamental information such as earnings, dividends, or overall productivity, are used by the second group to measure the expected equity risk premium. A third group adopts demand side models that derive the expected returns of equities through the payoff demanded by equity investors for bearing the additional risk. The opinions of financial professionals through broad surveys are relied upon by the fourth and final group.

This section is based upon the work by Roger G. Ibbotson and Peng Chen, who combined the first and second approaches to arrive at their forecast of the equity risk premium.[10] By proposing a new supply side methodology, the Ibbotson-Chen study challenges current arguments that future returns on stocks over bonds will be negative or close to zero. The results affirm the relationship between the stock market and the overall economy.

Supply Model

Long-term expected equity returns can be forecasted by the use of supply side models. The supply of stock market returns is generated by the productivity of the corporations in the real economy. Investors should not expect a much higher or lower return than that produced by the companies in the real economy. Thus, over the long run, equity return should be close to the long-run supply estimate.

Earnings, dividends, and capital gains are supplied by corporate productivity. Graph 11-8 illustrates that earnings and dividends have historically grown in tandem with the overall economy (GDP per capita). However, GDP per capita did not outpace the stock market. This is primarily because the P/E ratio increased 1.37 times during the same period. So, assuming that the economy will continue to grow, all three should continue to grow as well.

Forward-Looking Earnings Model

Roger G. Ibbotson and Peng Chen forecast the equity risk premium through a supply side model using historical data. They utilized an earnings model as the basis for their supply side estimate. The earnings model breaks the historical equity return into four pieces, with only three historically being supplied by companies: inflation, income return, and growth in real earnings per share. The growth in the P/E ratio, the fourth piece, is a reflection of investors' changing prediction of future earnings growth. The past supply of corporate growth is forecasted to continue; however, a change in investors' predictions is not. P/E rose dramatically from 1980 through 2001 because people believed that corporate earnings were going to grow faster in the future. This growth in P/E drove a small portion of the rise in equity returns over the same period.

Graph 11-8: Capital Gains, GDP Per Capita, Earnings, and Dividends
Index (Year-End 1925 = $1.00)

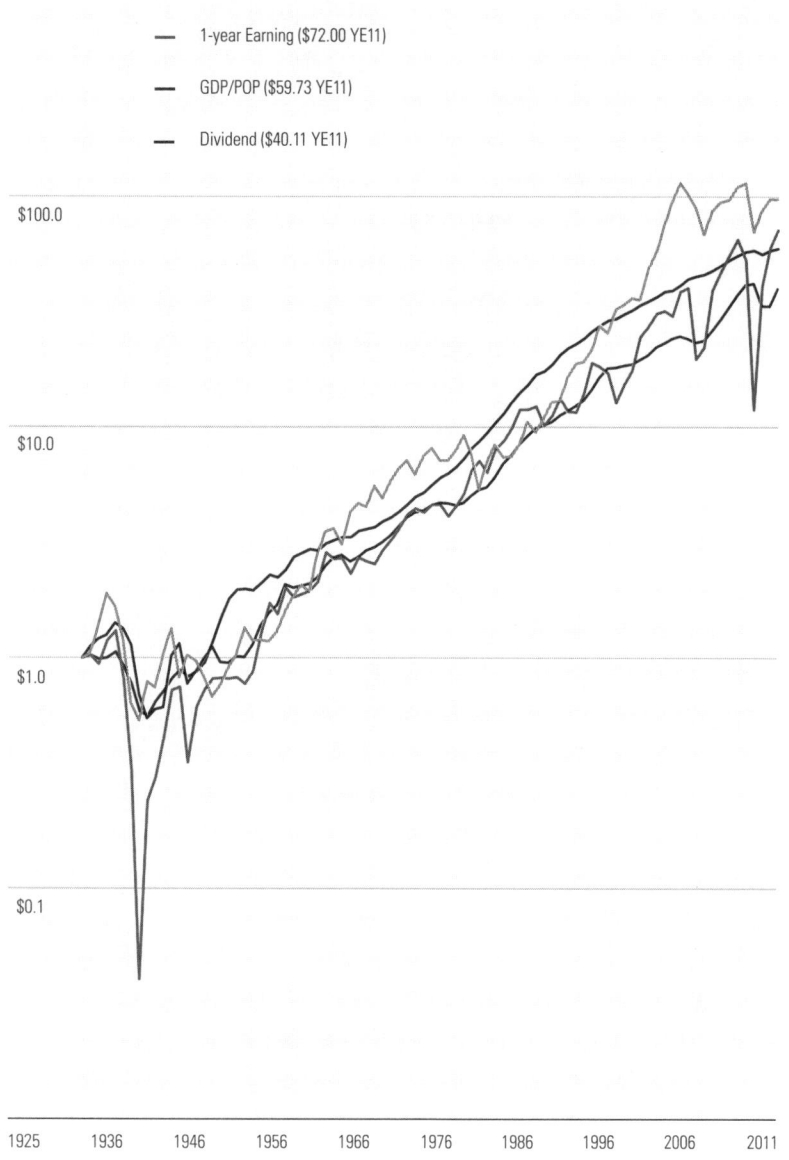

Graph 11-9 illustrates the price to earnings ratio from 1926 to 2011. The P/E ratio, using one-year average earnings, was 10.22 at the beginning of 1926 and ended the year 2011 at 13.99, an average increase of 0.37 percent per year. The highest P/E was 136.55 recorded in 1932, while the lowest was 7.07 recorded in 1948. Ibbotson Associates revised the calculation of the P/E ratio from a one-year to a three-year average earnings for use in equity forecasting.

This is because reported earnings are affected not only by the long-term productivity, but also by "one-time" items that do not necessarily have the same consistent impact year after year. The three-year average is more reflective of the long-term trend than the year-by-year numbers. The P/E ratio calculated using the three-year average of earnings had an increase of 0.33 percent per year.

Graph 11-9: Large Company Stocks P/E Ratio

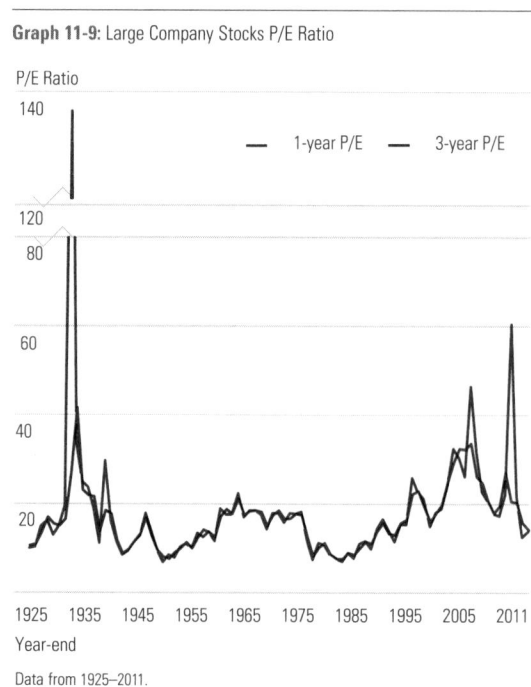

Data from 1925–2011.

The historical P/E growth factor, using three-year earnings, of 0.33 percent per year is subtracted from the equity forecast, because it is not believed that P/E will continue to increase in the future. The market serves as the cue. The current P/E ratio is the market's best guess for the future of corporate earnings and there is no reason to believe, at this time, that the market will change its mind. Using this top-down approach, the geometric supply-side equity risk premium is 4.08 percent, which equates to an arithmetic supply-side equity risk premium of 6.18 percent.

Another approach in calculating the premium would be to add up the components that comprise the supply of equity return, excluding the P/E component. Thus, the supply of equity return only includes inflation, the growth in real earnings per share, and income return. The forward-looking earnings model calculates the long-term supply of U.S. equity returns to be 9.43 percent:

$$SR = \left[(1+CPI)\times(1+g_{REPS})-1\right]+Inc+Rinv$$

$$9.43\%^* = \left[(1+2.99\%)\times(1+2.08\%)-1\right]+4.08\%+0.21\%$$

*difference due to rounding

where:

SR = the supply of the equity return;
CPI = Consumer Price Index (inflation);
g_{REPS} = the growth in real earning per share;
Inc = the income return;
$Rinv$ = the reinvestment return.

The equity risk premium, based on the supply-side earnings model, is calculated to be 4.10 percent on a geometric basis:

$$SERP = \frac{(1+SR)}{(1+CPI)\times(1+RRf)}-1$$

$$4.10\%^* = \frac{(1+9.43\%)}{(1+2.99\%)\times(1+2.07\%)}-1$$

*difference due to rounding

where:

$SERP$ = the supply-side equity risk premium;
SR = the supply of the equity return;
CPI = Consumer Price Index (inflation);
RRf = the real risk-free rate.

Converting the geometric average into an arithmetic average results in an equity risk premium of 6.16%:

$$R_A = R_G + \frac{\sigma^2}{2}$$

$$6.16\% = 4.10\% + \frac{20.30\%^2}{2}$$

where:

R_A = the arithmetic average;
R_G = the geometric average;
σ = the standard deviation of equity returns.

Long-Term Market Predictions

The supply side model estimates that stocks will continue to provide significant returns over the long run, averaging around 9.43 percent per year, assuming historical inflation rates. The equity risk premium, based on the top-down supply-side earnings model, is calculated to be 4.08 percent on a geometric basis and 6.18 percent on an arithmetic basis.

In the future, Ibbotson and Chen predict increased earnings growth that will offset lower dividend yields. The fact that earnings will grow as dividend payouts shrink is in line with the Miller and Modigliani Theory.

The forecasts for the market are in line with both the historical supply measures of public corporations (i.e. earnings) and overall economic productivity (GDP per capita). ▥

Endnotes

[1] The standard deviation is the square root of the variance; hence the term "mean-variance" in describing this form of the optimization problem.

[2] Markowitz, Harry M., Portfolio Selection: Efficient Diversification of Investments, New York: John Wiley & Sons, 1959.

[3] For more information about Morningstar *EnCorr*® software, refer to the Investment Tools and Resources page at the back of this book, or within the United States, call +1 866 910-0840. Outside the United States, call +44 020 3107-0020.

[4] It is also possible to conduct a simulation using entire data sets, that is, without estimating the statistical parameters of the data sets. Typically, in such a nonparametric simulation, the frequency of an event occurring in the simulated history is equal to the frequency of the event occurring in the actual history used to construct the data set.

[5] The expected capital gain on a par bond is self-evidently zero. For a zero-coupon (or other discount) bond, investors expect the price to rise as the bond ages, but the expected portion of this price increase should not be considered a capital gain. It is a form of income return.

[6] See Chapter 12, "Wealth Forecasting with Monte Carlo Simulation" for more information.

[7] See Markowitz and Usmen [2003].

[8] Ranking investment strategies by forecasted GM is sometimes described as applying the Kelly Criterion; an idea promoted by William Poundstone [2005].

[9] Other researchers have also proposed using GM and CVaR as the measures or reward and risk in an efficient frontier. See for example Sheikh and Qiao, [2009].

[10] "Long-Run Stock Returns: Participating in the Real Economy," Roger G. Ibbotson and Peng Chen, Financial Analysts Journal, January/February 2003.

Chapter 12

Wealth Forecasting With Monte Carlo Simulation

Meeting Today's Challenges

Comprehending and communicating various types of risk is one of the most challenging tasks facing advisors before, during, and after the planning process. With the number of complicated products growing and investors' level of sophistication increasing, advisors confront difficult issues each day in understanding and conveying risk effectively.

What Is Monte Carlo Simulation?

Monte Carlo simulation is a problem-solving technique utilized to approximate the probability of certain outcomes by performing multiple trial runs, called simulations, using random variables. The probability distribution of the results is calculated and analyzed in order to infer which outcomes are most likely to be produced. Monte Carlo derives its name from the city in Monaco, where casinos, which contain games of chance, serve as the primary attractions. Random behavior is exhibited in gambling games such as roulette, dice, and slot machines. The random behavior evident in games of chance is comparable to how Monte Carlo simulation selects variable values at random to simulate a model. When a die is rolled, it is certain that a 1, 2, 3, 4, 5, or 6 will result, but it is not known which for any particular roll. It's similar for variables that have a known range of values but an uncertain value for any particular time or event (e.g., interest rates, stock prices, weather conditions, or insurance).

Monte Carlo methods have been used for hundreds of years; however, it wasn't until the past several decades that they grew in popularity and application. Monte Carlo is currently utilized regularly in many different fields; it has particularly been widely embraced in fields that specialize in analyzing the financial markets.

Why Use Monte Carlo Simulation?

Real-life investing involves all sorts of interrelated decisions, ranging from saving, to spending, to tax issues, and more. When all of these complexities need to be considered, Monte Carlo simulation can be quite useful. The process starts with a set of assumptions about the estimated means, standard deviations, and correlations for a set of asset classes or investments. These assumptions are used to randomly generate thousands of possible future return scenarios—somewhat similar to drawing numbers out of a hat. When these returns are used in conjunction with a client's year-by-year cash flows, taxes, asset allocation, and financial product selections, a large number of possible "financial lives" for the client are produced. These "financial lives" can be used to answer a number of questions pertaining to the risk of the client's investment decisions. For example, how many times out of all of these lives did the client reach his goal versus running out of money? Used in this fashion, Monte Carlo techniques can calculate and display risk in a personalized way that is easy for investors to understand. The results from simulation are often used to construct and evaluate an appropriate asset allocation policy.

Types of Monte Carlo Simulation

The most crucial factor in simulation-based techniques is the generation of the future return scenarios. There are quite a few ways to generate simulations, some better than others. Certain methods use only historical data. Other techniques take into account just the mean and standard deviation of the assets involved, while ignoring the correlations. In other words, the value of a Monte Carlo-based tool is only as good as the quality and richness of the return scenarios it generates.

Non-Parametric

This method of Monte Carlo simulation uses purely historical data. The easiest way to describe it is to use this book as an example. Imagine if you were to take a page in this book that shows the annual returns for all of the asset classes (Appendix A) and create pieces of paper so that each piece has one year's total return numbers on it for all of the asset classes considered. The pieces are subsequently put into a hat. One of the pieces is drawn out of the hat, the return numbers on the piece are written down, the piece is dropped back into the hat, and the process is repeated for as many years in the future as you want to forecast. No distribution parameter assumptions need to be made and no parameter is estimated. The biggest problem with this technique is the limited amount of information it provides because only what has happened in the past can be drawn out of the hat. It is assumed that the future will resemble the past.

Parametric

A parametric model is based on the means, standard deviations, and correlations of the assets being forecast. These are the parameters that give this method its name. Once these parameters are set, a computer program is used to generate random samples from the bell curve that these parameters define. This provides a much richer set of results, since the program can draw from any number under the curve, not just numbers that have occurred in the past. It is very important to maintain the correlation across all asset classes in the simulation. This process generates a set of random numbers for all of the asset classes, thus maintaining the correlations.

Economic Modeling

This is the most complex method because it involves modeling the movements of the yield curve through time and then layering on various equity and fixed-income risk premia to derive returns. It is the most realistic simulation method, but unfortunately cannot be easily customized by each user.

In general, most Monte Carlo simulation models are constructed on the asset-class level, utilizing parametric modeling assumptions.

Wealth Forecasting

Simulation is used when a statistical property of the estimated variable is unknown or impossible to derive—in other words, when no analytical solution exists. Asset allocation policies are developed for the purpose of meeting financial needs, obligations, and goals. But because uncertainty is prevalent in the financial markets, it is not always clear whether these needs, obligations, and goals will be met. Monte Carlo simulation can help to illustrate this uncertainty with regard to wealth forecasting.

Wealth Forecasting Without Cash Flows

When forecasting the ending wealth level for a particular asset class or portfolio, the sequence of returns may or may not play a critical role in determining the ending wealth level. One situation in which the sequence of returns has no impact on the ending wealth value is when there are no cash flows in the analysis. Tables 12-1 and 12-2 illustrate this situation. In both cases the ending wealth value is $1,000,000. This case would not require the use of a simulation model. The use of a lognormal distribution model would be most appropriate. Using the lognormal model, it is fairly simple to form probabilistic forecasts of

both compound rates of return and ending period wealth values. Please refer to Chapter 11, Using Historical Data in Forecasting and Optimization, for more information.

Table 12-1: Wealth Forecasting without Cash Flows

Initial Investment		$1,000,000
Period 1	25% Return	+$250,000
Ending Wealth		$1,250,000
Period 2	-20% Return	-$250,000
Ending Wealth		$1,000,000

Table 12-2: Wealth Forecasting without Cash Flows

Initial Investment		$1,000,000
Period 1	-20% Return	-$200,000
Ending Wealth		$800,000
Period 2	25% Return	+$200,000
Ending Wealth		$1,000,000

Wealth Forecasting With Cash Flows

A situation in which the sequence of returns has an impact on the ending wealth value is when cash flows are present in the analysis. Tables 12-3 and 12-4 show a $1,000,000 investment with an outflow of $50,000 at the end of each period. In this situation the sequence of returns does have an impact on the ending wealth value. In Table 12-3 the ending wealth value in period 2 is $910,000, while in Table 12-4, the ending wealth value in period 2 is $887,500. That amounts to a $22,500 difference—when more years are taken into consideration, the difference can be greater. A simulation model would be required for situations of this nature.

Table 12-3: Wealth Forecasting with Cash Flows

Initial Investment		$1,000,000
Period 1	25% Return	+$250,000
	Cash Flow	-$50,000
Ending Wealth		$1,200,000
Period 2	-20% Return	-$240,000
	Cash Flow	-$50,000
Ending Wealth		$910,000

Table 12-4: Wealth Forecasting with Cash Flows

Initial Investment		$1,000,000
Period 1	-20% Return	-$200,000
	Cash Flow	-$50,000
Ending Wealth		750,000
Period 2	25% Return	+$187,500
	Cash Flow	-$50,000
Ending Wealth		$887,500

Steps in Monte Carlo Simulation

There are four key steps to follow when conducting a Monte Carlo simulation based on parametric modeling assumptions. The first step is to determine whether the random returns are to be generated on the asset class level or on the individual security level. An example of an asset class would be a large company stock index represented by the S&P 500 index, while an example of an individual security can be ABC International Growth Fund or IBM stock.

The fundamental characteristics of asset classes have remained fairly stable over time. Historically, equities have had a higher standard deviation than fixed income. Corporate bonds have had a higher level of default risk than their government counterparts. Due to this stability and consistency, a long historical data stream can be collected and analyzed in order to estimate the risk and return characteristics and the relationships across these asset classes. Conversely, the risk and return characteristics and the relationships across individual securities are highly dynamic and there is typically a rather short historical data stream. This dynamic nature of security-level data, as well as the limitation on available data, makes modeling their future returns extremely difficult. Confidence in security-level models and their ability to estimate risk and return is low when compared to asset class-level models.

Once this has been decided, the second step is to calculate the inputs around which the simulation will be run. These inputs consist of the arithmetic means, standard deviations, and correlations of the asset classes or portfolios for which the simulation results will be produced. The returns for each asset or portfolio are assumed to be lognormally distributed. The lognormal distribution is skewed to the right. That is, the expected value, or mean, is greater than the median. Furthermore, if returns are lognormally distributed, returns cannot fall below negative 100 percent.

The third step is to actually generate the random return scenarios. At this point the number of simulated runs to be conducted for each asset class or portfolio, for each period, needs to be determined. Some experts maintain that 500 simulations are sufficient; others prefer to run thousands or even hundreds of thousands of simulations. The fourth step is to analyze and evaluate the output and to make any necessary adjustments to the inputs. This is an extremely important step that should not be overlooked.

Case Study: Establishing Returns and Wealth Values

As mentioned earlier in the chapter, Monte Carlo simulation is a problem-solving technique utilized to approximate the probability of certain outcomes by performing multiple trial runs using random variables. Once the arithmetic means, standard deviations, and correlations for a set of asset classes or portfolios have been established, these assumptions are used to randomly generate thousands of possible future return scenarios.

Table 12-5 presents a snapshot from a parametric simulation that was run 100 times and produced 100 possible 35-year scenarios for the performance of a sample equity index. Table 12-6 shows a snapshot of the wealth values that were produced corresponding to the return values presented in Table 12-5. The entire table would consist of Year 1 through Year 35 and Simulation Run 1 through Simulation Run 100. The initial value of the portfolio is $1,000,000 and non-inflation-adjusted annual withdrawals of $50,000 are taken from the portfolio.

Calculation of Projected Wealth Values

The wealth values located in column Year 1 in Table 12-6 were calculated from the total returns found in column Year 1 in Table 12-5 using the following equation:

$$w_t = \left[(1+r_t)(w_0 - aw) \right]$$

(38)

where:

w_t = the wealth value as of year-end **t**;
r_t = the total return in period **t**;
w_0 = the wealth value as of year-end **0**;
aw = the annual withdrawal.

For example, the wealth value of $878,415, located in Table 12-6 under column Year 1 and next to row Simulation Run 1, was calculated using the total return -0.0754, found in the same location in Table 12-5, using equation 38 as follows:

$$\$878,415^* = \left[(1+(-0.0754))(\$1,000,000 - \$50,000) \right]$$

*difference due to rounding

Please keep in mind it is assumed that the investor retires at year zero and withdraws the required income need of $50,000 at the beginning of each year, beginning in year 1, in order to fund the investor's cash flow needs throughout the remainder of the year.

Table 12-5: Forecast Annual Returns (Sample Equity Index)

Simulation Run	Year 1	Year 2	Year 3	Year 4	Year 5			Year 35
1	**-0.0754**	**0.2524**	0.1827	0.0842	0.0950			0.2907
2	0.1865	0.0541	0.1773	0.2970	0.2218			0.1374
3	0.1701	0.4364	0.1221	0.2549	0.1967			0.0622
4	0.0368	0.3025	-0.2503	0.4014	-0.1414			0.3114
5	0.3224	0.1309	-0.2599	0.2620	0.2388			0.1464
100	-0.1174	0.1001	0.0997	-0.2605	0.2291			0.0012

Table 12-6: Forecast Wealth Values (Sample Equity Index)

Simulation Run	Year 1	Year 2	Year 3	Year 4	Year 5			Year 35
1	878415	1037492	1167907	1212008	1272410			11485008
2	1127176	1135500	1277910	1592550	1884636			12360234
3	1111636	1524922	1654959	2014004	2350415			33408922
4	984937	1217759	875473	1156831	950292			2602245
5	1256251	1364161	972614	1164311	1380388			29040376
100	838492	867457	898959	627797	710147			4112592

Table 12-7: Wealth Percentiles (Sample Equity Index)

Percentile	Year 1	Year 2	Year 3	Year 4	Year 5			Year 35
1	532406	598632	598431	503836	457332			0
2	600382	600719	635116	530389	585581			0
3	635013	671649	656676	556723	607811			215667
4	657177	687043	676242	627134	615185			246149
5	731704	719790	718042	627797	628094			474625
100	1509963	2078499	2718801	3424477	3823593			211427351

The wealth values located in columns Year 2 through Year 35 in Table 12-6 were calculated from the total returns found in columns Year 2 through Year 35 in Table 12-5 using the following equation:

$$w_t = \left[(1+r_t)(w_{t-1} - aw) \right] \tag{39}$$

where:
w_t = the wealth value as of year-end **t**;
r_t = the total return in period **t**;
w_{t-1} = the wealth value as of the previous year-end, **t−1**;
aw = the annual withdrawal.

For example, the wealth value of $1,037,492 located in Table 12-6 under column Year 2 and next to row Simulation Run 1 was calculated using the total return 0.2524, found in the same location in Table 12-5, using equation 39 as follows:

$$\$1,037,492^* = \left[(1+0.2524)(\$878,415 - \$50,000) \right]$$

*difference due to rounding

Establishing Wealth Percentiles

The values calculated and presented in Table 12-6 are the future projections of an investor's wealth level, and help determine whether or not the investor will be able to successfully fund his or her goal. The values for each year are subsequently sorted from smallest to largest and can be presented according to various wealth percentiles or probabilities.

For example, if you wanted to take the values from Table 12-6 and illustrate at certain probabilities how long the sample equity index may last into the future, you would start by sorting each column from the smallest wealth value to the largest wealth value. Table 12-7 shows the results after each column was sorted (keep in mind the table represents only a snapshot—the entire table actually has 100 simulation runs and 35 years). Since the table illustrates a snapshot of a simulation that was run 100 times, once the columns are sorted, each value alongside each percentile represents the corresponding probability. Take Percentile 5, for example. The investor has a 5 percent chance that the portfolio's future value will be less than $474,625 at the end of year 35. Correspondingly, there is a 95 percent chance that the portfolio's future value will be greater than $474,625 at the end of year 35.

Case Study: Asset-Class Forecasts

The asset classes chosen by an investor can affect how long his or her wealth may last or whether or not a particular goal may be sufficiently funded. Graph 12-1 is generated by means of a parametric simulation method using the asset-class input values displayed in Table 12-8. The table shows the arithmetic mean and standard deviation of each asset class from 1926 to 2011. For each asset class, the correlation to itself is 1.00.

Table 12-8: Simulation Inputs Arithmetic Mean and Standard Deviation

Asset Class	Arithmetic Mean (%)	Standard Deviation (%)
Large Company Stocks	11.8	20.3
Small Company Stocks	16.5	32.5
Long-Term Corporate Bonds	6.4	8.4
Long-Term Government Bonds	6.1	9.8
Cash (Treasury Bills)	3.6	3.1

Data from 1926–2011.

Each hypothetical portfolio has an initial starting value of $1 million. It is assumed that a person retires at year zero and makes a $50,000 withdrawal each year starting in year one (the $50,000 annual withdrawal is adjusted by the historical 1926–2011 inflation rate of 3.1 percent each year). Each simulation is run 5,000 times and produces 5,000 possible 35-year scenarios consistent with the characteristics of each asset class. Bucketing each of the resulting scenarios into a distribution enables us to estimate the length of time that investments in the various asset classes may last in retirement.

Graph 12-1 illustrates at a 90 percent confidence level the number of years that each asset class, with 100 percent allocation, may last. Examining results at the 90 percent confidence level enables us to focus on what many might consider "worst-case scenarios." In other words, the investment lasted longer than the time depicted in Graph 12-1 in 90 percent of the resulting scenarios for each of the asset classes examined, while the investment lasted a shorter time than depicted in Graph 12-1 in 10 percent of the resulting scenarios for each of the asset classes examined.

At the 90 percent confidence level, 10 percent of the resulting scenarios produced outcomes in which investments solely in any one of the asset classes experienced a shortfall between 17 years in the future (100 percent allocation to small stocks) and 20 years in the future (100 percent allocation to large company stocks or long-term corporate bonds). However, keep in mind that 90 percent of the resulting scenarios in investments in any one of the asset classes lasted longer than that depicted in Graph 12-1.

The investor in one of these portfolios may have to look into adding more money to the investment, shifting investment dollars into a different allocation, or withdrawing less in order to have a better chance of funding this need.

Case Study: Stock and Bond Portfolio Forecasts

Just as the assets one chooses to invest in can affect the length of time that investments will last in retirement or whether or not a particular goal may be sufficiently funded, the combination of asset classes that comprise a portfolio can also affect how long an investor's portfolio may last in retirement. Graph 12-2 is generated by means of a parametric simulation method using portfolios composed of various mixes of large company stocks and long-term government bonds (average maturity 20 years). The simulation's inputs are the arithmetic means, the standard deviations, and the correlations of the asset classes for which the simulation results will be produced.

Graph 12-1: Simulated Asset Class Performance
$50,000 Annual Inflation Adjusted Withdrawal (90% probability of lasting longer than shown)

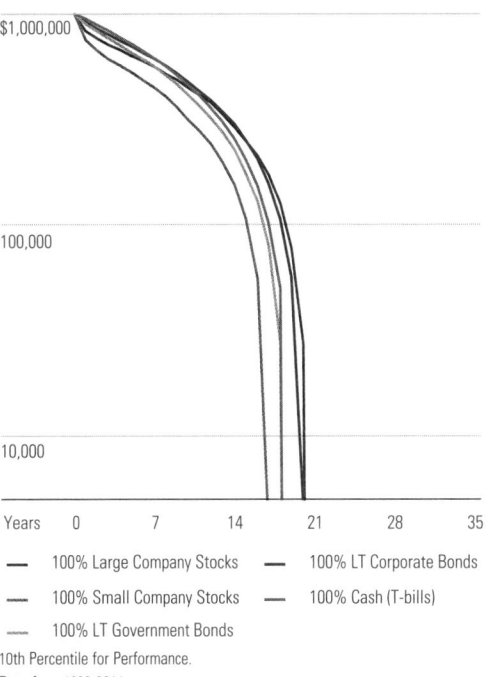

Years | 0 | 7 | 14 | 21 | 28 | 35

— 100% Large Company Stocks — 100% LT Corporate Bonds
— 100% Small Company Stocks — 100% Cash (T-bills)
--- 100% LT Government Bonds
10th Percentile for Performance.
Data from 1926-2011.

Table 12-8 shows the arithmetic mean and standard deviation of large company stocks and long-term government bonds from 1926 to 2011; the correlation between large company stocks and long-term government bonds is 0.03.

Each hypothetical stock/bond portfolio has an initial starting value of $1 million. It is assumed that a person retires at year zero and makes a $50,000 withdrawal each year starting in year one (the $50,000 annual withdrawal is adjusted by the historical 1926–2011 inflation rate of 3.1 percent each year). Each simulation is run 5,000 times and produces 5,000 possible 35-year scenarios, consistent with the characteristics of each portfolio. Bucketing each of the resulting scenarios into a distribution enables us to estimate the length of time a given portfolio mix may last in retirement.

Graph 12-2 shows the number of years a given portfolio mix is expected to last at a 90 percent confidence level. Examining results at the 90 percent confidence level enables us to focus on what many might consider "worst-case scenarios." In other words, the investment lasted longer than the time depicted in Graph 12-2 in 90 percent of the resulting scenarios for the respective portfolio mixes, while the investment lasted a shorter time than that depicted in Graph 12-2 in 10 percent of the resulting scenarios for the respective portfolios.

It is interesting to note that the diversified portfolios (those composed of both stocks and bonds) are forecast to last longer than the portfolios composed of only stocks or only bonds. This is not an unexpected result, as diversification has the potential to increase returns or lessen risk. All other things held the same, increased returns, lessened risk, or any combination of these two things will have the affect of increasing the number of years until the portfolio is exhausted.

Case Study: Ibbotson's National Savings Rate Guidelines for Individuals

New research by a team led by Professor Roger Ibbotson creates retirement savings guidelines for individuals based on age, current income level, and current savings.[1] The study utilizes Monte Carlo simulation to provide superior estimates than are possible with deterministic modeling, where parameters are determined by averages (and therefore not subject to the random fluctuations that are seen in the real world). Monte Carlo simulation, as opposed to deterministic modeling, enables savers to view projections of possible best- and worst-case scenarios, thus helping them achieve better financial decisions over long time horizons.

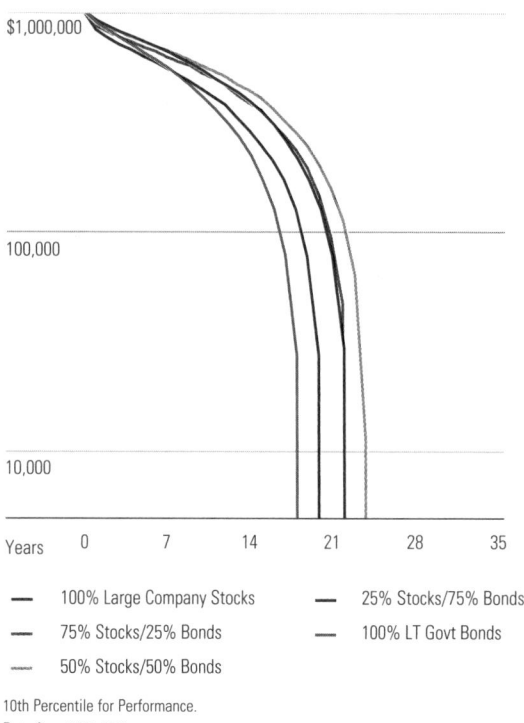

Graph 12-2: Simulated Portfolio Performance
$50,000 Annual Inflation-Adjusted Withdrawal (90% probability of lasting longer than shown)

— 100% Large Company Stocks   — 25% Stocks/75% Bonds
— 75% Stocks/25% Bonds   — 100% LT Govt Bonds
— 50% Stocks/50% Bonds

10th Percentile for Performance.
Data from 1926-2011.

Although savers are typically advised that they will need about 80% of their gross annual pre-retirement income for each year of retirement[2], Ibbotson's new research calculates annual retirement income needs as a percentage of net pre-retirement income. The study fairly assumes that the prospective retiree will continue to live off of approximately what he or she had been living off of prior to retiring—in other words, income minus savings. The study also takes into account Social Security income, inflation[3], and expected salary increases (limited to the expected inflation rate), but does not consider late-in-life medical costs. In addition, a retirement age of 65 at full Social Security benefits is also assumed[4], and a probability mortality rate model is used to calculate life expectancy.[5]

Creation of this analysis was very complex both in terms of the methodology and the selection of data used, but the results provide easy to use guidelines for annual saving requirements. The study addresses three major issues: retirement income needed (Table 12-9), savings rates guidelines (Table 12-10), and benchmarks against which savers can check their progress (Table 12-11).

Table 12-9: Calculation of Assets Needed at Age 65 to Provide Required Retirement Income

Step 1: Determine Annual Income Needed In Retirement

Pre-Retirement Income (Gross)		Annual savings		Income (Net)				Post-Retirement Income Needed (80% of Net)
$20,000	−	$1,720	=	$18,280	×	80%	=	$14,624
$40,000	−	$4,880	=	$35,120	×	80%	=	$28,096
$60,000	−	$8,760	=	$51,240	×	80%	=	$40,992
$80,000	−	$13,120	=	$66,880	×	80%	=	$53,504
$100,000	−	$17,600	=	$82,400	×	80%	=	$65,920
$120,000	−	$23,040	=	$96,960	×	80%	=	$77,568

Step 2: Determine Income Needed From Retirement Portfolio

Post-Retirement Income Needed* (Estimated)		Social Security Income Deficit		Annual Retirement Deficit		Retirement Portfolio Assets Needed to Generate (80% of Net)
$14,624	−	$11,242	=	$3,382		$64,946
$28,096	−	$17,798	=	$10,298		$190,647
$40,992	−	$22,177	=	$18,815	◄	$343,847
$53,504	−	$25,252	=	$28,252		$512,821
$65,920	−	$27,343	=	$38,577		$697,144
$77,568	−	$27,343	=	$50,225		$904,063

*80% of net, as determined in step 1.

Retirement Income Needed

Table 12-9 calculates the post-retirement income needed by future retirees based on what their pre-retirement income is, and also the total assets they will need to have saved to provide that income. Step 1 of Table 12-9 assumes that the annual post-retirement income needed is 80% of net pre-retirement income (gross pre-retirement income minus savings). Step 2 of Table 12-9 goes on to show how much of the required post-retirement income is forecast to come from Social Security benefits, with any annual income deficit necessarily being generated by the retirement portfolio. Finally, the total amount of assets needed in the retirement portfolio to generate the annual income deficit is calculated.[6]

Determining A Savings Rate

The study suggests adoption of the national savings rate guidelines shown in Table 12-10, which shows suggested savings rates for prospective retirees delineated by age, gross income, and the amount already saved. To determine the savings rate suggested for an individual's situation, locate the guideline savings rate in the row with their current age and income. Then, deduct the amount shown in column 4 for each $10,000 of retirement assets already accumulated.

For example, a 35 year old with no current savings and gross income of $40,000 per year needs to save 12.2 percent of his gross income. If, however, he had already saved $10,000, he could reduce the savings rate by 0.86 percent of his gross income (12.2%−0.86%), or 11.34 percent.

When the savings guidelines in Table 12-10 were used, 90 percent of the Monte Carlo simulations in the study resulted in total savings at age 65 capable of generating the retirement income deficit not covered by Social Security benefits.

Benchmarks for Checking Progress

Table 12-11 provides benchmarks against which future retirees can check their progress. The table shows the projected capital an individual should have accumulated depending on their current age and income level, and assumes that they had started saving at age 35 and followed the savings guidelines shown in Table 12-10.

The projections in Table 12-11 show the expected capital appreciated for the 90 percent confidence level, and should be considered the minimum someone should have accumulated (due to poor investment performance). In other words, 90 percent of the Monte Carlo simulations in the study resulted in a larger capital accumulation than is shown in Table 12-11, and ten percent resulted in a smaller capital accumulation than is shown.

For example, for 50 year old savers who started saving at age 35 and now have $80,000 in gross income, 90% will have saved more than $198,497 and 10 percent will have saved less than $198,497.

Limitations of Monte Carlo Simulation

While Monte Carlo simulation has its fair share of benefits, as with other mathematical models, it also has its limitations. Simulations can lead to misleading results if inappropriate inputs are entered into the model. As discussed earlier, in order to run simulations, the process begins with the entering of asset class returns, standard deviations, and correlations. When cash flows are added to the analysis they may be adjusted for inflation, which can present another possible problem if an unrealistic inflation rate is assumed. The burden clearly lies on the individual who sets up the simulation. The individual should be prepared to make the necessary adjustments if the results that are generated seem out of line.

Table 12-10: Savings Rates for Different Gross Income Levels with 80% Replacement of Net Pre-Retirement Income (90% probability of success)

Age	Gross Income ($)	Guideline Savings Rate (%)	Deductions for Each $10,000 of Current Savings(%)
25	20000	5.8	1.60
	40000	8.2	0.78
	60000	10.0	0.55
	80000	11.2	0.40
30	20000	7.0	1.65
	40000	10.0	0.79
	60000	11.8	0.54
	80000	13.6	0.42
35	20000	8.6	1.75
	40000	12.2	0.86
	60000	14.6	0.55
	80000	16.4	0.43
	100000	17.6	0.34
40	20000	10.2	1.67
	40000	14.8	0.86
	60000	17.6	0.57
	80000	19.8	0.42
	100000	21.4	0.35
45	20000	12.4	1.76
	40000	18.0	0.90
	60000	21.4	0.59
	80000	24.0	0.45
	100000	26.2	0.37
	120000	28.2	0.31
50	20000	15.0	1.87
	40000	22.0	0.97
	60000	26.2	0.64
	80000	29.8	0.48
	100000	32.2	0.39
	120000	35.0	0.33
55	20000	18.6	2.11
	40000	27.2	1.04
	60000	32.6	0.71
	80000	36.6	0.53
	100000	40.2	0.43
	120000	43.6	0.36
60	20000	23.8	2.39
	40000	34.4	1.23
	60000	41.2	0.81
	80000	46.8	0.61
	100000	51.4	0.50
	120000	55.4	0.41

Table 12-11: Minimum Projected Accumulated Wealth by Current Age for Various Income Levels with 80% Replacement of Net Pre-Retirement Income

Age	Income $20,000	$40,000	$60,000	$80,000	$100,000	$120,000
35	0	0	0	0	0	0
40	7,692	21,824	39,176	58,674	78,710	103,038
45	16,005	45,408	81,512	122,082	163,768	214,387
50	26,023	73,831	132,533	198,497	266,277	348,581
55	37,434	106,207	190,650	285,540	383,042	501,436
60	51,562	146,292	262,607	393,310	527,612	690,691
65	68,650	194,775	349,637	523,658	702,467	919,594

Some critics contend that Monte Carlo simulations cannot be taken too seriously because they make use of random numbers. They question how accurate Monte Carlo is in replicating the actual behavior of the capital markets. While Monte Carlo does a fine job of illustrating the wide variance of possible results and the probability of success or failure over thousands of "different market environments," it may not consider the consequences based on the "applicable market environment" that exists over an investor's lifetime. Investors rarely spend exactly what they say they will spend when they retire. Tax laws are highly unpredictable as well. Critics argue that there are a number of unknown factors that cannot truly be accounted for.

Conclusion

Monte Carlo simulation has been available for many years, but the forecasting method only recently grew in popularity and application due primarily to high-powered computers that are able to quickly handle the required calculations. One thing to keep in mind is that projecting the future is noeasy task—the future is unknowable. While Monte Carlo simulation can produce possible scenarios of the future and help investors make better decisions, it does not help investors make perfect decisions. It would be wise to use this type of simulation in conjunction with other forecasting techniques and compare the results. But there is an important point to remember when contemplating and choosing among the various simulation-based products. The quality of the forecast is directly related to the quality of the technique and the inputs used. ▥

Endnotes

[1] Roger Ibbotson, James Xiong, Robert P. Kreitler, Charles F. Kreitler, and Peng Chen. "National Savings Rate Guidelines for Individuals," *Journal of Financial Planning*, April 2007, pp. 50–61. To read the full research paper, go to: global.morningstar.com/US/IbbotsonResearch.

[2] Based on the AON Consulting/Georgia State University 2004 Retirement Income Replacement Ratio Study.

[3] Forecasted inflation of 2.5% was used, as assumed by Ibbotson Associates, December 2005.

[4] Age 65 was chosen to match the commonly accepted retirement age. Individuals should strongly consider delaying taking Social Security until they become eligible to receive the full benefit (currently age 67).

[5] Mortality rates calculated as the average of female and male mortality rates from the Society of Actuaries' 2000 mortality rate table.

[6] Total amount of assets needed in the retirement portfolio was calculated as the purchase price of an inflation-indexed lifetime fixed-payout annuity that would generate an annual income equal to annual income deficit (post-retirement income needed minus estimated Social Security benefits).

Chapter 13

Stock Market Returns From 1815–1925

Introduction

Studies on the long-horizon predictability of stock returns, by necessity, require a database of return information that dates as far back as possible. Ibbotson Associates® has been the leading producer and supplier of a broad set of historical returns on asset classes dating back to 1926. Researchers interested in the dynamics of the U.S. capital markets over earlier decades have had to rely upon indices of uneven quality. Roger Ibbotson and William N. Goetzmann, professors of finance, and Liang Peng, then a Ph.D. candidate in finance, all at Yale School of Management, have assembled a New York Stock Exchange database of annual returns for the periods prior to 1926. The first part of this chapter covers the sources and construction of this annual return database extending back to 1815.

The second part of this chapter introduces a new set of monthly real stock market total returns developed by Paul Kaplan, now director of European quantitative research at Morningstar. Kaplan uses these new returns to demonstrate that the severity of the financial crisis of 2008 was not unique, but was merely the latest chapter in a long history of market meltdowns.

While we firmly believe that a 1926 starting date was approximately when quality financial data came into existence, our hope is that the continuing development of these data sets will allow modern researchers of pre-1926 stock returns, along with future researchers, to test a broad range of hypotheses about the U.S. capital markets as well as open up new areas for more accurate analysis.

Data Sources and Collection Methods of the Ibbotson/Goetzmann/Peng Annual Data Series
Share Price Collection

End-of-month equity prices for companies listed on the New York Stock Exchange (NYSE) were hand-collected from three different sources published over the period January 1815 to December 1870. For the time period 1871 through 1925, end-of-month NYSE stock prices were collected from the major New York newspapers.

The New York Shipping List, later called *The New York Shipping and Commercial,* served as the "official" source for NYSE share price collection up until the early 1850s. In the mid-1850s, *The New York Shipping List* reported prices for fewer and fewer stocks. This led to the collection of price quotes from *The New York Herald* and *The New York Times.* While neither claimed to be the official list for the NYSE, the number of securities quoted by each far exceeded the number quoted by *The New York Shipping List.*

It is important to note that in instances where no transaction took place in December, the latest bid and ask prices were averaged to obtain a year-end price. In total, at least two prices from 664 companies were collected. From a low number of eight firms in 1815, the number of firms in the index reached a high point in May of 1883 with 114 listed firms.

One interesting observation was the fact that share prices for much of the period of analysis remained around 100. Graph 13-1 illustrates this point. The graph shows that the typical price of a share of stock was around 100. The distribution of stock prices is significantly skewed to the left with only a few trading above 200. Such a distribution suggests that management maintained a ceiling on stock prices by paying out most of earnings as dividends. No reports of stock splits over the period of data were discovered.

Graph 13-1: Distribution of Raw Stock Prices

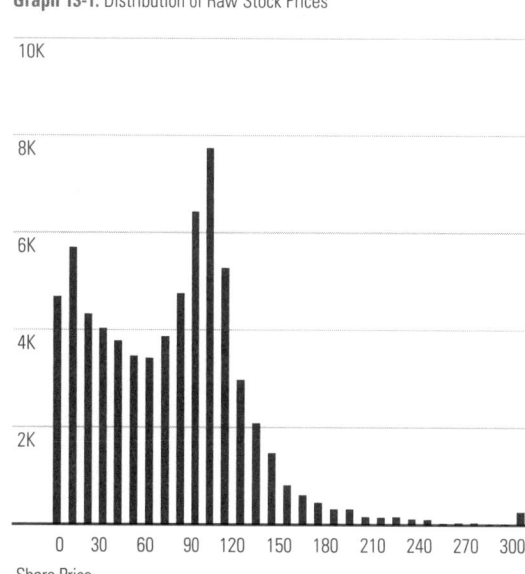

Share Price

Data from 1815–1925.

Dividend Collection

Dividend data was collected for the period 1825–1870 by identifying the semi-annual dividend announcements for equity securities as reported in *The New York Commercial, The Banker's Magazine, The New York Times,* and *The New York Herald.* From 1871 to 1925, aggregate dividend data from the Alfred Cowles[1] series was used. Whether or not the above publications reported dividends for all NYSE stocks is unknown. As a result, there is no way of knowing whether missing dividends meant that they were not paid or possibly not reported. Dividend records were collected for more than 500 stocks in the sample, and most stocks paid dividends semiannually.

In order to estimate the income return for each year, two approaches were implemented. The first approach, the low dividend return estimate, consisted of the summation of all of the dividends paid in a given year by firms whose prices were observed in the preceding year. This number is then divided by the sum of the last available preceding year prices for those firms. The second approach, the high dividend return estimate, focused solely on firms that paid regular dividends and for which price data was collected. The sample is restricted to firms that have two years of dividend payments (four semiannual dividends) and for which there was a price observation. Using the second approach, dividend yields tend to be quite high by modern standards.

It is important to note that when both a high and a low income return series were present, the average was computed. This holds true for the summary statistics table in this chapter as well as the graphs/tables presented throughout. Also, due to missing income return data for the year 1868, an average of the previous forty-three years was computed and used.

Price Index Estimation
Index Calculation Concerns

When attempting to construct an index without having market capitalization data readily available, one is left with one of two options: an equal-weighted index or a price-weighted index. One key concern with an equal-weighted index is the effect of a bid-ask bounce. Take for example an illiquid stock that trades at either $1.00 or $2.00 per share. When it rises in price from $1.00 to $2.00, it goes up by 100 percent. When it decreases in price from $2.00 to $1.00, it drops by 50 percent. Equally weighting these returns can produce a substantial upward bias. This led us to the construction of a price-weighted index.

Calculation of the Price-Weighted Index

The procedure used for calculating the price-weighted index is rather simple. For each month, returns are calculated for all stocks that trade in two consecutive periods. These returns are weighted by the price at the beginning of the two periods.

The return of the price-weighted index closely approximates the return to a "buy and hold" portfolio over the period. Buy and hold portfolios are not sensitive to bid-ask bounce bias. We believe that the price-weighted index does a fairly good job of avoiding such an upward bias.

It was found that companies were rather concentrated into specific industries. In 1815, the index was about evenly split between banks and insurance companies. Banks, transportation firms (primarily canals and railroads), and insurance companies made up the index by the 1850s. By the end of the sample period, the index was dominated by transport companies and other industrials.

A Look at the Historical Results

It is important to note that there are a few missing months of data that create gaps in the analysis. The NYSE was closed from July 1914 to December 1914 due to World War I. This is obviously an institutional gap. There are additional gaps. We are missing returns for 1822, part of 1848 and 1849, parts of 1866, all of 1867 and January 1868. We do not know whether the late 1860's missing records are due to the Civil War, but the NYSE was certainly open at that time—among other things, it was the era of heated speculation and stock price manipulation by legendary financiers Gould, Fisk and Drew. The number of available security records was quite lower after 1871. A change in the range of coverage by the financial press is the likely culprit for this. Further data collection efforts hopefully will allow these missing records to be filled in.

Table 13-1 illustrates summary statistics of annual returns of large company stocks for three different time periods. Note that the three different periods cover the pre-1926 data, the familiar 1926 to 2011 time period, and a combination of the two.

Price Returns

It is interesting to note that the price-weighted index in Table 13-1 has an annual geometric capital appreciation return from 1825 through 1925 of 1.3 percent. This number is significantly lower when compared to the 5.5 percent

Table 13-1: Large Company Stocks
Summary Statistics of Annual Returns

1825–1925	Geometric Mean (%)	Arithmetic Mean (%)	Standard Deviation (%)
Total Return	7.3%	8.4%	16.3%
Income Return	5.9	5.9	1.9
Capital Appreciation	1.3	2.5	16.1
1926–2011			
Total Return	9.8%	11.8%	20.3%
Income Return	4.1	4.1	1.6
Capital Appreciation	5.5	7.4	19.6
1825–2011			
Total Return	8.4%	10.0%	18.3%
Income Return	5.0	5.1	2.0
Capital Appreciation	3.2	4.8	17.9

annual capital appreciation return experienced by large company stocks over the period 1926 through 2011. This once again alludes to the suggestion that dividend policies have evolved over the past two centuries, and that management of old most likely paid out earnings and kept their stock prices lower. In today's financial world, capital appreciation is accepted as a substitute for dividend payments.

The rise in capital appreciation returns over the years is more evident when viewing returns on a twenty-year rolling period basis, as Graph 13-2 demonstrates.

Income Returns

Table 13-1 also illustrates the summary statistics for the annual income return series. The higher income return of 5.9 percent in the earlier period, and the fact the many stocks traded near par, once again suggest that most companies paid out a large share of their profits rather than retaining them.

Graph 13-3 shows the annual income returns for the period 1825 to 2011. In fact, when looking at the time distribution of dividend changes over the new time period, dividend decreases were only slightly less common than increases, suggesting that managers may have been less averse to cutting dividends than they are today. Perhaps in the pre-income tax environment of the nineteenth century, investors had a preference for income returns, as opposed to capital appreciation.

Graph 13-2: Large Company Stocks
20-Year Rolling Capital Appreciation Returns (%)

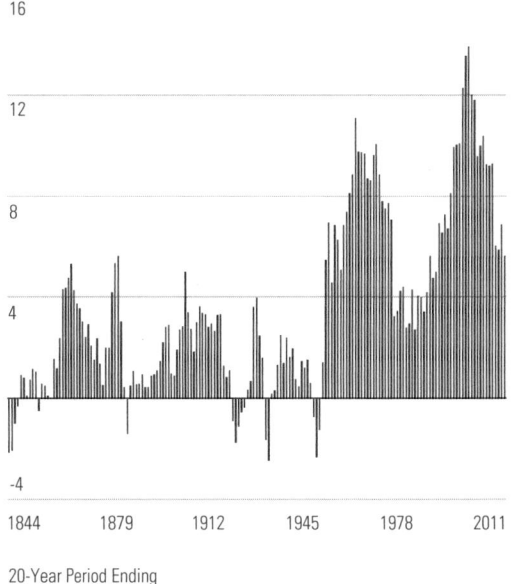

20-Year Period Ending

Data from 1844–2011.

Graph 13-3: Large Company Stocks Annual Income Returns (%)

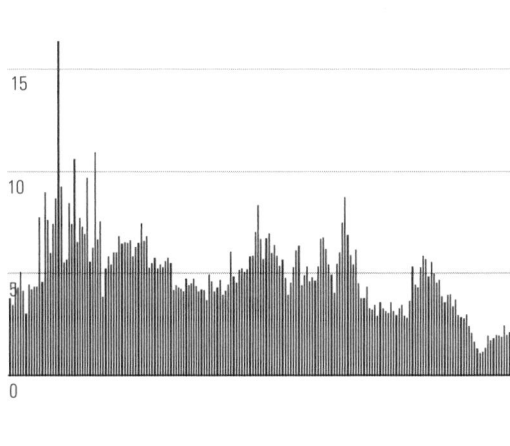

20-Year Period Ending

Data from 1825–2011.

Total Returns

Looking once again at the summary statistics in Table 13-1, it is interesting to notice that the annual geometric total return for large company stocks from 1825 to 1925 was 7.3 percent. This is quite low when compared to the 9.8 percent annual geometric total return of the commonly used

Table 13-2: Large Company Stocks Annual Capital Appreciation, Income, and Total Returns (%)

Year	Cap. App.	Avg. Income Ret.	Total Return	Year	Cap. App.	Avg. Income Ret.	Total Return
1815	-6.65	—	—	1871	3.34	5.86	9.20
1816	-1.93	—	—	1872	0.50	6.33	6.83
1817	19.43	—	—	1873	-17.70	6.51	-11.19
1818	-3.76	—	—	1874	-5.77	7.47	1.70
1819	-8.82	—	—	1875	-4.72	6.61	1.89
1820	9.59	—	—	1876	-13.31	6.86	-6.45
1821	3.34	—	—	1877	1.74	5.31	7.05
1822	-12.85	—	—	1878	10.50	5.54	16.04
1823	5.29	—	—	1879	51.31	5.80	57.10
1824	3.70	—	—	1880	19.83	5.28	25.12
1825	-12.99	3.81	-9.18	1881	1.88	5.48	7.36
1826	-1.22	3.48	2.27	1882	-9.54	5.32	-4.22
1827	-6.24	4.57	-1.67	1883	-15.04	5.65	-9.39
1828	-17.95	4.34	-13.61	1884	-24.28	5.81	-18.47
1829	10.33	5.10	15.43	1885	45.32	5.53	50.85
1830	27.31	4.20	31.51	1886	12.46	4.23	16.69
1831	-17.05	3.07	-13.98	1887	-12.13	4.43	-7.70
1832	8.60	4.48	13.08	1888	2.09	4.36	6.45
1833	-6.09	4.24	-1.85	1889	4.49	4.28	8.77
1834	8.84	4.40	13.24	1890	-10.72	4.14	-6.59
1835	-6.74	4.38	-2.36	1891	2.95	4.78	7.74
1836	4.33	7.76	12.09	1892	10.35	4.44	14.79
1837	-18.02	4.60	-13.43	1893	-16.86	4.54	-12.33
1838	12.20	8.99	21.19	1894	-2.82	4.76	1.94
1839	-26.62	7.64	-18.97	1895	2.14	4.42	6.56
1840	3.01	6.03	9.04	1896	0.69	4.17	4.86
1841	-23.52	7.46	-16.06	1897	14.15	4.27	18.41
1842	2.34	8.71	11.05	1898	12.17	4.21	16.38
1843	39.16	16.40	55.56	1899	4.17	3.72	7.89
1844	2.81	9.29	12.11	1900	17.99	4.98	22.97
1845	-11.61	5.56	-6.05	1901	24.60	4.66	29.26
1846	23.21	5.70	28.91	1902	5.29	4.15	9.44
1847	7.65	8.48	16.13	1903	-12.88	4.35	-8.53
1848	5.28	7.45	12.72	1904	14.94	4.72	19.66
1849	7.80	10.64	18.44	1905	6.67	4.00	10.67
1850	10.48	6.57	17.05	1906	-1.09	4.19	3.10
1851	-5.78	7.74	1.95	1907	-26.26	4.47	-21.79
1852	18.07	7.30	25.38	1908	28.47	6.09	34.56
1853	-8.15	6.94	-1.20	1909	18.12	4.87	22.99
1854	-20.34	9.71	-10.63	1910	-15.50	4.56	-10.94
1855	16.26	5.60	21.86	1911	2.17	5.19	7.37
1856	2.49	6.28	8.77	1912	0.03	5.27	5.30
1857	-24.22	10.99	-13.23	1913	-14.44	5.12	-9.32
1858	10.38	6.68	17.07	1914	-8.47	5.22	-3.25
1859	-0.62	7.56	6.94	1915	15.88	5.85	21.73
1860	-3.93	3.88	-0.06	1916	1.29	5.91	7.19
1861	-3.73	5.27	1.54	1917	-23.48	7.04	-16.44
1862	49.15	5.85	55.00	1918	2.88	8.38	11.27
1863	40.95	5.46	46.41	1919	9.38	6.71	16.09
1864	10.53	6.07	16.61	1920	-20.74	5.72	-15.02
1865	-1.33	6.08	4.75	1921	4.26	6.75	11.02
1866	0.46	6.85	7.31	1922	19.74	6.98	26.72
1867	-2.61	6.48	3.87	1923	-2.13	6.04	3.90
1868	1.52	6.56	8.08	1924	19.34	6.43	25.77
1869	-2.85	6.53	3.67	1925	23.22	5.91	29.12
1870	-1.44	6.66	5.22				

1926 to 2011 time period. For the entire period, the total return seems to fall somewhere in between.

The standard deviation of total returns is also slightly lower for the 1825 to 1925 time period (16.3 percent) versus the time period of 1926 to 2011 (20.3 percent).

Table 13-2 shows year-by-year capital appreciation, average income, and total returns from 1815 to 1925 of large company stocks. Table 13-3 shows the growth of a dollar invested in large company stocks over the period from the end of 1824 to the end of 2011.

One and a Quarter Centuries of Stock Market Drawdowns

Those familiar with the history of U.S. capital market history as documented in this book may have found former Federal Reserve Chairman Alan Greenspan characterization of the financial crisis of 2008 as a "once-in-a-century credit tsunami" quite surprising. A more appropriate statement may have been the one made by Leslie Rahl (founder of Capital Market Risk Advisors) more than year before the crisis when she said, "We seem to have a once-in-a-lifetime crisis every three or four years."[2] The contrast between Mr. Greenspan and Ms. Rahl's perspectives was the inspiration for an article in Morningstar Advisor magazine[3] on the history of market meltdowns titled "Déja Vu All Over Again."[4] In that article, Paul Kaplan illustrated the frequency and severity of the major drawdown for various countries using time series of stock market total returns. For the U.S., Kaplan naturally used the series on the S&P 500 that appear in the *Ibbotson® SBBI®* *Yearbooks*. The results of the study clearly demonstrate that the severity of the financial crisis of 2008 was not unique, but was merely the latest chapter in a long history of market meltdowns.

In 2009, a team of researchers at Morningstar expanded the analysis into a complete study on global equity market history as a contribution to the CFA Institute's book on the global history of market crashes.[5] In this study, the research team uses monthly *real* total returns[6] that go back into history as far as was possible with reasonably reliable data. The benefit of using real returns is to make meaningful return comparisons, as our study spans such a long period of time. The benefit of going further back in history is, of course, to give a longer-term and more robust historical perspective on market crashes, in terms of frequency, length, and magnitude.

Table 13-3: Large Company Stocks
Annual Capital Appreciation and Total Return Index Values

Year	Cap App	Total Return	Year	Cap App	Total Return	Year	Cap App	Total Return	Year	Cap App	Total Return
1824	1.00	1.00	1874	1.25	29.70	1924	3.10	926.09	1974	20.51	63,640.07
1825	0.87	0.91	1875	1.19	30.26	1925	3.82	1,195.79	1975	26.99	87,332.34
1826	0.86	0.93	1876	1.03	28.31	1926	4.04	1,334.79	1976	32.15	108,228.41
1827	0.81	0.91	1877	1.05	30.31	1927	5.28	1,835.18	1977	28.45	100,481.44
1828	0.66	0.79	1878	1.16	35.17	1928	7.29	2,635.47	1978	28.76	107,084.09
1829	0.73	0.91	1879	1.75	55.25	1929	6.42	2,413.68	1979	32.30	127,012.00
1830	0.93	1.20	1880	2.10	69.13	1930	4.59	1,812.75	1980	40.62	168,295.91
1831	0.77	1.03	1881	2.14	74.22	1931	2.43	1,027.17	1981	36.67	160,010.27
1832	0.84	1.16	1882	1.93	71.09	1932	2.06	943.01	1982	42.08	194,486.57
1833	0.79	1.14	1883	1.64	64.41	1933	3.02	1,452.15	1983	49.35	238,353.85
1834	0.86	1.29	1884	1.24	52.51	1934	2.84	1,431.20	1984	50.04	253,307.59
1835	0.80	1.26	1885	1.81	79.21	1935	4.02	2,113.43	1985	63.22	333,674.01
1836	0.83	1.42	1886	2.03	92.44	1936	5.14	2,830.34	1986	72.46	395,954.57
1837	0.68	1.23	1887	1.79	85.32	1937	3.16	1,838.97	1987	73.93	416,744.68
1838	0.77	1.49	1888	1.82	90.83	1938	3.95	2,411.28	1988	83.09	485,958.80
1839	0.56	1.20	1889	1.91	98.79	1939	3.74	2,401.38	1989	105.74	639,940.79
1840	0.58	1.31	1890	1.70	92.28	1940	3.17	2,166.42	1990	98.80	620,075.56
1841	0.44	1.10	1891	1.75	99.42	1941	2.60	1,915.28	1991	124.79	808,986.73
1842	0.45	1.22	1892	1.93	114.12	1942	2.92	2,304.86	1992	130.37	870,626.14
1843	0.63	1.90	1893	1.61	100.06	1943	3.49	2,901.81	1993	139.56	958,373.95
1844	0.65	2.14	1894	1.56	102.00	1944	3.97	3,474.99	1994	137.41	971,028.89
1845	0.57	2.01	1895	1.60	108.69	1945	5.19	4,741.15	1995	184.29	1,335,919.98
1846	0.71	2.59	1896	1.61	113.97	1946	4.58	4,358.47	1996	221.63	1,642,650.61
1847	0.76	3.00	1897	1.83	134.96	1947	4.58	4,607.25	1997	290.35	2,190,694.23
1848	0.80	3.39	1898	2.06	157.07	1948	4.55	4,860.71	1998	367.79	2,816,762.54
1849	0.86	4.01	1899	2.14	169.45	1949	5.01	5,774.16	1999	439.60	3,409,452.85
1850	0.95	4.69	1900	2.53	208.38	1950	6.11	7,605.31	2000	395.03	3,099,043.37
1851	0.90	4.78	1901	3.15	269.34	1951	7.11	9,431.83	2001	343.51	2,730,697.03
1852	1.06	6.00	1902	3.32	294.77	1952	7.95	11,164.22	2002	263.24	2,127,199.22
1853	0.97	5.93	1903	2.89	269.63	1953	7.42	11,053.79	2003	332.69	2,737,376.21
1854	0.78	5.30	1904	3.32	322.65	1954	10.77	16,870.69	2004	362.61	3,035,259.22
1855	0.90	6.45	1905	3.54	357.07	1955	13.61	22,195.54	2005	373.49	3,184,350.45
1856	0.92	7.02	1906	3.51	368.14	1956	13.96	23,650.66	2006	424.36	3,687,295.42
1857	0.70	6.09	1907	2.58	287.92	1957	11.97	21,100.54	2007	439.34	3,889,874.59
1858	0.77	7.13	1908	3.32	387.42	1958	16.52	30,250.51	2008	270.26	2,450,705.05
1859	0.77	7.63	1909	3.92	476.49	1959	17.92	33,866.99	2009	333.64	3,099,271.74
1860	0.74	7.62	1910	3.31	424.37	1960	17.39	34,026.04	2010	376.28	3,566,126.82
1861	0.71	7.74	1911	3.39	455.63	1961	21.41	43,175.12	2011	376.27	3,641,435.14
1862	1.06	12.00	1912	3.39	479.76	1962	18.88	39,406.58			
1863	1.49	17.56	1913	2.90	435.04	1963	22.45	48,391.75			
1864	1.65	20.48	1914	2.65	420.90	1964	25.36	56,368.02			
1865	1.63	21.45	1915	3.07	512.38	1965	27.66	63,386.42			
1866	1.64	23.02	1916	3.11	549.24	1966	24.03	57,007.67			
1867	1.59	23.91	1917	2.38	458.96	1967	28.86	70,675.64			
1868	1.62	25.84	1918	2.45	510.66	1968	31.08	78,493.36			
1869	1.57	26.79	1919	2.68	592.84	1969	27.54	71,817.85			
1870	1.55	28.19	1920	2.13	503.78	1970	27.57	74,587.78			
1871	1.60	30.78	1921	2.22	559.27	1971	30.50	85,254.09			
1872	1.61	32.89	1922	2.65	708.68	1972	35.32	101,448.06			
1873	1.32	29.21	1923	2.60	736.34	1973	29.19	86,546.56			

Peak		Trough		Decline (%)	Recovery		Event(s)
Aug.	1929	May	1932	79.00	Nov	1936	Crash of 1929, 1st part of Great Depression
Aug.	2000	Feb.	2009	54.00	TBD.	TBD	Dot-com bubble burst (00–02), Crash of 07–09
Dec.	1972	Sep.	1974	51.86	Dec.	1984	Inflationary Bear Market, Vietnam, Watergate
Jun.	1911	Dec.	1920	50.96	Dec.	1924	World War I, Postwar Auto Bubble Burst
Feb.	1937	Mar.	1938	49.93	Feb.	1945	2nd part of Great Depression, World War II
May	1946	Feb.	1948	37.18	Oct.	1950	Postwar Bear Market
Nov.	1968	Jun.	1970	35.46	Nov.	1972	Start of Inflationary Bear Market
Jan.	1906	Oct.	1907	34.22	Aug.	1908	Panic of 1907
Apr.	1899	Jun.	1900	30.41	Mar.	1901	Cornering of Northern Pacific Stock
Aug.	1987	Nov.	1987	30.16	Jul.	1989	Black Monday–Oct. 19, 1987
Oct.	1892	Jul.	1893	27.32	Mar.	1894	Silver Agitation
Dec.	1961	Jun.	1962	22.80	Apr.	1963	Height of the Cold War, Cuban Missile Crisis
Nov.	1886	Mar.	1888	22.04	May.	1889	Depression, Railroad strikes
Apr.	1903	Sep.	1903	21.67	Nov.	1904	Rich Man's Panic
Aug.	1897	Mar.	1898	21.13	Aug.	1898	Outbreak of Boer War
Sep.	1909	Jul.	1910	20.55	Feb.	1911	Enforcement of the Sherman Anti-Trust Act
May	1890	Jul.	1891	20.11	Feb.	1892	Baring Brothers Crisis

To complete the study, the research team needed to find monthly data from before 1925 on both stock returns and inflation, and calculate real returns. Since there was no such return series in existence, they had to create one out of readable available data.

Professor Robert Shiller of Yale posts a monthly history of U.S. stock market returns and inflation on his web site that goes back to 1871. Unfortunately, Professor Shiller's stock data is based on monthly average prices rather than month-end prices. So the research team could use his inflation data, but not his stock market data. Separately, Roger Ibbotson and some colleagues created an annual price and total return series for the NYSE that goes back to 1825.[7] However, annual returns are at too low a frequency to measure the largest drawdowns of the period, such as the large drop in the stock market during the panic of 1907. Fortunately, there is a book that contains daily price data on the Dow Jones Averages going back to 1885.[8] The team estimated the monthly price returns in the broader NYSE price index from the monthly price returns on the Dow Jones Averages and then interpolated the total returns by assuming that the level dividends remained constant during each year.

The Morningstar/Ibbotson team produced a time series of real total returns for the U.S. stock markets that runs from 1871 through the end of 2011. While for first 15 years there are only have annual returns, as a result of this research, we now have 126 years of monthly total real returns.

Truth in Numbers

The significance of this data is in the lessons that we can learn from it. Over the entire 141 year period, the Real US Stock Market Index grew from $1 to $7,136.52 in 1870 dollars. This is a compound annual real total return of 6.5%, almost the same as the post-1925 period. However, as Graph 13-4 shows, it was a very bumpy ride with a number of major drawdowns, some of which can be linked with specific economic and political events as the chart shows.

Graph 13-4 shows the growth of $1 invested in the U.S. stock market at the end of 1869 through December 2011 in real terms, along with a line that shows the highest level that the index had achieved as of that date (shown in burgundy). Whenever this line is above the cumulative value line (shown in gray), the index was amid a decline relative to its most recent peak. The bigger the gap, the more severe the decline; the wider the gap, the longer the time until the index returned to its peak. Wherever this line coincides with the index line, the index was climbing to a new peak.

Table 13-4 lists all of the drawdowns that exceeded 20%. In total, there were 17 such declines, including the present one from which we have yet to recover. Not surprisingly, the largest of all market declines started just before the Crash of 1929 and did not recover until toward the end of 1936. The U.S. stock market lost 79% of its real value in less than three years, and took more than five years to recover. What may be more sobering, however, is that not only are we currently in the second greatest decline, but it started nearly a decade ago. The combined effect of the crash of the Internet bubble in 2000 and the financial crisis of 2008 caused the U.S. stock market to lose 54% of its real value from August of 2000 to February 2009. How long it will take to recover from that, and when our next crisis will occur is anyone's guess.

The history of stock market drawdowns presented here shows that investing in stocks can be very risky business, and that the current crisis is hardly a "once-in-a-century" event. But to more than just state the obvious, we should use this data to better gauge the potential risks and long-term rewards of investing in risky assets such as stocks.

Graph 13-4: Largest Declines in U.S. Stock Market History

Index (Year-End 1869 = $1.00)

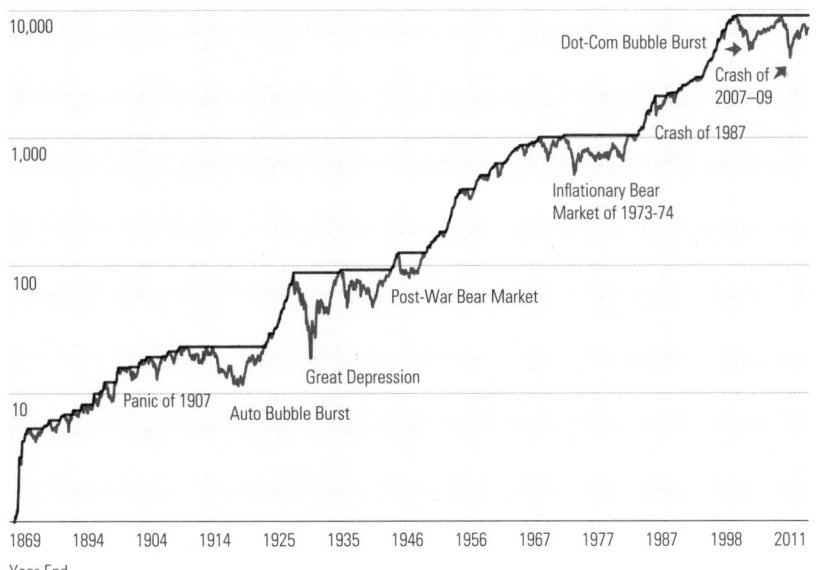

Year-End

Data from 1870–2011.

Endnotes

[1] Cowles, Alfred *Common Stock Indices*. Principia Press, Bloomington., 1939

[2] Christopher Wright, "Tail Tales," *CFA Institute Magazine*, March/April 2007.

[3] Morningstar Advisor magazine is a free publication for advisors. To subscribe to *Morningstar Advisor* magazine, go the MorningstarAdvisor.com or call 800-384-4000.

[4] Kaplan, Paul D. "Déjà All Over Again," *Morningstar Advisor*, February/April 2009.

[5] Kaplan, Paul D., Thomas Idzorek, Michele Gambera, Katsunari Yamaguchi, James Xiong, and David M. Blanchett. 2009. "The History and Economics of Stock Market Crashes." In Siegel, Laurence B., ed., Insights into the Global Financial Crisis, CFA Institute, Charlottesville, Va.

[6] That is, returns that include the reinvestment of dividends and are adjusted for inflation.

[7] Goetzmann, William N., Roger G. Ibbotson, and Liang Peng, "A New Historical Database for the NYSE 1815 to 1925: Performance and Predictability," Journal of Financial Markets, December 2000.

[8] Pierce, Phyllis, ed. 1982. The Dow Jones Averages 1885-1980. Dow Jones Irwin, Homewood, IL

Traditional measures of risk, such as standard deviation, can underestimate the risk associated with those events that are many standard deviations away from the mean (i.e. on the tails of a distribution). We suggest that these traditional measures of risk are supplemented with measures that better capture the "fat-tailed" nature of the historical returns and drawdowns as presented here. A complete discussion of incorporating fat-tailed distributions into risk measures is found in Chapter 11, "Using Historical Data in Forecasting and Optimization".

Conclusion

Data collection efforts have yielded a comprehensive database of New York Stock Exchange security prices for nearly the entire history of the NYSE. The goal of these studies is to assemble an NYSE database for the period prior to 1926. The 1926 starting date was approximately when high-quality financial data came into existence. However, with a pre-1926 database assembled, researchers can expand their analysis back to the early 1800s. It is our hope that the long time series outlined in this chapter will lead to a better understanding of how the U.S. stock market evolved from an emerging market at the turn of the eighteenth century to the largest capital market in the world today. ▮▮

Chapter 14
International Equity Investing

Discussion of International Investing

With the disappearance of trade barriers and the opening of foreign markets, the level of global business has increased considerably. Communism and other systems have essentially been discredited, leading to increasingly open markets in nations around the world. Investing internationally literally offers a world of opportunity. The opportunities available today are growing rapidly, encouraged by open markets and the accelerating economies of many nations. The evidence in favor of taking a global approach to investing, and the possible rewards an investor can reap, is plentiful. However, significant risks are present as well—risks that apply strictly to the international marketplace. In this chapter, we consider both the rewards and the risks associated with international investments.

Construction of the International Indices

Our analysis of international investing uses the indices created by Morgan Stanley Capital International, Inc. (MSCI®). The MSCI indices are designed to measure the performance of the developed and emerging stock markets of such countries and regions as the United States, Europe, Canada, Australasia, and the Far East, and that of industry groups. MSCI indices are designed to reflect the performance of the entire range of stocks available to investors in each local market.

From January 1970 to October 2001, inclusion in the MSCI indices was based upon market capitalization. Stocks chosen for the indices were required to have a target market representation of 60 percent of total market capitalization. MSCI has enhanced its index construction methodology by free float-adjusting constituents' index weights and increasing the target market representation. Target market representation is increased from 60 percent of total market capitalization to 85 percent of free float-adjusted market capitalization within each industry group, within each country. MSCI defines the free float of a security as the proportion of shares outstanding that is deemed to be available for purchase in the public equity markets by international investors.

The international stock series presented throughout this chapter is represented by the MSCI EAFE® (Europe, Australasia, Far East) index. The MSCI EAFE index consists of 22 developed equity markets outside of North America.

Benefits of Investing Internationally

The arguments for adding international investments to an investment portfolio can be rather powerful. Examples include participation in the more than 50 percent of the world's investable assets that exist outside the U.S., growth potential, diversification, and the improvement of the risk/reward trade-off.

Investment Opportunities

An investor who chooses to ignore investment opportunities outside of the United States is missing out on over half of the investable developed stock market opportunities in the world. Graph 14-1 presents the relative size of international and domestic markets as of year-end 2011. The international markets represented in the graph constitute countries having developed economies. In 2011, the total developed world stock market capitalization was $22.4 trillion, with $10.6 trillion representing international stock market capitalization.[1]

Graph 14-1: World Stock Market Capitalization: $22.4 Trillion

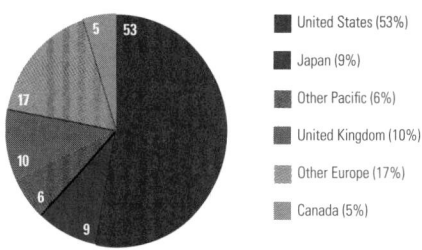

- United States (53%)
- Japan (9%)
- Other Pacific (6%)
- United Kingdom (10%)
- Other Europe (17%)
- Canada (5%)

Data as of year-end 2011. Note: Underlying data expressed in U.S. dollars.

Although the domestic (U.S.) stock market continues to account for the largest part of world stock market capitalization, an investor who chooses to exclude international investments from his or her portfolio is ignoring over half of the world's investable assets.

Many of the possible investment choices available to you outside the United States are with companies you already know and whose products you may in fact be using on a daily basis. From the car you drive to the technology you use, many of these products are produced by companies that call other countries home. Some examples include:

Graph 14-2: Global Investing
Index (Year-End 1969 = $1.00)

$100.0 ──	U.S. Large Company Stocks ($50.70 YE11)
	International Stocks ($46.13 YE11)
──	Long-Term Government Bonds ($38.62 YE11)
──	Treasury Bills ($9.18 YE11)
──	Inflation ($5.99 YE11)

$10.0

$1.0

| 1969 | 1978 | 1986 | 1994 | 2002 | 2011 |

Year-end

Data from 1969–2011. Note: Underlying data expressed in U.S. $

Daimler AG (Germany), Toyota (Japan), Nokia (Finland), and Samsung (Korea). If an investor were to limit the scope of his or her investments strictly to the U.S., many countries that are home to world class industries would be excluded. Switzerland has a major presence in the pharmaceutical industry, Germany in the automotive industry, and Japan in the consumer electronics industry. Globalization has helped to increase brand awareness with investors across the world. When looking at the names listed above, international investing suddenly seems a little less foreign.

Growth Potential

As markets have grown and international companies have thrived, the performance of many international stock markets has been impressive. Graph 14-2 depicts the growth of $1.00 invested in international stocks as well as U.S. large company stocks, long-term government bonds, Treasury bills, and a hypothetical asset returning the inflation rate over the period from the end of 1969 to the end of 2011. Of the asset classes shown, U.S. large company stocks accumulated the highest ending wealth by year-end 2011. International stocks had outperformed U.S. large company stocks on an annual basis from 2002 to 2010, with the exception of 2008. After dramatically improving in 2009 from the deep drop in 2008, the performance of both international and domestic slowed in 2010 only to see negative or low growth in 2011, respectively, with international stocks producing an -11.7 percent return and U.S. large company stocks producing a 2.1 percent return.

Graph 14-3 compares the performance of international and U.S. large company stocks over rolling 10-year holding periods ending 1979 through 2011. Although U.S. large company stocks outperformed international stocks in each of the ten-year holding periods ending 1995 through 2006, international stocks have outperformed U.S. large company stocks in the ten-year holding periods ending 2007 through 2011.

Graph 14-3: U.S. Large Company Stocks and International Stocks
10-Year Holding Period Annual Total Returns (%)

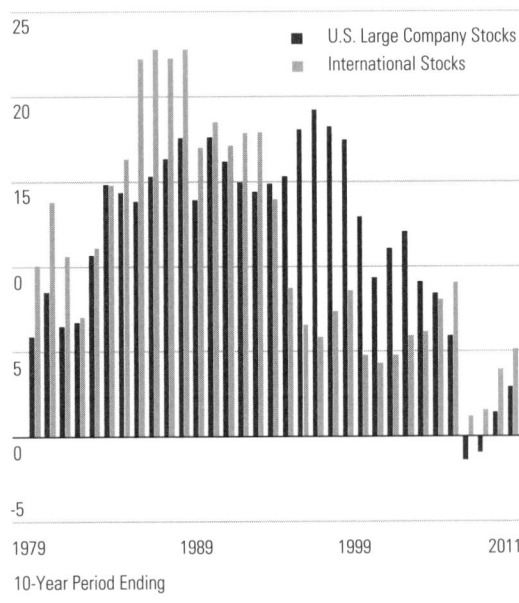

| ■ | U.S. Large Company Stocks |
| ■ | International Stocks |

| 1979 | 1989 | 1999 | 2011 |

10-Year Period Ending

Data from 1970-1979 through 2002-2011. Note: Underlying data expressed in U.S. $.

Graph 14-4: Benefits of Global Diversification

Index (Year-End 1969 = $1,000.00)

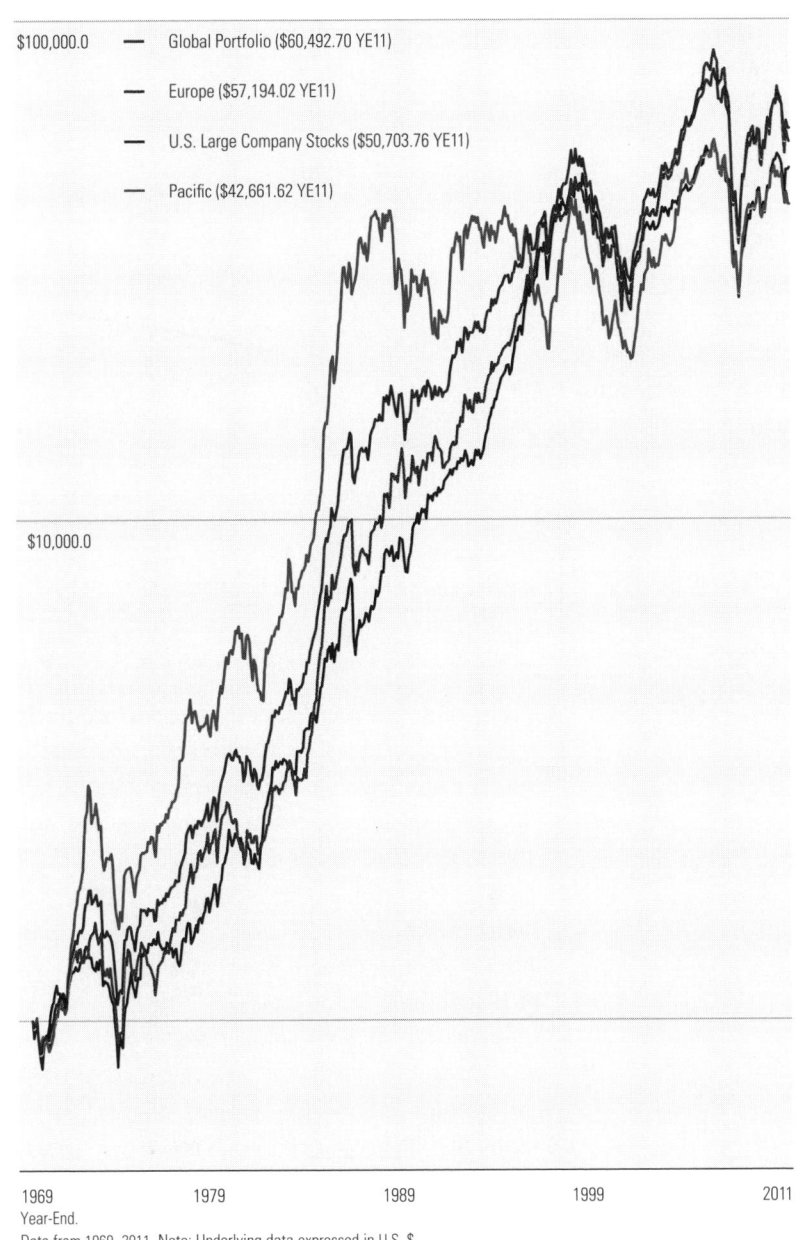

— Global Portfolio ($60,492.70 YE11)

— Europe ($57,194.02 YE11)

— U.S. Large Company Stocks ($50,703.76 YE11)

— Pacific ($42,661.62 YE11)

Year-End.

Data from 1969–2011. Note: Underlying data expressed in U.S. $.

Diversification

Diversification can be another important benefit of international investing. By spreading risks among foreign and U.S. stocks, investors can potentially lower overall investment risk and/or improve investment returns. Fluctuations may occur at different times for different markets, and if growth is slow in one country, international investing provides a means of seeking healthier prospects elsewhere. Investing abroad may help an investor balance such fluctuations. Since it is almost impossible to forecast which markets will be top performers in any given year, it can be very valuable to be invested in a portfolio diversified across several countries.

Graph 14-4 depicts the growth of $1,000 invested in U.S. large company stocks, European, and Pacific stocks as well as a global portfolio that represents an equally weighted mix of the aforementioned stocks. Notice that the Global portfolio was the top performer, followed in order of performance by the Europe, U.S. stock and Pacific indices at the end of the 41-year period. The European portfolio continues to outperform the U.S. portfolio in U.S. dollar terms when indexed from 1969. However, in 2011, the European portfolio produced an annual return of -10.5 percent while U.S. large company stocks produced a positive 2.1 percent return.

The cross-correlation coefficient between two series, covered in Chapter 6, measures the extent to which they are linearly related. The correlation coefficient measures the sensitivity of returns on one asset class or portfolio to the returns of another.

Graph 14-5 examines a 60-month rolling period correlation between international and U.S. large company stocks. This graph illustrates the recent rise in cross-correlation between the two, suggesting that the benefit of diversification has suffered in recent years. The maximum benefit to an investor would have come in the 60-month period ending July 1987, where the cross-correlation was 0.26. The least amount of diversification benefit would have come in the 60-month period ending October 2011, where the cross-correlation was 0.92. The monthly average over the entire time horizon has been 0.60.

Graph 14-5: Rolling 60-Month Correlations: Large Company Stocks and International Stocks

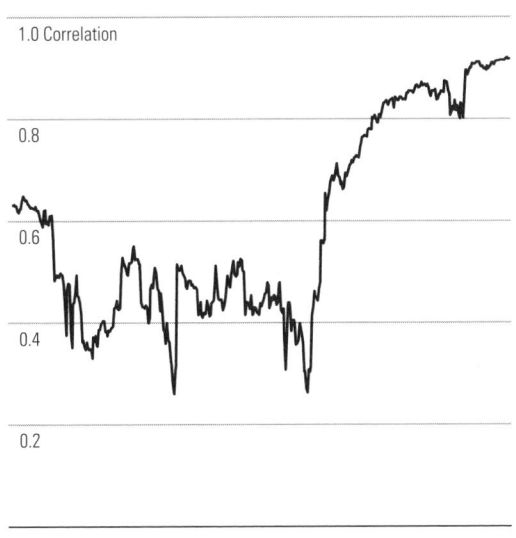

60-Month Period Ending

Data from 1970-1975 through 2007-2011. Note: Underlying data expressed in U.S. $.

Expanding the Efficient Range

Expanding a set of domestic portfolios to include securities from specific countries and regions can possibly improve the risk/return trade-off of investment opportunities. How would an efficient frontier be affected by such an expansion?

Graph 14-6 shows two efficient frontiers—one constructed entirely of domestic portfolios and the other constructed of global portfolios for the period 1970 to 1986. The comparison of the two efficient frontiers in this image makes a strong case for global diversification. An investor could have achieved higher returns at given levels of risk by expanding the set of domestic portfolios to include international stocks.

Graph 14-6: Efficient Frontier

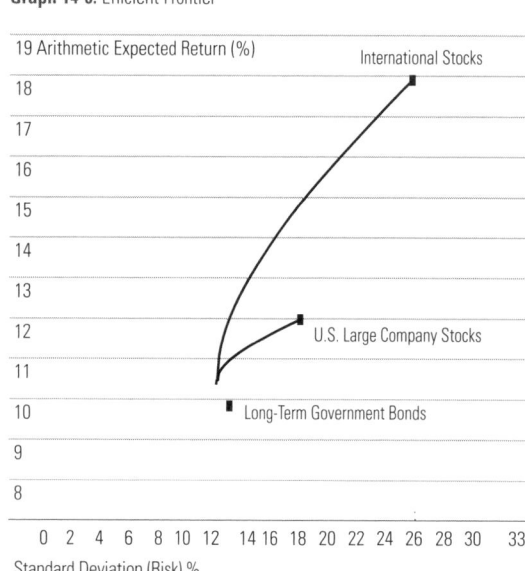

Data from 1970–1986. U.S. Large Company Stocks, Long-Term Government Bonds, and International Stocks. Note: Underlying data expressed in U.S. dollars

The time horizon is changed to cover the period 1987 to 2011 to construct the two efficient frontiers found in Graph 14-7. The comparison of the two efficient frontiers in this image makes a case for global diversification from the perspective of reducing risk. Although the diversification benefit and the risk/return trade-off have suffered of late, recent trends may not be indicative of future performance.

Risk Associated With International Investing

In addition to the potential rewards offered through international investing, significant risks apply as well. An investor assumes risk when investing in any type of stock.

Graph 14-7: Efficient Frontier

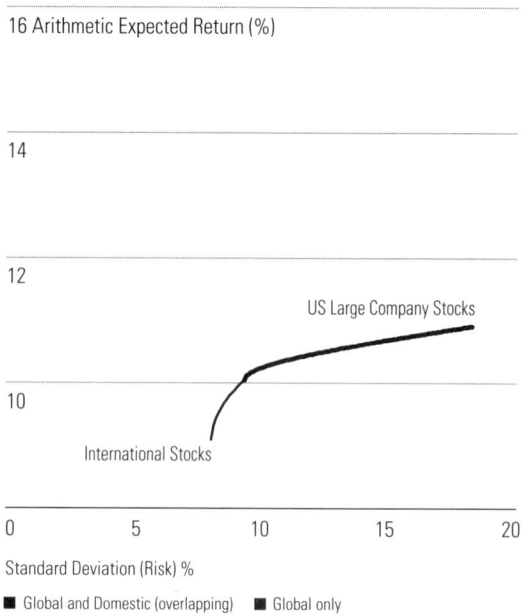

Data from 1987–2011. U.S. Large Company Stocks, Long-Term Government Bonds, and International Stocks. Note: Underlying data expressed in U.S. dollars

International investing, however, encompasses special risks—risks that should be carefully evaluated. Examples include currency risk, political and economic risk, liquidity risk, company information and accounting standards, market risk, and perhaps higher expenses.

Currency Risk

The risk of losing money when gains and losses are exchanged from foreign currencies into U.S. dollars is called currency risk. Exchange rates need to be considered with international stocks, and an investor should weigh the exchange rate risk (currency risk) in relation to the return benefit. Foreign exchange rates are continually fluctuating with changes in the supply and demand of each country's currency. Thus, returns realized by local investors are often quite different from the returns that U.S. investors attained—even though they are invested in the same security.

An investor purchases and trades foreign securities in the foreign country's local currency. When these securities are purchased by a U.S. investor, the investor's U.S. dollars must be converted to the foreign currency. When it is time to sell the securities or receive dividends, the currency is converted back to U.S. dollars. Movements in the foreign currency in relation to the U.S. dollar change the value of the foreign investment for the U.S. investor Thus, a strengthening dollar diminishes the value of foreign assets owned by U.S. investors, while a weakening dollar increases the value of the foreign investment owned by U.S. investors.

Table 14-1 illustrates the impact of currency conversion. Both the Canadian dollar and the Japanese yen appreciated relative to the U.S. dollar in 2004, translating into more dollars and a higher return for U.S. investors. For example, a local investor in Japan had a 10.87 percent return in 2004, while a U.S. investor would have realized a 16.23 percent return. Why? Because of the yen's increased value, the U.S. investor could purchase a greater number of U.S. dollars at the end of 2004 than he could have at the beginning of 2004 (with the same number of yen). In 2006 the opposite happened; both the Canadian dollar and the Japanese yen lost value relative to the U.S. dollar, and U.S. investors did not fare as well as their local counterparts. U.S. investors' yen purchased fewer dollars at the end of 2006 than they did at the beginning of 2006, thus lowering U.S. investors' return.

Table 14-1: Impact of Currency Conversion

Country	Year	Return to Local Investors (%)	Return to U.S. Investors (%)	Currency Impact (%)
Canada	2004	13.84	23.02	9.19
Japan	2004	10.87	16.23	5.37
Canada	2006	17.90	17.58	-0.32
Japan	2006	7.35	6.38	-0.97

Political/Economic Risk

Governmental and political environments abroad can be quite unstable at times. Political events pose a considerable hazard to the stability of returns from foreign markets. In emerging markets, macro-economic conditions remain exceptionally volatile and political risk is a fact of life. U.S. investors could be affected by economic policy changes such as currency controls, changes in taxation, restrictive trade policies, or seizure of foreigners' assets. Political instability and economic risk can lead to greater volatility, which can negatively affect investment markets/values.

Liquidity Risk

Liquidity risk refers to the potential that an asset will be difficult to buy or sell quickly and in large volume without substantially affecting the asset's price. Shares in large blue-chip stocks such as General Electric are liquid because they are actively traded and, therefore, the stock price will not be dramatically moved by a few buy or sell orders.

International markets, however, normally have much lower daily trading volumes when compared to the stock exchanges of the United States. Thus, a few large orders can have the potential to move the price of a security up or down rather sharply. This would go almost unnoticed in a large, established market. Also, a number of developing countries allow foreigners to buy only limited quantities of specified classes of shares.

Company Information/Accounting Standards

The type of information provided to investors from foreign companies often differs from the information U.S. public companies supply. Financial information concerning specific foreign companies can be much more difficult to obtain, since accounting and financial disclosure practices can vary widely from U.S. standards. Moreover, once the information is obtained, it may not be in English.

Market Risk

Just as U.S. stock prices fluctuate from one period to the next, prices of foreign stocks are subject to significant gains and declines. However, past returns from international stocks have fluctuated even more so than the returns of U.S. stocks. Annual ranges of returns provide an indication of the historical volatility (risk) experienced by investments in various markets.

Graph 14-8 illustrates the range of annual returns for domestic (U.S. large company stocks) and international composites, as well as the European and Pacific regional composites, over the period 1970 through 2011. Although all of the composites have similar compound returns over the 1970–2011 period, the three international composites exhibit greater volatility than the domestic composite. All investments have the potential of dramatic ups-and-downs; however, a long-term approach to investing may help reduce the pain of volatility.

Expenses

Lastly, for the reasons stated earlier, investments in foreign securities generally have higher associated expenses compared to investments in domestic securities, including transaction costs as well as sales charges. All of these expenses work to reduce the investor's return on the foreign security.

The risks associated with international investing should be carefully examined by an investor interested in or already partaking in the international marketplace. While the potential rewards of investing internationally are quite clear, an investor should weigh those along with the added risks.

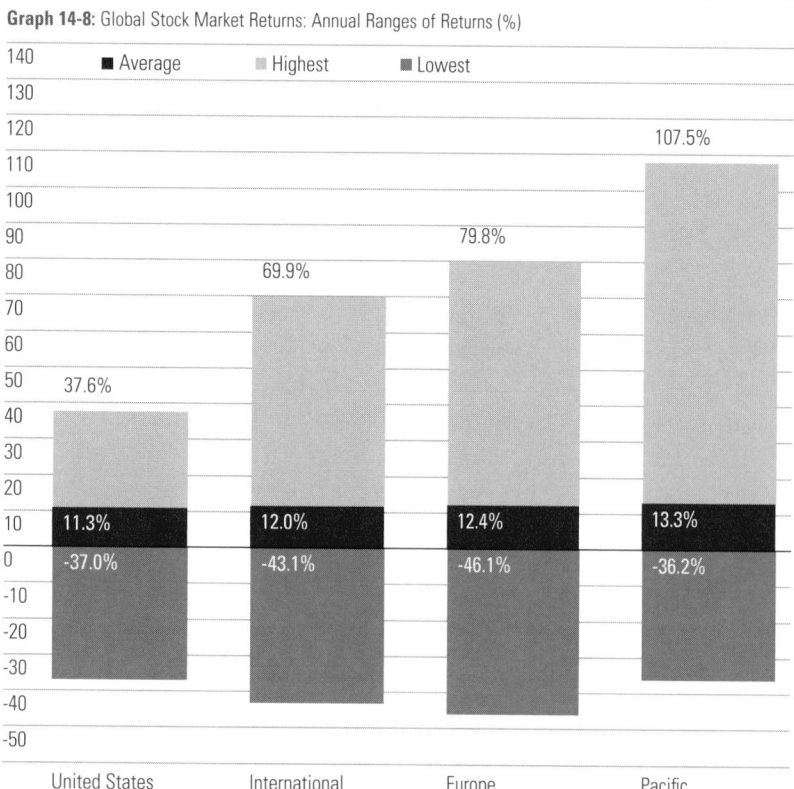

Graph 14-8: Global Stock Market Returns: Annual Ranges of Returns (%)

■ Average ▪ Highest ■ Lowest

Data from 1970–2011. Highest and Lowest Historical Annual Returns for Each Region.

Summary Statistics for International and Domestic Series

Table 14-2 shows summary statistics of annual total returns for various international regions and composites. The summary statistics presented are geometric mean, arithmetic mean, and standard deviation.

Over the period 1970 to 2011, the Pacific regional composite was the riskiest, with a standard deviation of 31.0 percent. The geometric mean of the Pacific regional composite was 9.3 percent, similar to EAFE and the World composite, which were considerably less risky.

Table 14-2: Summary Statistics of Annual Returns (%)

Series	Geometric Mean	Arithmetic Mean	Standard Deviation
Canada	10.1	12.3	22.1
Europe	10.1	12.4	22.4
Pacific	9.3	13.3	31.0
EAFE*	9.6	12.0	22.9
World	9.2	10.9	18.4
United States	9.8	11.3	17.8

Data from 1970–2011. Note: Underlying data expressed in U.S. dollars
*Europe, Australasia, Far East.

Table 14-3 shows the compound returns by decade for the various international regions and composites. The Pacific regional composite provided the highest compound annual rate of return in the first two decades but performed rather poorly in the 1990s as well as in the last two time periods. The 1990s were a good time period in which to be a domestic investor, with a compound annual rate of return of 18.2 percent.

Table 14-3: Compound Annual Rates of Return by Decade (%)

	1970s	1980s	1990s	2000s	2002–2011
Canada	11.0	11.7	9.9	9.2	11.7
Europe	8.6	18.5	14.5	2.4	4.9
Pacific	14.8	26.4	0.5	-0.3	5.8
EAFE*	10.1	22.8	7.3	1.6	5.1
World	7.0	19.9	12.0	0.2	4.2
U.S.	5.9	17.6	18.2	-0.9	2.9

Data from 1970–2011. Note: Underlying data expressed in U.S. dollars
*Europe, Australasia, Far East.

Table 14-4 shows the annualized monthly standard deviations by decade for the various international regions and composites. The World composite was the least risky asset in the 1970s, 1980s, and the 1990s. The Canadian index was the riskiest asset in the 2000s as well as the most recent decade. The domestic portfolio was the least risky asset in the most recent decade.

Table 14-4: Annualized Monthly Standard Deviation by Decade (%)

	1970s	1980s	1990s	2000s	2002–2011
Canada	20.6	24.8	18.6	25.9	25.1
Europe	18.6	21.5	16.8	20.4	22.5
Pacific	22.1	26.6	24.8	18.2	18.4
EAFE*	17.4	21.6	18.7	18.5	20.1
World	15.1	17.6	15.7	16.9	18.0
U.S.	17.2	19.4	15.9	16.3	16.6

Data from 1970–2011. Note: Underlying data expressed in U.S. dollars
*Europe, Australasia, Far East.

Table 14-5 presents annual cross-correlations and serial correlations from 1970 to 2011 for the six basic series and inflation as well as international stocks. International stocks, when compared to U.S. large company stocks, provided a higher cross-correlation than when compared to U.S. small company stocks. The serial correlation of international stocks suggests no pattern, and the return from period to period can best be interpreted as random or unpredictable.

Table 14-5: Basic Series and International Stocks: Serial and Cross-Correlations of Historical Annual Returns

Series	Intl Stocks	Large Co Stocks	Small Co Stocks	LT-Corp Bonds	LT-Gov't Bonds	Inter Gov't Bonds	U.S. T-Bills	Inflation
Intl Stocks	1.00							
Large Co Stocks	0.66	1.00						
Small Co Stocks	0.50	0.72	1.00					
LT-Corp Bonds	0.04	0.28	0.11	1.00				
LT-Govt Bonds	-0.12	0.06	-0.10	0.89	1.00			
IT-Govt Bonds	-0.14	0.08	-0.08	0.88	0.89	1.00		
Treasury Bills	0.00	0.10	0.04	0.00	0.00	0.30	1.00	
Inflation	-0.09	-0.10	0.05	-0.40	-0.35	-0.16	0.65	1.00
Serial Correlations	0.08	0.01	0.07	-0.09	-0.27	-0.07	0.85	0.72

Data from 1970–2011. Note: Underlying data expressed in U.S. dollars

Table 14-6: U.S. Large Company Stocks, International Stocks, Pacific Stocks, and Europe Stocks Annual Total Returns (%) from 1970 to 2011

Year	U.S. Large Company	International Stocks	Pacific Stocks	Europe Stocks
1970	3.86	-10.51	-11.99	-9.35
1971	14.30	31.21	38.75	28.04
1972	18.99	37.60	107.55	15.62
1973	-14.69	-14.17	-20.95	-7.73
1974	-26.47	-22.15	-20.94	-22.78
1975	37.23	37.10	26.73	43.90
1976	23.93	3.74	21.64	-6.37
1977	-7.16	19.42	13.69	23.92
1978	6.57	34.30	48.77	24.30
1979	18.61	6.18	-3.48	14.67
1980	32.50	24.43	36.38	14.53
1981	-4.92	-1.03	8.31	-10.45
1982	21.55	-0.86	-6.26	5.69
1983	22.56	24.61	26.42	22.38
1984	6.27	7.86	13.48	1.26
1985	31.73	56.72	39.39	79.79
1986	18.67	69.94	93.82	44.46
1987	5.25	24.93	39.85	4.10
1988	16.61	28.59	35.19	16.35
1989	31.69	10.80	2.68	29.06
1990	-3.10	-23.20	-34.29	-3.37
1991	30.47	12.50	11.54	13.66
1992	7.62	-11.85	-18.20	-4.25
1993	10.08	32.94	35.97	29.79
1994	1.32	8.06	13.03	2.66
1995	37.58	11.55	2.99	22.13
1996	22.96	6.36	-8.40	21.57
1997	33.36	2.06	-25.34	24.20
1998	28.58	20.33	2.64	28.91
1999	21.04	27.30	57.99	16.23
2000	-9.10	-13.96	-25.62	-8.14
2001	-11.89	-21.21	-25.22	-19.64
2002	-22.10	-15.66	-9.01	-18.09
2003	28.68	39.17	38.98	39.14
2004	10.88	20.70	19.30	21.39
2005	4.91	14.02	23.01	9.93
2006	15.79	26.86	12.51	34.36
2007	5.49	11.63	5.61	14.39
2008	-37.00	-43.06	-36.17	-46.08
2009	26.46	32.46	24.34	36.81
2010	15.06	8.21	16.08	4.49
2011	2.11	-11.73	-13.61	-10.50

Data from 1970–2011. Note: Underlying data expressed in U.S. dollars

Conclusion

International investments are no different than any other investment when it comes to information gathering. Investors interested in or already taking part in the international marketplace should learn as much as possible about the corresponding risks and rewards. International investments are not for everyone, and the most appropriate mix for an individual investor depends on his or her risk tolerance, investment goals, time horizon, and financial resources. ▥

Endnotes

[1] World Market Capitalization by County—Morgan Stanley Capital International Blue Book^{SM}.

Chapter 15
Lifecycle Investing

What is Lifecycle Investing

Lifecycle investing is focused on one objective: helping investors manage their retirement portfolios across a long and unpredictable lifetime. Complicating matters is the well-documented trend of corporate and government retirement income sources fading away. This has led to strong growth in lifecycle investing products as investors realize they alone are responsible for funding their own retirements.

Given the interest in the topic, the SBBI would like to introduce readers to an overview of lifecycle investing. The chapter starts by highlighting the challenges involved in lifecycle investing and summarizing how to approach an evaluation of a lifecycle methodology. The chapter then details Ibbotson's Lifetime Asset Allocation research to provide an in-depth example of a lifecycle methodology. The chapter concludes with performance data for a series of Morningstar asset allocation indexes specifically designed to benchmark lifecycle investing efforts.

Challenges Present in Lifecycle Investing

There are several aspects of investing over a lifetime that make it a challenge. Key challenges include long investment horizons, unpredictable cash flows, random market volatility, asset-to-income conversion costs, and portfolio management demands that cover a wide set of asset classes.

Investment Horizon

The first challenge in lifestyle investing is the investment horizon that the solution must cover. The timeline for funding an individual's retirement consumption liability is long, spanning approximately 40 years of employment. The time horizon for the post-retirement consumption that must be funded is also relatively long at 20 years plus. The duration of this liability is growing as medical and lifestyle advances (such as better cholesterol, diabetes and blood pressure control) lengthen average life-spans. The quality of the firm offering the solution also becomes important over these long horizons.

Cash Flow

The second challenge is cash flow. Forty years of inflows must be transformed overnight into a long series of outflows. Unemployment, health emergencies, family-member liabilities, and housing-related issues can all disrupt the contribution cash flow. Although some of these cash flow disruptions can be discretionary, many are out of the investor's control.

Market Volatility

The third challenge is market volatility. Market volatility can undermine performance and leave an investor short of the goal. Market volatility can also trigger behavioral responses in investors that are counter-productive. For example, research indicates investors tend to hold losing investments too long and sell investment winners too early. Withdrawing too much money in early retirement is another common behavior witnessed in retirement plans.

Conversion of Assets Into Income

A fourth key challenge is the conversion of assets into income at retirement. The ability to know how long one can work is quite diminished at this point in the lifecycle. The length of the income need remains quite variable at this point though. Inflation is yet another concern. Even modest inflation over 20 years leads to significant purchasing power degradation. Understanding optimal allocations to stocks, bonds and annuities at this point is a complex exercise.

Asset Allocation

A final challenge is asset allocation. On one level this is an important exercise in including not just domestic stocks and bonds, but international securities, or including real-return assets as a hedge against inflation. On another level this requires the inclusion of human capital, the present value of the remaining employment income stream at a point in time, into the portfolio planning process. Managing a portfolio this complex is hard enough for a professional, much less a novice investor.

Evaluating Lifecycle Investing Methodologies

Lifetime investing methodologies can be analyzed via their three major components: asset class diversity, security selection effectiveness, and de-risking effectiveness. Although lifestyle investing is a fairly new concept and does not have much performance data, it is still quite possible to perform meaningful evaluative analysis on the category as a whole.

Graph 15-1: Modern Portfolio Theory and the Market Portfolio

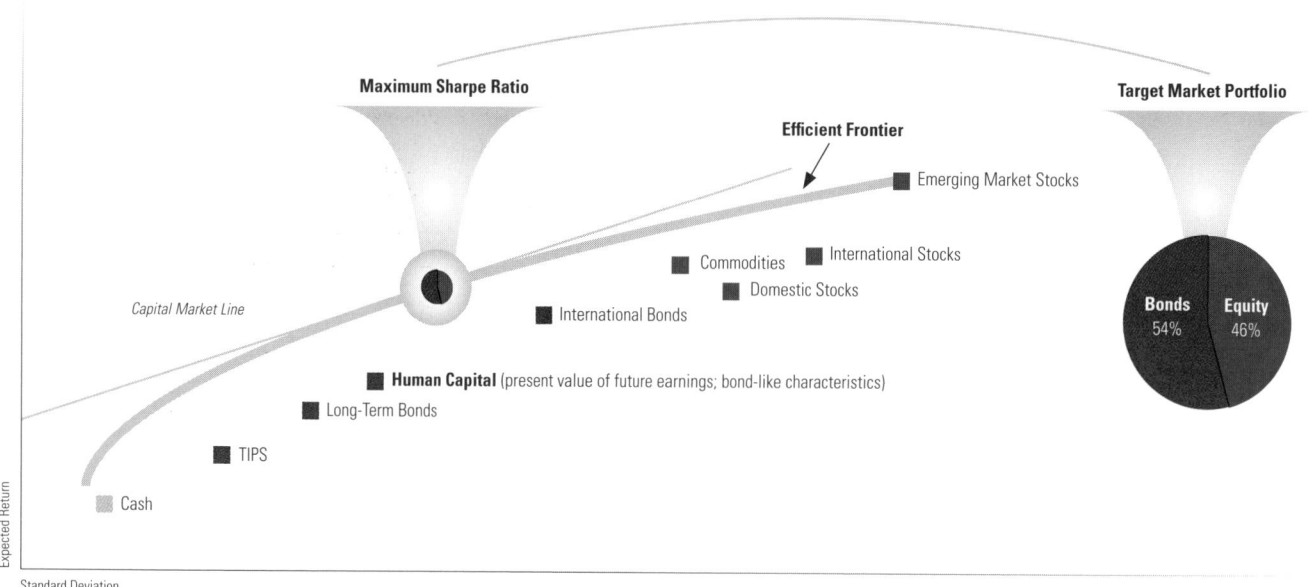

Asset Class Diversity

Time-tested financial theory has established that diversi-fication can improve an investor's portfolio by increasing return and decreasing risk. The optimal set of asset alloca-tion mixes for a particular set of asset classes is called the efficient frontier.[1]

For example, in Graph 15-1 all points on the efficient frontier have the highest possible return for the given amount of risk (or conversely, the lowest possible risk for the given expected return). Asset class diversification can improve an efficient frontier by either lowering the risk for a given return (a shift to the left), or increasing return for a given risk (a shift upwards).

Security Selection

Security selection within each chosen asset class is another major evaluation area for life cycle funds. Fund managers can select an active approach, where the best securities for each class are hand-picked, or a passive approach, where index rules drive security selection.

Evaluating a lifecycle fund's approach to security selec-tion usually focuses on risk-adjusted returns, net of fees. Measures that help separate market return from manager skill can be used to help determine if a fund's security selection process adds value. At a minimum, the security selection process should capture the beta of the asset class, as measured against an appropriate benchmark.

De-Risking Methodology (Glide Path)

Investors saving for retirement typically become more risk adverse the closer they get to retirement. This is driven by declines in human capital and increasingly limited control over their ability to work due to mandatory retirement rules, health issues and growing preference for leisure time. Their retirement nest egg represents a key source of retirement income and any impairment to that nest egg isn't easily fixed in the autumn of a career.

Levels of risk preference will vary among retirement investors however. Some investors will have well-funded pension plans and generally secure retirements. Others will be severely underfunded at retirement. Some will spend half their career in one situation, and due to a number of reasons, end up unexpectedly in the other situation.

The de-risking methodology, or glide path, simply repre-sents an effort to reduce market risk to synchronizing the fund's risk profile with the investor's risk profile. A glide path typically does this by reducing the equity market risk of the lifecycle portfolio at various rates over the fund's investment horizon.

Because risk-profiles will inevitably vary among investors, lifecycle funds today represent many different types of glide paths. Some dip steeply at retirement and then flat-line to provide as much protection as possible when account balances are the highest. Others slope gradually, well past the retirement date, to keep the portfolio growing as much as prudently possible to subsidize prolonged consumption. A key aim in lifecycle investing then should be to disclose as clearly as possible the nature of the de-risking methodology in use so investors can be matched to the glide path that best suites their situation and objectives.

Ibbotson's Lifetime Asset Allocation Methodology

The Ibbotson Lifetime Asset Allocation Methodology embraces the latest academic research regarding modern portfolio theory, the role of human capital, the application of liability-driven investing techniques to retirees, advanced optimization techniques, alternative asset class research, and 30 years of asset allocation thought leadership centered around human capital. The result is a methodology that can be used to create custom lifetime asset allocation solutions for individuals or specific demographic groups, such as employees from a specific company.

The creation of robust lifetime asset allocation solutions begins with an analysis of the changing risks investors face throughout their lifetimes. During the accumulation phase, investors are primarily concerned with expense risk, savings risk, mortality risk (dying too soon), and market risk. During the decumulation phase, or retirement phase, the primary risks are expense risk, longevity risk (living too long), bequest risk, and market risk. Just as the nature and magnitude of these risks evolve over time, so do the methods for controlling them. The changing nature of these risks is closely related to the size of the investor's financial and human capital.

Total Market Portfolio

Markowitz [1952, 1959] developed the idea of mean-variance efficiency, the notion that investors should select a portfolio that maximizes expected return for a given level of risk. Sharpe [1964] extended Markowitz's work to show that the optimum mean-variance efficient portfolio is the market portfolio. As Graph 15-1 illustrates, the theoretical market portfolio is the point on Markowitz's efficient frontier with the best risk-return trade-off and the maximum diversification possible.

Under Tobin's two-fund separation theorem, all investors should hold some portion of their wealth in the market portfolio and achieve their desired risk level with either a long or short position in the risk-free asset, often assumed to be cash. While in practice few investors fully adopt two-fund separation, the theoretical notion of a true, all-encompassing global market portfolio provides a compelling structure for strategic asset allocation.

The market portfolio is the cornerstone of modern portfolio theory and is at the heart of Markowitz's mean-variance optimization and Sharpe's CAPM. While an observable proxy is generally used for the market portfolio like the S&P 500 Index or the MSCI World Index, portfolio theory tells us that the unobservable, all-inclusive market portfolio includes all tradable assets, such as traditional capital assets, as well as non-tradable assets, such as human capital (see Roll 1977).

Human Capital Asset

Human capital is a precious asset that helps investors overcome many of the primary risks they face. Unlike financial assets, for which the rate which labor income is earned can be observed in monthly bank and brokerage statements, human capital's value is unobservable, its value must be estimated. The current value of any asset is the present value of the discounted cash flows the asset will generate. Considered in light of this asset valuation principle, and accounting for mortality risk, an individual's total human capital is the present value of all future labor income.

Composition of Human Capital

Recent Ibbotson research[2] on integrating human capital into modern portfolio theory includes "Human Capital, Asset Allocation, and Life Insurance," by Peng Chen, Roger Ibbotson, Moshe Milevsky, and Kevin X. Zhu, as well as the 2007 CFA Institute Research Foundation monograph by the same authors entitled "Lifetime Financial Advice."[3]

Based on this research, it is clear that when trying to consider human capital's impact on asset allocation choices, one must understand 1) human capital's role in both the hypothetical market portfolio and individual investor portfolios, and 2) human capital's systematic (or market-like) characteristics.

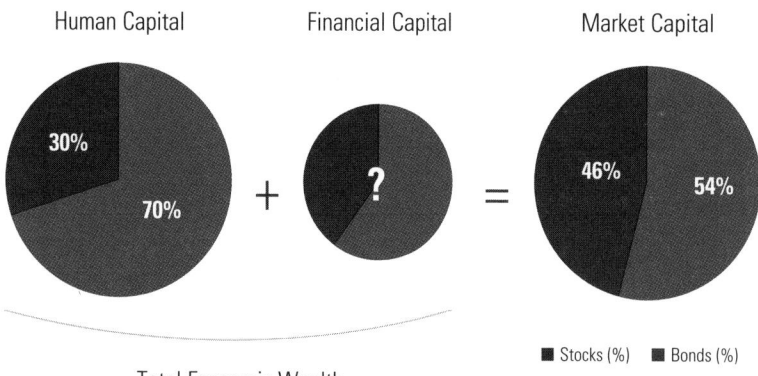

Human Capital   Financial Capital   Market Capital

Total Economic Wealth

■ Stocks (%)   ■ Bonds (%)

her overall economic situation is influenced by the same two sources that make up the bulk of the market portfolio: 1) financial capital (tradable assets) and 2) human capital (non-tradable assets).

Human capital fades over time as wages are earned, saved and spent. Graph 15-3 illustrates how the decline in the human capital asset can be offset by growth in the financial capital asset so an individual can smooth his or her consumption over the lifecycle. This asset mix shift is what drives the changing asset allocation inside the financial capital portfolio from risky to safe as the large bond-like human capital asset diminishes.

Graph 15-3: Relationship Between Human & Financial Capital Over Lifecycle

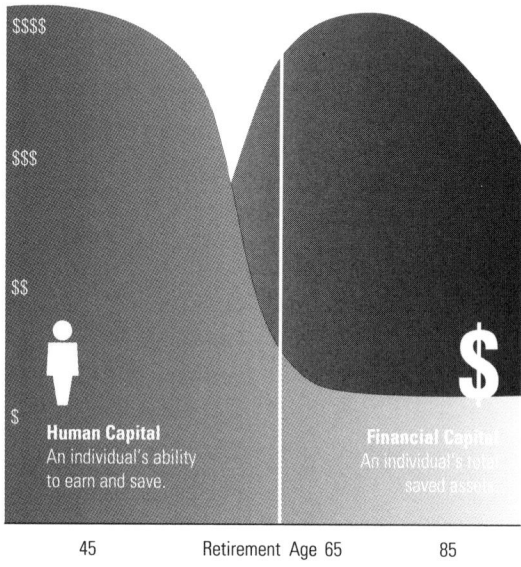

45   Retirement Age 65   85

■ Human Capital   ■ Financial Capital

Practitioners and academics alike are starting to acknowledge that human capital's return, risk, and correlation characteristics should be taken into account when building target asset allocations for investors. For example, Merton [2003] contents that it is important to include human capital's amount, volatility, and correlation (to other assets) into the asset allocation decision. To paraphrase the titles of recent works by Peng Chen and Moshe Milevsky (see Chen [2007] and Milevsky [2004]), is an investor a bond or a stock? This is a question we shall attempt to answer shortly.

The average investor's human capital is somewhere in between these two extremes. A typical investor's human capital is often described as a junk bond. During "normal" times junk bonds trade more like bonds, but during times of economic turmoil junk bonds trade more like equities. Overall, Ibbotson estimates that the typical investor's human capital is more bond-like than stock-like. Ibbotson models average human capital as 30% equities and 70% bonds. This decision was reached in June 1998 amongst members of Ibbotson's Advisory Board at the time. Members included Harry Markowitz, Daniel Kahneman, Jeff Jaffe, Shlomo Benartzi, John Carroll, and Richard Thaler.

The Human Capital/Financial Capital Relationship

In Graph 15-2, just as the hypothetical market portfolio includes an allocation to human capital, an individual investor's total portfolio also includes a non-tradable allocation to human capital. For an individual investor, his or

Liability-Driven Investing

For individuals, assets exist primarily to pay for their retirement income liability. As a result, the retirement income liability affects asset allocation policy throughout the investor's lifetime. Yet many asset allocations are based on an asset-only optimization framework, which focuses solely on a subset of the investor's portfolio. The retirement income liability's importance helps us to establish a glide path that is dependant on an investor's total financial health, and acknowledges that asset allocations need to evolve as human capital inevitably dwindles and its importance is superseded by financial capital.

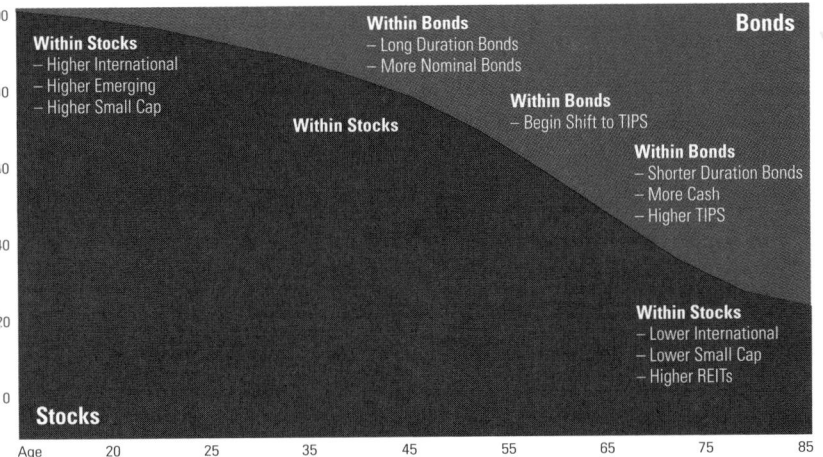

Human capital's systematic or "market-like" characteristics are different for different individuals. For example, tenured university professors most often have steady salaries that increase on an annual basis based on inflation with little chance of dramatic changes or interruptions. Correspondingly, their human capital is very bond-like and they have the capacity to embrace more risk in their financial capital portfolio. This type of stable income typically has a low correlation with equity markets. In contrast, brokers or commission-based salespeople have salaries that vary substantially from year to year and are usually highly correlated with the equity markets. Their human capital is very equity-like and they have a relatively lower capacity for risk in their financial capital portfolio.

Clearly then, there will not be a single "best" glide path. In order to design benchmark glide paths that meet the needs of most individuals, Morningstar has created three risk profiles: aggressive, moderate and conservative to cover the risk preference/risk capacity grid space. [See Graph 15-5].

Graph 15-5: Combining Capacity for Risk with Preference for Risk

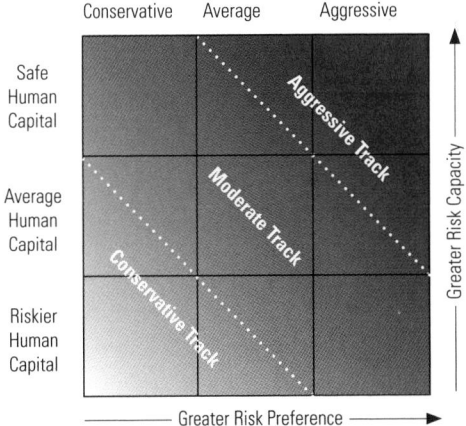

From a retirement liability perspective, as investors grow older, their financial asset allocations should adjust to match their retirement liability characteristics. For example, if retirement expenses are in dollars, the portfolio should end up being predominately in dollars at retirement. If most retirement expenses are sensitive to inflation, a very meaningful portion of the portfolio at retirement should be allocated to assets that move with inflation. These adjustments pertain to both the intra-stock and intra-bond allocations as illustrated in Graph 15-4. The implication for investors however is the possibility of some opportunity cost between the "optimal" portfolio and the "LDI" portfolio. The LDI portfolio for example may deliver lower expected returns by foregoing international equities and long-duration bonds in exchange for being synchronized to the investor's true retirement liability.

Investor Risk Profiles

When determining an appropriate target asset allocation for an individual investor's financial capital, one should look at the investor's capacity for risk, not just the investor's appetite for risk. An investor's risk capacity is governed by the investor's overall economic situation including income sensitivity to home-country capital markets, household net worth, flexibility of personal labor supply, and access to other income streams (pensions, social security, spouse, etc.). Of course these assets should be evaluated in the context of the investor's lifecycle liabilities—retirement income, out-of-pocket healthcare, college expenses, etc.

Conclusion

The goal of lifecycle investing is to fund individual retirements. Success requires many elements: adequate savings, reasonable product structures and investors with the discipline to stay with the program. There are many challenges that arise over a lifecycle that impact contributions, portfolio returns and withdrawals. These challenges include market volatility, longevity, inflation and liability matching. Lifecycle investing can guide investors through these challenges.

Graph 15-6: Morningstar Glide Paths vs. Target Date Market Glide Paths

Top 20 Largest Target Date Fund Families by AUM

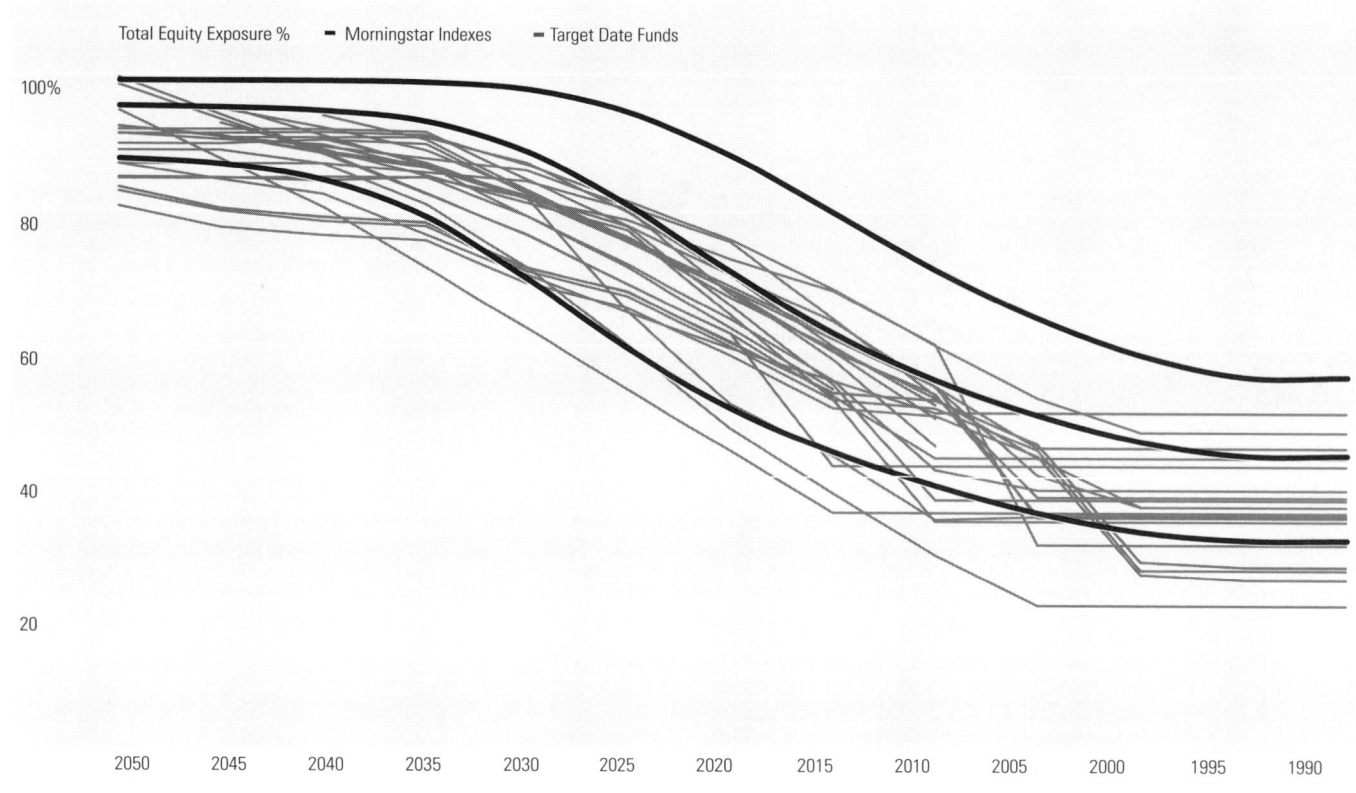

Source: Morningstar® Direct™

Evaluating a lifecycle investing methodology is a complex task, especially when one considers the risk to the investor of getting it wrong. A reasonable lifecycle investment methodology should have three key components: an adequate diversity of asset classes with meaningful allocations to each, a security-selection process that provides appropriate return for the risk it introduces, and a de-risking formula that is theoretically sound and keeps portfolio risk in sync with the target investor group.

The Morningstar/Ibbotson Lifetime Allocation Methodology is an example of a lifecycle investing methodology. It is distinctive in its use of human capital, asset allocation, liability-driven investing, and risk profile choice. When paired with the Morningstar asset-class index family, the Ibbotson research becomes a set of lifecycle investing benchmarks that relate well to the glide paths in many of the lifecycle products in the market today (see Graph 15-6).

Historical Performance

Investors considering a lifecycle methodology to convert assets to income should choose carefully. For example, the potential market risk inside the product should fit their objectives and sense of what would let them sleep at night. That evaluation process can start with a simple review of historical performance. The indexes, in Table 15-1, for example have markedly different annualized return histories and monthly standard deviations in categories considered close to retirement such as 2010 and 2005. ▮

Endnotes

[1] Please see Chapter 11, "Using Historical Data in Forecasting and Optimization", for a complete discussion of the efficient frontier.

[2] "Lifetime Asset Allocations: Methodologies for Target Maturity Funds", Ibbotson Associates Research Paper, February 11, 2008; Tom Idzorek, CFA, V.P., Director of Research and Product Development.

[3] In addition to Chen, Ibbotson, Milevsky, and Zhu [2006, 2007] other important works include Williams [1978], Bodie, Merton , and Samuelson [1992], Campbell and Viceira [2002], Milevsky [2004], and Chen [2007].

Table 15-1: Morningstar Lifetime Allocation Indexes

Index	Equity (%)	Three-Year Return	Three-Year Standard Deviation	Five-Year Return	Five-Year Standard Deviation	Annual Returns 2011	2010	2009	2008	2007
Morningstar Lifetime Aggressive Income	45	10.84	10.04	4.10	10.40	2.95	11.52	18.60	-18.06	9.56
Morningstar Lifetime Moderate Income	32	9.79	7.75	4.86	8.23	4.13	10.02	15.51	-12.67	9.72
Morningstar Lifetime Conservative Income	19	8.56	5.47	5.59	6.14	5.35	8.42	12.02	-6.60	9.86
Morningstar Lifetime Aggressive 2000	48	11.31	10.84	3.91	11.25	2.79	12.08	19.72	-19.84	9.55
Morningstar Lifetime Moderate 2000	34	10.18	8.29	4.82	8.81	4.17	10.50	16.20	-13.75	9.71
Morningstar Lifetime Conservative 2000	20	8.88	5.80	5.67	6.51	5.58	8.83	12.35	-7.08	9.84
Morningstar Lifetime Aggressive 2005	53	11.94	12.04	3.56	12.48	2.35	12.90	21.37	-22.47	9.54
Morningstar Lifetime Moderate 2005	38	10.71	9.15	4.67	9.69	4.01	11.17	17.36	-15.60	9.70
Morningstar Lifetime Conservative 2005	23	9.35	6.40	5.66	7.12	5.66	9.42	13.11	-8.30	9.82
Morningstar Lifetime Aggressive 2010	60	12.66	13.58	3.02	14.04	1.64	13.86	23.55	-25.89	9.52
Morningstar Lifetime Moderate 2010	43	11.34	10.30	4.37	10.85	3.61	11.96	18.98	-18.22	9.72
Morningstar Lifetime Conservative 2010	27	9.91	7.24	5.55	7.95	5.51	10.12	14.28	-10.16	9.82
Morningstar Lifetime Aggressive 2015	68	13.40	15.41	2.31	15.86	0.58	14.92	26.17	-29.79	9.49
Morningstar Lifetime Moderate 2015	50	12.09	11.82	3.85	12.39	2.90	12.90	21.22	-21.83	9.74
Morningstar Lifetime Conservative 2015	32	10.53	8.31	5.31	9.00	5.15	10.90	15.82	-12.69	9.85
Morningstar Lifetime Aggressive 2020	77	14.02	17.25	1.55	17.64	-0.71	15.90	28.81	-33.44	9.45
Morningstar Lifetime Moderate 2020	59	12.92	13.78	3.10	14.34	1.75	14.01	24.13	-26.27	9.74
Morningstar Lifetime Conservative 2020	39	11.28	9.71	4.87	10.40	4.50	11.78	17.99	-16.27	9.91
Morningstar Lifetime Aggressive 2025	85	14.39	18.71	0.95	19.00	-1.95	16.63	30.89	-36.02	9.46
Morningstar Lifetime Moderate 2025	70	13.65	15.87	2.26	16.36	0.24	15.15	27.18	-30.58	9.71
Morningstar Lifetime Conservative 2025	48	12.17	11.62	4.17	12.28	3.37	12.87	20.97	-20.95	9.96
Morningstar Lifetime Aggressive 2030	90	14.52	19.52	0.62	19.75	-2.84	17.00	32.13	-37.31	9.55
Morningstar Lifetime Moderate 2030	79	14.10	17.58	1.56	17.94	-1.23	16.04	29.62	-33.70	9.71
Morningstar Lifetime Conservative 2030	59	13.01	13.78	3.33	14.36	1.80	14.07	24.28	-25.78	9.96
Morningstar Lifetime Aggressive 2035	92	14.54	19.84	0.52	20.05	-3.34	17.11	32.76	-37.76	9.71
Morningstar Lifetime Moderate 2035	85	14.29	18.58	1.17	18.85	-2.28	16.53	31.08	-35.32	9.79
Morningstar Lifetime Conservative 2035	70	13.58	15.66	2.59	16.11	0.19	15.09	27.06	-29.46	9.96
Morningstar Lifetime Aggressive 2040	92	14.55	19.98	0.49	20.19	-3.65	17.13	33.21	-37.98	9.91
Morningstar Lifetime Moderate 2040	87	14.33	18.99	1.03	19.24	-2.85	16.71	31.81	-35.94	9.95
Morningstar Lifetime Conservative 2040	76	13.84	16.80	2.17	17.15	-0.96	15.70	28.72	-31.42	10.03
Morningstar Lifetime Aggressive 2045	92	14.56	20.07	0.48	20.31	-3.93	17.13	33.62	-38.15	10.11
Morningstar Lifetime Moderate 2045	88	14.36	19.19	0.98	19.44	-3.19	16.76	32.32	-36.27	10.14
Morningstar Lifetime Conservative 2045	79	13.92	17.34	1.99	17.65	-1.61	15.97	29.56	-32.27	10.20
Morningstar Lifetime Aggressive 2050	93	14.57	20.16	0.47	20.42	-4.19	17.12	34.03	-38.31	10.34
Morningstar Lifetime Moderate 2050	89	14.38	19.32	0.96	19.59	-3.47	16.78	32.76	-36.49	10.35
Morningstar Lifetime Conservative 2050	80	13.98	17.60	1.92	17.91	-1.96	16.06	30.15	-32.72	10.38
Morningstar Lifetime Aggressive 2055	93	14.56	20.24	0.44	20.50	-4.47	17.09	34.39	-38.44	10.46
Morningstar Lifetime Moderate 2055	89	14.36	19.40	0.93	19.67	-3.75	16.75	33.10	-36.62	10.47
Morningstar Lifetime Conservative 2055	81	13.96	17.75	1.87	18.04	-2.30	16.05	30.52	-32.92	10.49

Note: Underlying data expressed in U.S. dollars.

Appendix A

Basic Series

Real Riskless Rates of Return

from January 1926 to December 1970

Year	Jan	Feb	Mar	Apr	May	Jun	Jul	Aug	Sep	Oct	Nov	Dec	Year	Jan–Dec*
1926	0.0000	-0.0385	-0.0575	0.0253	0.0179	0.0457	0.0479	0.0248	0.0252	-0.0284	0.0347	0.0196	1926	0.1162
1927	-0.0193	0.0537	0.0087	0.0201	0.0607	-0.0067	0.0670	0.0515	0.0450	-0.0502	0.0721	0.0279	1927	0.3749
1928	-0.0040	-0.0125	0.1101	0.0345	0.0197	-0.0385	0.0141	0.0803	0.0259	0.0168	0.1292	0.0049	1928	0.4361
1929	0.0583	-0.0019	-0.0012	0.0176	-0.0362	0.1140	0.0471	0.1028	-0.0476	-0.1973	-0.1246	0.0282	1929	-0.0842
1930	0.0639	0.0259	0.0812	-0.0080	-0.0096	-0.1625	0.0386	0.0141	-0.1282	-0.0855	-0.0089	-0.0706	1930	-0.2490
1931	0.0502	0.1193	-0.0675	-0.0935	-0.1279	0.1421	-0.0722	0.0182	-0.2973	0.0896	-0.0798	-0.1400	1931	-0.4334
1932	-0.0271	0.0570	-0.1158	-0.1997	-0.2196	-0.0022	0.3815	0.3869	-0.0346	-0.1349	-0.0417	0.0565	1932	-0.0819
1933	0.0087	-0.1772	0.0353	0.4256	0.1683	0.1338	-0.0862	0.1206	-0.1118	-0.0855	0.1127	0.0253	1933	0.5399
1934	0.1069	-0.0322	0.0000	-0.0251	-0.0736	0.0229	-0.1132	0.0611	-0.0033	-0.0286	0.0942	-0.0010	1934	-0.0144
1935	-0.0411	-0.0341	-0.0286	0.0980	0.0409	0.0699	0.0850	0.0280	0.0256	0.0777	0.0474	0.0394	1935	0.4767
1936	0.0670	0.0224	0.0268	-0.0751	0.0545	0.0333	0.0701	0.0151	0.0031	0.0775	0.0134	-0.0029	1936	0.3392
1937	0.0390	0.0191	-0.0077	-0.0809	-0.0024	-0.0504	0.1045	-0.0483	-0.1403	-0.0981	-0.0866	-0.0459	1937	-0.3503
1938	0.0152	0.0674	-0.2487	0.1447	-0.0330	0.2503	0.0744	-0.0226	0.0166	0.0776	-0.0273	0.0401	1938	0.3112
1939	-0.0674	0.0390	-0.1339	-0.0027	0.0733	-0.0612	0.1105	-0.0648	0.1673	-0.0123	-0.0398	0.0270	1939	-0.0041
1940	-0.0336	0.0133	0.0124	-0.0024	-0.2289	0.0809	0.0341	0.0350	0.0123	0.0422	-0.0316	0.0009	1940	-0.0978
1941	-0.0463	-0.0060	0.0071	-0.0612	0.0183	0.0578	0.0579	0.0010	-0.0068	-0.0657	-0.0284	-0.0407	1941	-0.1159
1942	0.0161	-0.0159	-0.0652	-0.0399	0.0796	0.0221	0.0337	0.0164	0.0290	0.0678	-0.0021	0.0549	1942	0.2034
1943	0.0737	0.0583	0.0545	0.0035	0.0552	0.0223	-0.0526	0.0171	0.0263	-0.0108	-0.0654	0.0617	1943	0.2590
1944	0.0171	0.0042	0.0195	-0.0100	0.0505	0.0543	-0.0193	0.0157	-0.0008	0.0023	0.0133	0.0374	1944	0.1975
1945	0.0158	0.0683	-0.0441	0.0902	0.0195	-0.0007	-0.0180	0.0641	0.0438	0.0322	0.0396	0.0116	1945	0.3644
1946	0.0714	-0.0641	0.0480	0.0393	0.0288	-0.0370	-0.0239	-0.0674	-0.0997	-0.0060	-0.0027	0.0457	1946	-0.0807
1947	0.0255	-0.0077	-0.0149	-0.0363	0.0014	0.0554	0.0381	-0.0203	-0.0111	0.0238	-0.0175	0.0233	1947	0.0571
1948	-0.0379	-0.0388	0.0793	0.0292	0.0879	0.0054	-0.0508	0.0158	-0.0276	0.0710	-0.0961	0.0346	1948	0.0550
1949	0.0039	-0.0296	0.0328	-0.0179	-0.0258	0.0014	0.0650	0.0219	0.0263	0.0340	0.0175	0.0486	1949	0.1879
1950	0.0197	0.0199	0.0070	0.0486	0.0509	-0.0548	0.0119	0.0443	0.0592	0.0093	0.0169	0.0513	1950	0.3171
1951	0.0637	0.0157	-0.0156	0.0509	-0.0299	-0.0228	0.0711	0.0478	0.0013	-0.0103	0.0096	0.0424	1951	0.2402
1952	0.0181	-0.0282	0.0503	-0.0402	0.0343	0.0490	0.0196	-0.0071	-0.0176	0.0020	0.0571	0.0382	1952	0.1837
1953	-0.0049	-0.0106	-0.0212	-0.0237	0.0077	-0.0134	0.0273	-0.0501	0.0034	0.0540	0.0204	0.0053	1953	-0.0099
1954	0.0536	0.0111	0.0325	0.0516	0.0418	0.0031	0.0589	-0.0275	0.0851	-0.0167	0.0909	0.0534	1954	0.5262
1955	0.0197	0.0098	-0.0030	0.0396	0.0055	0.0841	0.0621	-0.0025	0.0130	-0.0284	0.0827	0.0015	1955	0.3156
1956	-0.0347	0.0413	0.0710	-0.0004	-0.0593	0.0409	0.0530	-0.0328	-0.0440	0.0066	-0.0050	0.0370	1956	0.0656
1957	-0.0401	-0.0264	0.0215	0.0388	0.0437	0.0004	0.0131	-0.0505	-0.0602	-0.0302	0.0231	-0.0395	1957	-0.1078
1958	0.0445	-0.0141	0.0328	0.0337	0.0212	0.0279	0.0449	0.0176	0.0501	0.0270	0.0284	0.0535	1958	0.4336
1959	0.0053	0.0049	0.0020	0.0402	0.0240	-0.0022	0.0363	-0.0102	-0.0443	0.0128	0.0186	0.0292	1959	0.1196
1960	-0.0700	0.0147	-0.0123	-0.0161	0.0326	0.0211	-0.0234	0.0317	-0.0590	-0.0007	0.0465	0.0479	1960	0.0047
1961	0.0645	0.0319	0.0270	0.0051	0.0239	-0.0275	0.0342	0.0243	-0.0184	0.0298	0.0447	0.0046	1961	0.2689
1962	-0.0366	0.0209	-0.0046	-0.0607	-0.0811	-0.0803	0.0652	0.0208	-0.0465	0.0064	0.1086	0.0153	1962	-0.0873
1963	0.0506	-0.0239	0.0370	0.0500	0.0193	-0.0188	-0.0022	0.0535	-0.0097	0.0339	-0.0046	0.0262	1963	0.2280
1964	0.0283	0.0147	0.0165	0.0075	0.0162	0.0178	0.0195	-0.0118	0.0301	0.0096	0.0005	0.0056	1964	0.1648
1965	0.0345	0.0031	-0.0133	0.0356	-0.0030	-0.0473	0.0147	0.0272	0.0334	0.0289	-0.0031	0.0106	1965	0.1245
1966	0.0062	-0.0131	-0.0205	0.0220	-0.0492	-0.0146	-0.0120	-0.0725	-0.0053	0.0494	0.0095	0.0002	1966	-0.1006
1967	0.0798	0.0072	0.0409	0.0437	-0.0477	0.0190	0.0468	-0.0070	0.0342	-0.0276	0.0065	0.0278	1967	0.2398
1968	-0.0425	-0.0261	0.0110	0.0834	0.0161	0.0105	-0.0172	0.0164	0.0400	0.0087	0.0531	-0.0402	1968	0.1106
1969	-0.0068	-0.0426	0.0359	0.0229	0.0026	-0.0542	-0.0587	0.0454	-0.0236	0.0459	-0.0297	-0.0177	1969	-0.0850
1970	-0.0743	0.0557	0.0044	-0.0875	-0.0578	-0.0466	0.0769	0.0478	0.0362	-0.0083	0.0506	0.0598	1970	0.0386

*Compound annual return

Table A-1 (Continued)

Large Company Stocks: Total Returns

from January 1971 to December 2011

Year	Jan	Feb	Mar	Apr	May	Jun	Jul	Aug	Sep	Oct	Nov	Dec	Year	Jan–Dec*
1971	0.0432	0.0117	0.0394	0.0389	-0.0391	0.0033	-0.0387	0.0388	-0.0044	-0.0391	0.0002	0.0888	1971	0.1430
1972	0.0206	0.0277	0.0083	0.0068	0.0197	-0.0194	0.0048	0.0369	-0.0025	0.0119	0.0481	0.0142	1972	0.1899
1973	-0.0149	-0.0352	0.0008	-0.0383	-0.0163	-0.0040	0.0407	-0.0341	0.0442	0.0002	-0.1109	0.0198	1973	-0.1469
1974	-0.0072	-0.0007	-0.0205	-0.0359	-0.0302	-0.0114	-0.0742	-0.0864	-0.1152	0.1681	-0.0489	-0.0156	1974	-0.2647
1975	0.1272	0.0638	0.0254	0.0510	0.0476	0.0477	-0.0644	-0.0176	-0.0312	0.0653	0.0282	-0.0081	1975	0.3723
1976	0.1217	-0.0084	0.0337	-0.0078	-0.0111	0.0443	-0.0048	-0.0018	0.0258	-0.0186	-0.0041	0.0561	1976	0.2393
1977	-0.0473	-0.0182	-0.0105	0.0042	-0.0196	0.0494	-0.0124	-0.0172	0.0015	-0.0389	0.0316	0.0075	1977	-0.0716
1978	-0.0574	-0.0203	0.0294	0.0902	0.0092	-0.0138	0.0583	0.0301	-0.0032	-0.0872	0.0215	0.0196	1978	0.0657
1979	0.0443	-0.0321	0.0596	0.0094	-0.0247	0.0435	0.0134	0.0577	0.0043	-0.0640	0.0475	0.0214	1979	0.1861
1980	0.0622	-0.0001	-0.0972	0.0462	0.0515	0.0316	0.0696	0.0101	0.0294	0.0202	0.1065	-0.0302	1980	0.3250
1981	-0.0418	0.0174	0.0400	-0.0193	0.0026	-0.0063	0.0021	-0.0577	-0.0493	0.0540	0.0413	-0.0256	1981	-0.0492
1982	-0.0131	-0.0559	-0.0052	0.0452	-0.0341	-0.0150	-0.0178	0.1214	0.0125	0.1151	0.0404	0.0193	1982	0.2155
1983	0.0372	0.0229	0.0369	0.0788	-0.0087	0.0389	-0.0295	0.0150	0.0138	-0.0116	0.0211	-0.0052	1983	0.2256
1984	-0.0056	-0.0352	0.0173	0.0095	-0.0554	0.0217	-0.0124	0.1104	0.0002	0.0039	-0.0112	0.0263	1984	0.0627
1985	0.0779	0.0122	0.0007	-0.0009	0.0578	0.0157	-0.0015	-0.0085	-0.0313	0.0462	0.0686	0.0484	1985	0.3173
1986	0.0056	0.0747	0.0558	-0.0113	0.0532	0.0169	-0.0559	0.0742	-0.0827	0.0577	0.0243	-0.0255	1986	0.1867
1987	0.1347	0.0395	0.0289	-0.0089	0.0087	0.0505	0.0507	0.0373	-0.0219	-0.2154	-0.0824	0.0761	1987	0.0525
1988	0.0421	0.0466	-0.0309	0.0111	0.0086	0.0459	-0.0038	-0.0339	0.0426	0.0278	-0.0143	0.0174	1988	0.1661
1989	0.0732	-0.0249	0.0233	0.0519	0.0405	-0.0057	0.0903	0.0195	-0.0041	-0.0232	0.0204	0.0240	1989	0.3169
1990	-0.0671	0.0129	0.0265	-0.0249	0.0975	-0.0067	-0.0032	-0.0904	-0.0487	-0.0043	0.0646	0.0279	1990	-0.0310
1991	0.0436	0.0715	0.0242	0.0024	0.0431	-0.0458	0.0466	0.0237	-0.0167	0.0134	-0.0403	0.1144	1991	0.3047
1992	-0.0186	0.0130	-0.0194	0.0294	0.0049	-0.0149	0.0409	-0.0205	0.0118	0.0035	0.0341	0.0123	1992	0.0762
1993	0.0084	0.0136	0.0211	-0.0242	0.0268	0.0029	-0.0040	0.0379	-0.0077	0.0207	-0.0095	0.0121	1993	0.1008
1994	0.0340	-0.0271	-0.0436	0.0128	0.0164	-0.0245	0.0328	0.0410	-0.0245	0.0225	-0.0364	0.0148	1994	0.0132
1995	0.0259	0.0390	0.0295	0.0294	0.0400	0.0232	0.0332	0.0025	0.0422	-0.0036	0.0439	0.0193	1995	0.3758
1996	0.0340	0.0093	0.0096	0.0147	0.0258	0.0038	-0.0442	0.0211	0.0563	0.0276	0.0756	-0.0198	1996	0.2296
1997	0.0625	0.0078	-0.0411	0.0597	0.0609	0.0448	0.0796	-0.0560	0.0548	-0.0334	0.0463	0.0172	1997	0.3336
1998	0.0111	0.0721	0.0512	0.0101	-0.0172	0.0406	-0.0106	-0.1446	0.0641	0.0813	0.0606	0.0576	1998	0.2858
1999	0.0418	-0.0311	0.0400	0.0387	-0.0236	0.0555	-0.0312	-0.0049	-0.0274	0.0633	0.0203	0.0589	1999	0.2104
2000	-0.0502	-0.0189	0.0978	-0.0301	-0.0205	0.0247	-0.0156	0.0621	-0.0528	-0.0042	-0.0788	0.0049	2000	-0.0910
2001	0.0355	-0.0912	-0.0634	0.0777	0.0067	-0.0243	-0.0098	-0.0626	-0.0808	0.0191	0.0767	0.0088	2001	-0.1189
2002	-0.0146	-0.0193	0.0376	-0.0606	-0.0074	-0.0712	-0.0780	0.0066	-0.1087	0.0880	0.0589	-0.0587	2002	-0.2210
2003	-0.0262	-0.0150	0.0097	0.0824	0.0527	0.0128	0.0176	0.0195	-0.0106	0.0566	0.0088	0.0524	2003	0.2868
2004	0.0184	0.0139	-0.0151	-0.0157	0.0137	0.0194	-0.0331	0.0040	0.0108	0.0153	0.0405	0.0340	2004	0.1088
2005	-0.0244	0.0210	-0.0177	-0.0190	0.0318	0.0014	0.0372	-0.0091	0.0081	-0.0167	0.0378	0.0003	2005	0.0491
2006	0.0265	0.0027	0.0124	0.0134	-0.0288	0.0014	0.0062	0.0238	0.0258	0.0326	0.0190	0.0140	2006	0.1579
2007	0.0151	-0.0196	0.0112	0.0443	0.0349	-0.0166	-0.0310	0.0150	0.0374	0.0159	-0.0418	-0.0069	2007	0.0549
2008	-0.0600	-0.0325	-0.0043	0.0487	0.0130	-0.0843	-0.0084	0.0145	-0.0891	-0.1679	-0.0718	0.0106	2008	-0.3700
2009	-0.0843	-0.1065	0.0876	0.0957	0.0559	0.0020	0.0756	0.0361	0.0373	-0.0186	0.0600	0.0193	2009	0.2646
2010	-0.0360	0.0310	0.0603	0.0158	-0.0799	-0.0523	0.0701	-0.0451	0.0892	0.0380	0.0001	0.0668	2010	0.1506
2011	0.0237	0.0343	0.0004	0.0296	-0.0113	-0.0167	-0.0203	-0.0543	-0.0703	0.1093	-0.0022	0.0102	2011	0.0211

*Compound annual return

from January 1926 to December 1970

Year	Jan	Feb	Mar	Apr	May	Jun	Jul	Aug	Sep	Oct	Nov	Dec	Year	Jan–Dec*
1926	0.0016	0.0055	0.0016	0.0026	0.0102	0.0025	0.0024	0.0078	0.0023	0.0030	0.0123	0.0030	1926	0.0541
1927	0.0015	0.0061	0.0022	0.0029	0.0085	0.0027	0.0020	0.0070	0.0018	0.0029	0.0105	0.0029	1927	0.0571
1928	0.0011	0.0051	0.0017	0.0021	0.0071	0.0020	0.0016	0.0062	0.0019	0.0023	0.0092	0.0021	1928	0.0481
1929	0.0012	0.0039	0.0012	0.0016	0.0066	0.0016	0.0014	0.0048	0.0013	0.0020	0.0091	0.0029	1929	0.0398
1930	0.0014	0.0044	0.0013	0.0016	0.0068	0.0020	0.0020	0.0066	0.0019	0.0032	0.0130	0.0036	1930	0.0457
1931	0.0013	0.0050	0.0017	0.0024	0.0093	0.0031	0.0020	0.0087	0.0022	0.0051	0.0180	0.0053	1931	0.0535
1932	0.0012	0.0063	0.0024	0.0027	0.0137	0.0067	0.0045	0.0115	0.0024	0.0037	0.0172	0.0046	1932	0.0616
1933	0.0015	0.0072	0.0018	0.0034	0.0096	0.0021	0.0018	0.0060	0.0018	0.0031	0.0100	0.0030	1933	0.0639
1934	0.0010	0.0045	0.0009	0.0019	0.0076	0.0021	0.0020	0.0069	0.0022	0.0033	0.0114	0.0031	1934	0.0446
1935	0.0011	0.0055	0.0023	0.0024	0.0086	0.0021	0.0020	0.0063	0.0018	0.0026	0.0080	0.0023	1935	0.0495
1936	0.0015	0.0056	0.0014	0.0020	0.0087	0.0028	0.0020	0.0063	0.0019	0.0025	0.0093	0.0029	1936	0.0536
1937	0.0012	0.0045	0.0017	0.0022	0.0079	0.0025	0.0019	0.0071	0.0019	0.0036	0.0146	0.0045	1937	0.0466
1938	0.0019	0.0065	0.0018	0.0035	0.0113	0.0032	0.0017	0.0048	0.0017	0.0016	0.0061	0.0024	1938	0.0483
1939	0.0015	0.0065	0.0016	0.0027	0.0110	0.0026	0.0018	0.0066	0.0027	0.0023	0.0094	0.0033	1939	0.0469
1940	0.0016	0.0066	0.0025	0.0024	0.0107	0.0043	0.0030	0.0087	0.0028	0.0028	0.0108	0.0038	1940	0.0536
1941	0.0019	0.0089	0.0030	0.0040	0.0140	0.0043	0.0030	0.0096	0.0029	0.0029	0.0137	0.0044	1941	0.0671
1942	0.0023	0.0091	0.0023	0.0037	0.0157	0.0037	0.0024	0.0093	0.0023	0.0034	0.0117	0.0032	1942	0.0679
1943	0.0020	0.0076	0.0018	0.0026	0.0104	0.0025	0.0016	0.0068	0.0025	0.0025	0.0101	0.0027	1943	0.0624
1944	0.0017	0.0068	0.0025	0.0025	0.0101	0.0032	0.0015	0.0071	0.0023	0.0023	0.0094	0.0023	1944	0.0548
1945	0.0015	0.0067	0.0021	0.0022	0.0081	0.0027	0.0020	0.0061	0.0019	0.0019	0.0072	0.0017	1945	0.0497
1946	0.0017	0.0054	0.0017	0.0017	0.0064	0.0021	0.0016	0.0056	0.0018	0.0020	0.0088	0.0027	1946	0.0409
1947	0.0020	0.0070	0.0019	0.0026	0.0103	0.0028	0.0020	0.0076	0.0026	0.0026	0.0110	0.0027	1947	0.0549
1948	0.0020	0.0082	0.0021	0.0027	0.0097	0.0024	0.0024	0.0082	0.0025	0.0032	0.0121	0.0041	1948	0.0608
1949	0.0026	0.0099	0.0027	0.0033	0.0115	0.0035	0.0028	0.0100	0.0026	0.0045	0.0162	0.0050	1949	0.0750
1950	0.0024	0.0100	0.0029	0.0035	0.0116	0.0032	0.0034	0.0118	0.0033	0.0051	0.0179	0.0051	1950	0.0877
1951	0.0024	0.0092	0.0028	0.0028	0.0107	0.0033	0.0024	0.0085	0.0021	0.0034	0.0122	0.0035	1951	0.0691
1952	0.0025	0.0083	0.0026	0.0029	0.0111	0.0029	0.0020	0.0075	0.0020	0.0029	0.0106	0.0027	1952	0.0593
1953	0.0023	0.0076	0.0023	0.0028	0.0110	0.0029	0.0021	0.0077	0.0021	0.0030	0.0114	0.0032	1953	0.0546
1954	0.0024	0.0084	0.0023	0.0026	0.0088	0.0024	0.0017	0.0065	0.0020	0.0028	0.0101	0.0026	1954	0.0621
1955	0.0017	0.0063	0.0019	0.0019	0.0068	0.0018	0.0015	0.0053	0.0016	0.0021	0.0078	0.0022	1955	0.0456
1956	0.0018	0.0066	0.0018	0.0016	0.0064	0.0018	0.0015	0.0053	0.0015	0.0015	0.0059	0.0018	1956	0.0383
1957	0.0017	0.0063	0.0018	0.0018	0.0068	0.0017	0.0017	0.0056	0.0018	0.0019	0.0071	0.0019	1957	0.0384
1958	0.0018	0.0065	0.0020	0.0019	0.0062	0.0018	0.0018	0.0057	0.0017	0.0016	0.0060	0.0015	1958	0.0438
1959	0.0014	0.0051	0.0014	0.0014	0.0050	0.0014	0.0014	0.0048	0.0013	0.0016	0.0054	0.0015	1959	0.0331
1960	0.0015	0.0056	0.0016	0.0014	0.0057	0.0016	0.0014	0.0056	0.0014	0.0017	0.0062	0.0016	1960	0.0326
1961	0.0014	0.0050	0.0014	0.0012	0.0047	0.0014	0.0014	0.0046	0.0013	0.0015	0.0054	0.0014	1961	0.0348
1962	0.0013	0.0046	0.0013	0.0013	0.0049	0.0015	0.0016	0.0055	0.0017	0.0020	0.0071	0.0018	1962	0.0298
1963	0.0014	0.0050	0.0016	0.0015	0.0050	0.0014	0.0013	0.0048	0.0014	0.0017	0.0059	0.0018	1963	0.0361
1964	0.0013	0.0048	0.0013	0.0014	0.0048	0.0014	0.0012	0.0044	0.0013	0.0015	0.0057	0.0017	1964	0.0333
1965	0.0013	0.0046	0.0013	0.0014	0.0047	0.0014	0.0013	0.0047	0.0014	0.0016	0.0056	0.0016	1965	0.0321
1966	0.0013	0.0047	0.0013	0.0015	0.0049	0.0015	0.0014	0.0053	0.0017	0.0018	0.0064	0.0017	1966	0.0311
1967	0.0016	0.0052	0.0015	0.0014	0.0048	0.0015	0.0014	0.0047	0.0014	0.0014	0.0054	0.0015	1967	0.0364
1968	0.0013	0.0051	0.0016	0.0014	0.0049	0.0014	0.0013	0.0049	0.0014	0.0015	0.0051	0.0014	1968	0.0318
1969	0.0013	0.0048	0.0014	0.0014	0.0048	0.0014	0.0014	0.0053	0.0015	0.0016	0.0056	0.0010	1969	0.0298
1970	0.0021	0.0031	0.0029	0.0030	0.0032	0.0034	0.0036	0.0033	0.0032	0.0031	0.0031	0.0030	1970	0.0333

*Compound annual return

from January 1971 to December 2011

Year	Jan	Feb	Mar	Apr	May	Jun	Jul	Aug	Sep	Oct	Nov	Dec	Year	Jan–Dec*
1971	0.0032	0.0022	0.0026	0.0035	0.0017	0.0026	0.0024	0.0029	0.0025	0.0041	0.0013	0.0041	1971	0.0349
1972	0.0011	0.0024	0.0023	0.0024	0.0041	0.0008	0.0024	0.0024	0.0023	0.0025	0.0025	0.0024	1972	0.0295
1973	0.0022	0.0022	0.0022	0.0025	0.0026	0.0026	0.0027	0.0026	0.0041	0.0015	0.0030	0.0032	1973	0.0286
1974	0.0029	0.0029	0.0028	0.0032	0.0033	0.0033	0.0036	0.0039	0.0042	0.0050	0.0043	0.0046	1974	0.0369
1975	0.0044	0.0039	0.0037	0.0037	0.0035	0.0034	0.0033	0.0035	0.0035	0.0037	0.0035	0.0034	1975	0.0537
1976	0.0034	0.0030	0.0030	0.0032	0.0032	0.0034	0.0033	0.0033	0.0032	0.0036	0.0037	0.0036	1976	0.0449
1977	0.0033	0.0034	0.0035	0.0040	0.0040	0.0041	0.0038	0.0038	0.0040	0.0045	0.0047	0.0046	1977	0.0435
1978	0.0041	0.0045	0.0045	0.0048	0.0044	0.0043	0.0044	0.0042	0.0041	0.0044	0.0048	0.0048	1978	0.0533
1979	0.0046	0.0044	0.0045	0.0077	0.0017	0.0048	0.0047	0.0046	0.0043	0.0046	0.0049	0.0046	1979	0.0589
1980	0.0045	0.0043	0.0046	0.0051	0.0049	0.0047	0.0046	0.0043	0.0043	0.0042	0.0042	0.0037	1980	0.0574
1981	0.0039	0.0041	0.0040	0.0041	0.0042	0.0041	0.0043	0.0044	0.0046	0.0048	0.0047	0.0044	1981	0.0488
1982	0.0045	0.0047	0.0049	0.0055	0.0047	0.0054	0.0051	0.0054	0.0049	0.0047	0.0043	0.0041	1982	0.0561
1983	0.0041	0.0039	0.0038	0.0040	0.0035	0.0037	0.0035	0.0037	0.0041	0.0032	0.0037	0.0036	1983	0.0504
1984	0.0036	0.0037	0.0038	0.0040	0.0040	0.0043	0.0040	0.0041	0.0037	0.0039	0.0039	0.0040	1984	0.0457
1985	0.0038	0.0036	0.0035	0.0037	0.0037	0.0035	0.0034	0.0035	0.0036	0.0036	0.0035	0.0033	1985	0.0472
1986	0.0032	0.0033	0.0030	0.0029	0.0030	0.0028	0.0028	0.0030	0.0028	0.0030	0.0027	0.0028	1986	0.0392
1987	0.0029	0.0026	0.0025	0.0026	0.0026	0.0026	0.0024	0.0024	0.0022	0.0023	0.0030	0.0032	1987	0.0364
1988	0.0016	0.0048	0.0024	0.0016	0.0055	0.0026	0.0016	0.0047	0.0029	0.0019	0.0046	0.0028	1988	0.0399
1989	0.0021	0.0040	0.0025	0.0018	0.0053	0.0023	0.0019	0.0040	0.0025	0.0020	0.0039	0.0026	1989	0.0403
1990	0.0017	0.0043	0.0022	0.0019	0.0055	0.0021	0.0020	0.0039	0.0025	0.0024	0.0047	0.0030	1990	0.0343
1991	0.0020	0.0042	0.0020	0.0020	0.0046	0.0021	0.0017	0.0040	0.0024	0.0016	0.0036	0.0028	1991	0.0376
1992	0.0013	0.0034	0.0024	0.0015	0.0039	0.0025	0.0015	0.0035	0.0026	0.0013	0.0038	0.0022	1992	0.0298
1993	0.0013	0.0031	0.0024	0.0012	0.0040	0.0022	0.0013	0.0035	0.0023	0.0013	0.0034	0.0020	1993	0.0291
1994	0.0015	0.0029	0.0021	0.0013	0.0040	0.0023	0.0013	0.0034	0.0025	0.0016	0.0031	0.0025	1994	0.0283
1995	0.0017	0.0029	0.0022	0.0015	0.0036	0.0020	0.0014	0.0028	0.0021	0.0014	0.0028	0.0018	1995	0.0304
1996	0.0014	0.0023	0.0017	0.0013	0.0029	0.0016	0.0016	0.0023	0.0021	0.0014	0.0022	0.0017	1996	0.0243
1997	0.0012	0.0019	0.0015	0.0013	0.0023	0.0013	0.0014	0.0014	0.0016	0.0011	0.0017	0.0014	1997	0.0210
1998	0.0009	0.0017	0.0013	0.0010	0.0016	0.0012	0.0010	0.0012	0.0017	0.0010	0.0015	0.0012	1998	0.0167
1999	0.0008	0.0012	0.0012	0.0008	0.0014	0.0011	0.0008	0.0013	0.0011	0.0007	0.0013	0.0011	1999	0.0136
2000	0.0007	0.0012	0.0011	0.0007	0.0014	0.0007	0.0007	0.0014	0.0007	0.0007	0.0012	0.0008	2000	0.0111
2001	0.0008	0.0011	0.0009	0.0009	0.0016	0.0007	0.0009	0.0015	0.0010	0.0010	0.0015	0.0012	2001	0.0118
2002	0.0010	0.0015	0.0009	0.0008	0.0017	0.0012	0.0010	0.0017	0.0013	0.0016	0.0018	0.0016	2002	0.0139
2003	0.0012	0.0020	0.0014	0.0013	0.0018	0.0014	0.0014	0.0016	0.0013	0.0016	0.0017	0.0017	2003	0.0199
2004	0.0011	0.0017	0.0013	0.0011	0.0016	0.0015	0.0012	0.0018	0.0015	0.0013	0.0019	0.0016	2004	0.0176
2005	0.0009	0.0021	0.0014	0.0011	0.0019	0.0016	0.0012	0.0021	0.0012	0.0011	0.0026	0.0013	2005	0.0184
2006	0.0010	0.0023	0.0014	0.0012	0.0021	0.0013	0.0011	0.0025	0.0012	0.0011	0.0025	0.0014	2006	0.0201
2007	0.0011	0.0023	0.0012	0.0010	0.0023	0.0012	0.0010	0.0021	0.0016	0.0011	0.0022	0.0017	2007	0.0196
2008	0.0012	0.0023	0.0016	0.0012	0.0023	0.0017	0.0015	0.0023	0.0017	0.0015	0.0031	0.0028	2008	0.0192
2009	0.0014	0.0035	0.0022	0.0018	0.0028	0.0018	0.0015	0.0025	0.0016	0.0012	0.0026	0.0015	2009	0.0248
2010	0.0010	0.0025	0.0016	0.0010	0.0021	0.0015	0.0013	0.0023	0.0017	0.0012	0.0024	0.0015	2010	0.0202
2011	0.0011	0.0023	0.0015	0.0011	0.0022	0.0016	0.0011	0.0025	0.0015	0.0016	0.0028	0.0017	2011	0.0213

*Compound annual return

Large Company Stocks: Capital Appreciation Returns

from January 1926 to December 1970

Year	Jan	Feb	Mar	Apr	May	Jun	Jul	Aug	Sep	Oct	Nov	Dec	Year	Jan–Dec*
1926	-0.0016	-0.0440	-0.0591	0.0227	0.0077	0.0432	0.0455	0.0171	0.0229	-0.0313	0.0223	0.0166	1926	0.0572
1927	-0.0208	0.0477	0.0065	0.0172	0.0522	-0.0094	0.0650	0.0445	0.0432	-0.0531	0.0616	0.0250	1927	0.3091
1928	-0.0051	-0.0176	0.1083	0.0324	0.0127	-0.0405	0.0125	0.0741	0.0240	0.0145	0.1199	0.0029	1928	0.3788
1929	0.0571	-0.0058	-0.0023	0.0161	-0.0428	0.1124	0.0456	0.0980	-0.0489	-0.1993	-0.1337	0.0253	1929	-0.1191
1930	0.0625	0.0215	0.0799	-0.0095	-0.0165	-0.1646	0.0367	0.0075	-0.1301	-0.0888	-0.0218	-0.0742	1930	-0.2848
1931	0.0489	0.1144	-0.0692	-0.0959	-0.1372	0.1390	-0.0742	0.0095	-0.2994	0.0844	-0.0978	-0.1453	1931	-0.4707
1932	-0.0283	0.0507	-0.1182	-0.2025	-0.2333	-0.0089	0.3770	0.3754	-0.0369	-0.1386	-0.0589	0.0519	1932	-0.1515
1933	0.0073	-0.1844	0.0336	0.4222	0.1587	0.1317	-0.0880	0.1146	-0.1136	-0.0885	0.1027	0.0223	1933	0.4659
1934	0.1059	-0.0367	-0.0009	-0.0270	-0.0813	0.0208	-0.1152	0.0541	-0.0055	-0.0319	0.0829	-0.0042	1934	-0.0594
1935	-0.0421	-0.0396	-0.0309	0.0956	0.0323	0.0678	0.0831	0.0217	0.0239	0.0751	0.0393	0.0371	1935	0.4137
1936	0.0655	0.0168	0.0254	-0.0771	0.0458	0.0306	0.0681	0.0088	0.0013	0.0750	0.0041	-0.0058	1936	0.2792
1937	0.0378	0.0146	-0.0094	-0.0831	-0.0103	-0.0529	0.1026	-0.0554	-0.1421	-0.1017	-0.1011	-0.0504	1937	-0.3859
1938	0.0133	0.0608	-0.2504	0.1412	-0.0443	0.2470	0.0727	-0.0274	0.0149	0.0760	-0.0334	0.0377	1938	0.2521
1939	-0.0689	0.0325	-0.1354	-0.0055	0.0623	-0.0638	0.1087	-0.0714	0.1646	-0.0146	-0.0491	0.0238	1939	-0.0545
1940	-0.0352	0.0066	0.0099	-0.0049	-0.2395	0.0766	0.0311	0.0262	0.0095	0.0394	-0.0424	-0.0028	1940	-0.1529
1941	-0.0482	-0.0149	0.0040	-0.0653	0.0043	0.0535	0.0548	-0.0087	-0.0097	-0.0686	-0.0421	-0.0451	1941	-0.1786
1942	0.0138	-0.0250	-0.0675	-0.0437	0.0640	0.0184	0.0313	0.0070	0.0267	0.0644	-0.0138	0.0517	1942	0.1243
1943	0.0716	0.0506	0.0527	0.0009	0.0449	0.0198	-0.0543	0.0103	0.0237	-0.0132	-0.0755	0.0590	1943	0.1945
1944	0.0154	-0.0025	0.0169	-0.0125	0.0404	0.0510	-0.0208	0.0087	-0.0031	0.0000	0.0039	0.0351	1944	0.1380
1945	0.0143	0.0616	-0.0462	0.0880	0.0115	-0.0033	-0.0201	0.0580	0.0419	0.0303	0.0324	0.0099	1945	0.3072
1946	0.0697	-0.0695	0.0463	0.0376	0.0224	-0.0391	-0.0255	-0.0729	-0.1015	-0.0080	-0.0115	0.0429	1946	-0.1187
1947	0.0235	-0.0147	-0.0169	-0.0389	-0.0089	0.0526	0.0362	-0.0279	-0.0137	0.0212	-0.0285	0.0207	1947	0.0000
1948	-0.0399	-0.0470	0.0771	0.0265	0.0782	0.0030	-0.0532	0.0076	-0.0301	0.0678	-0.1082	0.0305	1948	-0.0065
1949	0.0013	-0.0394	0.0301	-0.0212	-0.0373	-0.0021	0.0621	0.0120	0.0237	0.0295	0.0012	0.0436	1949	0.1026
1950	0.0173	0.0100	0.0041	0.0451	0.0393	-0.0580	0.0085	0.0325	0.0559	0.0041	-0.0010	0.0461	1950	0.2178
1951	0.0612	0.0065	-0.0183	0.0481	-0.0406	-0.0260	0.0687	0.0393	-0.0009	-0.0138	-0.0026	0.0389	1951	0.1646
1952	0.0156	-0.0365	0.0477	-0.0431	0.0232	0.0461	0.0176	-0.0146	-0.0196	-0.0008	0.0465	0.0355	1952	0.1178
1953	-0.0072	-0.0182	-0.0236	-0.0265	-0.0032	-0.0163	0.0253	-0.0578	0.0013	0.0510	0.0090	0.0020	1953	-0.0662
1954	0.0512	0.0027	0.0302	0.0490	0.0329	0.0007	0.0572	-0.0340	0.0831	-0.0195	0.0808	0.0508	1954	0.4502
1955	0.0181	0.0035	-0.0049	0.0377	-0.0013	0.0823	0.0607	-0.0078	0.0113	-0.0305	0.0749	-0.0007	1955	0.2640
1956	-0.0365	0.0347	0.0693	-0.0021	-0.0657	0.0392	0.0515	-0.0381	-0.0455	0.0051	-0.0110	0.0353	1956	0.0262
1957	-0.0418	-0.0326	0.0196	0.0370	0.0369	-0.0013	0.0114	-0.0561	-0.0619	-0.0321	0.0161	-0.0415	1957	-0.1431
1958	0.0428	-0.0206	0.0309	0.0318	0.0150	0.0261	0.0431	0.0119	0.0484	0.0254	0.0224	0.0520	1958	0.3806
1959	0.0038	-0.0002	0.0005	0.0388	0.0189	-0.0036	0.0349	-0.0150	-0.0456	0.0113	0.0132	0.0276	1959	0.0848
1960	-0.0715	0.0092	-0.0139	-0.0175	0.0269	0.0195	-0.0248	0.0261	-0.0604	-0.0024	0.0403	0.0463	1960	-0.0297
1961	0.0632	0.0269	0.0255	0.0038	0.0191	-0.0288	0.0328	0.0196	-0.0197	0.0283	0.0393	0.0032	1961	0.2313
1962	-0.0379	0.0163	-0.0059	-0.0620	-0.0860	-0.0818	0.0636	0.0153	-0.0482	0.0044	0.1016	0.0135	1962	-0.1181
1963	0.0491	-0.0289	0.0355	0.0485	0.0143	-0.0202	-0.0035	0.0487	-0.0110	0.0322	-0.0105	0.0244	1963	0.1889
1964	0.0269	0.0099	0.0152	0.0061	0.0115	0.0164	0.0182	-0.0162	0.0287	0.0081	-0.0052	0.0039	1964	0.1297
1965	0.0332	-0.0015	-0.0145	0.0342	-0.0077	-0.0486	0.0134	0.0225	0.0320	0.0273	-0.0088	0.0090	1965	0.0906
1966	0.0049	-0.0179	-0.0218	0.0205	-0.0541	-0.0161	-0.0135	-0.0778	-0.0070	0.0475	0.0031	-0.0015	1966	-0.1309
1967	0.0782	0.0020	0.0394	0.0422	-0.0524	0.0175	0.0453	-0.0117	0.0328	-0.0291	0.0011	0.0263	1967	0.2009
1968	-0.0438	-0.0312	0.0094	0.0819	0.0112	0.0091	-0.0185	0.0115	0.0385	0.0072	0.0480	-0.0416	1968	0.0766
1969	-0.0082	-0.0474	0.0344	0.0215	-0.0022	-0.0556	-0.0602	0.0401	-0.0250	0.0442	-0.0353	-0.0187	1969	-0.1136
1970	-0.0765	0.0527	0.0015	-0.0905	-0.0610	-0.0500	0.0733	0.0445	0.0330	-0.0114	0.0474	0.0568	1970	0.0010

*Compound annual return

from January 1971 to December 2011

Year	Jan	Feb	Mar	Apr	May	Jun	Jul	Aug	Sep	Oct	Nov	Dec	Year	Jan–Dec*
1971	0.0400	0.0095	0.0368	0.0354	-0.0407	0.0007	-0.0411	0.0359	-0.0070	-0.0432	-0.0011	0.0847	1971	0.1063
1972	0.0195	0.0253	0.0059	0.0044	0.0156	-0.0202	0.0023	0.0345	-0.0049	0.0093	0.0456	0.0118	1972	0.1579
1973	-0.0171	-0.0375	-0.0014	-0.0408	-0.0189	-0.0066	0.0380	-0.0367	0.0401	-0.0013	-0.1139	0.0166	1973	-0.1737
1974	-0.0100	-0.0036	-0.0233	-0.0391	-0.0336	-0.0147	-0.0778	-0.0903	-0.1193	0.1630	-0.0532	-0.0202	1974	-0.2972
1975	0.1228	0.0599	0.0217	0.0473	0.0441	0.0443	-0.0677	-0.0211	-0.0346	0.0616	0.0247	-0.0115	1975	0.3155
1976	0.1183	-0.0114	0.0307	-0.0110	-0.0144	0.0409	-0.0081	-0.0051	0.0226	-0.0222	-0.0078	0.0525	1976	0.1915
1977	-0.0505	-0.0217	-0.0140	0.0002	-0.0236	0.0454	-0.0162	-0.0210	-0.0025	-0.0434	0.0270	0.0028	1977	-0.1150
1978	-0.0615	-0.0248	0.0249	0.0854	0.0048	-0.0181	0.0539	0.0259	-0.0073	-0.0916	0.0166	0.0149	1978	0.0106
1979	0.0397	-0.0365	0.0552	0.0017	-0.0263	0.0387	0.0087	0.0531	0.0000	-0.0686	0.0426	0.0168	1979	0.1231
1980	0.0576	-0.0044	-0.1018	0.0411	0.0466	0.0270	0.0650	0.0058	0.0252	0.0160	0.1024	-0.0339	1980	0.2577
1981	-0.0457	0.0133	0.0360	-0.0235	-0.0017	-0.0104	-0.0022	-0.0621	-0.0538	0.0491	0.0366	-0.0301	1981	-0.0973
1982	-0.0175	-0.0606	-0.0101	0.0397	-0.0388	-0.0204	-0.0229	0.1160	0.0076	0.1104	0.0361	0.0152	1982	0.1476
1983	0.0331	0.0190	0.0331	0.0748	-0.0122	0.0352	-0.0330	0.0113	0.0097	-0.0148	0.0174	-0.0088	1983	0.1727
1984	-0.0092	-0.0389	0.0135	0.0055	-0.0594	0.0175	-0.0165	0.1063	-0.0035	-0.0001	-0.0151	0.0224	1984	0.0140
1985	0.0741	0.0086	-0.0029	-0.0046	0.0541	0.0121	-0.0048	-0.0120	-0.0348	0.0426	0.0651	0.0451	1985	0.2633
1986	0.0024	0.0715	0.0528	-0.0141	0.0502	0.0141	-0.0587	0.0712	-0.0854	0.0546	0.0216	-0.0283	1986	0.1462
1987	0.1318	0.0369	0.0264	-0.0115	0.0060	0.0479	0.0482	0.0350	-0.0242	-0.2176	-0.0853	0.0729	1987	0.0203
1988	0.0404	0.0418	-0.0333	0.0094	0.0032	0.0433	-0.0054	-0.0386	0.0397	0.0260	-0.0189	0.0147	1988	0.1240
1989	0.0711	-0.0289	0.0208	0.0501	0.0351	-0.0079	0.0884	0.0155	-0.0065	-0.0252	0.0165	0.0214	1989	0.2725
1990	-0.0688	0.0085	0.0243	-0.0269	0.0920	-0.0089	-0.0052	-0.0943	-0.0512	-0.0067	0.0599	0.0248	1990	-0.0656
1991	0.0415	0.0673	0.0222	0.0003	0.0386	-0.0479	0.0449	0.0196	-0.0191	0.0118	-0.0439	0.1116	1991	0.2631
1992	-0.0199	0.0096	-0.0218	0.0279	0.0010	-0.0174	0.0394	-0.0240	0.0091	0.0021	0.0303	0.0101	1992	0.0446
1993	0.0070	0.0105	0.0187	-0.0254	0.0227	0.0008	-0.0053	0.0344	-0.0100	0.0194	-0.0129	0.0101	1993	0.0706
1994	0.0325	-0.0300	-0.0457	0.0115	0.0124	-0.0268	0.0315	0.0376	-0.0269	0.0209	-0.0395	0.0123	1994	-0.0154
1995	0.0243	0.0361	0.0273	0.0280	0.0363	0.0213	0.0318	-0.0003	0.0401	-0.0050	0.0410	0.0174	1995	0.3411
1996	0.0326	0.0069	0.0079	0.0134	0.0229	0.0023	-0.0457	0.0188	0.0542	0.0261	0.0734	-0.0215	1996	0.2026
1997	0.0613	0.0059	-0.0426	0.0584	0.0586	0.0435	0.0781	-0.0574	0.0532	-0.0345	0.0446	0.0157	1997	0.3101
1998	0.0102	0.0704	0.0499	0.0091	-0.0188	0.0394	-0.0116	-0.1458	0.0624	0.0803	0.0591	0.0564	1998	0.2667
1999	0.0410	-0.0323	0.0388	0.0379	-0.0250	0.0544	-0.0320	-0.0063	-0.0286	0.0625	0.0191	0.0578	1999	0.1953
2000	-0.0509	-0.0201	0.0967	-0.0308	-0.0219	0.0239	-0.0163	0.0607	-0.0535	-0.0049	-0.0801	0.0041	2000	-0.1014
2001	0.0346	-0.0923	-0.0642	0.0768	0.0051	-0.0250	-0.0108	-0.0641	-0.0817	0.0181	0.0752	0.0076	2001	-0.1304
2002	-0.0156	-0.0208	0.0367	-0.0614	-0.0091	-0.0725	-0.0790	0.0049	-0.1100	0.0864	0.0571	-0.0603	2002	-0.2337
2003	-0.0274	-0.0170	0.0084	0.0810	0.0509	0.0113	0.0162	0.0179	-0.0119	0.0550	0.0071	0.0508	2003	0.2638
2004	0.0173	0.0122	-0.0164	-0.0168	0.0121	0.0180	-0.0343	0.0023	0.0094	0.0140	0.0386	0.0325	2004	0.0899
2005	-0.0253	0.0189	-0.0191	-0.0201	0.0300	-0.0001	0.0360	-0.0112	0.0069	-0.0177	0.0352	-0.0009	2005	0.0300
2006	0.0255	0.0005	0.0111	0.0122	-0.0309	0.0001	0.0051	0.0213	0.0246	0.0315	0.0165	0.0126	2006	0.1362
2007	0.0141	-0.0218	0.0100	0.0433	0.0326	-0.0178	-0.0320	0.0129	0.0358	0.0148	-0.0440	-0.0086	2007	0.0353
2008	-0.0612	-0.0348	-0.0060	0.0475	0.0107	-0.0860	-0.0099	0.0122	-0.0908	-0.1694	-0.0749	0.0078	2008	-0.3849
2009	-0.0857	-0.1099	0.0854	0.0939	0.0531	0.0002	0.0741	0.0336	0.0357	-0.0198	0.0574	0.0178	2009	0.2345
2010	-0.0370	0.0285	0.0588	0.0148	-0.0820	-0.0539	0.0688	-0.0475	0.0876	0.0369	-0.0023	0.0653	2010	0.1278
2011	0.0226	0.0320	-0.0011	0.0285	-0.0135	-0.0183	-0.0215	-0.0568	-0.0718	0.1077	-0.0051	0.0085	2011	0.0000

*Compound annual return

Table A-4
Small Company Stocks: Total Returns

from January 1926 to December 1970

Year	Jan	Feb	Mar	Apr	May	Jun	Jul	Aug	Sep	Oct	Nov	Dec	Year	Jan–Dec*
1926	0.0699	-0.0639	-0.1073	0.0179	-0.0066	0.0378	0.0112	0.0256	-0.0001	-0.0227	0.0207	0.0332	1926	0.0028
1927	0.0296	0.0547	-0.0548	0.0573	0.0734	-0.0303	0.0516	-0.0178	0.0047	-0.0659	0.0808	0.0316	1927	0.2210
1928	0.0482	-0.0236	0.0531	0.0910	0.0438	-0.0842	0.0059	0.0442	0.0890	0.0276	0.1147	-0.0513	1928	0.3969
1929	0.0035	-0.0026	-0.0200	0.0306	-0.1336	0.0533	0.0114	-0.0164	-0.0922	-0.2768	-0.1500	-0.0501	1929	-0.5136
1930	0.1293	0.0643	0.1007	-0.0698	-0.0542	-0.2168	0.0301	-0.0166	-0.1459	-0.1097	-0.0028	-0.1166	1930	-0.3815
1931	0.2103	0.2566	-0.0708	-0.2164	-0.1379	0.1819	-0.0557	-0.0763	-0.3246	0.0770	-0.1008	-0.2195	1931	-0.4975
1932	0.1019	0.0291	-0.1311	-0.2220	-0.1193	0.0033	0.3523	0.7346	-0.1320	-0.1775	-0.1227	-0.0492	1932	-0.0539
1933	-0.0083	-0.1278	0.1118	0.5038	0.6339	0.2617	-0.0550	0.0924	-0.1595	-0.1236	0.0654	0.0055	1933	1.4287
1934	0.3891	0.0166	-0.0012	0.0240	-0.1275	-0.0024	-0.2259	0.1546	-0.0167	0.0097	0.0948	0.0172	1934	0.2422
1935	-0.0328	-0.0592	-0.1189	0.0791	-0.0024	0.0305	0.0855	0.0545	0.0357	0.0994	0.1412	0.0598	1935	0.4019
1936	0.3009	0.0602	0.0066	-0.1795	0.0272	-0.0231	0.0873	0.0210	0.0542	0.0635	0.1400	0.0160	1936	0.6480
1937	0.1267	0.0658	0.0120	-0.1679	-0.0408	-0.1183	0.1235	-0.0736	-0.2539	-0.1093	-0.1453	-0.1694	1937	-0.5801
1938	0.0534	0.0343	-0.3600	0.2776	-0.0849	0.3498	0.1499	-0.1001	-0.0157	0.2136	-0.0689	0.0487	1938	0.3280
1939	-0.0848	0.0107	-0.2466	0.0142	0.1088	-0.1042	0.2535	-0.1590	0.5145	-0.0397	-0.1053	0.0422	1939	0.0035
1940	0.0009	0.0821	0.0632	0.0654	-0.3674	0.1051	0.0231	0.0255	0.0213	0.0545	0.0245	-0.0447	1940	-0.0516
1941	0.0025	-0.0288	0.0319	-0.0669	0.0044	0.0753	0.2165	-0.0060	-0.0469	-0.0672	-0.0495	-0.1204	1941	-0.0900
1942	0.1894	-0.0073	-0.0709	-0.0353	-0.0032	0.0336	0.0737	0.0325	0.0912	0.1087	-0.0511	0.0413	1942	0.4451
1943	0.2132	0.1931	0.1445	0.0933	0.1156	-0.0083	-0.1083	-0.0002	0.0428	0.0123	-0.1113	0.1241	1943	0.8837
1944	0.0641	0.0295	0.0749	-0.0532	0.0740	0.1384	-0.0299	0.0318	-0.0020	-0.0108	0.0499	0.0869	1944	0.5372
1945	0.0482	0.1009	-0.0861	0.1157	0.0500	0.0855	-0.0556	0.0557	0.0679	0.0701	0.1172	0.0171	1945	0.7361
1946	0.1562	-0.0637	0.0273	0.0696	0.0591	-0.0462	-0.0530	-0.0849	-0.1603	-0.0118	-0.0141	0.0373	1946	-0.1163
1947	0.0421	-0.0041	-0.0336	-0.1031	-0.0534	0.0552	0.0789	-0.0037	0.0115	0.0282	-0.0303	0.0359	1947	0.0092
1948	-0.0154	-0.0783	0.0986	0.0368	0.1059	0.0048	-0.0578	0.0006	-0.0526	0.0647	-0.1116	0.0088	1948	-0.0211
1949	0.0182	-0.0481	0.0629	-0.0336	-0.0564	-0.0096	0.0671	0.0256	0.0489	0.0472	0.0016	0.0690	1949	0.1975
1950	0.0492	0.0221	-0.0037	0.0411	0.0255	-0.0777	0.0591	0.0530	0.0521	-0.0059	0.0322	0.0953	1950	0.3875
1951	0.0830	0.0061	-0.0477	0.0367	-0.0331	-0.0529	0.0373	0.0605	0.0215	-0.0222	-0.0083	0.0044	1951	0.0780
1952	0.0191	-0.0300	0.0175	-0.0519	0.0032	0.0272	0.0112	-0.0006	-0.0161	-0.0103	0.0485	0.0160	1952	0.0303
1953	0.0409	0.0269	-0.0067	-0.0287	0.0141	-0.0486	0.0152	-0.0628	-0.0262	0.0292	0.0126	-0.0266	1953	-0.0649
1954	0.0756	0.0094	0.0183	0.0140	0.0451	0.0086	0.0808	0.0014	0.0410	0.0068	0.0779	0.1112	1954	0.6058
1955	0.0201	0.0479	0.0085	0.0150	0.0078	0.0293	0.0064	-0.0028	0.0109	-0.0170	0.0468	0.0163	1955	0.2044
1956	-0.0047	0.0278	0.0431	0.0047	-0.0398	0.0056	0.0283	-0.0134	-0.0260	0.0104	0.0053	0.0038	1956	0.0428
1957	0.0236	-0.0200	0.0167	0.0248	0.0075	0.0073	-0.0060	-0.0386	-0.0452	-0.0832	0.0113	-0.0481	1957	-0.1457
1958	0.1105	-0.0170	0.0471	0.0376	0.0387	0.0324	0.0492	0.0428	0.0518	0.0407	0.0496	0.0313	1958	0.6489
1959	0.0575	0.0295	0.0027	0.0117	0.0014	-0.0042	0.0327	-0.0088	-0.0431	0.0227	0.0222	0.0322	1959	0.1640
1960	-0.0306	0.0050	-0.0315	-0.0187	0.0204	0.0340	-0.0189	0.0525	-0.0738	-0.0401	0.0437	0.0332	1960	-0.0329
1961	0.0915	0.0589	0.0619	0.0127	0.0427	-0.0543	0.0031	0.0130	-0.0339	0.0262	0.0613	0.0079	1961	0.3209
1962	0.0136	0.0187	0.0057	-0.0777	-0.1009	-0.0785	0.0763	0.0289	-0.0659	-0.0373	0.1248	-0.0089	1962	-0.1190
1963	0.0906	0.0034	0.0149	0.0312	0.0436	-0.0118	0.0033	0.0517	-0.0163	0.0236	-0.0106	-0.0048	1963	0.2357
1964	0.0274	0.0365	0.0219	0.0093	0.0157	0.0163	0.0398	-0.0029	0.0402	0.0205	0.0011	-0.0112	1964	0.2352
1965	0.0529	0.0390	0.0238	0.0509	-0.0078	-0.0901	0.0449	0.0595	0.0347	0.0572	0.0371	0.0622	1965	0.4175
1966	0.0756	0.0311	-0.0192	0.0343	-0.0961	-0.0012	-0.0012	-0.1080	-0.0164	-0.0107	0.0491	0.0065	1966	-0.0701
1967	0.1838	0.0450	0.0615	0.0271	-0.0085	0.1017	0.0951	0.0020	0.0565	-0.0311	0.0117	0.0965	1967	0.8357
1968	0.0154	-0.0709	-0.0109	0.1461	0.0999	0.0030	-0.0345	0.0367	0.0599	0.0030	0.0764	0.0062	1968	0.3597
1969	-0.0166	-0.0990	0.0396	0.0395	0.0173	-0.1165	-0.1070	0.0732	-0.0261	0.0610	-0.0557	-0.0687	1969	-0.2505
1970	-0.0608	0.0387	-0.0285	-0.1728	-0.1031	-0.0929	0.0554	0.0949	0.1086	-0.0706	0.0137	0.0726	1970	-0.1743

*Compound annual return

Small Company Stocks: Total Returns

from January 1971 to December 2011

Year	Jan	Feb	Mar	Apr	May	Jun	Jul	Aug	Sep	Oct	Nov	Dec	Year	Jan–Dec*
1971	0.1592	0.0317	0.0564	0.0247	-0.0605	-0.0319	-0.0563	0.0583	-0.0226	-0.0551	-0.0373	0.1144	1971	0.1650
1972	0.1130	0.0296	-0.0143	0.0129	-0.0191	-0.0305	-0.0413	0.0186	-0.0349	-0.0175	0.0592	-0.0214	1972	0.0443
1973	-0.0432	-0.0799	-0.0208	-0.0621	-0.0811	-0.0290	0.1194	-0.0445	0.1064	0.0084	-0.1962	-0.0014	1973	-0.3090
1974	0.1326	-0.0085	-0.0074	-0.0464	-0.0793	-0.0147	-0.0219	-0.0681	-0.0653	0.1063	-0.0438	-0.0788	1974	-0.1995
1975	0.2767	0.0285	0.0618	0.0531	0.0663	0.0750	-0.0254	-0.0574	-0.0182	-0.0050	0.0320	-0.0197	1975	0.5282
1976	0.2684	0.1390	-0.0015	-0.0359	-0.0361	0.0459	0.0045	-0.0290	0.0104	-0.0209	0.0404	0.1180	1976	0.5738
1977	0.0450	-0.0039	0.0131	0.0228	-0.0028	0.0772	0.0030	-0.0107	0.0092	-0.0330	0.1086	0.0081	1977	0.2538
1978	-0.0189	0.0347	0.1032	0.0788	0.0820	-0.0189	0.0684	0.0939	-0.0032	-0.2427	0.0732	0.0168	1978	0.2346
1979	0.1321	-0.0282	0.1120	0.0387	0.0035	0.0472	0.0171	0.0756	-0.0344	-0.1154	0.0858	0.0588	1979	0.4346
1980	0.0836	-0.0284	-0.1778	0.0694	0.0750	0.0452	0.1323	0.0604	0.0418	0.0333	0.0766	-0.0338	1980	0.3988
1981	0.0207	0.0094	0.0943	0.0657	0.0422	0.0076	-0.0316	-0.0684	-0.0733	0.0742	0.0276	-0.0220	1981	0.1388
1982	-0.0196	-0.0296	-0.0086	0.0383	-0.0248	-0.0159	-0.0015	0.0698	0.0327	0.1305	0.0779	0.0132	1982	0.2801
1983	0.0628	0.0712	0.0525	0.0767	0.0870	0.0348	-0.0088	-0.0197	0.0133	-0.0568	0.0516	-0.0145	1983	0.3967
1984	-0.0008	-0.0645	0.0174	-0.0085	-0.0521	0.0300	-0.0420	0.0998	0.0027	-0.0217	-0.0336	0.0150	1984	-0.0667
1985	0.1059	0.0272	-0.0214	-0.0174	0.0276	0.0106	0.0260	-0.0072	-0.0544	0.0261	0.0620	0.0470	1985	0.2466
1986	0.0112	0.0719	0.0477	0.0064	0.0360	0.0026	-0.0710	0.0218	-0.0559	0.0346	-0.0031	-0.0262	1986	0.0685
1987	0.0943	0.0809	0.0233	-0.0313	-0.0039	0.0266	0.0364	0.0287	-0.0081	-0.2919	-0.0397	0.0520	1987	-0.0930
1988	0.0556	0.0760	0.0408	0.0209	-0.0179	0.0612	-0.0025	-0.0246	0.0227	-0.0123	-0.0437	0.0394	1988	0.2287
1989	0.0404	0.0083	0.0358	0.0279	0.0362	-0.0201	0.0407	0.0122	0.0000	-0.0604	-0.0051	-0.0134	1989	0.1018
1990	-0.0764	0.0187	0.0368	-0.0266	0.0561	0.0144	-0.0382	-0.1296	-0.0829	-0.0572	0.0450	0.0194	1990	-0.2156
1991	0.0841	0.1113	0.0680	0.0034	0.0334	-0.0485	0.0407	0.0261	0.0032	0.0317	-0.0276	0.0601	1991	0.4463
1992	0.1128	0.0452	-0.0249	-0.0403	-0.0014	-0.0519	0.0370	-0.0228	0.0131	0.0259	0.0885	0.0441	1992	0.2335
1993	0.0543	-0.0180	0.0289	-0.0306	0.0342	-0.0038	0.0166	0.0339	0.0316	0.0471	-0.0175	0.0194	1993	0.2098
1994	0.0618	-0.0023	-0.0446	0.0060	-0.0012	-0.0262	0.0184	0.0337	0.0105	0.0115	-0.0326	0.0002	1994	0.0311
1995	0.0283	0.0252	0.0145	0.0352	0.0298	0.0568	0.0645	0.0358	0.0195	-0.0487	0.0192	0.0239	1995	0.3446
1996	0.0028	0.0369	0.0228	0.0848	0.0749	-0.0582	-0.0943	0.0476	0.0291	-0.0175	0.0288	0.0204	1996	0.1762
1997	0.0420	-0.0206	-0.0490	-0.0276	0.1022	0.0498	0.0605	0.0509	0.0844	-0.0386	-0.0155	-0.0171	1997	0.2278
1998	-0.0059	0.0649	0.0481	0.0168	-0.0497	-0.0206	-0.0671	-0.2010	0.0369	0.0356	0.0758	0.0252	1998	-0.0731
1999	0.0279	-0.0687	-0.0379	0.0949	0.0387	0.0568	0.0092	-0.0191	-0.0221	-0.0087	0.0971	0.1137	1999	0.2979
2000	0.0595	0.2358	-0.0751	-0.1251	-0.0808	0.1368	-0.0322	0.0925	-0.0217	-0.0706	-0.1110	0.0189	2000	-0.0359
2001	0.1380	-0.0702	-0.0480	0.0731	0.0960	0.0359	-0.0254	-0.0295	-0.1278	0.0645	0.0674	0.0672	2001	0.2277
2002	0.0110	-0.0277	0.0884	0.0243	-0.0273	-0.0356	-0.1448	-0.0057	-0.0674	0.0257	0.0836	-0.0429	2002	-0.1328
2003	-0.0223	-0.0288	0.0111	0.0928	0.1162	0.0440	0.0738	0.0473	0.0009	0.0894	0.0430	0.0277	2003	0.6070
2004	0.0578	0.0050	0.0014	-0.0409	0.0000	0.0441	-0.0747	-0.0152	0.0501	0.0184	0.0897	0.0458	2004	0.1839
2005	-0.0410	0.0083	-0.0323	-0.0622	0.0603	0.0452	0.0763	-0.0139	0.0061	-0.0281	0.0453	0.0018	2005	0.0569
2006	0.0914	0.0025	0.0455	-0.0041	-0.0589	-0.0089	-0.0345	0.0278	0.0056	0.0545	0.0225	0.0161	2006	0.1617
2007	0.0115	-0.0050	0.0102	0.0150	0.0315	-0.0033	-0.0651	0.0116	0.0148	0.0170	-0.0842	-0.0006	2007	-0.0522
2008	-0.0765	-0.0314	0.0031	0.0207	0.0398	-0.0905	0.0448	0.0338	-0.0737	-0.2071	-0.1284	0.0566	2008	-0.3672
2009	-0.1191	-0.1311	0.0958	0.1739	0.0343	0.0276	0.0982	0.0273	0.0576	-0.0727	0.0178	0.0869	2009	0.2809
2010	-0.0294	0.0439	0.0808	0.0727	-0.0742	-0.0724	0.0714	-0.0798	0.1216	0.0434	0.0424	0.0819	2010	0.3126
2011	-0.0109	0.0587	0.0325	0.0168	-0.0192	-0.0216	-0.0269	-0.0893	-0.1058	0.1543	-0.0060	0.0086	2011	-0.0326

*Compound annual return

Table A-5

Long-Term Corporate Bonds: Total Returns

from January 1926 to December 1970

Year	Jan	Feb	Mar	Apr	May	Jun	Jul	Aug	Sep	Oct	Nov	Dec	Year	Jan–Dec*
1926	0.0072	0.0045	0.0084	0.0097	0.0044	0.0004	0.0057	0.0044	0.0057	0.0097	0.0057	0.0056	1926	0.0737
1927	0.0056	0.0069	0.0083	0.0055	-0.0011	0.0043	0.0003	0.0083	0.0149	0.0055	0.0068	0.0068	1927	0.0744
1928	0.0027	0.0068	0.0041	0.0014	-0.0078	-0.0024	-0.0010	0.0083	0.0030	0.0083	-0.0036	0.0084	1928	0.0284
1929	0.0043	0.0030	-0.0087	0.0019	0.0045	-0.0046	0.0020	0.0020	0.0034	0.0073	-0.0018	0.0192	1929	0.0327
1930	0.0059	0.0072	0.0138	0.0084	0.0057	0.0110	0.0056	0.0136	0.0108	0.0054	-0.0012	-0.0090	1930	0.0798
1931	0.0203	0.0068	0.0094	0.0067	0.0134	0.0052	0.0052	0.0012	-0.0014	-0.0363	-0.0189	-0.0286	1931	-0.0185
1932	-0.0052	-0.0238	0.0356	-0.0176	0.0107	-0.0009	0.0043	0.0436	0.0301	0.0074	0.0073	0.0139	1932	0.1082
1933	0.0547	-0.0523	0.0047	-0.0095	0.0588	0.0190	0.0161	0.0093	-0.0014	0.0040	-0.0248	0.0257	1933	0.1038
1934	0.0257	0.0146	0.0187	0.0104	0.0090	0.0158	0.0047	0.0047	-0.0061	0.0102	0.0129	0.0101	1934	0.1384
1935	0.0211	0.0141	0.0043	0.0112	0.0042	0.0112	0.0111	-0.0042	0.0000	0.0042	0.0069	0.0083	1935	0.0961
1936	0.0082	0.0054	0.0082	0.0026	0.0040	0.0082	0.0011	0.0067	0.0067	0.0025	0.0109	0.0010	1936	0.0674
1937	0.0024	-0.0046	-0.0114	0.0068	0.0040	0.0053	0.0039	-0.0017	0.0025	0.0067	0.0067	0.0067	1937	0.0275
1938	0.0038	0.0010	-0.0087	0.0138	0.0010	0.0095	0.0066	-0.0019	0.0109	0.0080	0.0037	0.0122	1938	0.0613
1939	0.0022	0.0064	0.0022	0.0064	0.0049	0.0035	-0.0007	-0.0392	0.0151	0.0237	0.0079	0.0078	1939	0.0397
1940	0.0049	0.0021	0.0049	-0.0092	-0.0021	0.0121	0.0021	0.0007	0.0092	0.0049	0.0063	-0.0023	1940	0.0339
1941	0.0006	0.0006	-0.0022	0.0078	0.0049	0.0063	0.0063	0.0034	0.0048	0.0034	-0.0094	0.0006	1941	0.0273
1942	0.0006	-0.0008	0.0063	0.0006	0.0020	0.0034	0.0020	0.0035	0.0020	0.0006	0.0006	0.0049	1942	0.0260
1943	0.0049	0.0006	0.0020	0.0049	0.0048	0.0048	0.0019	0.0019	0.0005	-0.0009	-0.0023	0.0049	1943	0.0283
1944	0.0020	0.0034	0.0048	0.0034	0.0005	0.0020	0.0034	0.0034	0.0019	0.0019	0.0048	0.0149	1944	0.0473
1945	0.0076	0.0046	0.0018	0.0018	-0.0011	0.0032	-0.0011	0.0004	0.0032	0.0032	0.0032	0.0133	1945	0.0408
1946	0.0128	0.0034	0.0034	-0.0043	0.0019	0.0019	-0.0012	-0.0088	-0.0026	0.0020	-0.0025	0.0113	1946	0.0172
1947	0.0005	0.0005	0.0067	0.0020	0.0020	0.0004	0.0020	-0.0071	-0.0131	-0.0099	-0.0098	0.0024	1947	-0.0234
1948	0.0024	0.0039	0.0115	0.0038	0.0008	-0.0083	-0.0052	0.0055	0.0024	0.0024	0.0085	0.0131	1948	0.0414
1949	0.0038	0.0038	0.0007	0.0023	0.0038	0.0084	0.0099	0.0037	0.0021	0.0067	0.0021	-0.0145	1949	0.0331
1950	0.0037	0.0007	0.0022	-0.0008	-0.0008	0.0023	0.0069	0.0038	-0.0039	-0.0008	0.0054	0.0023	1950	0.0212
1951	0.0019	-0.0044	-0.0237	-0.0009	-0.0015	-0.0093	0.0205	0.0114	-0.0057	-0.0145	-0.0061	0.0058	1951	-0.0269
1952	0.0199	-0.0085	0.0076	-0.0004	0.0031	0.0016	0.0016	0.0063	-0.0018	0.0039	0.0108	-0.0091	1952	0.0352
1953	-0.0080	-0.0040	-0.0033	-0.0248	-0.0030	0.0109	0.0177	-0.0085	0.0253	0.0227	-0.0073	0.0172	1953	0.0341
1954	0.0124	0.0198	0.0039	-0.0034	-0.0042	0.0063	0.0040	0.0018	0.0040	0.0040	0.0025	0.0017	1954	0.0539
1955	-0.0097	-0.0063	0.0092	-0.0001	-0.0018	0.0029	-0.0041	-0.0038	0.0076	0.0078	-0.0030	0.0063	1955	0.0048
1956	0.0104	0.0026	-0.0146	-0.0115	0.0052	-0.0018	-0.0093	-0.0208	0.0012	-0.0105	-0.0126	-0.0082	1956	-0.0681
1957	0.0197	0.0093	0.0050	-0.0066	-0.0075	-0.0322	-0.0110	-0.0009	0.0095	0.0023	0.0311	0.0685	1957	0.0871
1958	0.0099	-0.0008	-0.0046	0.0163	0.0031	-0.0038	-0.0153	-0.0320	-0.0096	0.0107	0.0105	-0.0058	1958	-0.0222
1959	-0.0028	0.0126	-0.0083	-0.0172	-0.0114	0.0044	0.0089	-0.0068	-0.0088	0.0165	0.0135	-0.0096	1959	-0.0097
1960	0.0107	0.0128	0.0191	-0.0022	-0.0021	0.0141	0.0257	0.0117	-0.0063	0.0008	-0.0070	0.0104	1960	0.0907
1961	0.0148	0.0210	-0.0029	-0.0116	0.0049	-0.0080	0.0040	-0.0018	0.0144	0.0127	0.0028	-0.0026	1961	0.0482
1962	0.0080	0.0052	0.0151	0.0142	0.0000	-0.0026	-0.0015	0.0143	0.0089	0.0068	0.0062	0.0023	1962	0.0795
1963	0.0059	0.0023	0.0026	-0.0051	0.0048	0.0043	0.0028	0.0035	-0.0023	0.0049	0.0015	-0.0034	1963	0.0219
1964	0.0087	0.0054	-0.0062	0.0040	0.0057	0.0048	0.0052	0.0037	0.0021	0.0050	-0.0004	0.0088	1964	0.0477
1965	0.0081	0.0009	0.0012	0.0021	-0.0008	0.0003	0.0019	-0.0006	-0.0015	0.0046	-0.0057	-0.0149	1965	-0.0046
1966	0.0022	-0.0113	-0.0059	0.0013	-0.0026	0.0030	-0.0098	-0.0259	0.0078	0.0261	-0.0020	0.0201	1966	0.0020
1967	0.0450	-0.0201	0.0117	-0.0071	-0.0254	-0.0223	0.0041	-0.0007	0.0094	-0.0281	-0.0272	0.0127	1967	-0.0495
1968	0.0361	0.0037	-0.0197	0.0048	0.0032	0.0122	0.0341	0.0206	-0.0053	-0.0160	-0.0226	-0.0233	1968	0.0257
1969	0.0139	-0.0160	-0.0200	0.0335	-0.0227	0.0035	0.0005	-0.0020	-0.0244	0.0127	-0.0471	-0.0134	1969	-0.0809
1970	0.0141	0.0401	-0.0045	-0.0250	-0.0163	0.0001	0.0556	0.0100	0.0139	-0.0096	0.0584	0.0372	1970	0.1837

*Compound annual return

from January 1971 to December 2011

Year	Jan	Feb	Mar	Apr	May	Jun	Jul	Aug	Sep	Oct	Nov	Dec	Year	Jan–Dec*
1971	0.0532	-0.0366	0.0258	-0.0236	-0.0161	0.0107	-0.0025	0.0554	-0.0102	0.0282	0.0029	0.0223	1971	0.1101
1972	-0.0033	0.0107	0.0024	0.0035	0.0163	-0.0068	0.0030	0.0072	0.0031	0.0101	0.0249	-0.0004	1972	0.0726
1973	-0.0054	0.0023	0.0045	0.0061	-0.0039	-0.0056	-0.0476	0.0356	0.0356	-0.0066	0.0078	-0.0089	1973	0.0114
1974	-0.0053	0.0009	-0.0307	-0.0341	0.0105	-0.0285	-0.0211	-0.0268	0.0174	0.0885	0.0117	-0.0075	1974	-0.0306
1975	0.0596	0.0137	-0.0247	-0.0052	0.0106	0.0304	-0.0030	-0.0175	-0.0126	0.0553	-0.0088	0.0442	1975	0.1464
1976	0.0188	0.0061	0.0167	-0.0015	-0.0103	0.0150	0.0149	0.0231	0.0167	0.0070	0.0319	0.0347	1976	0.1865
1977	-0.0303	-0.0020	0.0094	0.0100	0.0106	0.0175	-0.0005	0.0136	-0.0022	-0.0038	0.0061	-0.0105	1977	0.0171
1978	-0.0089	0.0051	0.0042	-0.0023	-0.0108	0.0023	0.0101	0.0257	-0.0048	-0.0205	0.0134	-0.0133	1978	-0.0007
1979	0.0184	-0.0128	0.0106	-0.0052	0.0228	0.0269	-0.0031	0.0006	-0.0179	-0.0890	0.0222	-0.0108	1979	-0.0418
1980	-0.0645	-0.0665	-0.0062	0.1376	0.0560	0.0341	-0.0429	-0.0445	-0.0237	-0.0159	0.0017	0.0248	1980	-0.0276
1981	-0.0130	-0.0269	0.0311	-0.0769	0.0595	0.0023	-0.0372	-0.0345	-0.0199	0.0521	0.1267	-0.0580	1981	-0.0124
1982	-0.0129	0.0312	0.0306	0.0338	0.0245	-0.0468	0.0540	0.0837	0.0623	0.0759	0.0201	0.0108	1982	0.4256
1983	-0.0094	0.0428	0.0072	0.0548	-0.0324	-0.0046	-0.0455	0.0051	0.0392	-0.0025	0.0142	-0.0033	1983	0.0626
1984	0.0270	-0.0172	-0.0235	-0.0073	-0.0483	0.0199	0.0586	0.0307	0.0314	0.0572	0.0212	0.0128	1984	0.1686
1985	0.0325	-0.0373	0.0179	0.0296	0.0820	0.0083	-0.0121	0.0260	0.0071	0.0329	0.0370	0.0469	1985	0.3009
1986	0.0045	0.0752	0.0256	0.0016	-0.0164	0.0218	0.0031	0.0275	-0.0114	0.0189	0.0233	0.0117	1986	0.1985
1987	0.0216	0.0058	-0.0087	-0.0502	-0.0052	0.0155	-0.0119	-0.0075	-0.0422	0.0507	0.0125	0.0212	1987	-0.0027
1988	0.0517	0.0138	-0.0188	-0.0149	-0.0057	0.0379	-0.0111	0.0054	0.0326	0.0273	-0.0169	0.0039	1988	0.1070
1989	0.0202	-0.0129	0.0064	0.0213	0.0379	0.0395	0.0178	-0.0163	0.0040	0.0276	0.0070	0.0006	1989	0.1623
1990	-0.0191	-0.0012	-0.0011	-0.0191	0.0385	0.0216	0.0102	-0.0292	0.0091	0.0132	0.0285	0.0167	1990	0.0678
1991	0.0150	0.0121	0.0108	0.0138	0.0039	-0.0018	0.0167	0.0275	0.0271	0.0043	0.0106	0.0436	1991	0.1989
1992	-0.0173	0.0096	-0.0073	0.0016	0.0254	0.0156	0.0308	0.0090	0.0099	-0.0156	0.0069	0.0228	1992	0.0939
1993	0.0250	0.0256	0.0025	0.0052	0.0020	0.0293	0.0100	0.0287	0.0043	0.0051	-0.0188	0.0067	1993	0.1319
1994	0.0202	-0.0286	-0.0383	-0.0097	-0.0062	-0.0081	0.0309	-0.0031	-0.0265	-0.0050	0.0018	0.0157	1994	-0.0576
1995	0.0256	0.0289	0.0095	0.0175	0.0631	0.0079	-0.0101	0.0214	0.0153	0.0185	0.0242	0.0228	1995	0.2720
1996	0.0014	-0.0373	-0.0130	-0.0160	0.0005	0.0172	0.0010	-0.0070	0.0259	0.0361	0.0263	-0.0186	1996	0.0140
1997	-0.0028	0.0028	-0.0221	0.0184	0.0128	0.0187	0.0528	-0.0240	0.0226	0.0191	0.0101	0.0163	1997	0.1295
1998	0.0137	-0.0007	0.0038	0.0053	0.0167	0.0115	-0.0056	0.0089	0.0413	-0.0190	0.0270	0.0010	1998	0.1076
1999	0.0123	-0.0401	0.0002	-0.0024	-0.0176	-0.0160	-0.0113	-0.0026	0.0093	0.0047	-0.0024	-0.0102	1999	-0.0745
2000	-0.0021	0.0092	0.0169	-0.0115	-0.0161	0.0326	0.0179	0.0135	0.0046	0.0045	0.0263	0.0270	2000	0.1287
2001	0.0359	0.0127	-0.0029	-0.0128	0.0132	0.0055	0.0361	0.0157	-0.0152	0.0437	-0.0188	-0.0090	2001	0.1065
2002	0.0175	0.0130	-0.0295	0.0253	0.0113	0.0073	0.0094	0.0452	0.0330	-0.0240	0.0103	0.0361	2002	0.1633
2003	0.0021	0.0264	-0.0080	0.0229	0.0471	-0.0143	-0.0881	0.0219	0.0503	-0.0203	0.0052	0.0139	2003	0.0527
2004	0.0187	0.0178	0.0118	-0.0534	-0.0071	0.0093	0.0184	0.0395	0.0101	0.0164	-0.0200	0.0257	2004	0.0872
2005	0.0277	-0.0112	-0.0125	0.0327	0.0295	0.0141	-0.0244	0.0233	-0.0310	-0.0204	0.0099	0.0225	2005	0.0587
2006	-0.0093	0.0128	-0.0404	-0.0224	-0.0020	0.0039	0.0237	0.0361	0.0183	0.0127	0.0246	-0.0232	2006	0.0324
2007	-0.0051	0.0287	-0.0231	0.0140	-0.0178	-0.0148	-0.0032	0.0152	0.0135	0.0088	0.0079	0.0028	2007	0.0260
2008	0.0017	-0.0071	-0.0059	0.0091	-0.0277	-0.0061	-0.0109	0.0121	-0.0863	-0.0450	0.1174	0.1560	2008	0.0878
2009	-0.0949	-0.0308	-0.0018	-0.0030	0.0489	0.0350	0.0565	0.0235	0.0273	0.0016	0.0044	-0.0275	2009	0.0302
2010	0.0096	0.0039	0.0045	0.0357	-0.0051	0.0519	0.0170	0.0473	-0.0144	-0.0203	-0.0057	-0.0036	2010	0.1244
2011	-0.0198	0.0157	-0.0072	0.0239	0.0257	-0.0210	0.0473	0.0240	0.0575	0.0094	-0.0356	0.0512	2011	0.1795

*Compound annual return

Table A-6

Long-Term Government Bonds: Total Returns

from January 1926 to December 1970

Year	Jan	Feb	Mar	Apr	May	Jun	Jul	Aug	Sep	Oct	Nov	Dec	Year	Jan–Dec*
1926	0.0138	0.0063	0.0041	0.0076	0.0014	0.0038	0.0004	0.0000	0.0038	0.0102	0.0160	0.0078	1926	0.0777
1927	0.0075	0.0088	0.0253	-0.0005	0.0109	-0.0069	0.0050	0.0076	0.0018	0.0099	0.0097	0.0072	1927	0.0893
1928	-0.0036	0.0061	0.0045	-0.0004	-0.0077	0.0041	-0.0217	0.0076	-0.0041	0.0158	0.0003	0.0004	1928	0.0010
1929	-0.0090	-0.0157	-0.0144	0.0275	-0.0162	0.0110	0.0000	-0.0034	0.0027	0.0382	0.0236	-0.0089	1929	0.0342
1930	-0.0057	0.0129	0.0083	-0.0016	0.0139	0.0051	0.0034	0.0013	0.0074	0.0035	0.0042	-0.0070	1930	0.0466
1931	-0.0121	0.0085	0.0104	0.0086	0.0145	0.0004	-0.0042	0.0012	-0.0281	-0.0330	0.0027	-0.0220	1931	-0.0531
1932	0.0034	0.0413	-0.0018	0.0604	-0.0188	0.0065	0.0481	0.0003	0.0057	-0.0017	0.0032	0.0131	1932	0.1684
1933	0.0148	-0.0258	0.0097	-0.0032	0.0303	0.0050	-0.0017	0.0044	0.0023	-0.0091	-0.0149	-0.0113	1933	-0.0007
1934	0.0257	0.0081	0.0197	0.0126	0.0131	0.0067	0.0040	-0.0118	-0.0146	0.0182	0.0037	0.0112	1934	0.1003
1935	0.0182	0.0092	0.0041	0.0079	-0.0057	0.0092	0.0046	-0.0133	0.0009	0.0061	0.0010	0.0070	1935	0.0498
1936	0.0055	0.0081	0.0106	0.0035	0.0040	0.0021	0.0060	0.0111	-0.0031	0.0006	0.0205	0.0038	1936	0.0752
1937	-0.0013	0.0086	-0.0411	0.0039	0.0053	-0.0018	0.0138	-0.0104	0.0045	0.0042	0.0096	0.0082	1937	0.0023
1938	0.0057	0.0052	-0.0037	0.0210	0.0044	0.0004	0.0043	0.0000	0.0022	0.0087	-0.0022	0.0080	1938	0.0553
1939	0.0059	0.0080	0.0125	0.0118	0.0171	-0.0027	0.0113	-0.0201	-0.0545	0.0410	0.0162	0.0145	1939	0.0594
1940	-0.0017	0.0027	0.0177	-0.0035	-0.0299	0.0258	0.0052	0.0028	0.0110	0.0031	0.0205	0.0067	1940	0.0609
1941	-0.0201	0.0020	0.0096	0.0129	0.0027	0.0066	0.0022	0.0018	-0.0012	0.0140	-0.0029	-0.0177	1941	0.0093
1942	0.0069	0.0011	0.0092	-0.0029	0.0075	0.0003	0.0018	0.0038	0.0003	0.0024	-0.0035	0.0049	1942	0.0322
1943	0.0033	-0.0005	0.0009	0.0048	0.0050	0.0018	-0.0001	0.0021	0.0011	0.0005	0.0000	0.0018	1943	0.0208
1944	0.0021	0.0032	0.0021	0.0013	0.0028	0.0008	0.0036	0.0027	0.0014	0.0012	0.0024	0.0042	1944	0.0281
1945	0.0127	0.0077	0.0021	0.0160	0.0056	0.0169	-0.0086	0.0026	0.0054	0.0104	0.0125	0.0194	1945	0.1073
1946	0.0025	0.0032	0.0010	-0.0135	-0.0012	0.0070	-0.0040	-0.0111	-0.0009	0.0074	-0.0054	0.0145	1946	-0.0010
1947	-0.0006	0.0021	0.0020	-0.0037	0.0033	0.0010	0.0063	0.0081	-0.0044	-0.0037	-0.0174	-0.0192	1947	-0.0262
1948	0.0020	0.0046	0.0034	0.0045	0.0141	-0.0084	-0.0021	0.0001	0.0014	0.0007	0.0076	0.0056	1948	0.0340
1949	0.0082	0.0049	0.0074	0.0011	0.0019	0.0167	0.0033	0.0111	-0.0011	0.0019	0.0021	0.0052	1949	0.0645
1950	-0.0061	0.0021	0.0008	0.0030	0.0033	-0.0025	0.0055	0.0014	-0.0072	-0.0048	0.0035	0.0016	1950	0.0006
1951	0.0058	-0.0074	-0.0157	-0.0063	-0.0069	-0.0062	0.0138	0.0099	-0.0080	0.0010	-0.0136	-0.0061	1951	-0.0393
1952	0.0028	0.0014	0.0111	0.0171	-0.0033	0.0003	-0.0020	-0.0070	-0.0130	0.0148	-0.0015	-0.0086	1952	0.0116
1953	0.0012	-0.0087	-0.0088	-0.0105	-0.0148	0.0223	0.0039	-0.0008	0.0299	0.0074	-0.0049	0.0206	1953	0.0364
1954	0.0089	0.0240	0.0058	0.0104	-0.0087	0.0163	0.0134	-0.0036	-0.0010	0.0006	-0.0025	0.0064	1954	0.0719
1955	-0.0241	-0.0078	0.0087	0.0001	0.0073	-0.0076	-0.0102	0.0004	0.0073	0.0144	-0.0045	0.0037	1955	-0.0129
1956	0.0083	-0.0002	-0.0149	-0.0113	0.0225	0.0027	-0.0209	-0.0187	0.0050	-0.0054	-0.0057	-0.0179	1956	-0.0559
1957	0.0346	0.0025	-0.0024	-0.0222	-0.0023	-0.0180	-0.0041	0.0002	0.0076	-0.0050	0.0533	0.0307	1957	0.0746
1958	-0.0084	0.0100	0.0102	0.0186	0.0001	-0.0160	-0.0278	-0.0435	-0.0117	0.0138	0.0120	-0.0181	1958	-0.0609
1959	-0.0080	0.0117	0.0017	-0.0117	-0.0005	0.0010	0.0060	-0.0041	-0.0057	0.0150	-0.0119	-0.0159	1959	-0.0226
1960	0.0112	0.0204	0.0282	-0.0170	0.0152	0.0173	0.0368	-0.0067	0.0075	-0.0028	-0.0066	0.0279	1960	0.1378
1961	-0.0107	0.0200	-0.0037	0.0115	-0.0046	-0.0075	0.0035	-0.0038	0.0129	0.0071	-0.0020	-0.0125	1961	0.0097
1962	-0.0014	0.0103	0.0253	0.0082	0.0046	-0.0076	-0.0109	0.0187	0.0061	0.0084	0.0021	0.0035	1962	0.0689
1963	-0.0001	0.0008	0.0009	-0.0012	0.0023	0.0019	0.0031	0.0021	0.0004	-0.0026	0.0051	-0.0006	1963	0.0121
1964	-0.0014	-0.0011	0.0037	0.0047	0.0050	0.0069	0.0008	0.0020	0.0050	0.0043	0.0017	0.0030	1964	0.0351
1965	0.0040	0.0014	0.0054	0.0036	0.0018	0.0047	0.0022	-0.0013	-0.0034	0.0027	-0.0062	-0.0078	1965	0.0071
1966	-0.0104	-0.0250	0.0296	-0.0063	-0.0059	-0.0016	-0.0037	-0.0206	0.0332	0.0228	-0.0148	0.0413	1966	0.0365
1967	0.0154	-0.0221	0.0198	-0.0291	-0.0039	-0.0312	0.0068	-0.0084	-0.0004	-0.0400	-0.0196	0.0192	1967	-0.0918
1968	0.0328	-0.0033	-0.0212	0.0227	0.0043	0.0230	0.0289	-0.0003	-0.0102	-0.0132	-0.0269	-0.0363	1968	-0.0026
1969	-0.0206	0.0042	0.0010	0.0427	-0.0490	0.0214	0.0079	-0.0069	-0.0531	0.0365	-0.0243	-0.0068	1969	-0.0507
1970	-0.0021	0.0587	-0.0068	-0.0413	-0.0468	0.0486	0.0319	-0.0019	0.0228	-0.0109	0.0791	-0.0084	1970	0.1211

*Compound annual return

from January 1971 to December 2011

Year	Jan	Feb	Mar	Apr	May	Jun	Jul	Aug	Sep	Oct	Nov	Dec	Year	Jan–Dec*
1971	0.0506	-0.0163	0.0526	-0.0283	-0.0006	-0.0159	0.0030	0.0471	0.0204	0.0167	-0.0047	0.0044	1971	0.1323
1972	-0.0063	0.0088	-0.0082	0.0027	0.0270	-0.0065	0.0216	0.0029	-0.0083	0.0234	0.0226	-0.0229	1972	0.0569
1973	-0.0321	0.0014	0.0082	0.0046	-0.0105	-0.0021	-0.0433	0.0391	0.0318	0.0215	-0.0183	-0.0082	1973	-0.0111
1974	-0.0083	-0.0024	-0.0292	-0.0253	0.0123	0.0045	-0.0029	-0.0232	0.0247	0.0489	0.0295	0.0171	1974	0.0435
1975	0.0225	0.0131	-0.0267	-0.0182	0.0212	0.0292	-0.0087	-0.0068	-0.0098	0.0475	-0.0109	0.0390	1975	0.0920
1976	0.0090	0.0062	0.0166	0.0018	-0.0158	0.0208	0.0078	0.0211	0.0145	0.0084	0.0339	0.0327	1976	0.1675
1977	-0.0388	-0.0049	0.0091	0.0071	0.0125	0.0164	-0.0070	0.0198	-0.0029	-0.0093	0.0093	-0.0168	1977	-0.0069
1978	-0.0080	0.0004	-0.0021	-0.0005	-0.0058	-0.0062	0.0143	0.0218	-0.0106	-0.0200	0.0189	-0.0130	1978	-0.0118
1979	0.0191	-0.0135	0.0129	-0.0112	0.0261	0.0311	-0.0085	-0.0035	-0.0122	-0.0841	0.0311	0.0057	1979	-0.0123
1980	-0.0741	-0.0467	-0.0315	0.1523	0.0419	0.0359	-0.0476	-0.0432	-0.0262	-0.0263	0.0100	0.0352	1980	-0.0395
1981	-0.0115	-0.0435	0.0384	-0.0518	0.0622	-0.0179	-0.0353	-0.0386	-0.0145	0.0829	0.1410	-0.0713	1981	0.0186
1982	0.0046	0.0182	0.0231	0.0373	0.0034	-0.0223	0.0501	0.0781	0.0618	0.0634	-0.0002	0.0312	1982	0.4036
1983	-0.0309	0.0492	-0.0094	0.0350	-0.0386	0.0039	-0.0486	0.0020	0.0505	-0.0132	0.0183	-0.0059	1983	0.0065
1984	0.0244	-0.0178	-0.0156	-0.0105	-0.0516	0.0150	0.0693	0.0266	0.0342	0.0561	0.0118	0.0091	1984	0.1548
1985	0.0364	-0.0493	0.0307	0.0242	0.0896	0.0142	-0.0180	0.0259	-0.0021	0.0338	0.0401	0.0541	1985	0.3097
1986	-0.0025	0.1145	0.0770	-0.0080	-0.0505	0.0613	-0.0108	0.0499	-0.0500	0.0289	0.0267	-0.0018	1986	0.2453
1987	0.0161	0.0202	-0.0223	-0.0473	-0.0105	0.0098	-0.0178	-0.0165	-0.0369	0.0623	0.0037	0.0165	1987	-0.0271
1988	0.0666	0.0052	-0.0307	-0.0160	-0.0102	0.0368	-0.0170	0.0058	0.0345	0.0308	-0.0196	0.0110	1988	0.0967
1989	0.0203	-0.0179	0.0122	0.0159	0.0401	0.0550	0.0238	-0.0259	0.0019	0.0379	0.0078	-0.0006	1989	0.1811
1990	-0.0343	-0.0025	-0.0044	-0.0202	0.0415	0.0230	0.0107	-0.0419	0.0117	0.0215	0.0402	0.0187	1990	0.0618
1991	0.0130	0.0030	0.0038	0.0140	0.0000	-0.0063	0.0157	0.0340	0.0303	0.0054	0.0082	0.0581	1991	0.1930
1992	-0.0324	0.0051	-0.0094	0.0016	0.0243	0.0200	0.0398	0.0067	0.0185	-0.0198	0.0010	0.0246	1992	0.0805
1993	0.0280	0.0354	0.0021	0.0072	0.0047	0.0449	0.0191	0.0434	0.0005	0.0096	-0.0259	0.0020	1993	0.1824
1994	0.0257	-0.0450	-0.0395	-0.0150	-0.0082	-0.0100	0.0363	-0.0086	-0.0331	-0.0025	0.0066	0.0161	1994	-0.0777
1995	0.0273	0.0287	0.0091	0.0169	0.0790	0.0139	-0.0168	0.0236	0.0175	0.0294	0.0249	0.0272	1995	0.3167
1996	-0.0011	-0.0483	-0.0210	-0.0165	-0.0054	0.0203	0.0018	-0.0139	0.0290	0.0404	0.0351	-0.0256	1996	-0.0093
1997	-0.0079	0.0005	-0.0252	0.0255	0.0095	0.0197	0.0626	-0.0317	0.0316	0.0341	0.0148	0.0184	1997	0.1585
1998	0.0200	-0.0072	0.0025	0.0026	0.0182	0.0228	-0.0040	0.0465	0.0395	-0.0218	0.0097	-0.0032	1998	0.1306
1999	0.0121	-0.0520	-0.0008	0.0021	-0.0185	-0.0078	-0.0079	-0.0051	0.0084	-0.0012	-0.0061	-0.0155	1999	-0.0896
2000	0.0228	0.0264	0.0367	-0.0076	-0.0054	0.0244	0.0173	0.0240	-0.0157	0.0187	0.0319	0.0243	2000	0.2148
2001	0.0005	0.0191	-0.0074	-0.0313	0.0037	0.0085	0.0376	0.0206	0.0081	0.0464	-0.0471	-0.0183	2001	0.0370
2002	0.0138	0.0115	-0.0436	0.0410	0.0015	0.0187	0.0303	0.0464	0.0417	-0.0294	-0.0122	0.0507	2002	0.1784
2003	-0.0106	0.0329	-0.0135	0.0102	0.0592	-0.0154	-0.0982	0.0166	0.0546	-0.0283	0.0027	0.0139	2003	0.0145
2004	0.0187	0.0230	0.0141	-0.0588	-0.0051	0.0121	0.0155	0.0395	0.0096	0.0154	-0.0234	0.0250	2004	0.0851
2005	0.0300	-0.0128	-0.0072	0.0373	0.0297	0.0167	-0.0288	0.0333	-0.0338	-0.0196	0.0076	0.0267	2005	0.0781
2006	-0.0118	0.0238	-0.0539	-0.0247	0.0010	0.0092	0.0199	0.0299	0.0170	0.0077	0.0207	-0.0236	2006	0.0119
2007	-0.0102	0.0335	-0.0145	0.0085	-0.0200	-0.0091	0.0284	0.0199	0.0012	0.0155	0.0468	-0.0029	2007	0.0988
2008	0.0213	0.0018	0.0106	-0.0288	-0.0164	0.0220	-0.0025	0.0242	0.0112	-0.0383	0.1443	0.0967	2008	0.2587
2009	-0.1124	-0.0056	0.0641	-0.0649	-0.0248	0.0083	0.0019	0.0231	0.0176	-0.0171	0.0208	-0.0584	2009	-0.1490
2010	0.0264	0.0032	-0.0179	0.0304	0.0437	0.0446	0.0024	0.0702	-0.0153	-0.0317	-0.0137	-0.0388	2010	0.1014
2011	-0.0196	0.0113	-0.0006	0.0199	0.0355	-0.0127	0.0526	0.0720	0.0684	-0.0274	0.0253	0.0324	2011	0.2823

*Compound annual return

from January 1926 to December 1970

Year	Jan	Feb	Mar	Apr	May	Jun	Jul	Aug	Sep	Oct	Nov	Dec	Year	Jan–Dec*
1926	0.0031	0.0028	0.0032	0.0030	0.0028	0.0033	0.0031	0.0031	0.0030	0.0030	0.0031	0.0030	1926	0.0373
1927	0.0030	0.0027	0.0029	0.0027	0.0028	0.0027	0.0027	0.0029	0.0027	0.0028	0.0027	0.0027	1927	0.0341
1928	0.0027	0.0025	0.0027	0.0026	0.0027	0.0027	0.0027	0.0029	0.0027	0.0030	0.0027	0.0029	1928	0.0322
1929	0.0029	0.0027	0.0028	0.0034	0.0030	0.0029	0.0032	0.0030	0.0032	0.0031	0.0026	0.0031	1929	0.0347
1930	0.0029	0.0026	0.0029	0.0027	0.0027	0.0029	0.0028	0.0026	0.0029	0.0027	0.0026	0.0028	1930	0.0332
1931	0.0028	0.0026	0.0029	0.0027	0.0026	0.0028	0.0027	0.0027	0.0027	0.0029	0.0031	0.0032	1931	0.0333
1932	0.0032	0.0032	0.0031	0.0030	0.0028	0.0028	0.0028	0.0028	0.0026	0.0027	0.0026	0.0027	1932	0.0369
1933	0.0027	0.0023	0.0027	0.0025	0.0028	0.0025	0.0026	0.0026	0.0025	0.0026	0.0025	0.0028	1933	0.0312
1934	0.0029	0.0024	0.0027	0.0025	0.0025	0.0024	0.0024	0.0024	0.0023	0.0027	0.0025	0.0025	1934	0.0318
1935	0.0025	0.0021	0.0022	0.0023	0.0023	0.0022	0.0024	0.0023	0.0023	0.0023	0.0024	0.0024	1935	0.0281
1936	0.0024	0.0023	0.0024	0.0022	0.0022	0.0024	0.0023	0.0023	0.0021	0.0023	0.0022	0.0022	1936	0.0277
1937	0.0021	0.0020	0.0022	0.0023	0.0022	0.0025	0.0024	0.0023	0.0023	0.0023	0.0024	0.0023	1937	0.0266
1938	0.0023	0.0021	0.0023	0.0022	0.0022	0.0021	0.0021	0.0022	0.0021	0.0022	0.0021	0.0022	1938	0.0264
1939	0.0021	0.0019	0.0021	0.0019	0.0020	0.0018	0.0019	0.0018	0.0019	0.0023	0.0020	0.0019	1939	0.0240
1940	0.0020	0.0018	0.0019	0.0018	0.0019	0.0019	0.0020	0.0019	0.0018	0.0018	0.0018	0.0017	1940	0.0223
1941	0.0016	0.0016	0.0018	0.0017	0.0017	0.0016	0.0016	0.0016	0.0016	0.0016	0.0014	0.0016	1941	0.0194
1942	0.0021	0.0019	0.0021	0.0020	0.0019	0.0021	0.0021	0.0021	0.0020	0.0021	0.0020	0.0021	1942	0.0246
1943	0.0020	0.0019	0.0021	0.0020	0.0019	0.0021	0.0021	0.0021	0.0020	0.0020	0.0021	0.0021	1943	0.0244
1944	0.0021	0.0020	0.0021	0.0020	0.0022	0.0020	0.0021	0.0021	0.0020	0.0021	0.0020	0.0020	1944	0.0246
1945	0.0021	0.0018	0.0020	0.0019	0.0019	0.0019	0.0018	0.0019	0.0018	0.0019	0.0018	0.0018	1945	0.0234
1946	0.0017	0.0015	0.0016	0.0017	0.0018	0.0016	0.0019	0.0017	0.0018	0.0019	0.0018	0.0019	1946	0.0204
1947	0.0018	0.0016	0.0018	0.0017	0.0017	0.0019	0.0018	0.0017	0.0018	0.0018	0.0017	0.0021	1947	0.0213
1948	0.0020	0.0019	0.0022	0.0020	0.0018	0.0021	0.0019	0.0021	0.0020	0.0019	0.0021	0.0020	1948	0.0240
1949	0.0020	0.0018	0.0019	0.0018	0.0020	0.0019	0.0017	0.0019	0.0017	0.0018	0.0017	0.0017	1949	0.0225
1950	0.0018	0.0016	0.0018	0.0016	0.0019	0.0017	0.0018	0.0018	0.0017	0.0019	0.0018	0.0018	1950	0.0212
1951	0.0020	0.0017	0.0019	0.0020	0.0021	0.0020	0.0023	0.0021	0.0019	0.0023	0.0021	0.0022	1951	0.0238
1952	0.0023	0.0021	0.0023	0.0022	0.0020	0.0022	0.0022	0.0021	0.0023	0.0023	0.0021	0.0024	1952	0.0266
1953	0.0023	0.0021	0.0025	0.0024	0.0024	0.0027	0.0025	0.0025	0.0025	0.0023	0.0024	0.0024	1953	0.0284
1954	0.0023	0.0022	0.0025	0.0022	0.0020	0.0025	0.0022	0.0023	0.0022	0.0021	0.0023	0.0023	1954	0.0279
1955	0.0022	0.0022	0.0024	0.0022	0.0025	0.0023	0.0023	0.0027	0.0024	0.0025	0.0024	0.0024	1955	0.0275
1956	0.0025	0.0023	0.0023	0.0026	0.0026	0.0023	0.0026	0.0026	0.0025	0.0029	0.0027	0.0028	1956	0.0299
1957	0.0029	0.0025	0.0026	0.0029	0.0029	0.0025	0.0033	0.0030	0.0031	0.0031	0.0029	0.0029	1957	0.0344
1958	0.0027	0.0025	0.0027	0.0026	0.0024	0.0027	0.0027	0.0027	0.0032	0.0032	0.0028	0.0033	1958	0.0327
1959	0.0031	0.0031	0.0035	0.0033	0.0033	0.0036	0.0035	0.0035	0.0034	0.0035	0.0035	0.0036	1959	0.0401
1960	0.0035	0.0037	0.0036	0.0032	0.0037	0.0034	0.0032	0.0034	0.0032	0.0033	0.0032	0.0033	1960	0.0426
1961	0.0033	0.0030	0.0031	0.0031	0.0034	0.0032	0.0033	0.0033	0.0032	0.0034	0.0032	0.0031	1961	0.0383
1962	0.0037	0.0032	0.0033	0.0033	0.0032	0.0030	0.0034	0.0034	0.0030	0.0035	0.0031	0.0032	1962	0.0400
1963	0.0032	0.0029	0.0031	0.0034	0.0033	0.0030	0.0036	0.0033	0.0034	0.0034	0.0032	0.0036	1963	0.0389
1964	0.0035	0.0032	0.0037	0.0035	0.0032	0.0038	0.0035	0.0035	0.0034	0.0034	0.0035	0.0035	1964	0.0415
1965	0.0033	0.0032	0.0038	0.0033	0.0033	0.0038	0.0034	0.0037	0.0035	0.0034	0.0037	0.0037	1965	0.0419
1966	0.0038	0.0034	0.0040	0.0036	0.0041	0.0039	0.0038	0.0043	0.0041	0.0040	0.0038	0.0039	1966	0.0449
1967	0.0040	0.0034	0.0039	0.0035	0.0043	0.0039	0.0043	0.0042	0.0040	0.0045	0.0045	0.0044	1967	0.0459
1968	0.0050	0.0042	0.0043	0.0049	0.0046	0.0042	0.0048	0.0042	0.0044	0.0045	0.0043	0.0049	1968	0.0550
1969	0.0050	0.0046	0.0047	0.0055	0.0047	0.0055	0.0052	0.0048	0.0055	0.0057	0.0049	0.0060	1969	0.0595
1970	0.0056	0.0052	0.0056	0.0054	0.0055	0.0064	0.0059	0.0057	0.0056	0.0055	0.0058	0.0053	1970	0.0674

*Compound annual return

from January 1971 to December 2011

Year	Jan	Feb	Mar	Apr	May	Jun	Jul	Aug	Sep	Oct	Nov	Dec	Year	Jan–Dec*
1971	0.0051	0.0046	0.0056	0.0048	0.0047	0.0056	0.0052	0.0055	0.0049	0.0047	0.0051	0.0050	1971	0.0632
1972	0.0050	0.0047	0.0049	0.0048	0.0055	0.0049	0.0051	0.0049	0.0047	0.0052	0.0048	0.0045	1972	0.0587
1973	0.0054	0.0051	0.0056	0.0057	0.0058	0.0055	0.0061	0.0062	0.0055	0.0063	0.0056	0.0060	1973	0.0651
1974	0.0061	0.0055	0.0058	0.0068	0.0068	0.0061	0.0072	0.0065	0.0071	0.0070	0.0062	0.0067	1974	0.0727
1975	0.0068	0.0060	0.0066	0.0067	0.0067	0.0070	0.0068	0.0065	0.0073	0.0072	0.0061	0.0074	1975	0.0799
1976	0.0065	0.0060	0.0071	0.0064	0.0059	0.0073	0.0065	0.0069	0.0064	0.0061	0.0066	0.0063	1976	0.0789
1977	0.0059	0.0057	0.0065	0.0061	0.0067	0.0062	0.0059	0.0067	0.0061	0.0063	0.0063	0.0062	1977	0.0714
1978	0.0069	0.0060	0.0069	0.0063	0.0075	0.0069	0.0073	0.0070	0.0065	0.0073	0.0071	0.0068	1978	0.0790
1979	0.0079	0.0065	0.0074	0.0076	0.0077	0.0071	0.0076	0.0073	0.0068	0.0082	0.0083	0.0083	1979	0.0886
1980	0.0083	0.0084	0.0099	0.0100	0.0087	0.0086	0.0084	0.0081	0.0097	0.0097	0.0091	0.0108	1980	0.0997
1981	0.0094	0.0088	0.0111	0.0101	0.0104	0.0109	0.0109	0.0110	0.0114	0.0117	0.0113	0.0100	1981	0.1155
1982	0.0108	0.0103	0.0124	0.0112	0.0101	0.0120	0.0114	0.0112	0.0100	0.0091	0.0094	0.0093	1982	0.1350
1983	0.0087	0.0081	0.0089	0.0085	0.0091	0.0090	0.0088	0.0103	0.0096	0.0095	0.0094	0.0094	1983	0.1038
1984	0.0103	0.0092	0.0098	0.0104	0.0103	0.0106	0.0116	0.0106	0.0094	0.0108	0.0091	0.0098	1984	0.1174
1985	0.0096	0.0082	0.0094	0.0102	0.0097	0.0080	0.0094	0.0085	0.0088	0.0089	0.0081	0.0086	1985	0.1125
1986	0.0079	0.0073	0.0071	0.0063	0.0062	0.0070	0.0066	0.0063	0.0065	0.0069	0.0059	0.0070	1986	0.0898
1987	0.0064	0.0059	0.0066	0.0065	0.0066	0.0075	0.0073	0.0075	0.0075	0.0079	0.0075	0.0078	1987	0.0792
1988	0.0072	0.0071	0.0072	0.0070	0.0078	0.0076	0.0071	0.0083	0.0076	0.0076	0.0070	0.0075	1988	0.0897
1989	0.0080	0.0069	0.0079	0.0070	0.0080	0.0070	0.0068	0.0066	0.0065	0.0072	0.0064	0.0064	1989	0.0881
1990	0.0073	0.0066	0.0071	0.0075	0.0075	0.0068	0.0074	0.0071	0.0069	0.0081	0.0071	0.0072	1990	0.0819
1991	0.0071	0.0064	0.0064	0.0076	0.0068	0.0063	0.0076	0.0068	0.0068	0.0065	0.0060	0.0068	1991	0.0822
1992	0.0061	0.0059	0.0067	0.0065	0.0061	0.0067	0.0063	0.0060	0.0058	0.0057	0.0061	0.0063	1992	0.0726
1993	0.0059	0.0055	0.0063	0.0057	0.0052	0.0062	0.0054	0.0056	0.0050	0.0049	0.0053	0.0055	1993	0.0717
1994	0.0055	0.0049	0.0058	0.0057	0.0063	0.0061	0.0060	0.0066	0.0061	0.0066	0.0064	0.0066	1994	0.0659
1995	0.0070	0.0059	0.0064	0.0058	0.0065	0.0054	0.0056	0.0057	0.0052	0.0057	0.0051	0.0049	1995	0.0760
1996	0.0054	0.0048	0.0052	0.0059	0.0058	0.0054	0.0062	0.0057	0.0060	0.0058	0.0052	0.0056	1996	0.0618
1997	0.0056	0.0051	0.0059	0.0059	0.0058	0.0059	0.0058	0.0049	0.0058	0.0054	0.0047	0.0054	1997	0.0664
1998	0.0048	0.0044	0.0052	0.0049	0.0048	0.0052	0.0049	0.0048	0.0044	0.0042	0.0045	0.0045	1998	0.0583
1999	0.0042	0.0040	0.0053	0.0048	0.0045	0.0055	0.0051	0.0054	0.0052	0.0050	0.0056	0.0055	1999	0.0557
2000	0.0057	0.0051	0.0054	0.0047	0.0056	0.0052	0.0052	0.0050	0.0046	0.0053	0.0048	0.0045	2000	0.0650
2001	0.0049	0.0042	0.0045	0.0047	0.0050	0.0047	0.0052	0.0046	0.0041	0.0048	0.0041	0.0046	2001	0.0553
2002	0.0048	0.0043	0.0043	0.0054	0.0049	0.0044	0.0051	0.0044	0.0042	0.0040	0.0040	0.0045	2002	0.0559
2003	0.0041	0.0038	0.0040	0.0040	0.0039	0.0036	0.0038	0.0042	0.0046	0.0041	0.0039	0.0047	2003	0.0480
2004	0.0042	0.0038	0.0043	0.0039	0.0040	0.0048	0.0043	0.0045	0.0040	0.0038	0.0041	0.0043	2004	0.0502
2005	0.0041	0.0035	0.0041	0.0039	0.0040	0.0036	0.0034	0.0040	0.0035	0.0039	0.0039	0.0039	2005	0.0469
2006	0.0040	0.0036	0.0039	0.0039	0.0048	0.0044	0.0045	0.0043	0.0039	0.0042	0.0039	0.0036	2006	0.0468
2007	0.0043	0.0038	0.0039	0.0042	0.0041	0.0040	0.0046	0.0042	0.0037	0.0043	0.0039	0.0037	2007	0.0486
2008	0.0040	0.0034	0.0037	0.0035	0.0037	0.0040	0.0039	0.0036	0.0039	0.0037	0.0036	0.0033	2008	0.0445
2009	0.0024	0.0030	0.0035	0.0029	0.0033	0.0038	0.0036	0.0036	0.0034	0.0033	0.0035	0.0034	2009	0.0347
2010	0.0036	0.0033	0.0040	0.0038	0.0034	0.0037	0.0031	0.0032	0.0026	0.0027	0.0032	0.0032	2010	0.0425
2011	0.0035	0.0032	0.0036	0.0034	0.0036	0.0032	0.0032	0.0033	0.0025	0.0022	0.0023	0.0022	2011	0.0381

*Compound annual return

Long-Term Government Bonds: Capital Appreciation Returns

from January 1926 to December 1970

Year	Jan	Feb	Mar	Apr	May	Jun	Jul	Aug	Sep	Oct	Nov	Dec	Year	Jan–Dec*
1926	0.0106	0.0035	0.0009	0.0046	-0.0014	0.0005	-0.0027	-0.0031	0.0007	0.0072	0.0129	0.0048	1926	0.0391
1927	0.0045	0.0061	0.0224	-0.0032	0.0081	-0.0096	0.0022	0.0047	-0.0009	0.0071	0.0071	0.0045	1927	0.0540
1928	-0.0063	0.0036	0.0019	-0.0029	-0.0104	0.0015	-0.0245	0.0047	-0.0067	0.0128	-0.0024	-0.0024	1928	-0.0312
1929	-0.0119	-0.0183	-0.0171	0.0242	-0.0192	0.0081	-0.0032	-0.0064	-0.0004	0.0351	0.0211	-0.0120	1929	-0.0020
1930	-0.0086	0.0102	0.0055	-0.0043	0.0113	0.0022	0.0007	-0.0013	0.0045	0.0008	0.0017	-0.0098	1930	0.0128
1931	-0.0149	0.0059	0.0076	0.0059	0.0119	-0.0024	-0.0069	-0.0015	-0.0307	-0.0360	-0.0004	-0.0252	1931	-0.0846
1932	0.0002	0.0382	-0.0049	0.0574	-0.0216	0.0037	0.0453	-0.0025	0.0031	-0.0044	0.0006	0.0104	1932	0.1294
1933	0.0122	-0.0282	0.0070	-0.0057	0.0274	0.0025	-0.0043	0.0018	-0.0002	-0.0117	-0.0174	-0.0140	1933	-0.0314
1934	0.0228	0.0057	0.0170	0.0101	0.0106	0.0043	0.0016	-0.0143	-0.0169	0.0155	0.0013	0.0087	1934	0.0676
1935	0.0157	0.0070	0.0019	0.0056	-0.0079	0.0070	0.0022	-0.0156	-0.0014	0.0038	-0.0014	0.0047	1935	0.0214
1936	0.0031	0.0059	0.0083	0.0013	0.0019	-0.0003	0.0037	0.0088	-0.0053	-0.0017	0.0183	0.0017	1936	0.0464
1937	-0.0034	0.0067	-0.0433	0.0016	0.0031	-0.0043	0.0114	-0.0128	0.0022	0.0019	0.0072	0.0059	1937	-0.0248
1938	0.0034	0.0031	-0.0059	0.0187	0.0022	-0.0016	0.0022	-0.0022	0.0001	0.0065	-0.0043	0.0059	1938	0.0283
1939	0.0038	0.0061	0.0105	0.0099	0.0151	-0.0045	0.0095	-0.0219	-0.0564	0.0386	0.0142	0.0125	1939	0.0348
1940	-0.0037	0.0009	0.0158	-0.0053	-0.0318	0.0239	0.0032	0.0009	0.0092	0.0013	0.0187	0.0050	1940	0.0377
1941	-0.0217	0.0004	0.0078	0.0112	0.0011	0.0050	0.0005	0.0002	-0.0028	0.0124	-0.0044	-0.0194	1941	-0.0101
1942	0.0048	-0.0008	0.0071	-0.0049	0.0056	-0.0018	-0.0003	0.0017	-0.0016	0.0004	-0.0055	0.0028	1942	0.0074
1943	0.0013	-0.0024	-0.0012	0.0028	0.0031	-0.0003	-0.0021	0.0000	-0.0009	-0.0015	-0.0021	-0.0003	1943	-0.0037
1944	0.0000	0.0012	0.0000	-0.0006	0.0006	-0.0012	0.0015	0.0006	-0.0006	-0.0009	0.0003	0.0022	1944	0.0032
1945	0.0105	0.0058	0.0001	0.0141	0.0037	0.0150	-0.0104	0.0007	0.0037	0.0085	0.0108	0.0177	1945	0.0827
1946	0.0008	0.0017	-0.0006	-0.0152	-0.0030	0.0054	-0.0058	-0.0129	-0.0028	0.0055	-0.0072	0.0126	1946	-0.0215
1947	-0.0024	0.0005	0.0002	-0.0054	0.0016	-0.0009	0.0044	0.0064	-0.0062	-0.0055	-0.0191	-0.0213	1947	-0.0470
1948	0.0000	0.0028	0.0013	0.0025	0.0123	-0.0105	-0.0041	-0.0019	-0.0006	-0.0012	0.0055	0.0036	1948	0.0096
1949	0.0062	0.0031	0.0055	-0.0006	0.0000	0.0148	0.0016	0.0092	-0.0029	0.0001	0.0004	0.0035	1949	0.0415
1950	-0.0080	0.0005	-0.0010	0.0014	0.0014	-0.0042	0.0037	-0.0004	-0.0089	-0.0067	0.0017	-0.0001	1950	-0.0206
1951	0.0038	-0.0091	-0.0176	-0.0083	-0.0090	-0.0082	0.0116	0.0077	-0.0098	-0.0012	-0.0157	-0.0083	1951	-0.0627
1952	0.0005	-0.0007	0.0088	0.0149	-0.0054	-0.0019	-0.0041	-0.0091	-0.0153	0.0124	-0.0036	-0.0110	1952	-0.0148
1953	-0.0011	-0.0108	-0.0113	-0.0129	-0.0171	0.0195	0.0014	-0.0033	0.0275	0.0051	-0.0073	0.0182	1953	0.0067
1954	0.0066	0.0218	0.0034	0.0081	-0.0107	0.0138	0.0113	-0.0059	-0.0031	-0.0015	-0.0048	0.0042	1954	0.0435
1955	-0.0264	-0.0100	0.0063	-0.0022	0.0048	-0.0099	-0.0125	-0.0022	0.0049	0.0119	-0.0069	0.0013	1955	-0.0407
1956	0.0058	-0.0025	-0.0172	-0.0139	0.0199	0.0004	-0.0234	-0.0213	0.0025	-0.0083	-0.0084	-0.0206	1956	-0.0846
1957	0.0317	0.0000	-0.0050	-0.0250	-0.0052	-0.0206	-0.0074	-0.0028	0.0045	-0.0081	0.0504	0.0277	1957	0.0382
1958	-0.0112	0.0075	0.0075	0.0160	-0.0023	-0.0187	-0.0305	-0.0463	-0.0149	0.0106	0.0092	-0.0213	1958	-0.0923
1959	-0.0111	0.0087	-0.0018	-0.0150	-0.0038	-0.0026	0.0025	-0.0076	-0.0091	0.0115	-0.0154	-0.0195	1959	-0.0620
1960	0.0077	0.0167	0.0246	-0.0202	0.0115	0.0139	0.0335	-0.0101	0.0043	-0.0061	-0.0098	0.0247	1960	0.0929
1961	-0.0140	0.0170	-0.0069	0.0085	-0.0080	-0.0106	0.0001	-0.0071	0.0097	0.0037	-0.0052	-0.0156	1961	-0.0286
1962	-0.0051	0.0071	0.0220	0.0049	0.0014	-0.0106	-0.0143	0.0153	0.0031	0.0049	-0.0010	0.0003	1962	0.0278
1963	-0.0033	-0.0022	-0.0022	-0.0046	-0.0010	-0.0011	-0.0005	-0.0011	-0.0029	-0.0060	0.0019	-0.0042	1963	-0.0270
1964	-0.0048	-0.0043	0.0000	0.0012	0.0018	0.0031	-0.0027	-0.0015	0.0015	0.0009	-0.0018	-0.0005	1964	-0.0072
1965	0.0007	-0.0018	0.0016	0.0003	-0.0015	0.0009	-0.0012	-0.0050	-0.0069	-0.0007	-0.0099	-0.0115	1965	-0.0345
1966	-0.0142	-0.0284	0.0256	-0.0099	-0.0100	-0.0054	-0.0074	-0.0249	0.0292	0.0188	-0.0187	0.0374	1966	-0.0106
1967	0.0115	-0.0255	0.0159	-0.0326	-0.0082	-0.0351	0.0026	-0.0126	-0.0045	-0.0445	-0.0241	0.0148	1967	-0.1355
1968	0.0278	-0.0075	-0.0254	0.0178	-0.0003	0.0188	0.0241	-0.0044	-0.0146	-0.0177	-0.0312	-0.0412	1968	-0.0551
1969	-0.0256	-0.0004	-0.0036	0.0371	-0.0537	0.0159	0.0027	-0.0117	-0.0586	0.0309	-0.0293	-0.0129	1969	-0.1083
1970	-0.0077	0.0535	-0.0124	-0.0467	-0.0523	0.0422	0.0260	-0.0076	0.0172	-0.0164	0.0733	-0.0137	1970	0.0484

*Compound annual return

from January 1971 to December 2011

Year	Jan	Feb	Mar	Apr	May	Jun	Jul	Aug	Sep	Oct	Nov	Dec	Year	Jan–Dec*
1971	0.0455	-0.0209	0.0470	-0.0331	-0.0053	-0.0214	-0.0022	0.0416	0.0154	0.0120	-0.0098	-0.0006	1971	0.0661
1972	-0.0114	0.0041	-0.0131	-0.0021	0.0215	-0.0113	0.0165	-0.0021	-0.0129	0.0182	0.0178	-0.0275	1972	-0.0035
1973	-0.0375	-0.0037	0.0026	-0.0012	-0.0162	-0.0076	-0.0495	0.0329	0.0263	0.0153	-0.0238	-0.0142	1973	-0.0770
1974	-0.0144	-0.0079	-0.0350	-0.0320	0.0055	-0.0016	-0.0101	-0.0298	0.0176	0.0419	0.0233	0.0105	1974	-0.0345
1975	0.0157	0.0071	-0.0333	-0.0248	0.0145	0.0222	-0.0155	-0.0133	-0.0171	0.0403	-0.0170	0.0316	1975	0.0073
1976	0.0025	0.0001	0.0094	-0.0046	-0.0217	0.0135	0.0013	0.0142	0.0081	0.0023	0.0273	0.0265	1976	0.0807
1977	-0.0447	-0.0106	0.0026	0.0010	0.0058	0.0102	-0.0130	0.0131	-0.0089	-0.0156	0.0031	-0.0230	1977	-0.0786
1978	-0.0149	-0.0056	-0.0090	-0.0068	-0.0133	-0.0132	0.0070	0.0148	-0.0171	-0.0273	0.0117	-0.0198	1978	-0.0905
1979	0.0112	-0.0200	0.0056	-0.0188	0.0184	0.0240	-0.0161	-0.0108	-0.0190	-0.0922	0.0229	-0.0026	1979	-0.0984
1980	-0.0824	-0.0551	-0.0413	0.1424	0.0332	0.0272	-0.0560	-0.0513	-0.0358	-0.0360	0.0009	0.0244	1980	-0.1400
1981	-0.0209	-0.0524	0.0274	-0.0618	0.0518	-0.0288	-0.0462	-0.0496	-0.0259	0.0712	0.1297	-0.0813	1981	-0.1033
1982	-0.0062	0.0079	0.0107	0.0262	-0.0067	-0.0343	0.0387	0.0669	0.0519	0.0543	-0.0097	0.0219	1982	0.2395
1983	-0.0396	0.0410	-0.0183	0.0265	-0.0477	-0.0051	-0.0574	-0.0083	0.0408	-0.0227	0.0089	-0.0152	1983	-0.0982
1984	0.0141	-0.0270	-0.0254	-0.0210	-0.0619	0.0044	0.0577	0.0160	0.0248	0.0453	0.0027	-0.0007	1984	0.0232
1985	0.0268	-0.0575	0.0212	0.0140	0.0798	0.0061	-0.0274	0.0173	-0.0109	0.0248	0.0320	0.0455	1985	0.1784
1986	-0.0105	0.1073	0.0699	-0.0142	-0.0567	0.0543	-0.0173	0.0437	-0.0565	0.0220	0.0208	-0.0087	1986	0.1499
1987	0.0096	0.0143	-0.0289	-0.0538	-0.0171	0.0023	-0.0251	-0.0239	-0.0443	0.0544	-0.0038	0.0088	1987	-0.1069
1988	0.0595	-0.0019	-0.0378	-0.0230	-0.0180	0.0292	-0.0241	-0.0025	0.0269	0.0232	-0.0266	0.0035	1988	0.0036
1989	0.0124	-0.0248	0.0044	0.0088	0.0321	0.0480	0.0170	-0.0325	-0.0046	0.0307	0.0014	-0.0070	1989	0.0862
1990	-0.0416	-0.0090	-0.0115	-0.0277	0.0340	0.0162	0.0033	-0.0490	0.0048	0.0135	0.0331	0.0114	1990	-0.0261
1991	0.0059	-0.0033	-0.0026	0.0065	-0.0068	-0.0126	0.0082	0.0272	0.0236	-0.0011	0.0022	0.0513	1991	0.1010
1992	-0.0385	-0.0008	-0.0161	-0.0049	0.0181	0.0133	0.0334	0.0007	0.0127	-0.0255	-0.0051	0.0183	1992	0.0034
1993	0.0222	0.0299	-0.0042	0.0015	-0.0006	0.0387	0.0138	0.0378	-0.0045	0.0048	-0.0312	-0.0035	1993	0.1071
1994	0.0202	-0.0498	-0.0453	-0.0208	-0.0146	-0.0161	0.0303	-0.0152	-0.0392	-0.0091	0.0002	0.0095	1994	-0.1429
1995	0.0203	0.0227	0.0028	0.0112	0.0725	0.0084	-0.0223	0.0179	0.0122	0.0237	0.0198	0.0223	1995	0.2304
1996	-0.0065	-0.0530	-0.0262	-0.0224	-0.0112	0.0149	-0.0045	-0.0196	0.0230	0.0345	0.0299	-0.0312	1996	-0.0737
1997	-0.0135	-0.0046	-0.0311	0.0196	0.0037	0.0138	0.0567	-0.0367	0.0258	0.0287	0.0101	0.0130	1997	0.0851
1998	0.0152	-0.0116	-0.0028	-0.0023	0.0135	0.0176	-0.0088	0.0416	0.0350	-0.0260	0.0052	-0.0077	1998	0.0689
1999	0.0079	-0.0560	-0.0061	-0.0028	-0.0230	-0.0133	-0.0130	-0.0105	0.0032	-0.0062	-0.0117	-0.0210	1999	-0.1435
2000	0.0171	0.0213	0.0312	-0.0123	-0.0111	0.0192	0.0120	0.0190	-0.0203	0.0135	0.0270	0.0198	2000	0.1436
2001	-0.0044	0.0149	-0.0119	-0.0360	-0.0013	0.0038	0.0324	0.0159	0.0040	0.0416	-0.0512	-0.0229	2001	-0.0189
2002	0.0090	0.0072	-0.0479	0.0355	-0.0034	0.0143	0.0252	0.0420	0.0374	-0.0334	-0.0161	0.0462	2002	0.1169
2003	-0.0147	0.0291	-0.0175	0.0062	0.0553	-0.0190	-0.1020	0.0124	0.0501	-0.0324	-0.0012	0.0093	2003	-0.0336
2004	0.0146	0.0192	0.0098	-0.0627	-0.0090	0.0074	0.0113	0.0350	0.0057	0.0115	-0.0275	0.0207	2004	0.0326
2005	0.0260	-0.0163	-0.0112	0.0334	0.0256	0.0131	-0.0322	0.0292	-0.0373	-0.0235	0.0037	0.0228	2005	0.0302
2006	-0.0157	0.0203	-0.0578	-0.0285	-0.0038	0.0048	0.0154	0.0256	0.0132	0.0035	0.0169	-0.0272	2006	-0.0364
2007	-0.0146	0.0297	-0.0184	0.0043	-0.0242	-0.0131	0.0238	0.0157	-0.0025	0.0112	0.0429	-0.0066	2007	0.0469
2008	0.0173	-0.0015	0.0069	-0.0324	-0.0202	0.0180	-0.0064	0.0206	0.0074	-0.0420	0.1407	0.0934	2008	0.2050
2009	-0.1149	-0.0086	0.0606	-0.0679	-0.0281	0.0046	-0.0018	0.0195	0.0142	-0.0203	0.0173	-0.0618	2009	-0.1825
2010	0.0228	-0.0002	-0.0219	0.0266	0.0403	0.0409	-0.0007	0.0670	-0.0180	-0.0344	-0.0169	-0.0420	2010	0.0589
2011	-0.0231	0.0081	-0.0042	0.0165	0.0318	-0.0160	0.0494	0.0688	0.0659	-0.0297	0.0230	0.0303	2011	0.2374

*Compound annual return

Table A-9

Long-Term Government Bonds: Yields

from January 1926 to December 1970

Year	Jan	Feb	Mar	Apr	May	Jun	Jul	Aug	Sep	Oct	Nov	Dec	Year	Jan–Dec*
1926	0.0374	0.0372	0.0371	0.0368	0.0369	0.0368	0.0370	0.0373	0.0372	0.0367	0.0358	0.0354	1926	0.0354
1927	0.0351	0.0347	0.0331	0.0333	0.0327	0.0334	0.0333	0.0329	0.0330	0.0325	0.0320	0.0316	1927	0.0316
1928	0.0321	0.0318	0.0317	0.0319	0.0327	0.0326	0.0344	0.0341	0.0346	0.0336	0.0338	0.0340	1928	0.0340
1929	0.0349	0.0363	0.0377	0.0358	0.0373	0.0367	0.0369	0.0375	0.0375	0.0347	0.0331	0.0340	1929	0.0340
1930	0.0347	0.0339	0.0335	0.0338	0.0329	0.0328	0.0327	0.0328	0.0324	0.0324	0.0322	0.0330	1930	0.0330
1931	0.0343	0.0338	0.0332	0.0327	0.0317	0.0319	0.0325	0.0326	0.0353	0.0385	0.0385	0.0407	1931	0.0407
1932	0.0390	0.0367	0.0370	0.0336	0.0349	0.0347	0.0320	0.0321	0.0319	0.0322	0.0322	0.0315	1932	0.0315
1933	0.0308	0.0325	0.0321	0.0325	0.0308	0.0306	0.0309	0.0308	0.0308	0.0315	0.0327	0.0336	1933	0.0336
1934	0.0321	0.0317	0.0307	0.0300	0.0292	0.0289	0.0288	0.0299	0.0310	0.0300	0.0299	0.0293	1934	0.0293
1935	0.0281	0.0275	0.0274	0.0269	0.0276	0.0270	0.0268	0.0281	0.0282	0.0279	0.0280	0.0276	1935	0.0276
1936	0.0285	0.0281	0.0275	0.0274	0.0273	0.0273	0.0271	0.0264	0.0268	0.0269	0.0257	0.0255	1936	0.0255
1937	0.0258	0.0253	0.0285	0.0284	0.0282	0.0285	0.0277	0.0286	0.0284	0.0283	0.0278	0.0273	1937	0.0273
1938	0.0271	0.0268	0.0273	0.0259	0.0257	0.0259	0.0257	0.0259	0.0259	0.0254	0.0257	0.0252	1938	0.0252
1939	0.0249	0.0245	0.0237	0.0229	0.0217	0.0221	0.0213	0.0231	0.0278	0.0247	0.0236	0.0226	1939	0.0226
1940	0.0229	0.0228	0.0215	0.0220	0.0246	0.0227	0.0224	0.0223	0.0215	0.0214	0.0199	0.0194	1940	0.0194
1941	0.0213	0.0213	0.0206	0.0196	0.0195	0.0191	0.0191	0.0190	0.0193	0.0182	0.0186	0.0204	1941	0.0204
1942	0.0247	0.0247	0.0244	0.0246	0.0243	0.0244	0.0244	0.0244	0.0244	0.0244	0.0247	0.0246	1942	0.0246
1943	0.0245	0.0246	0.0247	0.0246	0.0244	0.0244	0.0245	0.0245	0.0246	0.0247	0.0248	0.0248	1943	0.0248
1944	0.0248	0.0247	0.0247	0.0248	0.0247	0.0248	0.0247	0.0247	0.0247	0.0247	0.0247	0.0246	1944	0.0246
1945	0.0240	0.0236	0.0236	0.0228	0.0226	0.0217	0.0224	0.0223	0.0221	0.0216	0.0210	0.0199	1945	0.0199
1946	0.0199	0.0198	0.0198	0.0207	0.0209	0.0206	0.0209	0.0217	0.0219	0.0216	0.0220	0.0212	1946	0.0212
1947	0.0214	0.0214	0.0213	0.0217	0.0216	0.0216	0.0214	0.0210	0.0213	0.0217	0.0229	0.0243	1947	0.0243
1948	0.0243	0.0241	0.0241	0.0239	0.0231	0.0238	0.0241	0.0242	0.0242	0.0243	0.0239	0.0237	1948	0.0237
1949	0.0233	0.0231	0.0227	0.0227	0.0227	0.0217	0.0216	0.0210	0.0212	0.0212	0.0212	0.0209	1949	0.0209
1950	0.0215	0.0214	0.0215	0.0214	0.0213	0.0216	0.0214	0.0214	0.0220	0.0225	0.0224	0.0224	1950	0.0224
1951	0.0221	0.0228	0.0241	0.0248	0.0254	0.0259	0.0252	0.0246	0.0253	0.0254	0.0264	0.0269	1951	0.0269
1952	0.0268	0.0269	0.0263	0.0254	0.0257	0.0259	0.0261	0.0267	0.0277	0.0269	0.0272	0.0279	1952	0.0279
1953	0.0279	0.0287	0.0294	0.0303	0.0314	0.0301	0.0301	0.0303	0.0284	0.0281	0.0286	0.0274	1953	0.0274
1954	0.0291	0.0279	0.0278	0.0273	0.0279	0.0272	0.0266	0.0269	0.0271	0.0271	0.0274	0.0272	1954	0.0272
1955	0.0286	0.0292	0.0288	0.0290	0.0287	0.0293	0.0300	0.0301	0.0298	0.0292	0.0295	0.0295	1955	0.0295
1956	0.0292	0.0293	0.0303	0.0311	0.0299	0.0299	0.0313	0.0325	0.0324	0.0329	0.0333	0.0345	1956	0.0345
1957	0.0328	0.0328	0.0331	0.0345	0.0348	0.0361	0.0365	0.0367	0.0364	0.0369	0.0340	0.0323	1957	0.0323
1958	0.0330	0.0325	0.0321	0.0311	0.0313	0.0324	0.0343	0.0371	0.0380	0.0374	0.0368	0.0382	1958	0.0382
1959	0.0408	0.0402	0.0403	0.0414	0.0417	0.0419	0.0417	0.0423	0.0429	0.0421	0.0432	0.0447	1959	0.0447
1960	0.0441	0.0429	0.0411	0.0426	0.0417	0.0407	0.0382	0.0390	0.0387	0.0391	0.0399	0.0380	1960	0.0380
1961	0.0404	0.0392	0.0397	0.0391	0.0397	0.0404	0.0404	0.0410	0.0403	0.0400	0.0404	0.0415	1961	0.0415
1962	0.0419	0.0414	0.0398	0.0394	0.0393	0.0401	0.0412	0.0401	0.0398	0.0395	0.0396	0.0395	1962	0.0395
1963	0.0398	0.0400	0.0401	0.0405	0.0406	0.0407	0.0407	0.0408	0.0410	0.0415	0.0414	0.0417	1963	0.0417
1964	0.0421	0.0424	0.0424	0.0423	0.0422	0.0419	0.0421	0.0423	0.0421	0.0421	0.0422	0.0423	1964	0.0423
1965	0.0422	0.0424	0.0422	0.0422	0.0423	0.0423	0.0424	0.0428	0.0433	0.0433	0.0441	0.0450	1965	0.0450
1966	0.0457	0.0477	0.0460	0.0467	0.0473	0.0477	0.0482	0.0499	0.0480	0.0467	0.0480	0.0455	1966	0.0455
1967	0.0448	0.0465	0.0455	0.0477	0.0482	0.0507	0.0505	0.0514	0.0517	0.0549	0.0567	0.0556	1967	0.0556
1968	0.0536	0.0542	0.0560	0.0547	0.0547	0.0534	0.0517	0.0520	0.0531	0.0543	0.0566	0.0598	1968	0.0598
1969	0.0617	0.0618	0.0620	0.0593	0.0635	0.0623	0.0621	0.0630	0.0677	0.0653	0.0676	0.0687	1969	0.0687
1970	0.0693	0.0651	0.0661	0.0699	0.0743	0.0709	0.0687	0.0694	0.0680	0.0693	0.0637	0.0648	1970	0.0648

from January 1971 to December 2011

Year	Jan	Feb	Mar	Apr	May	Jun	Jul	Aug	Sep	Oct	Nov	Dec	Year	Jan–Dec*
1971	0.0612	0.0629	0.0593	0.0619	0.0624	0.0641	0.0643	0.0610	0.0598	0.0588	0.0596	0.0597	1971	0.0597
1972	0.0606	0.0602	0.0613	0.0615	0.0597	0.0607	0.0593	0.0595	0.0606	0.0591	0.0577	0.0599	1972	0.0599
1973	0.0685	0.0688	0.0686	0.0687	0.0703	0.0710	0.0760	0.0728	0.0703	0.0689	0.0712	0.0726	1973	0.0726
1974	0.0740	0.0748	0.0783	0.0816	0.0810	0.0812	0.0823	0.0855	0.0837	0.0795	0.0771	0.0760	1974	0.0760
1975	0.0796	0.0788	0.0824	0.0852	0.0836	0.0813	0.0829	0.0844	0.0862	0.0819	0.0838	0.0805	1975	0.0805
1976	0.0802	0.0802	0.0792	0.0797	0.0821	0.0807	0.0805	0.0790	0.0781	0.0779	0.0749	0.0721	1976	0.0721
1977	0.0764	0.0775	0.0772	0.0771	0.0765	0.0754	0.0768	0.0754	0.0764	0.0781	0.0777	0.0803	1977	0.0803
1978	0.0816	0.0822	0.0831	0.0838	0.0852	0.0865	0.0858	0.0843	0.0860	0.0889	0.0877	0.0898	1978	0.0898
1979	0.0886	0.0908	0.0902	0.0922	0.0903	0.0877	0.0895	0.0907	0.0927	0.1034	0.1009	0.1012	1979	0.1012
1980	0.1114	0.1186	0.1239	0.1076	0.1037	0.1006	0.1074	0.1140	0.1185	0.1231	0.1230	0.1199	1980	0.1199
1981	0.1211	0.1283	0.1248	0.1332	0.1265	0.1304	0.1370	0.1445	0.1482	0.1384	0.1220	0.1334	1981	0.1334
1982	0.1415	0.1402	0.1387	0.1348	0.1358	0.1412	0.1352	0.1254	0.1183	0.1112	0.1125	0.1095	1982	0.1095
1983	0.1113	0.1060	0.1083	0.1051	0.1112	0.1119	0.1198	0.1210	0.1157	0.1188	0.1176	0.1197	1983	0.1197
1984	0.1180	0.1217	0.1253	0.1284	0.1381	0.1374	0.1293	0.1270	0.1235	0.1173	0.1169	0.1170	1984	0.1170
1985	0.1127	0.1209	0.1181	0.1162	0.1062	0.1055	0.1091	0.1068	0.1082	0.1051	0.1011	0.0956	1985	0.0956
1986	0.0958	0.0841	0.0766	0.0782	0.0848	0.0790	0.0809	0.0763	0.0827	0.0803	0.0779	0.0789	1986	0.0789
1987	0.0778	0.0763	0.0795	0.0859	0.0880	0.0877	0.0907	0.0936	0.0992	0.0926	0.0931	0.0920	1987	0.0920
1988	0.0852	0.0854	0.0901	0.0929	0.0952	0.0917	0.0947	0.0950	0.0917	0.0889	0.0923	0.0918	1988	0.0918
1989	0.0903	0.0935	0.0929	0.0918	0.0878	0.0821	0.0801	0.0841	0.0847	0.0810	0.0808	0.0816	1989	0.0816
1990	0.0865	0.0876	0.0889	0.0924	0.0883	0.0864	0.0860	0.0920	0.0914	0.0898	0.0858	0.0844	1990	0.0844
1991	0.0837	0.0841	0.0844	0.0837	0.0845	0.0860	0.0850	0.0818	0.0790	0.0791	0.0789	0.0730	1991	0.0730
1992	0.0776	0.0777	0.0797	0.0803	0.0781	0.0765	0.0726	0.0725	0.0710	0.0741	0.0748	0.0726	1992	0.0726
1993	0.0725	0.0698	0.0702	0.0701	0.0701	0.0668	0.0656	0.0623	0.0627	0.0623	0.0651	0.0654	1993	0.0654
1994	0.0637	0.0682	0.0725	0.0745	0.0759	0.0774	0.0746	0.0761	0.0800	0.0809	0.0808	0.0799	1994	0.0799
1995	0.0780	0.0758	0.0755	0.0745	0.0677	0.0670	0.0691	0.0674	0.0663	0.0641	0.0623	0.0603	1995	0.0603
1996	0.0609	0.0659	0.0684	0.0706	0.0717	0.0703	0.0707	0.0726	0.0704	0.0671	0.0643	0.0673	1996	0.0673
1997	0.0689	0.0694	0.0723	0.0705	0.0701	0.0688	0.0637	0.0672	0.0649	0.0623	0.0614	0.0602	1997	0.0602
1998	0.0589	0.0599	0.0602	0.0604	0.0592	0.0576	0.0584	0.0547	0.0517	0.0540	0.0535	0.0542	1998	0.0542
1999	0.0536	0.0587	0.0592	0.0594	0.0615	0.0627	0.0639	0.0649	0.0646	0.0651	0.0662	0.0682	1999	0.0682
2000	0.0666	0.0646	0.0618	0.0630	0.0640	0.0622	0.0611	0.0594	0.0612	0.0600	0.0576	0.0558	2000	0.0558
2001	0.0562	0.0549	0.0559	0.0593	0.0594	0.0590	0.0561	0.0546	0.0542	0.0506	0.0553	0.0575	2001	0.0575
2002	0.0569	0.0563	0.0604	0.0575	0.0578	0.0566	0.0544	0.0510	0.0480	0.0508	0.0521	0.0484	2002	0.0484
2003	0.0495	0.0472	0.0486	0.0481	0.0436	0.0452	0.0542	0.0532	0.0490	0.0518	0.0519	0.0511	2003	0.0511
2004	0.0499	0.0483	0.0474	0.0531	0.0539	0.0532	0.0523	0.0493	0.0488	0.0478	0.0502	0.0484	2004	0.0484
2005	0.0465	0.0479	0.0488	0.0461	0.0440	0.0429	0.0456	0.0432	0.0464	0.0484	0.0481	0.0461	2005	0.0461
2006	0.0474	0.0457	0.0507	0.0532	0.0535	0.0531	0.0518	0.0496	0.0484	0.0481	0.0467	0.0491	2006	0.0491
2007	0.0502	0.0477	0.0493	0.0489	0.0510	0.0521	0.0501	0.0487	0.0489	0.0480	0.0445	0.0450	2007	0.0450
2008	0.0436	0.0438	0.0432	0.0458	0.0475	0.0460	0.0465	0.0449	0.0443	0.0478	0.0372	0.0303	2008	0.0303
2009	0.0394	0.0401	0.0355	0.0410	0.0432	0.0429	0.0430	0.0415	0.0403	0.0420	0.0406	0.0458	2009	0.0458
2010	0.0441	0.0441	0.0458	0.0437	0.0407	0.0376	0.0377	0.0327	0.0341	0.0367	0.0380	0.0414	2010	0.0414
2011	0.0432	0.0426	0.0429	0.0416	0.0391	0.0404	0.0366	0.0314	0.0265	0.0288	0.0271	0.0248	2011	0.0248

Intermediate-Term Government Bonds: Total Returns

from January 1926 to December 1970

Year	Jan	Feb	Mar	Apr	May	Jun	Jul	Aug	Sep	Oct	Nov	Dec	Year	Jan–Dec*
1926	0.0068	0.0032	0.0041	0.0090	0.0008	0.0027	0.0013	0.0009	0.0050	0.0054	0.0045	0.0089	1926	0.0538
1927	0.0057	0.0038	0.0038	0.0016	0.0020	0.0029	0.0043	0.0056	0.0060	-0.0034	0.0083	0.0037	1927	0.0452
1928	0.0046	-0.0004	0.0010	-0.0003	-0.0006	0.0017	-0.0089	0.0050	0.0028	0.0032	0.0019	-0.0007	1928	0.0092
1929	-0.0029	-0.0018	0.0005	0.0089	-0.0061	0.0107	0.0066	0.0052	-0.0014	0.0168	0.0180	0.0044	1929	0.0601
1930	-0.0041	0.0094	0.0161	-0.0071	0.0061	0.0142	0.0054	0.0022	0.0063	0.0076	0.0070	0.0024	1930	0.0672
1931	-0.0071	0.0099	0.0052	0.0083	0.0119	-0.0214	0.0016	0.0017	-0.0113	-0.0105	0.0049	-0.0159	1931	-0.0232
1932	-0.0032	0.0128	0.0078	0.0194	-0.0090	0.0108	0.0120	0.0124	0.0027	0.0045	0.0031	0.0118	1932	0.0881
1933	-0.0016	-0.0001	0.0099	0.0057	0.0199	0.0008	-0.0006	0.0073	0.0026	-0.0025	0.0027	-0.0253	1933	0.0183
1934	0.0130	0.0052	0.0189	0.0182	0.0120	0.0091	-0.0024	-0.0092	-0.0138	0.0190	0.0046	0.0125	1934	0.0900
1935	0.0114	0.0105	0.0125	0.0107	-0.0035	0.0113	0.0037	-0.0071	-0.0057	0.0109	0.0014	0.0120	1935	0.0701
1936	-0.0003	0.0069	0.0031	0.0024	0.0038	0.0012	0.0022	0.0050	0.0010	0.0025	0.0081	-0.0057	1936	0.0306
1937	-0.0031	0.0007	-0.0164	0.0047	0.0080	-0.0012	0.0059	-0.0043	0.0081	0.0032	0.0042	0.0062	1937	0.0156
1938	0.0085	0.0052	-0.0012	0.0230	0.0023	0.0075	0.0010	0.0015	-0.0013	0.0093	-0.0001	0.0052	1938	0.0623
1939	0.0029	0.0082	0.0081	0.0038	0.0095	0.0002	0.0040	-0.0147	-0.0262	0.0315	0.0074	0.0108	1939	0.0452
1940	-0.0014	0.0035	0.0088	0.0002	-0.0214	0.0187	0.0003	0.0043	0.0047	0.0036	0.0056	0.0028	1940	0.0296
1941	0.0001	-0.0047	0.0069	0.0033	0.0012	0.0056	0.0000	0.0011	0.0000	0.0023	-0.0092	-0.0016	1941	0.0050
1942	0.0074	0.0015	0.0023	0.0022	0.0016	0.0013	0.0000	0.0017	-0.0023	0.0017	0.0017	0.0000	1942	0.0194
1943	0.0039	0.0013	0.0021	0.0024	0.0057	0.0033	0.0021	0.0002	0.0014	0.0017	0.0015	0.0021	1943	0.0281
1944	0.0011	0.0016	0.0019	0.0028	0.0005	0.0007	0.0029	0.0024	0.0011	0.0011	0.0009	0.0010	1944	0.0180
1945	0.0052	0.0038	0.0004	0.0014	0.0012	0.0019	0.0000	0.0016	0.0017	0.0016	0.0010	0.0021	1945	0.0222
1946	0.0039	0.0048	-0.0038	-0.0020	0.0006	0.0033	-0.0010	0.0004	-0.0011	0.0026	-0.0008	0.0032	1946	0.0100
1947	0.0023	0.0006	0.0024	-0.0013	0.0008	0.0008	0.0006	0.0026	0.0000	-0.0023	0.0006	0.0021	1947	0.0091
1948	0.0015	0.0018	0.0018	0.0019	0.0053	-0.0008	-0.0002	-0.0004	0.0010	0.0013	0.0021	0.0032	1948	0.0185
1949	0.0028	0.0011	0.0025	0.0015	0.0023	0.0050	0.0020	0.0031	0.0008	0.0006	0.0002	0.0012	1949	0.0232
1950	-0.0005	0.0008	0.0000	0.0008	0.0020	0.0003	0.0020	-0.0007	-0.0004	0.0001	0.0018	0.0008	1950	0.0070
1951	0.0022	0.0007	-0.0127	0.0057	-0.0040	0.0050	0.0058	0.0036	-0.0057	0.0016	0.0032	-0.0016	1951	0.0036
1952	0.0038	-0.0020	0.0067	0.0054	0.0019	-0.0035	-0.0034	-0.0024	0.0019	0.0066	-0.0006	0.0019	1952	0.0163
1953	-0.0002	0.0003	-0.0017	-0.0096	-0.0117	0.0155	0.0056	-0.0008	0.0194	0.0038	0.0014	0.0103	1953	0.0323
1954	0.0065	0.0100	0.0027	0.0043	-0.0073	0.0125	-0.0005	0.0011	-0.0020	-0.0009	-0.0001	0.0005	1954	0.0268
1955	-0.0032	-0.0052	0.0024	0.0004	0.0001	-0.0036	-0.0071	0.0007	0.0082	0.0072	-0.0053	-0.0011	1955	-0.0065
1956	0.0105	0.0003	-0.0100	-0.0001	0.0112	0.0003	-0.0095	-0.0103	0.0092	-0.0019	-0.0047	0.0011	1956	-0.0042
1957	0.0237	-0.0012	0.0018	-0.0101	-0.0017	-0.0106	-0.0015	0.0109	0.0002	0.0043	0.0396	0.0215	1957	0.0784
1958	0.0034	0.0139	0.0053	0.0052	0.0060	-0.0068	-0.0091	-0.0356	-0.0017	0.0002	0.0132	-0.0061	1958	-0.0129
1959	-0.0013	0.0107	-0.0037	-0.0052	-0.0001	-0.0077	0.0034	-0.0078	0.0020	0.0174	-0.0092	-0.0020	1959	-0.0039
1960	0.0154	0.0072	0.0292	-0.0064	0.0031	0.0217	0.0267	-0.0004	0.0029	0.0016	-0.0094	0.0210	1960	0.1176
1961	-0.0059	0.0090	0.0037	0.0054	-0.0028	-0.0025	0.0007	0.0019	0.0079	0.0014	-0.0019	0.0018	1961	0.0185
1962	-0.0045	0.0155	0.0089	0.0025	0.0049	-0.0028	-0.0012	0.0125	0.0021	0.0051	0.0060	0.0056	1962	0.0556
1963	-0.0029	0.0017	0.0027	0.0030	0.0014	0.0014	0.0003	0.0019	0.0014	0.0011	0.0040	0.0003	1963	0.0164
1964	0.0033	0.0012	0.0016	0.0033	0.0081	0.0036	0.0027	0.0027	0.0045	0.0032	-0.0004	0.0058	1964	0.0404
1965	0.0042	0.0018	0.0043	0.0026	0.0035	0.0049	0.0017	0.0019	-0.0005	0.0000	0.0007	-0.0149	1965	0.0102
1966	0.0003	-0.0083	0.0187	-0.0019	0.0011	-0.0024	-0.0025	-0.0125	0.0216	0.0075	0.0027	0.0223	1966	0.0469
1967	0.0118	-0.0013	0.0183	-0.0089	0.0044	-0.0227	0.0133	-0.0036	0.0007	-0.0049	0.0028	0.0007	1967	0.0101
1968	0.0145	0.0040	-0.0026	-0.0016	0.0064	0.0167	0.0176	0.0021	0.0055	0.0009	-0.0013	-0.0173	1968	0.0454
1969	0.0086	-0.0013	0.0097	0.0079	-0.0082	-0.0084	0.0082	-0.0018	-0.0300	0.0333	-0.0047	-0.0193	1969	-0.0074
1970	0.0030	0.0439	0.0087	-0.0207	0.0110	0.0061	0.0152	0.0116	0.0196	0.0095	0.0451	0.0054	1970	0.1686

*Compound annual return

Table A-10 (Continued)
Intermediate-Term Government Bonds: Total Returns

from January 1971 to December 2011

Year	Jan	Feb	Mar	Apr	May	Jun	Jul	Aug	Sep	Oct	Nov	Dec	Year	Jan–Dec*
1971	0.0168	0.0224	0.0186	-0.0327	0.0011	-0.0187	0.0027	0.0350	0.0026	0.0220	0.0052	0.0110	1971	0.0872
1972	0.0106	0.0014	0.0015	0.0014	0.0016	0.0045	0.0015	0.0015	0.0014	0.0016	0.0045	0.0192	1972	0.0516
1973	-0.0006	-0.0075	0.0046	0.0064	0.0057	-0.0006	-0.0276	0.0254	0.0250	0.0050	0.0064	0.0040	1973	0.0461
1974	0.0009	0.0035	-0.0212	-0.0152	0.0130	-0.0087	0.0007	-0.0012	0.0319	0.0109	0.0236	0.0185	1974	0.0569
1975	0.0053	0.0148	-0.0059	-0.0186	0.0260	0.0027	-0.0030	-0.0009	0.0010	0.0366	-0.0010	0.0198	1975	0.0783
1976	0.0057	0.0084	0.0075	0.0116	-0.0145	0.0159	0.0119	0.0189	0.0076	0.0147	0.0321	0.0026	1976	0.1287
1977	-0.0190	0.0048	0.0055	0.0051	0.0056	0.0102	0.0001	0.0008	0.0015	-0.0060	0.0079	-0.0023	1977	0.0141
1978	0.0013	0.0017	0.0037	0.0024	-0.0002	-0.0021	0.0098	0.0079	0.0057	-0.0112	0.0092	0.0063	1978	0.0349
1979	0.0055	-0.0059	0.0112	0.0033	0.0193	0.0205	-0.0011	-0.0091	0.0006	-0.0468	0.0363	0.0087	1979	0.0409
1980	-0.0135	-0.0641	0.0143	0.1198	0.0490	-0.0077	-0.0106	-0.0387	-0.0038	-0.0152	0.0029	0.0171	1980	0.0391
1981	0.0032	-0.0235	0.0263	-0.0216	0.0245	0.0060	-0.0270	-0.0178	0.0164	0.0611	0.0624	-0.0142	1981	0.0945
1982	0.0050	0.0148	0.0042	0.0299	0.0146	-0.0135	0.0464	0.0469	0.0325	0.0531	0.0080	0.0185	1982	0.2910
1983	0.0007	0.0252	-0.0049	0.0259	-0.0122	0.0016	-0.0198	0.0081	0.0315	0.0019	0.0103	0.0047	1983	0.0741
1984	0.0177	-0.0064	-0.0035	-0.0003	-0.0250	0.0099	0.0393	0.0101	0.0202	0.0383	0.0192	0.0143	1984	0.1402
1985	0.0206	-0.0179	0.0166	0.0264	0.0485	0.0108	-0.0045	0.0148	0.0113	0.0162	0.0195	0.0257	1985	0.2033
1986	0.0082	0.0275	0.0338	0.0081	-0.0215	0.0276	0.0157	0.0266	-0.0110	0.0162	0.0113	0.0007	1986	0.1514
1987	0.0107	0.0059	-0.0031	-0.0244	-0.0038	0.0122	0.0025	-0.0038	-0.0141	0.0299	0.0083	0.0093	1987	0.0290
1988	0.0316	0.0123	-0.0086	-0.0044	-0.0049	0.0181	-0.0047	-0.0009	0.0196	0.0148	-0.0115	-0.0010	1988	0.0610
1989	0.0121	-0.0051	0.0049	0.0220	0.0212	0.0324	0.0235	-0.0246	0.0069	0.0237	0.0084	0.0012	1989	0.1329
1990	-0.0104	0.0007	0.0002	-0.0077	0.0261	0.0151	0.0174	-0.0092	0.0094	0.0171	0.0193	0.0161	1990	0.0973
1991	0.0107	0.0048	0.0023	0.0117	0.0059	-0.0023	0.0129	0.0247	0.0216	0.0134	0.0128	0.0265	1991	0.1546
1992	-0.0195	0.0022	-0.0079	0.0098	0.0222	0.0177	0.0242	0.0150	0.0194	-0.0182	-0.0084	0.0146	1992	0.0719
1993	0.0270	0.0243	0.0043	0.0088	-0.0009	0.0201	0.0005	0.0223	0.0056	0.0018	-0.0093	0.0032	1993	0.1124
1994	0.0138	-0.0258	-0.0257	-0.0105	-0.0002	-0.0028	0.0169	0.0026	-0.0158	-0.0023	-0.0070	0.0053	1994	-0.0514
1995	0.0182	0.0234	0.0063	0.0143	0.0369	0.0079	-0.0016	0.0086	0.0064	0.0121	0.0149	0.0095	1995	0.1680
1996	0.0006	-0.0138	-0.0118	-0.0050	-0.0032	0.0117	0.0025	-0.0005	0.0155	0.0183	0.0149	-0.0078	1996	0.0210
1997	0.0025	0.0002	-0.0114	0.0148	0.0077	0.0103	0.0264	-0.0098	0.0151	0.0150	-0.0001	0.0106	1997	0.0838
1998	0.0180	-0.0039	0.0026	0.0061	0.0070	0.0079	0.0027	0.0271	0.0330	0.0041	-0.0098	0.0037	1998	0.1021
1999	0.0055	-0.0262	0.0086	0.0021	-0.0147	0.0032	-0.0005	0.0015	0.0097	-0.0008	-0.0008	-0.0048	1999	-0.0177
2000	-0.0053	0.0078	0.0203	-0.0043	0.0052	0.0191	0.0072	0.0134	0.0096	0.0079	0.0174	0.0214	2000	0.1259
2001	0.0098	0.0105	0.0076	-0.0114	-0.0007	0.0066	0.0247	0.0095	0.0253	0.0180	-0.0171	-0.0082	2001	0.0762
2002	0.0036	0.0108	-0.0242	0.0239	0.0118	0.0169	0.0272	0.0167	0.0288	-0.0024	-0.0169	0.0279	2002	0.1293
2003	-0.0089	0.0179	-0.0007	0.0013	0.0273	-0.0035	-0.0319	-0.0027	0.0307	-0.0136	-0.0014	0.0109	2003	0.0240
2004	0.0052	0.0124	0.0100	-0.0334	-0.0049	0.0049	0.0082	0.0195	0.0012	0.0064	-0.0127	0.0067	2004	0.0225
2005	0.0026	-0.0111	-0.0038	0.0167	0.0103	0.0043	-0.0144	0.0161	-0.0124	-0.0063	0.0059	0.0061	2005	0.0136
2006	-0.0036	-0.0017	-0.0056	-0.0008	-0.0004	0.0022	0.0125	0.0135	0.0079	0.0052	0.0088	-0.0067	2006	0.0314
2007	-0.0020	0.0170	0.0024	0.0047	-0.0102	0.0011	0.0175	0.0185	0.0057	-0.0048	0.0425	0.0048	2007	0.1005
2008	0.0263	0.0234	0.0073	-0.0293	-0.0084	0.0075	0.0064	0.0104	0.0085	0.0146	0.0430	0.0160	2008	0.1311
2009	-0.0163	-0.0082	0.0186	-0.0166	-0.0132	-0.0076	0.0056	0.0097	0.0075	0.0030	0.0184	-0.0241	2009	-0.0240
2010	0.0194	0.0071	-0.0088	0.0094	0.0151	0.0129	0.0158	0.0128	0.0049	0.0064	-0.0082	-0.0171	2010	0.0712
2011	0.0062	-0.0053	-0.0005	0.0154	0.0179	0.0051	0.0189	0.0217	-0.0024	0.0167	-0.0127	0.0104	2011	0.0946

*Compound annual return

Intermediate-Term Government Bonds: Income Returns

from January 1926 to December 1970

Year	Jan	Feb	Mar	Apr	May	Jun	Jul	Aug	Sep	Oct	Nov	Dec	Year	Jan–Dec*
1926	0.0032	0.0032	0.0032	0.0031	0.0031	0.0031	0.0032	0.0032	0.0032	0.0031	0.0031	0.0030	1926	0.0378
1927	0.0029	0.0029	0.0029	0.0029	0.0029	0.0029	0.0029	0.0029	0.0028	0.0029	0.0028	0.0028	1927	0.0349
1928	0.0028	0.0028	0.0029	0.0029	0.0030	0.0030	0.0032	0.0032	0.0032	0.0032	0.0032	0.0033	1928	0.0364
1929	0.0034	0.0035	0.0036	0.0035	0.0037	0.0035	0.0035	0.0034	0.0035	0.0033	0.0030	0.0030	1929	0.0407
1930	0.0031	0.0030	0.0028	0.0030	0.0029	0.0027	0.0026	0.0026	0.0026	0.0025	0.0024	0.0024	1930	0.0330
1931	0.0026	0.0025	0.0024	0.0023	0.0021	0.0026	0.0026	0.0026	0.0028	0.0031	0.0031	0.0034	1931	0.0316
1932	0.0035	0.0034	0.0033	0.0030	0.0032	0.0031	0.0029	0.0027	0.0027	0.0027	0.0027	0.0025	1932	0.0363
1933	0.0026	0.0026	0.0025	0.0025	0.0021	0.0022	0.0022	0.0021	0.0021	0.0022	0.0022	0.0027	1933	0.0283
1934	0.0030	0.0024	0.0027	0.0024	0.0023	0.0021	0.0021	0.0021	0.0021	0.0026	0.0022	0.0023	1934	0.0293
1935	0.0021	0.0018	0.0018	0.0017	0.0016	0.0015	0.0015	0.0014	0.0015	0.0016	0.0015	0.0016	1935	0.0202
1936	0.0014	0.0013	0.0013	0.0012	0.0012	0.0013	0.0012	0.0012	0.0011	0.0011	0.0011	0.0010	1936	0.0144
1937	0.0010	0.0010	0.0012	0.0015	0.0013	0.0014	0.0014	0.0013	0.0014	0.0012	0.0012	0.0011	1937	0.0148
1938	0.0018	0.0016	0.0017	0.0017	0.0015	0.0014	0.0013	0.0014	0.0013	0.0014	0.0013	0.0013	1938	0.0182
1939	0.0013	0.0011	0.0012	0.0010	0.0011	0.0009	0.0009	0.0009	0.0011	0.0015	0.0010	0.0009	1939	0.0131
1940	0.0009	0.0008	0.0008	0.0007	0.0007	0.0010	0.0008	0.0008	0.0007	0.0007	0.0006	0.0005	1940	0.0090
1941	0.0006	0.0006	0.0008	0.0006	0.0006	0.0006	0.0005	0.0005	0.0005	0.0005	0.0004	0.0007	1941	0.0067
1942	0.0008	0.0006	0.0007	0.0006	0.0006	0.0006	0.0006	0.0006	0.0006	0.0006	0.0006	0.0006	1942	0.0076
1943	0.0014	0.0013	0.0014	0.0013	0.0013	0.0013	0.0013	0.0012	0.0012	0.0012	0.0012	0.0012	1943	0.0156
1944	0.0013	0.0012	0.0013	0.0012	0.0013	0.0012	0.0012	0.0012	0.0011	0.0012	0.0011	0.0011	1944	0.0144
1945	0.0012	0.0010	0.0010	0.0010	0.0010	0.0010	0.0010	0.0010	0.0009	0.0010	0.0009	0.0009	1945	0.0119
1946	0.0009	0.0008	0.0007	0.0009	0.0009	0.0009	0.0009	0.0009	0.0010	0.0010	0.0009	0.0010	1946	0.0108
1947	0.0010	0.0009	0.0010	0.0009	0.0010	0.0011	0.0010	0.0010	0.0010	0.0010	0.0010	0.0012	1947	0.0121
1948	0.0013	0.0012	0.0014	0.0013	0.0012	0.0013	0.0012	0.0013	0.0013	0.0013	0.0014	0.0013	1948	0.0156
1949	0.0013	0.0012	0.0013	0.0012	0.0013	0.0012	0.0010	0.0011	0.0010	0.0010	0.0010	0.0010	1949	0.0136
1950	0.0011	0.0010	0.0011	0.0010	0.0012	0.0011	0.0012	0.0011	0.0011	0.0013	0.0013	0.0013	1950	0.0139
1951	0.0016	0.0014	0.0015	0.0018	0.0017	0.0017	0.0018	0.0017	0.0015	0.0019	0.0017	0.0018	1951	0.0198
1952	0.0018	0.0017	0.0019	0.0017	0.0016	0.0017	0.0018	0.0018	0.0021	0.0020	0.0017	0.0021	1952	0.0219
1953	0.0019	0.0018	0.0021	0.0021	0.0022	0.0027	0.0024	0.0023	0.0023	0.0020	0.0020	0.0020	1953	0.0255
1954	0.0016	0.0014	0.0014	0.0013	0.0011	0.0016	0.0011	0.0012	0.0011	0.0012	0.0014	0.0014	1954	0.0160
1955	0.0018	0.0017	0.0020	0.0019	0.0021	0.0020	0.0020	0.0025	0.0023	0.0023	0.0021	0.0022	1955	0.0245
1956	0.0025	0.0021	0.0022	0.0026	0.0026	0.0023	0.0025	0.0027	0.0026	0.0030	0.0028	0.0030	1956	0.0305
1957	0.0030	0.0025	0.0026	0.0029	0.0030	0.0027	0.0036	0.0032	0.0032	0.0033	0.0031	0.0028	1957	0.0359
1958	0.0024	0.0021	0.0022	0.0021	0.0019	0.0021	0.0021	0.0022	0.0032	0.0032	0.0029	0.0032	1958	0.0293
1959	0.0031	0.0030	0.0033	0.0032	0.0033	0.0037	0.0038	0.0037	0.0039	0.0039	0.0038	0.0041	1959	0.0418
1960	0.0039	0.0039	0.0039	0.0032	0.0037	0.0035	0.0031	0.0030	0.0028	0.0029	0.0028	0.0031	1960	0.0415
1961	0.0030	0.0028	0.0029	0.0027	0.0030	0.0029	0.0031	0.0031	0.0030	0.0032	0.0030	0.0030	1961	0.0354
1962	0.0035	0.0031	0.0031	0.0031	0.0031	0.0029	0.0033	0.0032	0.0028	0.0033	0.0029	0.0030	1962	0.0373
1963	0.0030	0.0028	0.0029	0.0032	0.0031	0.0029	0.0034	0.0031	0.0033	0.0033	0.0031	0.0034	1963	0.0371
1964	0.0034	0.0030	0.0035	0.0033	0.0031	0.0036	0.0034	0.0033	0.0033	0.0033	0.0034	0.0034	1964	0.0400
1965	0.0033	0.0031	0.0037	0.0033	0.0033	0.0037	0.0034	0.0036	0.0034	0.0034	0.0038	0.0037	1965	0.0415
1966	0.0040	0.0036	0.0043	0.0038	0.0042	0.0040	0.0040	0.0047	0.0046	0.0044	0.0042	0.0042	1966	0.0493
1967	0.0041	0.0035	0.0039	0.0033	0.0042	0.0038	0.0045	0.0042	0.0041	0.0047	0.0046	0.0044	1967	0.0488
1968	0.0051	0.0043	0.0043	0.0049	0.0048	0.0043	0.0049	0.0042	0.0044	0.0044	0.0041	0.0047	1968	0.0549
1969	0.0054	0.0048	0.0049	0.0057	0.0050	0.0058	0.0059	0.0054	0.0061	0.0067	0.0056	0.0068	1969	0.0665
1970	0.0066	0.0061	0.0063	0.0059	0.0062	0.0067	0.0065	0.0062	0.0060	0.0057	0.0058	0.0050	1970	0.0749

*Compound annual return

from January 1971 to December 2011

Year	Jan	Feb	Mar	Apr	May	Jun	Jul	Aug	Sep	Oct	Nov	Dec	Year	Jan–Dec*
1971	0.0047	0.0043	0.0047	0.0040	0.0044	0.0053	0.0053	0.0056	0.0048	0.0046	0.0047	0.0046	1971	0.0575
1972	0.0048	0.0044	0.0046	0.0044	0.0052	0.0048	0.0049	0.0050	0.0047	0.0053	0.0051	0.0049	1972	0.0575
1973	0.0056	0.0048	0.0054	0.0056	0.0056	0.0053	0.0059	0.0064	0.0055	0.0060	0.0055	0.0056	1973	0.0658
1974	0.0057	0.0051	0.0054	0.0065	0.0067	0.0059	0.0073	0.0067	0.0072	0.0067	0.0061	0.0064	1974	0.0724
1975	0.0061	0.0055	0.0059	0.0060	0.0063	0.0063	0.0063	0.0061	0.0069	0.0068	0.0055	0.0067	1975	0.0735
1976	0.0060	0.0055	0.0066	0.0059	0.0054	0.0069	0.0060	0.0062	0.0056	0.0054	0.0058	0.0050	1976	0.0710
1977	0.0051	0.0050	0.0056	0.0053	0.0058	0.0055	0.0052	0.0059	0.0056	0.0059	0.0059	0.0059	1977	0.0649
1978	0.0066	0.0057	0.0066	0.0060	0.0071	0.0066	0.0070	0.0068	0.0065	0.0072	0.0072	0.0069	1978	0.0783
1979	0.0079	0.0066	0.0075	0.0077	0.0077	0.0070	0.0074	0.0073	0.0070	0.0084	0.0089	0.0086	1979	0.0904
1980	0.0086	0.0083	0.0107	0.0103	0.0081	0.0075	0.0079	0.0076	0.0097	0.0094	0.0096	0.0111	1980	0.1055
1981	0.0101	0.0095	0.0117	0.0106	0.0110	0.0118	0.0116	0.0120	0.0130	0.0129	0.0121	0.0108	1981	0.1297
1982	0.0107	0.0102	0.0122	0.0112	0.0101	0.0118	0.0113	0.0109	0.0097	0.0089	0.0087	0.0085	1982	0.1281
1983	0.0084	0.0079	0.0084	0.0081	0.0086	0.0085	0.0082	0.0103	0.0094	0.0092	0.0091	0.0091	1983	0.1035
1984	0.0096	0.0088	0.0095	0.0101	0.0104	0.0105	0.0113	0.0105	0.0095	0.0110	0.0093	0.0093	1984	0.1168
1985	0.0090	0.0081	0.0089	0.0097	0.0090	0.0073	0.0083	0.0081	0.0082	0.0081	0.0074	0.0078	1985	0.1029
1986	0.0071	0.0066	0.0068	0.0060	0.0060	0.0068	0.0062	0.0057	0.0058	0.0060	0.0052	0.0060	1986	0.0772
1987	0.0055	0.0052	0.0060	0.0058	0.0062	0.0071	0.0066	0.0068	0.0068	0.0073	0.0070	0.0070	1987	0.0747
1988	0.0065	0.0066	0.0064	0.0063	0.0072	0.0070	0.0064	0.0077	0.0072	0.0071	0.0067	0.0071	1988	0.0824
1989	0.0077	0.0066	0.0078	0.0071	0.0080	0.0070	0.0067	0.0061	0.0065	0.0071	0.0063	0.0060	1989	0.0846
1990	0.0071	0.0064	0.0069	0.0071	0.0075	0.0067	0.0072	0.0068	0.0065	0.0074	0.0067	0.0067	1990	0.0815
1991	0.0064	0.0059	0.0059	0.0070	0.0065	0.0059	0.0069	0.0062	0.0061	0.0058	0.0052	0.0056	1991	0.0743
1992	0.0052	0.0052	0.0060	0.0058	0.0056	0.0058	0.0053	0.0050	0.0047	0.0044	0.0050	0.0053	1992	0.0627
1993	0.0049	0.0045	0.0049	0.0045	0.0041	0.0050	0.0041	0.0044	0.0041	0.0038	0.0042	0.0043	1993	0.0553
1994	0.0045	0.0039	0.0048	0.0049	0.0058	0.0055	0.0055	0.0060	0.0055	0.0060	0.0061	0.0063	1994	0.0607
1995	0.0067	0.0056	0.0060	0.0054	0.0062	0.0050	0.0051	0.0051	0.0047	0.0052	0.0047	0.0043	1995	0.0669
1996	0.0046	0.0041	0.0045	0.0053	0.0054	0.0050	0.0058	0.0052	0.0056	0.0053	0.0047	0.0050	1996	0.0582
1997	0.0052	0.0047	0.0054	0.0055	0.0054	0.0055	0.0054	0.0046	0.0054	0.0050	0.0043	0.0052	1997	0.0614
1998	0.0046	0.0041	0.0049	0.0046	0.0045	0.0049	0.0047	0.0046	0.0041	0.0035	0.0036	0.0039	1998	0.0529
1999	0.0037	0.0035	0.0048	0.0043	0.0041	0.0052	0.0048	0.0051	0.0048	0.0046	0.0052	0.0052	1999	0.0530
2000	0.0054	0.0052	0.0056	0.0048	0.0059	0.0054	0.0053	0.0051	0.0047	0.0051	0.0047	0.0043	2000	0.0619
2001	0.0032	0.0026	0.0027	0.0033	0.0042	0.0040	0.0044	0.0039	0.0034	0.0035	0.0030	0.0035	2001	0.0427
2002	0.0038	0.0034	0.0034	0.0045	0.0039	0.0034	0.0037	0.0029	0.0027	0.0022	0.0022	0.0028	2002	0.0398
2003	0.0024	0.0024	0.0024	0.0023	0.0023	0.0019	0.0020	0.0025	0.0029	0.0022	0.0023	0.0029	2003	0.0285
2004	0.0026	0.0024	0.0026	0.0023	0.0027	0.0034	0.0030	0.0031	0.0026	0.0026	0.0027	0.0030	2004	0.0328
2005	0.0031	0.0028	0.0034	0.0033	0.0034	0.0031	0.0030	0.0037	0.0031	0.0035	0.0036	0.0036	2005	0.0392
2006	0.0037	0.0034	0.0039	0.0037	0.0044	0.0041	0.0043	0.0040	0.0036	0.0039	0.0036	0.0034	2006	0.0454
2007	0.0041	0.0036	0.0037	0.0038	0.0038	0.0038	0.0043	0.0038	0.0032	0.0037	0.0035	0.0028	2007	0.0444
2008	0.0031	0.0024	0.0022	0.0020	0.0025	0.0028	0.0028	0.0025	0.0026	0.0024	0.0020	0.0015	2008	0.0296
2009	0.0012	0.0014	0.0018	0.0014	0.0016	0.0021	0.0022	0.0021	0.0019	0.0018	0.0018	0.0015	2009	0.0201
2010	0.0022	0.0019	0.0021	0.0021	0.0018	0.0019	0.0015	0.0013	0.0010	0.0009	0.0009	0.0011	2010	0.0192
2011	0.0019	0.0017	0.0019	0.0019	0.0018	0.0014	0.0013	0.0011	0.0007	0.0007	0.0004	0.0007	2011	0.0158

*Compound annual return

Table A-12

Intermediate-Term Government Bonds: Capital Appreciation Returns

from January 1926 to December 1970

Year	Jan	Feb	Mar	Apr	May	Jun	Jul	Aug	Sep	Oct	Nov	Dec	Year	Jan–Dec*
1926	0.0036	0.0000	0.0009	0.0059	-0.0023	-0.0004	-0.0018	-0.0023	0.0018	0.0023	0.0014	0.0059	1926	0.0151
1927	0.0027	0.0009	0.0009	-0.0014	-0.0009	0.0000	0.0014	0.0027	0.0032	-0.0064	0.0055	0.0009	1927	0.0096
1928	0.0018	-0.0032	-0.0018	-0.0032	-0.0036	-0.0014	-0.0122	0.0018	-0.0004	0.0000	-0.0014	-0.0041	1928	-0.0273
1929	-0.0063	-0.0054	-0.0031	0.0054	-0.0098	0.0072	0.0031	0.0018	-0.0049	0.0135	0.0150	0.0014	1929	0.0177
1930	-0.0072	0.0064	0.0133	-0.0100	0.0032	0.0115	0.0028	-0.0005	0.0037	0.0051	0.0046	0.0000	1930	0.0330
1931	-0.0097	0.0074	0.0028	0.0060	0.0098	-0.0240	-0.0009	-0.0009	-0.0142	-0.0136	0.0018	-0.0193	1931	-0.0540
1932	-0.0067	0.0094	0.0045	0.0164	-0.0122	0.0077	0.0091	0.0096	0.0000	0.0018	0.0005	0.0092	1932	0.0502
1933	-0.0041	-0.0028	0.0074	0.0032	0.0178	-0.0014	-0.0028	0.0051	0.0005	-0.0047	0.0005	-0.0280	1933	-0.0099
1934	0.0100	0.0028	0.0162	0.0158	0.0097	0.0070	-0.0044	-0.0113	-0.0160	0.0164	0.0024	0.0102	1934	0.0597
1935	0.0093	0.0088	0.0107	0.0090	-0.0050	0.0098	0.0022	-0.0086	-0.0072	0.0093	-0.0002	0.0105	1935	0.0494
1936	-0.0017	0.0056	0.0018	0.0012	0.0026	-0.0001	0.0010	0.0038	-0.0001	0.0014	0.0070	-0.0067	1936	0.0160
1937	-0.0041	-0.0003	-0.0176	0.0032	0.0067	-0.0027	0.0045	-0.0056	0.0068	0.0020	0.0030	0.0051	1937	0.0005
1938	0.0067	0.0036	-0.0030	0.0214	0.0008	0.0061	-0.0003	0.0000	-0.0026	0.0079	-0.0014	0.0039	1938	0.0437
1939	0.0016	0.0071	0.0069	0.0028	0.0084	-0.0007	0.0030	-0.0155	-0.0273	0.0300	0.0063	0.0098	1939	0.0318
1940	-0.0023	0.0027	0.0080	-0.0005	-0.0221	0.0177	-0.0005	0.0035	0.0040	0.0030	0.0050	0.0023	1940	0.0204
1941	-0.0006	-0.0052	0.0061	0.0027	0.0006	0.0051	-0.0004	0.0006	-0.0004	0.0018	-0.0096	-0.0023	1941	-0.0017
1942	0.0066	0.0009	0.0016	0.0016	0.0010	0.0006	-0.0006	0.0011	-0.0029	0.0011	0.0011	-0.0006	1942	0.0117
1943	0.0025	0.0001	0.0007	0.0010	0.0044	0.0020	0.0008	-0.0010	0.0002	0.0005	0.0002	0.0008	1943	0.0123
1944	-0.0002	0.0004	0.0007	0.0016	-0.0008	-0.0005	0.0016	0.0012	0.0000	-0.0001	-0.0003	-0.0001	1944	0.0035
1945	0.0040	0.0028	-0.0005	0.0005	0.0002	0.0009	-0.0010	0.0006	0.0008	0.0006	0.0001	0.0012	1945	0.0102
1946	0.0030	0.0040	-0.0045	-0.0028	-0.0003	0.0024	-0.0019	-0.0005	-0.0020	0.0015	-0.0018	0.0022	1946	-0.0008
1947	0.0012	-0.0003	0.0014	-0.0022	-0.0002	-0.0003	-0.0004	0.0016	-0.0010	-0.0033	-0.0004	0.0008	1947	-0.0030
1948	0.0002	0.0006	0.0003	0.0006	0.0042	-0.0021	-0.0014	-0.0018	-0.0003	0.0000	0.0006	0.0019	1948	0.0027
1949	0.0015	0.0000	0.0012	0.0003	0.0010	0.0038	0.0010	0.0019	-0.0002	-0.0004	-0.0008	0.0002	1949	0.0095
1950	-0.0016	-0.0002	-0.0011	-0.0003	0.0007	-0.0008	0.0009	-0.0019	-0.0015	-0.0012	0.0005	-0.0004	1950	-0.0069
1951	0.0006	-0.0007	-0.0142	0.0040	-0.0058	0.0033	0.0040	0.0019	-0.0072	-0.0003	0.0015	-0.0033	1951	-0.0163
1952	0.0019	-0.0037	0.0048	0.0037	0.0004	-0.0052	-0.0052	-0.0042	-0.0002	0.0046	-0.0023	-0.0002	1952	-0.0057
1953	-0.0022	-0.0016	-0.0038	-0.0117	-0.0138	0.0129	0.0032	-0.0031	0.0171	0.0018	-0.0006	0.0083	1953	0.0061
1954	0.0049	0.0086	0.0013	0.0031	-0.0084	0.0109	-0.0016	-0.0001	-0.0032	-0.0021	-0.0015	-0.0010	1954	0.0108
1955	-0.0050	-0.0070	0.0004	-0.0014	-0.0019	-0.0057	-0.0091	-0.0018	0.0059	0.0050	-0.0074	-0.0033	1955	-0.0310
1956	0.0080	-0.0018	-0.0122	-0.0027	0.0086	-0.0020	-0.0120	-0.0130	0.0066	-0.0049	-0.0075	-0.0019	1956	-0.0345
1957	0.0207	-0.0037	-0.0009	-0.0130	-0.0047	-0.0133	-0.0051	0.0077	-0.0030	0.0010	0.0365	0.0188	1957	0.0405
1958	0.0010	0.0117	0.0031	0.0031	0.0041	-0.0088	-0.0112	-0.0378	-0.0048	-0.0029	0.0103	-0.0093	1958	-0.0417
1959	-0.0045	0.0078	-0.0070	-0.0084	-0.0033	-0.0113	-0.0004	-0.0116	-0.0019	0.0134	-0.0130	-0.0060	1959	-0.0456
1960	0.0115	0.0032	0.0253	-0.0096	-0.0006	0.0182	0.0236	-0.0034	0.0001	-0.0012	-0.0122	0.0180	1960	0.0742
1961	-0.0089	0.0063	0.0008	0.0026	-0.0058	-0.0054	-0.0024	-0.0012	0.0049	-0.0018	-0.0049	-0.0012	1961	-0.0172
1962	-0.0080	0.0124	0.0058	-0.0006	0.0018	-0.0056	-0.0045	0.0092	-0.0007	0.0018	0.0031	0.0026	1962	0.0173
1963	-0.0059	-0.0011	-0.0002	-0.0002	-0.0017	-0.0015	-0.0030	-0.0012	-0.0019	-0.0022	0.0008	-0.0032	1963	-0.0210
1964	-0.0001	-0.0019	-0.0019	0.0000	0.0049	0.0000	-0.0006	-0.0006	0.0012	0.0000	-0.0037	0.0024	1964	-0.0003
1965	0.0009	-0.0013	0.0006	-0.0007	0.0002	0.0012	-0.0016	-0.0017	-0.0039	-0.0033	-0.0031	-0.0186	1965	-0.0310
1966	-0.0037	-0.0120	0.0145	-0.0056	-0.0032	-0.0064	-0.0065	-0.0171	0.0170	0.0031	-0.0015	0.0180	1966	-0.0041
1967	0.0077	-0.0048	0.0144	-0.0122	0.0002	-0.0265	0.0089	-0.0078	-0.0035	-0.0095	-0.0018	-0.0038	1967	-0.0385
1968	0.0095	-0.0003	-0.0069	-0.0065	0.0015	0.0123	0.0128	-0.0021	0.0011	-0.0034	-0.0054	-0.0220	1968	-0.0099
1969	0.0032	-0.0061	0.0048	0.0021	-0.0131	-0.0142	0.0024	-0.0072	-0.0361	0.0266	-0.0103	-0.0260	1969	-0.0727
1970	-0.0035	0.0378	0.0024	-0.0266	0.0049	-0.0006	0.0087	0.0054	0.0136	0.0037	0.0393	0.0005	1970	0.0871

*Compound annual return

Intermediate-Term Government Bonds: Capital Appreciation Returns

from January 1971 to December 2011

Year	Jan	Feb	Mar	Apr	May	Jun	Jul	Aug	Sep	Oct	Nov	Dec	Year	Jan–Dec*
1971	0.0121	0.0181	0.0139	-0.0367	-0.0034	-0.0240	-0.0027	0.0294	-0.0022	0.0173	0.0005	0.0064	1971	0.0272
1972	0.0058	-0.0030	-0.0031	-0.0030	-0.0035	-0.0003	-0.0034	-0.0035	-0.0033	-0.0037	-0.0006	0.0143	1972	-0.0075
1973	-0.0062	-0.0123	-0.0008	0.0007	0.0001	-0.0059	-0.0336	0.0190	0.0195	-0.0010	0.0009	-0.0016	1973	-0.0219
1974	-0.0048	-0.0016	-0.0266	-0.0217	0.0063	-0.0147	-0.0066	-0.0078	0.0247	0.0043	0.0175	0.0120	1974	-0.0199
1975	-0.0008	0.0092	-0.0119	-0.0246	0.0197	-0.0035	-0.0093	-0.0070	-0.0059	0.0298	-0.0065	0.0131	1975	0.0012
1976	-0.0003	0.0028	0.0010	0.0057	-0.0200	0.0090	0.0059	0.0127	0.0019	0.0093	0.0264	-0.0024	1976	0.0525
1977	-0.0241	-0.0002	-0.0001	-0.0001	-0.0002	0.0048	-0.0051	-0.0052	-0.0041	-0.0118	0.0019	-0.0082	1977	-0.0515
1978	-0.0053	-0.0041	-0.0029	-0.0036	-0.0073	-0.0087	0.0028	0.0010	-0.0008	-0.0184	0.0020	-0.0005	1978	-0.0449
1979	-0.0024	-0.0125	0.0038	-0.0044	0.0116	0.0135	-0.0086	-0.0163	-0.0065	-0.0553	0.0274	0.0001	1979	-0.0507
1980	-0.0221	-0.0724	0.0036	0.1095	0.0409	-0.0152	-0.0185	-0.0463	-0.0135	-0.0246	-0.0067	0.0060	1980	-0.0681
1981	-0.0069	-0.0331	0.0146	-0.0322	0.0135	-0.0058	-0.0386	-0.0298	0.0034	0.0482	0.0502	-0.0250	1981	-0.0455
1982	-0.0057	0.0046	-0.0080	0.0186	0.0045	-0.0253	0.0351	0.0359	0.0228	0.0442	-0.0007	0.0100	1982	0.1423
1983	-0.0076	0.0173	-0.0133	0.0177	-0.0208	-0.0069	-0.0280	-0.0022	0.0220	-0.0073	0.0012	-0.0043	1983	-0.0330
1984	0.0081	-0.0153	-0.0129	-0.0104	-0.0353	-0.0007	0.0280	-0.0005	0.0106	0.0274	0.0099	0.0050	1984	0.0122
1985	0.0116	-0.0260	0.0077	0.0167	0.0395	0.0035	-0.0129	0.0067	0.0031	0.0081	0.0121	0.0178	1985	0.0901
1986	0.0011	0.0210	0.0270	0.0021	-0.0274	0.0208	0.0095	0.0209	-0.0168	0.0102	0.0061	-0.0053	1986	0.0699
1987	0.0051	0.0007	-0.0091	-0.0302	-0.0100	0.0051	-0.0040	-0.0105	-0.0209	0.0226	0.0013	0.0023	1987	-0.0475
1988	0.0251	0.0057	-0.0151	-0.0107	-0.0121	0.0111	-0.0111	-0.0086	0.0124	0.0077	-0.0182	-0.0081	1988	-0.0226
1989	0.0044	-0.0117	-0.0029	0.0149	0.0132	0.0254	0.0168	-0.0307	0.0004	0.0166	0.0021	-0.0048	1989	0.0434
1990	-0.0176	-0.0057	-0.0067	-0.0148	0.0186	0.0084	0.0102	-0.0160	0.0030	0.0096	0.0126	0.0095	1990	0.0102
1991	0.0042	-0.0011	-0.0036	0.0046	-0.0006	-0.0081	0.0060	0.0184	0.0155	0.0077	0.0076	0.0209	1991	0.0736
1992	-0.0247	-0.0030	-0.0139	0.0039	0.0166	0.0118	0.0189	0.0100	0.0147	-0.0226	-0.0134	0.0093	1992	0.0064
1993	0.0221	0.0198	-0.0006	0.0043	-0.0051	0.0152	-0.0036	0.0179	0.0015	-0.0020	-0.0135	-0.0011	1993	0.0556
1994	0.0093	-0.0297	-0.0306	-0.0154	-0.0060	-0.0084	0.0115	-0.0034	-0.0213	-0.0084	-0.0131	-0.0010	1994	-0.1114
1995	0.0115	0.0178	0.0003	0.0090	0.0307	0.0030	-0.0066	0.0035	0.0017	0.0069	0.0102	0.0052	1995	0.0966
1996	-0.0040	-0.0178	-0.0164	-0.0103	-0.0086	0.0067	-0.0033	-0.0057	0.0100	0.0129	0.0102	-0.0128	1996	-0.0390
1997	-0.0027	-0.0045	-0.0168	0.0093	0.0024	0.0048	0.0210	-0.0143	0.0098	0.0100	-0.0045	0.0054	1997	0.0195
1998	0.0134	-0.0080	-0.0024	0.0015	0.0025	0.0030	-0.0020	0.0225	0.0289	0.0006	-0.0134	-0.0002	1998	0.0466
1999	0.0018	-0.0297	0.0038	-0.0023	-0.0188	-0.0020	-0.0053	-0.0035	0.0049	-0.0054	-0.0060	-0.0100	1999	-0.0706
2000	-0.0107	0.0026	0.0147	-0.0091	-0.0007	0.0138	0.0019	0.0083	0.0049	0.0028	0.0127	0.0171	2000	0.0594
2001	0.0066	0.0079	0.0049	-0.0146	-0.0049	0.0025	0.0203	0.0056	0.0219	0.0145	-0.0201	-0.0117	2001	0.0323
2002	-0.0003	0.0073	-0.0276	0.0193	0.0079	0.0135	0.0234	0.0138	0.0261	-0.0046	-0.0191	0.0251	2002	0.0865
2003	-0.0113	0.0155	-0.0031	-0.0010	0.0250	-0.0054	-0.0339	-0.0053	0.0279	-0.0158	-0.0038	0.0080	2003	-0.0048
2004	0.0025	0.0100	0.0074	-0.0357	-0.0076	0.0015	0.0051	0.0164	-0.0014	0.0039	-0.0154	0.0036	2004	-0.0107
2005	-0.0005	-0.0139	-0.0073	0.0134	0.0069	0.0012	-0.0173	0.0124	-0.0155	-0.0098	0.0023	0.0026	2005	-0.0258
2006	-0.0073	-0.0051	-0.0095	-0.0045	-0.0049	-0.0019	0.0082	0.0095	0.0042	0.0012	0.0052	-0.0102	2006	-0.0151
2007	-0.0061	0.0134	-0.0012	0.0009	-0.0141	-0.0028	0.0132	0.0147	0.0026	-0.0085	0.0390	0.0021	2007	0.0533
2008	0.0231	0.0210	0.0051	-0.0314	-0.0110	0.0047	0.0036	0.0079	0.0058	0.0122	0.0410	0.0145	2008	0.0992
2009	-0.0175	-0.0096	0.0168	-0.0179	-0.0148	-0.0097	0.0034	0.0076	0.0056	0.0012	0.0166	-0.0256	2009	-0.0442
2010	0.0172	0.0052	-0.0109	0.0073	0.0133	0.0111	0.0143	0.0115	0.0039	0.0055	-0.0091	-0.0182	2010	0.0516
2011	0.0044	-0.0070	-0.0024	0.0136	0.0161	0.0037	0.0176	0.0206	-0.0031	0.0159	-0.0131	0.0097	2011	0.0779

*Compound annual return

from January 1926 to December 1970

Year	Jan	Feb	Mar	Apr	May	Jun	Jul	Aug	Sep	Oct	Nov	Dec	Year	Jan–Dec*
1926	0.0386	0.0386	0.0384	0.0371	0.0376	0.0377	0.0381	0.0386	0.0382	0.0377	0.0374	0.0361	1926	0.0361
1927	0.0355	0.0353	0.0351	0.0354	0.0356	0.0356	0.0353	0.0347	0.0340	0.0354	0.0342	0.0340	1927	0.0340
1928	0.0336	0.0343	0.0347	0.0354	0.0362	0.0365	0.0392	0.0388	0.0389	0.0389	0.0392	0.0401	1928	0.0401
1929	0.0415	0.0427	0.0434	0.0422	0.0444	0.0428	0.0421	0.0417	0.0428	0.0398	0.0365	0.0362	1929	0.0362
1930	0.0378	0.0364	0.0335	0.0357	0.0350	0.0325	0.0319	0.0320	0.0312	0.0301	0.0291	0.0291	1930	0.0291
1931	0.0312	0.0296	0.0290	0.0277	0.0256	0.0308	0.0310	0.0312	0.0343	0.0373	0.0369	0.0412	1931	0.0412
1932	0.0427	0.0406	0.0396	0.0360	0.0387	0.0370	0.0350	0.0329	0.0329	0.0325	0.0324	0.0304	1932	0.0304
1933	0.0313	0.0319	0.0303	0.0296	0.0258	0.0261	0.0267	0.0256	0.0255	0.0265	0.0264	0.0325	1933	0.0325
1934	0.0325	0.0321	0.0296	0.0272	0.0257	0.0246	0.0253	0.0271	0.0298	0.0271	0.0267	0.0249	1934	0.0249
1935	0.0233	0.0218	0.0199	0.0184	0.0193	0.0175	0.0171	0.0187	0.0201	0.0183	0.0183	0.0163	1935	0.0163
1936	0.0166	0.0155	0.0151	0.0149	0.0143	0.0143	0.0141	0.0133	0.0133	0.0130	0.0114	0.0129	1936	0.0129
1937	0.0134	0.0135	0.0184	0.0175	0.0156	0.0164	0.0151	0.0168	0.0147	0.0141	0.0131	0.0114	1937	0.0114
1938	0.0205	0.0200	0.0204	0.0174	0.0173	0.0164	0.0164	0.0164	0.0168	0.0156	0.0158	0.0152	1938	0.0152
1939	0.0149	0.0138	0.0127	0.0122	0.0108	0.0110	0.0105	0.0131	0.0180	0.0127	0.0116	0.0098	1939	0.0098
1940	0.0103	0.0098	0.0083	0.0084	0.0127	0.0092	0.0093	0.0086	0.0078	0.0072	0.0061	0.0057	1940	0.0057
1941	0.0077	0.0089	0.0075	0.0069	0.0067	0.0055	0.0056	0.0055	0.0056	0.0051	0.0076	0.0082	1941	0.0082
1942	0.0083	0.0081	0.0077	0.0074	0.0071	0.0070	0.0071	0.0069	0.0076	0.0073	0.0070	0.0072	1942	0.0072
1943	0.0166	0.0166	0.0164	0.0162	0.0153	0.0149	0.0147	0.0149	0.0149	0.0147	0.0147	0.0145	1943	0.0145
1944	0.0150	0.0150	0.0148	0.0143	0.0146	0.0147	0.0142	0.0139	0.0139	0.0139	0.0140	0.0140	1944	0.0140
1945	0.0127	0.0118	0.0120	0.0118	0.0117	0.0114	0.0118	0.0115	0.0112	0.0109	0.0109	0.0103	1945	0.0103
1946	0.0099	0.0087	0.0101	0.0111	0.0112	0.0103	0.0110	0.0112	0.0120	0.0114	0.0121	0.0112	1946	0.0112
1947	0.0116	0.0117	0.0112	0.0120	0.0121	0.0122	0.0124	0.0117	0.0121	0.0136	0.0138	0.0134	1947	0.0134
1948	0.0160	0.0158	0.0157	0.0155	0.0142	0.0149	0.0154	0.0160	0.0161	0.0161	0.0158	0.0151	1948	0.0151
1949	0.0153	0.0153	0.0148	0.0147	0.0144	0.0129	0.0125	0.0117	0.0118	0.0120	0.0124	0.0123	1949	0.0123
1950	0.0131	0.0132	0.0137	0.0138	0.0134	0.0139	0.0134	0.0145	0.0154	0.0162	0.0159	0.0162	1950	0.0162
1951	0.0179	0.0180	0.0211	0.0202	0.0215	0.0208	0.0199	0.0194	0.0212	0.0212	0.0209	0.0217	1951	0.0217
1952	0.0212	0.0222	0.0209	0.0199	0.0198	0.0213	0.0228	0.0241	0.0242	0.0227	0.0235	0.0235	1952	0.0235
1953	0.0242	0.0245	0.0253	0.0277	0.0307	0.0279	0.0272	0.0279	0.0241	0.0237	0.0238	0.0218	1953	0.0218
1954	0.0187	0.0157	0.0153	0.0142	0.0173	0.0131	0.0138	0.0138	0.0152	0.0161	0.0168	0.0172	1954	0.0172
1955	0.0227	0.0240	0.0240	0.0242	0.0246	0.0257	0.0276	0.0280	0.0267	0.0257	0.0273	0.0280	1955	0.0280
1956	0.0271	0.0275	0.0300	0.0305	0.0287	0.0292	0.0317	0.0346	0.0331	0.0342	0.0359	0.0363	1956	0.0363
1957	0.0326	0.0333	0.0334	0.0357	0.0366	0.0390	0.0399	0.0385	0.0390	0.0388	0.0320	0.0284	1957	0.0284
1958	0.0282	0.0259	0.0253	0.0246	0.0238	0.0250	0.0281	0.0365	0.0376	0.0382	0.0359	0.0381	1958	0.0381
1959	0.0395	0.0378	0.0393	0.0413	0.0420	0.0447	0.0448	0.0477	0.0482	0.0448	0.0482	0.0498	1959	0.0498
1960	0.0471	0.0464	0.0409	0.0431	0.0432	0.0390	0.0334	0.0343	0.0343	0.0346	0.0377	0.0331	1960	0.0331
1961	0.0363	0.0350	0.0348	0.0342	0.0355	0.0368	0.0373	0.0376	0.0365	0.0369	0.0381	0.0384	1961	0.0384
1962	0.0402	0.0377	0.0366	0.0367	0.0363	0.0375	0.0384	0.0365	0.0366	0.0362	0.0355	0.0350	1962	0.0350
1963	0.0368	0.0370	0.0370	0.0371	0.0374	0.0378	0.0385	0.0388	0.0392	0.0398	0.0396	0.0404	1963	0.0404
1964	0.0402	0.0407	0.0411	0.0411	0.0399	0.0399	0.0401	0.0402	0.0399	0.0399	0.0409	0.0403	1964	0.0403
1965	0.0413	0.0416	0.0414	0.0416	0.0415	0.0413	0.0416	0.0420	0.0429	0.0437	0.0444	0.0490	1965	0.0490
1966	0.0482	0.0507	0.0477	0.0489	0.0496	0.0510	0.0525	0.0565	0.0526	0.0519	0.0522	0.0479	1966	0.0479
1967	0.0459	0.0470	0.0437	0.0466	0.0465	0.0530	0.0508	0.0528	0.0537	0.0562	0.0566	0.0577	1967	0.0577
1968	0.0548	0.0549	0.0563	0.0577	0.0574	0.0547	0.0518	0.0523	0.0520	0.0528	0.0541	0.0596	1968	0.0596
1969	0.0637	0.0651	0.0640	0.0636	0.0666	0.0699	0.0693	0.0711	0.0799	0.0735	0.0761	0.0829	1969	0.0829
1970	0.0820	0.0730	0.0724	0.0790	0.0778	0.0780	0.0757	0.0743	0.0707	0.0697	0.0591	0.0590	1970	0.0590

from January 1971 to December 2011

Year	Jan	Feb	Mar	Apr	May	Jun	Jul	Aug	Sep	Oct	Nov	Dec	Year	Jan–Dec*
1971	0.0570	0.0526	0.0493	0.0585	0.0593	0.0656	0.0663	0.0585	0.0591	0.0545	0.0543	0.0525	1971	0.0525
1972	0.0556	0.0563	0.0570	0.0577	0.0586	0.0587	0.0595	0.0604	0.0613	0.0623	0.0625	0.0585	1972	0.0585
1973	0.0641	0.0671	0.0673	0.0671	0.0671	0.0686	0.0776	0.0725	0.0674	0.0677	0.0674	0.0679	1973	0.0679
1974	0.0687	0.0691	0.0751	0.0801	0.0786	0.0822	0.0838	0.0857	0.0797	0.0787	0.0743	0.0712	1974	0.0712
1975	0.0730	0.0709	0.0737	0.0798	0.0749	0.0758	0.0782	0.0800	0.0815	0.0736	0.0754	0.0719	1975	0.0719
1976	0.0743	0.0736	0.0733	0.0719	0.0771	0.0747	0.0732	0.0697	0.0692	0.0667	0.0594	0.0600	1976	0.0600
1977	0.0673	0.0673	0.0673	0.0674	0.0674	0.0662	0.0675	0.0689	0.0700	0.0733	0.0727	0.0751	1977	0.0751
1978	0.0773	0.0784	0.0791	0.0800	0.0820	0.0843	0.0836	0.0833	0.0835	0.0887	0.0882	0.0883	1978	0.0883
1979	0.0895	0.0928	0.0918	0.0929	0.0899	0.0864	0.0887	0.0933	0.0951	0.1112	0.1033	0.1033	1979	0.1033
1980	0.1093	0.1294	0.1285	0.1009	0.0903	0.0944	0.0996	0.1133	0.1171	0.1244	0.1264	0.1245	1980	0.1245
1981	0.1275	0.1371	0.1328	0.1427	0.1385	0.1404	0.1533	0.1636	0.1625	0.1472	0.1311	0.1396	1981	0.1396
1982	0.1397	0.1385	0.1406	0.1355	0.1343	0.1417	0.1315	0.1209	0.1144	0.1018	0.1020	0.0990	1982	0.0990
1983	0.1057	0.1010	0.1048	0.0997	0.1059	0.1080	0.1168	0.1175	0.1108	0.1131	0.1127	0.1141	1983	0.1141
1984	0.1137	0.1181	0.1219	0.1251	0.1363	0.1365	0.1274	0.1276	0.1242	0.1154	0.1121	0.1104	1984	0.1104
1985	0.1081	0.1152	0.1131	0.1084	0.0974	0.0963	0.1002	0.0982	0.0973	0.0949	0.0911	0.0855	1985	0.0855
1986	0.0870	0.0815	0.0743	0.0737	0.0816	0.0756	0.0728	0.0668	0.0718	0.0687	0.0669	0.0685	1986	0.0685
1987	0.0685	0.0683	0.0708	0.0793	0.0821	0.0806	0.0818	0.0849	0.0912	0.0844	0.0840	0.0832	1987	0.0832
1988	0.0782	0.0768	0.0807	0.0836	0.0870	0.0839	0.0871	0.0895	0.0859	0.0837	0.0892	0.0917	1988	0.0917
1989	0.0896	0.0927	0.0934	0.0895	0.0860	0.0791	0.0745	0.0834	0.0833	0.0786	0.0779	0.0794	1989	0.0794
1990	0.0842	0.0855	0.0871	0.0907	0.0864	0.0843	0.0819	0.0859	0.0851	0.0826	0.0795	0.0770	1990	0.0770
1991	0.0772	0.0774	0.0783	0.0772	0.0773	0.0793	0.0778	0.0732	0.0693	0.0673	0.0653	0.0597	1991	0.0597
1992	0.0683	0.0690	0.0720	0.0711	0.0674	0.0647	0.0604	0.0581	0.0547	0.0601	0.0634	0.0611	1992	0.0611
1993	0.0588	0.0547	0.0549	0.0540	0.0551	0.0517	0.0526	0.0486	0.0483	0.0488	0.0519	0.0522	1993	0.0522
1994	0.0515	0.0575	0.0638	0.0670	0.0682	0.0699	0.0675	0.0683	0.0730	0.0749	0.0778	0.0780	1994	0.0780
1995	0.0754	0.0708	0.0707	0.0685	0.0606	0.0598	0.0616	0.0606	0.0601	0.0582	0.0553	0.0538	1995	0.0538
1996	0.0528	0.0573	0.0614	0.0640	0.0663	0.0645	0.0654	0.0670	0.0643	0.0607	0.0578	0.0616	1996	0.0616
1997	0.0629	0.0639	0.0677	0.0656	0.0650	0.0639	0.0589	0.0624	0.0601	0.0576	0.0587	0.0573	1997	0.0573
1998	0.0545	0.0562	0.0567	0.0564	0.0558	0.0551	0.0556	0.0503	0.0435	0.0434	0.0467	0.0468	1998	0.0468
1999	0.0467	0.0535	0.0526	0.0532	0.0576	0.0581	0.0594	0.0602	0.0590	0.0604	0.0619	0.0645	1999	0.0645
2000	0.0675	0.0669	0.0636	0.0657	0.0658	0.0626	0.0621	0.0601	0.0589	0.0582	0.0551	0.0507	2000	0.0507
2001	0.0499	0.0482	0.0471	0.0504	0.0515	0.0510	0.0464	0.0450	0.0399	0.0365	0.0413	0.0442	2001	0.0442
2002	0.0459	0.0442	0.0504	0.0461	0.0443	0.0412	0.0358	0.0325	0.0265	0.0276	0.0323	0.0261	2002	0.0261
2003	0.0310	0.0276	0.0283	0.0285	0.0228	0.0240	0.0322	0.0335	0.0267	0.0307	0.0317	0.0297	2003	0.0297
2004	0.0315	0.0293	0.0276	0.0360	0.0378	0.0374	0.0362	0.0322	0.0326	0.0316	0.0356	0.0347	2004	0.0347
2005	0.0375	0.0405	0.0421	0.0392	0.0377	0.0374	0.0415	0.0385	0.0422	0.0446	0.0440	0.0434	2005	0.0434
2006	0.0449	0.0460	0.0481	0.0491	0.0502	0.0506	0.0487	0.0465	0.0455	0.0452	0.0439	0.0465	2006	0.0465
2007	0.0479	0.0448	0.0451	0.0449	0.0483	0.0490	0.0457	0.0420	0.0413	0.0435	0.0333	0.0328	2007	0.0328
2008	0.0301	0.0256	0.0245	0.0316	0.0340	0.0330	0.0322	0.0303	0.0289	0.0260	0.0161	0.0126	2008	0.0126
2009	0.0180	0.0202	0.0168	0.0206	0.0238	0.0259	0.0251	0.0234	0.0222	0.0219	0.0180	0.0242	2009	0.0242
2010	0.0242	0.0231	0.0254	0.0238	0.0208	0.0184	0.0151	0.0124	0.0115	0.0102	0.0124	0.0170	2010	0.0170
2011	0.0215	0.0229	0.0234	0.0206	0.0172	0.0164	0.0126	0.0081	0.0087	0.0052	0.0082	0.0059	2011	0.0059

Table A-14

U.S. Treasury Bills: Total Returns

from January 1926 to December 1970

Year	Jan	Feb	Mar	Apr	May	Jun	Jul	Aug	Sep	Oct	Nov	Dec	Year	Jan–Dec*
1926	0.0034	0.0027	0.0030	0.0034	0.0001	0.0035	0.0022	0.0025	0.0023	0.0032	0.0031	0.0028	1926	0.0327
1927	0.0025	0.0026	0.0030	0.0025	0.0030	0.0026	0.0030	0.0028	0.0021	0.0025	0.0021	0.0022	1927	0.0312
1928	0.0025	0.0033	0.0029	0.0022	0.0032	0.0031	0.0032	0.0032	0.0027	0.0041	0.0038	0.0006	1928	0.0356
1929	0.0034	0.0036	0.0034	0.0036	0.0044	0.0052	0.0033	0.0040	0.0035	0.0046	0.0037	0.0037	1929	0.0475
1930	0.0014	0.0030	0.0035	0.0021	0.0026	0.0027	0.0020	0.0009	0.0022	0.0009	0.0013	0.0014	1930	0.0241
1931	0.0015	0.0004	0.0013	0.0008	0.0009	0.0008	0.0006	0.0003	0.0003	0.0010	0.0017	0.0012	1931	0.0107
1932	0.0023	0.0023	0.0016	0.0011	0.0006	0.0002	0.0003	0.0003	0.0003	0.0002	0.0002	0.0001	1932	0.0096
1933	0.0001	-0.0003	0.0004	0.0010	0.0004	0.0002	0.0002	0.0003	0.0002	0.0001	0.0002	0.0002	1933	0.0030
1934	0.0005	0.0002	0.0002	0.0001	0.0001	0.0001	0.0001	0.0001	0.0001	0.0001	0.0001	0.0001	1934	0.0016
1935	0.0001	0.0002	0.0001	0.0001	0.0001	0.0001	0.0001	0.0001	0.0001	0.0001	0.0002	0.0001	1935	0.0017
1936	0.0001	0.0001	0.0002	0.0002	0.0002	0.0003	0.0001	0.0002	0.0001	0.0002	0.0001	0.0000	1936	0.0018
1937	0.0001	0.0002	0.0001	0.0003	0.0006	0.0003	0.0003	0.0002	0.0004	0.0002	0.0002	0.0000	1937	0.0031
1938	0.0000	0.0000	-0.0001	0.0001	0.0000	0.0000	-0.0001	0.0000	0.0002	0.0001	-0.0006	0.0000	1938	-0.0002
1939	-0.0001	0.0001	-0.0001	0.0000	0.0001	0.0001	0.0000	-0.0001	0.0001	0.0000	0.0000	0.0000	1939	0.0002
1940	0.0000	0.0000	0.0000	0.0000	-0.0002	0.0000	0.0001	-0.0001	0.0000	0.0000	0.0000	0.0000	1940	0.0000
1941	-0.0001	-0.0001	0.0001	-0.0001	0.0000	0.0000	0.0003	0.0001	0.0001	0.0000	0.0000	0.0001	1941	0.0006
1942	0.0002	0.0001	0.0001	0.0001	0.0003	0.0002	0.0003	0.0003	0.0003	0.0003	0.0003	0.0003	1942	0.0027
1943	0.0003	0.0003	0.0003	0.0003	0.0003	0.0003	0.0003	0.0003	0.0003	0.0003	0.0003	0.0003	1943	0.0035
1944	0.0003	0.0003	0.0002	0.0003	0.0003	0.0003	0.0003	0.0003	0.0002	0.0003	0.0003	0.0002	1944	0.0033
1945	0.0003	0.0002	0.0002	0.0003	0.0003	0.0002	0.0003	0.0003	0.0003	0.0003	0.0002	0.0003	1945	0.0033
1946	0.0003	0.0003	0.0003	0.0003	0.0003	0.0003	0.0003	0.0003	0.0003	0.0003	0.0003	0.0003	1946	0.0035
1947	0.0003	0.0003	0.0003	0.0003	0.0003	0.0003	0.0003	0.0003	0.0006	0.0006	0.0006	0.0008	1947	0.0050
1948	0.0007	0.0007	0.0009	0.0008	0.0008	0.0009	0.0008	0.0009	0.0004	0.0004	0.0004	0.0004	1948	0.0081
1949	0.0010	0.0009	0.0010	0.0009	0.0010	0.0010	0.0009	0.0009	0.0009	0.0009	0.0008	0.0009	1949	0.0110
1950	0.0009	0.0009	0.0010	0.0009	0.0010	0.0010	0.0010	0.0010	0.0010	0.0012	0.0011	0.0011	1950	0.0120
1951	0.0013	0.0010	0.0011	0.0013	0.0012	0.0012	0.0013	0.0013	0.0012	0.0016	0.0011	0.0012	1951	0.0149
1952	0.0015	0.0012	0.0011	0.0012	0.0013	0.0015	0.0015	0.0015	0.0016	0.0014	0.0010	0.0016	1952	0.0166
1953	0.0016	0.0014	0.0018	0.0016	0.0017	0.0018	0.0015	0.0017	0.0016	0.0013	0.0008	0.0013	1953	0.0182
1954	0.0011	0.0007	0.0008	0.0009	0.0005	0.0006	0.0005	0.0005	0.0009	0.0007	0.0006	0.0008	1954	0.0086
1955	0.0008	0.0009	0.0010	0.0010	0.0014	0.0010	0.0010	0.0016	0.0016	0.0018	0.0017	0.0018	1955	0.0157
1956	0.0022	0.0019	0.0015	0.0019	0.0023	0.0020	0.0022	0.0017	0.0018	0.0025	0.0020	0.0024	1956	0.0246
1957	0.0027	0.0024	0.0023	0.0025	0.0026	0.0024	0.0030	0.0025	0.0026	0.0029	0.0028	0.0024	1957	0.0314
1958	0.0028	0.0012	0.0009	0.0008	0.0011	0.0003	0.0007	0.0004	0.0019	0.0018	0.0011	0.0022	1958	0.0154
1959	0.0021	0.0019	0.0022	0.0020	0.0022	0.0025	0.0025	0.0019	0.0031	0.0030	0.0026	0.0034	1959	0.0295
1960	0.0033	0.0029	0.0035	0.0019	0.0027	0.0024	0.0013	0.0017	0.0016	0.0022	0.0013	0.0016	1960	0.0266
1961	0.0019	0.0014	0.0020	0.0017	0.0018	0.0020	0.0018	0.0014	0.0017	0.0019	0.0015	0.0019	1961	0.0213
1962	0.0024	0.0020	0.0020	0.0022	0.0024	0.0020	0.0027	0.0023	0.0021	0.0026	0.0020	0.0023	1962	0.0273
1963	0.0025	0.0023	0.0023	0.0025	0.0024	0.0023	0.0027	0.0025	0.0027	0.0029	0.0027	0.0029	1963	0.0312
1964	0.0030	0.0026	0.0031	0.0029	0.0026	0.0030	0.0030	0.0028	0.0028	0.0029	0.0029	0.0031	1964	0.0354
1965	0.0028	0.0030	0.0036	0.0031	0.0031	0.0035	0.0031	0.0033	0.0031	0.0031	0.0035	0.0033	1965	0.0393
1966	0.0038	0.0035	0.0038	0.0034	0.0041	0.0038	0.0035	0.0041	0.0040	0.0045	0.0040	0.0040	1966	0.0476
1967	0.0043	0.0036	0.0039	0.0032	0.0033	0.0027	0.0032	0.0031	0.0032	0.0039	0.0036	0.0033	1967	0.0421
1968	0.0040	0.0039	0.0038	0.0043	0.0045	0.0043	0.0048	0.0042	0.0043	0.0044	0.0042	0.0043	1968	0.0521
1969	0.0053	0.0046	0.0046	0.0053	0.0048	0.0051	0.0053	0.0050	0.0062	0.0060	0.0052	0.0064	1969	0.0658
1970	0.0060	0.0062	0.0057	0.0050	0.0053	0.0058	0.0052	0.0053	0.0054	0.0046	0.0046	0.0042	1970	0.0652

*Compound annual return

from January 1971 to December 2011

Year	Jan	Feb	Mar	Apr	May	Jun	Jul	Aug	Sep	Oct	Nov	Dec	Year	Jan–Dec*
1971	0.0038	0.0033	0.0030	0.0028	0.0029	0.0037	0.0040	0.0047	0.0037	0.0037	0.0037	0.0037	1971	0.0439
1972	0.0029	0.0025	0.0027	0.0029	0.0030	0.0029	0.0031	0.0029	0.0034	0.0040	0.0037	0.0037	1972	0.0384
1973	0.0044	0.0041	0.0046	0.0052	0.0051	0.0051	0.0064	0.0070	0.0068	0.0065	0.0056	0.0064	1973	0.0693
1974	0.0063	0.0058	0.0056	0.0075	0.0075	0.0060	0.0070	0.0060	0.0081	0.0051	0.0054	0.0070	1974	0.0800
1975	0.0058	0.0043	0.0041	0.0044	0.0044	0.0041	0.0048	0.0048	0.0053	0.0056	0.0041	0.0048	1975	0.0580
1976	0.0047	0.0034	0.0040	0.0042	0.0037	0.0043	0.0047	0.0042	0.0044	0.0041	0.0040	0.0040	1976	0.0508
1977	0.0036	0.0035	0.0038	0.0038	0.0037	0.0040	0.0042	0.0044	0.0043	0.0049	0.0050	0.0049	1977	0.0512
1978	0.0049	0.0046	0.0053	0.0054	0.0051	0.0054	0.0056	0.0055	0.0062	0.0068	0.0070	0.0078	1978	0.0718
1979	0.0077	0.0073	0.0081	0.0080	0.0082	0.0081	0.0077	0.0077	0.0083	0.0087	0.0099	0.0095	1979	0.1038
1980	0.0080	0.0089	0.0121	0.0126	0.0081	0.0061	0.0053	0.0064	0.0075	0.0095	0.0096	0.0131	1980	0.1124
1981	0.0104	0.0107	0.0121	0.0108	0.0115	0.0135	0.0124	0.0128	0.0124	0.0121	0.0107	0.0087	1981	0.1471
1982	0.0080	0.0092	0.0098	0.0113	0.0106	0.0096	0.0105	0.0076	0.0051	0.0059	0.0063	0.0067	1982	0.1054
1983	0.0069	0.0062	0.0063	0.0071	0.0069	0.0067	0.0074	0.0076	0.0076	0.0076	0.0070	0.0073	1983	0.0880
1984	0.0076	0.0071	0.0073	0.0081	0.0078	0.0075	0.0082	0.0083	0.0086	0.0100	0.0073	0.0064	1984	0.0985
1985	0.0065	0.0058	0.0062	0.0072	0.0066	0.0055	0.0062	0.0055	0.0060	0.0065	0.0061	0.0065	1985	0.0772
1986	0.0056	0.0053	0.0060	0.0052	0.0049	0.0052	0.0052	0.0046	0.0045	0.0046	0.0039	0.0049	1986	0.0616
1987	0.0042	0.0043	0.0047	0.0044	0.0038	0.0048	0.0046	0.0047	0.0045	0.0060	0.0035	0.0039	1987	0.0547
1988	0.0029	0.0046	0.0044	0.0046	0.0051	0.0049	0.0051	0.0059	0.0062	0.0061	0.0057	0.0063	1988	0.0635
1989	0.0055	0.0061	0.0067	0.0067	0.0079	0.0071	0.0070	0.0074	0.0065	0.0068	0.0069	0.0061	1989	0.0837
1990	0.0057	0.0057	0.0064	0.0069	0.0068	0.0063	0.0068	0.0066	0.0060	0.0068	0.0057	0.0060	1990	0.0781
1991	0.0052	0.0048	0.0044	0.0053	0.0047	0.0042	0.0049	0.0046	0.0046	0.0042	0.0039	0.0038	1991	0.0560
1992	0.0034	0.0028	0.0034	0.0032	0.0028	0.0032	0.0031	0.0026	0.0026	0.0023	0.0023	0.0028	1992	0.0351
1993	0.0023	0.0022	0.0025	0.0024	0.0022	0.0025	0.0024	0.0025	0.0026	0.0022	0.0025	0.0023	1993	0.0290
1994	0.0025	0.0021	0.0027	0.0027	0.0032	0.0031	0.0028	0.0037	0.0037	0.0038	0.0037	0.0044	1994	0.0390
1995	0.0042	0.0040	0.0046	0.0044	0.0054	0.0047	0.0045	0.0047	0.0043	0.0047	0.0042	0.0049	1995	0.0560
1996	0.0043	0.0039	0.0039	0.0046	0.0042	0.0040	0.0045	0.0041	0.0044	0.0042	0.0041	0.0046	1996	0.0521
1997	0.0045	0.0039	0.0043	0.0043	0.0049	0.0037	0.0043	0.0041	0.0044	0.0042	0.0039	0.0048	1997	0.0526
1998	0.0043	0.0039	0.0039	0.0043	0.0040	0.0041	0.0040	0.0043	0.0046	0.0032	0.0031	0.0038	1998	0.0486
1999	0.0035	0.0035	0.0043	0.0037	0.0034	0.0040	0.0038	0.0039	0.0039	0.0039	0.0036	0.0044	1999	0.0468
2000	0.0041	0.0043	0.0047	0.0046	0.0050	0.0040	0.0048	0.0050	0.0051	0.0056	0.0051	0.0050	2000	0.0589
2001	0.0054	0.0038	0.0042	0.0039	0.0032	0.0028	0.0030	0.0031	0.0028	0.0022	0.0017	0.0015	2001	0.0383
2002	0.0014	0.0013	0.0013	0.0015	0.0014	0.0013	0.0015	0.0014	0.0014	0.0014	0.0012	0.0011	2002	0.0165
2003	0.0010	0.0009	0.0010	0.0010	0.0009	0.0010	0.0007	0.0007	0.0008	0.0007	0.0007	0.0008	2003	0.0102
2004	0.0007	0.0006	0.0009	0.0008	0.0006	0.0008	0.0010	0.0011	0.0011	0.0011	0.0015	0.0016	2004	0.0120
2005	0.0016	0.0016	0.0021	0.0021	0.0024	0.0023	0.0024	0.0030	0.0029	0.0027	0.0031	0.0032	2005	0.0298
2006	0.0035	0.0034	0.0037	0.0036	0.0043	0.0040	0.0040	0.0042	0.0041	0.0041	0.0042	0.0040	2006	0.0480
2007	0.0044	0.0038	0.0043	0.0044	0.0041	0.0040	0.0040	0.0042	0.0032	0.0032	0.0034	0.0027	2007	0.0466
2008	0.0021	0.0013	0.0017	0.0018	0.0018	0.0017	0.0015	0.0013	0.0015	0.0008	0.0003	0.0000	2008	0.0160
2009	0.0000	0.0001	0.0002	0.0001	0.0000	0.0001	0.0001	0.0001	0.0001	0.0000	0.0000	0.0001	2009	0.0010
2010	0.0000	0.0000	0.0001	0.0001	0.0001	0.0001	0.0001	0.0001	0.0001	0.0001	0.0001	0.0001	2010	0.0012
2011	0.0001	0.0001	0.0001	0.0000	0.0000	0.0000	0.0000	0.0001	0.0000	0.0000	0.0000	0.0000	2011	0.0004

*Compound annual return

Table A-15

Inflation

from January 1926 to December 1970

Year	Jan	Feb	Mar	Apr	May	Jun	Jul	Aug	Sep	Oct	Nov	Dec	Year	Jan–Dec*
1926	0.0000	-0.0037	-0.0056	0.0094	-0.0056	-0.0075	-0.0094	-0.0057	0.0057	0.0038	0.0038	0.0000	1926	-0.0149
1927	-0.0076	-0.0076	-0.0058	0.0000	0.0077	0.0096	-0.0190	-0.0058	0.0058	0.0058	-0.0019	-0.0019	1927	-0.0208
1928	-0.0019	-0.0097	0.0000	0.0020	0.0058	-0.0078	0.0000	0.0020	0.0078	-0.0019	-0.0019	-0.0039	1928	-0.0097
1929	-0.0019	-0.0020	-0.0039	-0.0039	0.0059	0.0039	0.0098	0.0039	-0.0019	0.0000	-0.0019	-0.0058	1929	0.0020
1930	-0.0039	-0.0039	-0.0059	0.0059	-0.0059	-0.0059	-0.0139	-0.0060	0.0061	-0.0060	-0.0081	-0.0143	1930	-0.0603
1931	-0.0145	-0.0147	-0.0064	-0.0064	-0.0108	-0.0109	-0.0022	-0.0022	-0.0044	-0.0067	-0.0112	-0.0091	1931	-0.0952
1932	-0.0206	-0.0140	-0.0047	-0.0071	-0.0144	-0.0073	0.0000	-0.0123	-0.0050	-0.0075	-0.0050	-0.0101	1932	-0.1030
1933	-0.0153	-0.0155	-0.0079	-0.0027	0.0027	0.0106	0.0289	0.0102	0.0000	0.0000	0.0000	-0.0051	1933	0.0051
1934	0.0051	0.0076	0.0000	-0.0025	0.0025	0.0025	0.0000	0.0025	0.0150	-0.0074	-0.0025	-0.0025	1934	0.0203
1935	0.0149	0.0074	-0.0024	0.0098	-0.0048	-0.0024	-0.0049	0.0000	0.0049	0.0000	0.0049	0.0024	1935	0.0299
1936	0.0000	-0.0048	-0.0049	0.0000	0.0000	0.0098	0.0048	0.0072	0.0024	-0.0024	0.0000	0.0000	1936	0.0121
1937	0.0072	0.0024	0.0071	0.0047	0.0047	0.0023	0.0046	0.0023	0.0092	-0.0046	-0.0069	-0.0023	1937	0.0310
1938	-0.0139	-0.0094	0.0000	0.0047	-0.0047	0.0000	0.0024	-0.0024	0.0000	-0.0047	-0.0024	0.0024	1938	-0.0278
1939	-0.0048	-0.0048	-0.0024	-0.0024	0.0000	0.0000	0.0000	0.0000	0.0193	-0.0047	0.0000	-0.0048	1939	-0.0048
1940	-0.0024	0.0072	-0.0024	0.0000	0.0024	0.0024	-0.0024	-0.0024	0.0024	0.0000	0.0000	0.0048	1940	0.0096
1941	0.0000	0.0000	0.0047	0.0094	0.0070	0.0186	0.0046	0.0091	0.0180	0.0110	0.0087	0.0022	1941	0.0972
1942	0.0130	0.0085	0.0127	0.0063	0.0104	0.0021	0.0041	0.0061	0.0020	0.0101	0.0060	0.0080	1942	0.0929
1943	0.0000	0.0020	0.0158	0.0116	0.0077	-0.0019	-0.0076	-0.0038	0.0039	0.0038	-0.0019	0.0019	1943	0.0316
1944	-0.0019	-0.0019	0.0000	0.0058	0.0038	0.0019	0.0057	0.0038	0.0000	0.0000	0.0000	0.0038	1944	0.0211
1945	0.0000	-0.0019	0.0000	0.0019	0.0075	0.0093	0.0018	0.0000	-0.0037	0.0000	0.0037	0.0037	1945	0.0225
1946	0.0000	-0.0037	0.0074	0.0055	0.0055	0.0109	0.0590	0.0220	0.0116	0.0196	0.0240	0.0078	1946	0.1816
1947	0.0000	-0.0016	0.0218	0.0000	-0.0030	0.0076	0.0091	0.0105	0.0238	0.0000	0.0058	0.0130	1947	0.0901
1948	0.0114	-0.0085	-0.0028	0.0142	0.0070	0.0070	0.0125	0.0041	0.0000	-0.0041	-0.0068	-0.0069	1948	0.0271
1949	-0.0014	-0.0111	0.0028	0.0014	-0.0014	0.0014	-0.0070	0.0028	0.0042	-0.0056	0.0014	-0.0056	1949	-0.0180
1950	-0.0042	-0.0028	0.0043	0.0014	0.0042	0.0056	0.0098	0.0083	0.0069	0.0055	0.0041	0.0135	1950	0.0579
1951	0.0160	0.0118	0.0039	0.0013	0.0039	-0.0013	0.0013	0.0000	0.0064	0.0051	0.0051	0.0038	1951	0.0587
1952	0.0000	-0.0063	0.0000	0.0038	0.0013	0.0025	0.0076	0.0012	-0.0012	0.0012	0.0000	-0.0012	1952	0.0088
1953	-0.0025	-0.0050	0.0025	0.0013	0.0025	0.0038	0.0025	0.0025	0.0012	0.0025	-0.0037	-0.0012	1953	0.0062
1954	0.0025	-0.0012	-0.0012	-0.0025	0.0037	0.0012	0.0000	-0.0012	-0.0025	-0.0025	0.0012	-0.0025	1954	-0.0050
1955	0.0000	0.0000	0.0000	0.0000	0.0000	0.0000	0.0037	-0.0025	0.0037	0.0000	0.0012	-0.0025	1955	0.0037
1956	-0.0012	0.0000	0.0012	0.0012	0.0050	0.0062	0.0074	-0.0012	0.0012	0.0061	0.0000	0.0024	1956	0.0286
1957	0.0012	0.0036	0.0024	0.0036	0.0024	0.0060	0.0047	0.0012	0.0012	0.0000	0.0035	0.0000	1957	0.0302
1958	0.0059	0.0012	0.0070	0.0023	0.0000	0.0012	0.0012	-0.0012	0.0000	0.0000	0.0012	-0.0012	1958	0.0176
1959	0.0012	-0.0012	0.0000	0.0012	0.0012	0.0046	0.0023	-0.0011	0.0034	0.0034	0.0000	0.0000	1959	0.0150
1960	-0.0011	0.0011	0.0000	0.0057	0.0000	0.0023	0.0000	0.0000	0.0011	0.0045	0.0011	0.0000	1960	0.0148
1961	0.0000	0.0000	0.0000	0.0000	0.0000	0.0011	0.0045	-0.0011	0.0022	0.0000	0.0000	0.0000	1961	0.0067
1962	0.0000	0.0022	0.0022	0.0022	0.0000	0.0000	0.0022	0.0000	0.0055	-0.0011	0.0000	-0.0011	1962	0.0122
1963	0.0011	0.0011	0.0011	0.0000	0.0000	0.0044	0.0044	0.0000	0.0000	0.0011	0.0011	0.0022	1963	0.0165
1964	0.0011	-0.0011	0.0011	0.0011	0.0000	0.0022	0.0022	-0.0011	0.0022	0.0011	0.0021	0.0011	1964	0.0119
1965	0.0000	0.0000	0.0011	0.0032	0.0021	0.0053	0.0011	-0.0021	0.0021	0.0011	0.0021	0.0032	1965	0.0192
1966	0.0000	0.0063	0.0031	0.0042	0.0010	0.0031	0.0031	0.0051	0.0020	0.0041	0.0000	0.0010	1966	0.0335
1967	0.0000	0.0010	0.0020	0.0020	0.0030	0.0030	0.0050	0.0030	0.0020	0.0030	0.0030	0.0030	1967	0.0304
1968	0.0039	0.0029	0.0049	0.0029	0.0029	0.0058	0.0048	0.0029	0.0029	0.0057	0.0038	0.0028	1968	0.0472
1969	0.0028	0.0037	0.0084	0.0065	0.0028	0.0064	0.0046	0.0045	0.0045	0.0036	0.0054	0.0062	1969	0.0611
1970	0.0035	0.0053	0.0053	0.0061	0.0043	0.0052	0.0034	0.0017	0.0051	0.0051	0.0034	0.0051	1970	0.0549

*Compound annual rate

from January 1971 to December 2011

Year	Jan	Feb	Mar	Apr	May	Jun	Jul	Aug	Sep	Oct	Nov	Dec	Year	Jan–Dec*
1971	0.0008	0.0017	0.0033	0.0033	0.0050	0.0058	0.0025	0.0025	0.0008	0.0016	0.0016	0.0041	1971	0.0336
1972	0.0008	0.0049	0.0016	0.0024	0.0032	0.0024	0.0040	0.0016	0.0040	0.0032	0.0024	0.0032	1972	0.0341
1973	0.0031	0.0070	0.0093	0.0069	0.0061	0.0068	0.0023	0.0181	0.0030	0.0081	0.0073	0.0065	1973	0.0880
1974	0.0087	0.0129	0.0113	0.0056	0.0111	0.0096	0.0075	0.0128	0.0120	0.0086	0.0085	0.0071	1974	0.1220
1975	0.0045	0.0070	0.0038	0.0051	0.0044	0.0082	0.0106	0.0031	0.0049	0.0061	0.0061	0.0042	1975	0.0701
1976	0.0024	0.0024	0.0024	0.0042	0.0059	0.0053	0.0059	0.0047	0.0041	0.0041	0.0029	0.0029	1976	0.0481
1977	0.0057	0.0103	0.0062	0.0079	0.0056	0.0066	0.0044	0.0038	0.0038	0.0027	0.0049	0.0038	1977	0.0677
1978	0.0054	0.0069	0.0069	0.0090	0.0099	0.0103	0.0072	0.0051	0.0071	0.0080	0.0055	0.0055	1978	0.0903
1979	0.0089	0.0117	0.0097	0.0115	0.0123	0.0093	0.0130	0.0100	0.0104	0.0090	0.0093	0.0105	1979	0.1331
1980	0.0144	0.0137	0.0144	0.0113	0.0099	0.0110	0.0008	0.0065	0.0092	0.0087	0.0091	0.0086	1980	0.1240
1981	0.0081	0.0104	0.0072	0.0064	0.0082	0.0086	0.0114	0.0077	0.0101	0.0021	0.0029	0.0029	1981	0.0894
1982	0.0036	0.0032	-0.0011	0.0042	0.0098	0.0122	0.0055	0.0021	0.0017	0.0027	-0.0017	-0.0041	1982	0.0387
1983	0.0024	0.0003	0.0007	0.0072	0.0054	0.0034	0.0040	0.0033	0.0050	0.0027	0.0017	0.0013	1983	0.0380
1984	0.0056	0.0046	0.0023	0.0049	0.0029	0.0032	0.0032	0.0042	0.0048	0.0025	0.0000	0.0006	1984	0.0395
1985	0.0019	0.0041	0.0044	0.0041	0.0037	0.0031	0.0016	0.0022	0.0031	0.0031	0.0034	0.0025	1985	0.0377
1986	0.0031	-0.0027	-0.0046	-0.0021	0.0031	0.0049	0.0003	0.0018	0.0049	0.0009	0.0009	0.0009	1986	0.0113
1987	0.0060	0.0039	0.0045	0.0054	0.0030	0.0041	0.0021	0.0056	0.0050	0.0026	0.0014	-0.0003	1987	0.0441
1988	0.0026	0.0026	0.0043	0.0052	0.0034	0.0043	0.0042	0.0042	0.0067	0.0033	0.0008	0.0017	1988	0.0442
1989	0.0050	0.0041	0.0058	0.0065	0.0057	0.0024	0.0024	0.0016	0.0032	0.0048	0.0024	0.0016	1989	0.0465
1990	0.0103	0.0047	0.0055	0.0016	0.0023	0.0054	0.0038	0.0092	0.0084	0.0060	0.0022	0.0000	1990	0.0611
1991	0.0060	0.0015	0.0015	0.0015	0.0030	0.0029	0.0015	0.0029	0.0044	0.0015	0.0029	0.0007	1991	0.0306
1992	0.0015	0.0036	0.0051	0.0014	0.0014	0.0036	0.0021	0.0028	0.0028	0.0035	0.0014	-0.0007	1992	0.0290
1993	0.0049	0.0035	0.0035	0.0028	0.0014	0.0014	0.0000	0.0028	0.0021	0.0041	0.0007	0.0000	1993	0.0275
1994	0.0027	0.0034	0.0034	0.0014	0.0007	0.0034	0.0027	0.0040	0.0027	0.0007	0.0013	0.0000	1994	0.0267
1995	0.0040	0.0040	0.0033	0.0033	0.0020	0.0020	0.0000	0.0026	0.0020	0.0033	-0.0007	-0.0007	1995	0.0254
1996	0.0059	0.0032	0.0052	0.0039	0.0019	0.0006	0.0019	0.0019	0.0032	0.0032	0.0019	0.0000	1996	0.0332
1997	0.0032	0.0031	0.0025	0.0013	-0.0006	0.0012	0.0012	0.0019	0.0025	0.0025	-0.0006	-0.0012	1997	0.0170
1998	0.0019	0.0019	0.0019	0.0018	0.0018	0.0012	0.0012	0.0012	0.0012	0.0024	0.0000	-0.0006	1998	0.0161
1999	0.0024	0.0012	0.0030	0.0073	0.0000	0.0000	0.0030	0.0024	0.0048	0.0018	0.0006	0.0000	1999	0.0268
2000	0.0030	0.0059	0.0082	0.0006	0.0012	0.0052	0.0023	0.0000	0.0052	0.0017	0.0006	-0.0006	2000	0.0339
2001	0.0063	0.0040	0.0023	0.0040	0.0045	0.0017	-0.0028	0.0000	0.0045	-0.0034	-0.0017	-0.0039	2001	0.0155
2002	0.0023	0.0040	0.0056	0.0056	0.0000	0.0006	0.0011	0.0033	0.0017	0.0017	0.0000	-0.0022	2002	0.0238
2003	0.0044	0.0077	0.0060	-0.0022	-0.0016	0.0011	0.0011	0.0038	0.0033	-0.0011	-0.0027	-0.0011	2003	0.0188
2004	0.0049	0.0054	0.0064	0.0032	0.0059	0.0032	-0.0016	0.0005	0.0021	0.0053	0.0005	-0.0037	2004	0.0326
2005	0.0021	0.0058	0.0078	0.0067	-0.0010	0.0005	0.0046	0.0051	0.0122	0.0020	-0.0080	-0.0040	2005	0.0342
2006	0.0076	0.0020	0.0055	0.0085	0.0050	0.0020	0.0030	0.0020	-0.0049	-0.0054	-0.0015	0.0015	2006	0.0254
2007	0.0031	0.0054	0.0091	0.0065	0.0061	0.0019	-0.0003	-0.0018	0.0028	0.0021	0.0059	-0.0007	2007	0.0408
2008	0.0050	0.0029	0.0087	0.0061	0.0084	0.0101	0.0053	-0.0040	-0.0014	-0.0101	-0.0192	-0.0103	2008	0.0009
2009	0.0044	0.0050	0.0024	0.0025	0.0029	0.0086	-0.0016	0.0022	0.0006	0.0010	0.0007	-0.0018	2009	0.0272
2010	0.0034	0.0002	0.0041	0.0017	0.0008	-0.0010	0.0002	0.0014	0.0006	0.0012	0.0004	0.0017	2010	0.0150
2011	0.0048	0.0049	0.0098	0.0064	0.0047	-0.0011	0.0009	0.0028	0.0015	-0.0021	-0.0008	-0.0025	2011	0.0296

*Compound annual rate

Table A-16

U.S. Treasury Bills: Inflation-Adjusted Total Returns

from January 1926 to December 1970

Year	Jan	Feb	Mar	Apr	May	Jun	Jul	Aug	Sep	Oct	Nov	Dec	Year	Jan–Dec*
1926	0.0034	0.0064	0.0086	-0.0059	0.0057	0.0110	0.0118	0.0083	-0.0035	-0.0006	-0.0007	0.0028	1926	0.0483
1927	0.0101	0.0103	0.0088	0.0025	-0.0047	-0.0069	0.0224	0.0086	-0.0037	-0.0033	0.0040	0.0042	1927	0.0531
1928	0.0045	0.0131	0.0029	0.0003	-0.0026	0.0110	0.0032	0.0013	-0.0051	0.0060	0.0058	0.0045	1928	0.0457
1929	0.0054	0.0055	0.0074	0.0075	-0.0015	0.0013	-0.0064	0.0002	0.0055	0.0046	0.0057	0.0095	1929	0.0454
1930	0.0053	0.0069	0.0094	-0.0038	0.0085	0.0087	0.0161	0.0070	-0.0039	0.0069	0.0095	0.0159	1930	0.0898
1931	0.0162	0.0153	0.0077	0.0072	0.0118	0.0118	0.0028	0.0026	0.0047	0.0078	0.0130	0.0104	1931	0.1171
1932	0.0234	0.0166	0.0064	0.0083	0.0152	0.0076	0.0003	0.0127	0.0053	0.0077	0.0052	0.0103	1932	0.1255
1933	0.0157	0.0155	0.0084	0.0036	-0.0022	-0.0103	-0.0279	-0.0098	0.0002	0.0001	0.0002	0.0053	1933	-0.0021
1934	-0.0046	-0.0073	0.0002	0.0026	-0.0024	-0.0024	0.0001	-0.0024	-0.0147	0.0075	0.0026	0.0026	1934	-0.0183
1935	-0.0146	-0.0071	0.0026	-0.0095	0.0050	0.0026	0.0050	0.0001	-0.0047	0.0001	-0.0046	-0.0023	1935	-0.0273
1936	0.0001	0.0050	0.0051	0.0002	0.0002	-0.0094	-0.0047	-0.0070	-0.0023	0.0026	0.0001	0.0000	1936	-0.0102
1937	-0.0070	-0.0022	-0.0069	-0.0043	-0.0040	-0.0020	-0.0043	-0.0021	-0.0088	0.0048	0.0071	0.0024	1937	-0.0271
1938	0.0141	0.0095	-0.0001	-0.0046	0.0048	0.0000	-0.0024	0.0024	0.0002	0.0049	0.0018	-0.0024	1938	0.0284
1939	0.0047	0.0049	0.0023	0.0024	0.0001	0.0001	0.0000	-0.0001	-0.0189	0.0048	0.0000	0.0048	1939	0.0050
1940	0.0024	-0.0071	0.0024	0.0000	-0.0025	-0.0023	0.0025	0.0023	-0.0024	0.0000	0.0000	-0.0047	1940	-0.0094
1941	-0.0001	-0.0001	-0.0046	-0.0094	-0.0069	-0.0182	-0.0042	-0.0089	-0.0176	-0.0109	-0.0086	-0.0021	1941	-0.0880
1942	-0.0126	-0.0083	-0.0124	-0.0062	-0.0100	-0.0018	-0.0038	-0.0058	-0.0017	-0.0097	-0.0057	-0.0076	1942	-0.0825
1943	0.0003	-0.0017	-0.0152	-0.0112	-0.0074	0.0022	0.0080	0.0042	-0.0036	-0.0035	0.0022	-0.0016	1943	-0.0273
1944	0.0022	0.0022	0.0002	-0.0055	-0.0036	-0.0016	-0.0054	-0.0035	0.0002	0.0003	0.0003	-0.0035	1944	-0.0174
1945	0.0003	0.0021	0.0002	-0.0016	-0.0072	-0.0090	-0.0015	0.0003	0.0040	0.0003	-0.0034	-0.0034	1945	-0.0188
1946	0.0003	0.0040	-0.0070	-0.0052	-0.0051	-0.0105	-0.0554	-0.0212	-0.0111	-0.0189	-0.0232	-0.0075	1946	-0.1507
1947	0.0003	0.0018	-0.0210	0.0003	0.0033	-0.0073	-0.0087	-0.0101	-0.0226	0.0006	-0.0052	-0.0120	1947	-0.0780
1948	-0.0105	0.0093	0.0037	-0.0132	-0.0062	-0.0060	-0.0115	-0.0032	0.0004	0.0045	0.0073	0.0074	1948	-0.0185
1949	0.0023	0.0121	-0.0018	-0.0005	0.0024	-0.0004	0.0079	-0.0019	-0.0033	0.0065	-0.0006	0.0065	1949	0.0296
1950	0.0052	0.0037	-0.0033	-0.0006	-0.0032	-0.0046	-0.0087	-0.0073	-0.0058	-0.0043	-0.0030	-0.0123	1950	-0.0434
1951	-0.0145	-0.0107	-0.0028	0.0000	-0.0026	0.0025	0.0001	0.0013	-0.0052	-0.0035	-0.0040	-0.0026	1951	-0.0414
1952	0.0015	0.0075	0.0011	-0.0026	0.0000	-0.0010	-0.0060	0.0002	0.0029	0.0001	0.0010	0.0029	1952	0.0077
1953	0.0041	0.0064	-0.0007	0.0004	-0.0008	-0.0019	-0.0010	-0.0008	0.0004	-0.0012	0.0045	0.0025	1953	0.0119
1954	-0.0014	0.0019	0.0020	0.0034	-0.0032	-0.0007	0.0005	0.0017	0.0034	0.0032	-0.0006	0.0033	1954	0.0137
1955	0.0008	0.0009	0.0010	0.0010	0.0014	0.0010	-0.0027	0.0041	-0.0021	0.0018	0.0005	0.0043	1955	0.0119
1956	0.0035	0.0019	0.0003	0.0006	-0.0027	-0.0042	-0.0052	0.0029	0.0006	-0.0036	0.0020	0.0000	1956	-0.0039
1957	0.0015	-0.0012	-0.0001	-0.0011	0.0002	-0.0035	-0.0018	0.0013	0.0014	0.0029	-0.0008	0.0024	1957	0.0011
1958	-0.0031	0.0000	-0.0060	-0.0015	0.0011	-0.0009	-0.0005	0.0016	0.0019	0.0018	-0.0001	0.0034	1958	-0.0022
1959	0.0009	0.0030	0.0022	0.0008	0.0010	-0.0021	0.0002	0.0030	-0.0003	-0.0004	0.0026	0.0034	1959	0.0143
1960	0.0045	0.0017	0.0035	-0.0037	0.0027	0.0001	0.0013	0.0017	0.0005	-0.0023	0.0002	0.0016	1960	0.0117
1961	0.0019	0.0014	0.0020	0.0017	0.0018	0.0009	-0.0026	0.0025	-0.0006	0.0019	0.0015	0.0019	1961	0.0144
1962	0.0024	-0.0002	-0.0002	0.0000	0.0024	0.0020	0.0005	0.0023	-0.0034	0.0037	0.0020	0.0034	1962	0.0149
1963	0.0014	0.0012	0.0012	0.0025	0.0024	-0.0021	-0.0017	0.0025	0.0027	0.0018	0.0016	0.0008	1963	0.0144
1964	0.0019	0.0037	0.0020	0.0018	0.0026	0.0009	0.0008	0.0039	0.0006	0.0019	0.0008	0.0020	1964	0.0232
1965	0.0028	0.0030	0.0025	-0.0001	0.0010	-0.0018	0.0020	0.0054	0.0010	0.0021	0.0014	0.0002	1965	0.0197
1966	0.0038	-0.0028	0.0007	-0.0007	0.0031	0.0007	0.0005	-0.0010	0.0020	0.0005	0.0040	0.0030	1966	0.0136
1967	0.0043	0.0026	0.0019	0.0012	0.0003	-0.0004	-0.0019	0.0001	0.0012	0.0010	0.0006	0.0004	1967	0.0113
1968	0.0001	0.0009	-0.0011	0.0014	0.0015	-0.0015	0.0000	0.0013	0.0014	-0.0013	0.0005	0.0014	1968	0.0046
1969	0.0024	0.0009	-0.0037	-0.0011	0.0021	-0.0013	0.0008	0.0005	0.0017	0.0024	-0.0002	0.0002	1969	0.0045
1970	0.0025	0.0009	0.0004	-0.0011	0.0009	0.0006	0.0018	0.0036	0.0002	-0.0005	0.0012	-0.0008	1970	0.0098

*Compound annual return

from January 1971 to December 2011

Year	Jan	Feb	Mar	Apr	May	Jun	Jul	Aug	Sep	Oct	Nov	Dec	Year	Jan–Dec*
1971	0.0030	0.0016	-0.0004	-0.0006	-0.0020	-0.0020	0.0015	0.0022	0.0029	0.0020	0.0021	-0.0004	1971	0.0099
1972	0.0021	-0.0024	0.0011	0.0005	-0.0002	0.0005	-0.0009	0.0013	-0.0006	0.0008	0.0013	0.0006	1972	0.0041
1973	0.0012	-0.0029	-0.0047	-0.0017	-0.0010	-0.0017	0.0041	-0.0109	0.0038	-0.0016	-0.0017	-0.0002	1973	-0.0172
1974	-0.0024	-0.0070	-0.0057	0.0019	-0.0035	-0.0036	-0.0004	-0.0068	-0.0039	-0.0035	-0.0031	-0.0002	1974	-0.0374
1975	0.0013	-0.0027	0.0003	-0.0007	-0.0001	-0.0040	-0.0057	0.0017	0.0004	-0.0006	-0.0020	0.0006	1975	-0.0113
1976	0.0023	0.0010	0.0016	0.0000	-0.0022	-0.0010	-0.0012	-0.0005	0.0003	0.0000	0.0011	0.0012	1976	0.0026
1977	-0.0021	-0.0067	-0.0024	-0.0041	-0.0018	-0.0026	-0.0002	0.0006	0.0005	0.0022	0.0001	0.0011	1977	-0.0155
1978	-0.0005	-0.0023	-0.0016	-0.0036	-0.0048	-0.0049	-0.0016	0.0005	-0.0009	-0.0012	0.0015	0.0024	1978	-0.0169
1979	-0.0011	-0.0043	-0.0015	-0.0035	-0.0041	-0.0012	-0.0052	-0.0024	-0.0021	-0.0002	0.0005	-0.0010	1979	-0.0259
1980	-0.0063	-0.0048	-0.0023	0.0013	-0.0018	-0.0049	0.0045	-0.0001	-0.0017	0.0008	0.0005	0.0044	1980	-0.0103
1981	0.0022	0.0003	0.0048	0.0043	0.0033	0.0049	0.0010	0.0051	0.0023	0.0099	0.0078	0.0059	1981	0.0530
1982	0.0044	0.0060	0.0109	0.0070	0.0007	-0.0026	0.0050	0.0056	0.0034	0.0032	0.0081	0.0109	1982	0.0642
1983	0.0045	0.0058	0.0056	0.0000	0.0015	0.0033	0.0034	0.0043	0.0026	0.0049	0.0054	0.0059	1983	0.0482
1984	0.0020	0.0025	0.0050	0.0032	0.0049	0.0043	0.0050	0.0041	0.0038	0.0074	0.0073	0.0058	1984	0.0567
1985	0.0046	0.0017	0.0017	0.0031	0.0029	0.0024	0.0047	0.0033	0.0029	0.0034	0.0027	0.0040	1985	0.0381
1986	0.0025	0.0081	0.0106	0.0074	0.0019	0.0003	0.0049	0.0028	-0.0004	0.0037	0.0030	0.0040	1986	0.0498
1987	-0.0019	0.0004	0.0002	-0.0009	0.0008	0.0007	0.0025	-0.0009	-0.0004	0.0034	0.0020	0.0042	1987	0.0101
1988	0.0003	0.0020	0.0001	-0.0005	0.0016	0.0006	0.0008	0.0017	-0.0006	0.0028	0.0048	0.0047	1988	0.0185
1989	0.0005	0.0020	0.0009	0.0002	0.0022	0.0047	0.0045	0.0058	0.0033	0.0020	0.0045	0.0045	1989	0.0356
1990	-0.0046	0.0010	0.0010	0.0053	0.0044	0.0008	0.0029	-0.0026	-0.0024	0.0008	0.0034	0.0060	1990	0.0161
1991	-0.0008	0.0033	0.0029	0.0038	0.0018	0.0012	0.0034	0.0017	0.0002	0.0028	0.0010	0.0031	1991	0.0246
1992	0.0019	-0.0008	-0.0017	0.0018	0.0013	-0.0004	0.0009	-0.0002	-0.0003	-0.0012	0.0009	0.0035	1992	0.0059
1993	-0.0026	-0.0013	-0.0010	-0.0004	0.0008	0.0011	0.0024	-0.0003	0.0005	-0.0019	0.0018	0.0023	1993	0.0014
1994	-0.0002	-0.0013	-0.0007	0.0014	0.0025	-0.0003	0.0000	-0.0004	0.0010	0.0032	0.0023	0.0044	1994	0.0120
1995	0.0001	0.0000	0.0013	0.0011	0.0034	0.0027	0.0045	0.0020	0.0023	0.0014	0.0049	0.0055	1995	0.0298
1996	-0.0016	0.0007	-0.0012	0.0007	0.0023	0.0034	0.0026	0.0022	0.0012	0.0011	0.0022	0.0046	1996	0.0182
1997	0.0013	0.0007	0.0018	0.0031	0.0056	0.0024	0.0030	0.0022	0.0019	0.0017	0.0045	0.0060	1997	0.0349
1998	0.0024	0.0020	0.0021	0.0024	0.0022	0.0029	0.0028	0.0031	0.0033	0.0008	0.0031	0.0044	1998	0.0319
1999	0.0011	0.0023	0.0012	-0.0035	0.0034	0.0040	0.0008	0.0015	-0.0009	0.0021	0.0030	0.0044	1999	0.0195
2000	0.0017	-0.0016	-0.0035	0.0040	0.0045	-0.0018	0.0031	0.0039	-0.0001	0.0039	0.0045	0.0056	2000	0.0242
2001	0.0012	-0.0002	0.0019	0.0000	0.0039	-0.0013	0.0025	0.0050	-0.0017	0.0056	0.0034	0.0054	2001	0.0224
2002	-0.0009	-0.0026	-0.0043	-0.0040	0.0014	0.0007	0.0004	-0.0019	-0.0002	-0.0003	0.0012	0.0033	2002	-0.0071
2003	-0.0034	-0.0068	-0.0050	0.0032	0.0025	-0.0001	-0.0004	-0.0031	-0.0024	0.0018	0.0034	0.0019	2003	-0.0084
2004	-0.0042	-0.0048	-0.0055	-0.0024	-0.0052	-0.0023	0.0026	0.0006	-0.0010	-0.0041	0.0010	0.0053	2004	-0.0199
2005	-0.0005	-0.0041	-0.0057	-0.0046	0.0034	0.0018	-0.0022	-0.0021	-0.0093	0.0007	0.0113	0.0072	2005	-0.0042
2006	-0.0041	0.0013	-0.0019	-0.0049	-0.0006	0.0020	0.0010	0.0023	0.0090	0.0095	0.0057	0.0025	2006	0.0220
2007	0.0014	-0.0015	-0.0048	-0.0021	-0.0020	0.0020	0.0042	0.0060	0.0005	0.0011	-0.0025	0.0034	2007	0.0056
2008	0.0014	-0.0015	-0.0048	-0.0021	-0.0020	0.0020	0.0042	0.0060	0.0005	0.0011	-0.0025	0.0034	2008	0.0056
2009	-0.0043	-0.0048	-0.0023	-0.0024	-0.0029	-0.0084	0.0017	-0.0021	-0.0005	-0.0009	-0.0007	0.0018	2009	-0.0029
2010	-0.0034	-0.0002	-0.0040	-0.0016	-0.0007	0.0011	-0.0001	-0.0013	-0.0005	-0.0011	-0.0003	-0.0016	2010	-0.0135
2011	-0.0047	-0.0048	-0.0096	-0.0064	-0.0047	0.0011	-0.0009	-0.0027	-0.0015	0.0021	0.0008	0.0025	2011	-0.0284

*Compound annual return

Appendix B

Cumulative Wealth
Indices of Basic Series

Table B-1

Large Company Stocks: Total Return Index

from December 1925 to December 1970

Year	Jan	Feb	Mar	Apr	May	Jun	Jul	Aug	Sep	Oct	Nov	Dec	Yr-end	Index
1925												1.000	1925	1.000
1926	1.000	0.962	0.906	0.929	0.946	0.989	1.036	1.062	1.089	1.058	1.095	1.116	1926	1.116
1927	1.095	1.154	1.164	1.187	1.259	1.251	1.334	1.403	1.466	1.393	1.493	1.535	1927	1.535
1928	1.529	1.509	1.676	1.733	1.768	1.700	1.724	1.862	1.910	1.942	2.193	2.204	1928	2.204
1929	2.332	2.328	2.325	2.366	2.280	2.540	2.660	2.933	2.794	2.243	1.963	2.018	1929	2.018
1930	2.147	2.203	2.382	2.363	2.340	1.960	2.035	2.064	1.800	1.646	1.631	1.516	1930	1.516
1931	1.592	1.782	1.662	1.506	1.314	1.500	1.392	1.418	0.996	1.085	0.999	0.859	1931	0.859
1932	0.836	0.883	0.781	0.625	0.488	0.487	0.672	0.933	0.900	0.779	0.746	0.789	1932	0.789
1933	0.795	0.654	0.678	0.966	1.129	1.280	1.169	1.310	1.164	1.064	1.184	1.214	1933	1.214
1934	1.344	1.301	1.301	1.268	1.175	1.202	1.066	1.131	1.127	1.095	1.198	1.197	1934	1.197
1935	1.148	1.109	1.077	1.182	1.231	1.317	1.429	1.469	1.507	1.624	1.700	1.767	1935	1.767
1936	1.886	1.928	1.980	1.831	1.931	1.995	2.135	2.167	2.174	2.342	2.374	2.367	1936	2.367
1937	2.459	2.506	2.487	2.286	2.280	2.165	2.391	2.276	1.957	1.765	1.612	1.538	1937	1.538
1938	1.561	1.666	1.252	1.433	1.386	1.733	1.862	1.820	1.850	1.993	1.939	2.016	1938	2.016
1939	1.881	1.954	1.692	1.688	1.811	1.701	1.889	1.766	2.062	2.036	1.955	2.008	1939	2.008
1940	1.941	1.966	1.991	1.986	1.531	1.655	1.712	1.772	1.793	1.869	1.810	1.812	1940	1.812
1941	1.728	1.718	1.730	1.624	1.653	1.749	1.850	1.852	1.839	1.718	1.670	1.602	1941	1.602
1942	1.627	1.602	1.497	1.437	1.552	1.586	1.640	1.666	1.715	1.831	1.827	1.927	1942	1.927
1943	2.070	2.190	2.310	2.318	2.446	2.500	2.368	2.409	2.472	2.446	2.286	2.427	1943	2.427
1944	2.468	2.479	2.527	2.502	2.628	2.771	2.717	2.760	2.758	2.764	2.801	2.906	1944	2.906
1945	2.952	3.154	3.015	3.287	3.351	3.349	3.288	3.499	3.652	3.770	3.919	3.965	1945	3.965
1946	4.248	3.976	4.167	4.330	4.455	4.290	4.188	3.906	3.516	3.495	3.486	3.645	1946	3.645
1947	3.738	3.709	3.654	3.521	3.526	3.721	3.863	3.785	3.743	3.832	3.765	3.853	1947	3.853
1948	3.707	3.563	3.846	3.958	4.305	4.329	4.109	4.174	4.059	4.347	3.929	4.065	1948	4.065
1949	4.081	3.960	4.090	4.017	3.913	3.919	4.174	4.265	4.377	4.526	4.605	4.829	1949	4.829
1950	4.924	5.022	5.057	5.303	5.573	5.267	5.330	5.566	5.895	5.949	6.050	6.360	1950	6.360
1951	6.765	6.871	6.764	7.109	6.896	6.739	7.218	7.563	7.573	7.495	7.567	7.888	1951	7.888
1952	8.030	7.804	8.197	7.867	8.137	8.536	8.703	8.642	8.490	8.507	8.993	9.336	1952	9.336
1953	9.291	9.192	8.997	8.783	8.851	8.732	8.971	8.521	8.551	9.012	9.196	9.244	1953	9.244
1954	9.739	9.848	10.168	10.693	11.139	11.173	11.831	11.506	12.485	12.277	13.393	14.108	1954	14.108
1955	14.387	14.528	14.485	15.059	15.142	16.416	17.437	17.393	17.618	17.118	18.533	18.561	1955	18.561
1956	17.917	18.657	19.982	19.973	18.788	19.557	20.594	19.919	19.043	19.169	19.072	19.778	1956	19.778
1957	18.986	18.485	18.882	19.614	20.472	20.481	20.749	19.701	18.516	17.957	18.372	17.646	1957	17.646
1958	18.431	18.170	18.767	19.400	19.810	20.363	21.277	21.651	22.735	23.348	24.012	25.298	1958	25.298
1959	25.430	25.554	25.605	26.635	27.273	27.213	28.199	27.911	26.674	27.017	27.519	28.322	1959	28.322
1960	26.340	26.729	26.400	25.976	26.821	27.388	26.748	27.596	25.968	25.949	27.154	28.455	1960	28.455
1961	30.291	31.257	32.100	32.262	33.033	32.125	33.223	34.029	33.404	34.401	35.940	36.106	1961	36.106
1962	34.784	35.511	35.349	33.204	30.512	28.061	29.891	30.512	29.092	29.279	32.459	32.954	1962	32.954
1963	34.620	33.794	35.045	36.798	37.510	36.805	36.726	38.692	38.318	39.617	39.435	40.469	1963	40.469
1964	41.612	42.222	42.917	43.238	43.940	44.721	45.592	45.055	46.409	46.856	46.878	47.139	1964	47.139
1965	48.763	48.913	48.264	49.984	49.833	47.477	48.177	49.488	51.140	52.618	52.453	53.008	1965	53.008
1966	53.335	52.634	51.555	52.688	50.096	49.363	48.769	45.234	44.993	47.214	47.662	47.674	1966	47.674
1967	51.478	51.846	53.967	56.325	53.641	54.658	57.215	56.817	58.758	57.136	57.507	59.104	1967	59.104
1968	56.592	55.113	55.718	60.363	61.334	61.980	60.916	61.913	64.387	64.945	68.393	65.642	1968	65.642
1969	65.193	62.414	64.653	66.131	66.303	62.708	59.024	61.705	60.251	63.014	61.141	60.059	1969	60.059
1970	55.594	58.693	58.949	53.793	50.685	48.321	52.035	54.522	56.495	56.025	58.858	62.375	1970	62.375

Table B-1 (Continued)
Large Company Stocks: Total Return Index

from January 1971 to December 2011

Year	Jan	Feb	Mar	Apr	May	Jun	Jul	Aug	Sep	Oct	Nov	Dec	Yr-end	Index
1971	65.070	65.830	68.422	71.082	68.306	68.532	65.879	68.436	68.132	65.465	65.478	71.295	1971	71.295
1972	72.762	74.778	75.396	75.909	77.404	75.898	76.260	79.072	78.872	79.807	83.648	84.838	1972	84.838
1973	83.573	80.627	80.692	77.602	76.340	76.035	79.127	76.429	79.809	79.823	70.971	72.376	1973	72.376
1974	71.857	71.804	70.334	67.812	65.763	65.016	60.193	54.994	48.660	56.840	54.062	53.220	1974	53.220
1975	59.989	63.815	65.435	68.771	72.048	75.486	70.625	69.384	67.220	71.612	73.630	73.033	1975	73.033
1976	81.925	81.234	83.971	83.318	82.391	86.043	85.631	85.473	87.683	86.050	85.698	90.508	1976	90.508
1977	86.229	84.657	83.767	84.116	82.466	86.542	85.465	83.996	84.125	80.849	83.406	84.029	1977	84.029
1978	79.205	77.599	79.881	87.089	87.890	86.679	91.734	94.494	94.193	85.980	87.826	89.551	1978	89.551
1979	93.520	90.517	95.913	96.811	94.421	98.528	99.850	105.611	106.065	99.273	103.993	106.216	1979	106.216
1980	112.819	112.809	101.842	106.550	112.034	115.579	123.622	124.871	128.545	131.147	145.119	140.741	1980	140.741
1981	134.852	137.194	142.681	139.922	140.280	139.402	139.688	131.623	125.137	131.890	137.333	133.812	1981	133.812
1982	132.064	124.682	124.032	129.638	125.218	123.338	121.143	135.849	137.543	153.374	159.568	162.643	1982	162.643
1983	168.691	172.558	178.933	193.029	191.350	198.797	192.931	195.827	198.531	196.236	200.375	199.328	1983	199.328
1984	198.216	191.241	194.553	196.399	185.527	189.557	187.205	207.881	207.932	208.733	206.395	211.833	1984	211.833
1985	228.337	231.134	231.287	231.069	244.420	248.249	247.888	245.771	238.084	249.081	266.165	279.041	1985	279.041
1986	280.599	301.573	318.399	314.813	331.562	337.165	318.307	341.911	313.645	331.733	339.795	331.124	1986	331.124
1987	375.712	390.558	401.827	398.259	401.712	421.998	443.376	459.920	449.837	352.959	323.879	348.511	1987	348.511
1988	363.169	380.098	368.356	372.430	375.651	392.890	391.400	378.113	394.222	405.199	399.424	406.392	1988	406.392
1989	436.151	425.282	435.203	457.799	476.321	473.620	516.383	526.478	524.342	512.167	522.612	535.162	1989	535.162
1990	499.234	505.664	519.063	506.114	555.463	551.715	549.946	500.236	475.892	473.865	504.496	518.550	1990	518.550
1991	541.133	579.832	593.873	595.279	620.959	592.511	620.127	634.819	624.196	632.588	607.099	676.530	1991	676.530
1992	663.923	672.522	659.442	678.804	682.131	671.983	699.435	685.121	693.171	695.566	719.251	728.078	1992	728.078
1993	734.165	744.171	759.872	741.505	761.341	763.571	760.499	789.355	783.301	799.505	791.884	801.458	1993	801.458
1994	828.706	806.213	771.064	780.952	793.769	774.312	799.738	832.527	812.168	830.415	800.172	812.041	1994	812.041
1995	833.100	865.567	891.108	917.348	954.012	976.172	1008.544	1011.080	1053.750	1049.983	1096.076	1117.188	1995	1117.188
1996	1155.213	1165.924	1177.146	1194.502	1225.307	1229.982	1175.641	1200.440	1268.007	1302.979	1401.467	1373.698	1996	1373.698
1997	1459.520	1470.959	1410.520	1494.725	1585.730	1656.774	1788.599	1688.399	1780.866	1721.390	1801.078	1832.009	1997	1832.009
1998	1852.272	1985.867	2087.561	2108.563	2072.322	2156.497	2133.534	1825.072	1941.989	2099.953	2227.227	2355.571	1998	2355.571
1999	2454.072	2377.802	2472.935	2568.700	2508.044	2647.234	2564.575	2551.887	2481.930	2638.988	2692.634	2851.219	1999	2851.219
2000	2707.967	2656.707	2916.609	2828.860	2770.821	2839.130	2794.743	2968.337	2811.628	2799.741	2579.011	2591.633	2000	2591.633
2001	2683.582	2438.889	2284.385	2461.905	2478.399	2418.078	2394.274	2244.389	2063.149	2102.491	2263.765	2283.597	2001	2283.597
2002	2250.272	2206.875	2289.874	2151.043	2135.196	1983.107	1828.515	1840.520	1640.494	1784.883	1889.940	1778.910	2002	1778.910
2003	1732.309	1706.318	1722.885	1864.799	1963.051	1988.092	2023.145	2062.601	2040.697	2156.139	2175.110	2289.182	2003	2289.182
2004	2331.201	2363.603	2327.945	2291.401	2322.844	2368.012	2289.639	2298.900	2323.799	2359.299	2454.760	2538.293	2004	2538.293
2005	2476.422	2528.536	2483.761	2436.655	2514.186	2517.755	2611.386	2587.560	2608.518	2565.031	2662.046	2662.973	2005	2662.973
2006	2733.483	2740.899	2775.017	2812.279	2731.338	2735.041	2751.912	2817.388	2889.992	2984.166	3040.913	3083.570	2006	3083.570
2007	3130.204	3068.981	3103.307	3240.769	3353.856	3298.137	3195.879	3243.786	3365.100	3418.628	3275.706	3252.981	2007	3252.981
2008	3057.862	2958.525	2945.750	3089.217	3129.230	2865.425	2841.338	2882.437	2625.591	2184.628	2027.871	2049.448	2008	2049.448
2009	1876.707	1676.880	1823.766	1998.318	2110.089	2114.275	2274.193	2356.301	2444.227	2398.820	2542.710	2591.824	2009	2591.824
2010	2498.586	2575.985	2731.433	2774.556	2553.006	2419.361	2588.868	2471.996	2692.608	2795.060	2795.418	2982.240	2010	2982.240
2011	3052.924	3157.514	3158.770	3252.318	3215.504	3161.904	3097.607	2929.340	2723.410	3021.060	3014.384	3045.218	2011	3045.218

Table B-2

Large Company Stocks: Capital Appreciation Index

from December 1925 to December 1970

Year	Jan	Feb	Mar	Apr	May	Jun	Jul	Aug	Sep	Oct	Nov	Dec	Yr-end	Index
1925												1.000	1925	1.000
1926	0.998	0.955	0.898	0.918	0.926	0.966	1.009	1.027	1.050	1.017	1.040	1.057	1926	1.057
1927	1.035	1.085	1.092	1.111	1.168	1.158	1.233	1.288	1.343	1.272	1.350	1.384	1927	1.384
1928	1.377	1.353	1.499	1.548	1.567	1.504	1.523	1.636	1.675	1.699	1.903	1.908	1928	1.908
1929	2.017	2.005	2.001	2.033	1.946	2.165	2.263	2.485	2.364	1.893	1.640	1.681	1929	1.681
1930	1.786	1.824	1.970	1.951	1.919	1.603	1.662	1.675	1.457	1.328	1.299	1.202	1930	1.202
1931	1.261	1.405	1.308	1.183	1.020	1.162	1.076	1.086	0.761	0.825	0.745	0.636	1931	0.636
1932	0.618	0.650	0.573	0.457	0.350	0.347	0.478	0.658	0.633	0.545	0.513	0.540	1932	0.540
1933	0.544	0.444	0.458	0.652	0.755	0.855	0.780	0.869	0.770	0.702	0.774	0.792	1933	0.792
1934	0.875	0.843	0.842	0.820	0.753	0.769	0.680	0.717	0.713	0.690	0.748	0.745	1934	0.745
1935	0.713	0.685	0.664	0.727	0.751	0.802	0.868	0.887	0.908	0.976	1.015	1.053	1935	1.053
1936	1.121	1.140	1.169	1.079	1.129	1.163	1.242	1.253	1.255	1.349	1.354	1.346	1936	1.346
1937	1.397	1.418	1.404	1.288	1.274	1.207	1.331	1.257	1.078	0.969	0.871	0.827	1937	0.827
1938	0.838	0.889	0.666	0.760	0.726	0.906	0.972	0.945	0.959	1.032	0.998	1.035	1938	1.035
1939	0.964	0.995	0.861	0.856	0.909	0.851	0.944	0.876	1.020	1.005	0.956	0.979	1939	0.979
1940	0.944	0.951	0.960	0.955	0.726	0.782	0.806	0.828	0.835	0.868	0.832	0.829	1940	0.829
1941	0.789	0.777	0.781	0.730	0.733	0.772	0.814	0.807	0.799	0.745	0.713	0.681	1941	0.681
1942	0.690	0.673	0.628	0.600	0.639	0.650	0.671	0.676	0.694	0.738	0.728	0.766	1942	0.766
1943	0.821	0.862	0.908	0.908	0.949	0.968	0.915	0.925	0.947	0.934	0.864	0.915	1943	0.915
1944	0.929	0.926	0.942	0.930	0.968	1.017	0.996	1.005	1.002	1.002	1.005	1.041	1944	1.041
1945	1.056	1.121	1.069	1.163	1.176	1.172	1.149	1.216	1.266	1.305	1.347	1.361	1945	1.361
1946	1.455	1.354	1.417	1.470	1.503	1.444	1.408	1.305	1.172	1.163	1.150	1.199	1946	1.199
1947	1.227	1.209	1.189	1.143	1.132	1.192	1.235	1.201	1.184	1.209	1.175	1.199	1947	1.199
1948	1.151	1.097	1.182	1.213	1.308	1.312	1.242	1.252	1.214	1.296	1.156	1.191	1948	1.191
1949	1.193	1.146	1.180	1.155	1.112	1.110	1.179	1.193	1.221	1.257	1.259	1.313	1949	1.313
1950	1.336	1.350	1.355	1.416	1.472	1.386	1.398	1.444	1.524	1.531	1.529	1.600	1950	1.600
1951	1.697	1.708	1.677	1.758	1.687	1.643	1.755	1.824	1.823	1.798	1.793	1.863	1951	1.863
1952	1.892	1.823	1.910	1.828	1.870	1.956	1.991	1.962	1.923	1.922	2.011	2.082	1952	2.082
1953	2.067	2.030	1.982	1.929	1.923	1.892	1.940	1.828	1.830	1.923	1.940	1.944	1953	1.944
1954	2.044	2.049	2.111	2.215	2.288	2.289	2.420	2.338	2.532	2.483	2.683	2.820	1954	2.820
1955	2.871	2.881	2.867	2.975	2.971	3.216	3.411	3.384	3.422	3.318	3.567	3.564	1955	3.564
1956	3.434	3.553	3.799	3.792	3.542	3.681	3.871	3.723	3.554	3.572	3.533	3.658	1956	3.658
1957	3.505	3.390	3.457	3.585	3.717	3.712	3.755	3.544	3.324	3.218	3.270	3.134	1957	3.134
1958	3.268	3.201	3.299	3.404	3.455	3.545	3.698	3.742	3.923	4.023	4.113	4.327	1958	4.327
1959	4.343	4.342	4.345	4.513	4.599	4.582	4.742	4.671	4.458	4.508	4.567	4.694	1959	4.694
1960	4.358	4.398	4.337	4.261	4.375	4.461	4.350	4.464	4.194	4.184	4.353	4.554	1960	4.554
1961	4.842	4.972	5.099	5.118	5.216	5.066	5.232	5.335	5.230	5.378	5.589	5.607	1961	5.607
1962	5.395	5.483	5.451	5.113	4.673	4.291	4.563	4.633	4.410	4.429	4.879	4.945	1962	4.945
1963	5.188	5.038	5.217	5.470	5.549	5.437	5.418	5.682	5.619	5.800	5.739	5.879	1963	5.879
1964	6.038	6.097	6.190	6.227	6.299	6.402	6.519	6.413	6.597	6.650	6.616	6.642	1964	6.642
1965	6.862	6.852	6.752	6.984	6.929	6.592	6.681	6.832	7.050	7.243	7.179	7.244	1965	7.244
1966	7.279	7.149	6.993	7.136	6.750	6.641	6.552	6.042	6.000	6.285	6.305	6.295	1966	6.295
1967	6.788	6.801	7.069	7.368	6.981	7.103	7.426	7.339	7.579	7.359	7.367	7.560	1967	7.560
1968	7.229	7.003	7.069	7.648	7.734	7.804	7.660	7.748	8.046	8.104	8.493	8.140	1968	8.140
1969	8.073	7.690	7.955	8.126	8.108	7.658	7.197	7.485	7.298	7.621	7.352	7.215	1969	7.215
1970	6.663	7.014	7.024	6.389	5.999	5.699	6.117	6.389	6.600	6.524	6.834	7.222	1970	7.222

Table B-2 (Continued)
Large Company Stocks: Capital Appreciation Index

from January 1971 to December 2011

Year	Jan	Feb	Mar	Apr	May	Jun	Jul	Aug	Sep	Oct	Nov	Dec	Yr-end	Index
1971	7.511	7.582	7.861	8.140	7.808	7.814	7.492	7.761	7.707	7.374	7.366	7.990	1971	7.990
1972	8.146	8.352	8.401	8.438	8.570	8.397	8.416	8.706	8.664	8.745	9.143	9.252	1972	9.252
1973	9.093	8.752	8.740	8.383	8.225	8.171	8.481	8.170	8.498	8.487	7.520	7.645	1973	7.645
1974	7.568	7.541	7.365	7.078	6.840	6.740	6.216	5.654	4.980	5.792	5.484	5.373	1974	5.373
1975	6.033	6.394	6.533	6.842	7.143	7.460	6.955	6.809	6.573	6.978	7.150	7.068	1975	7.068
1976	7.904	7.814	8.054	7.966	7.851	8.172	8.107	8.065	8.248	8.064	8.002	8.422	1976	8.422
1977	7.996	7.823	7.713	7.715	7.533	7.875	7.747	7.584	7.565	7.237	7.432	7.453	1977	7.453
1978	6.995	6.821	6.991	7.589	7.625	7.487	7.890	8.095	8.036	7.300	7.422	7.532	1978	7.532
1979	7.832	7.545	7.962	7.975	7.765	8.065	8.136	8.567	8.567	7.980	8.320	8.459	1979	8.459
1980	8.947	8.908	8.001	8.330	8.718	8.953	9.535	9.591	9.832	9.990	11.013	10.640	1980	10.640
1981	10.153	10.288	10.658	10.408	10.391	10.283	10.260	9.623	9.105	9.553	9.902	9.604	1981	9.604
1982	9.436	8.864	8.774	9.122	8.768	8.589	8.393	9.366	9.437	10.479	10.857	11.022	1982	11.022
1983	11.387	11.603	11.988	12.884	12.727	13.175	12.740	12.884	13.009	12.817	13.041	12.926	1983	12.926
1984	12.806	12.309	12.475	12.543	11.799	12.005	11.807	13.063	13.017	13.017	12.820	13.107	1984	13.107
1985	14.078	14.199	14.158	14.093	14.855	15.035	14.962	14.783	14.268	14.876	15.844	16.558	1985	16.558
1986	16.597	17.784	18.723	18.458	19.385	19.658	18.505	19.822	18.129	19.119	19.531	18.979	1986	18.979
1987	21.480	22.273	22.861	22.599	22.735	23.825	24.973	25.846	25.222	19.733	18.049	19.364	1987	19.364
1988	20.147	20.989	20.289	20.480	20.546	21.434	21.318	20.495	21.310	21.863	21.450	21.765	1988	21.765
1989	23.313	22.638	23.109	24.267	25.119	24.920	27.122	27.543	27.363	26.674	27.115	27.696	1989	27.696
1990	25.790	26.010	26.641	25.925	28.310	28.058	27.912	25.279	23.985	23.825	25.252	25.879	1990	25.879
1991	26.954	28.767	29.406	29.416	30.551	29.088	30.393	30.990	30.397	30.756	29.406	32.687	1991	32.687
1992	32.036	32.343	31.637	32.520	32.551	31.986	33.245	32.448	32.743	32.812	33.805	34.147	1992	34.147
1993	34.387	34.748	35.397	34.498	35.281	35.308	35.120	36.329	35.966	36.664	36.191	36.556	1993	36.556
1994	37.744	36.610	34.935	35.338	35.776	34.818	35.914	37.264	36.261	37.018	35.556	35.993	1994	35.993
1995	36.867	38.197	39.241	40.338	41.803	42.692	44.049	44.035	45.800	45.572	47.443	48.271	1995	48.271
1996	49.845	50.191	50.588	51.267	52.439	52.557	50.153	51.097	53.865	55.272	59.328	58.052	1996	58.052
1997	61.611	61.977	59.336	62.801	66.480	69.369	74.788	70.492	74.238	71.679	74.875	76.053	1997	76.053
1998	76.825	82.237	86.344	87.128	85.488	88.859	87.827	75.022	79.703	86.103	91.194	96.335	1998	96.335
1999	100.286	97.048	100.813	104.638	102.025	107.580	104.132	103.481	100.526	106.813	108.849	115.145	1999	115.145
2000	109.284	107.087	117.444	113.827	111.333	113.997	112.134	118.941	112.580	112.022	103.053	103.471	2000	103.471
2001	107.054	97.174	90.935	97.920	98.419	95.958	94.924	88.839	81.579	83.055	89.299	89.975	2001	89.975
2002	88.574	86.735	89.921	84.398	83.632	77.572	71.444	71.793	63.894	69.417	73.379	68.952	2002	68.952
2003	67.061	65.921	66.472	71.859	75.517	76.372	77.611	78.998	78.054	82.344	82.931	87.141	2003	87.141
2004	88.647	89.729	88.261	86.779	87.828	89.408	86.342	86.539	87.350	88.574	91.992	94.978	2004	94.978
2005	92.576	94.326	92.523	90.663	93.378	93.365	96.723	95.638	96.302	94.593	97.922	97.829	2005	97.829
2006	100.320	100.366	101.476	102.713	99.537	99.546	100.052	102.180	104.691	107.990	109.768	111.152	2006	111.152
2007	112.715	110.253	111.353	116.173	119.955	117.818	114.050	115.517	119.651	121.425	116.077	115.076	2007	115.076
2008	108.037	104.282	103.660	108.589	109.748	100.314	99.325	100.535	91.408	75.921	70.238	70.788	2008	70.788
2009	64.724	57.609	62.529	68.402	72.033	72.048	77.389	79.987	82.843	81.206	85.863	87.390	2009	87.390
2010	84.158	86.558	91.647	93.000	85.376	80.776	86.331	82.235	89.435	92.731	92.519	98.560	2010	98.560
2011	100.792	104.013	103.904	106.865	105.422	103.497	101.275	95.524	88.668	98.220	97.723	98.557	2011	98.557

Table B-3
Small Company Stocks: Total Return Index

from December 1925 to December 1970

Year	Jan	Feb	Mar	Apr	May	Jun	Jul	Aug	Sep	Oct	Nov	Dec	Yr-end	Index
1925												1.000	1925	1.000
1926	1.070	1.001	0.894	0.910	0.904	0.938	0.949	0.973	0.973	0.951	0.971	1.003	1926	1.003
1927	1.032	1.089	1.029	1.088	1.168	1.133	1.191	1.170	1.176	1.098	1.187	1.224	1927	1.224
1928	1.283	1.253	1.319	1.440	1.503	1.376	1.384	1.445	1.574	1.617	1.803	1.710	1928	1.710
1929	1.716	1.712	1.677	1.729	1.498	1.578	1.596	1.569	1.425	1.030	0.876	0.832	1929	0.832
1930	0.939	1.000	1.101	1.024	0.968	0.758	0.781	0.768	0.656	0.584	0.583	0.515	1930	0.515
1931	0.623	0.783	0.727	0.570	0.491	0.581	0.548	0.507	0.342	0.368	0.331	0.259	1931	0.259
1932	0.285	0.293	0.255	0.198	0.175	0.175	0.237	0.411	0.357	0.293	0.257	0.245	1932	0.245
1933	0.243	0.212	0.235	0.354	0.578	0.729	0.689	0.753	0.633	0.555	0.591	0.594	1933	0.594
1934	0.825	0.839	0.838	0.858	0.749	0.747	0.578	0.667	0.656	0.663	0.726	0.738	1934	0.738
1935	0.714	0.672	0.592	0.639	0.637	0.656	0.713	0.751	0.778	0.855	0.976	1.035	1935	1.035
1936	1.346	1.427	1.436	1.179	1.211	1.183	1.286	1.313	1.384	1.472	1.678	1.705	1936	1.705
1937	1.921	2.047	2.072	1.724	1.654	1.458	1.638	1.517	1.132	1.008	0.862	0.716	1937	0.716
1938	0.754	0.780	0.499	0.638	0.584	0.788	0.906	0.815	0.802	0.974	0.907	0.951	1938	0.951
1939	0.870	0.879	0.663	0.672	0.745	0.667	0.837	0.704	1.066	1.023	0.915	0.954	1939	0.954
1940	0.955	1.033	1.099	1.171	0.741	0.818	0.837	0.859	0.877	0.925	0.947	0.905	1940	0.905
1941	0.907	0.881	0.909	0.848	0.852	0.916	1.115	1.108	1.056	0.985	0.936	0.823	1941	0.823
1942	0.979	0.972	0.903	0.872	0.869	0.898	0.964	0.995	1.086	1.204	1.143	1.190	1942	1.190
1943	1.444	1.723	1.971	2.155	2.404	2.384	2.126	2.126	2.217	2.244	1.994	2.242	1943	2.242
1944	2.385	2.456	2.640	2.499	2.684	3.055	2.964	3.059	3.053	3.020	3.170	3.446	1944	3.446
1945	3.612	3.977	3.634	4.055	4.257	4.621	4.364	4.607	4.920	5.265	5.882	5.983	1945	5.983
1946	6.917	6.476	6.653	7.117	7.537	7.189	6.808	6.230	5.232	5.170	5.097	5.287	1946	5.287
1947	5.509	5.487	5.303	4.756	4.502	4.750	5.125	5.106	5.165	5.311	5.150	5.335	1947	5.335
1948	5.254	4.842	5.320	5.515	6.099	6.128	5.774	5.778	5.474	5.828	5.177	5.223	1948	5.223
1949	5.318	5.062	5.380	5.199	4.906	4.859	5.185	5.318	5.578	5.841	5.851	6.254	1949	6.254
1950	6.562	6.706	6.682	6.956	7.134	6.580	6.969	7.338	7.720	7.675	7.922	8.677	1950	8.677
1951	9.398	9.455	9.004	9.334	9.026	8.548	8.867	9.403	9.606	9.392	9.314	9.355	1951	9.355
1952	9.533	9.248	9.410	8.922	8.950	9.193	9.296	9.291	9.142	9.047	9.486	9.638	1952	9.638
1953	10.032	10.302	10.233	9.939	10.079	9.589	9.735	9.123	8.884	9.143	9.258	9.013	1953	9.013
1954	9.694	9.786	9.965	10.104	10.561	10.651	11.512	11.528	12.000	12.082	13.024	14.473	1954	14.473
1955	14.764	15.471	15.602	15.837	15.960	16.428	16.533	16.487	16.667	16.384	17.152	17.431	1955	17.431
1956	17.348	17.830	18.598	18.685	17.942	18.042	18.552	18.303	17.827	18.013	18.108	18.177	1956	18.177
1957	18.607	18.234	18.540	19.000	19.143	19.283	19.167	18.427	17.595	16.131	16.314	15.529	1957	15.529
1958	17.245	16.952	17.750	18.418	19.131	19.752	20.722	21.610	22.730	23.655	24.828	25.605	1958	25.605
1959	27.076	27.875	27.951	28.277	28.315	28.196	29.118	28.863	27.619	28.245	28.873	29.804	1959	29.804
1960	28.891	29.034	28.120	27.594	28.158	29.116	28.565	30.064	27.844	26.728	27.896	28.823	1960	28.823
1961	31.460	33.314	35.376	35.825	37.355	35.326	35.436	35.898	34.682	35.590	37.772	38.072	1961	38.072
1962	38.591	39.314	39.537	36.464	32.786	30.213	32.518	33.458	31.254	30.087	33.842	33.540	1962	33.540
1963	36.580	36.705	37.251	38.412	40.088	39.613	39.744	41.799	41.118	42.090	41.642	41.444	1963	41.444
1964	42.581	44.134	45.099	45.520	46.234	46.985	48.857	48.715	50.676	51.716	51.772	51.193	1964	51.193
1965	53.902	56.003	57.335	60.252	59.782	54.398	56.837	60.220	62.310	65.876	68.319	72.567	1965	72.567
1966	78.051	80.479	78.935	81.645	73.797	73.709	73.617	65.669	64.595	63.902	67.041	67.479	1966	67.479
1967	79.884	83.475	88.606	91.003	90.232	99.411	108.862	109.085	115.244	111.662	112.965	123.870	1967	123.870
1968	125.779	116.861	115.586	132.468	145.698	146.137	141.088	146.266	155.034	155.505	167.388	168.429	1968	168.429
1969	165.634	149.238	155.142	161.265	164.063	144.954	129.449	138.925	135.301	143.552	135.552	126.233	1969	126.233
1970	118.554	123.145	119.641	98.970	88.762	80.519	84.975	93.037	103.140	95.856	97.170	104.226	1970	104.226

Table B-3 (Continued)
Small Company Stocks: Total Return Index

from January 1971 to December 2011

Year	Jan	Feb	Mar	Apr	May	Jun	Jul	Aug	Sep	Oct	Nov	Dec	Yr-end	Index
1971	120.820	124.647	131.676	134.923	126.760	122.710	115.802	122.555	119.780	113.180	108.954	121.423	1971	121.423
1972	135.142	139.141	137.144	138.912	136.257	132.100	126.645	129.005	124.506	122.329	129.576	126.807	1972	126.807
1973	121.329	111.635	109.318	102.527	94.211	91.476	102.398	97.837	108.242	109.155	87.737	87.618	1973	87.618
1974	99.238	98.393	97.661	93.129	85.745	84.485	82.637	77.009	71.978	79.629	76.143	70.142	1974	70.142
1975	89.551	92.105	97.799	102.990	109.821	118.053	115.056	108.456	106.488	105.954	109.341	107.189	1975	107.189
1976	135.960	154.854	154.626	149.081	143.698	150.298	150.976	146.592	148.123	145.028	150.881	168.691	1976	168.691
1977	176.275	175.587	177.880	181.941	181.434	195.445	196.028	193.924	195.715	189.249	209.804	211.500	1977	211.500
1978	207.502	214.707	236.868	255.528	276.484	271.254	289.807	317.010	316.002	239.303	256.811	261.120	1978	261.120
1979	295.623	287.279	319.448	331.805	332.955	348.676	354.642	381.457	368.351	325.827	353.796	374.614	1979	374.614
1980	405.926	394.411	324.303	346.795	372.814	389.666	441.224	467.894	487.473	503.725	542.326	523.992	1980	523.992
1981	534.839	539.866	590.776	629.590	656.158	661.145	640.253	596.460	552.739	593.752	610.140	596.717	1981	596.717
1982	585.021	567.705	562.822	584.378	569.886	560.825	559.983	599.070	618.660	699.395	753.878	763.829	1982	763.829
1983	811.793	869.617	915.267	985.448	1071.150	1108.462	1098.662	1077.054	1091.419	1029.455	1082.532	1066.828	1983	1066.828
1984	1065.974	997.219	1014.571	1005.947	953.537	982.143	940.893	1034.794	1037.588	1015.072	980.966	995.680	1984	995.680
1985	1101.123	1131.074	1106.869	1087.609	1117.627	1129.474	1158.840	1150.497	1087.910	1116.304	1185.515	1241.234	1985	1241.234
1986	1255.136	1345.380	1409.555	1418.576	1469.645	1473.466	1368.850	1398.691	1320.504	1366.193	1361.958	1326.275	1986	1326.275
1987	1451.342	1568.756	1605.308	1555.062	1548.997	1590.201	1648.084	1695.384	1681.651	1190.777	1143.503	1202.966	1987	1202.966
1988	1269.850	1366.359	1422.107	1451.829	1425.841	1513.102	1509.320	1472.190	1505.609	1487.090	1422.104	1478.135	1988	1478.135
1989	1537.852	1550.616	1606.128	1650.939	1710.703	1676.318	1744.544	1765.827	1765.827	1659.171	1650.710	1628.590	1989	1628.590
1990	1504.166	1532.294	1588.682	1546.423	1633.178	1656.695	1593.410	1386.904	1271.929	1199.175	1253.138	1277.449	1990	1277.449
1991	1384.882	1539.020	1643.673	1649.261	1704.347	1621.686	1687.688	1731.737	1737.279	1792.350	1742.882	1847.629	1991	1847.629
1992	2056.041	2148.974	2095.465	2011.018	2008.202	1903.977	1974.424	1929.407	1954.682	2005.308	2182.778	2279.039	1992	2279.039
1993	2402.790	2359.540	2427.731	2353.442	2433.930	2424.681	2464.931	2548.492	2629.024	2752.851	2704.676	2757.147	1993	2757.147
1994	2927.539	2920.806	2790.538	2807.281	2803.912	2730.450	2780.690	2874.399	2904.580	2937.983	2842.205	2842.773	1994	2842.773
1995	2923.224	2996.889	3040.344	3147.364	3241.155	3425.253	3646.182	3776.715	3850.361	3662.848	3733.175	3822.398	1995	3822.398
1996	3833.101	3974.542	4065.162	4409.887	4740.188	4464.309	4043.325	4235.787	4359.048	4282.765	4406.109	4495.993	1996	4495.993
1997	4684.825	4588.318	4363.490	4243.058	4676.698	4909.598	5206.628	5471.646	5933.453	5704.421	5616.003	5519.969	1997	5519.969
1998	5487.401	5843.534	6124.608	6227.501	5917.994	5796.084	5407.166	4320.326	4479.746	4639.225	4990.878	5116.648	1998	5116.648
1999	5259.403	4898.082	4712.445	5159.656	5359.334	5663.744	5715.851	5606.678	5482.771	5435.070	5962.816	6640.788	1999	6640.788
2000	7035.915	8694.984	8041.990	7035.937	6467.434	7352.179	7115.438	7773.616	7604.929	7068.021	6283.471	6402.228	2000	6402.228
2001	7285.736	6774.277	6449.112	6920.542	7584.914	7857.212	7657.639	7431.739	6481.963	6900.049	7365.112	7860.048	2001	7860.048
2002	7946.508	7726.390	8409.403	8613.752	8378.596	8080.318	6910.288	6870.899	6407.801	6572.481	7121.941	6816.409	2002	6816.409
2003	6664.404	6472.469	6544.313	7151.625	7982.644	8333.881	8948.921	9372.205	9380.640	10219.269	10658.698	10953.944	2003	10953.944
2004	11587.082	11645.017	11661.320	11184.372	11184.372	11677.603	10805.286	10641.046	11174.162	11379.767	12400.532	12968.476	2004	12968.476
2005	12436.768	12539.994	12134.952	11380.158	12066.381	12611.782	13574.061	13385.381	13467.032	13088.608	13681.522	13706.149	2005	13706.149
2006	14958.891	14996.288	15678.620	15614.337	14694.653	14563.870	14061.417	14452.324	14533.257	15325.320	15670.139	15922.429	2006	15922.429
2007	16105.537	16025.009	16188.464	16431.291	16948.877	16892.945	15793.215	15976.416	16212.867	16488.486	15100.155	15091.095	2007	15091.095
2008	13936.626	13499.016	13540.863	13821.159	14371.241	13070.644	13656.209	14117.788	13077.307	10368.997	9037.614	9548.944	2008	9548.944
2009	8411.664	7308.895	8009.087	9401.867	9724.351	9992.743	10974.031	11273.622	11922.982	11056.181	11252.981	12230.866	2009	12230.866
2010	11871.278	12392.427	13393.735	14367.460	13301.394	12338.373	13219.333	12164.431	13643.625	14235.759	14839.355	16054.698	2010	16054.698
2011	15879.702	16811.840	17358.225	17649.843	17310.966	16937.049	16481.443	15009.650	13421.629	15492.586	15399.631	15532.068	2011	15532.068

Table B-4

Long-Term Corporate Bonds: Total Return Index

from December 1925 to December 1970

Year	Jan	Feb	Mar	Apr	May	Jun	Jul	Aug	Sep	Oct	Nov	Dec	Yr-end	Index
1925												1.000	1925	1.000
1926	1.007	1.012	1.020	1.030	1.035	1.035	1.041	1.046	1.052	1.062	1.068	1.074	1926	1.074
1927	1.080	1.087	1.096	1.102	1.101	1.106	1.106	1.115	1.132	1.138	1.146	1.154	1927	1.154
1928	1.157	1.165	1.169	1.171	1.162	1.159	1.158	1.168	1.171	1.181	1.177	1.186	1928	1.186
1929	1.192	1.195	1.185	1.187	1.192	1.187	1.189	1.192	1.196	1.204	1.202	1.225	1929	1.225
1930	1.233	1.241	1.259	1.269	1.276	1.290	1.298	1.315	1.329	1.337	1.335	1.323	1930	1.323
1931	1.350	1.359	1.372	1.381	1.400	1.407	1.414	1.416	1.414	1.362	1.337	1.299	1931	1.299
1932	1.292	1.261	1.306	1.283	1.297	1.295	1.301	1.358	1.399	1.409	1.419	1.439	1932	1.439
1933	1.518	1.438	1.445	1.431	1.516	1.544	1.569	1.584	1.582	1.588	1.549	1.588	1933	1.588
1934	1.629	1.653	1.684	1.701	1.717	1.744	1.752	1.760	1.749	1.767	1.790	1.808	1934	1.808
1935	1.846	1.872	1.880	1.901	1.909	1.931	1.952	1.944	1.944	1.952	1.966	1.982	1935	1.982
1936	1.998	2.009	2.026	2.031	2.039	2.056	2.058	2.072	2.086	2.091	2.114	2.116	1936	2.116
1937	2.121	2.111	2.087	2.101	2.110	2.121	2.129	2.125	2.131	2.145	2.159	2.174	1937	2.174
1938	2.182	2.184	2.165	2.195	2.197	2.218	2.233	2.229	2.253	2.271	2.279	2.307	1938	2.307
1939	2.312	2.327	2.332	2.347	2.359	2.367	2.365	2.272	2.307	2.361	2.380	2.399	1939	2.399
1940	2.410	2.415	2.427	2.405	2.400	2.429	2.434	2.436	2.458	2.470	2.486	2.480	1940	2.480
1941	2.482	2.483	2.478	2.497	2.509	2.525	2.541	2.550	2.562	2.570	2.546	2.548	1941	2.548
1942	2.549	2.547	2.563	2.565	2.570	2.579	2.584	2.593	2.598	2.600	2.601	2.614	1942	2.614
1943	2.627	2.628	2.634	2.647	2.659	2.672	2.677	2.682	2.684	2.681	2.675	2.688	1943	2.688
1944	2.693	2.703	2.716	2.725	2.726	2.732	2.741	2.750	2.755	2.761	2.774	2.815	1944	2.815
1945	2.837	2.850	2.855	2.860	2.857	2.866	2.863	2.864	2.873	2.882	2.892	2.930	1945	2.930
1946	2.968	2.978	2.988	2.975	2.981	2.986	2.983	2.956	2.949	2.955	2.947	2.980	1946	2.980
1947	2.982	2.983	3.003	3.009	3.015	3.017	3.023	3.001	2.962	2.933	2.904	2.911	1947	2.911
1948	2.918	2.929	2.963	2.974	2.977	2.952	2.936	2.953	2.960	2.967	2.992	3.031	1948	3.031
1949	3.043	3.054	3.056	3.063	3.075	3.101	3.132	3.143	3.150	3.171	3.178	3.132	1949	3.132
1950	3.143	3.145	3.152	3.150	3.147	3.154	3.176	3.188	3.176	3.173	3.190	3.198	1950	3.198
1951	3.204	3.190	3.114	3.111	3.107	3.078	3.141	3.177	3.159	3.113	3.094	3.112	1951	3.112
1952	3.174	3.147	3.171	3.169	3.179	3.184	3.189	3.209	3.204	3.216	3.251	3.221	1952	3.221
1953	3.196	3.183	3.172	3.094	3.084	3.118	3.173	3.146	3.226	3.299	3.275	3.331	1953	3.331
1954	3.373	3.439	3.453	3.441	3.427	3.448	3.462	3.468	3.482	3.496	3.505	3.511	1954	3.511
1955	3.477	3.455	3.486	3.486	3.480	3.490	3.476	3.462	3.489	3.516	3.505	3.527	1955	3.527
1956	3.564	3.573	3.521	3.481	3.499	3.493	3.460	3.388	3.392	3.357	3.314	3.287	1956	3.287
1957	3.352	3.383	3.400	3.377	3.352	3.244	3.209	3.206	3.236	3.244	3.344	3.573	1957	3.573
1958	3.609	3.606	3.589	3.648	3.659	3.645	3.590	3.475	3.441	3.478	3.515	3.494	1958	3.494
1959	3.484	3.528	3.499	3.439	3.400	3.415	3.445	3.422	3.392	3.447	3.494	3.460	1959	3.460
1960	3.498	3.542	3.610	3.602	3.594	3.645	3.739	3.783	3.759	3.762	3.735	3.774	1960	3.774
1961	3.830	3.911	3.899	3.854	3.873	3.842	3.857	3.850	3.906	3.955	3.966	3.956	1961	3.956
1962	3.988	4.008	4.069	4.127	4.127	4.116	4.110	4.169	4.206	4.234	4.261	4.270	1962	4.270
1963	4.296	4.305	4.317	4.295	4.315	4.334	4.346	4.361	4.351	4.372	4.379	4.364	1963	4.364
1964	4.402	4.426	4.398	4.416	4.441	4.463	4.486	4.502	4.512	4.534	4.533	4.572	1964	4.572
1965	4.609	4.614	4.619	4.629	4.625	4.627	4.635	4.633	4.626	4.647	4.620	4.552	1965	4.552
1966	4.562	4.510	4.483	4.489	4.478	4.491	4.447	4.332	4.366	4.480	4.471	4.560	1966	4.560
1967	4.766	4.670	4.724	4.691	4.572	4.470	4.488	4.485	4.527	4.400	4.280	4.335	1967	4.335
1968	4.491	4.508	4.419	4.440	4.454	4.509	4.662	4.758	4.733	4.658	4.552	4.446	1968	4.446
1969	4.508	4.436	4.347	4.493	4.391	4.406	4.408	4.400	4.292	4.347	4.142	4.086	1969	4.086
1970	4.144	4.310	4.291	4.184	4.115	4.116	4.345	4.388	4.449	4.406	4.664	4.837	1970	4.837

from January 1971 to December 2011

Year	Jan	Feb	Mar	Apr	May	Jun	Jul	Aug	Sep	Oct	Nov	Dec	Yr-end	Index
1971	5.095	4.908	5.035	4.916	4.837	4.889	4.876	5.146	5.094	5.238	5.253	5.370	1971	5.370
1972	5.352	5.409	5.422	5.441	5.530	5.493	5.509	5.549	5.566	5.622	5.762	5.760	1972	5.760
1973	5.729	5.742	5.768	5.803	5.780	5.748	5.474	5.669	5.871	5.832	5.878	5.825	1973	5.825
1974	5.795	5.800	5.622	5.430	5.487	5.331	5.218	5.078	5.167	5.624	5.690	5.647	1974	5.647
1975	5.984	6.066	5.916	5.885	5.947	6.128	6.110	6.003	5.927	6.255	6.200	6.474	1975	6.474
1976	6.596	6.636	6.747	6.737	6.667	6.767	6.868	7.027	7.144	7.194	7.424	7.681	1976	7.681
1977	7.448	7.434	7.503	7.579	7.659	7.793	7.789	7.895	7.878	7.848	7.895	7.813	1977	7.813
1978	7.743	7.783	7.815	7.797	7.713	7.731	7.809	8.010	7.971	7.808	7.912	7.807	1978	7.807
1979	7.951	7.849	7.932	7.892	8.072	8.289	8.263	8.269	8.121	7.398	7.563	7.481	1979	7.481
1980	6.998	6.533	6.492	7.386	7.799	8.065	7.719	7.376	7.201	7.086	7.098	7.274	1980	7.274
1981	7.180	6.987	7.204	6.650	7.046	7.062	6.799	6.565	6.434	6.769	7.627	7.185	1981	7.185
1982	7.092	7.313	7.537	7.792	7.983	7.609	8.020	8.691	9.233	9.933	10.133	10.242	1982	10.242
1983	10.146	10.580	10.657	11.241	10.876	10.826	10.334	10.386	10.794	10.767	10.920	10.883	1983	10.883
1984	11.177	10.985	10.727	10.649	10.134	10.336	10.942	11.278	11.632	12.297	12.558	12.718	1984	12.718
1985	13.132	12.642	12.868	13.249	14.336	14.455	14.280	14.651	14.755	15.240	15.804	16.546	1985	16.546
1986	16.620	17.870	18.327	18.357	18.056	18.449	18.506	19.015	18.799	19.154	19.600	19.829	1986	19.829
1987	20.258	20.375	20.198	19.184	19.084	19.380	19.149	19.006	18.204	19.127	19.366	19.776	1987	19.776
1988	20.799	21.086	20.689	20.381	20.265	21.033	20.800	20.912	21.594	22.183	21.808	21.893	1988	21.893
1989	22.335	22.047	22.188	22.661	23.520	24.449	24.884	24.479	24.576	25.255	25.432	25.447	1989	25.447
1990	24.961	24.931	24.903	24.428	25.368	25.916	26.181	25.416	25.647	25.986	26.726	27.173	1990	27.173
1991	27.580	27.914	28.216	28.605	28.717	28.665	29.144	29.945	30.757	30.889	31.216	32.577	1991	32.577
1992	32.014	32.321	32.085	32.136	32.953	33.467	34.497	34.808	35.153	34.604	34.843	35.637	1992	35.637
1993	36.528	37.463	37.557	37.752	37.828	38.936	39.326	40.454	40.628	40.835	40.068	40.336	1993	40.336
1994	41.151	39.974	38.443	38.070	37.834	37.528	38.687	38.567	37.545	37.358	37.425	38.012	1994	38.012
1995	38.985	40.112	40.493	41.202	43.802	44.148	43.702	44.637	45.320	46.158	47.275	48.353	1995	48.353
1996	48.421	46.615	46.009	45.273	45.295	46.074	46.121	45.798	46.984	48.680	49.960	49.031	1996	49.031
1997	48.894	49.031	47.947	48.829	49.454	50.379	53.039	51.766	52.936	53.947	54.492	55.380	1997	55.380
1998	56.139	56.100	56.313	56.611	57.557	58.219	57.893	58.408	60.820	59.664	61.275	61.339	1998	61.339
1999	62.091	59.603	59.617	59.473	58.427	57.493	56.843	56.693	57.221	57.492	57.356	56.772	1999	56.772
2000	56.652	57.174	58.142	57.476	56.552	58.396	59.442	60.245	60.525	60.797	62.394	64.077	2000	64.077
2001	66.377	67.222	67.026	66.166	67.041	67.412	69.844	70.937	69.858	72.913	71.542	70.900	2001	70.900
2002	72.139	73.080	70.925	72.720	73.542	74.079	74.772	78.152	80.729	78.794	79.605	82.480	2002	82.480
2003	82.651	84.830	84.152	86.083	90.135	88.845	81.016	82.788	86.954	85.192	85.634	86.824	2003	86.824
2004	88.445	90.023	91.081	86.215	85.600	86.400	87.993	91.468	92.391	93.905	92.028	94.396	2004	94.396
2005	97.007	95.924	94.730	97.824	100.711	102.132	99.640	101.959	98.794	96.778	97.734	99.937	2005	99.937
2006	99.012	100.277	96.223	94.068	93.877	94.242	96.478	99.958	101.791	103.085	105.625	103.178	2006	103.178
2007	102.652	105.602	103.167	104.616	102.756	101.231	100.905	102.437	103.825	104.735	105.559	105.858	2007	105.858
2008	106.037	105.284	104.664	105.617	102.688	102.064	100.949	102.173	93.351	89.151	99.616	115.154	2008	115.154
2009	104.231	101.025	100.847	100.543	105.464	109.157	115.322	118.032	121.259	121.450	121.987	118.628	2009	118.628
2010	119.762	120.226	120.768	125.085	124.446	130.911	133.133	139.433	137.426	134.640	133.869	133.384	2010	133.384
2011	130.742	132.801	131.846	134.997	138.468	135.566	141.976	145.378	153.736	155.178	149.657	157.324	2011	157.324

Table B-5

Long-Term Government Bonds: Total Return Index

from December 1925 to December 1970

Year	Jan	Feb	Mar	Apr	May	Jun	Jul	Aug	Sep	Oct	Nov	Dec	Yr-end	Index
1925												1.000	1925	1.000
1926	1.014	1.020	1.024	1.032	1.034	1.038	1.038	1.038	1.042	1.053	1.069	1.078	1926	1.078
1927	1.086	1.095	1.123	1.122	1.135	1.127	1.132	1.141	1.143	1.154	1.166	1.174	1927	1.174
1928	1.170	1.177	1.182	1.182	1.173	1.178	1.152	1.161	1.156	1.174	1.175	1.175	1928	1.175
1929	1.165	1.146	1.130	1.161	1.142	1.155	1.155	1.151	1.154	1.198	1.226	1.215	1929	1.215
1930	1.208	1.224	1.234	1.232	1.249	1.256	1.260	1.262	1.271	1.276	1.281	1.272	1930	1.272
1931	1.257	1.267	1.280	1.291	1.310	1.311	1.305	1.307	1.270	1.228	1.231	1.204	1931	1.204
1932	1.208	1.258	1.256	1.332	1.307	1.315	1.379	1.379	1.387	1.385	1.389	1.407	1932	1.407
1933	1.428	1.391	1.405	1.400	1.443	1.450	1.447	1.454	1.457	1.444	1.422	1.406	1933	1.406
1934	1.442	1.454	1.483	1.501	1.521	1.531	1.537	1.519	1.497	1.524	1.530	1.547	1934	1.547
1935	1.575	1.590	1.596	1.609	1.600	1.615	1.622	1.600	1.602	1.611	1.613	1.624	1935	1.624
1936	1.633	1.647	1.664	1.670	1.677	1.680	1.690	1.709	1.704	1.705	1.740	1.746	1936	1.746
1937	1.744	1.759	1.687	1.693	1.702	1.699	1.723	1.705	1.712	1.720	1.736	1.750	1937	1.750
1938	1.760	1.770	1.763	1.800	1.808	1.809	1.817	1.817	1.821	1.837	1.833	1.847	1938	1.847
1939	1.858	1.873	1.896	1.919	1.951	1.946	1.968	1.929	1.824	1.898	1.929	1.957	1939	1.957
1940	1.954	1.959	1.994	1.987	1.927	1.977	1.987	1.993	2.015	2.021	2.062	2.076	1940	2.076
1941	2.034	2.039	2.058	2.085	2.090	2.104	2.109	2.113	2.110	2.140	2.133	2.096	1941	2.096
1942	2.110	2.112	2.132	2.126	2.142	2.142	2.146	2.154	2.155	2.160	2.152	2.163	1942	2.163
1943	2.170	2.169	2.171	2.181	2.192	2.196	2.196	2.201	2.203	2.204	2.204	2.208	1943	2.208
1944	2.213	2.220	2.224	2.227	2.234	2.235	2.243	2.249	2.253	2.255	2.261	2.270	1944	2.270
1945	2.299	2.317	2.321	2.358	2.372	2.412	2.391	2.397	2.410	2.435	2.466	2.514	1945	2.514
1946	2.520	2.528	2.531	2.497	2.493	2.511	2.501	2.473	2.471	2.489	2.475	2.511	1946	2.511
1947	2.510	2.515	2.520	2.511	2.519	2.522	2.537	2.558	2.547	2.537	2.493	2.445	1947	2.445
1948	2.450	2.462	2.470	2.481	2.516	2.495	2.490	2.490	2.494	2.496	2.514	2.529	1948	2.529
1949	2.549	2.562	2.581	2.584	2.589	2.632	2.641	2.670	2.667	2.672	2.678	2.692	1949	2.692
1950	2.675	2.681	2.683	2.691	2.700	2.693	2.708	2.712	2.692	2.679	2.689	2.693	1950	2.693
1951	2.709	2.689	2.646	2.630	2.612	2.596	2.632	2.657	2.636	2.639	2.603	2.587	1951	2.587
1952	2.595	2.598	2.627	2.672	2.663	2.664	2.658	2.640	2.606	2.644	2.640	2.617	1952	2.617
1953	2.620	2.598	2.575	2.548	2.510	2.566	2.576	2.574	2.651	2.671	2.658	2.713	1953	2.713
1954	2.737	2.802	2.819	2.848	2.823	2.869	2.908	2.897	2.894	2.896	2.889	2.907	1954	2.907
1955	2.837	2.815	2.840	2.840	2.861	2.839	2.810	2.811	2.832	2.872	2.859	2.870	1955	2.870
1956	2.894	2.893	2.850	2.818	2.881	2.889	2.829	2.776	2.790	2.775	2.759	2.710	1956	2.710
1957	2.803	2.810	2.804	2.741	2.735	2.686	2.675	2.675	2.696	2.682	2.825	2.912	1957	2.912
1958	2.887	2.916	2.946	3.001	3.001	2.953	2.871	2.746	2.714	2.751	2.785	2.734	1958	2.734
1959	2.712	2.744	2.749	2.717	2.715	2.718	2.734	2.723	2.708	2.748	2.716	2.673	1959	2.673
1960	2.702	2.757	2.835	2.787	2.829	2.878	2.984	2.964	2.986	2.978	2.958	3.041	1960	3.041
1961	3.008	3.068	3.057	3.092	3.078	3.055	3.065	3.054	3.093	3.115	3.109	3.070	1961	3.070
1962	3.066	3.098	3.176	3.202	3.217	3.192	3.158	3.217	3.236	3.263	3.270	3.282	1962	3.282
1963	3.281	3.284	3.287	3.283	3.290	3.297	3.307	3.314	3.315	3.307	3.324	3.322	1963	3.322
1964	3.317	3.313	3.326	3.341	3.358	3.381	3.384	3.390	3.407	3.422	3.428	3.438	1964	3.438
1965	3.452	3.457	3.475	3.488	3.494	3.511	3.518	3.514	3.502	3.511	3.490	3.462	1965	3.462
1966	3.427	3.341	3.440	3.418	3.398	3.393	3.380	3.310	3.420	3.498	3.447	3.589	1966	3.589
1967	3.644	3.564	3.634	3.528	3.515	3.405	3.428	3.399	3.398	3.262	3.198	3.259	1967	3.259
1968	3.366	3.355	3.284	3.359	3.373	3.451	3.550	3.549	3.513	3.466	3.373	3.251	1968	3.251
1969	3.184	3.197	3.201	3.337	3.174	3.242	3.267	3.245	3.073	3.185	3.107	3.086	1969	3.086
1970	3.079	3.260	3.238	3.104	2.959	3.103	3.202	3.196	3.269	3.233	3.489	3.460	1970	3.460

from January 1971 to December 2011

Year	Jan	Feb	Mar	Apr	May	Jun	Jul	Aug	Sep	Oct	Nov	Dec	Yr-end	Index
1971	3.634	3.575	3.763	3.657	3.655	3.597	3.607	3.777	3.854	3.918	3.900	3.917	1971	3.917
1972	3.892	3.927	3.895	3.905	4.011	3.985	4.071	4.082	4.049	4.143	4.237	4.140	1972	4.140
1973	4.007	4.013	4.046	4.064	4.021	4.013	3.839	3.989	4.116	4.205	4.128	4.094	1973	4.094
1974	4.060	4.050	3.932	3.833	3.880	3.897	3.886	3.796	3.890	4.080	4.200	4.272	1974	4.272
1975	4.368	4.426	4.308	4.229	4.319	4.445	4.407	4.377	4.334	4.539	4.490	4.665	1975	4.665
1976	4.707	4.736	4.815	4.824	4.747	4.846	4.884	4.987	5.059	5.102	5.274	5.447	1976	5.447
1977	5.236	5.210	5.257	5.295	5.361	5.449	5.411	5.518	5.502	5.451	5.502	5.410	1977	5.410
1978	5.366	5.368	5.357	5.355	5.323	5.290	5.366	5.483	5.425	5.316	5.416	5.346	1978	5.346
1979	5.448	5.375	5.444	5.383	5.524	5.696	5.647	5.627	5.559	5.091	5.250	5.280	1979	5.280
1980	4.889	4.660	4.514	5.201	5.419	5.613	5.346	5.115	4.982	4.851	4.899	5.071	1980	5.071
1981	5.013	4.795	4.979	4.721	5.015	4.925	4.751	4.568	4.502	4.875	5.562	5.166	1981	5.166
1982	5.189	5.284	5.406	5.608	5.627	5.501	5.777	6.228	6.613	7.033	7.031	7.251	1982	7.251
1983	7.027	7.372	7.303	7.558	7.267	7.295	6.940	6.954	7.305	7.209	7.341	7.298	1983	7.298
1984	7.476	7.343	7.228	7.152	6.782	6.884	7.361	7.557	7.816	8.254	8.352	8.427	1984	8.427
1985	8.734	8.304	8.558	8.766	9.551	9.686	9.512	9.759	9.738	10.067	10.471	11.037	1985	11.037
1986	11.009	12.270	13.215	13.109	12.447	13.210	13.068	13.720	13.034	13.410	13.769	13.745	1986	13.745
1987	13.966	14.247	13.930	13.271	13.132	13.260	13.024	12.810	12.337	13.106	13.154	13.372	1987	13.372
1988	14.263	14.337	13.897	13.675	13.536	14.035	13.797	13.876	14.355	14.796	14.506	14.665	1988	14.665
1989	14.963	14.695	14.875	15.111	15.717	16.582	16.977	16.537	16.569	17.198	17.332	17.322	1989	17.322
1990	16.728	16.686	16.613	16.278	16.954	17.344	17.530	16.796	16.992	17.358	18.056	18.392	1990	18.392
1991	18.632	18.689	18.760	19.023	19.024	18.904	19.202	19.855	20.458	20.569	20.738	21.942	1991	21.942
1992	21.231	21.339	21.140	21.173	21.687	22.121	23.001	23.155	23.584	23.117	23.140	23.709	1992	23.709
1993	24.374	25.237	25.290	25.472	25.591	26.739	27.251	28.433	28.448	28.722	27.979	28.034	1993	28.034
1994	28.755	27.462	26.378	25.981	25.767	25.508	26.435	26.209	25.342	25.280	25.447	25.856	1994	25.856
1995	26.561	27.322	27.572	28.039	30.255	30.675	30.161	30.873	31.413	32.337	33.143	34.044	1995	34.044
1996	34.007	32.366	31.687	31.163	30.994	31.622	31.678	31.237	32.142	33.440	34.612	33.727	1996	33.727
1997	33.459	33.476	32.633	33.465	33.783	34.448	36.603	35.441	36.560	37.807	38.366	39.074	1997	39.074
1998	39.856	39.570	39.668	39.771	40.497	41.421	41.256	43.173	44.876	43.896	44.320	44.178	1998	44.178
1999	44.713	42.390	42.355	42.444	41.660	41.337	41.012	40.803	41.147	41.099	40.849	40.218	1999	40.218
2000	41.135	42.220	43.768	43.437	43.200	44.254	45.018	46.100	45.376	46.227	47.699	48.856	2000	48.856
2001	48.882	49.816	49.447	47.899	48.079	48.488	50.309	51.343	51.758	54.160	51.607	50.662	2001	50.662
2002	51.361	51.951	49.686	51.721	51.798	52.769	54.368	56.888	59.258	57.517	56.817	59.699	2002	59.699
2003	59.065	61.011	60.186	60.798	64.397	63.406	57.178	58.129	61.306	59.573	59.732	60.564	2003	60.564
2004	61.699	63.117	64.007	60.244	59.939	60.666	61.609	64.040	64.657	65.649	64.115	65.717	2004	65.717
2005	67.691	66.826	66.348	68.820	70.862	72.047	69.973	72.302	69.860	68.489	69.010	70.852	2005	70.852
2006	70.018	71.687	67.821	66.148	66.213	66.819	68.148	70.186	71.383	71.932	73.425	71.694	2006	71.694
2007	70.961	73.335	72.272	72.887	71.428	70.782	72.790	74.235	74.323	75.476	79.009	78.779	2007	78.779
2008	80.460	80.608	81.460	79.111	77.812	79.526	79.330	81.251	82.164	79.016	90.416	99.161	2008	99.161
2009	88.012	87.518	93.129	87.081	84.921	85.629	85.790	87.769	89.314	87.790	89.620	84.383	2009	84.383
2010	86.608	86.881	85.328	87.921	91.762	95.851	96.085	102.831	101.255	98.041	96.696	92.942	2010	92.942
2011	91.121	92.152	92.095	93.929	97.261	96.022	101.074	108.355	115.765	112.589	115.437	119.183	2011	119.183

Table B-6

Long-Term Government Bonds: Capital Appreciation Index

from December 1925 to December 1970

Year	Jan	Feb	Mar	Apr	May	Jun	Jul	Aug	Sep	Oct	Nov	Dec	Yr-end	Index
1925												1.000	1925	1.000
1926	1.011	1.014	1.015	1.020	1.018	1.019	1.016	1.013	1.014	1.021	1.034	1.039	1926	1.039
1927	1.044	1.050	1.074	1.070	1.079	1.069	1.071	1.076	1.075	1.083	1.090	1.095	1927	1.095
1928	1.088	1.092	1.094	1.091	1.080	1.081	1.055	1.060	1.053	1.066	1.064	1.061	1928	1.061
1929	1.048	1.029	1.011	1.036	1.016	1.024	1.021	1.014	1.014	1.050	1.072	1.059	1929	1.059
1930	1.050	1.061	1.066	1.062	1.074	1.076	1.077	1.075	1.080	1.081	1.083	1.072	1930	1.072
1931	1.056	1.063	1.071	1.077	1.090	1.087	1.080	1.078	1.045	1.007	1.007	0.982	1931	0.982
1932	0.982	1.019	1.014	1.072	1.049	1.053	1.101	1.098	1.101	1.097	1.097	1.109	1932	1.109
1933	1.122	1.091	1.098	1.092	1.122	1.124	1.120	1.122	1.122	1.108	1.089	1.074	1933	1.074
1934	1.098	1.105	1.123	1.135	1.147	1.152	1.153	1.137	1.118	1.135	1.137	1.146	1934	1.146
1935	1.164	1.173	1.175	1.181	1.172	1.180	1.183	1.164	1.163	1.167	1.166	1.171	1935	1.171
1936	1.175	1.182	1.191	1.193	1.195	1.195	1.199	1.210	1.203	1.201	1.223	1.225	1936	1.225
1937	1.221	1.229	1.176	1.178	1.182	1.176	1.190	1.175	1.177	1.180	1.188	1.195	1937	1.195
1938	1.199	1.203	1.196	1.218	1.221	1.219	1.222	1.219	1.219	1.227	1.222	1.229	1938	1.229
1939	1.233	1.241	1.254	1.266	1.285	1.280	1.292	1.263	1.192	1.238	1.256	1.272	1939	1.272
1940	1.267	1.268	1.288	1.281	1.241	1.270	1.274	1.275	1.287	1.289	1.313	1.319	1940	1.319
1941	1.291	1.291	1.301	1.316	1.317	1.324	1.325	1.325	1.321	1.338	1.332	1.306	1941	1.306
1942	1.312	1.311	1.321	1.314	1.322	1.319	1.319	1.321	1.319	1.319	1.312	1.316	1942	1.316
1943	1.317	1.314	1.313	1.316	1.320	1.320	1.317	1.317	1.316	1.314	1.311	1.311	1943	1.311
1944	1.311	1.312	1.312	1.312	1.312	1.311	1.313	1.314	1.313	1.312	1.312	1.315	1944	1.315
1945	1.329	1.337	1.337	1.356	1.361	1.381	1.367	1.368	1.373	1.384	1.399	1.424	1945	1.424
1946	1.425	1.427	1.427	1.405	1.401	1.408	1.400	1.382	1.378	1.386	1.376	1.393	1946	1.393
1947	1.390	1.390	1.391	1.383	1.385	1.384	1.390	1.399	1.391	1.383	1.357	1.328	1947	1.328
1948	1.328	1.332	1.333	1.337	1.353	1.339	1.333	1.331	1.330	1.328	1.336	1.341	1948	1.341
1949	1.349	1.353	1.360	1.360	1.360	1.380	1.382	1.395	1.391	1.391	1.391	1.396	1949	1.396
1950	1.385	1.386	1.384	1.386	1.388	1.382	1.387	1.387	1.374	1.365	1.367	1.367	1950	1.367
1951	1.372	1.360	1.336	1.325	1.313	1.302	1.317	1.328	1.315	1.313	1.292	1.282	1951	1.282
1952	1.282	1.281	1.293	1.312	1.305	1.302	1.297	1.285	1.266	1.281	1.277	1.263	1952	1.263
1953	1.261	1.248	1.233	1.218	1.197	1.220	1.222	1.218	1.251	1.258	1.248	1.271	1953	1.271
1954	1.280	1.307	1.312	1.322	1.308	1.326	1.341	1.333	1.329	1.327	1.321	1.326	1954	1.326
1955	1.291	1.279	1.287	1.284	1.290	1.277	1.261	1.258	1.265	1.280	1.271	1.272	1955	1.272
1956	1.280	1.277	1.255	1.237	1.262	1.262	1.233	1.207	1.210	1.200	1.189	1.165	1956	1.165
1957	1.202	1.202	1.196	1.166	1.160	1.136	1.127	1.124	1.129	1.120	1.177	1.209	1957	1.209
1958	1.196	1.205	1.214	1.233	1.230	1.207	1.170	1.116	1.100	1.111	1.122	1.098	1958	1.098
1959	1.085	1.095	1.093	1.076	1.072	1.070	1.072	1.064	1.054	1.067	1.050	1.030	1959	1.030
1960	1.038	1.055	1.081	1.059	1.071	1.086	1.122	1.111	1.116	1.109	1.098	1.125	1960	1.125
1961	1.109	1.128	1.121	1.130	1.121	1.109	1.109	1.101	1.112	1.116	1.110	1.093	1961	1.093
1962	1.088	1.095	1.119	1.125	1.126	1.115	1.099	1.115	1.119	1.124	1.123	1.124	1962	1.124
1963	1.120	1.117	1.115	1.110	1.109	1.107	1.107	1.106	1.102	1.096	1.098	1.093	1963	1.093
1964	1.088	1.083	1.083	1.085	1.087	1.090	1.087	1.085	1.087	1.088	1.086	1.085	1964	1.085
1965	1.086	1.084	1.086	1.086	1.085	1.086	1.084	1.079	1.072	1.071	1.060	1.048	1965	1.048
1966	1.033	1.004	1.030	1.019	1.009	1.004	0.996	0.971	1.000	1.019	1.000	1.037	1966	1.037
1967	1.049	1.022	1.038	1.005	0.996	0.961	0.964	0.952	0.947	0.905	0.883	0.896	1967	0.896
1968	0.921	0.914	0.891	0.907	0.907	0.924	0.946	0.942	0.928	0.912	0.883	0.847	1968	0.847
1969	0.825	0.825	0.822	0.853	0.807	0.820	0.822	0.812	0.765	0.788	0.765	0.755	1969	0.755
1970	0.750	0.790	0.780	0.743	0.705	0.734	0.753	0.748	0.761	0.748	0.803	0.792	1970	0.792

from January 1971 to December 2011

Year	Jan	Feb	Mar	Apr	May	Jun	Jul	Aug	Sep	Oct	Nov	Dec	Yr-end	Index
1971	0.828	0.811	0.849	0.821	0.816	0.799	0.797	0.830	0.843	0.853	0.845	0.844	1971	0.844
1972	0.835	0.838	0.827	0.825	0.843	0.834	0.847	0.846	0.835	0.850	0.865	0.841	1972	0.841
1973	0.810	0.807	0.809	0.808	0.795	0.789	0.750	0.774	0.795	0.807	0.788	0.777	1973	0.777
1974	0.765	0.759	0.733	0.709	0.713	0.712	0.705	0.684	0.696	0.725	0.742	0.750	1974	0.750
1975	0.761	0.767	0.741	0.723	0.733	0.750	0.738	0.728	0.716	0.745	0.732	0.755	1975	0.755
1976	0.757	0.757	0.764	0.761	0.744	0.754	0.755	0.766	0.772	0.774	0.795	0.816	1976	0.816
1977	0.780	0.771	0.773	0.774	0.779	0.787	0.776	0.787	0.780	0.767	0.770	0.752	1977	0.752
1978	0.741	0.737	0.730	0.725	0.715	0.706	0.711	0.721	0.709	0.690	0.698	0.684	1978	0.684
1979	0.692	0.678	0.682	0.669	0.681	0.697	0.686	0.679	0.666	0.604	0.618	0.617	1979	0.617
1980	0.566	0.535	0.512	0.585	0.605	0.621	0.587	0.556	0.537	0.517	0.518	0.530	1980	0.530
1981	0.519	0.492	0.505	0.474	0.499	0.484	0.462	0.439	0.428	0.458	0.518	0.476	1981	0.476
1982	0.473	0.476	0.481	0.494	0.491	0.474	0.492	0.525	0.552	0.582	0.577	0.589	1982	0.589
1983	0.566	0.589	0.578	0.594	0.565	0.563	0.530	0.526	0.547	0.535	0.540	0.532	1983	0.532
1984	0.539	0.524	0.511	0.500	0.469	0.472	0.499	0.507	0.519	0.543	0.544	0.544	1984	0.544
1985	0.558	0.526	0.538	0.545	0.589	0.592	0.576	0.586	0.580	0.594	0.613	0.641	1985	0.641
1986	0.634	0.702	0.751	0.741	0.699	0.737	0.724	0.755	0.713	0.728	0.743	0.737	1986	0.737
1987	0.744	0.755	0.733	0.693	0.682	0.683	0.666	0.650	0.621	0.655	0.652	0.658	1987	0.658
1988	0.697	0.696	0.670	0.654	0.642	0.661	0.645	0.644	0.661	0.676	0.658	0.661	1988	0.661
1989	0.669	0.652	0.655	0.661	0.682	0.715	0.727	0.703	0.700	0.722	0.723	0.718	1989	0.718
1990	0.688	0.681	0.674	0.655	0.677	0.688	0.691	0.657	0.660	0.669	0.691	0.699	1990	0.699
1991	0.703	0.701	0.699	0.703	0.699	0.690	0.695	0.714	0.731	0.730	0.732	0.769	1991	0.769
1992	0.740	0.739	0.727	0.724	0.737	0.747	0.772	0.772	0.782	0.762	0.758	0.772	1992	0.772
1993	0.789	0.813	0.809	0.811	0.810	0.841	0.853	0.885	0.881	0.885	0.858	0.855	1993	0.855
1994	0.872	0.829	0.791	0.775	0.763	0.751	0.774	0.762	0.732	0.726	0.726	0.733	1994	0.733
1995	0.748	0.765	0.767	0.775	0.831	0.838	0.820	0.834	0.845	0.865	0.882	0.901	1995	0.901
1996	0.896	0.848	0.826	0.807	0.798	0.810	0.807	0.791	0.809	0.837	0.862	0.835	1996	0.835
1997	0.824	0.820	0.794	0.810	0.813	0.824	0.871	0.839	0.861	0.885	0.894	0.906	1997	0.906
1998	0.920	0.909	0.907	0.904	0.917	0.933	0.925	0.963	0.997	0.971	0.976	0.968	1998	0.968
1999	0.976	0.921	0.916	0.913	0.892	0.880	0.869	0.860	0.863	0.857	0.847	0.829	1999	0.829
2000	0.844	0.862	0.889	0.878	0.868	0.885	0.895	0.912	0.894	0.906	0.930	0.949	2000	0.949
2001	0.944	0.958	0.947	0.913	0.912	0.915	0.945	0.960	0.964	1.004	0.952	0.931	2001	0.931
2002	0.939	0.946	0.900	0.932	0.929	0.943	0.966	1.007	1.045	1.010	0.993	1.039	2002	1.039
2003	1.024	1.054	1.036	1.042	1.100	1.079	0.969	0.981	1.030	0.996	0.995	1.004	2003	1.004
2004	1.019	1.039	1.049	0.983	0.974	0.981	0.992	1.027	1.033	1.045	1.016	1.037	2004	1.037
2005	1.064	1.047	1.035	1.070	1.097	1.111	1.076	1.107	1.066	1.041	1.045	1.069	2005	1.069
2006	1.052	1.073	1.011	0.982	0.978	0.983	0.998	1.024	1.037	1.041	1.058	1.030	2006	1.030
2007	1.015	1.045	1.026	1.030	1.005	0.992	1.016	1.032	1.029	1.040	1.085	1.078	2007	1.078
2008	1.097	1.095	1.102	1.067	1.045	1.064	1.057	1.079	1.087	1.041	1.188	1.299	2008	1.299
2009	1.150	1.140	1.209	1.127	1.095	1.100	1.098	1.120	1.136	1.113	1.132	1.062	2009	1.062
2010	1.086	1.086	1.062	1.090	1.134	1.181	1.180	1.259	1.236	1.194	1.174	1.124	2010	1.124
2011	1.099	1.107	1.103	1.121	1.157	1.138	1.194	1.276	1.361	1.320	1.351	1.391	2011	1.391

Table B-7

Intermediate-Term Government Bonds: Total Return Index

from December 1925 to December 1970

Year	Jan	Feb	Mar	Apr	May	Jun	Jul	Aug	Sep	Oct	Nov	Dec	Yr-end	Index
1925												1.000	1925	1.000
1926	1.007	1.010	1.014	1.023	1.024	1.027	1.028	1.029	1.034	1.040	1.044	1.054	1926	1.054
1927	1.060	1.064	1.068	1.070	1.072	1.075	1.079	1.086	1.092	1.088	1.097	1.101	1927	1.101
1928	1.107	1.106	1.107	1.107	1.106	1.108	1.098	1.104	1.107	1.110	1.112	1.112	1928	1.112
1929	1.108	1.106	1.107	1.117	1.110	1.122	1.129	1.135	1.133	1.153	1.173	1.178	1929	1.178
1930	1.174	1.185	1.204	1.195	1.202	1.219	1.226	1.229	1.236	1.246	1.255	1.258	1930	1.258
1931	1.249	1.261	1.267	1.278	1.293	1.266	1.268	1.270	1.255	1.242	1.248	1.228	1931	1.228
1932	1.224	1.240	1.250	1.274	1.263	1.276	1.292	1.307	1.311	1.317	1.321	1.337	1932	1.337
1933	1.335	1.334	1.348	1.355	1.382	1.383	1.382	1.393	1.396	1.393	1.396	1.361	1933	1.361
1934	1.379	1.386	1.412	1.438	1.455	1.468	1.465	1.451	1.431	1.458	1.465	1.483	1934	1.483
1935	1.500	1.516	1.535	1.552	1.546	1.564	1.570	1.558	1.550	1.566	1.569	1.587	1935	1.587
1936	1.587	1.598	1.603	1.607	1.613	1.615	1.618	1.626	1.628	1.632	1.645	1.636	1936	1.636
1937	1.631	1.632	1.605	1.613	1.625	1.623	1.633	1.626	1.639	1.644	1.651	1.661	1937	1.661
1938	1.676	1.684	1.682	1.721	1.725	1.738	1.740	1.742	1.740	1.756	1.756	1.765	1938	1.765
1939	1.770	1.785	1.799	1.806	1.823	1.823	1.831	1.804	1.756	1.812	1.825	1.845	1939	1.845
1940	1.842	1.849	1.865	1.865	1.825	1.860	1.860	1.868	1.877	1.884	1.894	1.899	1940	1.899
1941	1.900	1.891	1.904	1.910	1.912	1.923	1.923	1.925	1.925	1.930	1.912	1.909	1941	1.909
1942	1.923	1.926	1.930	1.935	1.938	1.940	1.940	1.944	1.939	1.943	1.946	1.946	1942	1.946
1943	1.953	1.956	1.960	1.965	1.976	1.983	1.987	1.987	1.990	1.993	1.996	2.000	1943	2.000
1944	2.003	2.006	2.010	2.015	2.016	2.017	2.023	2.028	2.030	2.033	2.034	2.036	1944	2.036
1945	2.047	2.055	2.056	2.059	2.061	2.065	2.065	2.068	2.072	2.075	2.077	2.082	1945	2.082
1946	2.090	2.100	2.092	2.088	2.089	2.096	2.094	2.094	2.092	2.098	2.096	2.102	1946	2.102
1947	2.107	2.109	2.114	2.111	2.112	2.114	2.115	2.121	2.121	2.116	2.117	2.122	1947	2.122
1948	2.125	2.129	2.132	2.136	2.148	2.146	2.146	2.145	2.147	2.149	2.154	2.161	1948	2.161
1949	2.167	2.169	2.175	2.178	2.183	2.194	2.198	2.205	2.207	2.208	2.208	2.211	1949	2.211
1950	2.210	2.212	2.212	2.213	2.218	2.218	2.223	2.221	2.220	2.221	2.225	2.227	1950	2.227
1951	2.231	2.233	2.205	2.217	2.208	2.219	2.232	2.240	2.227	2.231	2.238	2.235	1951	2.235
1952	2.243	2.239	2.253	2.266	2.270	2.262	2.254	2.249	2.253	2.268	2.267	2.271	1952	2.271
1953	2.271	2.271	2.267	2.246	2.219	2.254	2.266	2.265	2.309	2.317	2.321	2.345	1953	2.345
1954	2.360	2.383	2.390	2.400	2.382	2.412	2.411	2.414	2.409	2.406	2.406	2.407	1954	2.407
1955	2.400	2.387	2.393	2.394	2.394	2.386	2.369	2.370	2.390	2.407	2.394	2.392	1955	2.392
1956	2.417	2.418	2.393	2.393	2.420	2.421	2.398	2.373	2.395	2.390	2.379	2.382	1956	2.382
1957	2.438	2.435	2.439	2.415	2.411	2.385	2.382	2.408	2.408	2.418	2.514	2.568	1957	2.568
1958	2.577	2.613	2.627	2.640	2.656	2.638	2.614	2.521	2.517	2.518	2.551	2.535	1958	2.535
1959	2.532	2.559	2.550	2.536	2.536	2.517	2.525	2.505	2.510	2.554	2.530	2.525	1959	2.525
1960	2.564	2.583	2.658	2.641	2.649	2.707	2.779	2.778	2.786	2.790	2.764	2.822	1960	2.822
1961	2.805	2.831	2.841	2.856	2.848	2.841	2.843	2.848	2.871	2.875	2.869	2.874	1961	2.874
1962	2.861	2.906	2.932	2.939	2.953	2.945	2.941	2.978	2.984	3.000	3.018	3.034	1962	3.034
1963	3.026	3.031	3.039	3.048	3.053	3.057	3.058	3.064	3.068	3.071	3.083	3.084	1963	3.084
1964	3.094	3.098	3.103	3.113	3.138	3.150	3.158	3.167	3.181	3.191	3.190	3.209	1964	3.209
1965	3.222	3.228	3.242	3.250	3.262	3.278	3.283	3.290	3.288	3.288	3.290	3.242	1965	3.242
1966	3.242	3.215	3.275	3.269	3.273	3.265	3.257	3.216	3.286	3.311	3.320	3.394	1966	3.394
1967	3.434	3.429	3.492	3.461	3.476	3.397	3.443	3.430	3.433	3.416	3.425	3.428	1967	3.428
1968	3.478	3.491	3.482	3.477	3.499	3.557	3.620	3.628	3.648	3.651	3.646	3.583	1968	3.583
1969	3.614	3.609	3.644	3.673	3.643	3.613	3.642	3.636	3.527	3.644	3.627	3.557	1969	3.557
1970	3.568	3.724	3.757	3.679	3.720	3.742	3.799	3.843	3.919	3.956	4.134	4.156	1970	4.156

from January 1971 to December 2011

Year	Jan	Feb	Mar	Apr	May	Jun	Jul	Aug	Sep	Oct	Nov	Dec	Yr-end	Index
1971	4.226	4.321	4.401	4.257	4.262	4.182	4.193	4.340	4.351	4.447	4.470	4.519	1971	4.519
1972	4.567	4.573	4.580	4.586	4.594	4.614	4.621	4.628	4.635	4.642	4.662	4.752	1972	4.752
1973	4.749	4.713	4.735	4.765	4.792	4.790	4.657	4.776	4.895	4.920	4.951	4.971	1973	4.971
1974	4.975	4.993	4.887	4.813	4.876	4.833	4.837	4.831	4.985	5.040	5.159	5.254	1974	5.254
1975	5.282	5.360	5.328	5.229	5.365	5.380	5.363	5.359	5.364	5.561	5.555	5.665	1975	5.665
1976	5.697	5.745	5.788	5.855	5.770	5.862	5.932	6.044	6.089	6.179	6.378	6.394	1976	6.394
1977	6.273	6.303	6.338	6.371	6.407	6.472	6.473	6.478	6.487	6.449	6.499	6.484	1977	6.484
1978	6.492	6.503	6.527	6.543	6.542	6.528	6.592	6.644	6.682	6.608	6.668	6.710	1978	6.710
1979	6.747	6.707	6.783	6.805	6.936	7.079	7.071	7.006	7.010	6.682	6.925	6.985	1979	6.985
1980	6.891	6.449	6.542	7.325	7.684	7.625	7.544	7.252	7.225	7.115	7.136	7.258	1980	7.258
1981	7.281	7.110	7.297	7.140	7.315	7.358	7.160	7.033	7.148	7.585	8.058	7.944	1981	7.944
1982	7.984	8.102	8.137	8.379	8.502	8.387	8.776	9.188	9.486	9.990	10.070	10.256	1982	10.256
1983	10.263	10.522	10.471	10.742	10.611	10.628	10.417	10.501	10.832	10.852	10.964	11.015	1983	11.015
1984	11.211	11.139	11.100	11.097	10.819	10.926	11.355	11.469	11.701	12.149	12.382	12.560	1984	12.560
1985	12.818	12.588	12.798	13.136	13.772	13.922	13.859	14.064	14.222	14.453	14.735	15.113	1985	15.113
1986	15.238	15.657	16.186	16.318	15.968	16.409	16.667	17.109	16.921	17.195	17.389	17.401	1986	17.401
1987	17.587	17.691	17.636	17.205	17.140	17.350	17.394	17.328	17.085	17.596	17.741	17.906	1987	17.906
1988	18.472	18.698	18.537	18.455	18.364	18.698	18.610	18.593	18.957	19.238	19.017	18.999	1988	18.999
1989	19.230	19.133	19.227	19.650	20.067	20.717	21.203	20.682	20.824	21.318	21.497	21.524	1989	21.524
1990	21.299	21.313	21.318	21.154	21.707	22.035	22.418	22.213	22.422	22.804	23.243	23.618	1990	23.618
1991	23.870	23.984	24.039	24.320	24.464	24.409	24.725	25.335	25.881	26.228	26.565	27.270	1991	27.270
1992	26.737	26.796	26.583	26.843	27.438	27.923	28.600	29.029	29.592	29.054	28.810	29.230	1992	29.230
1993	30.021	30.749	30.883	31.156	31.126	31.753	31.769	32.477	32.657	32.714	32.411	32.516	1993	32.516
1994	32.964	32.113	31.286	30.957	30.951	30.863	31.385	31.466	30.968	30.896	30.680	30.843	1994	30.843
1995	31.404	32.140	32.341	32.805	34.014	34.285	34.231	34.525	34.745	35.164	35.687	36.025	1995	36.025
1996	36.048	35.551	35.131	34.955	34.844	35.253	35.340	35.323	35.872	36.527	37.072	36.782	1996	36.782
1997	36.873	36.880	36.460	37.000	37.286	37.671	38.666	38.289	38.867	39.451	39.446	39.864	1997	39.864
1998	40.583	40.426	40.530	40.777	41.062	41.385	41.495	42.619	44.023	44.203	43.772	43.933	1998	43.933
1999	44.175	43.015	43.387	43.476	42.835	42.972	42.950	43.016	43.435	43.401	43.365	43.155	1999	43.155
2000	42.925	43.260	44.140	43.950	44.179	45.024	45.347	45.953	46.394	46.760	47.573	48.589	2000	48.589
2001	49.066	49.583	49.958	49.390	49.356	49.680	50.907	51.391	52.694	53.642	52.725	52.291	2001	52.291
2002	52.477	53.043	51.761	52.997	53.621	54.526	56.007	56.942	58.583	58.442	57.451	59.054	2002	59.054
2003	58.529	59.576	59.534	59.613	61.239	61.027	59.080	58.918	60.730	59.906	59.820	60.469	2003	60.469
2004	60.781	61.533	62.148	60.072	59.777	60.067	60.558	61.740	61.815	62.211	61.422	61.832	2004	61.832
2005	61.995	61.308	61.075	62.095	62.735	63.005	62.099	63.100	62.320	61.930	62.293	62.674	2005	62.674
2006	62.448	62.342	61.992	61.942	61.915	62.054	62.831	63.682	64.183	64.513	65.081	64.643	2006	64.643
2007	64.515	65.615	65.775	66.084	65.407	65.477	66.620	67.852	68.241	67.911	70.799	71.142	2007	71.142
2008	73.011	74.721	75.268	73.059	72.444	72.987	73.452	74.216	74.845	75.936	79.202	80.466	2008	80.466
2009	79.152	78.504	79.966	78.642	77.607	77.014	77.446	78.194	78.778	79.016	80.471	78.532	2009	78.532
2010	80.056	80.621	79.913	80.667	81.883	82.940	84.252	85.331	85.750	86.296	85.586	84.121	2010	84.121
2011	84.645	84.196	84.156	85.453	86.984	87.427	89.080	91.013	90.792	92.305	91.131	92.080	2011	92.080

Table B-8
Intermediate-Term Government Bonds: Capital Appreciation Index

from December 1925 to December 1970

Year	Jan	Feb	Mar	Apr	May	Jun	Jul	Aug	Sep	Oct	Nov	Dec	Yr-end	Index
1925												1.000	1925	1.000
1926	1.004	1.004	1.005	1.010	1.008	1.008	1.006	1.004	1.005	1.008	1.009	1.015	1926	1.015
1927	1.018	1.019	1.020	1.018	1.017	1.017	1.019	1.022	1.025	1.018	1.024	1.025	1927	1.025
1928	1.027	1.023	1.022	1.018	1.015	1.013	1.001	1.003	1.002	1.002	1.001	0.997	1928	0.997
1929	0.991	0.985	0.982	0.987	0.978	0.985	0.988	0.990	0.985	0.998	1.013	1.014	1929	1.014
1930	1.007	1.013	1.027	1.017	1.020	1.032	1.034	1.034	1.038	1.043	1.048	1.048	1930	1.048
1931	1.038	1.045	1.048	1.055	1.065	1.040	1.039	1.038	1.023	1.009	1.011	0.991	1931	0.991
1932	0.985	0.994	0.998	1.015	1.002	1.010	1.019	1.029	1.029	1.031	1.032	1.041	1932	1.041
1933	1.037	1.034	1.042	1.045	1.063	1.062	1.059	1.064	1.065	1.060	1.061	1.031	1933	1.031
1934	1.041	1.044	1.061	1.078	1.088	1.096	1.091	1.079	1.061	1.079	1.081	1.092	1934	1.092
1935	1.103	1.112	1.124	1.134	1.129	1.140	1.142	1.132	1.124	1.135	1.134	1.146	1935	1.146
1936	1.144	1.151	1.153	1.154	1.157	1.157	1.158	1.163	1.163	1.164	1.172	1.165	1936	1.165
1937	1.160	1.159	1.139	1.143	1.150	1.147	1.152	1.146	1.154	1.156	1.159	1.165	1937	1.165
1938	1.173	1.177	1.174	1.199	1.200	1.207	1.207	1.207	1.204	1.213	1.211	1.216	1938	1.216
1939	1.218	1.227	1.235	1.239	1.249	1.248	1.252	1.232	1.199	1.235	1.243	1.255	1939	1.255
1940	1.252	1.255	1.265	1.265	1.237	1.259	1.258	1.262	1.267	1.271	1.278	1.280	1940	1.280
1941	1.280	1.273	1.281	1.284	1.285	1.292	1.291	1.292	1.291	1.294	1.281	1.278	1941	1.278
1942	1.287	1.288	1.290	1.292	1.293	1.294	1.293	1.295	1.291	1.293	1.294	1.293	1942	1.293
1943	1.296	1.297	1.297	1.299	1.304	1.307	1.308	1.307	1.307	1.308	1.308	1.309	1943	1.309
1944	1.309	1.309	1.310	1.312	1.311	1.311	1.313	1.314	1.314	1.314	1.314	1.314	1944	1.314
1945	1.319	1.323	1.322	1.323	1.323	1.324	1.323	1.324	1.325	1.325	1.326	1.327	1945	1.327
1946	1.331	1.336	1.330	1.327	1.326	1.329	1.327	1.326	1.324	1.326	1.323	1.326	1946	1.326
1947	1.328	1.327	1.329	1.326	1.326	1.326	1.325	1.327	1.326	1.322	1.321	1.322	1947	1.322
1948	1.322	1.323	1.323	1.324	1.330	1.327	1.325	1.323	1.322	1.322	1.323	1.326	1948	1.326
1949	1.328	1.328	1.329	1.330	1.331	1.336	1.337	1.340	1.340	1.339	1.338	1.338	1949	1.338
1950	1.336	1.336	1.334	1.334	1.335	1.334	1.335	1.333	1.331	1.329	1.330	1.329	1950	1.329
1951	1.330	1.329	1.310	1.315	1.308	1.312	1.317	1.320	1.310	1.310	1.312	1.307	1951	1.307
1952	1.310	1.305	1.311	1.316	1.317	1.310	1.303	1.297	1.297	1.303	1.300	1.300	1952	1.300
1953	1.297	1.295	1.290	1.275	1.257	1.274	1.278	1.274	1.295	1.298	1.297	1.308	1953	1.308
1954	1.314	1.326	1.327	1.331	1.320	1.334	1.332	1.332	1.328	1.325	1.323	1.322	1954	1.322
1955	1.315	1.306	1.307	1.305	1.302	1.295	1.283	1.281	1.288	1.295	1.285	1.281	1955	1.281
1956	1.291	1.289	1.273	1.270	1.281	1.278	1.263	1.246	1.255	1.248	1.239	1.237	1956	1.237
1957	1.262	1.258	1.257	1.240	1.234	1.218	1.212	1.221	1.217	1.219	1.263	1.287	1957	1.287
1958	1.288	1.303	1.307	1.311	1.317	1.305	1.290	1.242	1.236	1.232	1.245	1.233	1958	1.233
1959	1.228	1.237	1.228	1.218	1.214	1.200	1.200	1.186	1.184	1.200	1.184	1.177	1959	1.177
1960	1.190	1.194	1.224	1.213	1.212	1.234	1.263	1.259	1.259	1.257	1.242	1.264	1960	1.264
1961	1.253	1.261	1.262	1.265	1.258	1.251	1.248	1.246	1.252	1.250	1.244	1.243	1961	1.243
1962	1.233	1.248	1.255	1.254	1.257	1.250	1.244	1.255	1.255	1.257	1.261	1.264	1962	1.264
1963	1.257	1.255	1.255	1.255	1.253	1.251	1.247	1.246	1.243	1.240	1.241	1.237	1963	1.237
1964	1.237	1.235	1.233	1.233	1.239	1.239	1.238	1.237	1.239	1.239	1.234	1.237	1964	1.237
1965	1.238	1.237	1.237	1.236	1.237	1.238	1.236	1.234	1.229	1.225	1.221	1.199	1965	1.199
1966	1.194	1.180	1.197	1.190	1.186	1.179	1.171	1.151	1.171	1.174	1.173	1.194	1966	1.194
1967	1.203	1.197	1.214	1.200	1.200	1.168	1.178	1.169	1.165	1.154	1.152	1.148	1967	1.148
1968	1.159	1.158	1.150	1.143	1.145	1.159	1.173	1.171	1.172	1.168	1.162	1.136	1968	1.136
1969	1.140	1.133	1.139	1.141	1.126	1.110	1.113	1.105	1.065	1.093	1.082	1.054	1969	1.054
1970	1.050	1.090	1.092	1.063	1.068	1.068	1.077	1.083	1.098	1.102	1.145	1.145	1970	1.145

Appendix B: Cumulative Wealth Indices of Basic Series

from January 1971 to December 2011

Year	Jan	Feb	Mar	Apr	May	Jun	Jul	Aug	Sep	Oct	Nov	Dec	Yr-end	Index
1971	1.159	1.180	1.197	1.153	1.149	1.121	1.118	1.151	1.149	1.169	1.169	1.177	1971	1.177
1972	1.183	1.180	1.176	1.173	1.169	1.168	1.164	1.160	1.156	1.152	1.151	1.168	1972	1.168
1973	1.161	1.146	1.145	1.146	1.146	1.140	1.101	1.122	1.144	1.143	1.144	1.142	1973	1.142
1974	1.137	1.135	1.105	1.081	1.088	1.072	1.065	1.056	1.083	1.087	1.106	1.120	1974	1.120
1975	1.119	1.129	1.116	1.088	1.110	1.106	1.095	1.088	1.081	1.114	1.106	1.121	1975	1.121
1976	1.121	1.124	1.125	1.131	1.109	1.119	1.125	1.139	1.142	1.152	1.183	1.180	1976	1.180
1977	1.151	1.151	1.151	1.151	1.151	1.156	1.150	1.144	1.140	1.126	1.128	1.119	1977	1.119
1978	1.113	1.109	1.105	1.101	1.093	1.084	1.087	1.088	1.087	1.067	1.069	1.069	1978	1.069
1979	1.066	1.053	1.057	1.052	1.064	1.079	1.069	1.052	1.045	0.987	1.015	1.015	1979	1.015
1980	0.992	0.920	0.924	1.025	1.067	1.051	1.031	0.983	0.970	0.946	0.940	0.946	1980	0.946
1981	0.939	0.908	0.921	0.892	0.904	0.898	0.864	0.838	0.841	0.881	0.926	0.903	1981	0.903
1982	0.897	0.902	0.894	0.911	0.915	0.892	0.923	0.956	0.978	1.021	1.021	1.031	1982	1.031
1983	1.023	1.041	1.027	1.045	1.023	1.016	0.988	0.986	1.007	1.000	1.001	0.997	1983	0.997
1984	1.005	0.990	0.977	0.967	0.933	0.932	0.958	0.958	0.968	0.994	1.004	1.009	1984	1.009
1985	1.021	0.994	1.002	1.019	1.059	1.063	1.049	1.056	1.059	1.068	1.081	1.100	1985	1.100
1986	1.101	1.124	1.155	1.157	1.125	1.149	1.160	1.184	1.164	1.176	1.183	1.177	1986	1.177
1987	1.183	1.184	1.173	1.138	1.126	1.132	1.127	1.116	1.092	1.117	1.118	1.121	1987	1.121
1988	1.149	1.156	1.138	1.126	1.112	1.125	1.112	1.103	1.116	1.125	1.105	1.096	1988	1.096
1989	1.100	1.088	1.085	1.101	1.115	1.144	1.163	1.127	1.128	1.146	1.149	1.143	1989	1.143
1990	1.123	1.117	1.109	1.093	1.113	1.122	1.134	1.116	1.119	1.130	1.144	1.155	1990	1.155
1991	1.160	1.158	1.154	1.160	1.159	1.150	1.156	1.178	1.196	1.205	1.214	1.240	1991	1.240
1992	1.209	1.206	1.189	1.193	1.213	1.228	1.251	1.263	1.282	1.253	1.236	1.248	1992	1.248
1993	1.275	1.301	1.300	1.305	1.299	1.318	1.314	1.337	1.339	1.336	1.318	1.317	1993	1.317
1994	1.329	1.290	1.250	1.231	1.224	1.213	1.227	1.223	1.197	1.187	1.171	1.170	1994	1.170
1995	1.184	1.205	1.205	1.216	1.253	1.257	1.249	1.253	1.255	1.264	1.277	1.283	1995	1.283
1996	1.278	1.255	1.235	1.222	1.212	1.220	1.216	1.209	1.221	1.237	1.249	1.233	1996	1.233
1997	1.230	1.225	1.204	1.215	1.218	1.224	1.250	1.232	1.244	1.256	1.251	1.257	1997	1.257
1998	1.274	1.264	1.261	1.263	1.266	1.270	1.267	1.296	1.333	1.334	1.316	1.316	1998	1.316
1999	1.318	1.279	1.284	1.281	1.257	1.255	1.248	1.244	1.250	1.243	1.235	1.223	1999	1.223
2000	1.210	1.213	1.231	1.220	1.219	1.236	1.238	1.248	1.254	1.258	1.274	1.296	2000	1.296
2001	1.304	1.315	1.321	1.302	1.295	1.298	1.325	1.332	1.361	1.381	1.353	1.338	2001	1.338
2002	1.337	1.347	1.310	1.335	1.346	1.364	1.396	1.415	1.452	1.445	1.418	1.453	2002	1.453
2003	1.437	1.459	1.455	1.453	1.489	1.481	1.431	1.424	1.463	1.440	1.435	1.446	2003	1.446
2004	1.450	1.464	1.475	1.423	1.412	1.414	1.421	1.444	1.442	1.448	1.426	1.431	2004	1.431
2005	1.430	1.410	1.400	1.419	1.429	1.430	1.405	1.423	1.401	1.387	1.390	1.394	2005	1.394
2006	1.384	1.377	1.364	1.357	1.351	1.348	1.359	1.372	1.378	1.380	1.387	1.373	2006	1.373
2007	1.364	1.383	1.381	1.382	1.363	1.359	1.377	1.397	1.401	1.389	1.443	1.446	2007	1.446
2008	1.479	1.511	1.518	1.471	1.455	1.461	1.467	1.478	1.487	1.505	1.567	1.589	2008	1.589
2009	1.562	1.547	1.573	1.545	1.522	1.507	1.512	1.523	1.532	1.534	1.559	1.519	2009	1.519
2010	1.545	1.553	1.537	1.548	1.568	1.586	1.608	1.627	1.633	1.642	1.627	1.598	2010	1.598
2011	1.605	1.593	1.590	1.611	1.637	1.643	1.672	1.706	1.701	1.728	1.705	1.722	2011	1.722

Table B-9

U.S. Treasury Bills: Total Return Index

from December 1925 to December 1970

Year	Jan	Feb	Mar	Apr	May	Jun	Jul	Aug	Sep	Oct	Nov	Dec	Yr-end	Index
1925												1.000	1925	1.000
1926	1.003	1.006	1.009	1.013	1.013	1.016	1.018	1.021	1.023	1.027	1.030	1.033	1926	1.033
1927	1.035	1.038	1.041	1.044	1.047	1.049	1.053	1.055	1.058	1.060	1.063	1.065	1927	1.065
1928	1.068	1.071	1.074	1.077	1.080	1.084	1.087	1.091	1.093	1.098	1.102	1.103	1928	1.103
1929	1.107	1.111	1.114	1.118	1.123	1.129	1.133	1.137	1.141	1.147	1.151	1.155	1929	1.155
1930	1.157	1.160	1.164	1.167	1.170	1.173	1.175	1.176	1.179	1.180	1.181	1.183	1930	1.183
1931	1.185	1.185	1.187	1.188	1.189	1.190	1.190	1.191	1.191	1.192	1.194	1.196	1931	1.196
1932	1.198	1.201	1.203	1.205	1.205	1.206	1.206	1.206	1.207	1.207	1.207	1.207	1932	1.207
1933	1.207	1.207	1.208	1.209	1.209	1.210	1.210	1.210	1.210	1.210	1.211	1.211	1933	1.211
1934	1.211	1.212	1.212	1.212	1.212	1.212	1.212	1.212	1.212	1.213	1.213	1.213	1934	1.213
1935	1.213	1.213	1.213	1.213	1.214	1.214	1.214	1.214	1.214	1.214	1.215	1.215	1935	1.215
1936	1.215	1.215	1.215	1.216	1.216	1.216	1.216	1.216	1.217	1.217	1.217	1.217	1936	1.217
1937	1.217	1.217	1.218	1.218	1.219	1.219	1.219	1.220	1.220	1.220	1.221	1.221	1937	1.221
1938	1.221	1.221	1.221	1.221	1.221	1.221	1.221	1.221	1.221	1.221	1.221	1.221	1938	1.221
1939	1.220	1.221	1.220	1.220	1.220	1.221	1.221	1.221	1.221	1.221	1.221	1.221	1939	1.221
1940	1.221	1.221	1.221	1.221	1.221	1.221	1.221	1.221	1.221	1.221	1.221	1.221	1940	1.221
1941	1.221	1.221	1.221	1.221	1.221	1.221	1.221	1.221	1.221	1.221	1.221	1.222	1941	1.222
1942	1.222	1.222	1.222	1.222	1.222	1.223	1.223	1.223	1.224	1.224	1.225	1.225	1942	1.225
1943	1.225	1.226	1.226	1.226	1.227	1.227	1.227	1.228	1.228	1.228	1.229	1.229	1943	1.229
1944	1.229	1.230	1.230	1.230	1.231	1.231	1.231	1.232	1.232	1.233	1.233	1.233	1944	1.233
1945	1.233	1.234	1.234	1.234	1.235	1.235	1.235	1.236	1.236	1.237	1.237	1.237	1945	1.237
1946	1.238	1.238	1.238	1.239	1.239	1.239	1.240	1.240	1.240	1.241	1.241	1.242	1946	1.242
1947	1.242	1.242	1.243	1.243	1.243	1.244	1.244	1.244	1.245	1.246	1.247	1.248	1947	1.248
1948	1.249	1.250	1.251	1.252	1.253	1.254	1.255	1.256	1.256	1.257	1.257	1.258	1948	1.258
1949	1.259	1.260	1.262	1.263	1.264	1.265	1.266	1.267	1.269	1.270	1.271	1.272	1949	1.272
1950	1.273	1.274	1.275	1.276	1.278	1.279	1.280	1.281	1.283	1.284	1.286	1.287	1950	1.287
1951	1.289	1.290	1.291	1.293	1.295	1.296	1.298	1.300	1.301	1.303	1.305	1.306	1951	1.306
1952	1.308	1.310	1.311	1.313	1.314	1.316	1.318	1.320	1.322	1.324	1.326	1.328	1952	1.328
1953	1.330	1.332	1.334	1.337	1.339	1.341	1.343	1.345	1.348	1.349	1.350	1.352	1953	1.352
1954	1.354	1.355	1.356	1.357	1.357	1.358	1.359	1.360	1.361	1.362	1.363	1.364	1954	1.364
1955	1.365	1.366	1.367	1.369	1.371	1.372	1.373	1.376	1.378	1.380	1.383	1.385	1955	1.385
1956	1.388	1.391	1.393	1.396	1.399	1.402	1.405	1.407	1.410	1.413	1.416	1.419	1956	1.419
1957	1.423	1.426	1.430	1.433	1.437	1.441	1.445	1.448	1.452	1.456	1.460	1.464	1957	1.464
1958	1.468	1.470	1.471	1.472	1.474	1.474	1.475	1.476	1.479	1.481	1.483	1.486	1958	1.486
1959	1.489	1.492	1.496	1.499	1.502	1.505	1.509	1.512	1.517	1.521	1.525	1.530	1959	1.530
1960	1.535	1.540	1.545	1.548	1.552	1.556	1.558	1.561	1.563	1.567	1.569	1.571	1960	1.571
1961	1.574	1.576	1.579	1.582	1.585	1.588	1.591	1.593	1.596	1.599	1.601	1.604	1961	1.604
1962	1.608	1.612	1.615	1.618	1.622	1.626	1.630	1.634	1.637	1.641	1.645	1.648	1962	1.648
1963	1.652	1.656	1.660	1.664	1.668	1.672	1.677	1.681	1.685	1.690	1.695	1.700	1963	1.700
1964	1.705	1.709	1.715	1.720	1.724	1.729	1.734	1.739	1.744	1.749	1.754	1.760	1964	1.760
1965	1.765	1.770	1.776	1.782	1.787	1.794	1.799	1.805	1.811	1.817	1.823	1.829	1965	1.829
1966	1.836	1.842	1.849	1.856	1.863	1.870	1.877	1.885	1.892	1.901	1.908	1.916	1966	1.916
1967	1.924	1.931	1.939	1.945	1.951	1.957	1.963	1.969	1.975	1.983	1.990	1.997	1967	1.997
1968	2.005	2.012	2.020	2.029	2.038	2.046	2.056	2.065	2.074	2.083	2.092	2.101	1968	2.101
1969	2.112	2.121	2.131	2.143	2.153	2.164	2.175	2.186	2.200	2.213	2.225	2.239	1969	2.239
1970	2.252	2.266	2.279	2.291	2.303	2.316	2.328	2.341	2.353	2.364	2.375	2.385	1970	2.385

Appendix B: Cumulative Wealth Indices of Basic Series

from January 1971 to December 2011

Year	Jan	Feb	Mar	Apr	May	Jun	Jul	Aug	Sep	Oct	Nov	Dec	Yr-end	Index
1971	2.394	2.402	2.409	2.416	2.423	2.432	2.442	2.453	2.462	2.471	2.480	2.490	1971	2.490
1972	2.497	2.503	2.510	2.517	2.525	2.532	2.540	2.547	2.556	2.566	2.575	2.585	1972	2.585
1973	2.596	2.607	2.619	2.633	2.646	2.660	2.677	2.695	2.714	2.732	2.747	2.764	1973	2.764
1974	2.782	2.798	2.813	2.835	2.856	2.873	2.893	2.911	2.934	2.949	2.965	2.986	1974	2.986
1975	3.003	3.016	3.028	3.042	3.055	3.067	3.082	3.097	3.113	3.131	3.144	3.159	1975	3.159
1976	3.174	3.184	3.197	3.210	3.222	3.237	3.252	3.265	3.280	3.293	3.306	3.319	1976	3.319
1977	3.331	3.343	3.356	3.368	3.381	3.394	3.408	3.423	3.438	3.455	3.472	3.489	1977	3.489
1978	3.506	3.522	3.541	3.560	3.578	3.597	3.618	3.638	3.660	3.685	3.711	3.740	1978	3.740
1979	3.769	3.796	3.827	3.858	3.889	3.921	3.951	3.981	4.014	4.049	4.089	4.128	1979	4.128
1980	4.161	4.198	4.248	4.302	4.336	4.363	4.386	4.414	4.447	4.489	4.532	4.592	1980	4.592
1981	4.639	4.689	4.746	4.797	4.852	4.917	4.978	5.042	5.105	5.166	5.221	5.267	1981	5.267
1982	5.309	5.358	5.411	5.472	5.530	5.583	5.641	5.684	5.713	5.747	5.783	5.822	1982	5.822
1983	5.862	5.899	5.936	5.978	6.020	6.060	6.105	6.151	6.198	6.245	6.289	6.335	1983	6.335
1984	6.383	6.428	6.475	6.528	6.579	6.629	6.683	6.738	6.796	6.864	6.914	6.959	1984	6.959
1985	7.004	7.044	7.088	7.138	7.186	7.225	7.271	7.311	7.355	7.403	7.448	7.496	1985	7.496
1986	7.538	7.578	7.623	7.663	7.700	7.741	7.781	7.817	7.852	7.889	7.919	7.958	1986	7.958
1987	7.991	8.025	8.063	8.099	8.129	8.169	8.206	8.245	8.282	8.331	8.360	8.393	1987	8.393
1988	8.418	8.456	8.493	8.532	8.576	8.617	8.661	8.712	8.766	8.819	8.869	8.926	1988	8.926
1989	8.975	9.030	9.090	9.152	9.224	9.289	9.354	9.423	9.485	9.549	9.614	9.673	1989	9.673
1990	9.728	9.783	9.846	9.914	9.981	10.043	10.111	10.178	10.238	10.308	10.366	10.429	1990	10.429
1991	10.483	10.533	10.579	10.635	10.685	10.730	10.782	10.832	10.881	10.928	10.970	11.012	1991	11.012
1992	11.049	11.081	11.118	11.154	11.185	11.221	11.255	11.285	11.314	11.340	11.366	11.398	1992	11.398
1993	11.425	11.450	11.479	11.506	11.531	11.561	11.588	11.617	11.647	11.673	11.702	11.728	1993	11.728
1994	11.758	11.783	11.814	11.846	11.884	11.921	11.954	11.998	12.042	12.088	12.132	12.186	1994	12.186
1995	12.237	12.286	12.342	12.397	12.464	12.522	12.579	12.638	12.692	12.752	12.806	12.868	1995	12.868
1996	12.923	12.974	13.025	13.084	13.140	13.192	13.252	13.306	13.365	13.421	13.476	13.538	1996	13.538
1997	13.599	13.652	13.710	13.769	13.837	13.888	13.948	14.005	14.067	14.127	14.182	14.250	1997	14.250
1998	14.311	14.367	14.423	14.485	14.544	14.603	14.662	14.725	14.792	14.840	14.886	14.942	1998	14.942
1999	14.994	15.048	15.112	15.168	15.219	15.280	15.338	15.397	15.457	15.517	15.573	15.641	1999	15.641
2000	15.706	15.774	15.848	15.920	16.001	16.064	16.141	16.223	16.305	16.397	16.480	16.563	2000	16.563
2001	16.652	16.715	16.784	16.850	16.905	16.952	17.004	17.056	17.103	17.142	17.172	17.197	2001	17.197
2002	17.221	17.243	17.266	17.293	17.318	17.340	17.367	17.391	17.416	17.440	17.460	17.480	2002	17.480
2003	17.497	17.512	17.530	17.547	17.563	17.580	17.592	17.604	17.619	17.631	17.644	17.659	2003	17.659
2004	17.671	17.682	17.697	17.711	17.722	17.737	17.754	17.774	17.794	17.814	17.842	17.871	2004	17.871
2005	17.900	17.930	17.968	18.005	18.048	18.089	18.132	18.186	18.238	18.288	18.345	18.403	2005	18.403
2006	18.468	18.530	18.598	18.664	18.745	18.819	18.894	18.974	19.051	19.128	19.209	19.287	2006	19.287
2007	19.372	19.447	19.529	19.615	19.694	19.773	19.851	19.934	19.998	20.063	20.131	20.186	2007	20.186
2008	20.229	20.256	20.291	20.326	20.363	20.398	20.429	20.455	20.486	20.503	20.509	20.509	2008	20.509
2009	20.509	20.512	20.515	20.518	20.518	20.520	20.522	20.525	20.527	20.527	20.527	20.529	2009	20.529
2010	20.529	20.529	20.531	20.533	20.535	20.538	20.541	20.544	20.546	20.549	20.551	20.553	2010	20.553
2011	20.555	20.557	20.559	20.560	20.560	20.561	20.560	20.562	20.562	20.562	20.562	20.562	2011	20.562

Table B-10

Inflation Index

from December 1925 to December 1970

Year	Jan	Feb	Mar	Apr	May	Jun	Jul	Aug	Sep	Oct	Nov	Dec	Yr-end	Index
1925												1.000	1925	1.000
1926	1.000	0.996	0.991	1.000	0.994	0.987	0.978	0.972	0.978	0.981	0.985	0.985	1926	0.985
1927	0.978	0.970	0.965	0.965	0.972	0.981	0.963	0.957	0.963	0.968	0.966	0.965	1927	0.965
1928	0.963	0.953	0.953	0.955	0.961	0.953	0.953	0.955	0.963	0.961	0.959	0.955	1928	0.955
1929	0.953	0.952	0.948	0.944	0.950	0.953	0.963	0.966	0.965	0.965	0.963	0.957	1929	0.957
1930	0.953	0.950	0.944	0.950	0.944	0.939	0.926	0.920	0.926	0.920	0.912	0.899	1930	0.899
1931	0.886	0.873	0.868	0.862	0.853	0.844	0.842	0.840	0.836	0.831	0.821	0.814	1931	0.814
1932	0.797	0.786	0.782	0.777	0.765	0.760	0.760	0.750	0.747	0.741	0.737	0.730	1932	0.730
1933	0.719	0.708	0.702	0.700	0.702	0.709	0.730	0.737	0.737	0.737	0.737	0.734	1933	0.734
1934	0.737	0.743	0.743	0.741	0.743	0.745	0.745	0.747	0.758	0.752	0.750	0.749	1934	0.749
1935	0.760	0.765	0.764	0.771	0.767	0.765	0.762	0.762	0.765	0.765	0.769	0.771	1935	0.771
1936	0.771	0.767	0.764	0.764	0.764	0.771	0.775	0.780	0.782	0.780	0.780	0.780	1936	0.780
1937	0.786	0.788	0.793	0.797	0.801	0.803	0.806	0.808	0.816	0.812	0.806	0.804	1937	0.804
1938	0.793	0.786	0.786	0.790	0.786	0.786	0.788	0.786	0.786	0.782	0.780	0.782	1938	0.782
1939	0.778	0.775	0.773	0.771	0.771	0.771	0.771	0.771	0.786	0.782	0.782	0.778	1939	0.778
1940	0.777	0.782	0.780	0.780	0.782	0.784	0.782	0.780	0.782	0.782	0.782	0.786	1940	0.786
1941	0.786	0.786	0.790	0.797	0.803	0.818	0.821	0.829	0.844	0.853	0.860	0.862	1941	0.862
1942	0.873	0.881	0.892	0.898	0.907	0.909	0.912	0.918	0.920	0.929	0.935	0.942	1942	0.942
1943	0.942	0.944	0.959	0.970	0.978	0.976	0.968	0.965	0.968	0.972	0.970	0.972	1943	0.972
1944	0.970	0.968	0.968	0.974	0.978	0.980	0.985	0.989	0.989	0.989	0.989	0.993	1944	0.993
1945	0.993	0.991	0.991	0.993	1.000	1.009	1.011	1.011	1.007	1.007	1.011	1.015	1945	1.015
1946	1.015	1.011	1.019	1.024	1.030	1.041	1.102	1.127	1.140	1.162	1.190	1.199	1946	1.199
1947	1.199	1.197	1.223	1.223	1.220	1.229	1.240	1.253	1.283	1.283	1.291	1.307	1947	1.307
1948	1.322	1.311	1.307	1.326	1.335	1.345	1.361	1.367	1.367	1.361	1.352	1.343	1948	1.343
1949	1.341	1.326	1.330	1.331	1.330	1.331	1.322	1.326	1.331	1.324	1.326	1.318	1949	1.318
1950	1.313	1.309	1.315	1.317	1.322	1.330	1.343	1.354	1.363	1.371	1.376	1.395	1950	1.395
1951	1.417	1.434	1.439	1.441	1.447	1.445	1.447	1.447	1.456	1.464	1.471	1.477	1951	1.477
1952	1.477	1.467	1.467	1.473	1.475	1.479	1.490	1.492	1.490	1.492	1.492	1.490	1952	1.490
1953	1.486	1.479	1.482	1.484	1.488	1.493	1.497	1.501	1.503	1.507	1.501	1.499	1953	1.499
1954	1.503	1.501	1.499	1.495	1.501	1.503	1.503	1.501	1.497	1.493	1.495	1.492	1954	1.492
1955	1.492	1.492	1.492	1.492	1.492	1.492	1.497	1.493	1.499	1.499	1.501	1.497	1955	1.497
1956	1.495	1.495	1.497	1.499	1.507	1.516	1.527	1.525	1.527	1.536	1.536	1.540	1956	1.540
1957	1.542	1.547	1.551	1.557	1.561	1.570	1.577	1.579	1.581	1.581	1.587	1.587	1957	1.587
1958	1.596	1.598	1.609	1.613	1.613	1.615	1.616	1.615	1.615	1.615	1.616	1.615	1958	1.615
1959	1.616	1.615	1.615	1.616	1.618	1.626	1.629	1.628	1.633	1.639	1.639	1.639	1959	1.639
1960	1.637	1.639	1.639	1.648	1.648	1.652	1.652	1.652	1.654	1.661	1.663	1.663	1960	1.663
1961	1.663	1.663	1.663	1.663	1.663	1.665	1.672	1.670	1.674	1.674	1.674	1.674	1961	1.674
1962	1.674	1.678	1.682	1.685	1.685	1.685	1.689	1.689	1.698	1.696	1.696	1.695	1962	1.695
1963	1.696	1.698	1.700	1.700	1.700	1.708	1.715	1.715	1.715	1.717	1.719	1.723	1963	1.723
1964	1.724	1.723	1.724	1.726	1.726	1.730	1.734	1.732	1.736	1.737	1.741	1.743	1964	1.743
1965	1.743	1.743	1.745	1.750	1.754	1.764	1.765	1.762	1.765	1.767	1.771	1.777	1965	1.777
1966	1.777	1.788	1.793	1.801	1.803	1.808	1.814	1.823	1.827	1.834	1.834	1.836	1966	1.836
1967	1.836	1.838	1.842	1.845	1.851	1.857	1.866	1.872	1.875	1.881	1.886	1.892	1967	1.892
1968	1.899	1.905	1.914	1.920	1.926	1.937	1.946	1.952	1.957	1.968	1.976	1.981	1968	1.981
1969	1.987	1.994	2.011	2.024	2.030	2.043	2.052	2.061	2.071	2.078	2.089	2.102	1969	2.102
1970	2.110	2.121	2.132	2.145	2.155	2.166	2.173	2.177	2.188	2.199	2.207	2.218	1970	2.218

Table B-10 (Continued)

Inflation Index

from January 1971 to December 2011

Year	Jan	Feb	Mar	Apr	May	Jun	Jul	Aug	Sep	Oct	Nov	Dec	Yr-end	Index
1971	2.220	2.223	2.231	2.238	2.250	2.263	2.268	2.274	2.276	2.279	2.283	2.292	1971	2.292
1972	2.294	2.305	2.309	2.315	2.322	2.328	2.337	2.341	2.350	2.358	2.363	2.371	1972	2.371
1973	2.378	2.395	2.417	2.434	2.449	2.466	2.471	2.516	2.523	2.544	2.562	2.579	1973	2.579
1974	2.602	2.635	2.665	2.680	2.710	2.736	2.756	2.791	2.825	2.849	2.873	2.894	1974	2.894
1975	2.907	2.927	2.939	2.953	2.967	2.991	3.022	3.032	3.047	3.065	3.084	3.097	1975	3.097
1976	3.104	3.112	3.119	3.132	3.151	3.168	3.186	3.201	3.214	3.227	3.237	3.246	1976	3.246
1977	3.264	3.298	3.318	3.345	3.363	3.386	3.400	3.413	3.426	3.436	3.453	3.466	1977	3.466
1978	3.484	3.508	3.533	3.564	3.600	3.637	3.663	3.682	3.708	3.737	3.758	3.778	1978	3.778
1979	3.812	3.857	3.894	3.939	3.987	4.024	4.076	4.117	4.160	4.197	4.237	4.281	1979	4.281
1980	4.343	4.402	4.466	4.516	4.561	4.611	4.615	4.644	4.687	4.728	4.771	4.812	1980	4.812
1981	4.851	4.901	4.937	4.968	5.009	5.052	5.110	5.149	5.201	5.212	5.227	5.242	1981	5.242
1982	5.261	5.278	5.272	5.294	5.346	5.412	5.441	5.453	5.462	5.477	5.467	5.445	1982	5.445
1983	5.458	5.460	5.464	5.503	5.533	5.551	5.574	5.592	5.620	5.635	5.644	5.652	1983	5.652
1984	5.683	5.710	5.723	5.750	5.767	5.786	5.805	5.829	5.857	5.872	5.872	5.875	1984	5.875
1985	5.886	5.911	5.937	5.961	5.983	6.002	6.011	6.024	6.043	6.061	6.082	6.097	1985	6.097
1986	6.115	6.099	6.071	6.058	6.076	6.106	6.108	6.119	6.149	6.155	6.160	6.166	1986	6.166
1987	6.203	6.227	6.255	6.289	6.307	6.333	6.346	6.382	6.413	6.430	6.439	6.438	1987	6.438
1988	6.454	6.471	6.499	6.532	6.555	6.583	6.610	6.638	6.683	6.705	6.711	6.722	1988	6.722
1989	6.756	6.783	6.822	6.867	6.906	6.923	6.940	6.951	6.973	7.007	7.023	7.034	1989	7.034
1990	7.107	7.140	7.180	7.191	7.207	7.246	7.274	7.341	7.403	7.447	7.464	7.464	1990	7.464
1991	7.509	7.520	7.531	7.542	7.564	7.587	7.598	7.620	7.654	7.665	7.687	7.693	1991	7.693
1992	7.704	7.732	7.771	7.782	7.793	7.821	7.838	7.860	7.882	7.910	7.921	7.916	1992	7.916
1993	7.955	7.983	8.011	8.033	8.044	8.055	8.055	8.078	8.094	8.128	8.133	8.133	1993	8.133
1994	8.156	8.184	8.212	8.223	8.228	8.256	8.278	8.312	8.334	8.340	8.351	8.351	1994	8.351
1995	8.384	8.418	8.446	8.474	8.490	8.507	8.507	8.529	8.546	8.574	8.569	8.563	1995	8.563
1996	8.613	8.641	8.686	8.719	8.736	8.741	8.758	8.775	8.803	8.831	8.847	8.847	1996	8.847
1997	8.875	8.903	8.926	8.937	8.931	8.942	8.953	8.970	8.993	9.015	9.009	8.998	1997	8.998
1998	9.015	9.032	9.048	9.065	9.082	9.093	9.104	9.115	9.126	9.149	9.149	9.143	1998	9.143
1999	9.165	9.177	9.204	9.271	9.271	9.271	9.299	9.322	9.366	9.383	9.389	9.389	1999	9.389
2000	9.416	9.472	9.550	9.556	9.567	9.617	9.640	9.640	9.690	9.707	9.712	9.707	2000	9.707
2001	9.768	9.807	9.829	9.868	9.913	9.930	9.902	9.902	9.946	9.913	9.896	9.857	2001	9.857
2002	9.879	9.919	9.974	10.030	10.030	10.036	10.047	10.080	10.097	10.114	10.114	10.091	2002	10.091
2003	10.136	10.214	10.276	10.253	10.237	10.248	10.259	10.298	10.331	10.320	10.292	10.281	2003	10.281
2004	10.331	10.387	10.454	10.488	10.549	10.582	10.566	10.571	10.594	10.649	10.655	10.616	2004	10.616
2005	10.638	10.700	10.783	10.856	10.845	10.850	10.900	10.956	11.090	11.112	11.023	10.978	2005	10.978
2006	11.062	11.084	11.146	11.241	11.296	11.319	11.352	11.375	11.319	11.257	11.241	11.257	2006	11.257
2007	11.292	11.352	11.456	11.530	11.600	11.623	11.620	11.599	11.631	11.655	11.725	11.717	2007	11.717
2008	11.775	11.809	11.912	11.984	12.085	12.207	12.271	12.222	12.205	12.081	11.850	11.728	2008	11.728
2009	11.779	11.837	11.866	11.896	11.930	12.032	12.013	12.040	12.048	12.059	12.068	12.047	2009	12.047
2010	12.088	12.091	12.141	12.162	12.171	12.159	12.162	12.178	12.186	12.201	12.206	12.227	2010	12.227
2011	12.285	12.346	12.466	12.546	12.605	12.592	12.603	12.638	12.657	12.631	12.620	12.589	2011	12.589

Appendix C

Rates of Return for All Yearly Holding Periods 1926–2011

Table C-1 (page 1 of 6)
Large Company Stocks: Total Returns
Rates of Return for all holding periods
Percent per annum compounded annually

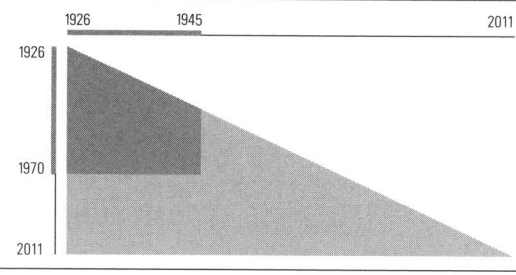

from 1926 to 2011

To the end of	From the beginning of 1926	1927	1928	1929	1930	1931	1932	1933	1934	1935	1936	1937	1938	1939	1940	1941	1942	1943	1944	1945
1926	11.6																			
1927	23.9	37.5																		
1928	30.1	40.5	43.6																	
1929	19.2	21.8	14.7	-8.4																
1930	8.7	8.0	-0.4	-17.1	-24.9															
1931	-2.5	-5.1	-13.5	-27.0	-34.8	-43.3														
1932	-3.3	-5.6	-12.5	-22.7	-26.9	-27.9	-8.2													
1933	2.5	1.2	-3.8	-11.2	-11.9	-7.1	18.9	54.0												
1934	2.0	0.9	-3.5	-9.7	-9.9	-5.7	11.7	23.2	-1.4											
1935	5.9	5.2	1.8	-3.1	-2.2	3.1	19.8	30.9	20.6	47.7										
1936	8.1	7.8	4.9	0.9	2.3	7.7	22.5	31.6	24.9	40.6	33.9									
1937	3.7	3.0	0.0	-3.9	-3.3	0.2	10.2	14.3	6.1	8.7	-6.7	-35.0								
1938	5.5	5.1	2.5	-0.9	0.0	3.6	13.0	16.9	10.7	13.9	4.5	-7.7	31.1							
1939	5.1	4.6	2.3	-0.8	-0.1	3.2	11.2	14.3	8.7	10.9	3.2	-5.3	14.3	-0.4						
1940	4.0	3.5	1.3	-1.6	-1.0	1.8	8.6	11.0	5.9	7.2	0.5	-6.5	5.6	-5.2	-9.8					
1941	3.0	2.4	0.3	-2.4	-1.9	0.5	6.4	8.2	3.5	4.3	-1.6	-7.5	1.0	-7.4	-10.7	-11.6				
1942	3.9	3.5	1.5	-1.0	-0.4	2.0	7.6	9.3	5.3	6.1	1.2	-3.4	4.6	-1.1	-1.4	3.1	20.3			
1943	5.0	4.7	2.9	0.6	1.3	3.7	9.0	10.8	7.2	8.2	4.0	0.4	7.9	3.8	4.8	10.2	23.1	25.9		
1944	5.8	5.5	3.8	1.7	2.5	4.8	9.8	11.5	8.3	9.3	5.7	2.6	9.5	6.3	7.7	12.5	22.0	22.8	19.8	
1945	7.1	6.9	5.4	3.5	4.3	6.6	11.5	13.2	10.4	11.5	8.4	5.9	12.6	10.1	12.0	17.0	25.4	27.2	27.8	36.4
1946	6.4	6.1	4.7	2.8	3.5	5.6	10.1	11.6	8.8	9.7	6.8	4.4	10.1	7.7	8.9	12.4	17.9	17.3	14.5	12.0
1947	6.3	6.1	4.7	3.0	3.7	5.6	9.8	11.2	8.6	9.4	6.7	4.5	9.6	7.5	8.5	11.4	15.8	14.9	12.3	9.9
1948	6.3	6.1	4.7	3.1	3.8	5.6	9.6	10.8	8.4	9.1	6.6	4.6	9.2	7.3	8.2	10.6	14.2	13.2	10.9	8.8
1949	6.8	6.6	5.3	3.8	4.5	6.3	10.1	11.2	9.0	9.7	7.4	5.6	10.0	8.3	9.2	11.5	14.8	14.0	12.2	10.7
1950	7.7	7.5	6.4	4.9	5.6	7.4	11.1	12.3	10.2	11.0	8.9	7.3	11.5	10.0	11.0	13.4	16.6	16.1	14.8	13.9
1951	8.3	8.1	7.1	5.7	6.4	8.2	11.7	12.9	11.0	11.7	9.8	8.4	12.4	11.1	12.1	14.3	17.3	16.9	15.9	15.3
1952	8.6	8.5	7.5	6.2	6.9	8.6	12.0	13.2	11.3	12.1	10.3	9.0	12.8	11.6	12.5	14.6	17.4	17.1	16.1	15.7
1953	8.3	8.1	7.2	5.9	6.5	8.2	11.4	12.4	10.7	11.4	9.6	8.3	11.9	10.7	11.5	13.4	15.7	15.3	14.3	13.7
1954	9.6	9.5	8.6	7.4	8.1	9.7	12.9	14.0	12.4	13.1	11.6	10.4	13.9	12.9	13.9	15.8	18.2	18.0	17.4	17.1
1955	10.2	10.2	9.3	8.2	8.9	10.5	13.7	14.7	13.2	13.9	12.5	11.4	14.8	13.9	14.9	16.8	19.1	19.0	18.5	18.4
1956	10.1	10.1	9.2	8.2	8.8	10.4	13.4	14.4	12.9	13.6	12.2	11.2	14.4	13.5	14.4	16.1	18.2	18.1	17.5	17.3
1957	9.4	9.3	8.5	7.4	8.1	9.5	12.3	13.2	11.8	12.4	11.0	10.0	13.0	12.1	12.8	14.3	16.2	15.9	15.2	14.9
1958	10.3	10.2	9.5	8.5	9.1	10.6	13.3	14.3	12.9	13.6	12.3	11.4	14.3	13.5	14.3	15.8	17.6	17.5	16.9	16.7
1959	10.3	10.3	9.5	8.6	9.2	10.6	13.3	14.2	12.9	13.5	12.3	11.4	14.2	13.4	14.1	15.6	17.3	17.1	16.6	16.4
1960	10.0	10.0	9.3	8.3	8.9	10.3	12.8	13.7	12.4	13.0	11.8	10.9	13.5	12.8	13.5	14.8	16.4	16.1	15.6	15.3
1961	10.5	10.4	9.7	8.8	9.4	10.8	13.3	14.1	12.9	13.4	12.3	11.5	14.1	13.4	14.0	15.3	16.9	16.7	16.2	16.0
1962	9.9	9.9	9.2	8.3	8.8	10.1	12.5	13.2	12.1	12.6	11.4	10.7	13.0	12.3	12.9	14.1	15.5	15.3	14.7	14.4
1963	10.2	10.2	9.5	8.7	9.2	10.5	12.8	13.5	12.4	12.9	11.8	11.1	13.4	12.7	13.3	14.5	15.8	15.6	15.1	14.9
1964	10.4	10.4	9.7	8.9	9.4	10.6	12.9	13.6	12.5	13.0	12.0	11.3	13.5	12.9	13.5	14.5	15.8	15.6	15.2	14.9
1965	10.4	10.4	9.8	9.0	9.5	10.7	12.9	13.6	12.5	13.0	12.0	11.3	13.5	12.9	13.4	14.5	15.7	15.5	15.0	14.8
1966	9.9	9.8	9.2	8.4	8.9	10.1	12.2	12.8	11.8	12.2	11.2	10.5	12.6	12.0	12.4	13.4	14.5	14.3	13.8	13.6
1967	10.2	10.2	9.6	8.8	9.3	10.4	12.5	13.1	12.1	12.5	11.6	10.9	12.9	12.4	12.8	13.8	14.9	14.7	14.2	14.0
1968	10.2	10.2	9.6	8.9	9.3	10.4	12.4	13.1	12.1	12.5	11.6	10.9	12.9	12.3	12.8	13.7	14.7	14.5	14.1	13.9
1969	9.8	9.7	9.1	8.4	8.9	9.9	11.8	12.4	11.4	11.8	10.9	10.3	12.1	11.6	12.0	12.8	13.8	13.6	13.1	12.9
1970	9.6	9.6	9.0	8.3	8.7	9.7	11.6	12.2	11.2	11.6	10.7	10.1	11.9	11.3	11.7	12.5	13.5	13.2	12.8	12.5

Table C-1 (page 2 of 6)
Large Company Stocks: Total Returns
Rates of Return for all holding periods
Percent per annum compounded annually

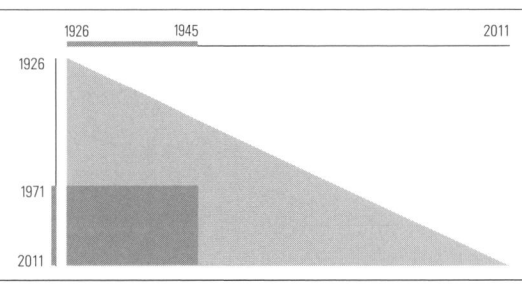

from 1926 to 2011

To the end of	From the beginning of 1926	1927	1928	1929	1930	1931	1932	1933	1934	1935	1936	1937	1938	1939	1940	1941	1942	1943	1944	1945
1971	9.7	9.7	9.1	8.4	8.9	9.8	11.7	12.2	11.3	11.7	10.8	10.2	11.9	11.4	11.8	12.6	13.5	13.3	12.8	12.6
1972	9.9	9.9	9.3	8.7	9.1	10.1	11.9	12.4	11.5	11.9	11.0	10.5	12.1	11.6	12.0	12.8	13.7	13.4	13.0	12.8
1973	9.3	9.3	8.7	8.1	8.5	9.4	11.1	11.7	10.8	11.1	10.3	9.7	11.3	10.8	11.1	11.8	12.6	12.4	12.0	11.7
1974	8.4	8.4	7.8	7.2	7.5	8.4	10.1	10.5	9.7	10.0	9.1	8.5	10.1	9.5	9.8	10.5	11.2	10.9	10.5	10.2
1975	9.0	8.9	8.4	7.7	8.1	9.0	10.6	11.1	10.2	10.5	9.8	9.2	10.7	10.2	10.5	11.1	11.9	11.6	11.2	11.0
1976	9.2	9.2	8.7	8.0	8.4	9.3	10.9	11.4	10.5	10.8	10.1	9.5	11.0	10.5	10.8	11.5	12.2	12.0	11.6	11.3
1977	8.9	8.8	8.3	7.7	8.1	8.9	10.5	10.9	10.1	10.4	9.6	9.1	10.5	10.0	10.3	10.9	11.6	11.4	11.0	10.7
1978	8.9	8.8	8.3	7.7	8.0	8.9	10.4	10.8	10.0	10.3	9.6	9.0	10.4	9.9	10.2	10.8	11.5	11.3	10.9	10.6
1979	9.0	9.0	8.5	7.9	8.2	9.1	10.6	11.0	10.2	10.5	9.8	9.2	10.6	10.2	10.4	11.0	11.7	11.4	11.1	10.8
1980	9.4	9.4	8.9	8.3	8.7	9.5	11.0	11.4	10.6	10.9	10.2	9.7	11.1	10.6	10.9	11.5	12.2	12.0	11.6	11.4
1981	9.1	9.1	8.6	8.1	8.4	9.2	10.6	11.0	10.3	10.6	9.9	9.4	10.7	10.2	10.5	11.1	11.7	11.5	11.1	10.9
1982	9.3	9.3	8.8	8.3	8.6	9.4	10.8	11.2	10.5	10.8	10.1	9.6	10.9	10.5	10.8	11.3	11.9	11.7	11.4	11.2
1983	9.6	9.5	9.1	8.5	8.9	9.6	11.0	11.5	10.7	11.0	10.3	9.9	11.2	10.7	11.0	11.6	12.2	12.0	11.7	11.5
1984	9.5	9.5	9.0	8.5	8.8	9.6	11.0	11.4	10.7	10.9	10.3	9.8	11.0	10.6	10.9	11.4	12.0	11.8	11.5	11.3
1985	9.8	9.8	9.4	8.9	9.2	9.9	11.3	11.7	11.0	11.3	10.7	10.2	11.4	11.1	11.3	11.8	12.4	12.3	12.0	11.8
1986	10.0	10.0	9.5	9.0	9.4	10.1	11.4	11.8	11.2	11.4	10.8	10.4	11.6	11.2	11.5	12.0	12.6	12.4	12.1	11.9
1987	9.9	9.9	9.5	9.0	9.3	10.0	11.3	11.7	11.0	11.3	10.7	10.3	11.5	11.1	11.3	11.8	12.4	12.2	12.0	11.8
1988	10.0	10.0	9.6	9.1	9.4	10.1	11.4	11.8	11.1	11.4	10.8	10.4	11.6	11.2	11.4	11.9	12.5	12.3	12.1	11.9
1989	10.3	10.3	9.9	9.4	9.7	10.5	11.7	12.1	11.5	11.7	11.2	10.8	11.9	11.6	11.8	12.3	12.9	12.7	12.4	12.3
1990	10.1	10.1	9.7	9.2	9.5	10.2	11.5	11.8	11.2	11.5	10.9	10.5	11.6	11.3	11.5	12.0	12.5	12.4	12.1	11.9
1991	10.4	10.4	10.0	9.5	9.8	10.5	11.8	12.1	11.5	11.8	11.2	10.8	11.9	11.6	11.8	12.3	12.9	12.7	12.4	12.3
1992	10.3	10.3	9.9	9.5	9.8	10.5	11.7	12.1	11.5	11.7	11.1	10.8	11.9	11.5	11.8	12.2	12.7	12.6	12.3	12.2
1993	10.3	10.3	9.9	9.5	9.8	10.5	11.7	12.0	11.4	11.7	11.1	10.8	11.8	11.5	11.7	12.2	12.7	12.6	12.3	12.2
1994	10.2	10.2	9.8	9.4	9.7	10.3	11.5	11.8	11.3	11.5	10.9	10.6	11.6	11.3	11.5	12.0	12.5	12.3	12.1	11.9
1995	10.5	10.5	10.2	9.7	10.0	10.7	11.9	12.2	11.6	11.9	11.3	11.0	12.0	11.7	11.9	12.4	12.9	12.8	12.5	12.4
1996	10.7	10.7	10.4	9.9	10.2	10.9	12.0	12.4	11.8	12.0	11.5	11.2	12.2	11.9	12.1	12.6	13.1	12.9	12.7	12.6
1997	11.0	11.0	10.7	10.2	10.5	11.2	12.3	12.7	12.1	12.3	11.9	11.5	12.5	12.2	12.5	12.9	13.4	13.3	13.1	12.9
1998	11.2	11.2	10.9	10.5	10.8	11.4	12.5	12.9	12.4	12.6	12.1	11.8	12.8	12.5	12.7	13.2	13.7	13.5	13.3	13.2
1999	11.3	11.3	11.0	10.6	10.9	11.5	12.7	13.0	12.5	12.7	12.2	11.9	12.9	12.6	12.9	13.3	13.8	13.7	13.5	13.3
2000	11.0	11.0	10.7	10.3	10.6	11.2	12.3	12.6	12.1	12.3	11.9	11.6	12.5	12.2	12.5	12.9	13.3	13.2	13.0	12.9
2001	10.7	10.7	10.4	10.0	10.3	10.9	11.9	12.2	11.7	11.9	11.5	11.2	12.1	11.8	12.0	12.4	12.9	12.7	12.5	12.4
2002	10.2	10.2	9.9	9.5	9.7	10.3	11.4	11.7	11.1	11.3	10.9	10.6	11.5	11.2	11.4	11.8	12.2	12.1	11.8	11.7
2003	10.4	10.4	10.1	9.7	10.0	10.5	11.6	11.9	11.4	11.6	11.1	10.8	11.7	11.4	11.6	12.0	12.4	12.3	12.1	12.0
2004	10.4	10.4	10.1	9.7	10.0	10.6	11.6	11.9	11.4	11.6	11.1	10.8	11.7	11.4	11.6	12.0	12.4	12.3	12.1	11.9
2005	10.4	10.3	10.0	9.7	9.9	10.5	11.5	11.8	11.3	11.5	11.0	10.7	11.6	11.3	11.5	11.9	12.3	12.2	12.0	11.8
2006	10.4	10.4	10.1	9.7	10.0	10.5	11.5	11.8	11.3	11.5	11.1	10.8	11.6	11.4	11.6	11.9	12.3	12.2	12.0	11.9
2007	10.4	10.3	10.0	9.7	9.9	10.5	11.5	11.7	11.3	11.4	11.0	10.7	11.6	11.3	11.5	11.8	12.2	12.1	11.9	11.8
2008	9.6	9.6	9.3	8.9	9.2	9.7	10.6	10.9	10.4	10.6	10.1	9.8	10.7	10.4	10.6	10.9	11.3	11.1	10.9	10.8
2009	9.8	9.8	9.5	9.1	9.4	9.9	10.8	11.1	10.6	10.8	10.4	10.1	10.9	10.6	10.8	11.1	11.5	11.4	11.1	11.0
2010	9.9	9.8	9.6	9.2	9.4	9.9	10.9	11.1	10.7	10.8	10.4	10.1	10.9	10.7	10.8	11.2	11.5	11.4	11.2	11.1
2011	9.8	9.8	9.5	9.1	9.3	9.8	10.8	11.0	10.6	10.7	10.3	10.0	10.8	10.5	10.7	11.0	11.4	11.3	11.1	10.9

Table C-1 (page 3 of 6)

Large Company Stocks: Total Returns
Rates of Return for all holding periods
Percent per annum compounded annually

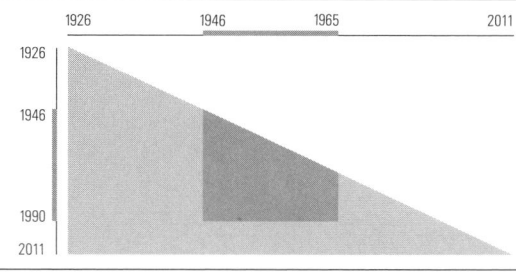

from 1926 to 2011

To the end of	From the beginning of																			
	1946	1947	1948	1949	1950	1951	1952	1953	1954	1955	1956	1957	1958	1959	1960	1961	1962	1963	1964	1965
1946	-8.1																			
1947	-1.4	5.7																		
1948	0.8	5.6	5.5																	
1949	5.1	9.8	11.9	18.8																
1950	9.9	14.9	18.2	25.1	31.7															
1951	12.1	16.7	19.6	24.7	27.8	24.0														
1952	13.0	17.0	19.4	23.1	24.6	21.2	18.4													
1953	11.2	14.2	15.7	17.9	17.6	13.3	8.3	-1.0												
1954	15.1	18.4	20.4	23.0	23.9	22.0	21.4	22.9	52.6											
1955	16.7	19.8	21.7	24.2	25.2	23.9	23.9	25.7	41.7	31.6										
1956	15.7	18.4	19.9	21.9	22.3	20.8	20.2	20.6	28.9	18.4	6.6									
1957	13.2	15.4	16.4	17.7	17.6	15.7	14.4	13.6	17.5	7.7	-2.5	-10.8								
1958	15.3	17.5	18.7	20.1	20.2	18.8	18.1	18.1	22.3	15.7	10.9	13.1	43.4							
1959	15.1	17.1	18.1	19.3	19.4	18.1	17.3	17.2	20.5	15.0	11.1	12.7	26.7	12.0						
1960	14.0	15.8	16.6	17.6	17.5	16.2	15.3	14.9	17.4	12.4	8.9	9.5	17.3	6.1	0.5					
1961	14.8	16.5	17.3	18.3	18.3	17.1	16.4	16.2	18.6	14.4	11.7	12.8	19.6	12.6	12.9	26.9				
1962	13.3	14.8	15.4	16.1	15.9	14.7	13.9	13.4	15.2	11.2	8.5	8.9	13.3	6.8	5.2	7.6	-8.7			
1963	13.8	15.2	15.8	16.6	16.4	15.3	14.6	14.3	15.9	12.4	10.2	10.8	14.8	9.9	9.3	12.5	5.9	22.8		
1964	13.9	15.3	15.9	16.6	16.4	15.4	14.7	14.4	16.0	12.8	10.9	11.5	15.1	10.9	10.7	13.5	9.3	19.6	16.5	
1965	13.8	15.1	15.7	16.3	16.2	15.2	14.6	14.3	15.7	12.8	11.1	11.6	14.7	11.1	11.0	13.2	10.1	17.2	14.4	12.5
1966	12.6	13.7	14.2	14.7	14.4	13.4	12.7	12.4	13.4	10.7	9.0	9.2	11.7	8.2	7.7	9.0	5.7	9.7	5.6	0.6
1967	13.1	14.2	14.6	15.1	14.9	14.0	13.4	13.1	14.2	11.6	10.1	10.5	12.8	9.9	9.6	11.0	8.6	12.4	9.9	7.8
1968	13.0	14.0	14.5	14.9	14.7	13.8	13.3	13.0	14.0	11.6	10.2	10.5	12.7	10.0	9.8	11.0	8.9	12.2	10.2	8.6
1969	12.0	13.0	13.3	13.7	13.4	12.5	11.9	11.6	12.4	10.1	8.7	8.9	10.7	8.2	7.8	8.7	6.6	9.0	6.8	5.0
1970	11.7	12.6	12.9	13.2	13.0	12.1	11.5	11.1	11.9	9.7	8.4	8.6	10.2	7.8	7.4	8.2	6.3	8.3	6.4	4.8
1971	11.8	12.6	12.9	13.3	13.0	12.2	11.6	11.3	12.0	10.0	8.8	8.9	10.5	8.3	8.0	8.7	7.0	9.0	7.3	6.1
1972	12.0	12.9	13.2	13.5	13.3	12.5	12.0	11.7	12.4	10.5	9.4	9.5	11.0	9.0	8.8	9.5	8.1	9.9	8.6	7.6
1973	10.9	11.7	11.9	12.2	11.9	11.2	10.6	10.2	10.8	9.0	7.9	7.9	9.2	7.3	6.9	7.4	6.0	7.4	6.0	4.9
1974	9.4	10.0	10.2	10.4	10.1	9.3	8.7	8.2	8.7	6.9	5.7	5.7	6.7	4.8	4.3	4.6	3.0	4.1	2.5	1.2
1975	10.2	10.9	11.1	11.3	11.0	10.3	9.7	9.4	9.9	8.1	7.1	7.1	8.2	6.4	6.1	6.5	5.2	6.3	5.0	4.1
1976	10.6	11.3	11.5	11.7	11.5	10.8	10.3	9.9	10.4	8.8	7.8	7.9	9.0	7.3	7.1	7.5	6.3	7.5	6.4	5.6
1977	10.0	10.7	10.8	11.0	10.7	10.0	9.5	9.2	9.6	8.1	7.1	7.1	8.1	6.5	6.2	6.6	5.4	6.4	5.4	4.5
1978	9.9	10.5	10.7	10.9	10.6	9.9	9.4	9.1	9.5	8.0	7.1	7.1	8.0	6.5	6.2	6.6	5.5	6.4	5.4	4.7
1979	10.2	10.8	10.9	11.1	10.9	10.2	9.7	9.4	9.8	8.4	7.5	7.6	8.5	7.1	6.8	7.2	6.2	7.1	6.2	5.6
1980	10.7	11.3	11.5	11.7	11.5	10.9	10.4	10.2	10.6	9.2	8.4	8.5	9.4	8.1	7.9	8.3	7.4	8.4	7.6	7.1
1981	10.3	10.8	11.0	11.2	10.9	10.3	9.9	9.6	10.0	8.7	7.9	7.9	8.8	7.5	7.3	7.7	6.8	7.7	6.9	6.3
1982	10.6	11.1	11.3	11.5	11.2	10.7	10.3	10.0	10.4	9.1	8.4	8.4	9.3	8.1	7.9	8.2	7.4	8.3	7.6	7.1
1983	10.9	11.4	11.6	11.8	11.6	11.0	10.6	10.4	10.8	9.6	8.8	8.9	9.8	8.6	8.5	8.8	8.1	8.9	8.3	7.9
1984	10.7	11.3	11.4	11.6	11.4	10.9	10.5	10.2	10.6	9.5	8.8	8.8	9.6	8.5	8.4	8.7	8.0	8.8	8.2	7.8
1985	11.2	11.8	11.9	12.1	11.9	11.4	11.1	10.8	11.2	10.1	9.5	9.6	10.4	9.3	9.2	9.6	8.9	9.7	9.2	8.8
1986	11.4	11.9	12.1	12.3	12.1	11.6	11.3	11.1	11.5	10.4	9.7	9.8	10.6	9.6	9.5	9.9	9.3	10.1	9.6	9.3
1987	11.2	11.8	11.9	12.1	11.9	11.4	11.1	10.9	11.3	10.2	9.6	9.7	10.5	9.5	9.4	9.7	9.1	9.9	9.4	9.1
1988	11.4	11.9	12.0	12.2	12.0	11.6	11.2	11.1	11.4	10.4	9.8	9.9	10.6	9.7	9.6	10.0	9.4	10.1	9.7	9.4
1989	11.8	12.3	12.5	12.6	12.5	12.0	11.7	11.6	11.9	10.9	10.4	10.5	11.3	10.3	10.3	10.6	10.1	10.9	10.4	10.2
1990	11.4	11.9	12.1	12.2	12.1	11.6	11.3	11.2	11.5	10.5	10.0	10.1	10.8	9.9	9.8	10.2	9.6	10.3	9.9	9.7

Table C-1 (page 4 of 6)

Large Company Stocks: Total Returns
Rates of Return for all holding periods
Percent per annum compounded annually

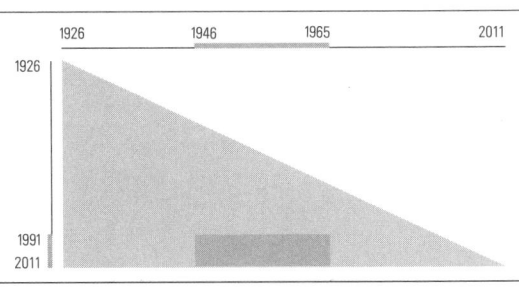

from 1926 to 2011

To the end of	From the beginning of 1946	1947	1948	1949	1950	1951	1952	1953	1954	1955	1956	1957	1958	1959	1960	1961	1962	1963	1964	1965
1991	11.8	12.3	12.5	12.6	12.5	12.1	11.8	11.6	12.0	11.0	10.5	10.6	11.3	10.5	10.4	10.8	10.3	11.0	10.6	10.4
1992	11.7	12.2	12.4	12.5	12.4	11.9	11.7	11.5	11.8	10.9	10.4	10.5	11.2	10.4	10.3	10.7	10.2	10.9	10.5	10.3
1993	11.7	12.2	12.3	12.5	12.3	11.9	11.6	11.5	11.8	10.9	10.4	10.5	11.2	10.4	10.3	10.6	10.2	10.8	10.5	10.3
1994	11.5	11.9	12.1	12.2	12.1	11.7	11.4	11.2	11.5	10.7	10.2	10.3	10.9	10.1	10.1	10.4	9.9	10.5	10.2	10.0
1995	11.9	12.4	12.5	12.7	12.6	12.2	11.9	11.8	12.1	11.3	10.8	10.9	11.5	10.8	10.7	11.1	10.6	11.3	10.9	10.8
1996	12.1	12.6	12.7	12.9	12.8	12.4	12.1	12.0	12.3	11.5	11.1	11.2	11.8	11.1	11.1	11.4	11.0	11.6	11.3	11.1
1997	12.5	13.0	13.1	13.3	13.2	12.8	12.6	12.4	12.8	12.0	11.6	11.7	12.3	11.6	11.6	11.9	11.5	12.2	11.9	11.7
1998	12.8	13.3	13.4	13.6	13.5	13.1	12.9	12.8	13.1	12.3	11.9	12.1	12.7	12.0	12.0	12.3	12.0	12.6	12.3	12.2
1999	13.0	13.4	13.5	13.7	13.6	13.3	13.1	12.9	13.3	12.5	12.1	12.3	12.9	12.2	12.2	12.5	12.2	12.8	12.5	12.4
2000	12.5	12.9	13.1	13.2	13.1	12.8	12.6	12.4	12.7	12.0	11.6	11.7	12.3	11.7	11.6	11.9	11.6	12.2	11.9	11.8
2001	12.0	12.4	12.6	12.7	12.6	12.2	12.0	11.9	12.2	11.4	11.0	11.1	11.7	11.0	11.0	11.3	10.9	11.5	11.2	11.1
2002	11.3	11.7	11.8	11.9	11.8	11.4	11.2	11.1	11.3	10.6	10.2	10.3	10.8	10.1	10.1	10.3	10.0	10.5	10.2	10.0
2003	11.6	12.0	12.1	12.2	12.1	11.7	11.5	11.4	11.7	10.9	10.6	10.6	11.2	10.5	10.5	10.7	10.4	10.9	10.6	10.5
2004	11.6	11.9	12.1	12.2	12.1	11.7	11.5	11.4	11.6	10.9	10.6	10.6	11.2	10.5	10.5	10.7	10.4	10.9	10.6	10.5
2005	11.5	11.8	11.9	12.0	11.9	11.6	11.4	11.3	11.5	10.8	10.4	10.5	11.0	10.4	10.4	10.6	10.3	10.8	10.5	10.3
2006	11.5	11.9	12.0	12.1	12.0	11.7	11.5	11.3	11.6	10.9	10.5	10.6	11.1	10.5	10.5	10.7	10.4	10.9	10.6	10.5
2007	11.4	11.8	11.9	12.0	11.9	11.6	11.4	11.2	11.5	10.8	10.4	10.5	11.0	10.4	10.4	10.6	10.3	10.7	10.5	10.3
2008	10.4	10.8	10.8	10.9	10.8	10.5	10.2	10.1	10.3	9.7	9.3	9.3	9.8	9.2	9.1	9.3	9.0	9.4	9.1	9.0
2009	10.7	11.0	11.1	11.2	11.0	10.7	10.5	10.4	10.6	9.9	9.6	9.6	10.1	9.5	9.5	9.6	9.3	9.7	9.5	9.3
2010	10.7	11.0	11.1	11.2	11.1	10.8	10.6	10.5	10.7	10.0	9.7	9.7	10.2	9.6	9.6	9.8	9.4	9.8	9.6	9.4
2011	10.6	10.9	11.0	11.1	11.0	10.6	10.4	10.3	10.5	9.9	9.5	9.6	10.0	9.5	9.4	9.6	9.3	9.7	9.4	9.3

Table C-1 (page 5 of 6)

Large Company Stocks: Total Returns
Rates of Return for all holding periods
Percent per annum compounded annually

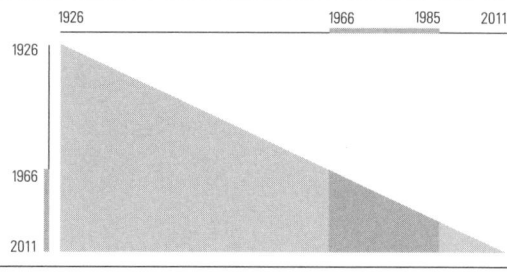

from 1926 to 2011

To the end of	From the beginning of 1966	1967	1968	1969	1970	1971	1972	1973	1974	1975	1976	1977	1978	1979	1980	1981	1982	1983	1984	1985
1966	-10.1																			
1967	5.6	24.0																		
1968	7.4	17.3	11.1																	
1969	3.2	8.0	0.8	-8.5																
1970	3.3	7.0	1.8	-2.5	3.9															
1971	5.1	8.4	4.8	2.8	9.0	14.3														
1972	6.9	10.1	7.5	6.6	12.2	16.6	19.0													
1973	4.0	6.1	3.4	2.0	4.8	5.1	0.8	-14.7												
1974	0.0	1.4	-1.5	-3.4	-2.4	-3.9	-9.3	-20.8	-26.5											
1975	3.3	4.9	2.7	1.5	3.3	3.2	0.6	-4.9	0.5	37.2										
1976	5.0	6.6	4.8	4.1	6.0	6.4	4.9	1.6	7.7	30.4	23.9									
1977	3.9	5.3	3.6	2.8	4.3	4.3	2.8	-0.2	3.8	16.4	7.3	-7.2								
1978	4.1	5.4	3.8	3.2	4.5	4.6	3.3	0.9	4.4	13.9	7.0	-0.5	6.6							
1979	5.1	6.4	5.0	4.5	5.9	6.1	5.1	3.3	6.6	14.8	9.8	5.5	12.4	18.6						
1980	6.7	8.0	6.9	6.6	8.0	8.5	7.8	6.5	10.0	17.6	14.0	11.7	18.8	25.4	32.5					
1981	6.0	7.1	6.0	5.6	6.9	7.2	6.5	5.2	8.0	14.1	10.6	8.1	12.3	14.3	12.2	-4.9				
1982	6.8	8.0	7.0	6.7	8.0	8.3	7.8	6.7	9.4	15.0	12.1	10.3	14.1	16.1	15.3	7.5	21.5			
1983	7.6	8.8	7.9	7.7	8.9	9.3	8.9	8.1	10.7	15.8	13.4	11.9	15.5	17.4	17.0	12.3	22.0	22.6		
1984	7.6	8.6	7.8	7.6	8.8	9.1	8.7	7.9	10.3	14.8	12.6	11.2	14.1	15.4	14.8	10.8	16.5	14.1	6.3	
1985	8.7	9.7	9.0	8.9	10.1	10.5	10.2	9.6	11.9	16.3	14.3	13.3	16.2	17.6	17.5	14.7	20.2	19.7	18.3	31.7
1986	9.1	10.2	9.5	9.4	10.6	11.0	10.8	10.2	12.4	16.5	14.7	13.8	16.5	17.8	17.6	15.3	19.9	19.5	18.4	25.0
1987	8.9	9.9	9.3	9.2	10.3	10.7	10.4	9.9	11.9	15.6	13.9	13.0	15.3	16.3	16.0	13.8	17.3	16.5	15.0	18.1
1988	9.3	10.2	9.6	9.5	10.6	11.0	10.8	10.3	12.2	15.6	14.1	13.3	15.4	16.3	16.1	14.2	17.2	16.5	15.3	17.7
1989	10.1	11.1	10.5	10.5	11.6	12.0	11.8	11.4	13.3	16.6	15.3	14.6	16.7	17.6	17.6	16.0	18.9	18.5	17.9	20.4
1990	9.6	10.5	9.9	9.9	10.8	11.2	11.0	10.6	12.3	15.3	14.0	13.3	15.0	15.8	15.5	13.9	16.2	15.6	14.6	16.1
1991	10.3	11.2	10.7	10.7	11.6	12.0	11.9	11.5	13.2	16.1	14.9	14.4	16.1	16.8	16.7	15.3	17.6	17.2	16.5	18.0
1992	10.2	11.1	10.6	10.5	11.5	11.8	11.7	11.3	12.9	15.6	14.5	13.9	15.5	16.1	16.0	14.7	16.6	16.2	15.5	16.7
1993	10.2	11.0	10.5	10.5	11.4	11.7	11.6	11.3	12.8	15.3	14.2	13.7	15.1	15.7	15.5	14.3	16.1	15.6	14.9	15.9
1994	9.9	10.7	10.2	10.2	11.0	11.3	11.2	10.8	12.2	14.6	13.5	13.0	14.3	14.8	14.5	13.3	14.9	14.3	13.6	14.4
1995	10.7	11.5	11.1	11.1	11.9	12.2	12.1	11.9	13.2	15.6	14.6	14.1	15.5	16.0	15.8	14.8	16.4	16.0	15.4	16.3
1996	11.1	11.9	11.5	11.5	12.3	12.6	12.6	12.3	13.7	15.9	15.0	14.6	15.8	16.4	16.3	15.3	16.8	16.5	16.0	16.9
1997	11.7	12.5	12.1	12.2	13.0	13.3	13.3	13.1	14.4	16.6	15.8	15.4	16.7	17.2	17.1	16.3	17.8	17.5	17.2	18.1
1998	12.2	13.0	12.6	12.7	13.5	13.8	13.8	13.6	14.9	17.1	16.3	16.0	17.2	17.8	17.7	16.9	18.4	18.2	17.9	18.8
1999	12.4	13.2	12.9	12.9	13.7	14.1	14.1	13.9	15.2	17.3	16.5	16.2	17.4	17.9	17.9	17.2	18.5	18.3	18.1	18.9
2000	11.8	12.5	12.1	12.2	12.9	13.2	13.2	13.0	14.2	16.1	15.3	15.0	16.1	16.5	16.4	15.7	16.9	16.6	16.3	16.9
2001	11.0	11.7	11.3	11.4	12.0	12.3	12.2	12.0	13.1	14.9	14.2	13.8	14.8	15.1	15.0	14.2	15.2	14.9	14.5	15.0
2002	10.0	10.6	10.2	10.2	10.8	11.0	10.9	10.7	11.7	13.4	12.6	12.1	13.0	13.3	13.0	12.2	13.1	12.7	12.2	12.5
2003	10.4	11.0	10.7	10.7	11.3	11.5	11.5	11.2	12.2	13.8	13.1	12.7	13.6	13.8	13.6	12.9	13.8	13.4	13.0	13.3
2004	10.4	11.0	10.7	10.7	11.3	11.5	11.4	11.2	12.2	13.7	13.0	12.6	13.5	13.7	13.5	12.8	13.6	13.3	12.9	13.2
2005	10.3	10.9	10.5	10.5	11.1	11.3	11.2	11.0	11.9	13.5	12.7	12.4	13.1	13.4	13.2	12.5	13.3	12.9	12.5	12.8
2006	10.4	11.0	10.7	10.7	11.2	11.4	11.4	11.1	12.0	13.5	12.8	12.5	13.2	13.5	13.3	12.6	13.4	13.0	12.6	12.9
2007	10.3	10.8	10.5	10.5	11.1	11.3	11.2	11.0	11.8	13.3	12.6	12.2	13.0	13.2	13.0	12.3	13.1	12.7	12.3	12.6
2008	8.9	9.4	9.0	9.0	9.5	9.6	9.5	9.2	10.0	11.3	10.6	10.2	10.9	11.0	10.7	10.0	10.6	10.2	9.8	9.9
2009	9.2	9.7	9.4	9.4	9.9	10.0	9.9	9.7	10.5	11.7	11.1	10.7	11.3	11.5	11.2	10.6	11.2	10.8	10.4	10.5
2010	9.4	9.9	9.5	9.5	10.0	10.2	10.0	9.8	10.6	11.8	11.2	10.8	11.4	11.6	11.4	10.7	11.3	10.9	10.5	10.7
2011	9.2	9.7	9.4	9.3	9.8	9.9	9.8	9.6	10.3	11.6	10.9	10.6	11.1	11.3	11.1	10.4	11.0	10.6	10.2	10.4

Table C-1 (page 6 of 6)-a
Large Company Stocks: Total Returns
Rates of Return for all holding periods
Percent per annum compounded annually

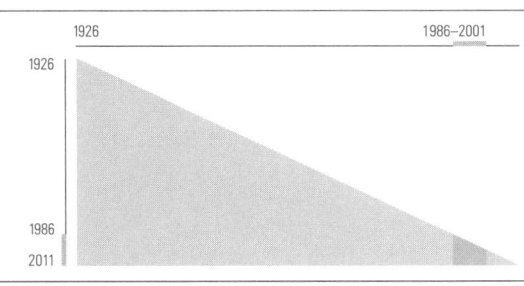

from 1926 to 2011

To the end of	From the beginning of 1986	1987	1988	1989	1990	1991	1992	1993	1994	1995	1996	1997	1998	1999	2000	2001
1986	18.7															
1987	11.8	5.3														
1988	13.4	10.8	16.6													
1989	17.7	17.4	23.9	31.7												
1990	13.2	11.9	14.2	13.0	-3.1											
1991	15.9	15.4	18.0	18.5	12.4	30.5										
1992	14.7	14.0	15.9	15.7	10.8	18.5	7.6									
1993	14.1	13.5	14.9	14.5	10.6	15.6	8.8	10.1								
1994	12.6	11.9	12.8	12.2	8.7	11.9	6.3	5.6	1.3							
1995	14.9	14.5	15.7	15.5	13.1	16.6	13.4	15.3	18.1	37.6						
1996	15.6	15.3	16.5	16.4	14.4	17.6	15.2	17.2	19.7	30.1	23.0					
1997	17.0	16.8	18.1	18.2	16.6	19.8	18.1	20.3	23.0	31.2	28.1	33.4				
1998	17.8	17.8	19.0	19.2	17.9	20.8	19.5	21.6	24.1	30.5	28.2	30.9	28.6			
1999	18.1	18.0	19.1	19.4	18.2	20.9	19.7	21.5	23.6	28.6	26.4	27.6	24.8	21.0		
2000	16.0	15.8	16.7	16.7	15.4	17.5	16.1	17.2	18.3	21.3	18.3	17.2	12.3	4.9	-9.1	
2001	14.0	13.7	14.4	14.2	12.9	14.4	12.9	13.5	14.0	15.9	12.7	10.7	5.7	-1.0	-10.5	-11.9
2002	11.5	11.1	11.5	11.1	9.7	10.8	9.2	9.3	9.3	10.3	6.9	4.4	-0.6	-6.8	-14.6	-17.2
2003	12.4	12.0	12.5	12.2	10.9	12.1	10.7	11.0	11.1	12.2	9.4	7.6	3.8	-0.6	-5.3	-4.1
2004	12.3	12.0	12.4	12.1	10.9	12.0	10.7	11.0	11.0	12.1	9.5	8.0	4.8	1.3	-2.3	-0.5
2005	11.9	11.6	12.0	11.7	10.5	11.5	10.3	10.5	10.5	11.4	9.1	7.6	4.8	1.8	-1.1	0.5
2006	12.1	11.8	12.2	11.9	10.9	11.8	10.6	10.9	10.9	11.8	9.7	8.4	6.0	3.4	1.1	2.9
2007	11.8	11.5	11.8	11.6	10.5	11.4	10.3	10.5	10.5	11.3	9.3	8.2	5.9	3.7	1.7	3.3
2008	9.1	8.6	8.8	8.4	7.3	7.9	6.7	6.7	6.5	6.8	4.8	3.4	1.0	-1.4	-3.6	-2.9
2009	9.7	9.4	9.5	9.2	8.2	8.8	7.7	7.8	7.6	8.0	6.2	5.0	2.9	0.9	-0.9	0.0
2010	9.9	9.6	9.8	9.5	8.5	9.1	8.1	8.1	8.0	8.5	6.8	5.7	3.8	2.0	0.4	1.4
2011	9.6	9.3	9.5	9.2	8.2	8.8	7.8	7.8	7.7	8.1	6.5	5.5	3.7	2.0	0.6	1.5

Table C-1 (page 6 of 6)-b
Large Company Stocks: Total Returns
Rates of Return for all holding periods
Percent per annum compounded annually

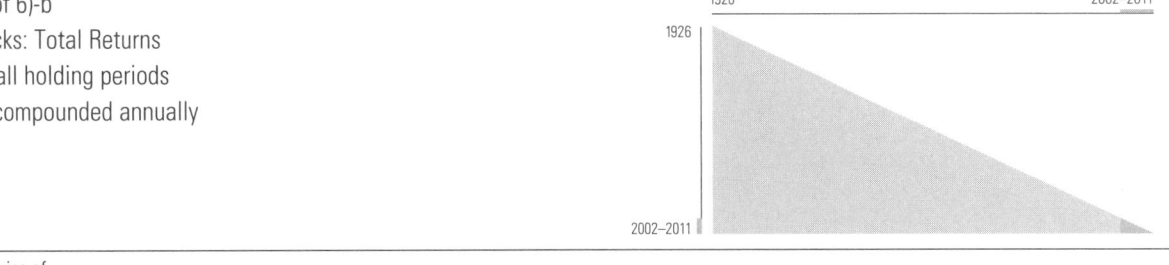

from 1926 to 2011

To the end of	From the beginning of 2002	2003	2004	2005	2006	2007	2008	2009	2010	2011
2002	-22.1									
2003	0.1	28.7								
2004	3.6	19.5	10.9							
2005	3.9	14.4	7.9	4.9						
2006	6.2	14.7	10.4	10.2	15.8					
2007	6.1	12.8	9.2	8.6	10.5	5.5				
2008	-1.5	2.4	-2.2	-5.2	-8.4	-18.5	-37.0			
2009	1.6	5.5	2.1	0.4	-0.7	-5.6	-10.7	26.5		
2010	3.0	6.7	3.9	2.7	2.3	-0.8	-2.9	20.6	15.1	
2011	2.9	6.2	3.6	2.6	2.3	-0.2	-1.6	14.1	8.4	2.1

Table C-2 (page 1 of 6)

Small Company Stocks: Total Returns
Rates of Return for all holding periods
Percent per annum compounded annually

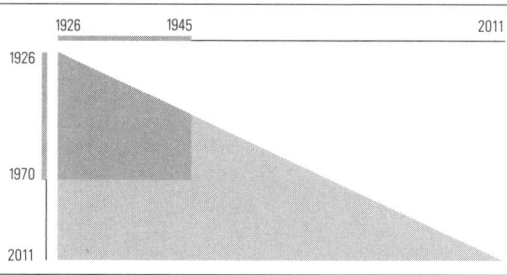

from 1926 to 2011

To the end of	From the beginning of 1926	1927	1928	1929	1930	1931	1932	1933	1934	1935	1936	1937	1938	1939	1940	1941	1942	1943	1944	1945
1926	0.3																			
1927	10.7	22.1																		
1928	19.6	30.6	39.7																	
1929	-4.5	-6.0	-17.6	-51.4																
1930	-12.4	-15.4	-25.1	-45.1	-38.1															
1931	-20.2	-23.7	-32.2	-46.7	-44.3	-49.8														
1932	-18.2	-21.0	-27.5	-38.5	-33.5	-31.1	-5.4													
1933	-6.3	-7.2	-11.4	-19.1	-8.1	4.9	51.6	142.9												
1934	-3.3	-3.8	-7.0	-13.1	-2.4	9.4	41.9	73.7	24.2											
1935	0.3	0.3	-2.1	-6.9	3.7	15.0	41.4	61.7	32.0	40.2										
1936	5.0	5.5	3.7	0.0	10.8	22.1	45.8	62.5	42.1	52.0	64.8									
1937	-2.7	-3.0	-5.2	-9.2	-1.9	4.8	18.5	24.0	4.8	-1.0	-16.8	-58.0								
1938	-0.4	-0.4	-2.3	-5.7	1.5	8.0	20.4	25.4	9.9	6.5	-2.8	-25.3	32.8							
1939	-0.3	-0.4	-2.1	-5.2	1.4	7.1	17.7	21.5	8.2	5.3	-2.0	-17.6	15.4	0.3						
1940	-0.7	-0.7	-2.3	-5.2	0.8	5.8	14.9	17.8	6.2	3.5	-2.6	-14.6	8.1	-2.4	-5.2					
1941	-1.2	-1.3	-2.8	-5.5	-0.1	4.4	12.3	14.4	4.2	1.6	-3.7	-13.5	3.6	-4.7	-7.1	-9.0				
1942	1.0	1.1	-0.2	-2.6	2.8	7.2	14.9	17.1	8.0	6.2	2.0	-5.8	10.7	5.8	7.6	14.7	44.5			
1943	4.6	4.8	3.9	1.8	7.3	12.0	19.7	22.3	14.2	13.1	10.1	4.0	21.0	18.7	23.8	35.3	65.0	88.4		
1944	6.7	7.1	6.3	4.5	9.9	14.5	22.0	24.7	17.3	16.7	14.3	9.2	25.2	23.9	29.3	39.7	61.1	70.2	53.7	
1945	9.4	9.9	9.2	7.6	13.1	17.8	25.2	27.9	21.2	21.0	19.2	15.0	30.4	30.1	35.8	45.9	64.2	71.3	63.4	73.6
1946	8.3	8.7	8.0	6.5	11.5	15.7	22.3	24.5	18.3	17.8	16.0	12.0	24.9	23.9	27.7	34.2	45.0	45.2	33.1	23.9
1947	7.9	8.3	7.6	6.2	10.9	14.7	20.8	22.8	17.0	16.4	14.6	10.9	22.2	21.1	24.0	28.8	36.5	35.0	24.2	15.7
1948	7.5	7.8	7.2	5.7	10.2	13.7	19.3	21.1	15.6	15.0	13.3	9.8	19.8	18.6	20.8	24.5	30.2	28.0	18.4	11.0
1949	7.9	8.3	7.7	6.4	10.6	14.0	19.4	21.0	15.8	15.3	13.7	10.5	19.8	18.7	20.7	24.0	28.8	26.7	18.6	12.7
1950	9.0	9.4	8.9	7.7	11.8	15.2	20.3	21.9	17.1	16.7	15.2	12.3	21.2	20.2	22.2	25.4	29.9	28.2	21.3	16.6
1951	9.0	9.3	8.8	7.7	11.6	14.8	19.7	21.1	16.5	16.1	14.8	12.0	20.1	19.2	21.0	23.7	27.5	25.7	19.6	15.3
1952	8.8	9.1	8.6	7.5	11.2	14.2	18.8	20.2	15.8	15.3	14.0	11.4	18.9	18.0	19.5	21.8	25.1	23.3	17.6	13.7
1953	8.2	8.5	8.0	6.9	10.4	13.3	17.5	18.7	14.6	14.1	12.8	10.3	17.2	16.2	17.4	19.3	22.1	20.2	14.9	11.3
1954	9.7	10.0	9.6	8.6	12.1	14.9	19.1	20.4	16.4	16.0	14.9	12.6	19.3	18.6	19.9	21.9	24.7	23.1	18.5	15.4
1955	10.0	10.3	9.9	9.0	12.4	15.1	19.2	20.4	16.6	16.3	15.2	13.0	19.4	18.7	19.9	21.8	24.4	22.9	18.6	15.9
1956	9.8	10.1	9.7	8.8	12.1	14.7	18.5	19.7	16.0	15.7	14.6	12.6	18.6	17.8	18.9	20.6	22.9	21.5	17.5	14.9
1957	8.9	9.2	8.8	7.9	11.0	13.4	17.1	18.1	14.6	14.2	13.1	11.1	16.6	15.8	16.8	18.2	20.1	18.7	14.8	12.3
1958	10.3	10.7	10.3	9.4	12.5	15.0	18.6	19.6	16.2	15.9	15.0	13.1	18.6	17.9	18.9	20.4	22.4	21.1	17.6	15.4
1959	10.5	10.8	10.5	9.7	12.7	15.0	18.5	19.5	16.3	15.9	15.0	13.2	18.5	17.8	18.8	20.2	22.1	20.9	17.6	15.5
1960	10.1	10.4	10.0	9.2	12.1	14.4	17.7	18.6	15.5	15.1	14.2	12.5	17.4	16.8	17.6	18.9	20.6	19.4	16.2	14.2
1961	10.6	10.9	10.6	9.9	12.7	14.9	18.1	19.0	16.0	15.7	14.9	13.2	18.0	17.4	18.2	19.5	21.1	20.0	17.0	15.2
1962	10.0	10.2	9.9	9.1	11.9	13.9	17.0	17.8	14.9	14.6	13.8	12.1	16.6	16.0	16.7	17.8	19.3	18.2	15.3	13.5
1963	10.3	10.6	10.3	9.5	12.2	14.2	17.2	18.0	15.2	14.9	14.1	12.5	16.9	16.3	17.0	18.1	19.5	18.4	15.7	14.0
1964	10.6	10.9	10.6	9.9	12.5	14.5	17.4	18.2	15.5	15.2	14.4	12.9	17.1	16.6	17.3	18.3	19.7	18.6	16.1	14.4
1965	11.3	11.6	11.3	10.7	13.2	15.2	18.0	18.8	16.2	16.0	15.2	13.8	17.9	17.4	18.1	19.2	20.5	19.6	17.1	15.6
1966	10.8	11.1	10.8	10.2	12.6	14.5	17.2	18.0	15.4	15.2	14.4	13.0	17.0	16.4	17.1	18.0	19.3	18.3	16.0	14.5
1967	12.2	12.5	12.2	11.6	14.1	16.0	18.7	19.5	17.0	16.8	16.1	14.8	18.7	18.3	19.0	20.0	21.3	20.4	18.2	16.9
1968	12.7	13.0	12.8	12.2	14.6	16.5	19.1	19.9	17.5	17.3	16.7	15.4	19.3	18.8	19.5	20.5	21.8	21.0	18.9	17.6
1969	11.6	11.9	11.7	11.1	13.4	15.2	17.7	18.4	16.1	15.8	15.2	13.9	17.5	17.1	17.7	18.6	19.7	18.9	16.8	15.5
1970	10.9	11.1	10.9	10.3	12.5	14.2	16.6	17.3	15.0	14.7	14.1	12.9	16.3	15.8	16.3	17.1	18.2	17.3	15.3	14.0

Table C-2 (page 2 of 6)

Small Company Stocks: Total Returns
Rates of Return for all holding periods
Percent per annum compounded annually

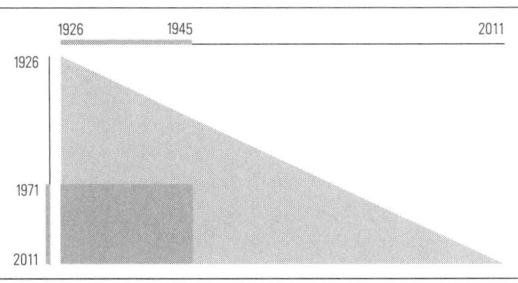

from 1926 to 2011

To the end of	From the beginning of 1926	1927	1928	1929	1930	1931	1932	1933	1934	1935	1936	1937	1938	1939	1940	1941	1942	1943	1944	1945
1971	11.0	11.2	11.0	10.4	12.6	14.3	16.6	17.3	15.0	14.8	14.2	13.0	16.3	15.8	16.4	17.1	18.1	17.3	15.3	14.1
1972	10.9	11.1	10.9	10.3	12.4	14.0	16.3	16.9	14.7	14.5	13.9	12.7	15.9	15.5	16.0	16.7	17.6	16.8	14.9	13.7
1973	9.8	10.0	9.7	9.1	11.2	12.7	14.9	15.4	13.3	13.0	12.4	11.2	14.3	13.8	14.2	14.9	15.7	14.9	13.0	11.8
1974	9.1	9.3	9.0	8.4	10.4	11.8	13.9	14.4	12.3	12.1	11.4	10.3	13.2	12.7	13.1	13.7	14.4	13.6	11.7	10.6
1975	9.8	10.0	9.8	9.2	11.1	12.6	14.7	15.2	13.2	12.9	12.3	11.2	14.1	13.6	14.0	14.6	15.4	14.6	12.8	11.7
1976	10.6	10.8	10.6	10.0	12.0	13.4	15.5	16.0	14.0	13.8	13.2	12.2	15.0	14.6	15.0	15.6	16.4	15.7	14.0	12.9
1977	10.8	11.1	10.9	10.3	12.2	13.7	15.7	16.2	14.3	14.1	13.5	12.5	15.3	14.9	15.3	15.9	16.7	16.0	14.3	13.3
1978	11.1	11.3	11.1	10.6	12.4	13.9	15.9	16.4	14.5	14.3	13.7	12.7	15.5	15.1	15.5	16.1	16.8	16.2	14.6	13.6
1979	11.6	11.8	11.6	11.1	13.0	14.4	16.4	16.9	15.0	14.8	14.3	13.4	16.1	15.7	16.1	16.7	17.5	16.8	15.3	14.3
1980	12.1	12.3	12.1	11.6	13.5	14.9	16.8	17.3	15.5	15.3	14.8	13.9	16.6	16.2	16.6	17.2	18.0	17.4	15.9	15.0
1981	12.1	12.3	12.1	11.7	13.5	14.8	16.8	17.3	15.5	15.3	14.8	13.9	16.5	16.2	16.6	17.2	17.9	17.3	15.8	14.9
1982	12.4	12.6	12.4	12.0	13.7	15.1	17.0	17.5	15.7	15.6	15.1	14.2	16.8	16.4	16.8	17.4	18.1	17.5	16.1	15.3
1983	12.8	13.0	12.9	12.4	14.2	15.5	17.4	17.9	16.2	16.0	15.6	14.7	17.2	16.9	17.3	17.9	18.6	18.0	16.7	15.8
1984	12.4	12.6	12.5	12.0	13.8	15.0	16.9	17.3	15.7	15.5	15.0	14.2	16.6	16.3	16.7	17.3	17.9	17.4	16.0	15.2
1985	12.6	12.8	12.7	12.3	13.9	15.2	17.0	17.5	15.8	15.7	15.2	14.4	16.8	16.5	16.9	17.4	18.1	17.5	16.2	15.4
1986	12.5	12.7	12.6	12.2	13.8	15.1	16.8	17.3	15.7	15.5	15.1	14.2	16.6	16.3	16.6	17.2	17.8	17.3	16.0	15.2
1987	12.1	12.3	12.2	11.8	13.4	14.6	16.3	16.7	15.1	15.0	14.5	13.7	16.0	15.7	16.0	16.5	17.2	16.6	15.4	14.6
1988	12.3	12.5	12.3	11.9	13.5	14.7	16.4	16.8	15.3	15.1	14.7	13.9	16.1	15.8	16.2	16.7	17.3	16.8	15.5	14.8
1989	12.2	12.5	12.3	11.9	13.5	14.6	16.3	16.7	15.2	15.0	14.6	13.8	16.0	15.7	16.0	16.5	17.1	16.6	15.4	14.7
1990	11.6	11.8	11.7	11.3	12.8	13.9	15.5	15.9	14.4	14.2	13.8	13.0	15.2	14.9	15.2	15.6	16.2	15.6	14.5	13.7
1991	12.1	12.3	12.1	11.7	13.2	14.4	15.9	16.3	14.9	14.7	14.3	13.5	15.7	15.4	15.7	16.1	16.7	16.2	15.0	14.3
1992	12.2	12.4	12.3	11.9	13.4	14.5	16.1	16.5	15.0	14.9	14.5	13.7	15.8	15.5	15.8	16.3	16.8	16.3	15.2	14.5
1993	12.4	12.5	12.4	12.0	13.5	14.6	16.1	16.5	15.1	15.0	14.6	13.8	15.9	15.6	15.9	16.3	16.9	16.4	15.3	14.6
1994	12.2	12.4	12.3	11.9	13.3	14.4	15.9	16.3	14.9	14.8	14.4	13.6	15.6	15.4	15.7	16.1	16.6	16.1	15.0	14.4
1995	12.5	12.7	12.6	12.2	13.6	14.7	16.2	16.6	15.2	15.1	14.7	14.0	15.9	15.7	16.0	16.4	16.9	16.5	15.4	14.7
1996	12.6	12.8	12.6	12.3	13.7	14.7	16.2	16.6	15.2	15.1	14.7	14.0	16.0	15.7	16.0	16.4	16.9	16.5	15.4	14.8
1997	12.7	12.9	12.8	12.4	13.8	14.9	16.3	16.7	15.3	15.2	14.8	14.2	16.1	15.8	16.1	16.5	17.0	16.6	15.6	14.9
1998	12.4	12.6	12.5	12.1	13.5	14.5	15.9	16.3	15.0	14.8	14.5	13.8	15.7	15.4	15.7	16.1	16.6	16.1	15.1	14.5
1999	12.6	12.8	12.7	12.3	13.7	14.7	16.1	16.5	15.2	15.0	14.7	14.0	15.9	15.6	15.9	16.3	16.8	16.3	15.3	14.7
2000	12.4	12.6	12.4	12.1	13.4	14.4	15.8	16.1	14.9	14.7	14.4	13.7	15.5	15.3	15.5	15.9	16.4	16.0	15.0	14.4
2001	12.5	12.7	12.6	12.2	13.6	14.5	15.9	16.2	15.0	14.8	14.5	13.9	15.6	15.4	15.7	16.0	16.5	16.1	15.1	14.5
2002	12.1	12.3	12.2	11.9	13.1	14.1	15.4	15.7	14.5	14.4	14.0	13.4	15.1	14.9	15.1	15.5	15.9	15.5	14.6	14.0
2003	12.7	12.8	12.7	12.4	13.7	14.6	15.9	16.3	15.1	14.9	14.6	14.0	15.7	15.5	15.7	16.1	16.6	16.1	15.2	14.6
2004	12.7	12.9	12.8	12.5	13.7	14.7	16.0	16.3	15.1	15.0	14.7	14.0	15.8	15.5	15.8	16.1	16.6	16.2	15.3	14.7
2005	12.6	12.8	12.7	12.4	13.6	14.6	15.8	16.2	15.0	14.8	14.5	13.9	15.6	15.4	15.6	16.0	16.4	16.0	15.1	14.6
2006	12.7	12.9	12.7	12.4	13.7	14.6	15.8	16.2	15.0	14.9	14.5	14.0	15.6	15.4	15.6	16.0	16.4	16.0	15.1	14.6
2007	12.5	12.6	12.5	12.2	13.4	14.3	15.5	15.8	14.7	14.6	14.2	13.7	15.3	15.0	15.3	15.6	16.0	15.6	14.8	14.2
2008	11.7	11.8	11.7	11.4	12.6	13.4	14.6	14.9	13.8	13.6	13.3	12.7	14.3	14.1	14.3	14.6	15.0	14.6	13.7	13.2
2009	11.9	12.0	11.9	11.6	12.7	13.6	14.8	15.1	14.0	13.8	13.5	12.9	14.5	14.3	14.5	14.8	15.2	14.8	13.9	13.4
2010	12.1	12.2	12.1	11.8	13.0	13.8	15.0	15.3	14.2	14.0	13.7	13.2	14.7	14.5	14.7	15.0	15.4	15.0	14.2	13.7
2011	11.9	12.0	11.9	11.6	12.7	13.6	14.7	15.0	13.9	13.8	13.5	12.9	14.4	14.2	14.4	14.7	15.1	14.7	13.9	13.4

Table C-2 (page 3 of 6)

Small Company Stocks: Total Returns
Rates of Return for all holding periods
Percent per annum compounded annually

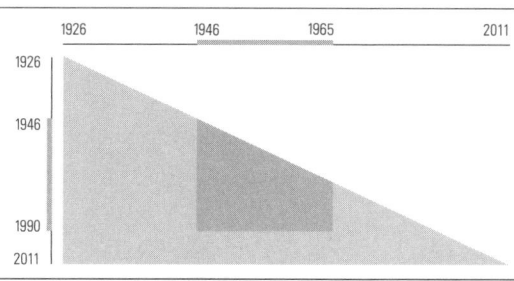

from 1926 to 2011

To the end of	From the beginning of 1946	1947	1948	1949	1950	1951	1952	1953	1954	1955	1956	1957	1958	1959	1960	1961	1962	1963	1964	1965
1946	-11.6																			
1947	-5.6	0.9																		
1948	-4.4	-0.6	-2.1																	
1949	1.1	5.8	8.3	19.7																
1950	7.7	13.2	17.6	28.9	38.7															
1951	7.7	12.1	15.1	21.4	22.3	7.8														
1952	7.0	10.5	12.6	16.6	15.5	5.4	3.0													
1953	5.3	7.9	9.1	11.5	9.6	1.3	-1.8	-6.5												
1954	10.3	13.4	15.3	18.5	18.3	13.6	15.7	22.5	60.6											
1955	11.3	14.2	15.9	18.8	18.6	15.0	16.8	21.8	39.1	20.4										
1956	10.6	13.1	14.6	16.9	16.5	13.1	14.2	17.2	26.3	12.1	4.3									
1957	8.3	10.3	11.3	12.9	12.0	8.7	8.8	10.0	14.6	2.4	-5.6	-14.6								
1958	11.8	14.0	15.3	17.2	17.0	14.5	15.5	17.7	23.2	15.3	13.7	18.7	64.9							
1959	12.2	14.2	15.4	17.2	16.9	14.7	15.6	17.5	22.1	15.5	14.4	17.9	38.5	16.4						
1960	11.1	12.9	13.9	15.3	14.9	12.8	13.3	14.7	18.1	12.2	10.6	12.2	22.9	6.1	-3.3					
1961	12.3	14.1	15.1	16.5	16.2	14.4	15.1	16.5	19.7	14.8	13.9	15.9	25.1	14.1	13.0	32.1				
1962	10.7	12.2	13.0	14.2	13.8	11.9	12.3	13.3	15.7	11.1	9.8	10.7	16.6	7.0	4.0	7.9	-11.9			
1963	11.4	12.9	13.7	14.8	14.5	12.8	13.2	14.2	16.5	12.4	11.4	12.5	17.8	10.1	8.6	12.9	4.3	23.6		
1964	12.0	13.4	14.2	15.3	15.0	13.5	14.0	14.9	17.1	13.5	12.7	13.8	18.6	12.2	11.4	15.4	10.4	23.5	23.5	
1965	13.3	14.8	15.6	16.7	16.6	15.2	15.8	16.8	19.0	15.8	15.3	16.6	21.3	16.0	16.0	20.3	17.5	29.3	32.3	41.8
1966	12.2	13.6	14.3	15.3	15.0	13.7	14.1	14.9	16.7	13.7	13.1	14.0	17.7	12.9	12.4	15.2	12.1	19.1	17.6	14.8
1967	14.8	16.2	17.0	18.1	18.0	16.9	17.5	18.6	20.6	18.0	17.8	19.1	23.1	19.1	19.5	23.2	21.7	29.9	31.5	34.3
1968	15.6	17.0	17.9	19.0	18.9	17.9	18.5	19.6	21.6	19.2	19.1	20.4	24.2	20.7	21.2	24.7	23.7	30.9	32.4	34.7
1969	13.5	14.8	15.5	16.4	16.2	15.1	15.6	16.3	17.9	15.5	15.2	16.1	19.1	15.6	15.5	17.8	16.2	20.8	20.4	19.8
1970	12.1	13.2	13.8	14.6	14.3	13.2	13.5	14.1	15.5	13.1	12.7	13.3	15.8	12.4	12.1	13.7	11.8	15.2	14.1	12.6
1971	12.3	13.4	13.9	14.7	14.4	13.4	13.7	14.3	15.5	13.3	12.9	13.5	15.8	12.7	12.4	14.0	12.3	15.4	14.4	13.1
1972	12.0	13.0	13.5	14.2	14.0	13.0	13.2	13.8	14.9	12.8	12.4	12.9	15.0	12.1	11.8	13.1	11.6	14.2	13.2	12.0
1973	10.1	11.0	11.4	11.9	11.6	10.6	10.7	11.1	12.0	9.9	9.4	9.7	11.4	8.5	8.0	8.9	7.2	9.1	7.8	6.2
1974	8.9	9.7	10.0	10.5	10.2	9.1	9.2	9.4	10.3	8.2	7.6	7.8	9.3	6.5	5.9	6.6	4.8	6.3	4.9	3.2
1975	10.1	10.9	11.3	11.8	11.5	10.6	10.7	11.0	11.9	10.0	9.5	9.8	11.3	8.8	8.3	9.2	7.7	9.3	8.2	6.9
1976	11.4	12.2	12.6	13.2	13.0	12.1	12.3	12.7	13.6	11.8	11.4	11.8	13.4	11.0	10.7	11.7	10.4	12.2	11.4	10.4
1977	11.8	12.6	13.1	13.6	13.4	12.6	12.7	13.1	14.1	12.4	12.0	12.4	13.9	11.8	11.5	12.4	11.3	13.1	12.3	11.5
1978	12.1	13.0	13.4	13.9	13.7	12.9	13.1	13.5	14.4	12.8	12.5	12.9	14.4	12.3	12.1	13.0	12.0	13.7	13.1	12.3
1979	12.9	13.8	14.2	14.8	14.6	13.9	14.1	14.5	15.4	13.9	13.6	14.1	15.6	13.6	13.5	14.5	13.5	15.3	14.8	14.2
1980	13.6	14.5	14.9	15.5	15.4	14.6	14.9	15.3	16.2	14.8	14.6	15.0	16.5	14.7	14.6	15.6	14.8	16.5	16.1	15.6
1981	13.6	14.5	14.9	15.4	15.3	14.6	14.9	15.3	16.2	14.8	14.6	15.0	16.4	14.7	14.6	15.5	14.8	16.4	16.0	15.5
1982	14.0	14.8	15.2	15.8	15.7	15.0	15.3	15.7	16.5	15.2	15.0	15.5	16.9	15.2	15.1	16.1	15.4	16.9	16.6	16.2
1983	14.6	15.4	15.9	16.4	16.3	15.7	16.0	16.4	17.2	16.0	15.8	16.3	17.7	16.1	16.1	17.0	16.4	17.9	17.6	17.3
1984	14.0	14.8	15.2	15.7	15.6	15.0	15.2	15.6	16.4	15.1	15.0	15.4	16.7	15.1	15.1	15.9	15.2	16.7	16.3	16.0
1985	14.3	15.0	15.4	15.9	15.8	15.2	15.5	15.9	16.6	15.4	15.3	15.7	16.9	15.5	15.4	16.2	15.6	17.0	16.7	16.4
1986	14.1	14.8	15.2	15.7	15.6	15.0	15.2	15.6	16.3	15.2	15.0	15.4	16.6	15.1	15.1	15.9	15.3	16.6	16.3	15.9
1987	13.5	14.2	14.5	15.0	14.8	14.3	14.4	14.8	15.5	14.3	14.1	14.5	15.6	14.2	14.1	14.8	14.2	15.4	15.1	14.7
1988	13.7	14.4	14.7	15.2	15.0	14.5	14.7	15.0	15.7	14.6	14.4	14.7	15.8	14.5	14.4	15.1	14.5	15.7	15.4	15.0
1989	13.6	14.3	14.6	15.0	14.9	14.4	14.5	14.9	15.5	14.4	14.3	14.6	15.7	14.3	14.3	14.9	14.4	15.5	15.2	14.8
1990	12.7	13.3	13.6	14.0	13.9	13.3	13.4	13.7	14.3	13.3	13.1	13.3	14.3	13.0	12.9	13.5	12.9	13.9	13.5	13.2

Table C-2 (page 4 of 6)
Small Company Stocks: Total Returns
Rates of Return for all holding periods
Percent per annum compounded annually

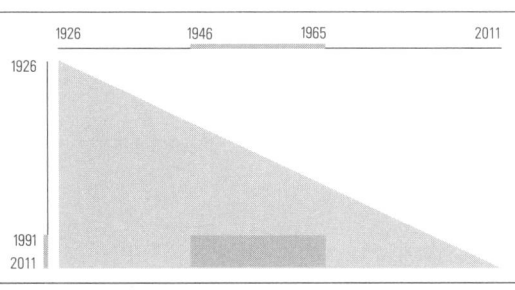

from 1926 to 2011

To the end of	From the beginning of 1946	1947	1948	1949	1950	1951	1952	1953	1954	1955	1956	1957	1958	1959	1960	1961	1962	1963	1964	1965
1991	13.3	13.9	14.2	14.6	14.5	14.0	14.1	14.4	15.0	14.0	13.8	14.1	15.1	13.8	13.8	14.4	13.8	14.8	14.5	14.2
1992	13.5	14.1	14.4	14.8	14.7	14.2	14.3	14.6	15.2	14.2	14.1	14.4	15.3	14.1	14.0	14.6	14.1	15.1	14.8	14.5
1993	13.6	14.2	14.5	14.9	14.8	14.3	14.5	14.8	15.4	14.4	14.3	14.5	15.5	14.3	14.2	14.8	14.3	15.3	15.0	14.7
1994	13.4	14.0	14.3	14.7	14.6	14.1	14.2	14.5	15.1	14.1	14.0	14.2	15.1	14.0	13.9	14.5	14.0	14.9	14.6	14.3
1995	13.8	14.4	14.7	15.1	15.0	14.5	14.6	14.9	15.5	14.6	14.4	14.7	15.6	14.5	14.4	15.0	14.5	15.4	15.2	14.9
1996	13.9	14.4	14.7	15.1	15.0	14.6	14.7	15.0	15.5	14.6	14.5	14.8	15.6	14.6	14.5	15.1	14.6	15.5	15.3	15.0
1997	14.0	14.6	14.9	15.3	15.2	14.7	14.9	15.2	15.7	14.8	14.7	15.0	15.8	14.8	14.7	15.3	14.8	15.7	15.5	15.2
1998	13.6	14.1	14.4	14.8	14.7	14.2	14.4	14.6	15.1	14.3	14.1	14.4	15.2	14.2	14.1	14.6	14.2	15.0	14.8	14.5
1999	13.9	14.4	14.7	15.0	15.0	14.5	14.7	14.9	15.4	14.6	14.5	14.7	15.5	14.5	14.5	15.0	14.5	15.4	15.1	14.9
2000	13.5	14.0	14.3	14.7	14.6	14.1	14.3	14.5	15.0	14.2	14.0	14.3	15.0	14.1	14.0	14.5	14.0	14.8	14.6	14.4
2001	13.7	14.2	14.5	14.8	14.7	14.3	14.4	14.7	15.1	14.3	14.2	14.4	15.2	14.2	14.2	14.7	14.3	15.0	14.8	14.6
2002	13.1	13.6	13.9	14.2	14.1	13.7	13.8	14.0	14.5	13.7	13.5	13.8	14.5	13.5	13.5	13.9	13.5	14.2	14.0	13.7
2003	13.8	14.3	14.6	14.9	14.8	14.4	14.6	14.8	15.3	14.5	14.4	14.6	15.3	14.4	14.4	14.8	14.4	15.2	15.0	14.8
2004	13.9	14.4	14.7	15.0	14.9	14.5	14.6	14.9	15.3	14.6	14.4	14.7	15.4	14.5	14.5	14.9	14.5	15.2	15.0	14.8
2005	13.8	14.3	14.5	14.8	14.7	14.3	14.5	14.7	15.1	14.4	14.3	14.5	15.2	14.3	14.3	14.7	14.3	15.0	14.8	14.6
2006	13.8	14.3	14.5	14.8	14.7	14.4	14.5	14.7	15.2	14.4	14.3	14.5	15.2	14.3	14.3	14.7	14.4	15.0	14.8	14.6
2007	13.5	13.9	14.2	14.5	14.4	14.0	14.1	14.3	14.7	14.0	13.9	14.1	14.7	13.9	13.9	14.2	13.9	14.5	14.3	14.1
2008	12.4	12.9	13.1	13.3	13.2	12.8	12.9	13.1	13.5	12.8	12.6	12.8	13.4	12.6	12.5	12.9	12.5	13.1	12.8	12.6
2009	12.6	13.1	13.3	13.6	13.5	13.1	13.2	13.4	13.7	13.0	12.9	13.1	13.7	12.9	12.8	13.1	12.8	13.4	13.2	12.9
2010	12.9	13.3	13.6	13.8	13.7	13.4	13.5	13.6	14.0	13.3	13.2	13.4	14.0	13.2	13.1	13.5	13.1	13.7	13.5	13.3
2011	12.7	13.1	13.3	13.5	13.4	13.1	13.2	13.3	13.7	13.0	12.9	13.1	13.6	12.9	12.8	13.1	12.8	13.3	13.1	12.9

Table C-2 (page 5 of 6)
Small Company Stocks: Total Returns
Rates of Return for all holding periods
Percent per annum compounded annually

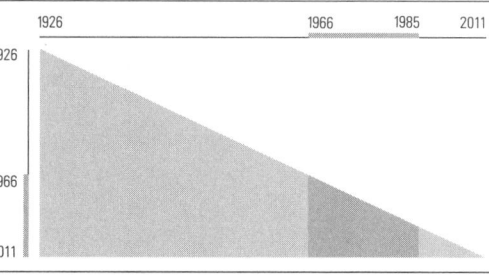

from 1926 to 2011

To the end of	From the beginning of 1966	1967	1968	1969	1970	1971	1972	1973	1974	1975	1976	1977	1978	1979	1980	1981	1982	1983	1984	1985
1966	-7.0																			
1967	30.7	83.6																		
1968	32.4	58.0	36.0																	
1969	14.8	23.2	0.9	-25.1																
1970	7.5	11.5	-5.6	-21.3	-17.4															
1971	9.0	12.5	-0.5	-10.3	-1.9	16.5														
1972	8.3	11.1	0.5	-6.9	0.2	10.3	4.4													
1973	2.4	3.8	-5.6	-12.3	-8.7	-5.6	-15.1	-30.9												
1974	-0.4	0.5	-7.8	-13.6	-11.1	-9.4	-16.7	-25.6	-19.9											
1975	4.0	5.3	-1.8	-6.3	-2.7	0.6	-3.1	-5.4	10.6	52.8										
1976	8.0	9.6	3.5	0.0	4.2	8.4	6.8	7.4	24.4	55.1	57.4									
1977	9.3	10.9	5.5	2.6	6.7	10.6	9.7	10.8	24.6	44.5	40.5	25.4								
1978	10.4	11.9	7.0	4.5	8.4	12.2	11.6	12.8	24.4	38.9	34.6	24.4	23.5							
1979	12.4	14.1	9.7	7.5	11.5	15.3	15.1	16.7	27.4	39.8	36.7	30.5	33.1	43.5						
1980	14.1	15.8	11.7	9.9	13.8	17.5	17.6	19.4	29.1	39.8	37.4	32.8	35.3	41.7	39.9					
1981	14.1	15.6	11.9	10.2	13.8	17.2	17.3	18.8	27.1	35.8	33.1	28.7	29.6	31.7	26.2	13.9				
1982	14.9	16.4	12.9	11.4	14.9	18.1	18.2	19.7	27.2	34.8	32.4	28.6	29.3	30.8	26.8	20.7	28.0			
1983	16.1	17.6	14.4	13.1	16.5	19.6	19.9	21.4	28.4	35.3	33.3	30.1	31.0	32.5	29.9	26.7	33.7	39.7		
1984	14.8	16.1	13.0	11.7	14.8	17.5	17.6	18.7	24.7	30.4	28.1	24.8	24.8	25.0	21.6	17.4	18.6	14.2	-6.7	
1985	15.3	16.6	13.7	12.5	15.4	18.0	18.1	19.2	24.7	29.9	27.8	24.8	24.8	24.9	22.1	18.8	20.1	17.6	7.9	24.7
1986	14.8	16.1	13.3	12.1	14.8	17.2	17.3	18.3	23.2	27.8	25.7	22.9	22.6	22.5	19.8	16.7	17.3	14.8	7.5	15.4
1987	13.6	14.7	12.0	10.9	13.3	15.5	15.4	16.2	20.6	24.4	22.3	19.6	19.0	18.5	15.7	12.6	12.4	9.5	3.0	6.5
1988	14.0	15.1	12.5	11.5	13.8	15.9	15.8	16.6	20.7	24.3	22.4	19.8	19.3	18.9	16.5	13.8	13.8	11.6	6.7	10.4
1989	13.8	14.8	12.4	11.4	13.6	15.6	15.5	16.2	20.0	23.3	21.5	19.1	18.5	18.1	15.8	13.4	13.4	11.4	7.3	10.3
1990	12.2	13.0	10.7	9.6	11.7	13.3	13.2	13.7	17.1	19.9	18.0	15.6	14.8	14.1	11.8	9.3	8.8	6.6	2.6	4.2
1991	13.3	14.2	11.9	11.0	13.0	14.7	14.6	15.1	18.5	21.2	19.5	17.3	16.7	16.2	14.2	12.1	12.0	10.3	7.1	9.2
1992	13.6	14.5	12.4	11.5	13.4	15.1	15.0	15.5	18.7	21.3	19.7	17.7	17.2	16.7	14.9	13.0	13.0	11.6	8.8	10.9
1993	13.9	14.7	12.7	11.8	13.7	15.3	15.3	15.8	18.8	21.3	19.8	17.9	17.4	17.0	15.3	13.6	13.6	12.4	10.0	12.0
1994	13.5	14.3	12.3	11.5	13.3	14.8	14.7	15.2	18.0	20.3	18.8	17.0	16.5	16.1	14.5	12.8	12.8	11.6	9.3	11.1
1995	14.1	14.9	13.0	12.3	14.0	15.5	15.5	16.0	18.7	21.0	19.6	17.8	17.4	17.1	15.6	14.2	14.2	13.2	11.2	13.0
1996	14.2	15.0	13.2	12.4	14.1	15.6	15.5	16.0	18.7	20.8	19.5	17.8	17.5	17.1	15.7	14.4	14.4	13.5	11.7	13.4
1997	14.5	15.3	13.5	12.8	14.4	15.8	15.8	16.3	18.8	20.9	19.6	18.1	17.7	17.4	16.1	14.9	14.9	14.1	12.5	14.1
1998	13.8	14.5	12.8	12.1	13.6	14.9	14.9	15.3	17.7	19.6	18.3	16.8	16.4	16.0	14.8	13.5	13.5	12.6	11.0	12.4
1999	14.2	14.9	13.3	12.6	14.1	15.4	15.4	15.8	18.1	20.0	18.8	17.3	17.0	16.7	15.5	14.3	14.3	13.6	12.1	13.5
2000	13.7	14.3	12.7	12.0	13.5	14.7	14.7	15.0	17.2	19.0	17.8	16.4	16.0	15.7	14.5	13.3	13.3	12.5	11.1	12.3
2001	13.9	14.6	13.0	12.4	13.8	15.0	14.9	15.3	17.4	19.1	18.0	16.6	16.3	16.0	14.8	13.8	13.8	13.1	11.7	12.9
2002	13.1	13.7	12.1	11.5	12.8	14.0	13.9	14.2	16.2	17.8	16.6	15.3	14.9	14.6	13.4	12.4	12.3	11.6	10.3	11.3
2003	14.1	14.7	13.3	12.7	14.0	15.1	15.1	15.5	17.5	19.0	18.0	16.7	16.4	16.1	15.1	14.1	14.1	13.5	12.4	13.5
2004	14.2	14.8	13.4	12.8	14.2	15.2	15.2	15.6	17.5	19.0	18.0	16.8	16.5	16.2	15.2	14.3	14.3	13.7	12.6	13.7
2005	14.0	14.6	13.2	12.6	13.9	15.0	14.9	15.2	17.1	18.5	17.6	16.4	16.1	15.8	14.8	13.9	14.0	13.4	12.3	13.3
2006	14.1	14.6	13.3	12.7	14.0	15.0	14.9	15.3	17.1	18.5	17.5	16.4	16.1	15.8	14.9	14.0	14.0	13.5	12.5	13.4
2007	13.6	14.1	12.8	12.2	13.4	14.4	14.3	14.6	16.4	17.7	16.7	15.6	15.3	15.0	14.1	13.3	13.2	12.7	11.7	12.5
2008	12.0	12.5	11.2	10.6	11.7	12.6	12.5	12.8	14.3	15.5	14.6	13.4	13.1	12.7	11.8	10.9	10.8	10.2	9.2	9.9
2009	12.4	12.9	11.6	11.0	12.1	13.0	12.9	13.1	14.7	15.9	15.0	13.9	13.5	13.2	12.3	11.5	11.4	10.8	9.8	10.6
2010	12.7	13.2	12.0	11.5	12.5	13.4	13.3	13.6	15.1	16.3	15.4	14.3	14.0	13.7	12.9	12.1	12.0	11.5	10.6	11.3
2011	12.4	12.8	11.6	11.1	12.1	13.0	12.9	13.1	14.6	15.7	14.8	13.8	13.5	13.2	12.3	11.6	11.5	10.9	10.0	10.7

Table C-2 (page 6 of 6)-a

Small Company Stocks: Total Returns

Rates of Return for all holding periods

Percent per annum compounded annually

from 1926 to 2011

To the end of	From the beginning of 1986	1987	1988	1989	1990	1991	1992	1993	1994	1995	1996	1997	1998	1999	2000	2001
1986	6.9															
1987	-1.6	-9.3														
1988	6.0	5.6	22.9													
1989	7.0	7.1	16.4	10.2												
1990	0.6	-0.9	2.0	-7.0	-21.6											
1991	6.9	6.9	11.3	7.7	6.5	44.6										
1992	9.1	9.4	13.6	11.4	11.9	33.6	23.3									
1993	10.5	11.0	14.8	13.3	14.1	29.2	22.2	21.0								
1994	9.6	10.0	13.1	11.5	11.8	22.1	15.4	11.7	3.1							
1995	11.9	12.5	15.5	14.5	15.3	24.5	19.9	18.8	17.7	34.5						
1996	12.4	13.0	15.8	14.9	15.6	23.3	19.5	18.5	17.7	25.8	17.6					
1997	13.2	13.8	16.5	15.8	16.5	23.3	20.0	19.4	19.0	24.8	20.2	22.8				
1998	11.5	11.9	14.1	13.2	13.6	18.9	15.7	14.4	13.2	15.8	10.2	6.7	-7.3			
1999	12.7	13.2	15.3	14.6	15.1	20.1	17.3	16.5	15.8	18.5	14.8	13.9	9.7	29.8		
2000	11.6	11.9	13.7	13.0	13.3	17.5	14.8	13.8	12.8	14.5	10.9	9.2	5.1	11.9	-3.6	
2001	12.2	12.6	14.3	13.7	14.0	18.0	15.6	14.7	14.0	15.6	12.8	11.8	9.2	15.4	8.8	22.8
2002	10.5	10.8	12.3	11.5	11.6	15.0	12.6	11.6	10.6	11.6	8.6	7.2	4.3	7.4	0.9	3.2
2003	12.9	13.2	14.8	14.3	14.6	18.0	16.0	15.3	14.8	16.2	14.1	13.6	12.1	16.4	13.3	19.6
2004	13.1	13.5	15.0	14.5	14.8	18.0	16.2	15.6	15.1	16.4	14.5	14.2	13.0	16.8	14.3	19.3
2005	12.8	13.1	14.5	14.0	14.2	17.1	15.4	14.8	14.3	15.4	13.6	13.2	12.0	15.1	12.8	16.4
2006	12.9	13.2	14.6	14.1	14.4	17.1	15.4	14.9	14.4	15.4	13.9	13.5	12.5	15.2	13.3	16.4
2007	12.0	12.3	13.5	13.0	13.2	15.6	14.0	13.4	12.9	13.7	12.1	11.6	10.6	12.8	10.8	13.0
2008	9.3	9.4	10.4	9.8	9.8	11.8	10.1	9.4	8.6	9.0	7.3	6.5	5.1	6.4	4.1	5.1
2009	10.0	10.1	11.1	10.6	10.6	12.6	11.1	10.4	9.8	10.2	8.7	8.0	6.9	8.2	6.3	7.5
2010	10.8	10.9	11.9	11.5	11.5	13.5	12.1	11.5	10.9	11.4	10.0	9.5	8.6	10.0	8.4	9.6
2011	10.2	10.3	11.2	10.8	10.8	12.6	11.2	10.6	10.1	10.5	9.2	8.6	7.7	8.9	7.3	8.4

Table C-2 (page 6 of 6)-b

Small Company Stocks: Total Returns

Rates of Return for all holding periods

Percent per annum compounded annually

from 1926 to 2011

To the end of	From the beginning of 2002	2003	2004	2005	2006	2007	2008	2009	2010	2011
2002	-13.3									
2003	18.1	60.7								
2004	18.2	37.9	18.4							
2005	14.9	26.2	11.9	5.7						
2006	15.2	23.6	13.3	10.8	16.2					
2007	11.5	17.2	8.3	5.2	4.9	-5.2				
2008	2.8	5.8	-2.7	-7.4	-11.3	-22.6	-36.7			
2009	5.7	8.7	1.9	-1.2	-2.8	-8.4	-10.0	28.1		
2010	8.3	11.3	5.6	3.6	3.2	0.2	2.1	29.7	31.3	
2011	7.0	9.6	4.5	2.6	2.1	-0.5	0.7	17.6	12.7	-3.3

Table C-3 (page 1 of 6)
Long-Term Corporate Bonds: Total Returns
Rates of Return for all holding periods
Percent per annum compounded annually

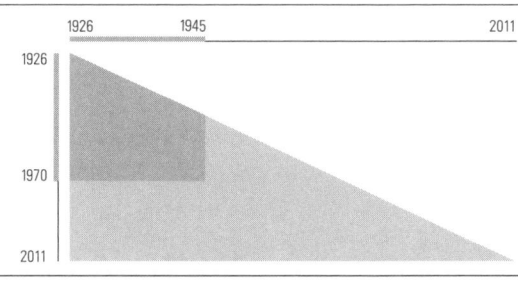

from 1926 to 2011

To the end of	From the beginning of 1926	1927	1928	1929	1930	1931	1932	1933	1934	1935	1936	1937	1938	1939	1940	1941	1942	1943	1944	1945
1926	7.4																			
1927	7.4	7.4																		
1928	5.9	5.1	2.8																	
1929	5.2	4.5	3.1	3.3																
1930	5.8	5.4	4.7	5.6	8.0															
1931	4.4	3.9	3.0	3.1	2.9	-1.9														
1932	5.3	5.0	4.5	4.9	5.5	4.3	10.8													
1933	6.0	5.8	5.5	6.0	6.7	6.3	10.6	10.4												
1934	6.8	6.7	6.6	7.3	8.1	8.1	11.7	12.1	13.8											
1935	7.1	7.0	7.0	7.6	8.3	8.4	11.2	11.3	11.7	9.6										
1936	7.1	7.0	7.0	7.5	8.1	8.1	10.3	10.1	10.0	8.2	6.7									
1937	6.7	6.6	6.5	7.0	7.4	7.4	9.0	8.6	8.2	6.3	4.7	2.7								
1938	6.6	6.6	6.5	6.9	7.3	7.2	8.6	8.2	7.8	6.3	5.2	4.4	6.1							
1939	6.4	6.4	6.3	6.6	6.9	6.8	8.0	7.6	7.1	5.8	4.9	4.3	5.0	4.0						
1940	6.2	6.2	6.1	6.3	6.6	6.5	7.5	7.0	6.6	5.4	4.6	4.1	4.5	3.7	3.4					
1941	6.0	5.9	5.8	6.1	6.3	6.1	7.0	6.6	6.1	5.0	4.3	3.8	4.0	3.4	3.1	2.7				
1942	5.8	5.7	5.6	5.8	6.0	5.8	6.6	6.2	5.7	4.7	4.0	3.6	3.8	3.2	2.9	2.7	2.6			
1943	5.6	5.5	5.4	5.6	5.8	5.6	6.3	5.8	5.4	4.5	3.9	3.5	3.6	3.1	2.9	2.7	2.7	2.8		
1944	5.6	5.5	5.4	5.5	5.7	5.5	6.1	5.8	5.3	4.5	4.0	3.6	3.8	3.4	3.3	3.2	3.4	3.8	4.7	
1945	5.5	5.4	5.3	5.5	5.6	5.4	6.0	5.6	5.2	4.5	4.0	3.7	3.8	3.5	3.4	3.4	3.6	3.9	4.4	4.1
1946	5.3	5.2	5.1	5.3	5.4	5.2	5.7	5.3	5.0	4.3	3.8	3.5	3.6	3.3	3.2	3.1	3.2	3.3	3.5	2.9
1947	5.0	4.9	4.7	4.8	4.9	4.7	5.2	4.8	4.4	3.7	3.3	2.9	3.0	2.6	2.4	2.3	2.2	2.2	2.0	1.1
1948	4.9	4.8	4.7	4.8	4.9	4.7	5.1	4.8	4.4	3.8	3.3	3.0	3.1	2.8	2.6	2.5	2.5	2.5	2.4	1.9
1949	4.9	4.8	4.6	4.7	4.8	4.6	5.0	4.7	4.3	3.7	3.3	3.1	3.1	2.8	2.7	2.6	2.6	2.6	2.6	2.2
1950	4.8	4.7	4.5	4.6	4.7	4.5	4.9	4.5	4.2	3.6	3.2	3.0	3.0	2.8	2.6	2.6	2.6	2.6	2.5	2.1
1951	4.5	4.3	4.2	4.3	4.3	4.2	4.5	4.1	3.8	3.2	2.9	2.6	2.6	2.3	2.2	2.1	2.0	2.0	1.8	1.4
1952	4.4	4.3	4.2	4.2	4.3	4.1	4.4	4.1	3.8	3.3	2.9	2.7	2.7	2.4	2.3	2.2	2.2	2.1	2.0	1.7
1953	4.4	4.3	4.2	4.2	4.3	4.1	4.4	4.1	3.8	3.3	2.9	2.7	2.7	2.5	2.4	2.3	2.3	2.2	2.2	1.9
1954	4.4	4.3	4.2	4.3	4.3	4.2	4.4	4.1	3.8	3.4	3.1	2.9	2.9	2.7	2.6	2.5	2.5	2.5	2.5	2.2
1955	4.3	4.2	4.1	4.1	4.2	4.0	4.3	4.0	3.7	3.2	2.9	2.7	2.7	2.5	2.4	2.4	2.4	2.3	2.3	2.1
1956	3.9	3.8	3.7	3.7	3.7	3.6	3.8	3.5	3.2	2.8	2.4	2.2	2.2	2.0	1.9	1.8	1.7	1.6	1.6	1.3
1957	4.1	4.0	3.8	3.9	3.9	3.7	4.0	3.7	3.4	3.0	2.7	2.5	2.5	2.3	2.2	2.2	2.1	2.1	2.1	1.9
1958	3.9	3.8	3.6	3.7	3.7	3.5	3.7	3.5	3.2	2.8	2.5	2.3	2.3	2.1	2.0	1.9	1.9	1.8	1.8	1.6
1959	3.7	3.6	3.5	3.5	3.5	3.4	3.6	3.3	3.0	2.6	2.3	2.2	2.1	1.9	1.8	1.8	1.7	1.7	1.6	1.4
1960	3.9	3.8	3.7	3.7	3.7	3.6	3.7	3.5	3.3	2.9	2.6	2.4	2.4	2.3	2.2	2.1	2.1	2.1	2.0	1.8
1961	3.9	3.8	3.7	3.7	3.7	3.6	3.8	3.5	3.3	2.9	2.7	2.5	2.5	2.4	2.3	2.2	2.2	2.2	2.2	2.0
1962	4.0	3.9	3.8	3.8	3.9	3.7	3.9	3.7	3.5	3.1	2.9	2.7	2.7	2.6	2.5	2.5	2.5	2.5	2.5	2.3
1963	4.0	3.9	3.8	3.8	3.8	3.7	3.9	3.6	3.4	3.1	2.9	2.7	2.7	2.6	2.5	2.5	2.5	2.5	2.5	2.3
1964	4.0	3.9	3.8	3.8	3.8	3.7	3.9	3.7	3.5	3.1	2.9	2.8	2.8	2.7	2.6	2.6	2.6	2.6	2.6	2.5
1965	3.9	3.8	3.7	3.7	3.7	3.6	3.8	3.6	3.3	3.0	2.8	2.7	2.7	2.5	2.5	2.5	2.4	2.4	2.4	2.3
1966	3.8	3.7	3.6	3.6	3.6	3.5	3.7	3.5	3.2	2.9	2.7	2.6	2.6	2.5	2.4	2.4	2.4	2.3	2.3	2.2
1967	3.6	3.5	3.4	3.4	3.4	3.3	3.4	3.2	3.0	2.7	2.5	2.3	2.3	2.2	2.1	2.1	2.1	2.0	2.0	1.9
1968	3.5	3.4	3.3	3.4	3.4	3.2	3.4	3.2	3.0	2.7	2.5	2.3	2.3	2.2	2.2	2.1	2.1	2.1	2.0	1.9
1969	3.3	3.2	3.1	3.1	3.1	2.9	3.1	2.9	2.7	2.4	2.2	2.0	2.0	1.9	1.8	1.7	1.7	1.7	1.6	1.5
1970	3.6	3.5	3.4	3.4	3.4	3.3	3.4	3.2	3.1	2.8	2.6	2.5	2.5	2.3	2.3	2.3	2.2	2.2	2.2	2.1

Table C-3 (page 2 of 6)

Long-Term Corporate Bonds: Total Returns
Rates of Return for all holding periods
Percent per annum compounded annually

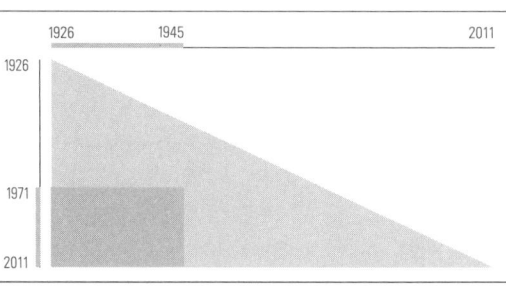

from 1926 to 2011

To the end of	From the beginning of 1926	1927	1928	1929	1930	1931	1932	1933	1934	1935	1936	1937	1938	1939	1940	1941	1942	1943	1944	1945
1971	3.7	3.6	3.6	3.6	3.6	3.5	3.6	3.4	3.3	3.0	2.8	2.7	2.7	2.6	2.6	2.5	2.5	2.5	2.5	2.4
1972	3.8	3.7	3.6	3.7	3.7	3.6	3.7	3.5	3.4	3.1	2.9	2.8	2.8	2.7	2.7	2.7	2.7	2.7	2.7	2.6
1973	3.7	3.7	3.6	3.6	3.6	3.5	3.6	3.5	3.3	3.0	2.9	2.8	2.8	2.7	2.6	2.6	2.6	2.6	2.6	2.5
1974	3.6	3.5	3.4	3.4	3.5	3.4	3.5	3.3	3.1	2.9	2.7	2.6	2.6	2.5	2.5	2.4	2.4	2.4	2.4	2.3
1975	3.8	3.7	3.7	3.7	3.7	3.6	3.7	3.6	3.4	3.2	3.0	2.9	2.9	2.8	2.8	2.8	2.8	2.8	2.8	2.7
1976	4.1	4.0	3.9	4.0	4.0	3.9	4.0	3.9	3.7	3.5	3.4	3.3	3.3	3.2	3.2	3.2	3.2	3.2	3.2	3.2
1977	4.0	4.0	3.9	3.9	3.9	3.9	4.0	3.8	3.7	3.5	3.3	3.2	3.2	3.2	3.2	3.1	3.2	3.2	3.2	3.1
1978	4.0	3.9	3.8	3.8	3.9	3.8	3.9	3.7	3.6	3.4	3.2	3.2	3.2	3.1	3.1	3.1	3.1	3.1	3.1	3.0
1979	3.8	3.7	3.7	3.7	3.7	3.6	3.7	3.6	3.4	3.2	3.1	3.0	3.0	2.9	2.9	2.9	2.9	2.9	2.9	2.8
1980	3.7	3.6	3.5	3.5	3.6	3.5	3.6	3.4	3.3	3.1	2.9	2.8	2.8	2.8	2.7	2.7	2.7	2.7	2.7	2.7
1981	3.6	3.5	3.4	3.5	3.5	3.4	3.5	3.3	3.2	3.0	2.8	2.8	2.8	2.7	2.6	2.6	2.6	2.6	2.6	2.6
1982	4.2	4.1	4.1	4.1	4.1	4.0	4.1	4.0	3.9	3.7	3.6	3.5	3.5	3.4	3.4	3.4	3.5	3.5	3.5	3.5
1983	4.2	4.1	4.1	4.1	4.1	4.1	4.2	4.0	3.9	3.7	3.6	3.5	3.6	3.5	3.5	3.5	3.5	3.5	3.6	3.5
1984	4.4	4.4	4.3	4.3	4.3	4.3	4.4	4.3	4.2	4.0	3.9	3.8	3.8	3.8	3.8	3.8	3.8	3.8	3.9	3.8
1985	4.8	4.7	4.7	4.7	4.8	4.7	4.8	4.7	4.6	4.4	4.3	4.3	4.3	4.3	4.3	4.3	4.3	4.4	4.4	4.4
1986	5.0	5.0	4.9	5.0	5.0	5.0	5.1	5.0	4.9	4.7	4.6	4.6	4.6	4.6	4.6	4.6	4.7	4.7	4.8	4.8
1987	4.9	4.9	4.8	4.9	4.9	4.9	5.0	4.9	4.8	4.6	4.5	4.5	4.5	4.5	4.5	4.5	4.6	4.6	4.6	4.6
1988	5.0	5.0	4.9	5.0	5.0	5.0	5.1	5.0	4.9	4.7	4.6	4.6	4.6	4.6	4.6	4.6	4.7	4.7	4.8	4.8
1989	5.2	5.2	5.1	5.2	5.2	5.1	5.3	5.2	5.1	4.9	4.8	4.8	4.8	4.8	4.8	4.9	4.9	5.0	5.0	5.0
1990	5.2	5.2	5.1	5.2	5.2	5.2	5.3	5.2	5.1	5.0	4.9	4.8	4.9	4.9	4.9	4.9	4.9	5.0	5.0	5.1
1991	5.4	5.4	5.4	5.4	5.4	5.4	5.5	5.4	5.3	5.2	5.1	5.1	5.1	5.1	5.1	5.2	5.2	5.3	5.3	5.3
1992	5.5	5.4	5.4	5.5	5.5	5.5	5.6	5.5	5.4	5.3	5.2	5.2	5.2	5.2	5.2	5.3	5.3	5.4	5.4	5.4
1993	5.6	5.6	5.5	5.6	5.6	5.6	5.7	5.6	5.5	5.4	5.3	5.3	5.4	5.3	5.4	5.4	5.5	5.5	5.6	5.6
1994	5.4	5.4	5.4	5.4	5.4	5.4	5.5	5.4	5.3	5.2	5.1	5.1	5.1	5.1	5.2	5.2	5.2	5.3	5.3	5.3
1995	5.7	5.7	5.6	5.7	5.7	5.7	5.8	5.7	5.7	5.5	5.5	5.4	5.5	5.5	5.5	5.5	5.6	5.7	5.7	5.7
1996	5.6	5.6	5.6	5.6	5.7	5.6	5.7	5.7	5.6	5.5	5.4	5.4	5.4	5.4	5.4	5.5	5.5	5.6	5.6	5.6
1997	5.7	5.7	5.7	5.7	5.8	5.7	5.9	5.8	5.7	5.6	5.5	5.5	5.5	5.5	5.6	5.6	5.7	5.7	5.8	5.8
1998	5.8	5.8	5.8	5.8	5.8	5.8	5.9	5.9	5.8	5.7	5.6	5.6	5.6	5.6	5.6	5.7	5.7	5.8	5.9	5.9
1999	5.6	5.6	5.6	5.6	5.6	5.6	5.7	5.6	5.6	5.4	5.4	5.4	5.4	5.4	5.4	5.5	5.5	5.6	5.6	5.6
2000	5.7	5.7	5.7	5.7	5.7	5.7	5.8	5.7	5.7	5.6	5.5	5.5	5.5	5.5	5.5	5.6	5.6	5.7	5.7	5.7
2001	5.8	5.7	5.7	5.8	5.8	5.8	5.9	5.8	5.7	5.6	5.6	5.6	5.6	5.6	5.6	5.7	5.7	5.8	5.8	5.8
2002	5.9	5.9	5.9	5.9	5.9	5.9	6.0	6.0	5.9	5.8	5.7	5.7	5.8	5.7	5.8	5.8	5.9	5.9	6.0	6.0
2003	5.9	5.9	5.9	5.9	5.9	5.9	6.0	5.9	5.9	5.8	5.7	5.7	5.7	5.7	5.8	5.8	5.9	5.9	6.0	6.0
2004	5.9	5.9	5.9	5.9	6.0	5.9	6.0	6.0	5.9	5.8	5.8	5.7	5.8	5.8	5.8	5.9	5.9	6.0	6.0	6.0
2005	5.9	5.9	5.9	5.9	6.0	5.9	6.0	6.0	5.9	5.8	5.8	5.7	5.8	5.8	5.8	5.9	5.9	6.0	6.0	6.0
2006	5.9	5.9	5.9	5.9	5.9	5.9	6.0	5.9	5.9	5.8	5.7	5.7	5.8	5.7	5.8	5.8	5.9	5.9	6.0	6.0
2007	5.9	5.8	5.8	5.8	5.9	5.9	6.0	5.9	5.8	5.7	5.7	5.7	5.7	5.7	5.7	5.8	5.8	5.9	5.9	5.9
2008	5.9	5.9	5.8	5.9	5.9	5.9	6.0	5.9	5.9	5.8	5.7	5.7	5.8	5.7	5.8	5.8	5.9	5.9	6.0	6.0
2009	5.9	5.8	5.8	5.8	5.9	5.9	6.0	5.9	5.8	5.7	5.7	5.7	5.7	5.7	5.7	5.8	5.8	5.9	5.9	5.9
2010	5.9	5.9	5.9	5.9	6.0	5.9	6.0	6.0	5.9	5.8	5.8	5.8	5.8	5.8	5.8	5.9	5.9	6.0	6.0	6.0
2011	6.1	6.0	6.0	6.1	6.1	6.1	6.2	6.1	6.1	6.0	5.9	5.9	6.0	6.0	6.0	6.0	6.1	6.1	6.2	6.2

Table C-3 (page 3 of 6)

Long-Term Corporate Bonds: Total Returns
Rates of Return for all holding periods
Percent per annum compounded annually

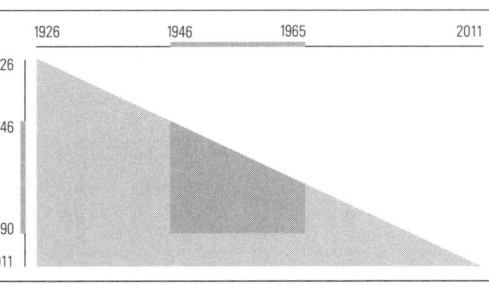

from 1926 to 2011

To the end of	From the beginning of 1946	1947	1948	1949	1950	1951	1952	1953	1954	1955	1956	1957	1958	1959	1960	1961	1962	1963	1964	1965
1946	1.7																			
1947	-0.3	-2.3																		
1948	1.1	0.8	4.1																	
1949	1.7	1.7	3.7	3.3																
1950	1.8	1.8	3.2	2.7	2.1															
1951	1.0	0.9	1.7	0.9	-0.3	-2.7														
1952	1.4	1.3	2.0	1.5	0.9	0.4	3.5													
1953	1.6	1.6	2.3	1.9	1.6	1.4	3.5	3.4												
1954	2.0	2.1	2.7	2.5	2.3	2.4	4.1	4.4	5.4											
1955	1.9	1.9	2.4	2.2	2.0	2.0	3.2	3.1	2.9	0.5										
1956	1.1	1.0	1.4	1.0	0.7	0.5	1.1	0.5	-0.4	-3.2	-6.8									
1957	1.7	1.7	2.1	1.8	1.7	1.6	2.3	2.1	1.8	0.6	0.7	8.7								
1958	1.4	1.3	1.7	1.4	1.2	1.1	1.7	1.4	1.0	-0.1	-0.3	3.1	-2.2							
1959	1.2	1.2	1.5	1.2	1.0	0.9	1.3	1.0	0.6	-0.3	-0.5	1.7	-1.6	-1.0						
1960	1.7	1.7	2.0	1.8	1.7	1.7	2.2	2.0	1.8	1.2	1.4	3.5	1.8	3.9	9.1					
1961	1.9	1.9	2.2	2.1	2.0	2.0	2.4	2.3	2.2	1.7	1.9	3.8	2.6	4.2	6.9	4.8				
1962	2.2	2.3	2.6	2.5	2.4	2.4	2.9	2.9	2.8	2.5	2.8	4.5	3.6	5.1	7.3	6.4	7.9			
1963	2.2	2.3	2.6	2.5	2.4	2.4	2.9	2.8	2.7	2.4	2.7	4.1	3.4	4.5	6.0	5.0	5.0	2.2		
1964	2.4	2.4	2.7	2.6	2.6	2.6	3.0	3.0	2.9	2.7	2.9	4.2	3.6	4.6	5.7	4.9	4.9	3.5	4.8	
1965	2.2	2.3	2.5	2.4	2.4	2.4	2.8	2.7	2.6	2.4	2.6	3.7	3.1	3.8	4.7	3.8	3.6	2.1	2.1	-0.5
1966	2.1	2.1	2.4	2.3	2.2	2.2	2.6	2.5	2.4	2.2	2.4	3.3	2.7	3.4	4.0	3.2	2.9	1.7	1.5	-0.1
1967	1.8	1.8	2.0	1.9	1.8	1.8	2.1	2.0	1.9	1.6	1.7	2.5	1.9	2.4	2.9	2.0	1.5	0.3	-0.2	-1.8
1968	1.8	1.8	2.0	1.9	1.9	1.8	2.1	2.0	1.9	1.7	1.8	2.5	2.0	2.4	2.8	2.1	1.7	0.7	0.4	-0.7
1969	1.4	1.4	1.6	1.4	1.3	1.3	1.5	1.4	1.3	1.0	1.1	1.7	1.1	1.4	1.7	0.9	0.4	-0.6	-1.1	-2.2
1970	2.0	2.0	2.2	2.1	2.1	2.1	2.3	2.3	2.2	2.0	2.1	2.8	2.4	2.7	3.1	2.5	2.3	1.6	1.5	0.9
1971	2.4	2.4	2.6	2.5	2.5	2.5	2.8	2.7	2.7	2.5	2.7	3.3	3.0	3.4	3.7	3.3	3.1	2.6	2.6	2.3
1972	2.5	2.6	2.8	2.7	2.7	2.7	3.0	2.9	2.9	2.8	2.9	3.6	3.2	3.6	4.0	3.6	3.5	3.0	3.1	2.9
1973	2.5	2.5	2.7	2.6	2.6	2.6	2.9	2.9	2.8	2.7	2.8	3.4	3.1	3.5	3.8	3.4	3.3	2.9	2.9	2.7
1974	2.3	2.3	2.5	2.4	2.4	2.4	2.6	2.6	2.5	2.4	2.5	3.1	2.7	3.0	3.3	2.9	2.8	2.4	2.4	2.1
1975	2.7	2.7	2.9	2.9	2.8	2.9	3.1	3.1	3.1	3.0	3.1	3.6	3.4	3.7	4.0	3.7	3.6	3.3	3.3	3.2
1976	3.2	3.2	3.4	3.4	3.4	3.4	3.7	3.7	3.7	3.6	3.8	4.3	4.1	4.5	4.8	4.5	4.5	4.3	4.4	4.4
1977	3.1	3.2	3.3	3.3	3.3	3.4	3.6	3.6	3.6	3.5	3.7	4.2	4.0	4.3	4.6	4.4	4.3	4.1	4.2	4.2
1978	3.0	3.1	3.2	3.2	3.2	3.2	3.5	3.5	3.5	3.4	3.5	4.0	3.8	4.1	4.4	4.1	4.1	3.8	4.0	3.9
1979	2.8	2.8	3.0	3.0	2.9	3.0	3.2	3.2	3.2	3.1	3.2	3.6	3.4	3.7	3.9	3.7	3.6	3.4	3.4	3.3
1980	2.6	2.7	2.8	2.8	2.8	2.8	3.0	3.0	2.9	2.8	2.9	3.4	3.1	3.4	3.6	3.3	3.3	3.0	3.1	2.9
1981	2.5	2.5	2.7	2.6	2.6	2.6	2.8	2.8	2.8	2.7	2.8	3.2	3.0	3.2	3.4	3.1	3.0	2.8	2.8	2.7
1982	3.4	3.5	3.7	3.6	3.7	3.7	3.9	3.9	3.9	3.9	4.0	4.5	4.3	4.6	4.8	4.6	4.6	4.5	4.6	4.6
1983	3.5	3.6	3.7	3.7	3.7	3.8	4.0	4.0	4.0	4.0	4.1	4.5	4.4	4.6	4.9	4.7	4.7	4.6	4.7	4.7
1984	3.8	3.9	4.1	4.1	4.1	4.1	4.4	4.4	4.4	4.4	4.5	5.0	4.8	5.1	5.3	5.2	5.2	5.1	5.2	5.2
1985	4.4	4.5	4.7	4.7	4.7	4.8	5.0	5.1	5.1	5.1	5.3	5.7	5.6	5.9	6.2	6.1	6.1	6.1	6.2	6.3
1986	4.8	4.9	5.0	5.1	5.1	5.2	5.4	5.5	5.6	5.6	5.7	6.2	6.1	6.4	6.7	6.6	6.7	6.6	6.8	6.9
1987	4.7	4.7	4.9	4.9	5.0	5.0	5.3	5.3	5.4	5.4	5.5	6.0	5.9	6.2	6.4	6.3	6.4	6.3	6.5	6.6
1988	4.8	4.9	5.0	5.1	5.1	5.2	5.4	5.5	5.5	5.5	5.7	6.1	6.0	6.3	6.6	6.5	6.5	6.5	6.7	6.7
1989	5.0	5.1	5.3	5.3	5.4	5.5	5.7	5.7	5.8	5.8	6.0	6.4	6.3	6.6	6.9	6.8	6.9	6.8	7.0	7.1
1990	5.1	5.2	5.3	5.4	5.4	5.5	5.7	5.8	5.8	5.8	6.0	6.4	6.3	6.6	6.9	6.8	6.9	6.8	7.0	7.1

Appendix C: Rates of Return for All Yearly Holding Periods 1926–2011

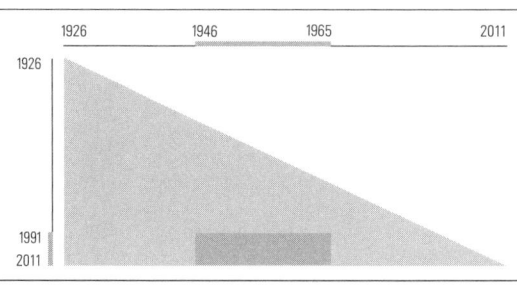

from 1926 to 2011

To the end of	From the beginning of 1946	1947	1948	1949	1950	1951	1952	1953	1954	1955	1956	1957	1958	1959	1960	1961	1962	1963	1964	1965
1991	5.4	5.5	5.6	5.7	5.7	5.8	6.0	6.1	6.2	6.2	6.4	6.8	6.7	7.0	7.3	7.2	7.3	7.3	7.4	7.5
1992	5.5	5.5	5.7	5.8	5.8	5.9	6.1	6.2	6.3	6.3	6.5	6.8	6.8	7.1	7.3	7.3	7.3	7.3	7.5	7.6
1993	5.6	5.7	5.9	5.9	6.0	6.1	6.3	6.4	6.4	6.5	6.6	7.0	7.0	7.2	7.5	7.4	7.5	7.5	7.7	7.8
1994	5.4	5.4	5.6	5.7	5.7	5.8	6.0	6.1	6.1	6.1	6.3	6.7	6.6	6.9	7.1	7.0	7.1	7.1	7.2	7.3
1995	5.8	5.9	6.0	6.1	6.1	6.2	6.4	6.5	6.6	6.6	6.8	7.1	7.1	7.4	7.6	7.6	7.6	7.6	7.8	7.9
1996	5.7	5.8	5.9	6.0	6.0	6.1	6.3	6.4	6.5	6.5	6.6	7.0	6.9	7.2	7.4	7.4	7.5	7.4	7.6	7.7
1997	5.8	5.9	6.1	6.1	6.2	6.3	6.5	6.5	6.6	6.6	6.8	7.1	7.1	7.3	7.6	7.5	7.6	7.6	7.8	7.9
1998	5.9	6.0	6.2	6.2	6.3	6.3	6.5	6.6	6.7	6.7	6.9	7.2	7.2	7.4	7.7	7.6	7.7	7.7	7.8	7.9
1999	5.6	5.7	5.9	5.9	6.0	6.0	6.2	6.3	6.4	6.4	6.5	6.9	6.8	7.0	7.2	7.2	7.3	7.2	7.4	7.5
2000	5.8	5.8	6.0	6.0	6.1	6.2	6.4	6.4	6.5	6.5	6.7	7.0	6.9	7.2	7.4	7.3	7.4	7.4	7.5	7.6
2001	5.9	5.9	6.1	6.1	6.2	6.3	6.5	6.5	6.6	6.6	6.7	7.1	7.0	7.3	7.5	7.4	7.5	7.5	7.6	7.7
2002	6.0	6.1	6.3	6.3	6.4	6.4	6.6	6.7	6.8	6.8	6.9	7.3	7.2	7.4	7.7	7.6	7.7	7.7	7.8	7.9
2003	6.0	6.1	6.3	6.3	6.3	6.4	6.6	6.7	6.7	6.8	6.9	7.2	7.2	7.4	7.6	7.6	7.6	7.6	7.8	7.8
2004	6.1	6.1	6.3	6.3	6.4	6.5	6.7	6.7	6.8	6.8	6.9	7.2	7.2	7.4	7.6	7.6	7.7	7.6	7.8	7.9
2005	6.1	6.1	6.3	6.3	6.4	6.5	6.6	6.7	6.8	6.8	6.9	7.2	7.2	7.4	7.6	7.6	7.6	7.6	7.7	7.8
2006	6.0	6.1	6.2	6.3	6.3	6.4	6.6	6.6	6.7	6.7	6.8	7.1	7.1	7.3	7.5	7.5	7.5	7.5	7.6	7.7
2007	6.0	6.0	6.2	6.2	6.3	6.3	6.5	6.6	6.6	6.6	6.8	7.0	7.0	7.2	7.4	7.4	7.4	7.4	7.5	7.6
2008	6.0	6.1	6.2	6.2	6.3	6.4	6.5	6.6	6.7	6.7	6.8	7.1	7.0	7.2	7.4	7.4	7.4	7.4	7.5	7.6
2009	6.0	6.0	6.2	6.2	6.2	6.3	6.5	6.5	6.6	6.6	6.7	7.0	7.0	7.2	7.3	7.3	7.3	7.3	7.4	7.5
2010	6.1	6.1	6.3	6.3	6.3	6.4	6.6	6.6	6.7	6.7	6.8	7.1	7.1	7.3	7.4	7.4	7.4	7.4	7.5	7.6
2011	6.2	6.3	6.4	6.5	6.5	6.6	6.8	6.8	6.9	6.9	7.0	7.3	7.3	7.4	7.6	7.6	7.6	7.6	7.8	7.8

Table C-3 (page 5 of 6)

Long-Term Corporate Bonds: Total Returns
Rates of Return for all holding periods
Percent per annum compounded annually

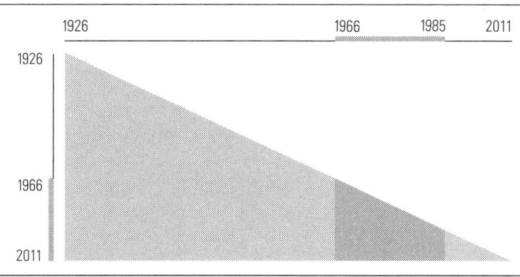

from 1926 to 2011

To the end of	From the beginning of 1966	1967	1968	1969	1970	1971	1972	1973	1974	1975	1976	1977	1978	1979	1980	1981	1982	1983	1984	1985
1966	0.2																			
1967	-2.4	-5.0																		
1968	-0.8	-1.3	2.6																	
1969	-2.7	-3.6	-2.9	-8.1																
1970	1.2	1.5	3.7	4.3	18.4															
1971	2.8	3.3	5.5	6.5	14.6	11.0														
1972	3.4	4.0	5.8	6.7	12.1	9.1	7.3													
1973	3.1	3.6	5.0	5.6	9.3	6.4	4.2	1.1												
1974	2.4	2.7	3.9	4.1	6.7	3.9	1.7	-1.0	-3.1											
1975	3.6	4.0	5.1	5.5	8.0	6.0	4.8	4.0	5.4	14.6										
1976	4.9	5.4	6.6	7.1	9.4	8.0	7.4	7.5	9.7	16.6	18.6									
1977	4.6	5.0	6.1	6.5	8.4	7.1	6.4	6.3	7.6	11.4	9.9	1.7								
1978	4.2	4.6	5.5	5.8	7.5	6.2	5.5	5.2	6.0	8.4	6.4	0.8	-0.1							
1979	3.6	3.9	4.7	4.8	6.2	5.0	4.2	3.8	4.3	5.8	3.7	-0.9	-2.1	-4.2						
1980	3.2	3.4	4.1	4.2	5.4	4.2	3.4	3.0	3.2	4.3	2.4	-1.4	-2.4	-3.5	-2.8					
1981	2.9	3.1	3.7	3.8	4.8	3.7	3.0	2.5	2.7	3.5	1.8	-1.3	-2.1	-2.7	-2.0	-1.2				
1982	4.9	5.2	5.9	6.1	7.3	6.5	6.0	5.9	6.5	7.7	6.8	4.9	5.6	7.0	11.0	18.7	42.6			
1983	5.0	5.2	5.9	6.1	7.2	6.4	6.1	6.0	6.4	7.6	6.7	5.1	5.7	6.9	9.8	14.4	23.1	6.3		
1984	5.6	5.9	6.5	6.8	7.9	7.1	6.9	6.8	7.4	8.5	7.8	6.5	7.2	8.5	11.2	15.0	21.0	11.4	16.9	
1985	6.7	7.0	7.7	8.0	9.1	8.5	8.4	8.5	9.1	10.3	9.8	8.9	9.8	11.3	14.1	17.9	23.2	17.3	23.3	30.1
1986	7.3	7.6	8.3	8.7	9.7	9.2	9.1	9.2	9.9	11.0	10.7	9.9	10.9	12.4	14.9	18.2	22.5	18.0	22.1	24.9
1987	6.9	7.2	7.9	8.2	9.2	8.6	8.5	8.6	9.1	10.1	9.8	9.0	9.7	10.9	12.9	15.4	18.4	14.1	16.1	15.9
1988	7.1	7.4	8.0	8.3	9.2	8.7	8.6	8.7	9.2	10.2	9.8	9.1	9.8	10.9	12.7	14.8	17.3	13.5	15.0	14.5
1989	7.4	7.8	8.4	8.7	9.6	9.1	9.0	9.1	9.7	10.6	10.3	9.7	10.3	11.3	13.0	14.9	17.1	13.9	15.2	14.9
1990	7.4	7.7	8.3	8.6	9.4	9.0	8.9	9.0	9.5	10.3	10.0	9.4	10.1	11.0	12.4	14.1	15.9	13.0	14.0	13.5
1991	7.9	8.2	8.8	9.0	9.9	9.5	9.4	9.5	10.0	10.9	10.6	10.1	10.7	11.6	13.0	14.6	16.3	13.7	14.7	14.4
1992	7.9	8.2	8.8	9.1	9.9	9.5	9.4	9.5	10.0	10.8	10.6	10.1	10.6	11.5	12.8	14.2	15.7	13.3	14.1	13.7
1993	8.1	8.4	9.0	9.2	10.0	9.7	9.6	9.7	10.2	10.9	10.7	10.2	10.8	11.6	12.8	14.1	15.5	13.3	14.0	13.7
1994	7.6	7.9	8.4	8.6	9.3	9.0	8.9	9.0	9.3	10.0	9.8	9.3	9.8	10.4	11.4	12.5	13.7	11.5	12.0	11.6
1995	8.2	8.5	9.0	9.2	10.0	9.6	9.6	9.7	10.1	10.8	10.6	10.2	10.7	11.3	12.4	13.5	14.6	12.7	13.2	12.9
1996	8.0	8.2	8.7	9.0	9.6	9.3	9.2	9.3	9.7	10.3	10.1	9.7	10.1	10.7	11.7	12.7	13.7	11.8	12.3	11.9
1997	8.1	8.4	8.9	9.1	9.8	9.4	9.4	9.5	9.8	10.4	10.2	9.9	10.3	10.9	11.8	12.7	13.6	11.9	12.3	12.0
1998	8.2	8.5	8.9	9.1	9.8	9.5	9.4	9.5	9.9	10.4	10.3	9.9	10.3	10.9	11.7	12.6	13.4	11.8	12.2	11.9
1999	7.7	7.9	8.4	8.6	9.2	8.9	8.8	8.8	9.2	9.7	9.5	9.1	9.4	9.9	10.7	11.4	12.2	10.6	10.9	10.5
2000	7.8	8.1	8.5	8.7	9.3	9.0	8.9	9.0	9.3	9.8	9.6	9.2	9.6	10.0	10.8	11.5	12.2	10.7	11.0	10.6
2001	7.9	8.2	8.6	8.8	9.3	9.0	9.0	9.0	9.3	9.8	9.6	9.3	9.6	10.1	10.8	11.5	12.1	10.7	11.0	10.6
2002	8.1	8.4	8.8	9.0	9.5	9.3	9.2	9.3	9.6	10.1	9.9	9.6	9.9	10.3	11.0	11.7	12.3	11.0	11.2	10.9
2003	8.1	8.3	8.7	8.9	9.4	9.1	9.1	9.1	9.4	9.9	9.7	9.4	9.7	10.1	10.8	11.4	12.0	10.7	10.9	10.6
2004	8.1	8.3	8.7	8.9	9.4	9.1	9.1	9.1	9.4	9.8	9.7	9.4	9.7	10.1	10.7	11.3	11.8	10.6	10.8	10.5
2005	8.0	8.2	8.6	8.8	9.3	9.0	9.0	9.0	9.3	9.7	9.6	9.3	9.5	9.9	10.5	11.0	11.6	10.4	10.6	10.3
2006	7.9	8.1	8.5	8.6	9.1	8.9	8.8	8.9	9.1	9.5	9.3	9.0	9.3	9.7	10.2	10.7	11.2	10.1	10.3	10.0
2007	7.8	8.0	8.3	8.5	8.9	8.7	8.6	8.7	8.9	9.3	9.1	8.8	9.1	9.4	9.9	10.4	10.9	9.8	9.9	9.7
2008	7.8	8.0	8.3	8.5	8.9	8.7	8.6	8.7	8.9	9.3	9.1	8.8	9.1	9.4	9.9	10.4	10.8	9.8	9.9	9.6
2009	7.7	7.9	8.2	8.3	8.8	8.6	8.5	8.5	8.7	9.1	8.9	8.6	8.9	9.2	9.6	10.1	10.5	9.5	9.6	9.3
2010	7.8	8.0	8.3	8.4	8.9	8.6	8.6	8.6	8.8	9.2	9.0	8.8	9.0	9.3	9.7	10.2	10.6	9.6	9.7	9.5
2011	8.0	8.2	8.5	8.6	9.1	8.9	8.8	8.9	9.1	9.4	9.3	9.0	9.2	9.5	10.0	10.4	10.8	9.9	10.0	9.8

Table C-3 (page 6 of 6)-a

Long-Term Corporate Bonds: Total Returns

Rates of Return for all holding periods

Percent per annum compounded annually

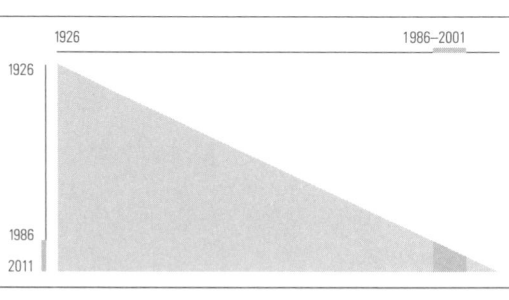

from 1926 to 2011

To the end of	From the beginning of 1986	1987	1988	1989	1990	1991	1992	1993	1994	1995	1996	1997	1998	1999	2000	2001
1986	19.8															
1987	9.3	-0.3														
1988	9.8	5.1	10.7													
1989	11.4	8.7	13.4	16.2												
1990	10.4	8.2	11.2	11.4	6.8											
1991	12.0	10.4	13.3	14.2	13.1	19.9										
1992	11.6	10.3	12.5	13.0	11.9	14.5	9.4									
1993	11.8	10.7	12.6	13.0	12.2	14.1	11.3	13.2								
1994	9.7	8.5	9.8	9.6	8.4	8.8	5.3	3.3	-5.8							
1995	11.3	10.4	11.8	12.0	11.3	12.2	10.4	10.7	9.5	27.2						
1996	10.4	9.5	10.6	10.6	9.8	10.3	8.5	8.3	6.7	13.6	1.4					
1997	10.6	9.8	10.8	10.9	10.2	10.7	9.2	9.2	8.2	13.4	7.0	12.9				
1998	10.6	9.9	10.8	10.9	10.3	10.7	9.5	9.5	8.7	12.7	8.3	11.8	10.8			
1999	9.2	8.4	9.2	9.0	8.4	8.5	7.2	6.9	5.9	8.4	4.1	5.0	1.2	-7.4		
2000	9.4	8.7	9.5	9.4	8.8	9.0	7.8	7.6	6.8	9.1	5.8	6.9	5.0	2.2	12.9	
2001	9.5	8.9	9.5	9.5	8.9	9.1	8.1	7.9	7.3	9.3	6.6	7.7	6.4	4.9	11.8	10.6
2002	9.9	9.3	10.0	9.9	9.5	9.7	8.8	8.8	8.3	10.2	7.9	9.1	8.3	7.7	13.3	13.5
2003	9.6	9.1	9.7	9.6	9.2	9.3	8.5	8.4	8.0	9.6	7.6	8.5	7.8	7.2	11.2	10.7
2004	9.6	9.1	9.6	9.6	9.1	9.3	8.5	8.5	8.0	9.5	7.7	8.5	7.9	7.4	10.7	10.2
2005	9.4	8.9	9.4	9.3	8.9	9.1	8.3	8.3	7.9	9.2	7.5	8.2	7.7	7.2	9.9	9.3
2006	9.1	8.6	9.1	9.0	8.6	8.7	8.0	7.9	7.5	8.7	7.1	7.7	7.2	6.7	8.9	8.3
2007	8.8	8.3	8.7	8.6	8.2	8.3	7.6	7.5	7.1	8.2	6.7	7.2	6.7	6.3	8.1	7.4
2008	8.8	8.3	8.8	8.7	8.3	8.4	7.7	7.6	7.2	8.2	6.9	7.4	6.9	6.5	8.2	7.6
2009	8.6	8.1	8.5	8.4	8.0	8.1	7.4	7.3	7.0	7.9	6.6	7.0	6.6	6.2	7.6	7.1
2010	8.7	8.3	8.7	8.6	8.2	8.3	7.7	7.6	7.3	8.2	7.0	7.4	7.0	6.7	8.1	7.6
2011	9.0	8.6	9.0	9.0	8.6	8.7	8.2	8.1	7.9	8.7	7.7	8.1	7.7	7.5	8.9	8.5

Table C-3 (page 6 of 6)-b

Long-Term Corporate Bonds: Total Returns

Rates of Return for all holding periods

Percent per annum compounded annually

from 1926 to 2011

To the end of	From the beginning of 2002	2003	2004	2005	2006	2007	2008	2009	2010	2011
2002	16.3									
2003	10.7	5.3								
2004	10.0	7.0	8.7							
2005	9.0	6.6	7.3	5.9						
2006	7.8	5.8	5.9	4.5	3.2					
2007	6.9	5.1	5.1	3.9	2.9	2.6				
2008	7.2	5.7	5.8	5.1	4.8	5.6	8.8			
2009	6.6	5.3	5.3	4.7	4.4	4.8	5.9	3.0		
2010	7.3	6.2	6.3	5.9	5.9	6.6	8.0	7.6	12.4	
2011	8.3	7.4	7.7	7.6	7.9	8.8	10.4	11.0	15.2	17.9

Table C-4 (page 1 of 6)

Long-Term Government Bonds: Total Returns
Rates of Return for all holding periods
Percent per annum compounded annually

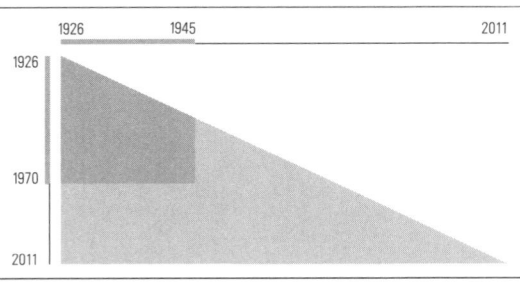

from 1926 to 2011

To the end of	From the beginning of 1926	1927	1928	1929	1930	1931	1932	1933	1934	1935	1936	1937	1938	1939	1940	1941	1942	1943	1944	1945
1926	7.8																			
1927	8.3	8.9																		
1928	5.5	4.4	0.1																	
1929	5.0	4.1	1.7	3.4																
1930	4.9	4.2	2.7	4.0	4.7															
1931	3.1	2.2	0.6	0.8	-0.5	-5.3														
1932	5.0	4.5	3.7	4.6	5.0	5.2	16.8													
1933	4.4	3.9	3.1	3.7	3.7	3.4	8.1	-0.1												
1934	5.0	4.6	4.0	4.7	4.9	5.0	8.7	4.9	10.0											
1935	5.0	4.7	4.1	4.7	5.0	5.0	7.8	4.9	7.5	5.0										
1936	5.2	4.9	4.5	5.1	5.3	5.4	7.7	5.5	7.5	6.2	7.5									
1937	4.8	4.5	4.1	4.5	4.7	4.7	6.4	4.5	5.6	4.2	3.8	0.2								
1938	4.8	4.6	4.2	4.6	4.8	4.8	6.3	4.6	5.6	4.5	4.4	2.8	5.5							
1939	4.9	4.7	4.4	4.7	4.9	4.9	6.3	4.8	5.7	4.8	4.8	3.9	5.7	5.9						
1940	5.0	4.8	4.5	4.9	5.0	5.0	6.2	5.0	5.7	5.0	5.0	4.4	5.9	6.0	6.1					
1941	4.7	4.5	4.2	4.5	4.6	4.6	5.7	4.5	5.1	4.4	4.3	3.7	4.6	4.3	3.5	0.9				
1942	4.6	4.5	4.2	4.5	4.5	4.5	5.5	4.4	4.9	4.3	4.2	3.6	4.3	4.0	3.4	2.1	3.2			
1943	4.5	4.3	4.0	4.3	4.4	4.3	5.2	4.2	4.6	4.0	3.9	3.4	3.9	3.6	3.1	2.1	2.6	2.1		
1944	4.4	4.2	4.0	4.2	4.3	4.2	5.0	4.1	4.5	3.9	3.8	3.3	3.8	3.5	3.0	2.3	2.7	2.4	2.8	
1945	4.7	4.6	4.3	4.6	4.6	4.6	5.4	4.6	5.0	4.5	4.5	4.1	4.6	4.5	4.3	3.9	4.7	5.1	6.7	10.7
1946	4.5	4.3	4.1	4.3	4.4	4.3	5.0	4.2	4.6	4.1	4.0	3.7	4.1	3.9	3.6	3.2	3.7	3.8	4.4	5.2
1947	4.1	4.0	3.7	3.9	4.0	3.9	4.5	3.8	4.0	3.6	3.5	3.1	3.4	3.2	2.8	2.4	2.6	2.5	2.6	2.5
1948	4.1	4.0	3.7	3.9	3.9	3.9	4.5	3.7	4.0	3.6	3.5	3.1	3.4	3.2	2.9	2.5	2.7	2.6	2.7	2.7
1949	4.2	4.1	3.8	4.0	4.1	4.0	4.6	3.9	4.1	3.8	3.7	3.4	3.7	3.5	3.2	2.9	3.2	3.2	3.4	3.5
1950	4.0	3.9	3.7	3.8	3.9	3.8	4.3	3.7	3.9	3.5	3.4	3.1	3.4	3.2	2.9	2.6	2.8	2.8	2.9	2.9
1951	3.7	3.6	3.3	3.5	3.5	3.4	3.9	3.3	3.4	3.1	3.0	2.7	2.8	2.6	2.4	2.0	2.1	2.0	2.0	1.9
1952	3.6	3.5	3.3	3.4	3.4	3.3	3.8	3.2	3.3	3.0	2.8	2.6	2.7	2.5	2.3	1.9	2.0	1.9	1.9	1.8
1953	3.6	3.5	3.3	3.4	3.4	3.3	3.8	3.2	3.3	3.0	2.9	2.6	2.8	2.6	2.4	2.1	2.2	2.1	2.1	2.0
1954	3.7	3.6	3.4	3.5	3.6	3.5	3.9	3.4	3.5	3.2	3.1	2.9	3.0	2.9	2.7	2.4	2.6	2.5	2.5	2.5
1955	3.6	3.4	3.2	3.4	3.4	3.3	3.7	3.1	3.3	3.0	2.9	2.6	2.8	2.6	2.4	2.2	2.3	2.2	2.2	2.2
1956	3.3	3.1	2.9	3.0	3.0	3.0	3.3	2.8	2.9	2.6	2.5	2.2	2.3	2.2	1.9	1.7	1.7	1.6	1.6	1.5
1957	3.4	3.3	3.1	3.2	3.2	3.1	3.5	3.0	3.1	2.8	2.7	2.5	2.6	2.4	2.2	2.0	2.1	2.0	2.0	1.9
1958	3.1	3.0	2.8	2.9	2.8	2.8	3.1	2.6	2.7	2.4	2.3	2.1	2.1	2.0	1.8	1.5	1.6	1.5	1.4	1.3
1959	2.9	2.8	2.6	2.7	2.7	2.6	2.9	2.4	2.5	2.2	2.1	1.9	1.9	1.8	1.6	1.3	1.4	1.3	1.2	1.1
1960	3.2	3.1	2.9	3.0	3.0	2.9	3.2	2.8	2.9	2.6	2.5	2.3	2.4	2.3	2.1	1.9	2.0	1.9	1.9	1.8
1961	3.2	3.0	2.9	3.0	2.9	2.9	3.2	2.7	2.8	2.6	2.5	2.3	2.4	2.2	2.1	1.9	1.9	1.9	1.8	1.8
1962	3.3	3.1	3.0	3.1	3.1	3.0	3.3	2.9	3.0	2.7	2.6	2.5	2.5	2.4	2.3	2.1	2.2	2.1	2.1	2.1
1963	3.2	3.1	2.9	3.0	3.0	3.0	3.2	2.8	2.9	2.7	2.6	2.4	2.5	2.4	2.2	2.1	2.1	2.1	2.1	2.0
1964	3.2	3.1	2.9	3.0	3.0	3.0	3.2	2.8	2.9	2.7	2.6	2.4	2.5	2.4	2.3	2.1	2.2	2.1	2.1	2.1
1965	3.2	3.0	2.9	3.0	3.0	2.9	3.2	2.8	2.9	2.6	2.6	2.4	2.5	2.4	2.2	2.1	2.1	2.1	2.1	2.0
1966	3.2	3.1	2.9	3.0	3.0	2.9	3.2	2.8	2.9	2.7	2.6	2.4	2.5	2.4	2.3	2.1	2.2	2.1	2.1	2.1
1967	2.9	2.7	2.6	2.7	2.6	2.6	2.8	2.4	2.5	2.3	2.2	2.0	2.1	2.0	1.8	1.7	1.7	1.7	1.6	1.6
1968	2.8	2.7	2.5	2.6	2.6	2.5	2.7	2.4	2.4	2.2	2.1	2.0	2.0	1.9	1.8	1.6	1.6	1.6	1.6	1.5
1969	2.6	2.5	2.3	2.4	2.4	2.3	2.5	2.1	2.2	2.0	1.9	1.7	1.8	1.7	1.5	1.4	1.4	1.3	1.3	1.2
1970	2.8	2.7	2.5	2.6	2.6	2.5	2.7	2.4	2.5	2.3	2.2	2.0	2.1	2.0	1.9	1.7	1.7	1.7	1.7	1.6

Table C-4 (page 2 of 6)

Long-Term Government Bonds: Total Returns
Rates of Return for all holding periods
Percent per annum compounded annually

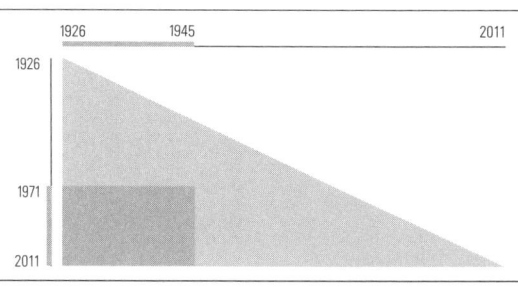

from 1926 to 2011

To the end of	From the beginning of 1926	1927	1928	1929	1930	1931	1932	1933	1934	1935	1936	1937	1938	1939	1940	1941	1942	1943	1944	1945
1971	3.0	2.9	2.8	2.8	2.8	2.8	3.0	2.7	2.7	2.5	2.5	2.3	2.4	2.3	2.2	2.1	2.1	2.1	2.1	2.0
1972	3.1	3.0	2.8	2.9	2.9	2.8	3.1	2.7	2.8	2.6	2.6	2.4	2.5	2.4	2.3	2.2	2.2	2.2	2.2	2.2
1973	3.0	2.9	2.8	2.8	2.8	2.8	3.0	2.6	2.7	2.5	2.5	2.3	2.4	2.3	2.2	2.1	2.1	2.1	2.1	2.1
1974	3.0	2.9	2.8	2.8	2.8	2.8	3.0	2.7	2.7	2.6	2.5	2.4	2.4	2.4	2.3	2.1	2.2	2.2	2.2	2.1
1975	3.1	3.0	2.9	3.0	3.0	2.9	3.1	2.8	2.9	2.7	2.7	2.6	2.6	2.5	2.4	2.3	2.4	2.4	2.4	2.4
1976	3.4	3.3	3.2	3.2	3.2	3.2	3.4	3.1	3.2	3.0	3.0	2.9	3.0	2.9	2.8	2.7	2.8	2.8	2.8	2.8
1977	3.3	3.2	3.1	3.2	3.2	3.1	3.3	3.0	3.1	3.0	2.9	2.8	2.9	2.8	2.7	2.6	2.7	2.7	2.7	2.7
1978	3.2	3.1	3.0	3.1	3.1	3.0	3.2	2.9	3.0	2.9	2.8	2.7	2.8	2.7	2.6	2.5	2.6	2.5	2.6	2.6
1979	3.1	3.0	2.9	3.0	3.0	2.9	3.1	2.9	2.9	2.8	2.7	2.6	2.7	2.6	2.5	2.4	2.5	2.4	2.5	2.4
1980	3.0	2.9	2.8	2.9	2.8	2.8	3.0	2.7	2.8	2.6	2.6	2.5	2.5	2.4	2.3	2.3	2.3	2.3	2.3	2.3
1981	3.0	2.9	2.8	2.8	2.8	2.8	3.0	2.7	2.7	2.6	2.5	2.4	2.5	2.4	2.3	2.2	2.3	2.3	2.3	2.2
1982	3.5	3.5	3.4	3.4	3.4	3.4	3.6	3.3	3.4	3.3	3.2	3.1	3.2	3.2	3.1	3.0	3.1	3.1	3.1	3.1
1983	3.5	3.4	3.3	3.4	3.4	3.4	3.5	3.3	3.3	3.2	3.2	3.1	3.2	3.1	3.0	3.0	3.0	3.0	3.0	3.0
1984	3.7	3.6	3.5	3.6	3.6	3.6	3.7	3.5	3.6	3.4	3.4	3.3	3.4	3.4	3.3	3.2	3.3	3.3	3.3	3.3
1985	4.1	4.0	3.9	4.0	4.0	4.0	4.2	4.0	4.0	3.9	3.9	3.8	3.9	3.9	3.8	3.8	3.8	3.9	3.9	3.9
1986	4.4	4.3	4.3	4.3	4.3	4.3	4.5	4.3	4.4	4.3	4.3	4.2	4.3	4.3	4.2	4.2	4.3	4.3	4.3	4.4
1987	4.3	4.2	4.1	4.2	4.2	4.2	4.4	4.2	4.3	4.2	4.1	4.1	4.2	4.1	4.1	4.0	4.1	4.1	4.2	4.2
1988	4.4	4.3	4.2	4.3	4.3	4.3	4.5	4.3	4.4	4.3	4.2	4.2	4.3	4.2	4.2	4.2	4.2	4.2	4.3	4.3
1989	4.6	4.5	4.4	4.5	4.5	4.5	4.7	4.5	4.6	4.5	4.5	4.4	4.5	4.5	4.5	4.4	4.5	4.5	4.6	4.6
1990	4.6	4.5	4.5	4.5	4.6	4.6	4.7	4.5	4.6	4.5	4.5	4.5	4.5	4.5	4.5	4.5	4.5	4.6	4.6	4.7
1991	4.8	4.7	4.7	4.8	4.8	4.8	5.0	4.8	4.9	4.8	4.8	4.7	4.8	4.8	4.8	4.7	4.8	4.8	4.9	4.9
1992	4.8	4.8	4.7	4.8	4.8	4.8	5.0	4.8	4.9	4.8	4.8	4.8	4.9	4.8	4.8	4.8	4.9	4.9	5.0	5.0
1993	5.0	5.0	4.9	5.0	5.0	5.0	5.2	5.0	5.1	5.0	5.0	5.0	5.1	5.1	5.1	5.0	5.1	5.2	5.2	5.3
1994	4.8	4.8	4.7	4.8	4.8	4.8	5.0	4.8	4.9	4.8	4.8	4.8	4.8	4.8	4.8	4.8	4.9	4.9	4.9	5.0
1995	5.2	5.1	5.1	5.2	5.2	5.2	5.4	5.2	5.3	5.2	5.2	5.2	5.3	5.2	5.2	5.2	5.3	5.3	5.4	5.5
1996	5.1	5.0	5.0	5.1	5.1	5.1	5.3	5.1	5.2	5.1	5.1	5.1	5.1	5.1	5.1	5.1	5.2	5.2	5.3	5.3
1997	5.2	5.2	5.1	5.2	5.2	5.2	5.4	5.2	5.3	5.3	5.3	5.2	5.3	5.3	5.3	5.3	5.4	5.4	5.5	5.5
1998	5.3	5.3	5.2	5.3	5.3	5.4	5.5	5.4	5.4	5.4	5.4	5.3	5.4	5.4	5.4	5.4	5.5	5.5	5.6	5.7
1999	5.1	5.1	5.0	5.1	5.1	5.1	5.3	5.1	5.2	5.1	5.1	5.1	5.2	5.2	5.2	5.2	5.2	5.3	5.3	5.4
2000	5.3	5.3	5.2	5.3	5.3	5.4	5.5	5.4	5.4	5.4	5.4	5.3	5.4	5.4	5.4	5.4	5.5	5.5	5.6	5.6
2001	5.3	5.3	5.2	5.3	5.3	5.3	5.5	5.3	5.4	5.3	5.4	5.3	5.4	5.4	5.4	5.4	5.5	5.5	5.6	5.6
2002	5.5	5.4	5.4	5.5	5.5	5.5	5.7	5.5	5.6	5.5	5.5	5.5	5.6	5.6	5.6	5.6	5.6	5.7	5.7	5.8
2003	5.4	5.4	5.3	5.4	5.4	5.4	5.6	5.4	5.5	5.5	5.5	5.4	5.5	5.5	5.5	5.5	5.6	5.6	5.7	5.7
2004	5.4	5.4	5.4	5.4	5.5	5.5	5.6	5.5	5.6	5.5	5.5	5.5	5.6	5.6	5.6	5.5	5.6	5.7	5.7	5.8
2005	5.5	5.4	5.4	5.5	5.5	5.5	5.7	5.5	5.6	5.5	5.5	5.5	5.6	5.6	5.6	5.6	5.7	5.7	5.8	5.8
2006	5.4	5.4	5.3	5.4	5.4	5.4	5.6	5.5	5.5	5.5	5.5	5.5	5.5	5.5	5.5	5.5	5.6	5.6	5.7	5.7
2007	5.5	5.4	5.4	5.5	5.5	5.5	5.7	5.5	5.6	5.5	5.5	5.5	5.6	5.6	5.6	5.6	5.6	5.7	5.7	5.8
2008	5.7	5.7	5.6	5.7	5.7	5.7	5.9	5.8	5.8	5.8	5.8	5.8	5.9	5.9	5.9	5.9	5.9	6.0	6.0	6.1
2009	5.4	5.4	5.4	5.4	5.4	5.5	5.6	5.5	5.5	5.5	5.5	5.5	5.5	5.5	5.5	5.5	5.6	5.6	5.7	5.7
2010	5.5	5.4	5.4	5.5	5.5	5.5	5.7	5.5	5.6	5.5	5.5	5.5	5.6	5.6	5.6	5.6	5.6	5.7	5.7	5.8
2011	5.7	5.7	5.7	5.7	5.8	5.8	5.9	5.8	5.9	5.8	5.8	5.8	5.9	5.9	5.9	5.9	5.9	6.0	6.0	6.1

Table C-4 (page 3 of 6)

Long-Term Government Bonds: Total Returns
Rates of Return for all holding periods
Percent per annum compounded annually

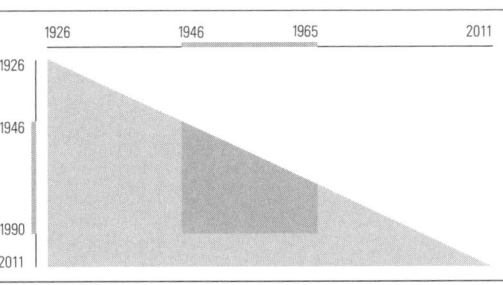

from 1926 to 2011

To the end of	From the beginning of 1946	1947	1948	1949	1950	1951	1952	1953	1954	1955	1956	1957	1958	1959	1960	1961	1962	1963	1964	1965
1946	-0.1																			
1947	-1.4	-2.6																		
1948	0.2	0.3	3.4																	
1949	1.7	2.3	4.9	6.4																
1950	1.4	1.8	3.3	3.2	0.1															
1951	0.5	0.6	1.4	0.8	-2.0	-3.9														
1952	0.6	0.7	1.4	0.9	-0.9	-1.4	1.2													
1953	1.0	1.1	1.7	1.4	0.2	0.2	2.4	3.6												
1954	1.6	1.8	2.5	2.4	1.6	1.9	4.0	5.4	7.2											
1955	1.3	1.5	2.0	1.8	1.1	1.3	2.6	3.1	2.9	-1.3										
1956	0.7	0.8	1.1	0.9	0.1	0.1	0.9	0.9	0.0	-3.5	-5.6									
1957	1.2	1.4	1.8	1.6	1.0	1.1	2.0	2.2	1.8	0.0	0.7	7.5								
1958	0.6	0.7	1.0	0.8	0.2	0.2	0.8	0.7	0.2	-1.5	-1.6	0.5	-6.1							
1959	0.4	0.5	0.7	0.5	-0.1	-0.1	0.4	0.3	-0.2	-1.7	-1.8	-0.5	-4.2	-2.3						
1960	1.3	1.4	1.7	1.5	1.1	1.2	1.8	1.9	1.6	0.7	1.2	2.9	1.5	5.5	13.8					
1961	1.3	1.3	1.6	1.5	1.1	1.2	1.7	1.8	1.6	0.8	1.1	2.5	1.3	3.9	7.2	1.0				
1962	1.6	1.7	2.0	1.9	1.5	1.7	2.2	2.3	2.1	1.5	1.9	3.2	2.4	4.7	7.1	3.9	6.9			
1963	1.6	1.7	1.9	1.8	1.5	1.6	2.1	2.2	2.0	1.5	1.8	3.0	2.2	4.0	5.6	3.0	4.0	1.2		
1964	1.7	1.8	2.0	1.9	1.6	1.8	2.2	2.3	2.2	1.7	2.0	3.0	2.4	3.9	5.2	3.1	3.8	2.4	3.5	
1965	1.6	1.7	2.0	1.9	1.6	1.7	2.1	2.2	2.1	1.6	1.9	2.8	2.2	3.4	4.4	2.6	3.1	1.8	2.1	0.7
1966	1.7	1.8	2.0	2.0	1.7	1.8	2.2	2.3	2.2	1.8	2.1	2.9	2.4	3.5	4.3	2.8	3.2	2.3	2.6	2.2
1967	1.2	1.2	1.4	1.3	1.1	1.1	1.5	1.5	1.3	0.9	1.1	1.7	1.1	2.0	2.5	1.0	1.0	-0.1	-0.5	-1.8
1968	1.1	1.2	1.4	1.3	1.0	1.1	1.4	1.4	1.2	0.8	1.0	1.5	1.0	1.7	2.2	0.8	0.8	-0.2	-0.4	-1.4
1969	0.9	0.9	1.1	1.0	0.7	0.7	1.0	1.0	0.8	0.4	0.5	1.0	0.5	1.1	1.4	0.2	0.1	-0.9	-1.2	-2.1
1970	1.3	1.3	1.5	1.4	1.2	1.3	1.5	1.6	1.4	1.1	1.3	1.8	1.3	2.0	2.4	1.3	1.3	0.7	0.6	0.1
1971	1.7	1.8	2.0	1.9	1.7	1.8	2.1	2.1	2.1	1.8	2.0	2.5	2.1	2.8	3.2	2.3	2.5	2.0	2.1	1.9
1972	1.9	1.9	2.1	2.1	1.9	2.0	2.3	2.3	2.3	2.0	2.2	2.7	2.4	3.0	3.4	2.6	2.8	2.4	2.5	2.3
1973	1.8	1.8	2.0	1.9	1.8	1.8	2.1	2.2	2.1	1.8	2.0	2.5	2.2	2.7	3.1	2.3	2.4	2.0	2.1	2.0
1974	1.8	1.9	2.1	2.0	1.9	1.9	2.2	2.3	2.2	1.9	2.1	2.6	2.3	2.8	3.2	2.5	2.6	2.2	2.3	2.2
1975	2.1	2.2	2.3	2.3	2.1	2.2	2.5	2.5	2.5	2.3	2.5	2.9	2.7	3.2	3.5	2.9	3.0	2.7	2.9	2.8
1976	2.5	2.6	2.8	2.8	2.6	2.7	3.0	3.1	3.1	2.9	3.1	3.6	3.4	3.9	4.3	3.7	3.9	3.7	3.9	3.9
1977	2.4	2.5	2.7	2.7	2.5	2.6	2.9	2.9	2.9	2.7	2.9	3.3	3.1	3.7	4.0	3.4	3.6	3.4	3.5	3.5
1978	2.3	2.4	2.6	2.5	2.4	2.5	2.7	2.8	2.8	2.6	2.7	3.1	2.9	3.4	3.7	3.2	3.3	3.1	3.2	3.2
1979	2.2	2.3	2.4	2.4	2.3	2.3	2.6	2.6	2.6	2.4	2.6	2.9	2.7	3.2	3.5	2.9	3.1	2.8	2.9	2.9
1980	2.0	2.1	2.2	2.2	2.1	2.1	2.3	2.4	2.3	2.2	2.3	2.6	2.4	2.8	3.1	2.6	2.7	2.4	2.5	2.5
1981	2.0	2.1	2.2	2.2	2.1	2.1	2.3	2.4	2.3	2.2	2.3	2.6	2.4	2.8	3.0	2.6	2.6	2.4	2.5	2.4
1982	2.9	3.0	3.2	3.1	3.0	3.1	3.4	3.5	3.4	3.3	3.5	3.9	3.7	4.1	4.4	4.0	4.2	4.0	4.2	4.2
1983	2.8	2.9	3.1	3.1	3.0	3.1	3.3	3.4	3.4	3.2	3.4	3.7	3.6	4.0	4.3	3.9	4.0	3.9	4.0	4.0
1984	3.2	3.2	3.4	3.4	3.3	3.4	3.6	3.7	3.7	3.6	3.8	4.1	4.0	4.4	4.7	4.3	4.5	4.4	4.5	4.6
1985	3.8	3.9	4.0	4.1	4.0	4.1	4.4	4.5	4.5	4.4	4.6	5.0	4.9	5.3	5.6	5.3	5.5	5.4	5.6	5.7
1986	4.2	4.3	4.5	4.6	4.5	4.6	4.9	5.0	5.0	5.0	5.2	5.6	5.5	5.9	6.3	6.0	6.2	6.1	6.4	6.5
1987	4.1	4.2	4.3	4.4	4.3	4.4	4.7	4.8	4.8	4.7	4.9	5.3	5.2	5.6	5.9	5.6	5.8	5.8	6.0	6.1
1988	4.2	4.3	4.5	4.5	4.4	4.6	4.8	4.9	4.9	4.9	5.1	5.4	5.4	5.8	6.0	5.8	6.0	5.9	6.1	6.2
1989	4.5	4.6	4.8	4.8	4.8	4.9	5.1	5.2	5.3	5.2	5.4	5.8	5.7	6.1	6.4	6.2	6.4	6.4	6.6	6.7
1990	4.5	4.6	4.8	4.8	4.8	4.9	5.2	5.3	5.3	5.3	5.5	5.8	5.7	6.1	6.4	6.2	6.4	6.3	6.5	6.7

Table C-4 (page 4 of 6)
Long-Term Government Bonds: Total Returns
Rates of Return for all holding periods
Percent per annum compounded annually

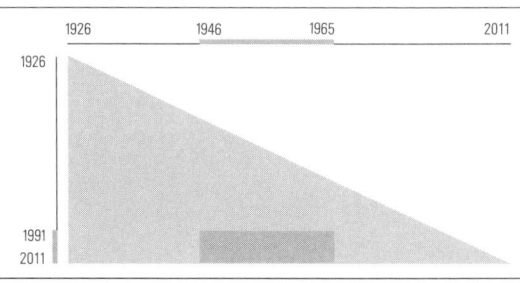

from 1926 to 2011

To the end of	From the beginning of 1946	1947	1948	1949	1950	1951	1952	1953	1954	1955	1956	1957	1958	1959	1960	1961	1962	1963	1964	1965
1991	4.8	4.9	5.1	5.2	5.1	5.2	5.5	5.6	5.7	5.6	5.8	6.2	6.1	6.5	6.8	6.6	6.8	6.8	7.0	7.1
1992	4.9	5.0	5.2	5.2	5.2	5.3	5.6	5.7	5.7	5.7	5.9	6.2	6.2	6.6	6.8	6.6	6.8	6.8	7.0	7.1
1993	5.2	5.3	5.4	5.5	5.5	5.6	5.8	6.0	6.0	6.0	6.2	6.5	6.5	6.9	7.2	7.0	7.2	7.2	7.4	7.5
1994	4.9	5.0	5.1	5.2	5.2	5.3	5.5	5.6	5.7	5.6	5.8	6.1	6.1	6.4	6.7	6.5	6.7	6.7	6.8	7.0
1995	5.3	5.5	5.6	5.7	5.7	5.8	6.0	6.1	6.2	6.2	6.4	6.7	6.7	7.1	7.3	7.1	7.3	7.3	7.5	7.7
1996	5.2	5.3	5.5	5.5	5.5	5.6	5.9	6.0	6.0	6.0	6.2	6.5	6.5	6.8	7.1	6.9	7.1	7.1	7.3	7.4
1997	5.4	5.5	5.7	5.7	5.7	5.9	6.1	6.2	6.3	6.2	6.4	6.7	6.7	7.1	7.3	7.1	7.3	7.3	7.5	7.6
1998	5.6	5.7	5.8	5.9	5.9	6.0	6.2	6.3	6.4	6.4	6.6	6.9	6.9	7.2	7.5	7.3	7.5	7.5	7.7	7.8
1999	5.3	5.4	5.5	5.6	5.6	5.7	5.9	6.0	6.0	6.0	6.2	6.5	6.5	6.8	7.0	6.8	7.0	7.0	7.2	7.3
2000	5.5	5.7	5.8	5.9	5.8	6.0	6.2	6.3	6.3	6.3	6.5	6.8	6.8	7.1	7.3	7.2	7.4	7.4	7.5	7.7
2001	5.5	5.6	5.8	5.8	5.8	5.9	6.1	6.2	6.3	6.3	6.4	6.7	6.7	7.0	7.3	7.1	7.3	7.3	7.4	7.5
2002	5.7	5.8	6.0	6.0	6.0	6.1	6.3	6.5	6.5	6.5	6.7	7.0	6.9	7.3	7.5	7.3	7.5	7.5	7.7	7.8
2003	5.6	5.7	5.9	5.9	5.9	6.0	6.3	6.4	6.4	6.4	6.6	6.8	6.8	7.1	7.4	7.2	7.4	7.4	7.5	7.6
2004	5.7	5.8	5.9	6.0	6.0	6.1	6.3	6.4	6.4	6.4	6.6	6.9	6.9	7.2	7.4	7.2	7.4	7.4	7.6	7.7
2005	5.7	5.8	6.0	6.0	6.0	6.1	6.3	6.4	6.5	6.5	6.6	6.9	6.9	7.2	7.4	7.2	7.4	7.4	7.6	7.7
2006	5.6	5.7	5.9	5.9	5.9	6.0	6.2	6.3	6.4	6.4	6.5	6.8	6.8	7.0	7.2	7.1	7.3	7.3	7.4	7.5
2007	5.7	5.8	6.0	6.0	6.0	6.1	6.3	6.4	6.4	6.4	6.6	6.8	6.8	7.1	7.3	7.2	7.3	7.3	7.5	7.6
2008	6.0	6.1	6.3	6.3	6.3	6.4	6.6	6.7	6.8	6.8	6.9	7.2	7.2	7.4	7.7	7.5	7.7	7.7	7.8	7.9
2009	5.6	5.7	5.9	5.9	5.9	6.0	6.2	6.3	6.3	6.3	6.5	6.7	6.7	7.0	7.1	7.0	7.1	7.2	7.3	7.4
2010	5.7	5.8	5.9	6.0	6.0	6.1	6.3	6.3	6.4	6.4	6.5	6.8	6.8	7.0	7.2	7.1	7.2	7.2	7.3	7.4
2011	6.0	6.1	6.3	6.3	6.3	6.4	6.6	6.7	6.7	6.7	6.9	7.1	7.1	7.4	7.6	7.5	7.6	7.6	7.7	7.8

Table C-4 (page 5 of 6)

Long-Term Government Bonds: Total Returns
Rates of Return for all holding periods
Percent per annum compounded annually

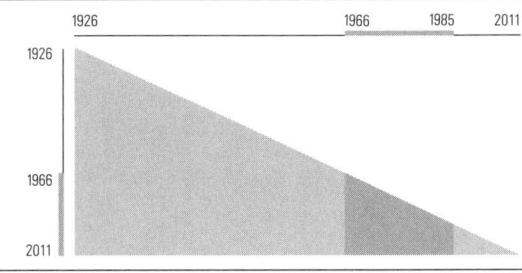

from 1926 to 2011

To the end of	From the beginning of 1966	1967	1968	1969	1970	1971	1972	1973	1974	1975	1976	1977	1978	1979	1980	1981	1982	1983	1984	1985
1966	3.7																			
1967	-3.0	-9.2																		
1968	-2.1	-4.8	-0.3																	
1969	-2.8	-4.9	-2.7	-5.1																
1970	0.0	-0.9	2.0	3.2	12.1															
1971	2.1	1.8	4.7	6.4	12.7	13.2														
1972	2.6	2.4	4.9	6.2	10.3	9.4	5.7													
1973	2.1	1.9	3.9	4.7	7.3	5.8	2.2	-1.1												
1974	2.4	2.2	3.9	4.7	6.7	5.4	2.9	1.6	4.4											
1975	3.0	3.0	4.6	5.3	7.1	6.2	4.5	4.1	6.7	9.2										
1976	4.2	4.3	5.9	6.7	8.5	7.9	6.8	7.1	10.0	12.9	16.8									
1977	3.8	3.8	5.2	5.8	7.3	6.6	5.5	5.5	7.2	8.2	7.7	-0.7								
1978	3.4	3.4	4.6	5.1	6.3	5.6	4.5	4.4	5.5	5.8	4.6	-0.9	-1.2							
1979	3.1	3.0	4.1	4.5	5.5	4.8	3.8	3.5	4.3	4.3	3.1	-1.0	-1.2	-1.2						
1980	2.6	2.5	3.5	3.8	4.6	3.9	2.9	2.6	3.1	2.9	1.7	-1.8	-2.1	-2.6	-3.9					
1981	2.5	2.5	3.3	3.6	4.4	3.7	2.8	2.5	2.9	2.7	1.7	-1.1	-1.1	-1.1	-1.1	1.9				
1982	4.4	4.5	5.5	5.9	6.8	6.4	5.8	5.8	6.6	6.8	6.5	4.9	6.0	7.9	11.2	19.6	40.4			
1983	4.2	4.3	5.2	5.5	6.3	5.9	5.3	5.3	6.0	6.1	5.8	4.3	5.1	6.4	8.4	12.9	18.9	0.7		
1984	4.8	4.9	5.7	6.1	6.9	6.6	6.1	6.1	6.8	7.0	6.8	5.6	6.5	7.9	9.8	13.5	17.7	7.8	15.5	
1985	6.0	6.1	7.0	7.5	8.3	8.0	7.7	7.8	8.6	9.0	9.0	8.2	9.3	10.9	13.1	16.8	20.9	15.0	23.0	31.0
1986	6.8	6.9	7.9	8.3	9.2	9.0	8.7	8.9	9.8	10.2	10.3	9.7	10.9	12.5	14.6	18.1	21.6	17.3	23.5	27.7
1987	6.3	6.5	7.3	7.7	8.5	8.3	8.0	8.1	8.8	9.2	9.2	8.5	9.5	10.7	12.3	14.9	17.2	13.0	16.3	16.6
1988	6.5	6.6	7.4	7.8	8.5	8.4	8.1	8.2	8.9	9.2	9.2	8.6	9.5	10.6	12.0	14.2	16.1	12.5	15.0	14.9
1989	6.9	7.1	7.9	8.3	9.0	8.8	8.6	8.8	9.4	9.8	9.8	9.3	10.2	11.3	12.6	14.6	16.3	13.2	15.5	15.5
1990	6.9	7.0	7.8	8.2	8.9	8.7	8.5	8.6	9.2	9.6	9.6	9.1	9.9	10.8	12.0	13.7	15.2	12.3	14.1	13.9
1991	7.4	7.5	8.3	8.7	9.3	9.2	9.0	9.2	9.8	10.1	10.2	9.7	10.5	11.5	12.6	14.2	15.6	13.1	14.8	14.6
1992	7.4	7.5	8.3	8.6	9.3	9.1	9.0	9.1	9.7	10.0	10.0	9.6	10.4	11.2	12.2	13.7	14.9	12.6	14.0	13.8
1993	7.8	7.9	8.6	9.0	9.6	9.5	9.4	9.5	10.1	10.4	10.5	10.1	10.8	11.7	12.7	14.1	15.1	13.1	14.4	14.3
1994	7.2	7.3	8.0	8.3	8.9	8.7	8.6	8.7	9.2	9.4	9.4	9.0	9.6	10.4	11.2	12.3	13.2	11.2	12.2	11.9
1995	7.9	8.1	8.7	9.1	9.7	9.6	9.4	9.6	10.1	10.4	10.4	10.1	10.8	11.5	12.4	13.5	14.4	12.6	13.7	13.5
1996	7.6	7.8	8.4	8.7	9.3	9.2	9.0	9.1	9.6	9.8	9.9	9.5	10.1	10.8	11.5	12.6	13.3	11.6	12.5	12.3
1997	7.9	8.0	8.6	9.0	9.5	9.4	9.2	9.4	9.9	10.1	10.1	9.8	10.4	11.0	11.8	12.8	13.5	11.9	12.7	12.5
1998	8.0	8.2	8.8	9.1	9.6	9.5	9.4	9.5	10.0	10.2	10.3	10.0	10.5	11.1	11.8	12.8	13.5	12.0	12.8	12.6
1999	7.5	7.6	8.2	8.5	8.9	8.8	8.7	8.8	9.2	9.4	9.4	9.1	9.5	10.1	10.7	11.5	12.1	10.6	11.3	11.0
2000	7.9	8.0	8.5	8.8	9.3	9.2	9.1	9.2	9.6	9.8	9.9	9.6	10.0	10.6	11.2	12.0	12.6	11.2	11.8	11.6
2001	7.7	7.9	8.4	8.7	9.1	9.0	8.9	9.0	9.4	9.6	9.6	9.3	9.8	10.3	10.8	11.6	12.1	10.8	11.4	11.1
2002	8.0	8.1	8.7	8.9	9.4	9.3	9.2	9.3	9.7	9.9	9.9	9.6	10.1	10.6	11.1	11.9	12.4	11.1	11.7	11.5
2003	7.8	7.9	8.5	8.7	9.2	9.1	8.9	9.0	9.4	9.6	9.6	9.3	9.7	10.2	10.7	11.4	11.8	10.6	11.2	10.9
2004	7.8	8.0	8.5	8.7	9.1	9.0	8.9	9.0	9.4	9.5	9.6	9.3	9.7	10.1	10.6	11.3	11.7	10.5	11.0	10.8
2005	7.8	7.9	8.4	8.7	9.1	9.0	8.9	9.0	9.3	9.5	9.5	9.2	9.6	10.0	10.5	11.1	11.5	10.4	10.9	10.7
2006	7.7	7.8	8.2	8.5	8.9	8.8	8.7	8.7	9.1	9.2	9.2	9.0	9.3	9.7	10.1	10.7	11.1	10.0	10.4	10.2
2007	7.7	7.8	8.3	8.5	8.9	8.8	8.7	8.8	9.1	9.2	9.2	9.0	9.3	9.7	10.1	10.7	11.0	10.0	10.4	10.2
2008	8.1	8.2	8.7	8.9	9.3	9.2	9.1	9.2	9.5	9.7	9.7	9.5	9.8	10.2	10.6	11.2	11.6	10.6	11.0	10.8
2009	7.5	7.6	8.1	8.3	8.6	8.5	8.4	8.5	8.8	8.9	8.9	8.7	9.0	9.3	9.7	10.2	10.5	9.5	9.9	9.7
2010	7.6	7.7	8.1	8.3	8.7	8.6	8.5	8.5	8.8	8.9	8.9	8.7	9.0	9.3	9.7	10.2	10.5	9.5	9.9	9.7
2011	8.0	8.1	8.5	8.7	9.1	9.0	8.9	9.0	9.3	9.4	9.4	9.2	9.5	9.9	10.2	10.7	11.0	10.1	10.5	10.3

Table C-4 (page 6 of 6)-a
Long-Term Government Bonds: Total Returns
Rates of Return for all holding periods
Percent per annum compounded annually

from 1926 to 2011

To the end of	From the beginning of 1986	1987	1988	1989	1990	1991	1992	1993	1994	1995	1996	1997	1998	1999	2000	2001
1986	24.5															
1987	10.1	-2.7														
1988	9.9	3.3	9.7													
1989	11.9	8.0	13.8	18.1												
1990	10.8	7.6	11.2	12.0	6.2											
1991	12.1	9.8	13.2	14.4	12.6	19.3										
1992	11.5	9.5	12.1	12.8	11.0	13.5	8.1									
1993	12.4	10.7	13.1	13.8	12.8	15.1	13.0	18.2								
1994	9.9	8.2	9.9	9.9	8.3	8.9	5.6	4.4	-7.8							
1995	11.9	10.6	12.4	12.8	11.9	13.1	11.6	12.8	10.2	31.7						
1996	10.7	9.4	10.8	11.0	10.0	10.6	9.0	9.2	6.4	14.2	-0.9					
1997	11.1	10.0	11.3	11.5	10.7	11.4	10.1	10.5	8.7	14.8	7.1	15.9				
1998	11.3	10.2	11.5	11.7	11.0	11.6	10.5	10.9	9.5	14.3	9.1	14.4	13.1			
1999	9.7	8.6	9.6	9.6	8.8	9.1	7.9	7.8	6.2	9.2	4.3	6.0	1.5	-9.0		
2000	10.4	9.5	10.5	10.5	9.9	10.3	9.3	9.5	8.3	11.2	7.5	9.7	7.7	5.2	21.5	
2001	10.0	9.1	10.0	10.0	9.4	9.6	8.7	8.8	7.7	10.1	6.8	8.5	6.7	4.7	12.2	3.7
2002	10.4	9.6	10.5	10.5	10.0	10.3	9.5	9.7	8.8	11.0	8.4	10.0	8.8	7.8	14.1	10.5
2003	9.9	9.1	9.9	9.9	9.4	9.6	8.8	8.9	8.0	9.9	7.5	8.7	7.6	6.5	10.8	7.4
2004	9.8	9.1	9.8	9.8	9.3	9.5	8.8	8.9	8.1	9.8	7.6	8.7	7.7	6.8	10.3	7.7
2005	9.7	9.0	9.7	9.7	9.2	9.4	8.7	8.8	8.0	9.6	7.6	8.6	7.7	7.0	9.9	7.7
2006	9.3	8.6	9.2	9.2	8.7	8.9	8.2	8.2	7.5	8.9	7.0	7.8	7.0	6.2	8.6	6.6
2007	9.3	8.7	9.3	9.3	8.8	8.9	8.3	8.3	7.7	8.9	7.2	8.0	7.3	6.6	8.8	7.1
2008	10.0	9.4	10.0	10.0	9.6	9.8	9.3	9.4	8.8	10.1	8.6	9.4	8.8	8.4	10.5	9.3
2009	8.8	8.2	8.7	8.7	8.2	8.3	7.8	7.8	7.1	8.2	6.7	7.3	6.6	6.1	7.7	6.3
2010	8.9	8.3	8.8	8.8	8.3	8.4	7.9	7.9	7.3	8.3	6.9	7.5	6.9	6.4	7.9	6.6
2011	9.6	9.0	9.5	9.5	9.2	9.3	8.8	8.9	8.4	9.4	8.1	8.8	8.3	7.9	9.5	8.4

Table C-4 (page 6 of 6)-b
Long-Term Government Bonds: Total Returns
Rates of Return for all holding periods
Percent per annum compounded annually

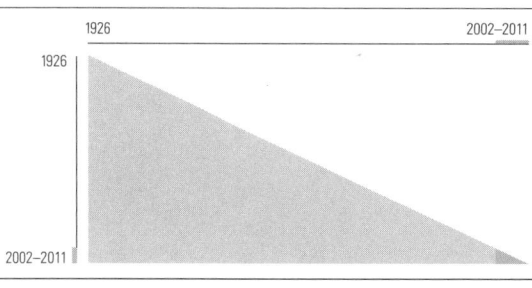

1926 2002–2011

1926

2002–2011

from 1926 to 2011

To the end of	From the beginning of 2002	2003	2004	2005	2006	2007	2008	2009	2010	2011
2002	17.8									
2003	9.3	1.4								
2004	9.1	4.9	8.5							
2005	8.7	5.9	8.2	7.8						
2006	7.2	4.7	5.8	4.4	1.2					
2007	7.6	5.7	6.8	6.2	5.4	9.9				
2008	10.1	8.8	10.4	10.8	11.9	17.6	25.9			
2009	6.6	5.1	5.7	5.1	4.5	5.6	3.5	-14.9		
2010	7.0	5.7	6.3	5.9	5.6	6.7	5.7	-3.2	10.1	
2011	8.9	8.0	8.8	8.9	9.1	10.7	10.9	6.3	18.8	28.2

Table C-5 (page 1 of 6)

Intermediate-Term Government Bonds: Total Returns
Rates of Return for all holding periods
Percent per annum compounded annually

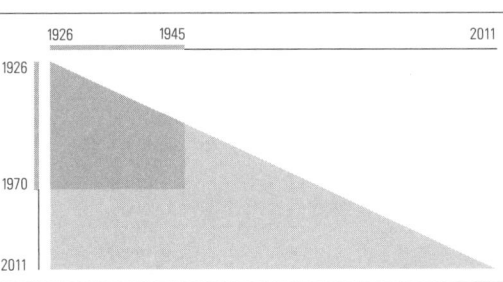

from 1926 to 2011

To the end of	From the beginning of 1926	1927	1928	1929	1930	1931	1932	1933	1934	1935	1936	1937	1938	1939	1940	1941	1942	1943	1944	1945
1926	5.4																			
1927	4.9	4.5																		
1928	3.6	2.7	0.9																	
1929	4.2	3.8	3.4	6.0																
1930	4.7	4.5	4.5	6.4	6.7															
1931	3.5	3.1	2.8	3.4	2.1	-2.3														
1932	4.2	4.0	3.9	4.7	4.3	3.1	8.8													
1933	3.9	3.7	3.6	4.1	3.7	2.7	5.3	1.8												
1934	4.5	4.4	4.3	4.9	4.7	4.2	6.5	5.4	9.0											
1935	4.7	4.7	4.7	5.2	5.1	4.8	6.6	5.9	8.0	7.0										
1936	4.6	4.5	4.5	4.9	4.8	4.5	5.9	5.2	6.3	5.0	3.1									
1937	4.3	4.2	4.2	4.6	4.4	4.1	5.2	4.4	5.1	3.8	2.3	1.6								
1938	4.5	4.4	4.4	4.7	4.6	4.3	5.3	4.7	5.3	4.4	3.6	3.9	6.2							
1939	4.5	4.4	4.4	4.7	4.6	4.3	5.2	4.7	5.2	4.5	3.8	4.1	5.4	4.5						
1940	4.4	4.3	4.3	4.6	4.4	4.2	5.0	4.5	4.9	4.2	3.7	3.8	4.6	3.7	3.0					
1941	4.1	4.0	4.0	4.2	4.1	3.9	4.5	4.0	4.3	3.7	3.1	3.1	3.5	2.6	1.7	0.5				
1942	4.0	3.9	3.9	4.1	3.9	3.7	4.3	3.8	4.1	3.4	3.0	2.9	3.2	2.5	1.8	1.2	1.9			
1943	3.9	3.8	3.8	4.0	3.9	3.6	4.1	3.7	3.9	3.4	2.9	2.9	3.1	2.5	2.0	1.7	2.4	2.8		
1944	3.8	3.7	3.7	3.9	3.7	3.5	4.0	3.6	3.7	3.2	2.8	2.8	2.9	2.4	2.0	1.8	2.2	2.3	1.8	
1945	3.7	3.6	3.6	3.8	3.6	3.4	3.8	3.5	3.6	3.1	2.7	2.7	2.9	2.4	2.0	1.8	2.2	2.3	2.0	2.2
1946	3.6	3.5	3.5	3.6	3.5	3.3	3.6	3.3	3.4	2.9	2.6	2.5	2.7	2.2	1.9	1.7	2.0	2.0	1.7	1.6
1947	3.5	3.4	3.3	3.5	3.3	3.1	3.5	3.1	3.2	2.8	2.4	2.4	2.5	2.1	1.8	1.6	1.8	1.7	1.5	1.4
1948	3.4	3.3	3.3	3.4	3.2	3.1	3.4	3.0	3.1	2.7	2.4	2.3	2.4	2.0	1.8	1.6	1.8	1.8	1.6	1.5
1949	3.4	3.3	3.2	3.3	3.2	3.0	3.3	3.0	3.1	2.7	2.4	2.3	2.4	2.1	1.8	1.7	1.9	1.8	1.7	1.7
1950	3.3	3.2	3.1	3.2	3.1	2.9	3.2	2.9	2.9	2.6	2.3	2.2	2.3	2.0	1.7	1.6	1.7	1.7	1.5	1.5
1951	3.1	3.1	3.0	3.1	3.0	2.8	3.0	2.7	2.8	2.4	2.2	2.1	2.1	1.8	1.6	1.5	1.6	1.5	1.4	1.3
1952	3.1	3.0	2.9	3.0	2.9	2.7	3.0	2.7	2.7	2.4	2.1	2.1	2.1	1.8	1.6	1.5	1.6	1.6	1.4	1.4
1953	3.1	3.0	2.9	3.0	2.9	2.7	3.0	2.7	2.8	2.4	2.2	2.1	2.2	1.9	1.7	1.6	1.7	1.7	1.6	1.6
1954	3.1	3.0	2.9	3.0	2.9	2.7	3.0	2.7	2.8	2.5	2.2	2.2	2.2	2.0	1.8	1.7	1.8	1.8	1.7	1.7
1955	2.9	2.9	2.8	2.9	2.8	2.6	2.8	2.6	2.6	2.3	2.1	2.0	2.0	1.8	1.6	1.5	1.6	1.6	1.5	1.5
1956	2.8	2.8	2.7	2.8	2.6	2.5	2.7	2.4	2.5	2.2	2.0	1.9	1.9	1.7	1.5	1.4	1.5	1.5	1.4	1.3
1957	3.0	2.9	2.9	2.9	2.8	2.7	2.9	2.6	2.7	2.4	2.2	2.2	2.2	2.0	1.9	1.8	1.9	1.9	1.8	1.8
1958	2.9	2.8	2.7	2.8	2.7	2.5	2.7	2.5	2.5	2.3	2.1	2.0	2.0	1.8	1.7	1.6	1.7	1.7	1.6	1.6
1959	2.8	2.7	2.6	2.7	2.6	2.4	2.6	2.4	2.4	2.2	2.0	1.9	1.9	1.7	1.6	1.5	1.6	1.5	1.5	1.4
1960	3.0	2.9	2.9	3.0	2.9	2.7	2.9	2.7	2.7	2.5	2.3	2.3	2.3	2.2	2.0	2.0	2.1	2.1	2.0	2.1
1961	3.0	2.9	2.9	2.9	2.8	2.7	2.9	2.7	2.7	2.5	2.3	2.3	2.3	2.1	2.0	2.0	2.1	2.1	2.0	2.0
1962	3.0	3.0	2.9	3.0	2.9	2.8	3.0	2.8	2.8	2.6	2.4	2.4	2.4	2.3	2.2	2.2	2.2	2.2	2.2	2.2
1963	3.0	2.9	2.9	3.0	2.9	2.8	2.9	2.7	2.8	2.6	2.4	2.4	2.4	2.3	2.2	2.1	2.2	2.2	2.2	2.2
1964	3.0	3.0	2.9	3.0	2.9	2.8	3.0	2.8	2.8	2.6	2.5	2.4	2.5	2.3	2.2	2.2	2.3	2.3	2.3	2.3
1965	3.0	2.9	2.9	2.9	2.9	2.7	2.9	2.7	2.7	2.6	2.4	2.4	2.4	2.3	2.2	2.2	2.2	2.2	2.2	2.2
1966	3.0	3.0	2.9	3.0	2.9	2.8	2.9	2.8	2.8	2.6	2.5	2.5	2.5	2.4	2.3	2.3	2.3	2.3	2.3	2.3
1967	3.0	2.9	2.9	2.9	2.8	2.7	2.9	2.7	2.8	2.6	2.4	2.4	2.4	2.3	2.2	2.2	2.3	2.3	2.3	2.3
1968	3.0	3.0	2.9	3.0	2.9	2.8	2.9	2.8	2.8	2.6	2.5	2.5	2.5	2.4	2.3	2.3	2.4	2.4	2.4	2.4
1969	2.9	2.9	2.8	2.9	2.8	2.7	2.8	2.7	2.7	2.5	2.4	2.4	2.4	2.3	2.2	2.2	2.2	2.3	2.2	2.3
1970	3.2	3.2	3.1	3.2	3.1	3.0	3.2	3.0	3.1	2.9	2.8	2.8	2.8	2.7	2.7	2.6	2.7	2.7	2.7	2.8

Table C-5 (page 2 of 6)

Intermediate-Term Government Bonds: Total Returns
Rates of Return for all holding periods
Percent per annum compounded annually

from 1926 to 2011

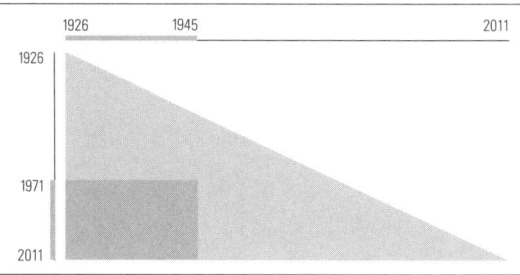

To the end of	From the beginning of 1926	1927	1928	1929	1930	1931	1932	1933	1934	1935	1936	1937	1938	1939	1940	1941	1942	1943	1944	1945
1971	3.3	3.3	3.3	3.3	3.3	3.2	3.3	3.2	3.2	3.1	2.9	2.9	3.0	2.9	2.8	2.8	2.9	2.9	3.0	3.0
1972	3.4	3.3	3.3	3.4	3.3	3.2	3.4	3.2	3.3	3.1	3.0	3.0	3.0	3.0	2.9	2.9	3.0	3.0	3.0	3.1
1973	3.4	3.4	3.3	3.4	3.3	3.2	3.4	3.3	3.3	3.1	3.0	3.0	3.1	3.0	3.0	3.0	3.0	3.1	3.1	3.1
1974	3.4	3.4	3.4	3.4	3.4	3.3	3.4	3.3	3.3	3.2	3.1	3.1	3.2	3.1	3.0	3.0	3.1	3.2	3.2	3.2
1975	3.5	3.5	3.5	3.5	3.5	3.4	3.5	3.4	3.5	3.3	3.2	3.2	3.3	3.2	3.2	3.2	3.3	3.3	3.3	3.4
1976	3.7	3.7	3.7	3.7	3.7	3.6	3.7	3.6	3.7	3.5	3.5	3.5	3.5	3.4	3.4	3.4	3.5	3.6	3.6	3.6
1977	3.7	3.6	3.6	3.7	3.6	3.6	3.7	3.6	3.6	3.5	3.4	3.4	3.5	3.4	3.4	3.4	3.5	3.5	3.5	3.6
1978	3.7	3.6	3.6	3.7	3.6	3.6	3.7	3.6	3.6	3.5	3.4	3.4	3.5	3.4	3.4	3.4	3.5	3.5	3.5	3.6
1979	3.7	3.6	3.6	3.7	3.6	3.6	3.7	3.6	3.6	3.5	3.4	3.4	3.5	3.4	3.4	3.4	3.5	3.5	3.5	3.6
1980	3.7	3.6	3.6	3.7	3.6	3.6	3.7	3.6	3.6	3.5	3.4	3.4	3.5	3.4	3.4	3.4	3.5	3.5	3.5	3.6
1981	3.8	3.7	3.7	3.8	3.7	3.7	3.8	3.7	3.7	3.6	3.6	3.6	3.6	3.6	3.5	3.6	3.6	3.7	3.7	3.7
1982	4.2	4.1	4.1	4.2	4.2	4.1	4.2	4.2	4.2	4.1	4.0	4.1	4.1	4.1	4.1	4.1	4.2	4.2	4.3	4.3
1983	4.2	4.2	4.2	4.3	4.2	4.2	4.3	4.2	4.3	4.2	4.1	4.1	4.2	4.2	4.1	4.2	4.3	4.3	4.4	4.4
1984	4.4	4.4	4.4	4.4	4.4	4.4	4.5	4.4	4.5	4.4	4.3	4.3	4.4	4.4	4.4	4.4	4.5	4.5	4.6	4.7
1985	4.6	4.6	4.6	4.7	4.7	4.6	4.8	4.7	4.7	4.7	4.6	4.6	4.7	4.7	4.7	4.7	4.8	4.9	4.9	5.0
1986	4.8	4.8	4.8	4.9	4.8	4.8	4.9	4.9	4.9	4.8	4.8	4.8	4.9	4.9	4.9	4.9	5.0	5.1	5.2	5.2
1987	4.8	4.8	4.8	4.8	4.8	4.8	4.9	4.8	4.9	4.8	4.8	4.8	4.9	4.8	4.8	4.9	5.0	5.1	5.1	5.2
1988	4.8	4.8	4.8	4.8	4.8	4.8	4.9	4.9	4.9	4.8	4.8	4.8	4.9	4.9	4.9	4.9	5.0	5.1	5.1	5.2
1989	4.9	4.9	4.9	5.0	5.0	4.9	5.1	5.0	5.1	5.0	4.9	5.0	5.0	5.0	5.0	5.1	5.2	5.2	5.3	5.4
1990	5.0	5.0	5.0	5.1	5.0	5.0	5.1	5.1	5.1	5.1	5.0	5.1	5.1	5.1	5.1	5.2	5.3	5.3	5.4	5.5
1991	5.1	5.1	5.1	5.2	5.2	5.2	5.3	5.2	5.3	5.2	5.2	5.2	5.3	5.3	5.3	5.4	5.5	5.5	5.6	5.7
1992	5.2	5.2	5.2	5.2	5.2	5.2	5.3	5.3	5.3	5.3	5.2	5.3	5.4	5.3	5.4	5.4	5.5	5.6	5.6	5.7
1993	5.3	5.3	5.3	5.3	5.3	5.3	5.4	5.4	5.4	5.4	5.3	5.4	5.5	5.4	5.5	5.5	5.6	5.7	5.7	5.8
1994	5.1	5.1	5.1	5.2	5.2	5.1	5.2	5.2	5.2	5.2	5.2	5.2	5.3	5.2	5.3	5.3	5.4	5.5	5.5	5.6
1995	5.3	5.3	5.3	5.3	5.3	5.3	5.4	5.4	5.4	5.4	5.3	5.4	5.4	5.4	5.5	5.5	5.6	5.7	5.7	5.8
1996	5.2	5.2	5.2	5.3	5.3	5.2	5.4	5.3	5.4	5.3	5.3	5.3	5.4	5.4	5.4	5.4	5.5	5.6	5.6	5.7
1997	5.3	5.3	5.3	5.3	5.3	5.3	5.4	5.4	5.4	5.4	5.3	5.4	5.4	5.4	5.4	5.4	5.5	5.6	5.6	5.7	5.8
1998	5.3	5.3	5.3	5.4	5.4	5.4	5.5	5.4	5.5	5.4	5.4	5.4	5.5	5.5	5.5	5.5	5.6	5.7	5.7	5.8	5.9
1999	5.2	5.2	5.2	5.3	5.3	5.3	5.4	5.3	5.4	5.3	5.3	5.3	5.4	5.4	5.4	5.4	5.5	5.6	5.6	5.7
2000	5.3	5.3	5.3	5.4	5.4	5.4	5.5	5.4	5.5	5.4	5.4	5.4	5.5	5.5	5.5	5.6	5.6	5.7	5.8	5.8
2001	5.3	5.3	5.4	5.4	5.4	5.4	5.5	5.5	5.5	5.5	5.4	5.5	5.5	5.5	5.5	5.6	5.7	5.7	5.8	5.9
2002	5.4	5.4	5.5	5.5	5.5	5.5	5.6	5.6	5.6	5.6	5.5	5.6	5.6	5.6	5.7	5.7	5.8	5.9	5.9	6.0
2003	5.4	5.4	5.4	5.5	5.5	5.4	5.6	5.5	5.6	5.5	5.5	5.5	5.6	5.6	5.6	5.6	5.7	5.8	5.8	5.9
2004	5.4	5.4	5.4	5.4	5.4	5.4	5.5	5.5	5.5	5.5	5.5	5.5	5.5	5.5	5.6	5.6	5.7	5.7	5.8	5.9
2005	5.3	5.3	5.3	5.4	5.4	5.3	5.5	5.4	5.5	5.4	5.4	5.4	5.5	5.5	5.5	5.5	5.6	5.7	5.7	5.8
2006	5.3	5.3	5.3	5.3	5.3	5.3	5.4	5.4	5.4	5.4	5.4	5.4	5.4	5.4	5.5	5.5	5.6	5.6	5.7	5.7
2007	5.3	5.3	5.3	5.4	5.4	5.4	5.5	5.4	5.5	5.4	5.4	5.4	5.5	5.5	5.5	5.5	5.6	5.6	5.7	5.7	5.8
2008	5.4	5.4	5.4	5.5	5.5	5.5	5.6	5.5	5.6	5.5	5.5	5.6	5.6	5.6	5.6	5.7	5.7	5.8	5.8	5.9
2009	5.3	5.3	5.3	5.4	5.4	5.4	5.5	5.4	5.5	5.4	5.4	5.4	5.5	5.5	5.5	5.5	5.6	5.7	5.7	5.8
2010	5.4	5.4	5.4	5.4	5.4	5.4	5.5	5.5	5.5	5.5	5.4	5.5	5.5	5.5	5.5	5.6	5.6	5.7	5.7	5.8
2011	5.4	5.4	5.4	5.5	5.5	5.4	5.5	5.5	5.6	5.5	5.5	5.5	5.6	5.6	5.6	5.6	5.7	5.7	5.8	5.9

Table C-5 (page 3 of 6)

Intermediate-Term Government Bonds: Total Returns
Rates of Return for all holding periods
Percent per annum compounded annually

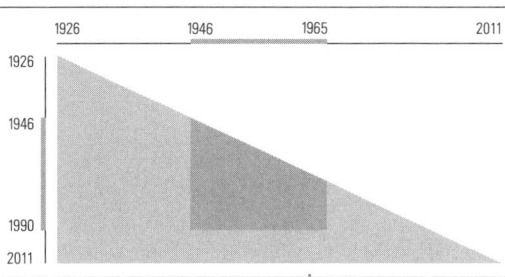

from 1926 to 2011

To the end of	From the beginning of 1946	1947	1948	1949	1950	1951	1952	1953	1954	1955	1956	1957	1958	1959	1960	1961	1962	1963	1964	1965
1946	1.0																			
1947	1.0	0.9																		
1948	1.3	1.4	1.8																	
1949	1.5	1.7	2.1	2.3																
1950	1.4	1.4	1.6	1.5	0.7															
1951	1.2	1.2	1.3	1.1	0.5	0.4														
1952	1.3	1.3	1.4	1.3	0.9	1.0	1.6													
1953	1.5	1.6	1.7	1.6	1.5	1.7	2.4	3.2												
1954	1.6	1.7	1.8	1.8	1.7	2.0	2.5	3.0	2.7											
1955	1.4	1.4	1.5	1.5	1.3	1.4	1.7	1.7	1.0	-0.7										
1956	1.2	1.3	1.3	1.2	1.1	1.1	1.3	1.2	0.5	-0.5	-0.4									
1957	1.8	1.8	1.9	1.9	1.9	2.1	2.3	2.5	2.3	2.2	3.6	7.8								
1958	1.5	1.6	1.6	1.6	1.5	1.6	1.8	1.9	1.6	1.3	2.0	3.2	-1.3							
1959	1.4	1.4	1.5	1.4	1.3	1.4	1.5	1.5	1.2	1.0	1.4	2.0	-0.8	-0.4						
1960	2.1	2.1	2.2	2.3	2.2	2.4	2.6	2.8	2.7	2.7	3.4	4.3	3.2	5.5	11.8					
1961	2.0	2.1	2.2	2.2	2.2	2.3	2.5	2.7	2.6	2.6	3.1	3.8	2.9	4.3	6.7	1.8				
1962	2.2	2.3	2.4	2.5	2.5	2.6	2.8	2.9	2.9	2.9	3.5	4.1	3.4	4.6	6.3	3.7	5.6			
1963	2.2	2.3	2.4	2.4	2.4	2.5	2.7	2.8	2.8	2.8	3.2	3.8	3.1	4.0	5.1	3.0	3.6	1.6		
1964	2.3	2.4	2.5	2.5	2.5	2.6	2.8	2.9	2.9	2.9	3.3	3.8	3.2	4.0	4.9	3.3	3.7	2.8	4.0	
1965	2.2	2.3	2.4	2.4	2.4	2.5	2.7	2.8	2.7	2.7	3.1	3.5	3.0	3.6	4.2	2.8	3.1	2.2	2.5	1.0
1966	2.4	2.4	2.5	2.5	2.6	2.7	2.8	2.9	2.9	2.9	3.2	3.6	3.1	3.7	4.3	3.1	3.4	2.8	3.2	2.8
1967	2.3	2.4	2.4	2.5	2.5	2.6	2.7	2.8	2.8	2.8	3.0	3.4	2.9	3.4	3.9	2.8	3.0	2.5	2.7	2.2
1968	2.4	2.5	2.5	2.6	2.6	2.7	2.8	2.9	2.9	2.9	3.2	3.5	3.1	3.5	4.0	3.0	3.2	2.8	3.0	2.8
1969	2.3	2.3	2.4	2.4	2.4	2.5	2.6	2.7	2.6	2.6	2.9	3.1	2.8	3.1	3.5	2.6	2.7	2.3	2.4	2.1
1970	2.8	2.9	3.0	3.0	3.1	3.2	3.3	3.4	3.4	3.5	3.8	4.1	3.8	4.2	4.6	3.9	4.2	4.0	4.4	4.4
1971	3.0	3.1	3.2	3.3	3.3	3.4	3.6	3.7	3.7	3.8	4.1	4.4	4.1	4.5	5.0	4.4	4.6	4.5	4.9	5.0
1972	3.1	3.2	3.3	3.3	3.4	3.5	3.7	3.8	3.8	3.9	4.1	4.4	4.2	4.6	5.0	4.4	4.7	4.6	4.9	5.0
1973	3.2	3.2	3.3	3.4	3.4	3.6	3.7	3.8	3.8	3.9	4.1	4.4	4.2	4.6	5.0	4.5	4.7	4.6	4.9	5.0
1974	3.2	3.3	3.4	3.5	3.5	3.6	3.8	3.9	3.9	4.0	4.2	4.5	4.3	4.7	5.0	4.5	4.7	4.7	5.0	5.1
1975	3.4	3.5	3.6	3.6	3.7	3.8	4.0	4.1	4.1	4.2	4.4	4.7	4.5	4.8	5.2	4.8	5.0	4.9	5.2	5.3
1976	3.7	3.8	3.9	4.0	4.0	4.1	4.3	4.4	4.5	4.5	4.8	5.1	4.9	5.3	5.6	5.2	5.5	5.5	5.8	5.9
1977	3.6	3.7	3.8	3.9	3.9	4.0	4.2	4.3	4.3	4.4	4.6	4.9	4.7	5.1	5.4	5.0	5.2	5.2	5.5	5.6
1978	3.6	3.7	3.8	3.8	3.9	4.0	4.2	4.3	4.3	4.4	4.6	4.8	4.7	5.0	5.3	4.9	5.1	5.1	5.3	5.4
1979	3.6	3.7	3.8	3.9	3.9	4.0	4.2	4.2	4.3	4.4	4.6	4.8	4.7	4.9	5.2	4.9	5.1	5.0	5.2	5.3
1980	3.6	3.7	3.8	3.9	3.9	4.0	4.1	4.2	4.3	4.3	4.5	4.8	4.6	4.9	5.2	4.8	5.0	5.0	5.2	5.2
1981	3.8	3.9	4.0	4.0	4.1	4.2	4.3	4.4	4.5	4.5	4.7	4.9	4.8	5.1	5.3	5.1	5.2	5.2	5.4	5.5
1982	4.4	4.5	4.6	4.7	4.8	4.9	5.0	5.2	5.2	5.3	5.5	5.8	5.7	6.0	6.3	6.0	6.2	6.3	6.5	6.7
1983	4.5	4.6	4.7	4.8	4.8	5.0	5.1	5.2	5.3	5.4	5.6	5.8	5.8	6.1	6.3	6.1	6.3	6.3	6.6	6.7
1984	4.7	4.8	4.9	5.0	5.1	5.2	5.4	5.5	5.6	5.7	5.9	6.1	6.1	6.3	6.6	6.4	6.6	6.7	6.9	7.1
1985	5.1	5.2	5.3	5.4	5.5	5.6	5.8	5.9	6.0	6.1	6.3	6.6	6.5	6.8	7.1	6.9	7.2	7.2	7.5	7.7
1986	5.3	5.4	5.5	5.6	5.7	5.9	6.0	6.2	6.3	6.4	6.6	6.9	6.8	7.1	7.4	7.2	7.5	7.5	7.8	8.0
1987	5.3	5.4	5.5	5.6	5.7	5.8	6.0	6.1	6.2	6.3	6.5	6.7	6.7	7.0	7.2	7.1	7.3	7.4	7.6	7.8
1988	5.3	5.4	5.5	5.6	5.7	5.8	6.0	6.1	6.2	6.3	6.5	6.7	6.7	6.9	7.2	7.0	7.2	7.3	7.5	7.7
1989	5.5	5.6	5.7	5.8	5.9	6.0	6.1	6.3	6.4	6.5	6.7	6.9	6.9	7.1	7.4	7.3	7.5	7.5	7.8	7.9
1990	5.5	5.7	5.8	5.9	5.9	6.1	6.2	6.4	6.4	6.5	6.8	7.0	7.0	7.2	7.5	7.3	7.5	7.6	7.8	8.0

Table C-5 (page 4 of 6)

Intermediate-Term Government Bonds: Total Returns
Rates of Return for all holding periods
Percent per annum compounded annually

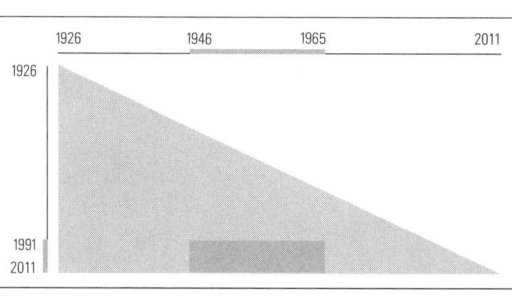

from 1926 to 2011

To the end of	From the beginning of 1946	1947	1948	1949	1950	1951	1952	1953	1954	1955	1956	1957	1958	1959	1960	1961	1962	1963	1964	1965
1991	5.8	5.9	6.0	6.1	6.2	6.3	6.5	6.6	6.7	6.8	7.0	7.2	7.2	7.5	7.7	7.6	7.8	7.9	8.1	8.2
1992	5.8	5.9	6.0	6.1	6.2	6.3	6.5	6.6	6.7	6.8	7.0	7.2	7.2	7.5	7.7	7.6	7.8	7.8	8.1	8.2
1993	5.9	6.0	6.1	6.2	6.3	6.4	6.6	6.7	6.8	6.9	7.1	7.3	7.3	7.6	7.8	7.7	7.9	8.0	8.2	8.3
1994	5.7	5.8	5.9	5.9	6.0	6.2	6.3	6.4	6.5	6.6	6.8	7.0	6.9	7.2	7.4	7.3	7.5	7.5	7.7	7.8
1995	5.9	6.0	6.1	6.2	6.3	6.4	6.5	6.6	6.7	6.8	7.0	7.2	7.2	7.4	7.7	7.5	7.7	7.8	8.0	8.1
1996	5.8	5.9	6.0	6.1	6.2	6.3	6.4	6.5	6.6	6.7	6.9	7.1	7.1	7.3	7.5	7.4	7.6	7.6	7.8	7.9
1997	5.8	5.9	6.0	6.1	6.2	6.3	6.5	6.6	6.7	6.7	6.9	7.1	7.1	7.3	7.5	7.4	7.6	7.6	7.8	7.9
1998	5.9	6.0	6.1	6.2	6.3	6.4	6.5	6.7	6.7	6.8	7.0	7.2	7.2	7.4	7.6	7.5	7.6	7.7	7.9	8.0
1999	5.8	5.9	6.0	6.0	6.1	6.2	6.4	6.5	6.5	6.6	6.8	7.0	6.9	7.2	7.4	7.2	7.4	7.4	7.6	7.7
2000	5.9	6.0	6.1	6.2	6.2	6.4	6.5	6.6	6.7	6.8	6.9	7.1	7.1	7.3	7.5	7.4	7.5	7.6	7.7	7.8
2001	5.9	6.0	6.1	6.2	6.3	6.4	6.5	6.6	6.7	6.8	6.9	7.1	7.1	7.3	7.5	7.4	7.5	7.6	7.7	7.8
2002	6.0	6.1	6.2	6.3	6.4	6.5	6.6	6.7	6.8	6.9	7.1	7.2	7.2	7.4	7.6	7.5	7.7	7.7	7.9	8.0
2003	6.0	6.1	6.2	6.2	6.3	6.4	6.5	6.6	6.7	6.8	7.0	7.1	7.1	7.3	7.5	7.4	7.5	7.6	7.7	7.8
2004	5.9	6.0	6.1	6.2	6.2	6.3	6.5	6.6	6.6	6.7	6.9	7.0	7.0	7.2	7.4	7.3	7.4	7.4	7.6	7.7
2005	5.8	5.9	6.0	6.1	6.2	6.3	6.4	6.5	6.5	6.6	6.7	6.9	6.9	7.1	7.2	7.1	7.3	7.3	7.4	7.5
2006	5.8	5.9	6.0	6.0	6.1	6.2	6.3	6.4	6.5	6.5	6.7	6.8	6.8	7.0	7.1	7.0	7.2	7.2	7.3	7.4
2007	5.9	5.9	6.0	6.1	6.2	6.3	6.4	6.5	6.5	6.6	6.7	6.9	6.9	7.0	7.2	7.1	7.2	7.3	7.4	7.5
2008	6.0	6.1	6.1	6.2	6.3	6.4	6.5	6.6	6.6	6.7	6.9	7.0	7.0	7.2	7.3	7.2	7.3	7.4	7.5	7.6
2009	5.8	5.9	6.0	6.1	6.1	6.2	6.3	6.4	6.5	6.5	6.7	6.8	6.8	7.0	7.1	7.0	7.1	7.2	7.3	7.4
2010	5.9	5.9	6.0	6.1	6.1	6.2	6.3	6.4	6.5	6.6	6.7	6.8	6.8	7.0	7.1	7.0	7.1	7.2	7.3	7.4
2011	5.9	6.0	6.1	6.1	6.2	6.3	6.4	6.5	6.5	6.6	6.7	6.9	6.9	7.0	7.2	7.1	7.2	7.2	7.3	7.4

Table C-5 (page 5 of 6)

Intermediate-Term Government Bonds: Total Returns

Rates of Return for all holding periods

Percent per annum compounded annually

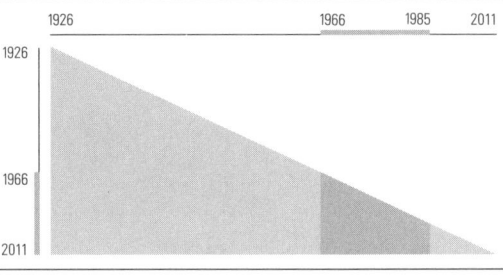

from 1926 to 2011

To the end of	From the beginning of 1966	1967	1968	1969	1970	1971	1972	1973	1974	1975	1976	1977	1978	1979	1980	1981	1982	1983	1984	1985
1966	4.7																			
1967	2.8	1.0																		
1968	3.4	2.8	4.5																	
1969	2.3	1.6	1.9	-0.7																
1970	5.1	5.2	6.6	7.7	16.9															
1971	5.7	5.9	7.2	8.0	12.7	8.7														
1972	5.6	5.8	6.8	7.3	10.1	6.9	5.2													
1973	5.5	5.6	6.4	6.8	8.7	6.1	4.9	4.6												
1974	5.5	5.6	6.3	6.6	8.1	6.0	5.2	5.1	5.7											
1975	5.7	5.9	6.5	6.8	8.1	6.4	5.8	6.0	6.8	7.8										
1976	6.4	6.5	7.2	7.5	8.7	7.4	7.2	7.7	8.8	10.3	12.9									
1977	5.9	6.1	6.6	6.8	7.8	6.6	6.2	6.4	6.9	7.3	7.0	1.4								
1978	5.8	5.8	6.3	6.5	7.3	6.2	5.8	5.9	6.2	6.3	5.8	2.4	3.5							
1979	5.6	5.7	6.1	6.3	7.0	5.9	5.6	5.7	5.8	5.9	5.4	3.0	3.8	4.1						
1980	5.5	5.6	5.9	6.1	6.7	5.7	5.4	5.4	5.6	5.5	5.1	3.2	3.8	4.0	3.9					
1981	5.8	5.8	6.2	6.3	6.9	6.1	5.8	5.9	6.0	6.1	5.8	4.4	5.2	5.8	6.6	9.5				
1982	7.0	7.2	7.6	7.8	8.5	7.8	7.7	8.0	8.4	8.7	8.8	8.2	9.6	11.2	13.7	18.9	29.1			
1983	7.0	7.2	7.6	7.8	8.4	7.8	7.7	7.9	8.3	8.6	8.7	8.1	9.2	10.4	12.1	14.9	17.8	7.4		
1984	7.4	7.5	7.9	8.2	8.8	8.2	8.2	8.4	8.8	9.1	9.2	8.8	9.9	11.0	12.5	14.7	16.5	10.7	14.0	
1985	8.0	8.2	8.6	8.8	9.5	9.0	9.0	9.3	9.7	10.1	10.3	10.0	11.2	12.3	13.7	15.8	17.4	13.8	17.1	20.3
1986	8.3	8.5	8.9	9.2	9.8	9.4	9.4	9.7	10.1	10.5	10.7	10.5	11.6	12.6	13.9	15.7	17.0	14.1	16.5	17.7
1987	8.1	8.2	8.6	8.8	9.4	9.0	9.0	9.2	9.6	9.9	10.1	9.8	10.7	11.5	12.5	13.8	14.5	11.8	12.9	12.5
1988	8.0	8.1	8.5	8.7	9.2	8.8	8.8	9.0	9.4	9.6	9.8	9.5	10.3	11.0	11.8	12.8	13.3	10.8	11.5	10.9
1989	8.2	8.4	8.7	8.9	9.4	9.0	9.1	9.3	9.6	9.9	10.0	9.8	10.5	11.2	11.9	12.8	13.3	11.2	11.8	11.4
1990	8.3	8.4	8.8	8.9	9.4	9.1	9.1	9.3	9.6	9.8	10.0	9.8	10.5	11.1	11.7	12.5	12.9	11.0	11.5	11.1
1991	8.5	8.7	9.0	9.2	9.7	9.4	9.4	9.6	9.9	10.2	10.3	10.2	10.8	11.4	12.0	12.8	13.1	11.5	12.0	11.7
1992	8.5	8.6	9.0	9.1	9.6	9.3	9.3	9.5	9.8	10.0	10.1	10.0	10.6	11.1	11.6	12.3	12.6	11.0	11.5	11.1
1993	8.6	8.7	9.0	9.2	9.7	9.4	9.4	9.6	9.8	10.1	10.2	10.0	10.6	11.1	11.6	12.2	12.5	11.1	11.4	11.1
1994	8.1	8.2	8.5	8.6	9.0	8.7	8.7	8.9	9.1	9.3	9.3	9.1	9.6	10.0	10.4	10.9	11.0	9.6	9.8	9.4
1995	8.4	8.5	8.8	8.9	9.3	9.0	9.0	9.2	9.4	9.6	9.7	9.5	10.0	10.4	10.8	11.3	11.4	10.1	10.4	10.1
1996	8.2	8.3	8.5	8.7	9.0	8.7	8.7	8.9	9.1	9.2	9.3	9.1	9.6	9.9	10.3	10.7	10.8	9.6	9.7	9.4
1997	8.2	8.3	8.5	8.7	9.0	8.7	8.7	8.9	9.1	9.2	9.3	9.1	9.5	9.8	10.2	10.5	10.6	9.5	9.6	9.3
1998	8.2	8.3	8.6	8.7	9.1	8.8	8.8	8.9	9.1	9.3	9.3	9.2	9.5	9.9	10.2	10.5	10.6	9.5	9.7	9.4
1999	7.9	8.0	8.2	8.4	8.7	8.4	8.4	8.5	8.7	8.8	8.8	8.7	9.0	9.3	9.5	9.8	9.9	8.8	8.9	8.6
2000	8.0	8.1	8.4	8.5	8.8	8.5	8.5	8.7	8.8	8.9	9.0	8.8	9.2	9.4	9.7	10.0	10.0	9.0	9.1	8.8
2001	8.0	8.1	8.3	8.5	8.8	8.5	8.5	8.6	8.8	8.9	8.9	8.8	9.1	9.3	9.6	9.9	9.9	9.0	9.0	8.8
2002	8.2	8.3	8.5	8.6	8.9	8.6	8.6	8.8	8.9	9.0	9.1	8.9	9.2	9.5	9.7	10.0	10.0	9.1	9.2	9.0
2003	8.0	8.1	8.3	8.4	8.7	8.5	8.4	8.6	8.7	8.8	8.8	8.7	9.0	9.2	9.4	9.7	9.7	8.8	8.9	8.6
2004	7.9	7.9	8.1	8.2	8.5	8.3	8.3	8.3	8.5	8.6	8.6	8.4	8.7	8.9	9.1	9.3	9.3	8.5	8.6	8.3
2005	7.7	7.8	7.9	8.0	8.3	8.1	8.0	8.1	8.2	8.3	8.3	8.2	8.4	8.6	8.8	9.0	9.0	8.2	8.2	8.0
2006	7.6	7.6	7.8	7.9	8.2	7.9	7.9	8.0	8.1	8.2	8.2	8.0	8.3	8.4	8.6	8.8	8.7	8.0	8.0	7.7
2007	7.6	7.7	7.9	8.0	8.2	8.0	8.0	8.0	8.1	8.2	8.2	8.1	8.3	8.5	8.6	8.8	8.8	8.1	8.1	7.8
2008	7.8	7.8	8.0	8.1	8.3	8.1	8.1	8.2	8.3	8.4	8.4	8.2	8.5	8.6	8.8	9.0	9.0	8.2	8.3	8.0
2009	7.5	7.6	7.7	7.8	8.0	7.8	7.8	7.9	8.0	8.0	8.0	7.9	8.1	8.3	8.4	8.6	8.5	7.8	7.8	7.6
2010	7.5	7.6	7.7	7.8	8.0	7.8	7.8	7.9	7.9	8.0	8.0	7.9	8.1	8.2	8.4	8.5	8.5	7.8	7.8	7.6
2011	7.5	7.6	7.8	7.8	8.1	7.8	7.8	7.9	8.0	8.0	8.1	7.9	8.1	8.3	8.4	8.5	8.5	7.9	7.9	7.7

Table C-5 (page 6 of 6)-a

Intermediate-Term Government Bonds: Total Returns
Rates of Return for all holding periods
Percent per annum compounded annually

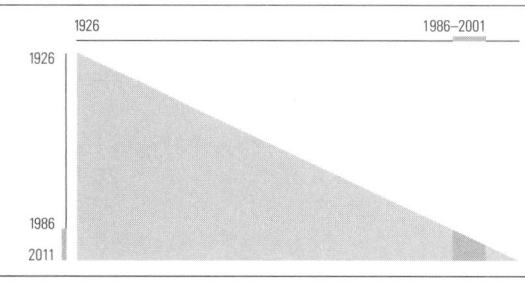

from 1926 to 2011

To the end of	From the beginning of															
	1986	**1987**	**1988**	**1989**	**1990**	**1991**	**1992**	**1993**	**1994**	**1995**	**1996**	**1997**	**1998**	**1999**	**2000**	**2001**
1986	15.1															
1987	8.8	2.9														
1988	7.9	4.5	6.1													
1989	9.2	7.3	9.6	13.3												
1990	9.3	7.9	9.7	11.5	9.7											
1991	10.3	9.4	11.1	12.8	12.6	15.5										
1992	9.9	9.0	10.3	11.4	10.7	11.2	7.2									
1993	10.1	9.3	10.5	11.3	10.9	11.2	9.2	11.2								
1994	8.2	7.4	8.1	8.4	7.5	6.9	4.2	2.7	-5.1							
1995	9.1	8.4	9.1	9.6	9.0	8.8	7.2	7.2	5.3	16.8						
1996	8.4	7.8	8.3	8.6	8.0	7.7	6.2	5.9	4.2	9.2	2.1					
1997	8.4	7.8	8.3	8.6	8.0	7.8	6.5	6.4	5.2	8.9	5.2	8.4				
1998	8.6	8.0	8.5	8.7	8.3	8.1	7.1	7.0	6.2	9.2	6.8	9.3	10.2			
1999	7.8	7.2	7.6	7.7	7.2	6.9	5.9	5.7	4.8	6.9	4.6	5.5	4.0	-1.8		
2000	8.1	7.6	8.0	8.1	7.7	7.5	6.6	6.6	5.9	7.9	6.2	7.2	6.8	5.2	12.6	
2001	8.1	7.6	8.0	8.1	7.7	7.5	6.7	6.7	6.1	7.8	6.4	7.3	7.0	6.0	10.1	7.6
2002	8.3	7.9	8.3	8.4	8.1	7.9	7.3	7.3	6.9	8.5	7.3	8.2	8.2	7.7	11.0	10.2
2003	8.0	7.6	7.9	8.0	7.7	7.5	6.9	6.8	6.4	7.8	6.7	7.4	7.2	6.6	8.8	7.6
2004	7.7	7.3	7.6	7.7	7.3	7.1	6.5	6.4	6.0	7.2	6.2	6.7	6.5	5.9	7.5	6.2
2005	7.4	7.0	7.2	7.3	6.9	6.7	6.1	6.0	5.6	6.7	5.7	6.1	5.8	5.2	6.4	5.2
2006	7.2	6.8	7.0	7.0	6.7	6.5	5.9	5.8	5.4	6.4	5.5	5.8	5.5	4.9	5.9	4.9
2007	7.3	6.9	7.1	7.2	6.9	6.7	6.2	6.1	5.8	6.6	5.8	6.2	6.0	5.5	6.4	5.6
2008	7.5	7.2	7.4	7.5	7.2	7.0	6.6	6.5	6.2	7.1	6.4	6.7	6.6	6.2	7.2	6.5
2009	7.1	6.8	7.0	7.0	6.7	6.5	6.1	6.0	5.7	6.4	5.7	6.0	5.8	5.4	6.2	5.5
2010	7.1	6.8	7.0	7.0	6.7	6.6	6.1	6.0	5.8	6.5	5.8	6.1	5.9	5.6	6.3	5.6
2011	7.2	6.9	7.1	7.1	6.8	6.7	6.3	6.2	6.0	6.6	6.0	6.3	6.2	5.9	6.5	6.0

Table C-5 (page 6 of 6)-b

Intermediate-Term Government Bonds: Total Returns
Rates of Return for all holding periods
Percent per annum compounded annually

from 1926 to 2011

To the end of	From the beginning of									
	2002	**2003**	**2004**	**2005**	**2006**	**2007**	**2008**	**2009**	**2010**	**2011**
2002	12.9									
2003	7.5	2.4								
2004	5.7	2.3	2.3							
2005	4.6	2.0	1.8	1.4						
2006	4.3	2.3	2.3	2.2	3.1					
2007	5.3	3.8	4.1	4.8	6.5	10.1				
2008	6.4	5.3	5.9	6.8	8.7	11.6	13.1			
2009	5.2	4.2	4.5	4.9	5.8	6.7	5.1	-2.4		
2010	5.4	4.5	4.8	5.3	6.1	6.8	5.7	2.2	7.1	
2011	5.8	5.1	5.4	5.9	6.6	7.3	6.7	4.6	8.3	9.5

Table C-6 (page 1 of 6)

U.S. Treasury Bills: Total Returns

Rates of Return for all holding periods

Percent per annum compounded annually

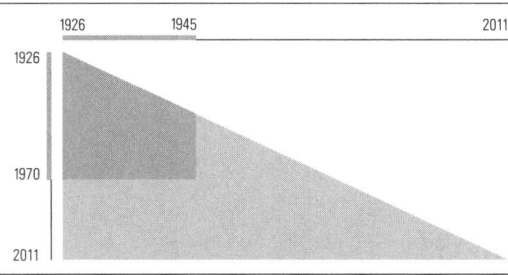

from 1926 to 2011

To the end of	From the beginning of 1926	1927	1928	1929	1930	1931	1932	1933	1934	1935	1936	1937	1938	1939	1940	1941	1942	1943	1944	1945
1926	3.3																			
1927	3.2	3.1																		
1928	3.3	3.3	3.6																	
1929	3.7	3.8	4.2	4.7																
1930	3.4	3.5	3.6	3.6	2.4															
1931	3.0	3.0	2.9	2.7	1.7	1.1														
1932	2.7	2.6	2.5	2.3	1.5	1.0	1.0													
1933	2.4	2.3	2.2	1.9	1.2	0.8	0.6	0.3												
1934	2.2	2.0	1.9	1.6	1.0	0.6	0.5	0.2	0.2											
1935	2.0	1.8	1.7	1.4	0.8	0.5	0.4	0.2	0.2	0.2										
1936	1.8	1.7	1.5	1.2	0.7	0.5	0.4	0.2	0.2	0.2	0.2									
1937	1.7	1.5	1.4	1.1	0.7	0.4	0.3	0.2	0.2	0.2	0.2	0.3								
1938	1.5	1.4	1.2	1.0	0.6	0.4	0.3	0.2	0.2	0.2	0.2	0.1	0.0							
1939	1.4	1.3	1.1	0.9	0.6	0.3	0.3	0.2	0.1	0.1	0.1	0.1	0.0	0.0						
1940	1.3	1.2	1.1	0.9	0.5	0.3	0.2	0.1	0.1	0.1	0.1	0.1	0.0	0.0	0.0					
1941	1.3	1.1	1.0	0.8	0.5	0.3	0.2	0.1	0.1	0.1	0.1	0.1	0.0	0.0	0.0	0.1				
1942	1.2	1.1	0.9	0.8	0.5	0.3	0.2	0.1	0.1	0.1	0.1	0.1	0.1	0.1	0.1	0.2	0.3			
1943	1.2	1.0	0.9	0.7	0.4	0.3	0.2	0.2	0.2	0.1	0.1	0.1	0.1	0.1	0.2	0.2	0.3	0.3		
1944	1.1	1.0	0.9	0.7	0.4	0.3	0.2	0.2	0.2	0.2	0.2	0.2	0.1	0.2	0.2	0.3	0.3	0.3	0.3	
1945	1.1	1.0	0.8	0.7	0.4	0.3	0.2	0.2	0.2	0.2	0.2	0.2	0.2	0.2	0.2	0.3	0.3	0.3	0.3	0.3
1946	1.0	0.9	0.8	0.7	0.4	0.3	0.3	0.2	0.2	0.2	0.2	0.2	0.2	0.2	0.2	0.3	0.3	0.3	0.3	0.3
1947	1.0	0.9	0.8	0.7	0.4	0.3	0.3	0.2	0.2	0.2	0.2	0.2	0.2	0.2	0.3	0.3	0.4	0.4	0.4	0.4
1948	1.0	0.9	0.8	0.7	0.4	0.3	0.3	0.3	0.3	0.3	0.3	0.3	0.3	0.3	0.3	0.4	0.4	0.4	0.5	0.5
1949	1.0	0.9	0.8	0.7	0.5	0.4	0.3	0.3	0.3	0.3	0.3	0.3	0.3	0.3	0.4	0.4	0.5	0.5	0.6	0.6
1950	1.0	0.9	0.8	0.7	0.5	0.4	0.4	0.4	0.4	0.4	0.4	0.4	0.4	0.4	0.5	0.5	0.6	0.6	0.7	0.7
1951	1.0	0.9	0.9	0.7	0.6	0.5	0.4	0.4	0.4	0.4	0.5	0.5	0.5	0.5	0.6	0.6	0.7	0.7	0.8	0.8
1952	1.1	1.0	0.9	0.8	0.6	0.5	0.5	0.5	0.5	0.5	0.5	0.5	0.6	0.6	0.6	0.7	0.8	0.8	0.9	0.9
1953	1.1	1.0	0.9	0.8	0.7	0.6	0.6	0.5	0.6	0.6	0.6	0.6	0.6	0.7	0.7	0.8	0.8	0.9	1.0	1.0
1954	1.1	1.0	0.9	0.8	0.7	0.6	0.6	0.6	0.6	0.6	0.6	0.6	0.7	0.7	0.7	0.8	0.9	0.9	0.9	1.0
1955	1.1	1.0	0.9	0.8	0.7	0.6	0.6	0.6	0.6	0.6	0.7	0.7	0.7	0.7	0.8	0.8	0.9	1.0	1.0	1.1
1956	1.1	1.1	1.0	0.9	0.8	0.7	0.7	0.7	0.7	0.7	0.7	0.8	0.8	0.8	0.9	0.9	1.0	1.1	1.1	1.2
1957	1.2	1.1	1.1	1.0	0.8	0.8	0.8	0.8	0.8	0.8	0.9	0.9	0.9	1.0	1.0	1.1	1.1	1.2	1.3	1.3
1958	1.2	1.1	1.1	1.0	0.9	0.8	0.8	0.8	0.8	0.9	0.9	0.9	0.9	1.0	1.0	1.1	1.2	1.2	1.3	1.3
1959	1.3	1.2	1.1	1.1	0.9	0.9	0.9	0.9	0.9	0.9	1.0	1.0	1.0	1.1	1.1	1.2	1.3	1.3	1.4	1.4
1960	1.3	1.2	1.2	1.1	1.0	1.0	0.9	0.9	1.0	1.0	1.0	1.1	1.1	1.2	1.2	1.3	1.3	1.4	1.5	1.5
1961	1.3	1.3	1.2	1.1	1.0	1.0	1.0	1.0	1.0	1.0	1.1	1.1	1.1	1.2	1.3	1.3	1.4	1.4	1.5	1.6
1962	1.4	1.3	1.3	1.2	1.1	1.0	1.0	1.0	1.1	1.1	1.1	1.2	1.2	1.3	1.3	1.4	1.4	1.5	1.6	1.6
1963	1.4	1.4	1.3	1.2	1.1	1.1	1.1	1.1	1.1	1.2	1.2	1.2	1.3	1.3	1.4	1.4	1.5	1.6	1.6	1.7
1964	1.5	1.4	1.4	1.3	1.2	1.2	1.2	1.2	1.2	1.2	1.3	1.3	1.4	1.4	1.5	1.5	1.6	1.7	1.7	1.8
1965	1.5	1.5	1.4	1.4	1.3	1.3	1.3	1.3	1.3	1.3	1.4	1.4	1.5	1.5	1.6	1.6	1.7	1.8	1.8	1.9
1966	1.6	1.6	1.5	1.5	1.4	1.3	1.4	1.4	1.4	1.4	1.5	1.5	1.6	1.6	1.7	1.7	1.8	1.9	1.9	2.0
1967	1.7	1.6	1.6	1.5	1.5	1.4	1.4	1.4	1.5	1.5	1.6	1.6	1.7	1.7	1.8	1.8	1.9	2.0	2.0	2.1
1968	1.7	1.7	1.7	1.6	1.5	1.5	1.5	1.6	1.6	1.6	1.7	1.7	1.8	1.8	1.9	2.0	2.0	2.1	2.2	2.2
1969	1.8	1.8	1.8	1.7	1.7	1.6	1.7	1.7	1.7	1.8	1.8	1.9	1.9	2.0	2.0	2.1	2.2	2.3	2.3	2.4
1970	2.0	1.9	1.9	1.9	1.8	1.8	1.8	1.8	1.8	1.9	1.9	2.0	2.1	2.1	2.2	2.3	2.3	2.4	2.5	2.6

Appendix C: Rates of Return for All Yearly Holding Periods 1926–2011

Table C-6 (page 2 of 6)
U.S. Treasury Bills: Total Returns
Rates of Return for all holding periods
Percent per annum compounded annually

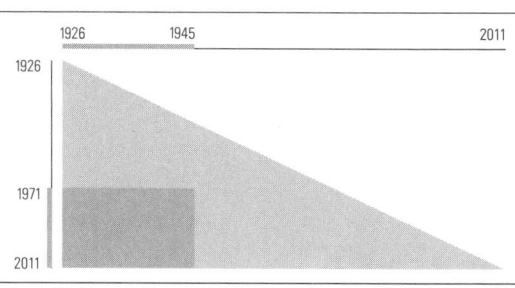

from 1926 to 2011

To the end of	From the beginning of 1926	1927	1928	1929	1930	1931	1932	1933	1934	1935	1936	1937	1938	1939	1940	1941	1942	1943	1944	1945
1971	2.0	2.0	1.9	1.9	1.8	1.8	1.9	1.9	1.9	2.0	2.0	2.1	2.1	2.2	2.3	2.3	2.4	2.5	2.6	2.6
1972	2.0	2.0	2.0	2.0	1.9	1.9	1.9	1.9	2.0	2.0	2.1	2.1	2.2	2.2	2.3	2.4	2.4	2.5	2.6	2.7
1973	2.1	2.1	2.1	2.1	2.0	2.0	2.0	2.0	2.1	2.1	2.2	2.2	2.3	2.4	2.4	2.5	2.6	2.7	2.7	2.8
1974	2.3	2.2	2.2	2.2	2.1	2.1	2.2	2.2	2.2	2.3	2.3	2.4	2.4	2.5	2.6	2.7	2.7	2.8	2.9	3.0
1975	2.3	2.3	2.3	2.3	2.2	2.2	2.2	2.3	2.3	2.4	2.4	2.5	2.5	2.6	2.7	2.8	2.8	2.9	3.0	3.1
1976	2.4	2.4	2.3	2.3	2.3	2.3	2.3	2.3	2.4	2.4	2.5	2.5	2.6	2.7	2.7	2.8	2.9	3.0	3.1	3.1
1977	2.4	2.4	2.4	2.4	2.3	2.3	2.4	2.4	2.4	2.5	2.5	2.6	2.7	2.7	2.8	2.9	3.0	3.0	3.1	3.2
1978	2.5	2.5	2.5	2.5	2.4	2.4	2.5	2.5	2.5	2.6	2.6	2.7	2.8	2.8	2.9	3.0	3.1	3.1	3.2	3.3
1979	2.7	2.6	2.6	2.6	2.6	2.6	2.6	2.7	2.7	2.8	2.8	2.9	2.9	3.0	3.1	3.2	3.3	3.3	3.4	3.5
1980	2.8	2.8	2.8	2.8	2.7	2.7	2.8	2.8	2.9	2.9	3.0	3.1	3.1	3.2	3.3	3.4	3.5	3.5	3.6	3.7
1981	3.0	3.0	3.0	3.0	3.0	3.0	3.0	3.1	3.1	3.2	3.2	3.3	3.4	3.5	3.5	3.6	3.7	3.8	3.9	4.0
1982	3.1	3.1	3.1	3.1	3.1	3.1	3.2	3.2	3.3	3.3	3.4	3.5	3.5	3.6	3.7	3.8	3.9	4.0	4.1	4.2
1983	3.2	3.2	3.2	3.2	3.2	3.2	3.3	3.3	3.4	3.4	3.5	3.6	3.6	3.7	3.8	3.9	4.0	4.1	4.2	4.3
1984	3.3	3.3	3.3	3.3	3.3	3.3	3.4	3.4	3.5	3.6	3.6	3.7	3.8	3.9	3.9	4.0	4.1	4.2	4.3	4.4
1985	3.4	3.4	3.4	3.4	3.4	3.4	3.5	3.5	3.6	3.6	3.7	3.8	3.9	3.9	4.0	4.1	4.2	4.3	4.4	4.5
1986	3.5	3.5	3.5	3.5	3.4	3.5	3.5	3.6	3.6	3.7	3.8	3.8	3.9	4.0	4.1	4.2	4.3	4.3	4.4	4.5
1987	3.5	3.5	3.5	3.5	3.5	3.5	3.5	3.6	3.7	3.7	3.8	3.9	3.9	4.0	4.1	4.2	4.3	4.4	4.5	4.6
1988	3.5	3.5	3.5	3.5	3.5	3.5	3.6	3.6	3.7	3.8	3.8	3.9	4.0	4.1	4.1	4.2	4.3	4.4	4.5	4.6
1989	3.6	3.6	3.6	3.6	3.6	3.6	3.7	3.7	3.8	3.8	3.9	4.0	4.1	4.1	4.2	4.3	4.4	4.5	4.6	4.7
1990	3.7	3.7	3.7	3.7	3.7	3.7	3.7	3.8	3.8	3.9	4.0	4.1	4.1	4.2	4.3	4.4	4.5	4.6	4.7	4.8
1991	3.7	3.7	3.7	3.7	3.7	3.7	3.8	3.8	3.9	3.9	4.0	4.1	4.2	4.2	4.3	4.4	4.5	4.6	4.7	4.8
1992	3.7	3.7	3.7	3.7	3.7	3.7	3.8	3.8	3.9	3.9	4.0	4.1	4.1	4.2	4.3	4.4	4.5	4.6	4.7	4.7
1993	3.7	3.7	3.7	3.7	3.7	3.7	3.8	3.8	3.9	3.9	4.0	4.1	4.1	4.2	4.3	4.4	4.4	4.5	4.6	4.7
1994	3.7	3.7	3.7	3.7	3.7	3.7	3.8	3.8	3.9	3.9	4.0	4.1	4.1	4.2	4.3	4.4	4.4	4.5	4.6	4.7
1995	3.7	3.7	3.7	3.7	3.7	3.7	3.8	3.8	3.9	3.9	4.0	4.1	4.1	4.2	4.3	4.4	4.5	4.5	4.6	4.7
1996	3.7	3.7	3.8	3.8	3.7	3.8	3.8	3.8	3.9	4.0	4.0	4.1	4.2	4.2	4.3	4.4	4.5	4.5	4.6	4.7
1997	3.8	3.8	3.8	3.8	3.8	3.8	3.8	3.9	3.9	4.0	4.1	4.1	4.2	4.3	4.3	4.4	4.5	4.6	4.6	4.7
1998	3.8	3.8	3.8	3.8	3.8	3.8	3.8	3.9	3.9	4.0	4.1	4.1	4.2	4.3	4.3	4.4	4.5	4.6	4.6	4.7
1999	3.8	3.8	3.8	3.8	3.8	3.8	3.9	3.9	4.0	4.0	4.1	4.1	4.2	4.3	4.3	4.4	4.5	4.6	4.6	4.7
2000	3.8	3.8	3.8	3.8	3.8	3.8	3.9	3.9	4.0	4.0	4.1	4.2	4.2	4.3	4.4	4.4	4.5	4.6	4.7	4.7
2001	3.8	3.8	3.8	3.8	3.8	3.8	3.9	3.9	4.0	4.0	4.1	4.2	4.2	4.3	4.4	4.4	4.5	4.6	4.7	4.7
2002	3.8	3.8	3.8	3.8	3.8	3.8	3.9	3.9	3.9	4.0	4.1	4.1	4.2	4.2	4.3	4.4	4.5	4.5	4.6	4.7
2003	3.7	3.8	3.8	3.8	3.8	3.8	3.8	3.9	3.9	4.0	4.0	4.1	4.1	4.2	4.3	4.3	4.4	4.5	4.5	4.6
2004	3.7	3.7	3.7	3.7	3.7	3.7	3.8	3.8	3.9	3.9	4.0	4.0	4.1	4.2	4.2	4.3	4.4	4.4	4.5	4.6
2005	3.7	3.7	3.7	3.7	3.7	3.7	3.8	3.8	3.9	3.9	4.0	4.0	4.1	4.1	4.2	4.3	4.3	4.4	4.5	4.5
2006	3.7	3.7	3.7	3.7	3.7	3.7	3.8	3.8	3.9	3.9	4.0	4.0	4.1	4.1	4.2	4.3	4.3	4.4	4.5	4.5
2007	3.7	3.7	3.7	3.7	3.7	3.8	3.8	3.8	3.9	3.9	4.0	4.0	4.1	4.2	4.2	4.3	4.3	4.4	4.5	4.5
2008	3.7	3.7	3.7	3.7	3.7	3.7	3.8	3.8	3.8	3.9	3.9	4.0	4.1	4.1	4.2	4.2	4.3	4.4	4.4	4.5
2009	3.7	3.7	3.7	3.7	3.7	3.7	3.7	3.7	3.8	3.8	3.9	3.9	4.0	4.1	4.1	4.2	4.2	4.3	4.4	4.4
2010	3.6	3.6	3.6	3.6	3.6	3.6	3.7	3.7	3.7	3.8	3.8	3.9	3.9	4.0	4.1	4.1	4.2	4.2	4.3	4.4
2011	3.6	3.6	3.6	3.6	3.6	3.6	3.6	3.7	3.7	3.7	3.8	3.8	3.9	3.9	4.0	4.1	4.1	4.2	4.2	4.3

Table C-6 (page 3 of 6)

U.S. Treasury Bills: Total Returns

Rates of Return for all holding periods

Percent per annum compounded annually

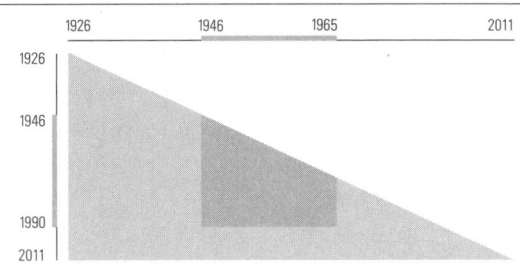

from 1926 to 2011

To the end of	From the beginning of 1946	1947	1948	1949	1950	1951	1952	1953	1954	1955	1956	1957	1958	1959	1960	1961	1962	1963	1964	1965
1946	0.4																			
1947	0.4	0.5																		
1948	0.6	0.7	0.8																	
1949	0.7	0.8	1.0	1.1																
1950	0.8	0.9	1.0	1.1	1.2															
1951	0.9	1.0	1.2	1.3	1.3	1.5														
1952	1.0	1.1	1.3	1.4	1.4	1.6	1.7													
1953	1.1	1.2	1.3	1.5	1.5	1.7	1.7	1.8												
1954	1.1	1.2	1.3	1.4	1.4	1.5	1.4	1.3	0.9											
1955	1.1	1.2	1.3	1.4	1.4	1.5	1.5	1.4	1.2	1.6										
1956	1.3	1.3	1.4	1.5	1.6	1.6	1.7	1.7	1.6	2.0	2.5									
1957	1.4	1.5	1.6	1.7	1.8	1.9	1.9	2.0	2.0	2.4	2.8	3.1								
1958	1.4	1.5	1.6	1.7	1.7	1.8	1.9	1.9	1.9	2.2	2.4	2.3	1.5							
1959	1.5	1.6	1.7	1.8	1.9	1.9	2.0	2.0	2.1	2.3	2.5	2.5	2.2	3.0						
1960	1.6	1.7	1.8	1.9	1.9	2.0	2.1	2.1	2.2	2.4	2.5	2.6	2.4	2.8	2.7					
1961	1.6	1.7	1.8	1.9	2.0	2.0	2.1	2.1	2.2	2.3	2.5	2.5	2.3	2.6	2.4	2.1				
1962	1.7	1.8	1.9	1.9	2.0	2.1	2.1	2.2	2.2	2.4	2.5	2.5	2.4	2.6	2.5	2.4	2.7			
1963	1.8	1.9	2.0	2.0	2.1	2.2	2.2	2.3	2.3	2.5	2.6	2.6	2.5	2.7	2.7	2.7	2.9	3.1		
1964	1.9	2.0	2.0	2.1	2.2	2.3	2.3	2.4	2.4	2.6	2.7	2.7	2.7	2.9	2.8	2.9	3.1	3.3	3.5	
1965	2.0	2.1	2.1	2.2	2.3	2.4	2.4	2.5	2.5	2.7	2.8	2.9	2.8	3.0	3.0	3.1	3.3	3.5	3.7	3.9
1966	2.1	2.2	2.3	2.4	2.4	2.5	2.6	2.7	2.7	2.9	3.0	3.0	3.0	3.2	3.3	3.4	3.6	3.8	4.1	4.3
1967	2.2	2.3	2.4	2.5	2.5	2.6	2.7	2.8	2.8	3.0	3.1	3.2	3.2	3.3	3.4	3.5	3.7	3.9	4.1	4.3
1968	2.3	2.4	2.5	2.6	2.7	2.8	2.8	2.9	3.0	3.1	3.3	3.3	3.3	3.5	3.6	3.7	3.9	4.1	4.3	4.5
1969	2.5	2.6	2.7	2.8	2.9	3.0	3.0	3.1	3.2	3.4	3.5	3.6	3.6	3.8	3.9	4.0	4.3	4.5	4.7	4.9
1970	2.7	2.8	2.9	3.0	3.0	3.1	3.2	3.3	3.4	3.6	3.7	3.8	3.8	4.0	4.1	4.3	4.5	4.7	5.0	5.2
1971	2.7	2.8	2.9	3.0	3.1	3.2	3.3	3.4	3.4	3.6	3.7	3.8	3.9	4.0	4.1	4.3	4.5	4.7	4.9	5.1
1972	2.8	2.9	3.0	3.0	3.1	3.2	3.3	3.4	3.5	3.6	3.7	3.8	3.9	4.0	4.1	4.2	4.4	4.6	4.8	4.9
1973	2.9	3.0	3.1	3.2	3.3	3.4	3.5	3.6	3.6	3.8	3.9	4.0	4.1	4.2	4.3	4.4	4.6	4.8	5.0	5.1
1974	3.1	3.2	3.3	3.4	3.5	3.6	3.7	3.8	3.8	4.0	4.1	4.2	4.3	4.5	4.6	4.7	4.9	5.1	5.3	5.4
1975	3.2	3.3	3.4	3.5	3.6	3.7	3.7	3.8	3.9	4.1	4.2	4.3	4.4	4.5	4.6	4.8	5.0	5.1	5.3	5.5
1976	3.2	3.3	3.4	3.5	3.6	3.7	3.8	3.9	4.0	4.1	4.2	4.3	4.4	4.6	4.7	4.8	5.0	5.1	5.3	5.4
1977	3.3	3.4	3.5	3.6	3.7	3.8	3.9	3.9	4.0	4.2	4.3	4.4	4.4	4.6	4.7	4.8	5.0	5.1	5.3	5.4
1978	3.4	3.5	3.6	3.7	3.8	3.9	4.0	4.1	4.2	4.3	4.4	4.5	4.6	4.7	4.8	4.9	5.1	5.3	5.4	5.5
1979	3.6	3.7	3.8	3.9	4.0	4.1	4.2	4.3	4.4	4.5	4.7	4.8	4.8	5.0	5.1	5.2	5.4	5.5	5.7	5.8
1980	3.8	3.9	4.0	4.1	4.2	4.3	4.4	4.5	4.6	4.8	4.9	5.0	5.1	5.3	5.4	5.5	5.7	5.9	6.0	6.2
1981	4.1	4.2	4.3	4.4	4.5	4.7	4.8	4.9	5.0	5.1	5.3	5.4	5.5	5.7	5.8	5.9	6.1	6.3	6.5	6.7
1982	4.3	4.4	4.5	4.6	4.7	4.8	4.9	5.1	5.2	5.3	5.5	5.6	5.7	5.9	6.0	6.1	6.3	6.5	6.7	6.9
1983	4.4	4.5	4.6	4.7	4.8	4.9	5.1	5.2	5.3	5.4	5.6	5.7	5.8	6.0	6.1	6.2	6.4	6.6	6.8	7.0
1984	4.5	4.6	4.8	4.9	5.0	5.1	5.2	5.3	5.4	5.6	5.7	5.8	5.9	6.1	6.2	6.4	6.6	6.8	6.9	7.1
1985	4.6	4.7	4.8	4.9	5.1	5.2	5.3	5.4	5.5	5.7	5.8	5.9	6.0	6.2	6.3	6.4	6.6	6.8	7.0	7.1
1986	4.6	4.8	4.9	5.0	5.1	5.2	5.3	5.4	5.5	5.7	5.8	5.9	6.0	6.2	6.3	6.4	6.6	6.8	6.9	7.1
1987	4.7	4.8	4.9	5.0	5.1	5.2	5.3	5.4	5.5	5.7	5.8	5.9	6.0	6.2	6.3	6.4	6.6	6.7	6.9	7.0
1988	4.7	4.8	4.9	5.0	5.1	5.2	5.3	5.4	5.5	5.7	5.8	5.9	6.0	6.2	6.3	6.4	6.6	6.7	6.9	7.0
1989	4.8	4.9	5.0	5.1	5.2	5.3	5.4	5.5	5.6	5.8	5.9	6.0	6.1	6.2	6.3	6.5	6.6	6.8	6.9	7.1
1990	4.9	5.0	5.1	5.2	5.3	5.4	5.5	5.6	5.7	5.8	5.9	6.0	6.1	6.3	6.4	6.5	6.7	6.8	6.9	7.1

Appendix C: Rates of Return for All Yearly Holding Periods 1926–2011

Table C-6 (page 4 of 6)

U.S. Treasury Bills: Total Returns

Rates of Return for all holding periods

Percent per annum compounded annually

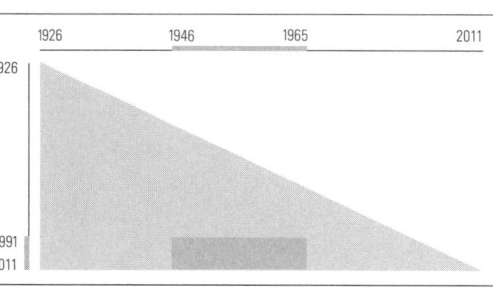

from 1926 to 2011

To the end of	From the beginning of 1946	1947	1948	1949	1950	1951	1952	1953	1954	1955	1956	1957	1958	1959	1960	1961	1962	1963	1964	1965
1991	4.9	5.0	5.1	5.2	5.3	5.4	5.5	5.6	5.7	5.8	5.9	6.0	6.1	6.3	6.4	6.5	6.6	6.8	6.9	7.0
1992	4.8	4.9	5.0	5.1	5.2	5.3	5.4	5.5	5.6	5.7	5.9	6.0	6.0	6.2	6.3	6.4	6.5	6.7	6.8	6.9
1993	4.8	4.9	5.0	5.1	5.2	5.3	5.4	5.5	5.5	5.7	5.8	5.9	6.0	6.1	6.2	6.3	6.4	6.5	6.7	6.8
1994	4.8	4.9	5.0	5.1	5.2	5.2	5.3	5.4	5.5	5.6	5.7	5.8	5.9	6.0	6.1	6.2	6.3	6.5	6.6	6.7
1995	4.8	4.9	5.0	5.1	5.2	5.2	5.3	5.4	5.5	5.6	5.7	5.8	5.9	6.0	6.1	6.2	6.3	6.4	6.5	6.6
1996	4.8	4.9	5.0	5.1	5.2	5.2	5.3	5.4	5.5	5.6	5.7	5.8	5.9	6.0	6.1	6.2	6.3	6.4	6.5	6.6
1997	4.8	4.9	5.0	5.1	5.2	5.2	5.3	5.4	5.5	5.6	5.7	5.8	5.9	6.0	6.0	6.1	6.3	6.4	6.5	6.5
1998	4.8	4.9	5.0	5.1	5.2	5.2	5.3	5.4	5.5	5.6	5.7	5.8	5.8	5.9	6.0	6.1	6.2	6.3	6.4	6.5
1999	4.8	4.9	5.0	5.1	5.1	5.2	5.3	5.4	5.5	5.6	5.7	5.7	5.8	5.9	6.0	6.1	6.2	6.3	6.4	6.4
2000	4.8	4.9	5.0	5.1	5.2	5.2	5.3	5.4	5.5	5.6	5.7	5.7	5.8	5.9	6.0	6.1	6.2	6.3	6.3	6.4
2001	4.8	4.9	5.0	5.1	5.1	5.2	5.3	5.4	5.4	5.5	5.6	5.7	5.8	5.9	5.9	6.0	6.1	6.2	6.3	6.4
2002	4.8	4.8	4.9	5.0	5.1	5.1	5.2	5.3	5.4	5.5	5.5	5.6	5.7	5.8	5.8	5.9	6.0	6.1	6.2	6.2
2003	4.7	4.8	4.8	4.9	5.0	5.1	5.1	5.2	5.3	5.4	5.4	5.5	5.6	5.7	5.7	5.8	5.9	6.0	6.0	6.1
2004	4.6	4.7	4.8	4.9	4.9	5.0	5.1	5.1	5.2	5.3	5.4	5.4	5.5	5.6	5.6	5.7	5.8	5.8	5.9	6.0
2005	4.6	4.7	4.7	4.8	4.9	5.0	5.0	5.1	5.1	5.2	5.3	5.4	5.4	5.5	5.6	5.6	5.7	5.8	5.8	5.9
2006	4.6	4.7	4.8	4.8	4.9	5.0	5.0	5.1	5.1	5.2	5.3	5.4	5.4	5.5	5.5	5.6	5.7	5.7	5.8	5.9
2007	4.6	4.7	4.7	4.8	4.9	4.9	5.0	5.1	5.1	5.2	5.3	5.3	5.4	5.5	5.5	5.6	5.7	5.7	5.8	5.8
2008	4.6	4.6	4.7	4.8	4.8	4.9	4.9	5.0	5.1	5.1	5.2	5.3	5.3	5.4	5.4	5.5	5.6	5.6	5.7	5.7
2009	4.5	4.6	4.6	4.7	4.7	4.8	4.9	4.9	5.0	5.1	5.1	5.2	5.2	5.3	5.3	5.4	5.5	5.5	5.6	5.6
2010	4.4	4.5	4.5	4.6	4.7	4.7	4.8	4.8	4.9	5.0	5.0	5.1	5.1	5.2	5.2	5.3	5.3	5.4	5.4	5.5
2011	4.4	4.4	4.5	4.5	4.6	4.6	4.7	4.8	4.8	4.9	4.9	5.0	5.0	5.1	5.1	5.2	5.2	5.3	5.3	5.4

Table C-6 (page 5 of 6)

U.S. Treasury Bills: Total Returns
Rates of Return for all holding periods
Percent per annum compounded annually

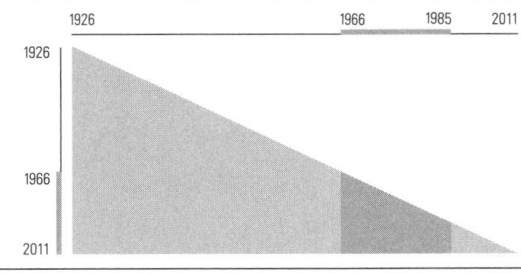

from 1926 to 2011

To the end of	From the beginning of 1966	1967	1968	1969	1970	1971	1972	1973	1974	1975	1976	1977	1978	1979	1980	1981	1982	1983	1984	1985
1966	4.8																			
1967	4.5	4.2																		
1968	4.7	4.7	5.2																	
1969	5.2	5.3	5.9	6.6																
1970	5.5	5.6	6.1	6.6	6.5															
1971	5.3	5.4	5.7	5.8	5.5	4.4														
1972	5.1	5.1	5.3	5.3	4.9	4.1	3.8													
1973	5.3	5.4	5.6	5.6	5.4	5.0	5.4	6.9												
1974	5.6	5.7	5.9	6.0	5.9	5.8	6.2	7.5	8.0											
1975	5.6	5.7	5.9	6.0	5.9	5.8	6.1	6.9	6.9	5.8										
1976	5.6	5.6	5.8	5.9	5.8	5.7	5.9	6.4	6.3	5.4	5.1									
1977	5.5	5.6	5.7	5.8	5.7	5.6	5.8	6.2	6.0	5.3	5.1	5.1								
1978	5.7	5.7	5.9	5.9	5.9	5.8	6.0	6.3	6.2	5.8	5.8	6.1	7.2							
1979	6.0	6.1	6.2	6.3	6.3	6.3	6.5	6.9	6.9	6.7	6.9	7.5	8.8	10.4						
1980	6.3	6.4	6.6	6.7	6.7	6.8	7.0	7.4	7.5	7.4	7.8	8.5	9.6	10.8	11.2					
1981	6.8	7.0	7.2	7.3	7.4	7.5	7.8	8.2	8.4	8.4	8.9	9.7	10.8	12.1	13.0	14.7				
1982	7.0	7.2	7.4	7.6	7.6	7.7	8.0	8.5	8.6	8.7	9.1	9.8	10.8	11.7	12.1	12.6	10.5			
1983	7.1	7.3	7.5	7.6	7.7	7.8	8.1	8.5	8.6	8.7	9.1	9.7	10.4	11.1	11.3	11.3	9.7	8.8		
1984	7.3	7.4	7.6	7.8	7.9	7.9	8.2	8.6	8.8	8.8	9.2	9.7	10.4	10.9	11.0	11.0	9.7	9.3	9.8	
1985	7.3	7.4	7.6	7.8	7.8	7.9	8.2	8.5	8.7	8.7	9.0	9.5	10.0	10.4	10.5	10.3	9.2	8.8	8.8	7.7
1986	7.3	7.4	7.5	7.7	7.7	7.8	8.1	8.4	8.5	8.5	8.8	9.1	9.6	9.9	9.8	9.6	8.6	8.1	7.9	6.9
1987	7.2	7.3	7.4	7.6	7.6	7.7	7.9	8.2	8.3	8.3	8.5	8.8	9.2	9.4	9.3	9.0	8.1	7.6	7.3	6.4
1988	7.1	7.2	7.4	7.5	7.6	7.6	7.8	8.1	8.1	8.1	8.3	8.6	8.9	9.1	8.9	8.7	7.8	7.4	7.1	6.4
1989	7.2	7.3	7.4	7.5	7.6	7.6	7.8	8.1	8.1	8.2	8.3	8.6	8.9	9.0	8.9	8.6	7.9	7.5	7.3	6.8
1990	7.2	7.3	7.5	7.6	7.6	7.7	7.8	8.1	8.1	8.1	8.3	8.5	8.8	8.9	8.8	8.5	7.9	7.6	7.4	7.0
1991	7.1	7.2	7.4	7.5	7.5	7.6	7.7	7.9	8.0	8.0	8.1	8.3	8.6	8.7	8.5	8.3	7.7	7.3	7.2	6.8
1992	7.0	7.1	7.2	7.3	7.3	7.4	7.5	7.7	7.7	7.7	7.8	8.0	8.2	8.3	8.1	7.9	7.3	6.9	6.7	6.4
1993	6.9	6.9	7.0	7.1	7.1	7.2	7.3	7.5	7.5	7.5	7.6	7.7	7.9	7.9	7.7	7.5	6.9	6.6	6.4	6.0
1994	6.8	6.8	6.9	7.0	7.0	7.0	7.1	7.3	7.3	7.3	7.4	7.5	7.6	7.7	7.5	7.2	6.7	6.3	6.1	5.8
1995	6.7	6.8	6.9	6.9	7.0	7.0	7.1	7.2	7.2	7.2	7.3	7.4	7.5	7.5	7.4	7.1	6.6	6.3	6.1	5.7
1996	6.7	6.7	6.8	6.9	6.9	6.9	7.0	7.1	7.2	7.1	7.2	7.3	7.4	7.4	7.2	7.0	6.5	6.2	6.0	5.7
1997	6.6	6.7	6.8	6.8	6.8	6.8	6.9	7.1	7.1	7.0	7.1	7.2	7.3	7.3	7.1	6.9	6.4	6.1	6.0	5.7
1998	6.6	6.6	6.7	6.8	6.8	6.8	6.9	7.0	7.0	6.9	7.0	7.1	7.2	7.2	7.0	6.8	6.3	6.1	5.9	5.6
1999	6.5	6.6	6.6	6.7	6.7	6.7	6.8	6.9	6.9	6.8	6.9	7.0	7.1	7.1	6.9	6.7	6.2	6.0	5.8	5.5
2000	6.5	6.5	6.6	6.7	6.7	6.7	6.8	6.9	6.9	6.8	6.9	6.9	7.0	7.0	6.8	6.6	6.2	6.0	5.8	5.6
2001	6.4	6.5	6.5	6.6	6.6	6.6	6.7	6.8	6.7	6.7	6.7	6.8	6.9	6.9	6.7	6.5	6.1	5.9	5.7	5.5
2002	6.3	6.3	6.4	6.4	6.4	6.4	6.5	6.6	6.6	6.5	6.5	6.6	6.7	6.6	6.5	6.3	5.9	5.7	5.5	5.3
2003	6.1	6.2	6.2	6.3	6.3	6.3	6.3	6.4	6.4	6.3	6.3	6.4	6.4	6.4	6.2	6.0	5.7	5.4	5.3	5.0
2004	6.0	6.1	6.1	6.1	6.1	6.1	6.2	6.2	6.2	6.1	6.2	6.2	6.2	6.2	6.0	5.8	5.5	5.2	5.1	4.8
2005	5.9	6.0	6.0	6.0	6.0	6.0	6.1	6.1	6.1	6.0	6.1	6.1	6.1	6.1	5.9	5.7	5.4	5.1	5.0	4.7
2006	5.9	5.9	6.0	6.0	6.0	6.0	6.0	6.1	6.1	6.0	6.0	6.0	6.1	6.0	5.9	5.7	5.3	5.1	5.0	4.7
2007	5.9	5.9	6.0	6.0	6.0	5.9	6.0	6.0	6.0	6.0	6.0	6.0	6.0	6.0	5.8	5.6	5.3	5.1	4.9	4.7
2008	5.8	5.8	5.8	5.9	5.8	5.8	5.9	5.9	5.9	5.8	5.8	5.9	5.9	5.8	5.7	5.5	5.2	5.0	4.8	4.6
2009	5.6	5.7	5.7	5.7	5.7	5.7	5.7	5.8	5.7	5.7	5.7	5.7	5.7	5.6	5.5	5.3	5.0	4.8	4.6	4.4
2010	5.5	5.5	5.6	5.6	5.6	5.5	5.6	5.6	5.6	5.5	5.5	5.5	5.5	5.5	5.3	5.1	4.8	4.6	4.5	4.3
2011	5.4	5.4	5.4	5.4	5.4	5.4	5.4	5.5	5.4	5.4	5.3	5.3	5.4	5.3	5.1	5.0	4.6	4.4	4.3	4.1

Table C-6 (page 6 of 6)-a

U.S. Treasury Bills: Total Returns

Rates of Return for all holding periods

Percent per annum compounded annually

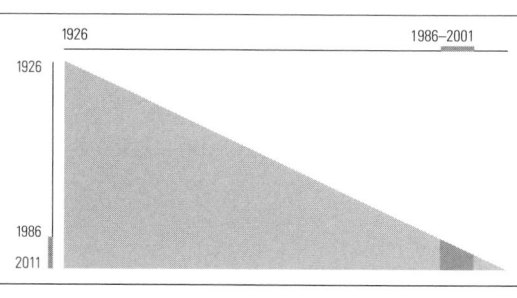

from 1926 to 2011

To the end of	From the beginning of 1986	1987	1988	1989	1990	1991	1992	1993	1994	1995	1996	1997	1998	1999	2000	2001
1986	6.2															
1987	5.8	5.5														
1988	6.0	5.9	6.3													
1989	6.6	6.7	7.4	8.4												
1990	6.8	7.0	7.5	8.1	7.8											
1991	6.6	6.7	7.0	7.3	6.7	5.6										
1992	6.2	6.2	6.3	6.3	5.6	4.5	3.5									
1993	5.8	5.7	5.7	5.6	4.9	4.0	3.2	2.9								
1994	5.5	5.5	5.5	5.3	4.7	4.0	3.4	3.4	3.9							
1995	5.6	5.5	5.5	5.4	4.9	4.3	4.0	4.1	4.7	5.6						
1996	5.5	5.5	5.5	5.3	4.9	4.4	4.2	4.4	4.9	5.4	5.2					
1997	5.5	5.4	5.4	5.3	5.0	4.6	4.4	4.6	5.0	5.4	5.2	5.3				
1998	5.4	5.4	5.4	5.3	5.0	4.6	4.5	4.6	5.0	5.2	5.1	5.1	4.9			
1999	5.4	5.3	5.3	5.2	4.9	4.6	4.5	4.6	4.9	5.1	5.0	4.9	4.8	4.7		
2000	5.4	5.4	5.4	5.3	5.0	4.7	4.6	4.8	5.1	5.2	5.2	5.2	5.1	5.3	5.9	
2001	5.3	5.3	5.3	5.2	4.9	4.7	4.6	4.7	4.9	5.0	5.0	4.9	4.8	4.8	4.9	3.8
2002	5.1	5.0	5.0	4.9	4.7	4.4	4.3	4.4	4.5	4.6	4.5	4.4	4.2	4.0	3.8	2.7
2003	4.9	4.8	4.8	4.7	4.4	4.1	4.0	4.1	4.2	4.2	4.0	3.9	3.6	3.4	3.1	2.2
2004	4.7	4.6	4.5	4.4	4.2	3.9	3.8	3.8	3.9	3.9	3.7	3.5	3.3	3.0	2.7	1.9
2005	4.6	4.5	4.5	4.3	4.1	3.9	3.7	3.8	3.8	3.8	3.6	3.5	3.2	3.0	2.7	2.1
2006	4.6	4.5	4.5	4.4	4.1	3.9	3.8	3.8	3.9	3.9	3.7	3.6	3.4	3.2	3.0	2.6
2007	4.6	4.5	4.5	4.4	4.2	4.0	3.9	3.9	4.0	4.0	3.8	3.7	3.5	3.4	3.2	2.9
2008	4.5	4.4	4.3	4.2	4.0	3.8	3.7	3.7	3.8	3.8	3.7	3.5	3.4	3.2	3.1	2.7
2009	4.3	4.2	4.1	4.0	3.8	3.6	3.5	3.5	3.6	3.5	3.4	3.3	3.1	2.9	2.8	2.4
2010	4.1	4.0	4.0	3.9	3.7	3.5	3.3	3.3	3.4	3.3	3.2	3.0	2.9	2.7	2.5	2.2
2011	4.0	3.9	3.8	3.7	3.5	3.3	3.2	3.2	3.2	3.1	3.0	2.8	2.7	2.5	2.3	2.0

Table C-6 (page 6 of 6)-b

U.S. Treasury Bills: Total Returns

Rates of Return for all holding periods

Percent per annum compounded annually

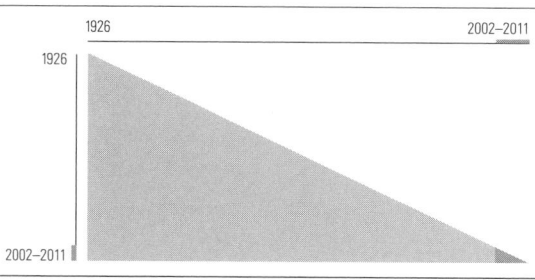

from 1926 to 2011

To the end of	From the beginning of 2002	2003	2004	2005	2006	2007	2008	2009	2010	2011
2002	1.6									
2003	1.3	1.0								
2004	1.3	1.1	1.2							
2005	1.7	1.7	2.1	3.0						
2006	2.3	2.5	3.0	3.9	4.8					
2007	2.7	2.9	3.4	4.1	4.7	4.7				
2008	2.5	2.7	3.0	3.5	3.7	3.1	1.6			
2009	2.2	2.3	2.5	2.8	2.8	2.1	0.8	0.1		
2010	2.0	2.0	2.2	2.4	2.2	1.6	0.6	0.1	0.1	
2011	1.8	1.8	1.9	2.0	1.9	1.3	0.5	0.1	0.1	0.0

Table C-7 (page 1 of 6)

Inflation

Rates of Return for all holding periods

Percent per annum compounded annually

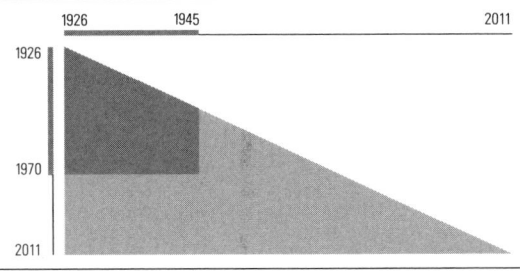

from 1926 to 2011

To the end of	From the beginning of 1926	1927	1928	1929	1930	1931	1932	1933	1934	1935	1936	1937	1938	1939	1940	1941	1942	1943	1944	1945
1926	-1.5																			
1927	-1.8	-2.1																		
1928	-1.5	-1.5	-1.0																	
1929	-1.1	-1.0	-0.4	0.2																
1930	-2.1	-2.2	-2.3	-3.0	-6.0															
1931	-3.4	-3.7	-4.2	-5.2	-7.8	-9.5														
1932	-4.4	-4.9	-5.4	-6.5	-8.6	-9.9	-10.3													
1933	-3.8	-4.1	-4.5	-5.1	-6.4	-6.6	-5.0	0.5												
1934	-3.2	-3.4	-3.6	-4.0	-4.8	-4.5	-2.7	1.3	2.0											
1935	-2.6	-2.7	-2.8	-3.0	-3.5	-3.0	-1.3	1.8	2.5	3.0										
1936	-2.2	-2.3	-2.3	-2.5	-2.9	-2.3	-0.8	1.7	2.1	2.1	1.2									
1937	-1.8	-1.8	-1.8	-1.9	-2.1	-1.6	-0.2	2.0	2.3	2.4	2.2	3.1								
1938	-1.9	-1.9	-1.9	-2.0	-2.2	-1.7	-0.6	1.2	1.3	1.1	0.5	0.1	-2.8							
1939	-1.8	-1.8	-1.8	-1.8	-2.0	-1.6	-0.6	0.9	1.0	0.8	0.2	-0.1	-1.6	-0.5						
1940	-1.6	-1.6	-1.6	-1.6	-1.8	-1.3	-0.4	0.9	1.0	0.8	0.4	0.2	-0.8	0.2	1.0					
1941	-0.9	-0.9	-0.8	-0.8	-0.9	-0.4	0.6	1.9	2.0	2.0	1.9	2.0	1.7	3.3	5.2	9.7				
1942	-0.3	-0.3	-0.2	-0.1	-0.1	0.4	1.3	2.6	2.8	2.9	2.9	3.2	3.2	4.8	6.6	9.5	9.3			
1943	-0.2	-0.1	0.0	0.1	0.1	0.6	1.5	2.6	2.9	2.9	2.9	3.2	3.2	4.4	5.7	7.3	6.2	3.2		
1944	0.0	0.0	0.2	0.2	0.2	0.7	1.5	2.6	2.8	2.9	2.8	3.1	3.0	4.1	5.0	6.0	4.8	2.6	2.1	
1945	0.1	0.2	0.3	0.4	0.4	0.8	1.6	2.6	2.7	2.8	2.8	3.0	2.9	3.8	4.5	5.2	4.2	2.5	2.2	2.3
1946	0.9	1.0	1.2	1.3	1.3	1.8	2.6	3.6	3.9	4.0	4.1	4.4	4.5	5.5	6.4	7.3	6.8	6.2	7.3	9.9
1947	1.2	1.4	1.5	1.7	1.7	2.2	3.0	4.0	4.2	4.4	4.5	4.8	5.0	5.9	6.7	7.5	7.2	6.8	7.7	9.6
1948	1.3	1.4	1.6	1.7	1.8	2.3	3.0	3.9	4.1	4.3	4.4	4.6	4.8	5.6	6.2	6.9	6.5	6.1	6.7	7.8
1949	1.2	1.3	1.4	1.5	1.6	2.0	2.7	3.5	3.7	3.8	3.9	4.1	4.2	4.9	5.4	5.9	5.5	4.9	5.2	5.8
1950	1.3	1.5	1.6	1.7	1.8	2.2	2.9	3.7	3.9	4.0	4.0	4.2	4.3	4.9	5.4	5.9	5.5	5.0	5.3	5.8
1951	1.5	1.6	1.8	1.9	2.0	2.4	3.0	3.8	4.0	4.1	4.1	4.3	4.4	5.0	5.5	5.9	5.5	5.1	5.4	5.8
1952	1.5	1.6	1.8	1.9	1.9	2.3	2.9	3.6	3.8	3.9	4.0	4.1	4.2	4.7	5.1	5.5	5.1	4.7	4.9	5.2
1953	1.5	1.6	1.7	1.8	1.9	2.2	2.8	3.5	3.6	3.7	3.8	3.9	4.0	4.4	4.8	5.1	4.7	4.3	4.4	4.7
1954	1.4	1.5	1.6	1.7	1.8	2.1	2.7	3.3	3.4	3.5	3.5	3.7	3.7	4.1	4.4	4.7	4.3	3.9	4.0	4.2
1955	1.4	1.5	1.6	1.7	1.7	2.1	2.6	3.2	3.3	3.4	3.4	3.5	3.5	3.9	4.2	4.4	4.0	3.6	3.7	3.8
1956	1.4	1.5	1.6	1.7	1.8	2.1	2.6	3.2	3.3	3.3	3.3	3.5	3.5	3.8	4.1	4.3	3.9	3.6	3.6	3.7
1957	1.5	1.5	1.7	1.8	1.8	2.1	2.6	3.2	3.3	3.3	3.3	3.4	3.5	3.8	4.0	4.2	3.9	3.5	3.6	3.7
1958	1.5	1.6	1.7	1.8	1.8	2.1	2.6	3.1	3.2	3.3	3.3	3.4	3.4	3.7	3.9	4.1	3.8	3.4	3.4	3.5
1959	1.5	1.6	1.7	1.8	1.8	2.1	2.5	3.0	3.1	3.2	3.2	3.3	3.3	3.6	3.8	3.9	3.6	3.3	3.3	3.4
1960	1.5	1.6	1.7	1.7	1.8	2.1	2.5	3.0	3.1	3.1	3.1	3.2	3.2	3.5	3.7	3.8	3.5	3.2	3.2	3.3
1961	1.4	1.5	1.6	1.7	1.8	2.0	2.4	2.9	3.0	3.0	3.0	3.1	3.1	3.4	3.5	3.7	3.4	3.1	3.1	3.1
1962	1.4	1.5	1.6	1.7	1.7	2.0	2.4	2.8	2.9	3.0	3.0	3.0	3.0	3.3	3.4	3.6	3.3	3.0	3.0	3.0
1963	1.4	1.5	1.6	1.7	1.7	2.0	2.4	2.8	2.9	2.9	2.9	3.0	3.0	3.2	3.4	3.5	3.2	2.9	2.9	2.9
1964	1.4	1.5	1.6	1.7	1.7	2.0	2.3	2.8	2.8	2.9	2.9	2.9	2.9	3.1	3.3	3.4	3.1	2.8	2.8	2.9
1965	1.4	1.5	1.6	1.7	1.7	2.0	2.3	2.7	2.8	2.8	2.8	2.9	2.9	3.1	3.2	3.3	3.1	2.8	2.8	2.8
1966	1.5	1.6	1.7	1.7	1.8	2.0	2.4	2.8	2.8	2.8	2.8	2.9	2.9	3.1	3.2	3.3	3.1	2.8	2.8	2.8
1967	1.5	1.6	1.7	1.8	1.8	2.0	2.4	2.8	2.8	2.8	2.8	2.9	2.9	3.1	3.2	3.3	3.1	2.8	2.8	2.8
1968	1.6	1.7	1.8	1.8	1.9	2.1	2.4	2.8	2.9	2.9	2.9	3.0	3.0	3.1	3.3	3.4	3.1	2.9	2.9	2.9
1969	1.7	1.8	1.9	1.9	2.0	2.2	2.5	2.9	3.0	3.0	3.0	3.0	3.0	3.2	3.4	3.5	3.2	3.0	3.0	3.0
1970	1.8	1.9	2.0	2.0	2.1	2.3	2.6	3.0	3.0	3.1	3.1	3.1	3.1	3.3	3.4	3.5	3.3	3.1	3.1	3.1

Table C-7 (page 2 of 6)

Inflation

Rates of Return for all holding periods

Percent per annum compounded annually

from 1926 to 2011

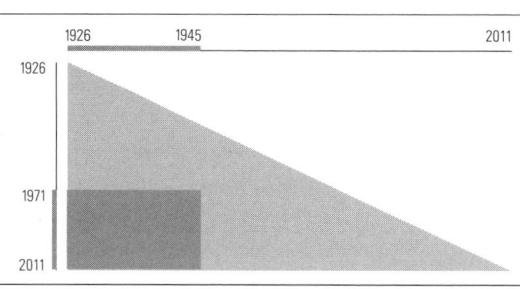

To the end of	From the beginning of 1926	1927	1928	1929	1930	1931	1932	1933	1934	1935	1936	1937	1938	1939	1940	1941	1942	1943	1944	1945
1971	1.8	1.9	2.0	2.1	2.1	2.3	2.6	3.0	3.0	3.1	3.1	3.1	3.1	3.3	3.4	3.5	3.3	3.1	3.1	3.1
1972	1.9	1.9	2.0	2.1	2.1	2.3	2.6	3.0	3.1	3.1	3.1	3.1	3.1	3.3	3.4	3.5	3.3	3.1	3.1	3.2
1973	2.0	2.1	2.2	2.2	2.3	2.5	2.8	3.1	3.2	3.2	3.2	3.3	3.3	3.5	3.6	3.7	3.5	3.3	3.3	3.3
1974	2.2	2.3	2.4	2.4	2.5	2.7	3.0	3.3	3.4	3.4	3.4	3.5	3.5	3.7	3.8	3.9	3.7	3.6	3.6	3.6
1975	2.3	2.4	2.5	2.5	2.6	2.8	3.1	3.4	3.5	3.5	3.5	3.6	3.6	3.8	3.9	4.0	3.8	3.7	3.7	3.7
1976	2.3	2.4	2.5	2.6	2.6	2.8	3.1	3.4	3.5	3.6	3.6	3.6	3.6	3.8	3.9	4.0	3.9	3.7	3.7	3.8
1977	2.4	2.5	2.6	2.7	2.7	2.9	3.2	3.5	3.6	3.6	3.6	3.7	3.7	3.9	4.0	4.1	3.9	3.8	3.8	3.9
1978	2.5	2.6	2.7	2.8	2.8	3.0	3.3	3.6	3.7	3.7	3.8	3.8	3.8	4.0	4.1	4.2	4.1	3.9	4.0	4.0
1979	2.7	2.8	2.9	3.0	3.0	3.2	3.5	3.8	3.9	4.0	4.0	4.0	4.1	4.2	4.4	4.4	4.3	4.2	4.2	4.3
1980	2.9	3.0	3.1	3.2	3.2	3.4	3.7	4.0	4.1	4.1	4.2	4.2	4.2	4.4	4.5	4.6	4.5	4.4	4.4	4.5
1981	3.0	3.1	3.2	3.3	3.3	3.5	3.8	4.1	4.2	4.2	4.3	4.3	4.4	4.5	4.6	4.7	4.6	4.5	4.5	4.6
1982	3.0	3.1	3.2	3.3	3.3	3.5	3.8	4.1	4.2	4.2	4.2	4.3	4.3	4.5	4.6	4.7	4.6	4.5	4.5	4.6
1983	3.0	3.1	3.2	3.3	3.3	3.5	3.8	4.1	4.2	4.2	4.2	4.3	4.3	4.5	4.6	4.7	4.6	4.5	4.5	4.6
1984	3.0	3.1	3.2	3.3	3.4	3.5	3.8	4.1	4.2	4.2	4.2	4.3	4.3	4.5	4.6	4.7	4.6	4.5	4.5	4.5
1985	3.1	3.1	3.2	3.3	3.4	3.5	3.8	4.1	4.2	4.2	4.2	4.3	4.3	4.5	4.6	4.7	4.5	4.4	4.5	4.5
1986	3.0	3.1	3.2	3.3	3.3	3.5	3.8	4.0	4.1	4.1	4.2	4.2	4.2	4.4	4.5	4.6	4.5	4.4	4.4	4.4
1987	3.0	3.1	3.2	3.3	3.3	3.5	3.8	4.0	4.1	4.1	4.2	4.2	4.2	4.4	4.5	4.6	4.5	4.4	4.4	4.4
1988	3.1	3.1	3.2	3.3	3.4	3.5	3.8	4.0	4.1	4.1	4.2	4.2	4.3	4.4	4.5	4.6	4.5	4.4	4.4	4.4
1989	3.1	3.2	3.3	3.3	3.4	3.5	3.8	4.1	4.1	4.2	4.2	4.2	4.3	4.4	4.5	4.6	4.5	4.4	4.4	4.4
1990	3.1	3.2	3.3	3.4	3.4	3.6	3.8	4.1	4.2	4.2	4.2	4.3	4.3	4.4	4.5	4.6	4.5	4.4	4.4	4.5
1991	3.1	3.2	3.3	3.4	3.4	3.6	3.8	4.1	4.1	4.2	4.2	4.2	4.3	4.4	4.5	4.6	4.5	4.4	4.4	4.5
1992	3.1	3.2	3.3	3.4	3.4	3.6	3.8	4.1	4.1	4.2	4.2	4.2	4.2	4.4	4.5	4.5	4.4	4.3	4.4	4.4
1993	3.1	3.2	3.3	3.3	3.4	3.6	3.8	4.0	4.1	4.1	4.1	4.2	4.2	4.3	4.4	4.5	4.4	4.3	4.3	4.4
1994	3.1	3.2	3.3	3.3	3.4	3.5	3.8	4.0	4.1	4.1	4.1	4.2	4.2	4.3	4.4	4.5	4.4	4.3	4.3	4.4
1995	3.1	3.2	3.3	3.3	3.4	3.5	3.7	4.0	4.0	4.1	4.1	4.1	4.2	4.3	4.4	4.4	4.3	4.3	4.3	4.3
1996	3.1	3.2	3.3	3.3	3.4	3.5	3.7	4.0	4.0	4.1	4.1	4.1	4.1	4.3	4.4	4.4	4.3	4.2	4.3	4.3
1997	3.1	3.2	3.2	3.3	3.4	3.5	3.7	3.9	4.0	4.0	4.0	4.1	4.1	4.2	4.3	4.4	4.3	4.2	4.2	4.2
1998	3.1	3.1	3.2	3.3	3.3	3.5	3.7	3.9	4.0	4.0	4.0	4.0	4.1	4.2	4.3	4.3	4.2	4.1	4.2	4.2
1999	3.1	3.1	3.2	3.3	3.3	3.5	3.7	3.9	3.9	4.0	4.0	4.0	4.0	4.2	4.2	4.3	4.2	4.1	4.1	4.2
2000	3.1	3.1	3.2	3.3	3.3	3.5	3.7	3.9	3.9	4.0	4.0	4.0	4.0	4.1	4.2	4.3	4.2	4.1	4.1	4.2
2001	3.1	3.1	3.2	3.2	3.3	3.4	3.6	3.8	3.9	3.9	3.9	4.0	4.0	4.1	4.2	4.2	4.1	4.1	4.1	4.1
2002	3.0	3.1	3.2	3.2	3.3	3.4	3.6	3.8	3.9	3.9	3.9	4.0	4.0	4.1	4.2	4.2	4.1	4.0	4.0	4.1
2003	3.0	3.1	3.2	3.2	3.3	3.4	3.6	3.8	3.8	3.9	3.9	3.9	3.9	4.0	4.1	4.2	4.1	4.0	4.0	4.0
2004	3.0	3.1	3.2	3.2	3.3	3.4	3.6	3.8	3.8	3.9	3.9	3.9	3.9	4.0	4.1	4.2	4.1	4.0	4.0	4.0
2005	3.0	3.1	3.2	3.2	3.3	3.4	3.6	3.8	3.8	3.9	3.9	3.9	3.9	4.0	4.1	4.1	4.1	4.0	4.0	4.0
2006	3.0	3.1	3.2	3.2	3.3	3.4	3.6	3.8	3.8	3.8	3.8	3.9	3.9	4.0	4.1	4.1	4.0	4.0	4.0	4.0
2007	3.0	3.1	3.2	3.2	3.3	3.4	3.6	3.8	3.8	3.8	3.9	3.9	3.9	4.0	4.1	4.1	4.0	4.0	4.0	4.0
2008	3.0	3.1	3.1	3.2	3.2	3.3	3.5	3.7	3.8	3.8	3.8	3.8	3.8	3.9	4.0	4.1	4.0	3.9	3.9	3.9
2009	3.0	3.1	3.1	3.2	3.2	3.3	3.5	3.7	3.8	3.8	3.8	3.8	3.8	3.9	4.0	4.0	4.0	3.9	3.9	3.9
2010	3.0	3.0	3.1	3.2	3.2	3.3	3.5	3.7	3.7	3.7	3.8	3.8	3.8	3.9	4.0	4.0	3.9	3.8	3.8	3.9
2011	3.0	3.0	3.1	3.2	3.2	3.3	3.5	3.7	3.7	3.7	3.7	3.8	3.8	3.9	3.9	4.0	3.9	3.8	3.8	3.9

Table C-7 (page 3 of 6)

Inflation

Rates of Return for all holding periods

Percent per annum compounded annually

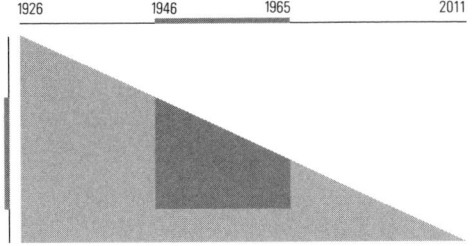

from 1926 to 2011

To the end of	From the beginning of 1946	1947	1948	1949	1950	1951	1952	1953	1954	1955	1956	1957	1958	1959	1960	1961	1962	1963	1964	1965
1946	18.2																			
1947	13.5	9.0																		
1948	9.8	5.8	2.7																	
1949	6.8	3.2	0.4	-1.8																
1950	6.6	3.8	2.2	1.9	5.8															
1951	6.5	4.3	3.1	3.2	5.8	5.9														
1952	5.6	3.7	2.6	2.6	4.2	3.3	0.9													
1953	5.0	3.2	2.3	2.2	3.3	2.4	0.8	0.6												
1954	4.4	2.8	1.9	1.8	2.5	1.7	0.3	0.1	-0.5											
1955	4.0	2.5	1.7	1.6	2.1	1.4	0.3	0.2	-0.1	0.4										
1956	3.9	2.5	1.8	1.7	2.2	1.7	0.8	0.8	0.9	1.6	2.9									
1957	3.8	2.6	2.0	1.9	2.3	1.9	1.2	1.3	1.4	2.1	2.9	3.0								
1958	3.6	2.5	1.9	1.9	2.3	1.8	1.3	1.3	1.5	2.0	2.5	2.4	1.8							
1959	3.5	2.4	1.9	1.8	2.2	1.8	1.3	1.4	1.5	1.9	2.3	2.1	1.6	1.5						
1960	3.3	2.4	1.9	1.8	2.1	1.8	1.3	1.4	1.5	1.8	2.1	1.9	1.6	1.5	1.5					
1961	3.2	2.2	1.8	1.7	2.0	1.7	1.3	1.3	1.4	1.7	1.9	1.7	1.4	1.2	1.1	0.7				
1962	3.1	2.2	1.7	1.7	1.9	1.6	1.3	1.3	1.4	1.6	1.8	1.6	1.3	1.2	1.1	0.9	1.2			
1963	3.0	2.2	1.7	1.7	1.9	1.6	1.3	1.3	1.4	1.6	1.8	1.6	1.4	1.3	1.3	1.2	1.4	1.6		
1964	2.9	2.1	1.7	1.6	1.9	1.6	1.3	1.3	1.4	1.6	1.7	1.6	1.4	1.3	1.2	1.2	1.4	1.4	1.2	
1965	2.8	2.1	1.7	1.7	1.9	1.6	1.3	1.4	1.4	1.6	1.7	1.6	1.4	1.4	1.4	1.3	1.5	1.6	1.6	1.9
1966	2.9	2.2	1.8	1.8	2.0	1.7	1.5	1.5	1.6	1.7	1.9	1.8	1.6	1.6	1.6	1.7	1.9	2.0	2.2	2.6
1967	2.9	2.2	1.9	1.8	2.0	1.8	1.6	1.6	1.7	1.8	2.0	1.9	1.8	1.8	1.8	1.9	2.1	2.2	2.4	2.8
1968	3.0	2.3	2.0	2.0	2.2	2.0	1.7	1.8	1.9	2.0	2.2	2.1	2.0	2.1	2.1	2.2	2.4	2.6	2.8	3.3
1969	3.1	2.5	2.2	2.2	2.4	2.2	2.0	2.0	2.1	2.3	2.5	2.4	2.4	2.4	2.5	2.6	2.9	3.1	3.4	3.8
1970	3.2	2.6	2.3	2.3	2.5	2.3	2.2	2.2	2.3	2.5	2.7	2.6	2.6	2.7	2.8	2.9	3.2	3.4	3.7	4.1
1971	3.2	2.6	2.4	2.4	2.5	2.4	2.2	2.3	2.4	2.6	2.7	2.7	2.7	2.7	2.8	3.0	3.2	3.4	3.6	4.0
1972	3.2	2.7	2.4	2.4	2.6	2.4	2.3	2.3	2.4	2.6	2.7	2.7	2.7	2.8	2.9	3.0	3.2	3.4	3.6	3.9
1973	3.4	2.9	2.6	2.6	2.8	2.7	2.6	2.6	2.8	2.9	3.1	3.1	3.1	3.2	3.3	3.4	3.7	3.9	4.1	4.4
1974	3.7	3.2	3.0	3.0	3.2	3.1	3.0	3.1	3.2	3.4	3.5	3.6	3.6	3.7	3.9	4.0	4.3	4.6	4.8	5.2
1975	3.8	3.3	3.1	3.1	3.3	3.2	3.1	3.2	3.4	3.5	3.7	3.7	3.8	3.9	4.1	4.2	4.5	4.7	5.0	5.4
1976	3.8	3.4	3.2	3.2	3.4	3.3	3.2	3.3	3.4	3.6	3.8	3.8	3.8	4.0	4.1	4.3	4.5	4.8	5.0	5.3
1977	3.9	3.5	3.3	3.3	3.5	3.4	3.3	3.4	3.6	3.7	3.9	3.9	4.0	4.1	4.2	4.4	4.7	4.9	5.1	5.4
1978	4.1	3.7	3.5	3.5	3.7	3.6	3.5	3.6	3.8	3.9	4.1	4.2	4.2	4.3	4.5	4.7	4.9	5.1	5.4	5.7
1979	4.3	3.9	3.8	3.8	4.0	3.9	3.9	4.0	4.1	4.3	4.5	4.5	4.6	4.8	4.9	5.1	5.4	5.6	5.9	6.2
1980	4.5	4.2	4.0	4.1	4.3	4.2	4.2	4.3	4.4	4.6	4.8	4.9	4.9	5.1	5.3	5.5	5.7	6.0	6.2	6.6
1981	4.7	4.3	4.2	4.2	4.4	4.4	4.3	4.4	4.6	4.8	4.9	5.0	5.1	5.3	5.4	5.6	5.9	6.1	6.4	6.7
1982	4.6	4.3	4.2	4.2	4.4	4.3	4.3	4.4	4.5	4.7	4.9	5.0	5.1	5.2	5.4	5.5	5.8	6.0	6.2	6.5
1983	4.6	4.3	4.2	4.2	4.4	4.3	4.3	4.4	4.5	4.7	4.9	4.9	5.0	5.1	5.3	5.5	5.7	5.9	6.1	6.4
1984	4.6	4.3	4.1	4.2	4.4	4.3	4.3	4.4	4.5	4.7	4.8	4.9	5.0	5.1	5.2	5.4	5.6	5.8	6.0	6.3
1985	4.6	4.3	4.1	4.2	4.3	4.3	4.3	4.4	4.5	4.6	4.8	4.9	4.9	5.0	5.2	5.3	5.5	5.7	5.9	6.1
1986	4.5	4.2	4.1	4.1	4.3	4.2	4.2	4.3	4.4	4.5	4.7	4.7	4.8	4.9	5.0	5.2	5.4	5.5	5.7	5.9
1987	4.5	4.2	4.1	4.1	4.3	4.2	4.2	4.3	4.4	4.5	4.7	4.7	4.8	4.9	5.0	5.1	5.3	5.5	5.6	5.8
1988	4.5	4.2	4.1	4.1	4.3	4.2	4.2	4.3	4.4	4.5	4.7	4.7	4.8	4.9	5.0	5.1	5.3	5.4	5.6	5.8
1989	4.5	4.2	4.1	4.1	4.3	4.2	4.2	4.3	4.4	4.5	4.7	4.7	4.8	4.9	5.0	5.1	5.3	5.4	5.6	5.7
1990	4.5	4.2	4.1	4.2	4.3	4.3	4.2	4.3	4.4	4.6	4.7	4.8	4.8	4.9	5.0	5.1	5.3	5.4	5.6	5.8

Table C-7 (page 4 of 6)

Inflation
Rates of Return for all holding periods
Percent per annum compounded annually

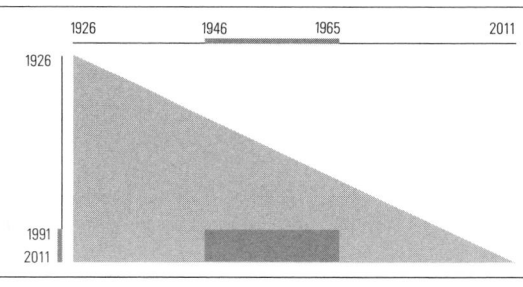

from 1926 to 2011

To the end of	From the beginning of 1946	1947	1948	1949	1950	1951	1952	1953	1954	1955	1956	1957	1958	1959	1960	1961	1962	1963	1964	1965
1991	4.5	4.2	4.1	4.1	4.3	4.3	4.2	4.3	4.4	4.5	4.7	4.7	4.8	4.8	5.0	5.1	5.2	5.4	5.5	5.7
1992	4.5	4.2	4.1	4.1	4.3	4.2	4.2	4.3	4.4	4.5	4.6	4.7	4.7	4.8	4.9	5.0	5.1	5.3	5.4	5.6
1993	4.4	4.2	4.1	4.1	4.2	4.2	4.1	4.2	4.3	4.4	4.6	4.6	4.6	4.7	4.8	4.9	5.1	5.2	5.3	5.5
1994	4.4	4.1	4.0	4.1	4.2	4.2	4.1	4.2	4.3	4.4	4.5	4.5	4.6	4.7	4.8	4.9	5.0	5.1	5.2	5.4
1995	4.4	4.1	4.0	4.0	4.2	4.1	4.1	4.2	4.2	4.4	4.5	4.5	4.5	4.6	4.7	4.8	4.9	5.0	5.1	5.3
1996	4.3	4.1	4.0	4.0	4.1	4.1	4.1	4.1	4.2	4.3	4.4	4.5	4.5	4.6	4.7	4.8	4.9	5.0	5.1	5.2
1997	4.3	4.0	3.9	4.0	4.1	4.0	4.0	4.1	4.2	4.3	4.4	4.4	4.4	4.5	4.6	4.7	4.8	4.9	5.0	5.1
1998	4.2	4.0	3.9	3.9	4.0	4.0	4.0	4.0	4.1	4.2	4.3	4.3	4.4	4.4	4.5	4.6	4.7	4.8	4.9	5.0
1999	4.2	4.0	3.9	3.9	4.0	4.0	3.9	4.0	4.1	4.2	4.3	4.3	4.3	4.4	4.5	4.5	4.6	4.7	4.8	4.9
2000	4.2	3.9	3.9	3.9	4.0	4.0	3.9	4.0	4.1	4.2	4.2	4.3	4.3	4.4	4.4	4.5	4.6	4.7	4.8	4.9
2001	4.1	3.9	3.8	3.8	3.9	3.9	3.9	3.9	4.0	4.1	4.2	4.2	4.2	4.3	4.4	4.4	4.5	4.6	4.7	4.8
2002	4.1	3.9	3.8	3.8	3.9	3.9	3.8	3.9	4.0	4.1	4.1	4.2	4.2	4.3	4.3	4.4	4.5	4.6	4.6	4.7
2003	4.1	3.8	3.8	3.8	3.9	3.8	3.8	3.9	3.9	4.0	4.1	4.1	4.1	4.2	4.3	4.3	4.4	4.5	4.6	4.7
2004	4.1	3.8	3.7	3.8	3.9	3.8	3.8	3.8	3.9	4.0	4.1	4.1	4.1	4.2	4.2	4.3	4.4	4.5	4.5	4.6
2005	4.0	3.8	3.7	3.8	3.9	3.8	3.8	3.8	3.9	4.0	4.1	4.1	4.1	4.2	4.2	4.3	4.4	4.4	4.5	4.6
2006	4.0	3.8	3.7	3.7	3.8	3.8	3.8	3.8	3.9	4.0	4.0	4.1	4.1	4.1	4.2	4.2	4.3	4.4	4.5	4.5
2007	4.0	3.8	3.7	3.7	3.8	3.8	3.8	3.8	3.9	4.0	4.0	4.1	4.1	4.1	4.2	4.2	4.3	4.4	4.5	4.5
2008	4.0	3.7	3.7	3.7	3.8	3.7	3.7	3.8	3.8	3.9	4.0	4.0	4.0	4.0	4.1	4.2	4.2	4.3	4.4	4.4
2009	3.9	3.7	3.6	3.7	3.8	3.7	3.7	3.7	3.8	3.9	3.9	4.0	4.0	4.0	4.1	4.1	4.2	4.3	4.3	4.4
2010	3.9	3.7	3.6	3.6	3.7	3.7	3.6	3.7	3.7	3.8	3.9	3.9	3.9	4.0	4.0	4.1	4.1	4.2	4.3	4.3
2011	3.9	3.7	3.6	3.6	3.7	3.7	3.6	3.7	3.7	3.8	3.9	3.9	3.9	4.0	4.0	4.0	4.1	4.2	4.2	4.3

Table C-7 (page 5 of 6)

Inflation

Rates of Return for all holding periods

Percent per annum compounded annually

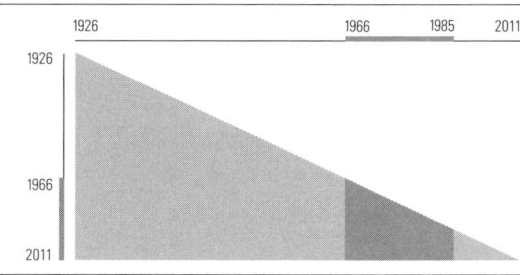

from 1926 to 2011

To the end of	From the beginning of 1966	1967	1968	1969	1970	1971	1972	1973	1974	1975	1976	1977	1978	1979	1980	1981	1982	1983	1984	1985
1966	3.4																			
1967	3.2	3.0																		
1968	3.7	3.9	4.7																	
1969	4.3	4.6	5.4	6.1																
1970	4.5	4.8	5.4	5.8	5.5															
1971	4.3	4.5	4.9	5.0	4.4	3.4														
1972	4.2	4.3	4.6	4.6	4.1	3.4	3.4													
1973	4.8	5.0	5.3	5.4	5.2	5.2	6.1	8.8												
1974	5.6	5.9	6.3	6.5	6.6	6.9	8.1	10.5	12.2											
1975	5.7	6.0	6.4	6.6	6.7	6.9	7.8	9.3	9.6	7.0										
1976	5.6	5.9	6.2	6.4	6.4	6.6	7.2	8.2	8.0	5.9	4.8									
1977	5.7	5.9	6.2	6.4	6.4	6.6	7.1	7.9	7.7	6.2	5.8	6.8								
1978	6.0	6.2	6.5	6.7	6.7	6.9	7.4	8.1	7.9	6.9	6.9	7.9	9.0							
1979	6.5	6.7	7.0	7.3	7.4	7.6	8.1	8.8	8.8	8.1	8.4	9.7	11.1	13.3						
1980	6.9	7.1	7.4	7.7	7.8	8.1	8.6	9.3	9.3	8.8	9.2	10.3	11.6	12.9	12.4					
1981	7.0	7.2	7.6	7.8	7.9	8.1	8.6	9.2	9.3	8.9	9.2	10.1	10.9	11.5	10.7	8.9				
1982	6.8	7.0	7.3	7.5	7.6	7.8	8.2	8.7	8.7	8.2	8.4	9.0	9.5	9.6	8.3	6.4	3.9			
1983	6.6	6.8	7.1	7.2	7.3	7.5	7.8	8.2	8.2	7.7	7.8	8.2	8.5	8.4	7.2	5.5	3.8	3.8		
1984	6.5	6.7	6.9	7.0	7.1	7.2	7.5	7.9	7.8	7.3	7.4	7.7	7.8	7.6	6.5	5.1	3.9	3.9	4.0	
1985	6.4	6.5	6.7	6.8	6.9	7.0	7.2	7.5	7.4	7.0	7.0	7.3	7.3	7.1	6.1	4.8	3.8	3.8	3.9	3.8
1986	6.1	6.2	6.4	6.5	6.5	6.6	6.8	7.1	6.9	6.5	6.5	6.6	6.6	6.3	5.3	4.2	3.3	3.2	2.9	2.4
1987	6.0	6.2	6.3	6.4	6.4	6.5	6.7	6.9	6.8	6.3	6.3	6.4	6.4	6.1	5.2	4.2	3.5	3.4	3.3	3.1
1988	6.0	6.1	6.2	6.3	6.3	6.4	6.5	6.7	6.6	6.2	6.1	6.3	6.2	5.9	5.1	4.3	3.6	3.6	3.5	3.4
1989	5.9	6.0	6.2	6.2	6.2	6.3	6.4	6.6	6.5	6.1	6.0	6.1	6.1	5.8	5.1	4.3	3.7	3.7	3.7	3.7
1990	5.9	6.0	6.1	6.2	6.2	6.3	6.4	6.6	6.5	6.1	6.0	6.1	6.1	5.8	5.2	4.5	4.0	4.0	4.1	4.1
1991	5.8	5.9	6.0	6.1	6.1	6.1	6.2	6.4	6.3	5.9	5.9	5.9	5.9	5.6	5.0	4.4	3.9	3.9	3.9	3.9
1992	5.7	5.8	5.9	5.9	5.9	6.0	6.1	6.2	6.1	5.7	5.7	5.7	5.7	5.4	4.8	4.2	3.8	3.8	3.8	3.8
1993	5.6	5.7	5.8	5.8	5.8	5.8	5.9	6.0	5.9	5.6	5.5	5.6	5.5	5.2	4.7	4.1	3.7	3.7	3.7	3.7
1994	5.5	5.6	5.7	5.7	5.7	5.7	5.8	5.9	5.8	5.4	5.4	5.4	5.3	5.1	4.6	4.0	3.6	3.6	3.6	3.6
1995	5.4	5.5	5.5	5.6	5.5	5.6	5.6	5.7	5.6	5.3	5.2	5.2	5.2	4.9	4.4	3.9	3.6	3.5	3.5	3.5
1996	5.3	5.4	5.5	5.5	5.5	5.5	5.6	5.6	5.5	5.2	5.1	5.1	5.1	4.8	4.4	3.9	3.6	3.5	3.5	3.5
1997	5.2	5.3	5.3	5.4	5.3	5.3	5.4	5.5	5.3	5.1	5.0	5.0	4.9	4.7	4.2	3.8	3.4	3.4	3.4	3.3
1998	5.1	5.1	5.2	5.2	5.2	5.2	5.3	5.3	5.2	4.9	4.8	4.8	4.7	4.5	4.1	3.6	3.3	3.3	3.3	3.2
1999	5.0	5.1	5.1	5.1	5.1	5.1	5.2	5.2	5.1	4.8	4.7	4.7	4.6	4.4	4.0	3.6	3.3	3.3	3.2	3.2
2000	5.0	5.0	5.1	5.1	5.1	5.0	5.1	5.2	5.0	4.8	4.7	4.7	4.6	4.4	4.0	3.6	3.3	3.3	3.2	3.2
2001	4.9	4.9	5.0	5.0	4.9	4.9	5.0	5.0	4.9	4.6	4.6	4.5	4.5	4.3	3.9	3.5	3.2	3.2	3.1	3.1
2002	4.8	4.8	4.9	4.9	4.9	4.8	4.9	4.9	4.8	4.6	4.5	4.5	4.4	4.2	3.8	3.4	3.2	3.1	3.1	3.1
2003	4.7	4.8	4.8	4.8	4.8	4.8	4.8	4.8	4.7	4.5	4.4	4.4	4.3	4.1	3.7	3.4	3.1	3.1	3.0	3.0
2004	4.7	4.7	4.8	4.8	4.7	4.7	4.8	4.8	4.7	4.4	4.3	4.3	4.2	4.1	3.7	3.4	3.1	3.1	3.0	3.0
2005	4.7	4.7	4.7	4.7	4.7	4.7	4.7	4.8	4.6	4.4	4.3	4.3	4.2	4.0	3.7	3.4	3.1	3.1	3.1	3.0
2006	4.6	4.6	4.7	4.7	4.6	4.6	4.7	4.7	4.6	4.3	4.3	4.2	4.1	4.0	3.6	3.3	3.1	3.1	3.0	3.0
2007	4.6	4.6	4.7	4.7	4.6	4.6	4.6	4.7	4.6	4.3	4.2	4.2	4.1	4.0	3.7	3.4	3.1	3.1	3.1	3.0
2008	4.5	4.5	4.6	4.6	4.5	4.5	4.5	4.5	4.4	4.2	4.1	4.1	4.0	3.8	3.5	3.2	3.0	3.0	3.0	2.9
2009	4.4	4.5	4.5	4.5	4.5	4.4	4.5	4.5	4.4	4.2	4.1	4.1	4.0	3.8	3.5	3.2	3.0	3.0	3.0	2.9
2010	4.4	4.4	4.4	4.4	4.4	4.4	4.4	4.4	4.3	4.1	4.0	4.0	3.9	3.7	3.4	3.2	3.0	2.9	2.9	2.9
2011	4.3	4.4	4.4	4.4	4.4	4.3	4.4	4.4	4.3	4.1	4.0	3.9	3.9	3.7	3.4	3.2	3.0	2.9	2.9	2.9

Appendix C: Rates of Return for All Yearly Holding Periods 1926–2011

Table C-7 (page 6 of 6)-a

Inflation

Rates of Return for all holding periods

Percent per annum compounded annually

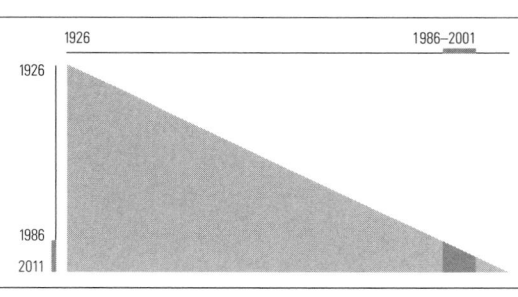

1926   1986–2001

from 1926 to 2011

To the end of	From the beginning of 1986	1987	1988	1989	1990	1991	1992	1993	1994	1995	1996	1997	1998	1999	2000	2001
1986	1.1															
1987	2.8	4.4														
1988	3.3	4.4	4.4													
1989	3.6	4.5	4.5	4.6												
1990	4.1	4.9	5.1	5.4	6.1											
1991	4.0	4.5	4.6	4.6	4.6	3.1										
1992	3.8	4.3	4.2	4.2	4.0	3.0	2.9									
1993	3.7	4.0	4.0	3.9	3.7	2.9	2.8	2.7								
1994	3.6	3.9	3.8	3.7	3.5	2.8	2.8	2.7	2.7							
1995	3.5	3.7	3.6	3.5	3.3	2.8	2.7	2.7	2.6	2.5						
1996	3.4	3.7	3.6	3.5	3.3	2.9	2.8	2.8	2.8	2.9	3.3					
1997	3.3	3.5	3.4	3.3	3.1	2.7	2.6	2.6	2.6	2.5	2.5	1.7				
1998	3.2	3.3	3.2	3.1	3.0	2.6	2.5	2.4	2.4	2.3	2.2	1.7	1.6			
1999	3.1	3.3	3.2	3.1	2.9	2.6	2.5	2.5	2.4	2.4	2.3	2.0	2.1	2.7		
2000	3.1	3.3	3.2	3.1	3.0	2.7	2.6	2.6	2.6	2.5	2.5	2.3	2.6	3.0	3.4	
2001	3.0	3.2	3.1	3.0	2.9	2.6	2.5	2.5	2.4	2.4	2.4	2.2	2.3	2.5	2.5	1.6
2002	3.0	3.1	3.0	2.9	2.8	2.5	2.5	2.5	2.4	2.4	2.4	2.2	2.3	2.5	2.4	2.0
2003	2.9	3.1	3.0	2.9	2.7	2.5	2.4	2.4	2.4	2.3	2.3	2.2	2.2	2.4	2.3	1.9
2004	3.0	3.1	3.0	2.9	2.8	2.5	2.5	2.5	2.5	2.4	2.4	2.3	2.4	2.5	2.5	2.3
2005	3.0	3.1	3.0	2.9	2.8	2.6	2.6	2.5	2.5	2.5	2.5	2.4	2.5	2.6	2.6	2.5
2006	3.0	3.1	3.0	2.9	2.8	2.6	2.6	2.5	2.5	2.5	2.5	2.4	2.5	2.6	2.6	2.5
2007	3.0	3.1	3.0	3.0	2.9	2.7	2.7	2.6	2.6	2.6	2.6	2.6	2.7	2.8	2.8	2.7
2008	2.9	3.0	2.9	2.8	2.7	2.5	2.5	2.5	2.5	2.5	2.4	2.4	2.4	2.5	2.5	2.4
2009	2.9	3.0	2.9	2.8	2.7	2.6	2.5	2.5	2.5	2.5	2.5	2.4	2.5	2.5	2.5	2.4
2010	2.8	2.9	2.8	2.8	2.7	2.5	2.5	2.4	2.4	2.4	2.4	2.3	2.4	2.4	2.4	2.3
2011	2.8	2.9	2.8	2.8	2.7	2.5	2.5	2.5	2.5	2.4	2.4	2.4	2.4	2.5	2.5	2.4

Table C-7 (page 6 of 6)-b

Inflation

Rates of Return for all holding periods

Percent per annum compounded annually

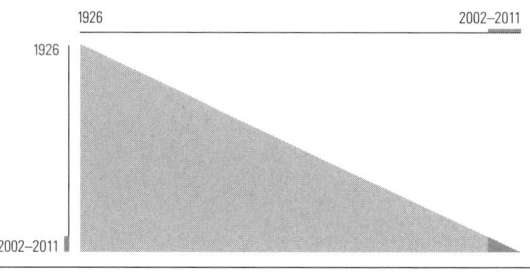

1926   2002–2011

from 1926 to 2011

To the end of	From the beginning of 2002	2003	2004	2005	2006	2007	2008	2009	2010	2011
2002	2.4									
2003	2.1	1.9								
2004	2.5	2.6	3.3							
2005	2.7	2.8	3.3	3.4						
2006	2.7	2.8	3.1	3.0	2.5					
2007	2.9	3.0	3.3	3.3	3.3	4.1				
2008	2.5	2.5	2.7	2.5	2.2	2.1	0.1			
2009	2.5	2.6	2.7	2.6	2.3	2.3	1.4	2.7		
2010	2.4	2.4	2.5	2.4	2.2	2.1	1.4	2.1	1.4	
2011	2.5	2.5	2.6	2.5	2.3	2.3	1.8	2.4	2.2	3.0

Glossary

Glossary

Arbitrage Pricing Theory (APT)
A model in which multiple betas and multiple risk premia are used to generate the expected return of a security.

Arithmetic Mean Return
A simple average of a series of returns.

Asset Allocation
The process of dividing a portfolio among major asset classes, such as stocks, bonds, or cash. Investing in a combination of investments can reduce risk and enhance returns through diversification.

Asset Class
A grouping of securities with similar characteristics and properties. As a group, these securities will tend to react in a specific way to economic factors (e.g., stocks, bonds, and real estate are all asset classes).

Balanced Mutual Fund
Fund that seeks both income and capital appreciation by investing in a generally fixed combination of stocks and bonds.

Basic Series
The seven primary time series representing Stocks, Bonds, Bills and Inflation: large company stocks, small company stocks, long-term corporate bonds, long-term government bonds, intermediate-term government bonds, U.S. Treasury bills, and inflation.

Beta
The systematic risk of a security as estimated by regressing the security's returns against the market portfolio's returns. The slope of the regression is beta.

Book-to-Market Ratio
The ratio of total book value to total market capitalization. Value companies have a high book-to-market ratio, while growth companies have a low book-to-market ratio.

Callable Bonds
Bonds that the issuer has the right to redeem (or call) prior to maturity at a specified price.

Capital Appreciation Return
The component of total return which results from the price change of an asset class over a given period.

Capital Asset Pricing Model (CAPM)
A model in which the cost of capital for any security or portfolio of securities equals the riskless rate plus a risk premium that is proportionate to the amount of systematic risk of the security or portfolio.

Commodity
Any basic substance for which there is demand and supply and which exhibits no differentiating characteristics.

Convexity
The property of a bond that its price does not change in proportion to changes in its yield. A bond with positive convexity will rise in price faster than the rate at which yields decline, and will fall in price slower than the rate at which yields rise.

Correlation Coefficient
The degree of association or strength between two variables. A value of +1 indicates a perfectly positive relationship, -1 indicates a perfectly inverse relationship, and 0 indicates no relationship between the variables.

Cost of Capital
The discount rate which should be used to derive the present value of an asset's future cash flows.

Coupon
The periodic interest payment on a bond.

Currency Risk

The risk of losing money when gains and losses are exchanged from foreign currencies into U.S. dollars. Also known as exchange rate risk.

Decile

One of 10 portfolios formed by ranking a set of securities by some criteria and dividing them into 10 equally populated subsets. The New York Stock Exchange market capitalization deciles are formed by ranking the stocks traded on the Exchange by their market capitalization.

Derived Series

The components or elemental parts of the returns of the seven primary Stocks, Bonds, Bills, and Inflation asset classes. The two categories of derived series are: risk premia, or payoffs for taking various types of risk, and inflation-adjusted asset returns.

Discount Rate

The rate used to convert a series of future cash flows to a single present value.

Dow Jones Industrial Average

The oldest stock price index beginning in 1896 with 12 stocks; currently consisting of 30 representative large stocks.

Duration (Macauley Duration)

The weighted average term-to-maturity of a bond's cash flows. The weights are the present values of each cash flow as a percentage of the present value of all cash flows. Can be used to estimate price sensitivity to interest rate changes.

Efficient Frontier

The set of portfolios that provides the highest expected returns for their respective risk levels. The efficient frontier is calculated for a given set of assets with estimates of expected return and standard deviation for each asset, and a correlation coefficient for each pair of asset returns.

Equity REITs

Companies that own and operate income-generating real estate.

Europe Stocks

Morgan Stanley Capital International Europe Index.

FF Large Growth Stocks

A portfolio of stocks constructed by setting a book-to-market ratio cutoff at the bottom 30 percent of NYSE stocks and a market capitalization cutoff at the median of NYSE stocks and selecting all NYSE, NYSE Amex, and NASDAQ stocks with a book-to-market ratio lower than the book-to-market cutoff and a market capitalization greater than the market capitalization cutoff. Data supplied by Eugene Fama and Ken French.

FF Large Value Stocks

A portfolio of stocks constructed by setting a book-to-market ratio cutoff at the top 30 percent of NYSE stocks and a market capitalization cutoff at the median of NYSE stocks and selecting all NYSE, NYSE Amex, and NASDAQ stocks with a book-to-market ratio higher than the book-to-market cutoff and a market capitalization greater than the market capitalization cutoff. Data supplied by Eugene Fama and Ken French.

FF Small Growth Stocks

A portfolio of stocks constructed by setting a book-to-market ratio cutoff at the bottom 30 percent of NYSE stocks and a market capitalization cutoff at the median of NYSE stocks and selecting all NYSE, NYSE Amex, and NASDAQ stocks with a book-to-market ratio lower than the book-to-market cutoff and a market capitalization smaller than the market capitalization cutoff. Data supplied by Eugene Fama and Ken French.

FF Small Value Stocks

A portfolio of stocks constructed by setting a book-to-market ratio cutoff at the top 30 percent of NYSE stocks and a market capitalization cutoff at the median of NYSE stocks and selecting all NYSE, NYSE Amex, and NASDAQ stocks with a book-to-market ratio higher than the book-to-market cutoff and a market capitalization smaller than the market capitalization cutoff. Data supplied by Eugene Fama and Ken French.

Free Float

The number of shares outstanding adjusted for block ownership to reflect only shares available for investment. The types of block ownership that are considered during float adjustment are cross ownership, government ownership, private ownership, and restricted shares.

Geometric Mean Return

The compound rate of return. The geometric mean of a return series is a measure of the actual average performance of a portfolio over a given time period.

Histogram

A bar graph in which the frequency of occurrence for each class of data is represented by the relative height of the bars.

IA All Growth Stocks

A portfolio of stocks constructed using the lagged market capitalization-weighted returns of the large-, mid-, and small-cap growth series.

IA All Value Stocks

A portfolio of stocks constructed using the lagged market capitalization-weighted returns of the large-, mid-, and small-cap value series.

IA Large-cap Growth Stocks

A portfolio of stocks constructed by first selecting deciles 1-2 of the NYSE universe. Once these breakpoints are established, similar-sized NYSE Amex and NASDAQ companies are assigned to the corresponding portfolios. The companies are then ranked by book-to-price, creating a growth portfolio (low B/P) where the total market capitalization of the growth and value indices are equal within each portfolio.

IA Large-cap Value Stocks

A portfolio of stocks constructed by first selecting deciles 1-2 of the NYSE universe. Once these breakpoints are established, similar-sized NYSE Amex and NASDAQ companies are assigned to the corresponding portfolios. The companies are then ranked by book-to-price, creating a value portfolio (high B/P) where the total market capitalization of the growth and value indices are equal within each portfolio.

IA Mid-cap Growth Stocks

A portfolio of stocks constructed by first selecting deciles 3-5 of the NYSE universe. Once these breakpoints are established, similar-sized NYSE Amex and NASDAQ companies are assigned to the corresponding portfolios. The companies are then ranked by book-to-price, creating a growth portfolio (low B/P) where the total market capitalization of the growth and value indices are equal within each portfolio.

IA Mid-cap Value Stocks

A portfolio of stocks constructed by first selecting deciles 3-5 of the NYSE universe. Once these breakpoints are established, similar-sized NYSE Amex and NASDAQ companies are assigned to the corresponding portfolios. The companies are then ranked by book-to-price, creating a value portfolio (high B/P) where the total market capitalization of the growth and value indices are equal within each portfolio.

IA Small-cap Growth Stocks

A portfolio of stocks constructed by first selecting deciles 6-8 of the NYSE universe. Once these breakpoints are established, similar-sized NYSE Amex and NASDAQ companies are assigned to the corresponding portfolios. The companies are then ranked by book-to-price, creating a growth portfolio (low B/P) where the total market capitalization of the growth and value indices are equal within each portfolio.

IA Small-cap Value Stocks

A portfolio of stocks constructed by first selecting deciles 6-8 of the NYSE universe. Once these breakpoints are established, similar-sized NYSE Amex and NASDAQ companies are assigned to the corresponding portfolios. The companies are then ranked by book-to-price, creating a value portfolio (high B/P) where the total market capitalization of the growth and value indices are equal within each portfolio

Income Return

The component of total return which results from a periodic cash flow, such as dividends.

Index Value

The cumulative value of returns on a dollar amount invested. It is used when measuring investment performance and computing returns over non-calendar periods.

Inflation

The rate of change in consumer prices. The Consumer Price Index for All Urban Consumers (CPI-U), not seasonally adjusted, is used to measure inflation. Prior to January 1978, the CPI (as compared with CPI-U) was used. Both inflation measures are constructed by the U.S. Department of Labor, Bureau of Labor Statistics, Washington.

Inflation-Adjusted Returns

Asset class returns in real terms. The inflation-adjusted return of an asset is calculated by geometrically subtracting inflation from the asset's nominal return.

Intermediate-Term Government Bonds

A one-bond portfolio with a maturity near 5 years.

International Stocks

Morgan Stanley Capital International EAFE® (Europe, Australasia, Far East) Index. Represents 21 developed equity markets outside of North America.

Large Company Stocks

The Standard and Poor's 500 Stock Composite Index® (S&P 500).

Lifecycle Investing

An investment style focused on helping investors manage their retirement portfolios across a long and unpredictable lifetime.

Liquidity

The ease of executing trades in securities.

Liquidity Premium

The excess valuation that a liquid security has relative to an illiquid security. In other words, illiquid securities are valued at an illiquidity discount relative to liquid securities, and consequently illiquid securities have higher expected returns.

Liquidity Risk

The risk that an asset will be difficult to buy or sell quickly and in large volume without substantially affecting the asset's price.

Logarithmic Scale

A scale in which equal percentage changes are represented by equal distances.

Lognormal Distribution

The distribution of a random variable whose natural logarithm is normally distributed. A lognormal distribution is skewed so that a higher proportion of possible returns exceed the expected value versus falling short of the expected value. In the lognormal forecasting model, one plus the total return has a lognormal distribution.

Long-Term Corporate Bonds

Citigroup long-term, high-grade corporate bond total return index.

Long-Term Government Bonds

A one-bond portfolio with a maturity near 20 years.

Low-cap Stocks

The portfolio of stocks comprised of the 6-8th deciles of the New York Stock Exchange, including similar-sized NYSE Amex and NASDAQ companies.

Market Capitalization

The current market price of a security determined by the most recently recorded trade multiplied by the number of issues outstanding of that security. For equities, market capitalization is computed by taking the share price of a stock times the number of shares outstanding.

Markowitz 2.0

An improved version of traditional mean variance optimization which takes into account fat-tailed probability distributions, forward looking geometric rates of return, conditional value at risk, and Monte Carlo simulation.

Mean-Variance Optimization (MVO)

The process of identifying portfolios that have the highest possible return for a given level of risk or the lowest possible risk for a given return. The inputs for MVO are return, standard deviation, and the correlation coefficients of returns for each pair of asset classes.

Micro-cap Stocks

The portfolio of stocks comprised of the 9-10th deciles of the New York Stock Exchange, including similar-sized NYSE Amex and NASDAQ companies.

Mid-cap Stocks

The portfolio of stocks comprised of the 3-5th deciles of the New York Stock Exchange, including similar-sized NYSE Amex and NASDAQ companies.

Monte Carlo Simulation

A technique that starts with a set of assumptions about the estimated mean, standard deviation, and correlations for a set of asset classes or investments. These assumptions are used to randomly generate hundreds of possible future return scenarios. These returns can then be used in conjunction with a client's year-by-year cash flows, taxes, asset allocation, and financial product selections. A large number of possible "financial lives" for the client can be produced.

NAREIT

National Association of Real Estate Investment Trusts®. Membership includes U.S. REITs and publicly traded real estate companies worldwide

National Association of Securities Dealers Automated Quotation System (NASDAQ)

A computerized system showing current bid and asked prices for stocks traded on the Over-the-Counter market, as well as some New York Stock Exchange listed stocks.

New York Stock Exchange (NYSE)

The largest and oldest stock exchange in the United States, founded in 1792.

Non-Parametric

A type of Monte Carlo simulation that uses purely historical data.

NYSE Amex (AMEX)

Formerly known as the American Stock Exchange (AMEX), the NYSE Amex is one of the largest stock exchanges in the U.S. Securities traded on this exchange are generally of small to medium-size companies.

Over-the-Counter Market (OTC)

A market in which assets are not traded on an organized exchange like the New York Stock Exchange, but rather through various dealers or market makers who are linked electronically.

Pacific Stocks

Morgan Stanley Capital International Pacific Index.

Parametric

A type of Monte Carlo simulation that is based on the mean, standard deviation, and correlations for the assets being forecast. These are the parameters that give this method its name. Once these parameters are set, a computer program is used to generate random samples from the bell curve that these parameters define.

Portfolio

A group of assets, such as stocks and bonds, that are held by an investor.

Price-Weighted Index

An index in which component stocks are weighted by their price. Thus, higher-priced stocks have a greater percentage impact on the index than lower-priced stocks.

Quintile

One of 5 portfolios formed by ranking a set of securities by some criteria and dividing them into 5 equally populated subsets. The micro-cap stocks are a market capitalization quintile.

R-squared

Measures the "goodness of fit" of the regression line and describes the percentage of variation in the dependent variable that is explained by the independent variable. The R-squared measure may vary from zero to one.

Real Estate Investment Trusts (REITs)

Companies that own and operate, as well as finance, income-generating real estate. To qualify as a REIT, a company is obligated to pay out at least 90 percent of its taxable profit to shareholders on an annual basis.

Return

see Total Return

Risk

The extent to which an investment is subject to uncertainty. Risk may be measured by standard deviation.

Riskless Rate of Return

The return on a riskless investment; it is the rate of return an investor can obtain without taking market risk.

Risk Premium

The reward which investors require to accept the uncertain outcomes associated with securities. The size of the risk premium will depend upon the type and extent of the risk.

Rolling Period Returns

A series of overlapping contiguous periods of returns defined by the frequency of the data under examination. In examining 5-year rolling periods of returns for annual data that starts in 1970, the first rolling period would be 1970–1974, the second rolling period would be 1971–1975, the third rolling period would be 1972–1976, etc.

Rolling Period Standard Deviation

A series of overlapping contiguous periods of standard deviations defined by the frequency of the data under examination. In examining 5-year rolling periods of standard deviation for annual data that starts in 1970, the first rolling period would be 1970–1974, the second rolling period would be 1971–1975, the third rolling period would be 1972–1976, etc.

Serial Correlation (Autocorrelation)

The degree to which the return of a given series is related from period to period. A serial correlation near +1 or -1 indicates that returns are predictable from one period to the next; a serial correlation near zero indicates returns are random or unpredictable.

Small Company Stocks

A portfolio of stocks represented by the fifth capitalization quintile of stocks on the NYSE for 1926–1981. For January 1982 to March 2001, the series is represented by the DFA U.S. 9–10 Small Company Portfolio and the DFA U.S. Micro Cap Portfolio thereafter.

S&P 500®

Stock index including 500 of the largest stocks (in terms of stock market value) in the United States representing 88 separate industries. Prior to 1957, it consisted of 90 of the largest stocks.

Standard Deviation

A measure of the dispersion of returns of an asset, or the extent to which returns vary from the arithmetic mean. It represents the volatility or risk of an asset. The greater the degree of dispersion, the greater the risk associated with the asset.

Systematic Risk

The risk that is unavoidable according to CAPM. It is the risk that is common to all risky securities and cannot be eliminated through diversification. The amount of an asset's systematic risk is measured by its beta.

Total Return

A measure of performance of an asset class over a designated time period. It is comprised of income return, reinvestment of income return and capital appreciation return components.

Treasury Bills

A one-bill portfolio containing, at the beginning of each month, the bill having the shortest maturity not less than one month.

Unsystematic Risk

The portion of total risk specific to an individual security that can be avoided through diversification.

Volatility

The extent to which an asset's returns fluctuate from period to period.

World Stocks

Morgan Stanley Capital International World Index.

Yield

The yield to maturity is the internal rate of return that equates the bond's price with the stream of cash flows promised to the bondholder. The yield on a stock is the percentage rate of return paid in dividends.

Index

Index

Investment Tools and Resources

2012 Ibbotson® Stocks, Bonds, Bills, and Inflation® (SBBI®) Classic Yearbook

The 2012 Ibbotson SBBI Classic Yearbook provides a comprehensive, historical view of the performance of capital markets in the United States dating back to 1926.

2012 Ibbotson® SBBI® Classic Yearbook $175

Cost of Capital Resources

global.morningstar.com/US/CofCResources
(Historical archives available online for all reports except individual company tax rates)
- ▶Ibbotson® **Industry Cost of Capital data** is available for more than 300 industries with the same extensive analysis utilized in the Cost of Capital Yearbook, including: industry betas, multiples, cost of equity estimates, weighted average cost of capital, and much more. $100 per industry
- ▶Ibbotson® **Company Beta Reports** available for approximately 5,000 U.S. companies, provide statistics critical for calculating cost of equity with the CAPM and the Fama-French 3-factor model.
- ▶Ibbotson® **International Cost of Capital Report** contains up to six-cost of equity estimates for 170+ countries from the perspective of U.S. investors. $250
- ▶Ibbotson® **International Cost of Capital Perspectives Report** contains cost of equity estimates for 170+ countries from the perspective of international investors. $150
- ▶Ibbotson® **International Equity Risk Premia Report** contains historical equity risk premia for 16 countries. $150
- ▶Ibbotson® **Risk Premia Over Time Report** provides equity and size premia over your choice of historical time periods from 1926–2011. $130
- ▶**Individual Tax Rates** are available for approximately 5,000 U.S. companies. $50 per company

Morningstar® Peer Group Builder

An easy-to-use tool that helps professionals build a custom industry utilizing all of the same methodologies and features of the Ibbotson Cost of Capital Yearbook.
- ▶Create your peer group from screening on more than 10,000 U.S.-based companies in multiple SIC codes
- ▶Compare your peer group's characteristics to your subject company using data such as sales, net income, margins, and market multiples
- ▶Calculate automatically the cost of capital for your custom group (including cost of equity, WACC, as well as raw, adjusted, and levered betas)

For more information call (888) 298-3647 or visit our Web site:
global.morningstar.com/US/CofCResources

2012 Ibbotson® Cost of Capital Yearbook

Providing data on more than 400 industries, the Ibbotson Cost of Capital Yearbook is a comprehensive source of market comparables. The yearbook includes:
- ▶Five separate measures of cost of equity.
- ▶Weighted average cost of capital.
- ▶Detailed statistics for sales, profitability, capitalization, beta, multiples, ratios, equity returns and capital structure.

Published annually, the Ibbotson Cost of Capital Yearbook is updated with data through March 2012 (ships in June). For the most frequent data available, subscribe to quarterly Cost of Capital Updates to complement your 2012 Ibbotson Cost of Capital Yearbook. Updates are made available on line with data through June, September, and December 2012.

2012 Ibbotson® Cost of Capital Yearbook $465

2012 Ibbotson® Stocks, Bonds, Bills, and Inflation® (SBBI®) Valuation Yearbook

The industry standard in business valuation reference materials, the Ibbotson SBBI Valuation Yearbook will help you make the most informed decisions when estimating the cost of capital. It features a comparison of the buildup method, the Capital Asset Pricing Model, the Fama-French three-factor model, and the discounted cash flow approach.
- ▶Key Variables in Estimating the Cost of Capital table
- ▶Nearly 500 industry risk premia
- ▶Annual returns for decile portfolios dating back to 1926
- ▶Discussion on estimating the cost of capital for international markets

2012 Ibbotson® SBBI® Valuation Yearbook $175

For more information or to request a product catalog, call (888) 298-3647 or visit our Web site:
global.morningstar.com/SBBIYearbooks

Note: Archived editions (2011 and prior) of Ibbotson publications are available in limited quantities. Please call Product Sales at the number listed above to check availability and pricing.

Ibbotson Associates®

Ibbotson Associates is a leading authority on asset allocation with expertise in capital market expectations and portfolio implementation. Its experienced consultants and portfolio managers serve mutual fund firms, banks, broker-dealers, and insurance companies worldwide. Ibbotson Associates' methodologies and services address all investment phases, from accumulation to retirement and the transition between the two.

Visit Ibbotson.com for contact information, published research, product fact sheets and other information.

Morningstar® Indexes

Morningstar Indexes include a broad range of equity, fixed income and commodity indexes that can be used for asset allocation, bench-marking, or to serve as the basis for investment product creation and market monitoring purposes.

Visit http://indexes.morningstar.com for more information.

Morningstar® Principia®

Principia is one of the most widely used resources in the financial planning industry. With a powerful research database that includes mutual funds, stocks, variable annuities, closed-end funds, and separate accounts, advisors can conduct advanced research and analysis, monitor portfolios, and propose investment strategies.

Specialized Principia Modules include the Defined Contribution Plans module and the Asset Allocation module. The Defined Contribution module was designed to help advisors and plan sponsors build, monitor and manage 401(k), 403(b) and other types of retirement plan lineups. With the Asset Allocation module, advisors can build better portfolios for their clients by determining the asset mix most likely to achieve the highest return for a given risk level. Advanced features like efficient frontier graphing and Monte Carlo wealth forecasting help create individualized asset allocation strategies based on a client's risk tolerance, current assets, future needs, and other factors.

Morningstar Principia® Presentations and Education 2012

This library encompasses a collection of communication resources developed to assist advisors during client interactions. Specialized Microsoft® PowerPoint® presentations formerly known as Ibbotson's Asset Allocation Library introduce time-tested investment principles. Investor brochures available as PDF files address common retirement risks. Advisors can also search and download white papers on a broad range of research. This library may be purchased separately or as part of the Principia® Suite.

For more information on Principia Presentations and Education 2012 call: 866-608-9571 or visit:

http://global.morningstar.com/US/PresentationMaterials

Morningstar Workstation Office Edition®

Office Edition is Morningstar's complete office system for independent advisors. This single, all-inclusive platform is designed so that advisors can use it to run their entire practice. Office Edition features the most current Morningstar research data, sophisticated planning tools, complete portfolio accounting, client management tools, e-mail and calendar functions, batch reporting, archiving, and more.

For more information on Workstation Office Edition call 1-800-886-1749 or visit http://global.morningstar.com/Office

Ibbotson® SBBI® Print Kit

This collection of print materials based on the popular Stocks, Bonds, Bills, and Inflation graph demonstrates both the value of asset allocation and the benefits of long-term investing.

Ibbotson® SBBI® Print Kit: $105 (includes one poster, two market charts, and three chart pads)

Morningstar® Newsletter Builder℠

A web-based platform that provides access to timely FINRA-reviewed Morningstar articles that cover a variety of investment topics, Newsletter Builder is extremely intuitive and allows advisors to create and distribute customized newsletters in minutes. Advisors can search and sort pre-written Morningstar articles by length, topic or keyword. Once an article has been selected, advisors can seamlessly drag-and-drop each article into their chosen newsletter format.

Professionally designed layout templates allow advisors to integrate their own content, and 'Article Sidebar' comments are available for users to enter talking points, highlight key findings, offer product solutions, or recommend portfolio strategies.

12-month Newsletter Builder subscription (single user license) $399

For more product information please call (866) 608-9571 or visit www.morningstar.com/goto/nws.

Morningstar® Andex® Charts

Richly detailed, FINRA-reviewed Andex Charts are powerful resources for highlighting the relationship between world events and historical market performance. Available in both handout and wallchart formats, this in-depth perspective shows the growth of $1 invested in six major asset classes, plus one hypothetical balanced portfolio, and inflation since 1926.

Wallchart (25" × 38") $35
Handouts (11" × 16.5" folds to 8.5" × 11") $16.50
Bulk discounts available.
Customization available for orders of 500 or more.

For more product information please call (866) 608-9571 or visit www.morningstar.com/goto/andex.

Morningstar® EnCorr®

Institutions worldwide use Morningstar® EnCorr® to research, create, analyze, and implement optimal asset allocation strategies within a single software. This advanced analytical software unites proven financial models, sophisticated Ibbotson methodologies, and comprehensive Morningstar investment data.

An innovative solution for conducting advanced statistical and graphical analyses, Morningstar EnCorr helps build portfolios designed to generate robust returns at varying risk levels. The software provides invaluable support to institutional investment professionals conducting in-depth portfolio research, including analysts, investment consultants, Registered Investment Advisors, and portfolio managers.

Morningstar® Direct®

Morningstar Direct is a global, multi-currency institutional research platform that provides in-depth performance and holdings analysis of investments. This web-based solution unites continuous data updates with powerful analytics to help institutions worldwide with product development, competitive analysis, marketing, investment selection, and performance evaluation.

For more information about Morningstar EnCorr or Morningstar Direct within the United States call +1 866 910 0840.

Outside the United States, please contact your local office:
Asia (excluding mainland China): +852 2973 4633
Australia: +61 2 9276 4445 or +61 414 819 354;
Canada: +1 416 484-7818; China: +86 755 8826 3088;
Europe: +44 020 3107 0020.